T0331740

Integrating Video into Pre–Service and In–Service Teacher Training

Pier Giuseppe Rossi
University of Macerata, Italy

Laura Fedeli
University of Macerata, Italy

A volume in the Advances in Higher Education and Professional Development (AHEPD) Book Series

www.igi-global.com

Published in the United States of America by
   IGI Global
   Information Science Reference (an imprint of IGI Global)
   701 E. Chocolate Avenue
   Hershey PA, USA 17033
   Tel: 717-533-8845
   Fax: 717-533-8661
   E-mail: cust@igi-global.com
   Web site: http://www.igi-global.com

Copyright © 2017 by IGI Global. All rights reserved. No part of this publication may be reproduced, stored or distributed in
any form or by any means, electronic or mechanical, including photocopying, without written permission from the publisher.
Product or company names used in this set are for identification purposes only. Inclusion of the names of the products or
companies does not indicate a claim of ownership by IGI Global of the trademark or registered trademark.
                    Library of Congress Cataloging-in-Publication Data

Names: Rossi, Pier Giuseppe, editor. | Fedeli, Laura, 1958- editor.
Title: Integrating video into pre-service and in-service teacher training /
   Pier Giuseppe Rossi and Laura Fedeli, editors.
Description: Hershey PA : Information Science Reference, [2017] | Series:
   Advances in higher education and professional development | Includes
   bibliographical references and index.
Identifiers: LCCN 2016024313| ISBN 9781522507116 (hardcover) | ISBN
   9781522507123 (ebook)
Subjects: LCSH: Teachers--Training of--Audio-visual aids.
Classification: LCC LB1731 .I569 2017 | DDC 370.71/1--dc23 LC record available at https://lccn.loc.gov/2016024313

This book is published in the IGI Global book series Advances in Higher Education and Professional Development
(AHEPD) (ISSN: 2327-6983; eISSN: 2327-6991)

British Cataloguing in Publication Data
A Cataloguing in Publication record for this book is available from the British Library.

All work contributed to this book is new, previously-unpublished material. The views expressed in this book are those of the
authors, but not necessarily of the publisher.

For electronic access to this publication, please contact: eresources@igi-global.com.

Advances in Higher Education and Professional Development (AHEPD) Book Series

Jared Keengwe
University of North Dakota, USA

ISSN: 2327-6983
EISSN: 2327-6991

Mission

As world economies continue to shift and change in response to global financial situations, job markets have begun to demand a more highly-skilled workforce. In many industries a college degree is the minimum requirement and further educational development is expected to advance. With these current trends in mind, the **Advances in Higher Education & Professional Development (AHEPD) Book Series** provides an outlet for researchers and academics to publish their research in these areas and to distribute these works to practitioners and other researchers.

AHEPD encompasses all research dealing with higher education pedagogy, development, and curriculum design, as well as all areas of professional development, regardless of focus.

Coverage

- Adult Education
- Assessment in Higher Education
- Career Training
- Coaching and Mentoring
- Continuing Professional Development
- Governance in Higher Education
- Higher Education Policy
- Pedagogy of Teaching Higher Education
- Vocational Education

IGI Global is currently accepting manuscripts for publication within this series. To submit a proposal for a volume in this series, please contact our Acquisition Editors at Acquisitions@igi-global.com or visit: http://www.igi-global.com/publish/.

The Advances in Higher Education and Professional Development (AHEPD) Book Series (ISSN 2327-6983) is published by IGI Global, 701 E. Chocolate Avenue, Hershey, PA 17033-1240, USA, www.igi-global.com. This series is composed of titles available for purchase individually; each title is edited to be contextually exclusive from any other title within the series. For pricing and ordering information please visit http://www.igi-global.com/book-series/advances-higher-education-professional-development/73681. Postmaster: Send all address changes to above address. Copyright © 2017 IGI Global. All rights, including translation in other languages reserved by the publisher. No part of this series may be reproduced or used in any form or by any means – graphics, electronic, or mechanical, including photocopying, recording, taping, or information and retrieval systems – without written permission from the publisher, except for non commercial, educational use, including classroom teaching purposes. The views expressed in this series are those of the authors, but not necessarily of IGI Global.

Titles in this Series

For a list of additional titles in this series, please visit: www.igi-global.com

Handbook of Research on Learner-Centered Pedagogy in Teacher Education and Professional Development
Jared Keengwe (University of North Dakota, USA) and Grace Onchwari (University of North Dakota, USA)
Information Science Reference • copyright 2017 • 451pp • H/C (ISBN: 9781522508922) • US $265.00 (our price)

Accelerated Opportunity Education Models and Practices
Rene Cintron (Louisiana Community & Technical College System, USA) Jeanne C. Samuel (Delgado Community College, USA) and Janice M. Hinson (University of North Carolina at Charlotte, USA)
Information Science Reference • copyright 2017 • 316pp • H/C (ISBN: 9781522505280) • US $180.00 (our price)

Preparing Foreign Language Teachers for Next-Generation Education
Chin-Hsi Lin (Michigan State University, USA) Dongbo Zhang (Michigan State University, USA) and Binbin Zheng (Michigan State University, USA)
Information Science Reference • copyright 2017 • 313pp • H/C (ISBN: 9781522504832) • US $185.00 (our price)

Innovative Practices for Higher Education Assessment and Measurement
Elena Cano (University of Barcelona, Spain) and Georgeta Ion (Universitat Autònoma de Barcelona, Spain)
Information Science Reference • copyright 2017 • 471pp • H/C (ISBN: 9781522505310) • US $215.00 (our price)

Handbook of Research on Study Abroad Programs and Outbound Mobility
Donna M. Velliaris (Eynesbury Institute of Business & Technology, Australia) and Deb Coleman-George (University of Adelaide, Australia)
Information Science Reference • copyright 2016 • 754pp • H/C (ISBN: 9781522501695) • US $335.00 (our price)

Setting a New Agenda for Student Engagement and Retention in Historically Black Colleges and Universities
Charles B. W. Prince (Howard University, USA) and Rochelle L. Ford (Syracuse University, USA)
Information Science Reference • copyright 2016 • 343pp • H/C (ISBN: 9781522503088) • US $185.00 (our price)

Handbook of Research on Professional Development for Quality Teaching and Learning
Teresa Petty (University of North Carolina at Charlotte, USA) Amy Good (University of North Carolina at Charlotte, USA) and S. Michael Putman (University of North Carolina at Charlotte, USA)
Information Science Reference • copyright 2016 • 824pp • H/C (ISBN: 9781522502043) • US $310.00 (our price)

Administrative Challenges and Organizational Leadership in Historically Black Colleges and Universities
Charles B. W. Prince (Howard University, USA) and Rochelle L. Ford (Syracuse University, USA)
Information Science Reference • copyright 2016 • 301pp • H/C (ISBN: 9781522503118) • US $170.00 (our price)

www.igi-global.com

701 E. Chocolate Ave., Hershey, PA 17033
Order online at www.igi-global.com or call 717-533-8845 x100
To place a standing order for titles released in this series, contact: cust@igi-global.com
Mon-Fri 8:00 am - 5:00 pm (est) or fax 24 hours a day 717-533-8661

Table of Contents

Detailed Table of Contents

Using a Narrative-based Review approach in this chapter we aim to provide a system perspective on the use of videos in supporting teachers' professional development, with specific regard to professional vision. We first look at the 'affordances' of video: the capacities that it adds to the toolkits of teacher educators. We then look specifically at evidence for the development of specific abilities related to the professional vision through video: capacity for reflection, noticing and other potential benefits. Later, we focus on how to analyse video so as to develop reflective practice in teachers by presenting meaningful experiences and studies. Lastly, we propose an in-depth view of the possibilities related to collaborative analysis for professional vision development paying specific attention to the more widely used and validated methodologies such as lesson-study, teaching video club, and the dialogic video cycle.

Chapter 2

Awareness of the centrality of education and training in a knowledge society, the need for Lifelong Learning, and, connected to these, the search for recursive processes between theory and practice, require educators to look for training models suitable for emerging professionals and their development. Specifically, training models appear to be necessary; models that can activate a holistic approach, starting from initial training. Those models should be present in the different training steps (training for pre-service, newly hired and in-service teachers) and could build bridges among the different training steps so that the approach to knowledge and the development of professionality can become a habitus and a deeply-rooted personal drive. Learning paths in which videos are used can ensure those goals. The chapter describes a university training path for pre-service primary teachers in which class video recordings are used as binding objects whose discussion involves students, university professors and school teachers. Such process proposes Lifelong Learning also as interaction among different training levels.

Chapter 3

This chapter explores the possibility and potential of using video devices as recording instruments for didactic practices, within the context of the discussion of lines of analysis, aimed at the development of didactic models, as artefacts produced by pedagogic research in support of teaching processes and the professionalization of teachers. The main theoretical references are cited which analyse the validity of didactic models in teaching innovation processes and which point to possible new avenues for research in this field, with specific attention focused on practice-based approaches. Exploring and developing the potentiality of video research in line with directions specifically corresponding to the problems of analysis in the education field is clearly important. The same is discussed starting from an analysis of specific research experience.

Chapter 4

Video is increasingly used in professional development programs for teachers. Several studies have shown that the ability to notice and analyze pertinent classroom elements is the mark of an expert teacher, but little research has focused on how to use video to bring about real transformations in teachers' classroom activity. A research program was therefore developed to address this issue, drawing on Dewey's notion of collaborative inquiry and key concepts from work analysis. The research revealed three processes of professional development that video-artifacts can bring to the fore and enrich: mimetic engagement, the comparison and cross-fertilization between activities, and the deconstruction-reconstruction of activity. On the basis of these processes, the researchers designed a program called the Collaborative Video Learning Laboratory, which has yielded promising preliminary results for professional development. The advantages and challenges of this program are discussed and the new perspectives for professional development programs for teachers are presented.

Chapter 5

Observing teaching-learning situations in order to better understand them, such was the OPEN project (Altet, Bru and Blanchard-Laville, 2012). This project has been transformed into the research federative structure of OPÉEN&ReForm (the passage from observation by research to observation for training being at stake). In this chapter, the resort to the video aiming at analyzing the activity is carried out according to an approach of professional didactics (Pastré, 2011; Vinatier, 2013) with the purpose to help the professionals in their development (Vinatier, 2013). The authors introduce the case study of a co-analysis approach of the video traces of a teacher activity, according to her point of view, in a collaborative research (Vinatier et al., 2012) in French Polynesia, what seems to constitute for her a potential situation of professional development (Mayen, 1999), in her authorizing herself to try out new ways to lead her teaching.

Rossella Santagata, University of California, Irvine, USA
Janette Jovel, Independent Researcher, USA
Cathery Yeh, Chapman University, USA

Research that focuses on understanding pre-service teachers' learning processes as they engage in video-based activities is still limited. This study investigates pre-service teachers' group conversations around videos of mathematics teaching. Conversations of two groups attending a ten-week video-based course introducing standards-based instruction were videotaped, transcribed, and analyzed. Pre-service teachers' discussions included elements of an analysis framework used to guide their viewing: mathematics content, analysis of teaching and of student thinking and learning, and suggestions for instructional improvement. Analyses became more elaborated over the duration of the course. In addition, pre-service teachers discussed standards-based mathematics teaching by increasingly valorizing its characteristics. Findings highlighted important dimensions for working with video in teacher collaborative settings: the purpose, viewing lens, group dynamics, and facilitator role.

Giorgio Bolondi, Alma Mater Studiorum Università di Bologna, Italy
Federica Ferretti, Alma Mater Studiorum Università di Bologna, Italy
Alessandro Gimigliano, Alma Mater Studiorum Università di Bologna, Italy
Stefania Lovece, Alma Mater Studiorum Università di Bologna, Italy
Ira Vannini, Alma Mater Studiorum Università di Bologna, Italy

The purpose of this chapter is to present a systematic observational research on the math teachers' assessment practices in the classroom. This research is a specific phase of an international project (FAMT&L - Comenius Multilateral Project) and it is aimed to promote the use of formative assessment in teaching mathematics to students aged from 11 to 16. The observational study is carried out by a plan of systematic observations of teachers' behaviour in the classroom with the help of video recording. Thanks to a specific tool of video analysis (a structured grid), developed using indications from international literature and experiences of teacher training in the five Partner countries involved (Italy, France, Holland, Switzerland and Cyprus), we managed to gather many different indicators on good and bad practices for the formative assessment of mathematics teachers. Furthermore, the analysed video will be used in in-service teacher training courses in order to promote a correct use of formative assessment and to improve achievements in learning mathematics.

What role has video analysis today in activating, supporting and guiding this professional development process? In this chapter, we will try to provide some answers and open up research paths that can provide suggestions for redirecting training and joint-training processes. The use of video-analysis as a tool for self-comparison was found to be vital; it was however decided to not give it an exclusive role, but include it as part of a more complex training device. The interest of the study was aimed at understanding action, in its planning, the contextualised situation, a review of the action and perception of oneself before and after the intervention. The research in question is based on a holistic case study that was selected for its representative nature within the group of teachers in the research-training, and can therefore be defined as an "emblematic case".

This research is born of a dual interest: on one hand in the concept of didactic transposition, i.e., the work done to manufacture a teaching object out of an object of knowledge," (Chevallard, 1985, p. 39), and on the other hand, for studying practical research and training methods for teachers, based on observation and on the study of teaching practices. This paper describes a case study in which several filmed lessons of a primary school teacher have been analysed by the author using a model to study didactic transposition that was developed following an advanced theoretical study. By then combining the video films with interviews between the researcher and teacher, the results of lesson analysis were provided to the teacher in order to raise his awareness of some of the characteristic aspects of the way in he performed the didactic transposition for the subject of history. The training aim is followed by a research aim, i.e., "assessment" by the researcher, of the training or educational route achieved by the teacher. This assessment is the linchpin of this paper.

Chapter 10

Video-research, which represents a multi-methodological practice and an interdisciplinary study area, responds to various knowledge problems created by the complexity of the didactic phenomena to be investigated, and proposes instruments and technologies that have a very high potential about phenomena description, reproduction and comprehension, not only for researchers but also for teachers themselves who are the protagonists of those phenomena. Starting by these preliminary remarks, this chapter will be focused on the introduction of the preliminary results of a video-research itinerary achieved by the DidaSco group (School Didactics) throughout a project itinerary that involved six infant, primary and secondary (first degree only) schools in Bari and its province, working on History didactics intermediary processes. In the meantime, in this chapter a particular attention will be paid to the introduction of a video analysis form which was realized by the authors.

This paper discusses the relationship between cinema and education based on opportunities for the fruition, analysis and production of video in educational contexts. To do so, it locates different approaches to cinema in schools and analyzes the importance of principles and proposals for working with audiovisual materials in the education of teachers and students. Based on the media-education perspective and on multiliteracies, the paper addresses aspects of an experience with audiovisual production in the initial education of teachers, with students in at a teacher's college, based on the Lumière Minute proposal and the Situated Learning Episodes methodology. Finally, the paper indicates some challenges and possibilities for working with video in education.

Chapter 12

This chapter is proposed with the primary aim of analysing the massive incorporation of the video in social networking sites, as a narrative resource support in those platforms. At the same time, and more specifically, it aims to show how they are able to be used in teacher training, since social networking sites appear as enhancing the use of video possibilities in open teacher training. However, in the educational field are shown as an aspect that still needs to explore and deepen this line of research. First, this chapter presents the phenomenon of the incorporation of video into social networking sites. Second, we present a systematization of the research work on the pedagogical value of videos and social networking sites in teacher training. This new scenario favours knowledge democratization and involves a reformulation of teacher training models and professional identity.

Chapter 13

Teachers are the main foundations of the education system, and their professional development during their working life is vital in ensuring the success of any attempts to change that system. It is for this reason that in-service training is high on the agenda of most countries, although previous studies have shown that teachers are unable to transfer the knowledge they gain through in-service training to in-class activities, as more long-lasting help is required. One way in which teachers can be provided help in this regard is through the use of technology in line with a strong instructional design theory. This chapter aims to address this issue by showing how videos can be used in the professional development of teachers as part of an expertise-based training (XBT) program. The chapter is compiled in seven main parts: 1) Introduction 2) Background 3) Main Focus of the Chapter 5) Solutions and Recommendations 6) Future Research Directions, and finally, 7) Conclusions.

Beverly B. Ray, Idaho State University, USA
Angiline Powell, University of Memphis, USA

Having teachers who can demonstrate and document teaching effectiveness, ethical behavior, professional obligations, and willingness to embrace continuous learning is important to for the well-being of the field. Video serves as a viable means of addressing these concerns. In particular, use of video in teacher training promotes a disposition for reflection on and documentation of emerging practice. It also serves to document transfer of classroom based knowledge into teaching even as it provides a tool for the documentation of growth across time. The chapter provides an outline of best practices in the use of video in teacher training, focusing on problems and techniques of video production that support quality recording and production of videos in class and in the field. Various categories of video appropriate for use in Teacher Training programs are addressed and examples of use are provided. Directions for getting started are provided along with a process for implementation using both hard and soft scaffolding.

Preface

The volume addresses the need to focus on two specific aspects related to the use of class video recordings in educational contexts, that is, the pedagogical finality of the use of videos, and the types of videos that are used to train pre-service and in-service teachers.

The shared goals when using videos in teacher training (as highlighted by the different researchers in terms of disciplines and regarding different levels of school context) are the need to foster dialogue and the connection between theory and practice. Different modalities are used to reach these goals. Here we mean (as commonly meant by most researchers in the field), using videos to provide teachers with given models considered successful by the trainer; using videos to foster reflection on videoed teaching practices with different teachers from the ones being trained; and using videos of the teachers who are being trained to make them aware of their habitus so as to be able to modify it, thus building their own models while taking into account theoretical references.

If we start from the assumption that models of successful practice need to be observed and acquired through videos, and that self-reflective teaching considerations can be initiated as a result, we have a convergence between the teacher's habitus and best practice.

We can activate a personal modelling, rather than compliance to a template, by enhancing teachers' awareness of their teaching habitus through identifying their choices and reasons why specific decisions were taken. We also aim to check whether their actual intentions were followed by actions consistent with those intentions. Teachers who are encouraged to watch and reflect upon their recorded videos can thus identify the acted theorems, analyse and take into account the didactical principles acquired from the theoretical reference literature, and re-shape their own teaching habitus - not to satisfy a given model, but to build their own in order to activate this process. To this end, it is necessary that the teacher is shown his/her own video recordings and that he/she is available to discuss them.

The second aspect of our focus mentioned above is directly connected to the first, that is using videos showing colleagues/unknown teachers as well as videos of the teacher currently in training. If we consider the latter option, that is using videos that involve the teacher in training, we need to highlight that the studies on the "analyse plurielle," (of francophone origin, Vinatier, Altet, 2008), have deepened the relevance of multiple diverse viewpoints when observing, discussing and reflecting on videos. The "plurality" here is meant as the opportunity to share training with student-teachers, newly hired teachers, in-service teachers and researchers. The presence of multiple professional perspectives can offer rich reflective inputs for each professional profile, independent of their level of expertise. Moreover, the "plurality of analysis" can also be seen in the different theoretical approaches. In order to effectively analyse the teacher's practice, longitudinal studies can be successful strategies to adopt. Teachers who are exposed to their own video recordings over a period of years, are able to trace a path of self-observation and reflection which can modify their habitus, again, not to comply with a given model, but to optimize it, due to an acquired awareness of consistencies between objectives and actual actions in class.

This volume presents different operational strategies. The contributions are organized into three main sections addressing the following issues: teacher professionalism; disciplines and didactics; and the processes and techniques related to video making.

The first 5 chapters are related to teacher professionalism. Giuseppina Rita Mangione, Maria Chiara Pettenati, and Alessia Rosa report from a professional perspective, a narrative review in which they aim to provide a systems perspective on the use of videos in supporting teachers' professional development, with specific regard to professionalism theory. Pier Giuseppe Rossi and Laura Fedeli, by presenting a university training path for pre-service teachers, highlight the relevance of using video to involve students in direct discussion with the school teacher (actor in the video) and the university professor, thus activating a triangulation process. Daniela Maccario explores the potential of using video devices as recording instruments for didactic practices, discussing analytic processes aimed at the development of didactic models as artefacts produced by pedagogic research and then used to support teaching processes and the professionalisation of teachers. Valérie Lussi Borer and Alain Muller describe the research program called the *Collaborative Video Learning Laboratory* that was developed to address the real transformations in teachers' classroom activity. Amélie Alletru and Grégory Munoz introduce the case study of a co-analysis approach of video traces of a teacher's activity, according to her point of view, in collaborative research within the OPEEN and ReForm project.

Disciplines and didactics are the main focus of the following 5 chapters. Rossella Santagata, Janette Jovel and Cathery Yeh investigate pre-service teachers' group conversations around videos of mathematics teaching, which findings have highlighted important dimensions for working with video in teacher collaborative settings. Giorgio Bolondi, Federica Ferretti, Alessandro Gimigliano, Stefania Lovece, and Ira Vannini present a systematic observational research on the Maths teachers' assessment practices in the classroom, developed within the international project FAMT and aimed at promoting the use of formative assessment in teaching Mathematics to students aged from 11 to 16 years. Patrizia Magnoler and Maila Pentucci present a study aimed at understanding the didactical activity in an example where the use of video-analysis as a tool for self-comparison was revealed to be vital. Ljuba Pezzimenti addresses the concept of didactic transposition and presents a case study in which several filmed lessons of a primary school teacher were used to reflect on the transposition for the subject of history. Finally, Loredana Perla and Nunzia Schiavone focus on the introduction of the preliminary results of a video-research itinerary achieved by the DidaSco group through a project that involved infant, primary and secondary schools working on History didactics and intermediary processes.

The last section of the volume is aimed at describing processes and techniques of video making, sharing, and usage. Monica Fantin discusses the relationship between cinema and education based on opportunities for the application, analysis and production of video in educational contexts. She presents different approaches and analyses principles and proposals for working with audiovisual materials in the education of teachers and students. Juan De Pablos-Pons, Pilar Colás-Bravo, Teresa González-Ramírez, Jesús Conde-Jimenez, Salvador Reyes-de-Cózar, and Jose Antonio Contreras-Rosado analyse the increased incorporation of videos into social networking sites and show how they could be used in training, elaborating how such social networking sites can enhance the possibilities of the use of video in open teacher training. The chapter by Hatice Sancar Tokmak aims at showing how videos can be used in the professional development of teachers as part of an expertise-based training (XBT) program in which teachers can be supported through the use of technology, in line with strong instructional design theory. Beverly B. Ray and Angiline Powell close the volume with a contribution that provides an outline of best practices in the use of video in teacher training, focusing on problems, techniques of video production that support quality recording, and production of videos in class and in the field.

REFERENCES

Vinatier, I., & Altet, M. (Eds.). (2008). *Analyser et comprendre la pratique enseignante*. Rennes: PUR.

Chapter 1
Professional Vision Narrative Review:
The Use of Videos to Support the Development of Teachers' Reflective Practice

Giuseppina Rita Mangione
INDIRE, Istituto Nazionale di Documentazione, Innovazione e Ricerca Educativa, Italy

Maria Chiara Pettenati
INDIRE, Istituto Nazionale di Documentazione, Innovazione e Ricerca Educativa, Italy

Alessia Rosa
INDIRE, Istituto Nazionale di Documentazione, Innovazione e Ricerca Educativa, Italy

ABSTRACT

Using a Narrative-based Review approach in this chapter we aim to provide a system perspective on the use of videos in supporting teachers' professional development, with specific regard to professional vision. We first look at the 'affordances' of video: the capacities that it adds to the toolkits of teacher educators. We then look specifically at evidence for the development of specific abilities related to the professional vision through video: capacity for reflection, noticing and other potential benefits. Later, we focus on how to analyse video so as to develop reflective practice in teachers by presenting meaningful experiences and studies. Lastly, we propose an in-depth view of the possibilities related to collaborative analysis for professional vision development paying specific attention to the more widely used and validated methodologies such as lesson-study, teaching video club, and the dialogic video cycle.

DOI: 10.4018/978-1-5225-0711-6.ch001

Copyright © 2017, IGI Global. Copying or distributing in print or electronic forms without written permission of IGI Global is prohibited.

NARRATIVE-BASED REVIEW: METHOD AND RESEARCH QUESTIONS

In the last few years, professional vision activities have been the subject of a large number of empirical research activities and analytical reflections which have highlighted their worth, through the use of both synchronous and asynchronous video products, to support teacher professional development.

The professional vision studies described in the present chapter illustrate the potential of such practice in supporting the development of critical observation, analysis, and reflection competences in relation to teaching practices of teachers who can, thus, re-think their action process within an analytical, critical, virtuous, and shared circuit. Moreover, theories related to professional vision highlight how such practice permits/enables teachers to: connect their practical and theoretical knowledge more easily, acquire a sharper/more precise and contextualized language, and, lastly, improve collaboration competences through shared vision practices. This is not a question of providing a possible extemporaneous education & training offer; rather, it is a long-term critical approach to one's own professional activity whose values and possible limitations we intend to highlight in the present contribution.

Given the growing availability of studies in this area, the need to develop a stronger theoretical framework in this context arises: a place of reflection for the research community which permits the broadening of one's knowledge horizons which goes beyond the single studies on the topic.

Providing greater clarity on how epistemic knowledge is developed and used can make its role more transparent in relation to the other domains of knowledge (Gough, 2007). Systematic synthesis is a set of formal processes to bring together different types of evidence so as to clarify what we know from research and how we know it (Gough & Elbourne, 2002; Gough, 2004). More specifically, the review or synthesis, aka "research synthesis", or secondary research is based on the basis of (the reporting of) the observation of single studies, the setting-up of the same, the critical evaluation and the synthesis of results from primary research studies in an integrated approach. Currently, there are different study types in systematic reviews (Harden & Thomas, 2005; Elliott, 2001, Egger, 2003).

More specifically, the methodology on which this review is developed is of a qualitative nature (Estabrooks, 1994) which is characterized by combining information gathered from the different studies and the description of the results in a "narrative form" (Montù, 2011) by identifying similarities and strands of thought. Moreover, the specific approach followed is that of the emergent or iterative method in which the different phases of analyses emerge en route, in constant dialogue with the Literature analysed. The latter can be modified or repeated if necessary. Even in the case of an emergent method of reviewing, it is, nonetheless, necessary to preserve the systematic nature of the analysis by exemplifying, in a rigorous manner, the choices made and the actions employed.

The preparatory work for the Literature Review involved the selection of topics, the delimitation of the research field, and the choice of questions. This preparatory stage guided the choice of studies to be analysed as well as the identification of new studies on the basis of citations and coherence with the initial questions in a continuous integration process.

Figure 1 presents in a schematic way the workflow for a literature review. It identifies relevant research related to the specific questions and themes posed in the form of specific research questions: what are the macro functions/objectives of the use of video practices? What is the professional vision and can teacher competence be defined? and, if so, in what way? Which abilities are characteristic of the professional vision? What processes support the professional vision? Professional vision is a competence which develops individually or can it avail of video-based collaborative strategies? and, if so, of what type?

Figure 1. Literature review narrative process

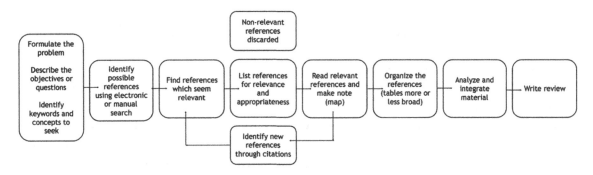

We aim here to review the international literature base in order to evaluate what is currently known about the impact of video technology upon the development of teacher professional vision. We first look at the 'affordances' of video: the capacities that it adds to the toolkits of teacher educators. We then look specifically at evidence for the development of specific abilities related to the professional vision through video: capacity for reflection, noticing and other potential benefits. Later, we focus on how to analyse video so as to develop reflective practice in teachers by presenting meaningful experiences and studies. Lastly, we propose an in-depth view of the possibilities related to collaborative analysis for professional vision development paying specific attention to the more widely used and validated methodologies such as lesson-study, teaching video club, and the dialogic video cycle.

Our conclusions include implications for teacher training and accompanying activities which can learn from videos by using them in "contexts" which aim at continuously developing professional vision in teaching practices. Our intention is to provide a structure capable of highlighting the relevance of the themes addressed.

BACKGROUND: VIDEO IN TEACHER TRAINING

The use of video in teacher training has for a long time been considered a useful technique for the professional development of personnel engaged in educational contexts. Despite the fact that there are a multitude of theories on the theme, it is possible to define three macro aims/objectives in the use of videos which are not to be conceived of as closed spaces but as aspects related to video practices:

1. The first macro-group includes video production activities which are primarily documentaries in which the video production aims to capture the complexity of the educational action/event (Borko et al., 2008; Santagata, 2009; Rosaen et al., 2010; Santagata & Guarino, 2011), so as to reflect on an activity in which it was difficult to grasp the nuances while in the context (and in reality also during the external observation activities). Such a use of video practices has been highlighted both for the analysis of one's work (Borko et al., 2008; Sherin & van Es, 2009) and in relation to that of others (Bliss & Reynolds, 2004). In this respect, the video allows comparative analysis of the teaching methodology practices both over time and in relation to the different teachers. When the videos can acquire both video and audio tracks (through the use of microphones) thus permitting

the analysis of both the gestural and verbal interactions, the video becomes what Zhang et al. (2011) define as the 'window into practice'.

2. Videos realized with the intention of stimulating shared discussion and reflection between the teachers Hiebert, Gallimore, and Stigler (2002) belong to the second macro-group. Videos provide concrete examples of instructional practices that avoid much of the ambiguity of written descriptions. Because the educational community lacks a shared language for describing teaching, key phrases such as 'problem solving' or 'language experience' often mean different things to different teachers. Videotapes of lessons can illustrate concretely what a teacher has in mind (Hiebert, Gallimore, and Stigler, 2002). Viewing videos enables colleagues to be able to compare and contrast by having the whole group concentrate on limited/restricted areas of interaction which would probably go unnoticed in F2F observation contexts. This happens because when sharing views on F2F observation contexts memory acquires an important role because it relies on what those involved remember as well as how information is selected (Brophy, 2004). Instead, with videos, one can view specific things over and over again, despite the fact that, in the literature, there is a lot of debate about the actual usefulness of the repeated re-viewing of material. Indeed, some studies (Zhang et al., 2011; Tripp & Rich, 2011) suggest the saturation point is reached after just three or four viewings.

3. The third macro-group highlights the superiority of the video image over the spoken word. The video frees us of the narration of the facts by one of those involved. Moreover, the events may be more clearly and powerfully demonstrated by 'real people in real situations' than by the abstraction of a teacher educator at one remove from the classroom activity (Marsh & Mitchell 2014). Such "truth" in the material permits the exemplification and the sharing of so-called "best practices" as well as the mediocre ones which, according to Mitchell et al. (2010) demonstrated that for beginning teachers at least there was a perceived value in viewing mediocre and even 'bad' practice as it afforded insights into 'real classrooms'; into the practice of teachers facing real-life dilemmas and decisions. As stated by Schwartz and Hartman (2007), video can equally be employed to support problem-based learning approaches to teacher education (Marsh & Mitchell, 2014).

Despite being convinced of the high potential of using videos in training, it is important to remember that whatever recording one is viewing only presents a limited part of the real situation which is determined by the part chosen, by the lighting, and by the fact that there is always a director of the production (Marsh, Mitchell, & Adamczyk, 2010; Mitchell et al., 2010). Thus, it is not the video per se, but the use that is made of it in the planning of training initiatives, in relation to the final objectives and the intended outcomes. Provide broad definitions and discussions of the topic and incorporate views of others (literature review) into the discussion to support, refute, or demonstrate your position on the topic.

PROFESSIONAL VISION: DEFINITIONS AND PROCESSES

In contemporary research, the idea of the teacher as a "reflective practitioner" promoted by Schon (1983) in relation to the concept of "action" has placed the attention on the importance of the "professional vision" as the key competence of the teacher.

The concept was first introduced by Goodwin (1994) who defines it as "socially organized ways of seeing and understanding events that are answerable to the distinctive interests of a particular social group" (p. 606). Today, it is considered a prerequisite for effective teaching practice (Grossman et al.,

2009; Sherin, 2001), and a competence objective in teacher education and training contexts (Berliner, 1986; Putnam & Borko, 2000; Sherin, 2004; Carbonneau & Hétu, 2006).

Pedagogical research has adapted Goodwin's concept applying it to the professional context of reference for the teaching corps: the teaching room (Lefstein & Snell, 2011). The professional vision is recognised as "competence" (Lefstein & Snell, 2011) or better still as the "ability to notice and interpret significant features of classroom or classroom events relevant for student learning" (Sherin, 2001; van Es & Sherin, 2002; Sherin, 2007). This ability enables teachers to perceive situations, answer students flexibly, understanding them and reasoning with them so as to provide efficient learning opportunities (Berliner, 1983), remodulate the action in terms of the objectives (Kersting, Givvin, Sotelo & Stigler, 2010; Roth, 2009).

The importance of the concept emerges as a result of the science and mathematics educational reforms which focused the attention of the teacher on the student's critical thinking and on the flexible adaptation of the lessons in answer to the ideas and the formulation of solutions to the problems (van Es e Sherin, 2008). The success of such pedagogical reforms was linked to the ability of the teachers to note and interpret what is happening around them in their classes and re-examine their own teaching methodology in a new way.

Over the years, research has demonstrated some systematic differences between "experienced" and "inexperienced" teachers by making reference, in point of fact, to the professional vision (Gruber, 2001; Putnam & Borko 2000; Shulman 1987). Indeed, the literature demonstrates that the teachers who observe their teaching practices are capable of activating contextualized Knowledge in relation to the class observed and can put better teaching practices in place (Borko et al., 2008; Goldman, 2007). More specifically, what emerges from these studies is that teachers with expertise are capable of noticing critical situations in a classroom and can draw on their conceptual knowledge to reason about these situations (Palmer et al., 2005). On the contrary, teachers without a strong expertise tend to describe situations in class in a limited manner and use rather naive terms (Carter et al., 1987). They are not able to identify the relevant events or explain or foresee their effects, whereas more expert teachers can (Seidel e Prenzel, 2007). It is presumed that the professional vision is an ability that can be promoted during the education and training of teachers with specific reference to initial training (Darling-Hammond, 2010; Kee, 2012; Zeichner, 2010).

The study of the professional vision of teachers poses some specific challenges (Sharin et al., 2008). The application of the professional vision comes about in a fleeting manner, and is distributed throughout different educational moments. Given the ongoing nature of education, one cannot expect to put teaching activities momentarily in 'pause mode' and ask a teacher to review what (s)he did and then continue without any interruptions. To tackle this problem, we based our research on videos as a tool to support professional vision. We asked teachers to retrospectively look at short video extracts we collected during their teaching or that of others.

Recent studies conducted by Roth (2009), and by Kersting, Givvin, Sotelo and Stigler (2010), have shown how this ability can be supported by means of the use of video. Video can improve teachers' situated awareness by placing the teacher in the condition in which (s)he can predict the impact(s) of a specific teaching strategy in relation to the objectives (Star & Strickland, 2008; van Es & Sherin, 2002). Teachers who have little or no experience with video analysis cannot critically evaluate the recordings which show specific class situations (Atkins, 1998; Friel & Carboni, 2000; Krajcik et al., 1996; Rosaen et al., 2002). On the other hand, teachers experienced in the analysis of the practices shown in the videos can benefit from the same in terms of practical teaching methods and the improvement of the same

(Schwindt, 2008; Seidel & Prenzel, 2007). Our research demonstrates that in-service teachers consider video analysis as a motivating and fascinating experience (Areglado, 1999; Roth, 2007)

Based on what teachers maintain, at least three great advantages from the use of video-analysis can be identified: authenticity, repetition and reflection mediated at a "distance".

With regard to the first point, authenticity, video can capture the complex school reality in an authentic and important way (Schwan & Riempp, 2004; Spiro, Collins & Ramchandran, 2007) highlighting the multiple actions which take place in the same place simultaneously. Observers can draw more/several connections with their own practices and achieve a deeper level of commitment and involvement (Goldman, 2007). From this perspective, observing videos provides "a vivid secondhand experience" because the viewers can immerge themselves individually in situations (Miller & Zhou, 2007). Video offers teachers the possibility to access the necessary information so as to envisage themselves "inside" the event. Goldman (2007) uses the term "immersion" to describe the effect that video has on a deep level of commitment and involvement on a theme, and expresses the ability of a teacher to make connections with the situation by creating a resonance effect, capturing the early stages of the "daily operations" involved in their profession (Kazemi, Franke & Lampert, 2009).

Secondly, videos provide a permanent recording which can be viewed many times, repeatedly. Thus, diversely to any "live" moment whatsoever in teaching which is finished from a temporal perspective, videos allow us to preserve the interaction and subject it to subsequent analysis and considerations. Moreover, observers can pause the video or re-view scenes over and over again to reflect on situations also from different perspectives.

Thirdly, video observers have the opportunity to examine situations at a certain "distance". There is no need to respond with the immediacy typically required during teaching. By observing the video, it is possible to analyse teaching in a systematic way, at a moment when it is distanced from the interaction situation with the environment and the learners (Sherin, 2004; Sherin & van Es, 2009). The complex classroom situations can be observed in micro-moments, from the more manageable dimensions (Le Fevre, 2004), thus, favoring a better harmonisation of the theories with educational practices (Orland-Barak e Yinon, 2007).

The professional vision demands, on the part of the teacher, a knowledge of teaching processes, and the ability to apply this knowledge in observed situations (Borko, 2004; Berliner, 1991; Sherin & van Es, 2009). These considerations have led to the conceptualization of the professional vision of teachers as the interaction of two giant macro-processes:

1. Noticing, and
2. Knowledge-based reasoning (Sherin & van Es, 2009; van Es & Sherin, 2008).

The ability to "notice" recalls the sub processes of selective attention in complex educational environments such as classes. It recalls the ability to identify the situations in class which, from a professional viewpoint, are decisive for an efficient teaching practice. Previously, researchers (Frederiksen, Sipusic, Sherin & Wolfe; 1998) had introduced the term "call out" to refer to those moments which teachers note as something important to investigate. Also Jacobs and Morita (2002) refer to a specific term i.e., "stopping point" to describe the moments in which teachers take a break and comment on the events which have taken place in class.

The opportunity to view the videos of the classroom situations is extremely important for the teachers because it provides the opportunity to clarify those aspects which during the action in the classroom had attracted their attention and which can be of specific importance for the learning of the student and improve the ways in which learners learn other subjects (Borko et al, 2008; Kersting, 2008; Kobarg, 2009; Krammer et al., 2006; Miller & Zhou, 2007; Santagata, 2009; Sherin & van Es, 2009; Star & Strickland, 2008). Research on "Teaching effectiveness" (Seidel et al., 2010; Seidel and Shavelson, 2007; Hattie, 2009) stresses the importance of:

1.   Goal clarity and coherence;
2.   Teacher support by means of elicitation, guidance, and feedback;
3.   A positive and supportive learning climate.

The ability to notice impacts therefore on o teaching methodology practices and on its efficacy, and can be considered a support to the functional teacher to review and align strategies and objectives and to improve the class climate (Star & Strickland 2008).

Once the events which took place in class have been "notified", teachers begin to reason on the bases of their conscience. The Knowledge-based reasoning is the ability to process and interpret the situations which have taken place on the basis of the knowledge one has on teaching and learning (Borko, 2004; Sherin, 2007; van Es & Sherin, 2002). In the modelling of the processes we can identify three different aspects (Seidel & Stürmer, 2013):

1.   Description,
2.   Explanation, and
3.   Forecast.

The description reflects the ability to identify and distinguish between events which are more or less relevant without the need to request further judgements. The explanation refers to ability to use what one knows to reason efficiently on a specific situation. This relies on the ability to connect class events to the collective consciousness and classify the situations on the basis of the dimensions of the teaching involved. The forecast refers to the ability to foresee the consequences of the events observed in terms of the impact on student learning. This is based on a broader knowledge of teaching and learning as in its application in teaching practices.

The two macro processes of noticing and knowledge-based reasoning should not be seen as isolated moments of a linear process. Rather, they are to be seen and presented through a "circular interplay". This type of interaction will very probably influence the way in which they look at the situations which take place in class and at the same time on the ability to reason about those events (Sherin & van Es, 2009).

VIDEO FOR THE DEVELOPMENT OF REFLECTIVE ACTIVITIES AND CRITICAL ANALYSES

Basically, three types of video are used in teacher training and professional development (Gaudi & Chali, 2015): videos of unknown teachers (Hatch & Grossman, 2009), videos of colleagues (Sherin e Han, 2004), and videos of one's own activities (Rosaen, Lundeberg, Cooper, Fritzen & Terpstra, 2008). In the present contribution we focus on the last of the list the objective of which is to develop in teachers the ability to analyse what happens in class and to reflect on their practices so as to improve their teaching activities.

Even if it does not become a systematic operation (Kleinknecht & Schneider, 2013) reviewing one's own actions with the support of video allows us to develop authentic immersion practices motivating honest and sincere forms of comparison (Borko et al., 2008; Rosaen et al., 2008; Seidel et al., 2011) but also forms of destructuring (Downey, 2008; Pastore & Hannafin, 2009), our own actions recognising ourselves from a professional viewpoint and learning how to identify elements in their teaching practices which can be improved (Borko et al., 2008). Such practices have demonstrated important reference points on the development of teacher professionalism both when they are used as individual confrontation as well as in the perspective of the video study group. These two approaches can be held complementary and reciprocally enriching starting with the individual self-confrontation which we can define as "like having a mirror placed in my face" (Zhang et al., 2011).

Learning to look at one's self as if one were an external observer allows one to implement, even in a classroom context one's own observation, analysis and interpretation abilities, in the same way as one's classroom intervention ability which is the result of a wider reflection (Coffey, 2014; Krammer et al., 2006; Sherin & van Es, 2009; Star & Stirkland, 2008).

By viewing the video supports it is actually possible to gather a series of dynamics which are sometimes lost during the normal course of one's own lessons (Borko et al., 2008, 2011; Coffey, 2014; Romano & Schwartz, 2005; Zhang et al., 2011). Indeed, research shows that the practices of video recording allow us to pay more attention to the "non-verbal behaviours" (Bergman, 2015), and to the "movements around the classroom", and the perception of the "curricular value" of lessons (Bruce & Chiu, 2015) the reasons can be the most varied; for example, sometimes the teacher concentrates attention observing students with most difficulties, at other times, from a more banal viewpoint, some students are outside the teacher's visual field (Snoeyink, 2010). This is in line with further studies which indicate in "live classroom observation" the way to reduce "reactivity" i.e., "observer effect" (Liang, 2015). Video recording is also indicated as a strategy of "Digital Memory work" (Strong-Wilson et al., 2014) making teachers agents of change through a "looking forward through looking back" process.

The objective of this type of video is to develop a descriptive and critical reflection as a means to reprocess and delineate the thinking processes which led to the realization of a specific teaching activity so as to: gain greater knowledge of the procedures enacted to accomplish a specific activity and which more generally speaking characterize one's profession (for this phase verbalization and writing are two important aspects).

It is possible to identify another functional aspect for the use of such a practice, that is it is to be found in the acquisition of new critical approaches which lead to a greater care in making judgements about the practices of others (Baecher & Kung, 2011). This process of identification of the reasons and the phases which led to the choices made in first person to support those processes of destructing of action which can then be attributed also outside and in the praxis of others.

Such practice is not without side-effects and sometimes seeing oneself can create situations of dissonance when the perception and the idea of one's own actions appear too far removed from what one observes with the video (Baecher e Kung, 2011; Harlin, 2014; Rosaen et al., 2008).

To contrast the tendency to phenomena of negationism (Eraut, 2000; Krone, Hamborg & Gediga, 2002; Borko et al., 2008; Sherin & Han, 2004), just as in the case of excessive self-criticism, sharing between peers can be useful as an important support mechanism. Colleagues can, in these cases, absolve the "double mirror" function (Downey, 2008; Snoeyink, 2010; Wu & Kao, 2008; van Es, 2012; Zhang et al., 2011) according to the most recent studies, video capture can permit the creation of a "collaborative space for teacher preparation", a space in which the traditional hierarchies and borders between actors and roles (student teacher, school mentor, and university tutor) and knowledge (academic, professional, and practical) are disrupted (Youens, Smethem, & Sullivan, 2014). In some ways, reciprocal vision places everyone in the same situation of reflective self-criticism and professional growth. In such cases, the community represents a reassuring and functional element (Borko et al., 2008; Coyle, 2004; Lasagabaster & Sierra, 2011; Sherin & Han, 2004).

Present your perspective on the issues, controversies, problems, etc., as they relate to theme and arguments supporting your position. Compare and contrast with what has been, or is currently being done as it relates to the chapter's specific topic and the main theme of the book.

THE FORMS OF VIDEO GROUP STUDY IN PROFESSIONAL VISION

The individual analysis of one's own practices using video implies, according to some scientific studies refer to the presence of several risks and negative effects. More specifically, an individual vision can limit and compromise constructive reflection on "critical incidents" recorded in the classroom.

Recent studies (Seidel, Stürmer, Blomberg & Schwindt, 2011; Gaudin & Chalies, 2015) show how the use of video is functional to the development of sub-processes, previously described; however, the immersion, resonance, authenticity and motivation elements which are central to this approach, can find huge obstacles in the "self-defense mechanisms" which impede a critical analysis and objective judgement of one's own teaching methodology approach (Seidel, Stürmer, Blomberg & Schwindt, 2011).

Indeed, it is hypothesized that the knowledge-based reasoning, sub-process of the professional vision, can be negatively influenced by the activation of "self-related knowledge" (Fiske, 1995), and consequently, by self-defense mechanisms which impede critical articulation and reflection (Eraut, 2000; Krone Hamborg & Gediga, 2002).

The case presented by (Seidel, Stürmer, Blomberg & Schwindt, 2011) found how teachers called upon to evaluate their own practice tend to comment in a less critical way indicating, where the critical aspects are encountered, consequences of minor impact or few changes to the teaching methodological aspects with respect to the to the teachers called to evaluate the performance of other colleagues.

So, we highlight the importance of a collaborative and comparative dimension which, supported by the shared norms for video analyses of practices and their discussion, can facilitate professional growth based on critical argumentation of one's practice and, consequently, improve teaching in the classroom. Research on "teacher professional development" (TPD) emphasises the role of participatory collaboration as an indispensable component which ought to be present in all training initiatives (initial, induction and in-service) (Butler et al., 2004; Cordingley et al., 2003; Desimone, 2009; Guskey, 2002). More specifically, the collaborative dimension and that of the co-evolution of teacher professionalism is at the attention of international programmes and is supported by international organisations such as the National Council for the Accreditation of Teacher Education (NCATE). Also the thematic networks such as the Teacher Induction Network (TIN) show much interest in the professional learning communities (PLC) such as spaces which help the training of teachers during one's school activities.

The evolution of the use of video in Teacher Education is characterised by the passage from the Behaviourist vision, represented for example by microteaching actions (Acheson and Zigler, 1971; Allen and Clark, 1967; Limbacher, 1971) to the Cognitivist one linked to movements such as the "Learning to notice framework" of Sherin and Russ (2004; 2014), and the "Framework of reflection-for-action" by

McFadden (McFadden et al., 2014) in which videos contribute to the collaborative dimension of teacher education programmes both online and F2F.

The use of video in a collaborative mode by teachers can be represented on a continuum in which, according to Borko, Koellner, Jacobs & Seago (2011), at the extremes, one finds, on the one hand, the approaches of the "highly adaptive" type (e.g., Video study group) and on the other, the "highly specified" approach types (e.g., Problem-Solving Cycle, LTG- Learning and Teaching Geometry). In the Literature, the "highly adaptive" are concerned with "goals and resources derived from the local context and facilitation based on general guidelines rather than specific activities and materials" (pp. 77), while in the "highly specified" ones, apart from a greater characterization of a disciplinary type, the "goals, resources and facilitation materials are specified for a particular predetermined professional experience" (pp.177).

Despite being aware of the importance and the functionality of different approaches in this contribution, we focus on the "highly adaptive" approach in which the attention is on the change in practices and on reflection which guides this change so as to improve both the professional vision and students' learning opportunity. In general, approaches of this type can be traced to the "Video Study Group" and to the forms of co-professional development in which teachers share videos of their own class and discuss aspects of their teaching practice which they consider to be of specific interest (Sherin & Han, 2004).

In the past few years, and in line with the reflection framework, numerous video study group programs such as "Problem-Solving Cycle" (Borko et al., 2008), "Video Based Quality Circle" (Gärtner, 2008), Lesson study (Maltinti, 2014), "Video Club" (Sherin & van Es, 2009) and, more recently, "Dialogic Video Cycle" (Seidel, Pehmer & Kiemer, 2014) can be identified; these share the idea that teachers and facilitators need to work together to plan lessons, identify some routines, and reflect on practices.

Based on the objectives which these experiences primarily focus on, the following three approaches can be identified:

1. Primary importance is given to the demonstration of teaching practices to support teacher interpretation and reflection (Teacher Video Club or Video Based Quality Circle), or those in which
2. Observation is closely focused on student learning and not on teacher performance (typically Lesson Study in which what changes is the lesson plan not the teacher praxis), or experiences in which
3. Facilitator guidance is essential for "noticing skills" and the improvement of teaching practices based on peer trust (Video Club and Dialogic).

For reasons of synthesis, we present a technique which represents the three macro approaches identified as being characteristic of the video group study. More specifically, we focus our attention on the reflection of practices accompanied by the figure of the facilitator according to three different perspectives: one is linked to the ability to guide analysis of class interaction; another is more oriented towards redefining lesson plans, and the last one is linked to the concept of "mindfulness-based moves".

Teacher Video Club

Quite similar to the teacher study group and focus group (Arbaugh, 2003; Van Es, 2012), as well as to the less recent teacher inquiry group (Hammerman, 1999), in the past few years the asynchronous video club (Sherin, 2004) has become important in the context of professional vision development.

These video clubs are also made up of groups of teachers. In this case, the groups meet to analyze short video clips from the classes of the participating teachers with specific attention to the analysis of student reasoning and learning. During the video club meetings teachers, guided by a facilitator, learn to develop the ability of "noticing" the interactions which take place in class (Santagata, Zannoni & Stigler, 2007; Star & Strickland, 2007; van Es & Sherin, 2008) and to observe "student thinking" (Webster-Wright, 2009; van Es & Sherin, 2010).

A typical setting related to this way of working among teachers envisages a facilitator who records class participation during the teacher's lesson and together with the teacher selects a short video clip to show during the group meeting. During the video club meeting, teachers view short video clips and discuss those issues or situations which they deem important or critical. While the majority of video club experience cases, it is a researcher or expert facilitator who acts as facilitator, there are also cases in which a single teacher fills this role for the group, or else a group of teachers take turns in leading.

The video clubs have been designed to involve teachers in collaborative reflection (Gwyn-Paquette, 2001) for a definition of teaching practice in a period of sharing and analysis which is much slower than the time of action which the class context demands. Moreover, video clubs promote a process of inquiry among teachers not only about the single video, but also as regards the practices of the video club itself and on themes to be addressed and on which to pose questions and learn (Tochon, 1999; Sipusic, 1994). The very concept of "critical colleagueship" is an integral part of the structure of these collaboration model (Wineburg & Grossman, 1998) not aimed at the evaluation of the practices but at improving the teaching, and there, the learning processes.

Studies in the field show that the architecture of the video club meeting which is characterised by a social and collaborative dimension supports the development of Selective Attention and Knowledge-Based Reasoning. In the last few years, research has led to the development of a framework to develop these collaborative models based on videos.

Framework for the Development of a Teacher Learning Community in a Video Club proposed by van Es (2012) presents the structure of a video club in terms of the working processes and models which enable the analysis of the recording(s) of teaching practices. However, there are some limitations that need to be pointed out so as to improve the structure and guarantee reliability. In particular, one needs to remember that the videos which are the subject of discussion are only a short extract of what happens in class (Miller & Zhou, 2007). This is an important aspect because otherwise the teachers that view the video-clips can jump too quickly to conclusions without valuing the fact that one is dealing with particular moments in teaching time (for this novice teachers are often accompanied with moments of "rehearsal" for qualitative analysis of their practice as showed in Lambert et al., 2013) and with one single indicator compared to the whole lot of the structures which make up the corpus to be analysed including also the task results and types of support and the help which teachers use in their own class(es) (Le Fevre, 2004).

This type of group reflection based on shared video is useful for the co-evolution of teachers for curriculum enactment (Kazemi & Hubbard, 2008). To date, the research carried out has specifically explored how teachers view the video-clips and the role of the participants (Sherin et al. 2009; van Es 2009) which influences group discussion. How the context of the teacher video clubs supports the development of teacher community has also been analysed, as well as the way in which this work form can help define video club objectives (van Es, 2007). A further research theme is the way in which the facilitator establishes rules or procedures of video analysis so as to improve the interpretation and the actions of the teacher and the thinking process of the student.

Lesson Study

At the centre of Lesson Study research interpreted as activities for Teacher Professional Development (TPD), and therefore as professionalising practices realized, constructed, discussed, in a collaborative manner, with groups of teachers, the objective is to improve the effective aspect of learning (Lewis & Perry, 2006).

Indeed, in Lesson Study, individuals work together to analyse in a specific manner lesson planning and presentation, also referred to as research lesson, and make an impact on professional practice so as to improve both individual and collective results (Calvani et al., 2013).

Researchers distinguish between four and eight phases associated with the Lesson Study programme. Catherine Lewis, the American researcher who, with Lynn Liptak, Tad Watanabe and Makoto Yoshida, is among the pioneers of Lesson Study who define its structure. The entire process has four key moments: i) definition of an objective which the teachers intend their learners to achieve; this initial phase also envisages the study of curriculum and the exploration of strategies and resources; ii) planning of the lesson which is written in detail; iii) leading a research lesson, which envisages observation by group members and external observers; iv) reflection (which may include reviewing the lesson in video or repeating the lesson), comparison and, to follow, publication of the results.

The teacher conducting the research lesson (which is open to many observers), announces, recites the written script in collaboration with other teachers. The observation focuses on student reactions and not on teacher performance, and the attention is on how students interact, learn and participate. Often the observation is supported by the "guides" that help teachers understand the students' behavior and answer questions on reasoning from them implemented. Among the most authoritative guides us recall the «Lesson Analysis Framework» (Santagata, 2010). Some of the guide questions to observation are:

The students have made progress towards the goal of learning? How do we know we have made progress? What data do we have? What data do we lack? How could you improve the lesson to make it more effective in terms of student learning?

After sharing in group, centered on the reactions of the students and not on the performance of the teacher, teachers decide whether it is appropriate to revise the video lesson or repeat it with the changes proposed by members. If the strategies proposed do not allow the expected results to be achieved, the lesson plan is then modified.

In the UK, there is a growing interest and, with government support, Lesson Study is used as a powerful form of professional development (Dudley, 2012). It has also been introduced into Indonesia and Malaysia, as in South America, South Africa, Australia, Canada, Hong Kong, Sweden, Thailand, and Vietnam. Korea and Singapore, as well as China, which like Japan, has a long tradition in improving teaching and learning through communities of practice in schools known as Teacher Research Groups, are no exception. In Japan, Lesson Study has played an important role in improving syllabuses, textbooks, teacher materials for student learning which are usually produced by the teachers themselves. Teachers improve through mutual reflections and the mutual learning of lessons (Saito & Atencio, 2013) giving rise to the building of community learning spaces (Wenger, 1998).

Through a continuous analysis of the relations created within the class and of the consequent learning, the teacher has the possibility to improve the structure of the lesson, indirectly intervening on teaching effectiveness in order to obtain a positive effect on student results.

Dialogic Video Cycle

More recently, "Dialogic Video Cycle" (DVC) model has emerged; this is based on the concept of "mindfulness" for teacher professional development, as well as on how to improve the process of critical dialogue among groups of trainee teachers. Research on "mindfulness in teacher education" shows that the mindfulness-based approaches can favour stress reduction (Jennings & Greenberg, 2009), well-being (Brown & Ryan, 2003), and so facilitate "positive changes" in class (Napoli, 2004).

If, on the one hand, the perspective of mindfulness in teacher training programmes has been strongly oriented down through the years to favour of an "introspective model" (e.g., meditation, yoga, body scans, etc.) capable of supporting the intra-individual learning processes and improve the student-teacher relationship in class (Napoli 2004; Roeser, Skinner, Beers & Jennings,2012), the Dialogic Video Cycle approach refers to an "extrospective model" of the mindfulness dimension in Professional Teaching Development (PTD) programmes in which the way to teach is shared through the discussion of the video-clips of teaching practice and directed thanks to discussions and reflections among peers.

The research by Seidel, Pehmer and Kiemer (2014) well describes this type of approach and allows the facilitator and his/her actions (i.e., "moves") to emerge because they are "mindful" in guiding teachers in the exchange of knowledge and reflection on practices used in class. In agreement with Borko, Koellner & Jacobs (2014), the "facilitation moves" can be interpreted as "each instructional action of a professional facilitator to clarify rules, introduce new knowledge about productive classroom dialogue, and structure the discussion among teachers to productively transfer knowledge and experiences with regard to classroom instruction and student thinking" (Borko, Koellner & Jacobs, 2014).

In a "Dialogic Video Cycle" the central dimension is that linked to the development and maintaining of a professional learning community in which teachers work together to improve how they activate dialogic processes in class.

Teachers are called on to identify a lesson they want to improve by including elements of productive dialogue in class, and by bringing specific lesson plans to the first class meeting. In a practical collaborative manner together with the facilitator (phase 1), these plans are readapted by inserting teaching strategies of a conversational type to use in class (e.g., through the inclusion of open-ended questions or a request for feedback, and a moment for sharing ideas). Next (phase 2), teachers bring these modified lesson plans into class, and are videoed while teaching and while doing their routines. Thereafter (phase 3), the facilitator selects some parts of the video recordings (using guiding criteria for a productive dialogic praxis in class), and prepares the basis for reflection with the teacher(s). Using a workshop-type model, teachers are asked to carefully watch the selected video-clips, and share their questions regarding the "productive class dialogue", and to reflect on their experiences (Gröschner, Seidel, Kiemer & Pehmer, 2014).

As emerges concisely here from the different phases, the focus of these PTD models is primarily on "describing" what is observed by the teaching community (Seidel et al., 2009). This practice of describing observations before offering an explanation about what has been observed and predicting how what has been observed in the video can influence student learning is extremely important in video-based research, as well as for the teacher's professional development. Significant discussions and reflections among teachers emerge by following this script.

By means of "facilitation moves", the facilitator guides exchanges between participants towards analysis and reflection, and, in line with a mindfulness-based approach, encourages them to actively take part in the discussion and to improve their awareness of teaching practices. There are nine facilitation moves in all, and these are divided into two macro types. The first four moves are support actions for individual review which the teacher undertakes in relation to his/her own classroom lessons by including productive dialogue elements. By so doing, routines and teaching approaches become visible, as do the ideas that teachers have in relation to "good" teaching" and "effective" interactional practice". Instead, facilitation moves five to nine are interventions based on video and script rules of observation related to how to comment these videos together with the teachers and provide peer feedback.

In accordance with other studies in this field (Borko, Koellner & Jacobs, 2014; van Es, 2012), there are some central "features" which provide feedback as to the actual role of the facilitator, and which can help to improve the process of the dialogic moments based on the video. These include: a trustful atmosphere in which issues and criticisms are raised and addressed; mature reflection by the teacher about one's own practices through the viewing of one's own outputs and openness to new perspectives; the acceptance of shared viewpoints; and the entering into discussions with others (Gröschner et al., 2014).

DISCUSSION AND FUTURE WORKS

The majority of the research examined in this narrative type review presents experiences of the development of the professional vision, a competence stimulated by the viewing and analysis of their teaching practices of both individual (Rosaen et al., 2008; Yerrick, Ross & Molebash, 2005) and groups of teachers through peer confrontations (Borko et al., 2008; Harford & MacRuairc, 2008).

The two macro processes of noticing and knowledge-based reasoning which characterise this competence are based on the observation of video recordings of classroom situations and on the ability to process and interpret the situations identified, and by distinguishing between more or less relevant events, reasoning in a more effective manner on the specific situation by connecting it to prior knowledge and experiences, anticipating the consequences of the events observed.

Much data allows us to state that the real success lies in the consequential union of individual and collaborative practices (Roche & Gal-Petitfaux, 2014; Zhang et al., 2011) in which awareness of one's own way of acting passes first through a subjective critical analysis and then through a reasoned discussion with peers which contributes to the overcoming of conditions of "self-related knowledge" of self-defense as regards one's own actions and which feeds that sense of trust which is at the basis of the teacher learning communities (Hatch & Grossman, 2009; Sherin, 2007; van Es, 2012) and teaching innovation.

In the future it will be interesting not only to focus on videos of one's own activities, but also on the videos of colleagues and unknown teachers, in order to understand how the comparison between practices can promote the real "lab change" in the teaching profession. This discussion and the development of different abilities underlying processes of problematization, negotiation, cross-fertilization and transformation can drive the development of "prescriptive and training paths" and improve teacher curriculum competencies able to support innovation at school.

REFERENCES

Anne, M. (2014). Using video to develop skills in reflection in teacher education students. *Australian Journal of Teacher Education, 39*(9), 6.

Areglado, N. (1999). I became convinced. *Journal of Staff Development, 20*(1), 35–37.

Atkins, S. (1998). Best practice: Preservice teachers' perceptions of videodisc vs. videotape of classroom practices in a methods course. *Journal of Technology and Teacher Education, 6,* 51–59.

Baecher, L., & Kung, S. C. (2011). Jumpstarting Novice Teachers' Ability to Analyze Classroom Video: Affordances of an Online Workshop. *Journal of Digital Learning in Teacher Education, 28*(1), 16–26. doi:10.1080/21532974.2011.10784676

Bergman, D. (2015). Comparing the Effects of Classroom Audio-Recording and Video-Recording on Preservice Teachers' Reflection of Practice. *Teacher Educator, 50*(2), 127–144. doi:10.1080/0887873 0.2015.1010054

Berliner, D. C. (1983). Developing conceptions of classroom environments: Some light on the T in classroom studies of ATI. *Educational Psychologist, 18*(1), 1–13. doi:10.1080/00461528309529256

Bliss, T., & Reynolds, A. (2004). Quality visions and focused imagination. In J. Brophy (Ed.), *Using video in teacher education* (pp. 29–52). Oxford, UK: Elsevier.

Borko, H. (2004). Professional development and teacher learning: Mapping the terrain. *Educational Researcher, 33*(8), 3–15. doi:10.3102/0013189X033008003

Borko, H., Jacobs, J. K., Eiteljorg, E., & Pittman, M. E. (2008). Video as a tool for fostering productive discussions in mathematics professional development. *Teaching and Teacher Education, 24*(2), 417–436. doi:10.1016/j.tate.2006.11.012

Borko, H., Koellner, K., & Jacobs, J. (2014). Examining novice teacher leaders' facilitation of mathematics professional development. *The Journal of Mathematical Behavior, 33,* 149–167. doi:10.1016/j.jmathb.2013.11.003

Borko, H., Koellner, K., Jacobs, J., & Seago, N. (2011). Using video representations of teaching in practice-based professional development programs. *ZDM, 43*(1), 175–187. doi:10.1007/s11858-010-0302-5

Brophy, J. (2004). *Using video in teacher education.* Amsterdam, Netherlands: Elsevier.

Brown, K. W., & Ryan, R. M. (2003). The benefits of being present: Mindfulness and its role in psychological well-being. *Journal of Personality and Social Psychology, 84*(4), 822–848. doi:10.1037/0022-3514.84.4.822 PMID:12703651

Bruce, D. L., & Chiu, M. M. (2015). Composing With New Technology Teacher Reflections on Learning Digital Video. *Journal of Teacher Education, 66*(3), 272–287. doi:10.1177/0022487115574291

Calvani, A., Biagioli, R., Maltinti, C., Menichetti, L., & Micheletta, S. (2013). Formarsi nei media: Nuovi scenari per la formazione dei maestri in una società digitale. *Formazione, Lavoro. Persona, 3*(8), 1–2.

Carbonneau, M., & Hétu, J. C. (2006). Formazione pratica degli insegnanti e nascita di un'intelligenza professionale. In M. Altet, E. Charlier, L. Paquay, & P. Perrenoud (Eds.), *Formare gli insegnanti professionisti. Quali strategie? Quali competenze? Armando editore* (pp. 77–95). Roma.

Carter, K., Sabers, D., Cushing, K., Pinnegar, P., & Berliner, D. C. (1987). Processing and using information about students: A study of expert, novice and postulant teachers. *Teaching and Teacher Education, 3*(2), 147–157. doi:10.1016/0742-051X(87)90015-1

Coyle, D. (2004). Redefining Classroom Boundaries: Learning to Teach Using New Technologies. *Canadian Journal of Educational Administration and Policy, 32.*

Darling-Hammond, L. (2010). Teacher education and the American future. *Journal of Teacher Education, 61*(1–2), 35–47. doi:10.1177/0022487109348024

Dobie, T. E., & Anderson, E. R. (2015). Interaction in teacher communities: Three forms teachers use to express contrasting ideas in video clubs. *Teaching and Teacher Education, 47*, 230–240. doi:10.1016/j.tate.2015.01.003

Egger, M., Juni, P., Bartlett, C., Holenstein, F., & Sterne, J. (2003). How important are comprehensive literature searches and the assessment of trial quality in systematic reviews? Empirical study. *Health technology assessment (Winchester, England), 7*(1), 1–82. PMID:12583822

Elliott, J. (2001). Making evidence-based practice educational. *British Educational Research Journal, 27*(5), 555–574. doi:10.1080/01411920120095735

Eraut, M. (2000). Non-formal learning and tacit knowledge in professional work. *The British Journal of Educational Psychology, 70*(1), 113–136. doi:10.1348/000709900158001 PMID:10765570

Estabrooks, C. A., Field, P. A., & Morse, J. M. (1994). Aggregating qualitative findings: An approach to theory development. *Qualitative Health Research, 4*(4), 503–511. doi:10.1177/104973239400400410

Friel, S., & Carboni, L. (2000). Using video-based pedagogy in an elementary mathematics methods course. *School Science and Mathematics, 100*(3), 118–127. doi:10.1111/j.1949-8594.2000.tb17247.x

Gaudin, C., & Chaliès, S. (2015). Video viewing in teacher education and professional development: A literature review. *Educational Research Review, 16*, 41–67. doi:10.1016/j.edurev.2015.06.001

Goldman, R., Pea, R., Barron, B., & Denny, S. J. (Eds.). (2007). *Video research in the learning sciences.* Mahwah, NJ: Lawrence Erlbaum.

Goodwin, C. (1994). Professional vision. *American Anthropologist, 96*(3), 606–633. doi:10.1525/aa.1994.96.3.02a00100

Gough, D. (2007). Weight of evidence: A framework for the appraisal of the quality and relevance of evidence. *Research Papers in Education, 22*(2), 213–228. doi:10.1080/02671520701296189

Gough, D., & Elbourne, D. (2002). Systematic research synthesis to inform policy, practice and democratic debate. *Social Policy and Society, 1*(3), 225–236. doi:10.1017/S147474640200307X

Gröschner, A., Seidel, T., Kiemer, K., & Pehmer, A. K. (2014). Through the lens of teacher professional development components: the 'Dialogic Video Cycle' as an innovative program to foster classroom dialogue. *Professional Development in Education.*

Grossman, P., Compton, C., Igra, D., Ronfeldt, M., Shahan, E., & Williamson, P. W. (2009). Teaching practice: A cross-professional perspective. *Teachers College Record, 111*(9), 2055–2100.

Gruber, H. (2001). Acquisition of expertise. In J. Smelser & P. B. Baltes (Eds.), *International encyclopedia of the social and behavioral sciences* (pp. 5145–5150). Amsterdam: Elsevier. doi:10.1016/B0-08-043076-7/02371-8

Harden, A., & Thomas, J. (2005). Methodological issues in combining diverse study types in systematic reviews. *International Journal of Social Research Methodology, 8*(3), 257–271. doi:10.1080/13645570500155078

Harford, J., & MacRuairc, G. (2008). Engaging student teachers in meaningful reflective practice. *Teaching and Teacher Education, 24*(7), 1884–1892. doi:10.1016/j.tate.2008.02.010

Harlin, E. M. (2014). Watching oneself teach–long-term effects of teachers' reflections on their video-recorded teaching. *Technology, Pedagogy and Education, 23*(4), 507–521. doi:10.1080/1475939X.2013.822413

Hatch, T., & Grossman, P. (2009). Learning to look beyond the boundaries of representation. *Journal of Teacher Education, 60*(1), 70–85. doi:10.1177/0022487108328533

Hattie, J. (2009). *Visible learning: A synthesis of over 800 meta-analyses relating to achievement.* New York: Routledge.

Hiebert, J., Gallimore, R., & Stigler, J. W. (2002). A knowledge base for the teaching profession: What would it look like and how can we get one? *Educational Researcher, 31*(5), 3–15. doi:10.3102/0013189X031005003

Jennings, P. A., & Greenberg, M. (2009). The prosocial classroom: Teacher social and emotional competence in relation to child and classroom outcomes. *Review of Educational Research, 79*(1), 491–525. doi:10.3102/0034654308325693

Kazemi, E., Franke, M., & Lampert, M. (2009). Developing pedagogies in teacher education to support novice teachers' ability to enact ambitious instruction. In *Crossing divides:Proceedings of the 32nd annual conference of the Mathematics Education Research Group of Australasia* (*Vol. 1*, pp. 12-30).

Kee, A. N. (2012). Feelings of preparedness among alternatively certified teachers: What is the role of program features? *Journal of Teacher Education, 63*(1), 23–38. doi:10.1177/0022487111421933

Kersting, N. (2008). Using video clips of mathematics classroom instruction as item prompts to measure teachers' knowledge of teaching mathematics. *Educational and Psychological Measurement, 68*(5), 845–861. doi:10.1177/0013164407313369

Kersting, N. B., Givvin, K. B., Sotclo, F. L., & Stigler, J. W. (2010). Teachers' analyses of classroom video predict student learning of mathematics: Further explorations of a novel measure of teacher knowledge. *Journal of Teacher Education, 61*(1-2), 172–181. doi:10.1177/0022487109347875

Kleinknecht, M., & Schneider, J. (2013). What do teachers think and feel when analyzing videos of themselves and other teachers teaching? *Teaching and Teacher Education, 33*, 13–23. doi:10.1016/j.tate.2013.02.002

Kobarg, M., Seidel, T., Prenzel, M., McCrae, B., & Walker, M. (2009, September). Patterns of science teaching and learning in an international comparison. In *PISA Research Conference*, Kiel (pp. 14–16).

Koellner, K., Jacobs, J., Borko, H., Schneider, C., Pittman, M. E., Eiteljorg, E., & Frykholm, J. (2007). The Problem-Solving Cycle: A model to support the development of teachers' professional knowledge. *Mathematical Thinking and Learning, 9*(3), 273–303. doi:10.1080/10986060701360944

Krajcik, J., Soloway, E., Blumenfeld, P., Marx, R. W., Ladewski, B. L., & Bos, N. D. et al.. (1996). The casebook of project practices: An example of an interactive multimedia system for professional development. *Journal of Computers in Mathematics and Science Teaching, 15*, 119–135.

Krammer, K., Ratzka, N., Klieme, E., Lipowsky, F., Pauli, C., & Reusser, K. (2006). Learning with classroom videos: Conception and first results of an online teacher-training program. *Zeitschrift für Didaktik der Mathematik, 38*(5), 422–432. doi:10.1007/BF02652803

Krone, A., Hamborg, K. C., & Gediga, G. (2002). About error-related emotional reactions in human-computer interaction. *Zeitschrift für Arbeits- und Organisationspsychologie, 46*(4), 185–200. doi:10.1026//0932-4089.46.4.185

Lampert, M. (2010). Learning Teaching in, from, and for Practice: What Do We Mean? *Journal of Teacher Education, 61*(1-2), 21–34. doi:10.1177/0022487109347321

Lampert, M., Franke, M. L., Kazemi, E., Ghousseini, H., Turrou, A. C., Beasley, H., & Crowe, K. (2013). Keeping It Complex: Using Rehearsals to Support Novice Teacher Learning of Ambitious Teaching. *Journal of Teacher Education, 64*(3), 226–243. doi:10.1177/0022487112473837

Lasagabaster, D., & Sierra, J. M. (2011). Classroom observation: Desirable conditions established by teachers. *European Journal of Teacher Education, 34*(4), 449–463. doi:10.1080/02619768.2011.587113

Le Fevre, D. M. (2004). Designing for teacher learning: video-based curriculum design. In J. Brophy (Ed.), *Using video in teacher education. Advances in research on teaching* (Vol. 10, pp. 235–258). Amsterdam: Elsevier. doi:10.1016/S1479-3687(03)10009-0

Lefstein, A., & Snell, J. (in press). Classroom discourse: the promise and complexity of dialogic practice. In S. Ellis, E. McCartney, & J. Bourne (Eds.), *Insight and impact: Applied linguistics and the primary school*. Cambridge: Cambridge University Press. doi:10.1017/CBO9780511921605.018

Liang, J. (2015). Live video classroom observation: an effective approach to reducing reactivity in collecting observational information for teacher professional development. *Journal of Education for Teaching*.

Maltinti, C. (2014). Il Lesson Study giapponese: un efficace modello cross-cultural. *Form@ re-Open Journal per la formazione in rete, 14*(2), 87–97.

Marsh, B., & Mitchell, N. (2014). The role of video in teacher professional development. *Teacher Development, 18*(3), 403–417. doi:10.1080/13664530.2014.938106

Marsh, B., Mitchell, N., & Adamczyk, P. (2010). Interactive video technology: Enhancing professional learning in initial teacher education. *Computers & Education*, *54*(3), 742–748. doi:10.1016/j.compedu.2009.09.011

Miller, K., & Zhou, X. (2007). Learning from classroom video: what makes it compelling and what makes it hard. In R. Goldmann, R. Pea, B. Barron, & S. J. Derry (Eds.), *Video research in the learning sciences* (pp. 321–334). Mahwah, NJ: Lawrence Erlbaum.

Mitchell, N., Marsh, B., Hobson, A. J., & Sorensen, P. (2010). 'Bringing theory to life': Findings from an evaluation of the use of interactive video within an initial teacher preparation programme. *Teacher Development*, *14*(1), 15–27. doi:10.1080/13664531003696543

Montù, V. (2015). La costruzione di una systematic review sulla ricerca con i bambini. *Formazione & Insegnamento. Rivista internazionale di Scienze dell'educazione e della formazione*, *9*(1), 211–218.

Napoli, M. (2004). Mindfulness training for teachers: A pilot program. *Complementary Health Practice Review*, *9*(1), 31–42.

Orland-Barak, L., & Yinon, H. (2007). When theory meets practice: What student teachers learn from guided reflection on their own classroom discourse. *Teaching and Teacher Education*, *23*(6), 957–969. doi:10.1016/j.tate.2006.06.005

Palmer, D. J., Stough, L. M., Burdenski, T. K. Jr, & Gonzales, M. (2005). Identifying teacher expertise: An examination of researchers' decision making. *Educational Psychologist*, *40*(1), 13–25. doi:10.1207/s15326985ep4001_2

Putnam, R. T., & Borko, H. (2000). What do new views of knowledge and thinking have to say about research on teacher learning? *Educational Researcher*, *29*(1), 4–15. doi:10.3102/0013189X029001004

Roche, L., & Gal-Petitfaux, N. (2014, March). Design of an audiovisual device for preservice teachers' training. In *Society for Information Technology & Teacher Education International Conference* (Vol. 2014, No. 1, pp. 1313–1316).

Roeser, R. W., Skinner, E., Beers, J., & Jennings, P. A. (2012). Mindfulness training and teachers' professional development: An emerging area of research and practice. *Child Development Perspectives*, *6*(2), 167–173. doi:10.1111/j.1750-8606.2012.00238.x

Romano, M., & Schwartz, J. (2005). Exploring technology as a tool for eliciting and encouraging beginning teacher reflection. *Contemporary Issues in Technology & Teacher Education*, *5*(2), 149–168.

Rosaen, C., Schram, P., & Herbel-Eisenmann, B. (2002). Using hypermedia technology to explore connections among mathematics, language, and literacy in teacher education. *Contemporary Issues in Technology & Teacher Education*, *2*, 2–31.

Rosaen, C. L., Lundeberg, M., Cooper, M., Fritzen, A., & Terpstra, M. (2008). Noticing How Does Investigation of Video Records Change How Teachers Reflect on Their Experiences? *Journal of Teacher Education*, *59*(4), 347–360. doi:10.1177/0022487108322128

Roth, K. J. (2009). Using video studies to transform science teaching and learning: results from the STeLLA professional development program. In T. Janik & T. Seidel (Eds.), *The power of video studies in investigating teaching and learning in the classroom* (pp. 243–258). Münster: Waxmann.

Roth, W. M. (2007). Epistemic mediation: Video data as filters for the objectification of teaching by teachers. In R. Goldman, R. Pea, B. Barron, & S. J. Derry (Eds.), *Video research in the learning sciences* (pp. 367–382). Mahwah, NJ: Lawrence Erlbaum Ass.

Santagata, R. (2009). Designing video-based professional development for mathematics teachers in low-performing schools. *Journal of Teacher Education*, *60*(1), 38–51. doi:10.1177/0022487108328485

Santagata, R. (2010), From Teacher Noticing to a Framework for Analyzing and Improving Classroom Lessons. In M. Sherin, R. Phillip e V. Jacobs (Eds.), Mathematics teacher noticing: Seeing through teachers' eyes (152-168). New York: Routledge.

Santagata, R., & Guarino, J. (2011), Using video to teach future teachers to learn from teaching, in ZDM the International Journal of Mathematics Education, 43(1), 133–145. doi:10.1007/s11858-010-0292-3

Santagata, R., Zannoni, C., & Stigler, J. (2007). The role of lesson analysis in pre-service teacher education: An empirical investigation of teacher learning from a virtual video-based field experience. *Journal of Mathematics Teacher Education*, *10*(2), 123–140. doi:10.1007/s10857-007-9029-9

Schon, D. A. (1983). *How professionals think in action. The Reflective Practitioner*. New York: Basic Books.

Schwan, S., & Riempp, R. (2004). The cognitive benefits of interactive videos: Learning to tie nautical knots. *Learning and Instruction*, *14*(3), 293–305. doi:10.1016/j.learninstruc.2004.06.005

Schwindt, K. (2008). *Teachers observe instruction: Criteria for competent perception of instruction*. Münster, Germany: Waxmann.

Seidel, T., Pehmer, A. K., & Kiemer, K. (2014). Facilitating collaborative teacher learning: The role of "mindfulness" in video-based teacher professional development programs. *Gruppendynamik und Organisationsberatung*, *45*(3), 273–290. doi:10.1007/s11612-014-0248-0

Seidel, T., & Prenzel, M. (2007). How teachers perceive lessons- Assessing educational competencies by means of videos. *Zeitschrift fur Erziehungswissenschaft*, *10*, 201–216.

Seidel, T., & Shavelson, R. J. (2007). Teaching effectiveness research in the past decade: The role of theory and research design in disentangling meta-analysis results. *Review of Educational Research*, *77*(4), 454–499. doi:10.3102/0034654307310317

Seidel, T., & Stürmer, K. (2014). Modeling and Measuring the Structure of Professional Vision in Preservice Teachers. *American Educational Research Journal*, *51*(4), 739–771. doi:10.3102/0002831214531321

Seidel, T., Stürmer, K., & Blomberg, G. (2010). *Observer: video-based tool to diagnose teachers' professional vision*. Munich: Technische Universität München.

Seidel, T., Stürmer, K., Blomberg, G., Kobarg, M., & Schwindt, K. (2011). Teacher learning from analysis of videotaped classroom situations: Does it make a difference whether teachers observe their own teaching or that of others? *Teaching and Teacher Education, 27*(2), 259–267. doi:10.1016/j.tate.2010.08.009

Seidel, T., Stürmer, K., Blomberg, G., Kobarg, M., & Schwindt, K. (2011). Teacher learning from analysis of videotaped classroom situations: Does it make a difference whether teachers observe their own teaching or that of others? *Teaching and Teacher Education, 27*(2), 259–267. doi:10.1016/j.tate.2010.08.009

Seidel, T., Stürmer, K., Blomberg, G., Kobarg, M., & Schwindt, K. (2011). Teacher learning from analysis of videotaped classroom situations: Does it make a difference whether teachers observe their own teaching or that of others? *Teaching and Teacher Education, 27*(2), 259–267. doi:10.1016/j.tate.2010.08.009

Sherin, M. G. (2001). Developing a professional vision of classroom events. In T. Wood, B. Scott Nelson, & J. Warfield (Eds.), Beyond classical pedagogy: Teaching elementary school mathematics (pp. 75–93). Hillsdale, NJ: Erlbaum

Sherin, M. G. (2007). The development of teachers' professional vision in video clubs. In R. Goldman, R. Pea, B. Barron, & S. Derry (Eds.), *Video research in the learning sciences* (pp. 383–395). Hillsdale, NJ: Erlbaum.

Sherin, M. G., & Han, S. Y. (2004). Teacher learning in the context of a video club. *Teaching and Teacher Education, 20*(2), 163–183. doi:10.1016/j.tate.2003.08.001

Sherin, M. G., Linsenmeier, K. A., & van Es, E. A. (2009). Issues in the design of video clubs: Selecting video clips for teacher learning. *Journal of Teacher Education, 60*(3), 213–230. doi:10.1177/0022487109336967

Sherin, M. G., Russ, R. S., Sherin, B. L., & Colestock, A. (2008). Professional Vision in Action: An Exploratory Study. *Issues in Teacher Education, 17*(2), 27–46.

Sherin, M. G., & van Es, E. A. (2008). Effects of video club participation on teachers' professional vision. *Journal of Teacher Education, 60*(1), 20–37. doi:10.1177/0022487108328155

Shulman, L. S. (1987). Knowledge and teaching: Foundations of the new reform. *Harvard Educational Review, 57*(1), 1–22. doi:10.17763/haer.57.1.j463w79r56455411

Snoeyink, R. (2010). Using video self-analysis to improve the "withitness" of student teachers. *Journal of Computing in Teacher Education, 26*(3), 101–110.

Spiro, R. J., Collins, B. P., & Ramchandran, A. (2007). Reflections on a post-Gutenberg epistemology of video use in ill-structured domains: fostering complex learning and cognitive flexibility. In R. Goldman, R. Pea, B. Barron, & S. J. Derry (Eds.), *Video research in the learning sciences* (pp. 93–100). Mahwah, NJ: Lawrence Erlbaum.

Star, J. R., & Strickland, S. K. (2008). Learning to observe: Using video to improve preservice mathematics teachers' ability to notice. *Journal of Mathematics Teacher Education, 11*(2), 107–125. doi:10.1007/s10857-007-9063-7

Strong-Wilson, T., Mitchell, C., Morrison, C., Radford, L., & Pithouse-Morgan, K. (2014). Looking Forward Through Looking Back: Using Digital Memory-work in Teaching for Transformation. In *Becoming teacher: Sites for teacher development in Canadian Teacher Education*, 442.

Stürmer, K., Seidel, T., & Schäfer, S. (2013). Changes in professional vision in the context of practice. *Gruppendynamik und Organisationsberatung*, *44*(3), 339–355. doi:10.1007/s11612-013-0216-0

Tripp, T., & Rich, P. (2012). Using video to analyze one's own teaching. *British Journal of Educational Technology*, *43*(4), 678–704. doi:10.1111/j.1467-8535.2011.01234.x

van Es, E. A. (2009). Participants' Roles in the Context of a Video Club. *Journal of the Learning Sciences*, *18*(1), 100–137. doi:10.1080/10508400802581668

van Es, E. A. (2012). Examining the development of a teacher learning community: The case of a video club. *Teaching and Teacher Education*, *28*(2), 182–192. doi:10.1016/j.tate.2011.09.005

Wu, C. C., & Kao, H. C. (2008). Streaming videos in peer assessment to support training pre-service teachers. *Journal of Educational Technology & Society*, *11*(1), 45–55.

Yerrick, R., Ross, D., & Molebash, P. (2005). Too close for comfort: Real-time science teaching reflections via digital video editing. *Journal of Science Teacher Education*, *16*(4), 351–375. doi:10.1007/s10972-005-1105-3

Youens, B., Smethem, L., & Sullivan, S. (2014). Promoting collaborative practice and reciprocity in initial teacher education: Realising a 'dialogic space' through video capture analysis. *Journal of Education for Teaching*, *40*(2), 101–113. doi:10.1080/02607476.2013.871163

Zeichner, K. (2010). Rethinking the connections between campus courses and field experiences in college and university-based teacher education. *Journal of Teacher Education*, *61*(1), 89–99. doi:10.1177/0022487109347671

Zhang, M., Lundeberg, M., Koehler, M. J., & Eberhardt, J. (2011). Understanding affordances and challenges of three types of video for teacher professional development. *Teaching and Teacher Education*, *27*(2), 454–462. doi:10.1016/j.tate.2010.09.015

KEY TERMS AND DEFINITIONS

Dialogic Video Cycle: A specific kind of video group study where the central point is the development and preservation of a professional learning community where teachers work together in order to improve their way to start dialogic processes in their class.

Knowledge Based Reasoning: Ability to process and understand the occurring situations on the base of the knowledge about teaching and learning.

Lesson Study: A specific kind of video group study where research lesson is focused on student reactions rather than on teacher performance.

Narrative Review: Emergent method of reviewing where various analysis phases emerge during the process, in a constant relationship with the analyzed literature.

Noticing: Ability that recalls the sub-processes of selective attention in a complex environment as a classroom.

Professional Vision: Ability to notice and interpret significant features of classroom events relevant for student learning.

Self-Defense Mechanisms: Individual strategies that undermine critical articulation and reflection.

Teacher Video Club: A specific kind of video group study where teacher groups meet together to analyze short video fragments recorded in classrooms with a particular interest towards student thinking and learning.

Video Group Study: Forms of *co-professional development* where teachers share videos of their classes and discuss relevant aspects of their teaching activity.

Chapter 2

The Use of Videos in the Triangulation Process among Professors, School Teachers, and Students:
Promoting Permeability between Pre-Service and In-Service Training

Pier Giuseppe Rossi
University of Macerata, Italy

Laura Fedeli
University of Macerata, Italy

ABSTRACT

Awareness of the centrality of education and training in a knowledge society, the need for Lifelong Learning, and, connected to these, the search for recursive processes between theory and practice, require educators to look for training models suitable for emerging professionals and their development. Specifically, training models appear to be necessary; models that can activate a holistic approach, starting from initial training. Those models should be present in the different training steps (training for pre-service, newly hired and in-service teachers) and could build bridges among the different training steps so that the approach to knowledge and the development of professionality can become a habitus and a deeply-rooted personal drive. Learning paths in which videos are used can ensure those goals. The chapter describes a university training path for pre-service primary teachers in which class video recordings are used as binding objects whose discussion involves students, university professors and school teachers. Such process proposes Lifelong Learning also as interaction among different training levels.

DOI: 10.4018/978-1-5225-0711-6.ch002

Copyright © 2017, IGI Global. Copying or distributing in print or electronic forms without written permission of IGI Global is prohibited.

INTRODUCTION

Research on the use of videos in professional training has had a strong impact over the last two decades. The aspects being highlighted in those studies are: to introduce a professional vision (Sherin & van Es, 2009), to map teacher activity (van Es & Sherin, 2002), to avoid practice shock (Stokking, Leenders, de Jong, & van Tartwijk, 2003), to improve the quality of teaching (Blomberg, Sherin, Renkl, Glogger, & Seidel, 2014). These goals can have an impact both on pre-service training, and on in-service training and can foster in both cases a reflection on the practices that help acquiring a conscious professionalism.

However, most of those approaches don't highlight one aspect that we consider relevant in the current context, this is connected to the evolution of the concept of professionalism and to the centrality of training in the knowledge society also to the role of Lifelong Learning in the development of professional and personal identity.

Lifelong Learning is widely used today, but it's not always clear that such an approach also requires the overcoming of the division still present, mostly in Italy, among pre and in service training and research requires the creation of procedures for mixing the steps as well. In fact, there are some *dispositifs[1]* that, often indirectly, can foster a different interaction between the training steps. Alternation (Vanhule, Merhan, & Ronveaux, 2007), both as theoretical concept in recursivity theory-practice, and as a *dispositif* for school-work in pre- and in-service training is one of the example of this process.

The proposal described in the present contribution identifies as central:

1. The presence of *dispositifs* that can foster permeability among pre-service, in service training, and research,
2. The presence of processes of mediation among different paths and roles,
3. The presence of boundary objects, that is, artifacts which act as a bridge connecting the two training paths (pre- and in- service), for example the videos of didactical activities to be used during in pre-service, in-service training and in research,
4. The presence of triangulation among students, expert school teachers and university professors.

We need to define the three profiles. Students here are meant as those who enrolled on a degree course to become primary school teachers. In Italy such a learning path lasts 5 years and can be accessed after secondary school. Students are normally 19 years old when they enroll in the university, even though you can find older students who wish to restart studying after an interruption due to work or graduates who wish to get an additional degree. Expert school teachers are here meant as primary school teachers with at least 5 years of work experience and available to participate in an academic experience to reflect on his/her professionalism, valorize it and offer their expertise to young students. Professors are here meant as university professors who are in charge of both the pre- and in- service teacher training. In such a last case, in relation to the situations described in the following paragraphs, the approach of the professor is the one of the Collaborative Research[2] (Desgagné, 1998; Desgagné & Larouche, 2010, Vinatier, 2011b), that is, the professor develops his/her work along with a school teacher making him/her express his/her practices and fostering reflection on them.

From the perspective of a strong division between pre-service training and in-service training, the educational relation requires a two-tier relationship in pre-service training between the student and the professor and a different two-tier relation in in-service training, the one between the professor and the school teacher as a professional. If we want to overcome the strong division between the two educational steps we need to plan the use of *dispositifs* in which the synchronous presence of the three actors (student, professor, school teacher), in some of the phases of the training path, makes possible the activation of processes of mediation among competences and different perspectives.

The presence of three profiles creates an interaction between possible worlds and the current world, between daily practices and the need to adjust them to the needs of the new generations and of continuous innovation; even because the need for Lifelong training generates from the obsolescence of the knowledge and from the necessity to activate research processes. Videos become, in this process, boundary objects, that is, objects that are able to open the dialogue between the current practices and a reflection on them, between immersion in action and reflective distancing.

If the role of the school teacher is to propose the experience and problems of daily routines, the role of the student is to propose a different perspective, naive and ambitious at the same time. The professor is in charge of mediation between what is potential and what is sustainable. Even if he/she knows both the needs and the most up-to-date experiences, and the difficulties of the context, his/her role cannot express itself in making synthesis, that is, to identify solutions and apply them to the two contexts. This is related to the enactive rationale of the learning process, that is, the uselessness of instructivist paths. The new practices arise from the old ones and from a systematization and reorganization of the previous experiences and concepts, this process can be carried out only by those who are in a learning process and only if they start from real problems with an inter-spatial perspective. The professor's task is to act as a mediator between the past and the present, between the possible and the sustainable.

The proposed *dispositif* here consists in the analysis of *video-verité* (Carbonneau & Hétu, 2006) in which the class activity run by the expert school teacher is shown to students in a context of pre-service training at university. The professor and the students analyze, along with the expert school teacher the video and ask her/him to make explicit the choices made in class. As will be reported, the students' questions are different from the professor's ones. Their perspectives are different as, is their knowledge background. But those "provocations", that can activate interesting discussions, are allowed by the divergence caused by the lack of knowledge about the context and about the concepts. This happens because students are not expert yet, like the school teacher is, but they have a tacit knowledge of the teaching/learning processes, since they have experienced them as students for more than 15 years.

The analysis of the video is the space-time of the crossing of different perspectives. At the same time the video ties the perspective to the activities, but guaranteeing that distancing which is at the heart of a process of future projection. In the analysis of videos, thanks to the three perspectives (professor, school teacher, student), we try to understand how the school teacher made her/his choice and managed this process, rather than trying to highlight good practices. But, we also have the visible emotional involvement of the school teacher with her/his difficulties and strokes of genius, the teacher as *bricoleur* (Paquay, Altet, Charlier, & Perrenoud, 1996).

The relationship involves three profiles, this is different from both the dual relation typical of pre-service training (student-professor) and of in-service training (professor-school teacher). In the first case (student-professor) the professor proposes his/her knowledge, already mediated and generalized and meant as an absolute reference - but often also lacking of "life" for the student who has no tools to put that knowledge under discussion. In the second case (professor-school teacher) the discussion focusses on contingent issues with the difficulty of seeing them from a broader perspective.

BACKGROUND

Video recording and the techniques of video analysis of teaching/learning situations can draw on a wide reference literature on pre-service training and professional school teacher in-service training. The works by Fenstermacher (1990) and Shulman (2004) highlight the relationship between the two levels of training and the teacher's thinking.

Recently there have been new interests in this direction (Seidel, Stürmer, Blomberg, Kobarg, & Schwindt, 2011; Shanahan & Tochelli, 2014; Sherin, Jacobs, & Philipp, 2011; West, 2012; van Es & Sherin, 2002; Santagata & Stürmer, 2014) and not just in the field of teacher training[3].

As indicated by the previous references such a stimulus is connected with studies on professionalism and the attention to professional identity and its development. Thinking about professionalism as a trajectory requires paths of principle of alternation (alternation of education and work) (Schuetze & Sweet, 2003; Vanhulle, 2007) that is, the alternation can be seen as both a concept, (the alternation between theory and praxis), and as a *dispositif* (the alternation between immersion in action and reflective distancing). In both cases it requires that the involved actors have a posture that lets them observe and store the practices and retain the general overview from the details, and that can also activate constructive processes, that is, the activity aimed at improving the competences in the action, typical of the teacher, and productive processes, that is, the activities aimed at improving oneself as a professional, taking care of one's own awareness activating proper training choices (Altet, 2012) that are able to create a recursive and generative relation between theory and practice.

Professionalism cannot be acquired neither just with theoretical classes, nor with mere immersion in action. Vicariant paths of practices such as the simulations and the analysis of videos of professional actions are, thus, necessary along with paths in which the subject in training is guided in action.

The analysis of video can have several goals. Investigations into the use of video recordings and video analysis in pre-service primary teacher training address both the different skills tied to the approach of a specific discipline, such as for example math, science, foreign languages (Abell & Cennamo, 2004; Haynes & Judith, 2015; Llinares & Valls, 2009) and classroom management skills (McCormack, 2001) which contribute to reaching a holistic approach (Masats & Dooly, 2011).

Acquiring a holistic approach is of paramount importance since, as explained in the introduction, being a primary school teacher today means be able to manage the complexity of the current cultural and social reality in order to be able to offer students all the knowledge and expertise needed to successfully become citizens in their local context and in the global one as well.

To be able to reach a holistic approach the student-teacher needs to develop a "professional vision". As stated by Rhine and Bryant (2007) the aim of training courses should "strive for pre-service and in-service teachers to see beyond the day-to-day requirements of teaching and to develop an ability to think intuitively, critically, and reflectively about the social, emotional, and intellectual elements of schools and classrooms." (p. 345).

In such a direction the use of class videos in teacher training can have the following goals:

- To immerse the novice in the complexity of professional practices and avoid what in literature is called "practice shock" (Stokking, Leenders, de Jong, & van Tartwijk, 2003);
- To inform and train the novice on school routines, proposing also innovative procedures;
- To activate processes of analysis that are able to give meaning to the observed practices, creating recursive processes between theory and practice;

- To activate reflective processes in which the professional rethinks his/her own practice with a detached view and starts a revision of his/her professional identity.

The studies by Santagata and Stürmer (2014) are not dissimilar, they recall Blomberg, Sherin, Renkl, Glogger and Seidel (2014), and propose the following goals in the use of videos:

1. The description of teaching practices,
2. The development of interpretation and reflection competences able to make teachers attribute meanings to didactical practices, and
3. Guiding and mentoring to facilitate change and improvement of didactical practices.

Many of the previous mentioned studies agree in stating that at the centre of the use of videos in the pre-service teacher training is the goal related to the acquisition of a "professional vision" that, according to the conceptualization by Sherin and van Es (2009), implies not only the skill to identify, through the video, relevant events, but to be also able to "describe" and "explain" the didactical action and "suppose" the effects of the action itself on the student learning; to summarize, the skill to acquire the competence to understand the decision processes made by the teacher, his/her motivations and the effects on his/her action. The concept of "professional vision", recurrent in the literature, is meant by Goodwin (1994) as a key process of professional expertise in which a socially situated body of practices is the means through which "the objects of knowledge which animate the discourse of a profession are constructed and shaped." (Goodwin, 1994, 605). "Seeing" or "noticing" (van Es & Sherin, 2008) as a training practice, thus, should include an interactive flow of viewpoints by different involved actors. Goodwin explains that "the ability to see relevant entities is not lodged in the individual mind, but instead within a community of competent practitioners (626)".

Acquiring a professional vision seems to synthetize competences within the key concepts expressed by the phrases "teacher quality" and "teaching quality" that Riley (2009) describes as:

Teacher quality — what teachers do — refers to the ability of teachers to develop strong skills in pedagogy and theory in order to devise and implement a broad range of instructional strategies. A deep knowledge of content, teaching methods and curriculum standards are critical components... Teaching quality— what children learn — focuses on the instructional strategies teachers use on a daily basis to improve student achievement in the classroom. Other evidence of teaching quality involves implementing current, significant curriculum changes — i.e., 21st-century skills — and creating classroom opportunities for all children based on their existing skill levels (p. 7).

Van Es and Sherin highlighted, already in 2002, that:

Current programs of teacher education often do not focus on helping teachers to interpret classroom interactions. They focus on helping teachers learn to act, often providing them with instruction concerning new pedagogical techniques and new activities that they can use (Berliner, 2000; Day, 1999; Huling, Resta, & Rainwater, 2001; Niess, 2001; Putnam & Borko, 2000; Taylor, 2000): Although these techniques and activities are certainly important resources for new teachers, they do not necessarily ensure that teachers will learn to interpret classroom interactions in ways that allow for flexibility in their approach to teaching (2002, p. 572).

The previous citations highlight how necessary it is to put the concept of professionalism in the centre of a holistic vision of the teacher with his/her professional knowledge, beliefs, motivations and self-regulation skills (Seidel, 2013) and it's possible to perceive two directions (not conflicting and equally valid) in the analysis's methodology, the first one mostly present in Anglophone studies, the second in the Francophone ones, even if, as will be shown, it is the starting points that seem different rather than the general characteristics of the paths.

In the Anglophone studies the starting point seems to be practice and, specifically, single specific didactical situations from which the analysis starts to, in a later step, analyze professionalism in its comprehensiveness. In the Francophone studies, instead, researchers seem to start from *habitus* and identity to, in a later step, also analyze specific situations and didactical *dispositifs*. The attention on the processes of *co-explicitation* (professor-teacher) seems to be more directed to decisional processes and analysis of the event created by the teacher (Vinatier, 2011a).

The attention of the Anglophone researchers in their studies seems to be mostly focussed on the connection between teacher professionalism and quality of teaching. The difference between the two approaches could come from the history of the two scientific communities and the origins of the research on practices: the Francophone research mostly derives from ergonomic studies which originated from professional didactics (Lussi Borer, Durand & Yvon, 2015). In the Anglophone field, instead the research was originally based on studies about limitations and problems in teacher training and the quality of learning (Santagata & Stürmer, 2014; Seidel, et al., 2011; Sherin & van Es, 2009).

The difference seems to be in the double function within pre-service training: to promote professionalism and to promote professional practices. The two functions are interwoven and it becomes central to understand how to organize and connect them, knowing that training can never be exhaustive and cover all professional situations, also because many of them could come in relation to specific contexts and many could also come thanks to the future evolution of the complex structures in which we live. An additional double function is, then, between training about frequent and predictable situations and acquiring competences to face unpredictable situations.

Both cases seem to recall the continuity needed between pre-service and in-service training as indicated in the introduction.

A different aspect to be taken into consideration is connected to the concept of professionalism in the second decade of the third millennium.

This concept has radically changed at the end of the last century, a change that can be described with the shift from technical rationality to reflective rationality (Shön, 1993). In the second decade of the current millennium there was an additional change and it's used to talk, instead, about the evolution from *professionalization* to *professionalisme*. Veyrunes (2015) states that many of the expectations, born in the Anglophone field in which *professionalization* was a positive movement, were partly disappointed by the recent evolution of the teacher's job: its uncertainty, the relative impoverishment of teachers, the extension of the assessment culture, the request for accountability, and the increase of regulations don't allow positive developments towards major autonomy and self-regulation of the professional. According to the author, who aims at basing professional school training on the culture of the profession, collective cultural, historical dimensions create the profession of 'teacher'. Autonomy centered in single subjects would end in the loss of those dimensions because of current economic policies.

On one hand the new direction indicates a generalization of the concept of professionalism, that crosses all professional activities from the most complex to the simplest ones (to be more explicit we refer also to routine and repetitive jobs, which today require taking into account complex variables), on the other hand it shows the activation of a process that could create, mainly in some professions, a decrease in the quality of professionalism and autonomy. The two processes are interconnected. Specifically, in the field of training this double process was accompanied and, maybe, fostered by institutional interventions, aimed at identifying indicators for assessment that cannot avoid becoming prescriptive and eroding the chance of self-regulation that the competent action requires.

Again, the route to the new direction may evolve positively or, better, less negatively, and avoid a regression towards less autonomous forms. A major mechanism in the processes, could, we argue, be the more organic presence of training in job processes and the presence of better continuity between pre-service and in-service training, making the two steps strongly synergistic to foster a culture of professionalism. Here, similar *dispositif*, present in the two steps, could be interesting. The video and a modality to analyze, annotate and catch the meanings could be an example of a common *dispositif*. A different *dispositif* could be the e-portfolio that accompanies the student during his/her work and fosters the professionalization process from university (Rossi et al., 2015).

The use of videos should be explored as a boundary artefact between pre-service and in-service training. As will be described in this chapter the same videos can be examined in paths where both school teachers and student-teachers are involved.

As highlighted in the review by Gaudin and Chaliès (2015) in which 255 studies (including article, book chapters, proceedings published from 2003) are analyzed, the potentialities in the use of videos in teacher training are also based on the chance to create a collaborative space in which different actors can contribute to the student development of a professional identity.

The objective of the chapter is twofold, on one hand we aim to describe a teaching/learning path that can support the acquisition of a professional vision through the use of videos, and on the other hand we wish to highlight how the video can represent an opportunity for triangulation among the professor, the students and the school teachers and be an artefact which bridges pre-service and in-service training.

THE WORKSHOP IN GENERAL DIDACTICS: A CASE-STUDY

The degree course in primary teacher training in Italy is aimed at training pre-school teachers (age range of target students: 3-6 years old children) and primary school teachers (age range of target students: 6-11 years old children). The structure of the course, defined by a national law, implies the organization of lectures, workshops and internships[4]. The course lasts five years and, starting from the second year, each student must undertake practice in a school. The activities run during the internship are also discussed with a supervisor in seminars.

The course developed at the University of Macerata implies the use of videos in different phases of the learning path. The workshop of the first and of the third year and the seminar activities connected to the internship, along with lectures classes take advantage of videos recorded at primary schools.

The present contribution will deal with the use of videos in the first year workshop of the degree course. The workshop is connected with the course of General Didactics that is developed in 48 hours of lectures in which basic topics are addressed such as terminology like "teaching" and "learning", their meaning, the indicators of didactics and the main models for macro and micro design. The course is connected with the workshop, which lasts 20 hours and is organized around six meetings.

In the first meeting the students make a collage (drawings and pasting images taken from magazines in a poster), a metaphor of what they mean by teaching and being a teacher. In such a way they can make explicit their naive conceptions about the two concepts. The work done by students is not commented on by the professor or the supervisor.

From the second meeting to the fifth students analyze and discuss the videos. Each meeting is organized in two phases: in the first step a 10/15 minute video is collectively watched and then analyzed by the professor, by the school teacher (actor in the video) and by the supervisors present in the workshop. The debate is organized around: the identification of objectives, goals, the events that occurred and the interactions. Moreover, the activities are analyzed according to four perspectives: epistemological, psycho-pedagogical, the one tied to instructional design and the one connected to values. Specifically the epistemological perspective is connected to the addressed conceptual nodes, the challenges tied to the disciplines, the misconceptions; the psycho-pedagogical perspective is related to the way the cognitive maturity of the student was taken into account; the instructional design is connected to the didactical strategies and the formats, the choice of the mediators and of the media support; the ethical perspective, finally, takes into account the addressed values related to the respect of the others, of the environment, of the self as family and socio-cultural identity, and how the attention to values has directed the choice and the way the discipline was approached. Special attention was dedicated to the connections and interactions among the different rationales. It was, in fact, underlined how difficult was, in some cases, to distinguish in the same action the different perspectives, but being focused on them let the actors comprehend the teacher's professionalism.

After this first phase a second video is watched and students in small group of four analyze it. The results of such analysis are, then, discussed again with the whole classroom, the professor and the school teachers. Each of the four meetings connected to videos is focused on a typology of activities: frontal class, dialogic class, group class. Moreover, the videos are selected from those which deal with the discipline of History.

In the final meeting the students are required to comment on the collage done in the first meeting and to identify what they would change or keep considering the path they took during the workshop. As highlighted in a previous paper (Rossi et al., 2015) in the experience of the last three years' workshops students show that they tend to keep their original idea, correct some aspects that they consider to be in contrast with the professional awareness that they have acquired and, most of all, build significant bridges between their starting ideas and the theories they have learnt.

In the present contribution we focus on the workshop of the first year and specifically we deal with the central meetings (2-5) in which the videos are used.

THE ROLE OF THE VIDEO AND THE RESEARCH METHODOLOGY

The design of the training workshop is based on the use of video recordings of classes run by some school teachers during their usual teaching activity at school and may include disciplinary history classes (second cycle of primary school with student aged 8-10). Video analysis lets university students focus on open-ended, ill-defined tasks that require them to make an effort in assuming several perspectives and face issues that have no 'right' answers, but which require the student to discuss different solutions through a process of inquiry.

The workshop can represent an explorative case-study (Hancock & Algozzine, 2006) in which the video recordings of the different classes are analysed using a phenomenological approach to holistically interpret the data, the approach lets the researcher[5] take into account the fact that the students' assumptions about the teaching process are based on their previous learning experiences (Biggs 1993; Entwistle & Peterson, 2004; Laurillard, 2014; Pajares, 1992).

The objective is to increase awareness about the opinions and decisions made by the professor and the school teachers through an in-depth view of the videos and the analysis of the interviews.

The research questions wish to investigate mainly the effects of the contemporary presence of students, professors and school teachers (implying also the supervisors) in the analysis of a boundary object, as the video is. As said in the introduction those effects are not to be seen in one direction (that is capturing the contribution of the professor in the professional development of the student), but in two directions (that is, checking how the students' questions can activate reflections in the professor). The proposed enactive approach wishes to investigate how the discussion can promote questions and observations that create a deeper knowledge of the video recorded class interaction and how this interaction can connect with the professional identity of the professor and the novice identity of the students.

The focus of the video analysis of the main actors involved in the workshop follows four paths:

- The analysis of students starts from their questions;
- The analysis of the school teacher (actor in the primary class video recording) starts from what she/he did and what she/he believes is correctly done;
- The analysis of the supervisors starts from what should be captured.

The video of selected activities/events is shown to students and then discussed in presence of the university professor and the teacher according to the "video-viewing" and "video modelling" methodology (Masats & Dooly, 2011): "Video-viewing is often used as a method to focus student-teachers' attention on certain topics and to set up a base for class discussion and assignments. Videomodelling is a means of getting student-teachers' to focus their attention on target skills or behaviour" (p. 1152).

After the collective vision of the video, student-teachers are invited to ask questions to the teacher and the analysis made during the here reported and past experimentations (Rossi et al., 2015) show that questions are mainly focused on contextual issues. Student-teachers, in fact, ask information about the class as a whole (number of pupils, presence of immigrants, presence of pupils with special needs, etc.) and about specific pupils who intervene in the video sequences or who appear to have a significant behaviour (level of competence, family history, specific traits such as the presence of an emotional and psychological trauma, etc.), those questions enable students to better understand the complexity of the didactical event.

But they also ask for a deeper understanding of the strategies used by the teacher. It may happen that students also focus their attentions on details that are not strictly connected with the objectives of the class, insignificant issues that are, however, relevant for them to start understanding the communication and interaction relationships in the classroom.

The students' questions about the video are an opportunity to discuss and reflect on the choices made by the teacher during the class that has been recorded, the analysis of the reasons that led to a specific action visible in the video. Students can see what happens in the class, but only the school teacher can tell students why he/she behaved in a specific way and what the pupils' background is.

The university professor acts as a guide, he introduces the video and encourages students to express their voice even if they are not sure. His objective is to train them in acquiring a professional vision directing them with open questions to observe aspects tied to the didactical transposition (Damiano, 2013).

The school teacher replies to student's questions giving detailed information about his/her strategy, his/her choices and the way he/she managed the class. He/she aims at demonstrating her audience the consistence between what the objective (disciplinary or organizational) of the class and what she decided and actually did during class.

The presence of the school teacher is necessary to go deeper in the video analysis. Videos shows de-contextualized events where the effect or consequences of the student interaction is shown, but the video itself cannot provide all the background data which can frame the different actions into a complex event. The video doesn't show neither the past nor the future of the class nor the motivations of the teacher.

The school teacher's reasoning process during the design and the development of the lesson can be made explicit only by him/her and that's why his/her presence is a necessary reference for students. Students ask questions and wish to understand the reason why certain things happen and why some choices worked and others not. The university professor plays, instead, a connecting role putting into relation the languages of the two actors and the languages of the practice with the language of theory. Moreover, the professor asks mirror questions in order to go deeper in the discussion, but he rarely expresses judgements that could stop the process of knowledge.

The workshop highlights the benefits of video viewing for the three actors:

- The students can take advantage of the participation of the teacher to contextualize the events in the video and disambiguate complex situations and, most of all, to understand how the teacher chooses and plans the actions;
- The school teacher can acquire inputs by students and avoid self-reference in the video self-analysis;
- The university professor can optimize the professional teaching-learning path for the student offering a holistic approach, he can get feedback on what student-teachers were able to capture and what was not understandable by them.

An additional remark can be made about the presence of the supervisors and whose interventions show their professional perspectives on facts they didn't experience in the first person, but that they can interpret and can enrich with examples taken from their experience. Being external to the video, they can offer students an additional value.

In order to elicit both the university professor and the teacher perspectives on the workshop and, specifically, on the use of video recorded classroom as an initial input to train students a semi-structured interview was used at the end of the course.

The interviews involved the actors who participated in the workshop of the academic year 2014-2015 and was carried out by one of the authors. The analysis included the class video recordings made at school and the audio recording of the workshop. Moreover, the audio recorded interview to the school teacher was analyzed and discussed by both authors. The analysis of the interactions in the workshop and the interviews were used with the purpose of gathering personal opinions and perceptions on the effectiveness of the use of video in the workshop in which there was the active participation of the interviewee.

Open ended questions were built to understand the respondent's point of view and get useful inputs/insights on aspects the interviewer might not have considered. Questions consisted of: *descriptive questions* (are meant to get the description of a situation/status) and *structural questions* (are meant to get information about processes and dynamics activated in the institution).

The interview was developed passing through the following steps:

- Perceptions about the role in the workshop: How do you feel coordinating the workshop with the university professor? How do you see your professional relationship with him/her?
- Actions taken during the workshop: what did you highlight during the discussion with students? When (and why) did you choose to go deeper in explaining certain aspects?
- Opinions about the effect of the workshop on professionalism: did the students' questions somehow have an impact on your idea about the video recorded class? How did the workshop affect student-teachers' professional vision?

The feedback received shows that the design of the workshop which includes more teaching professionals coming from different contexts (academic and primary school contexts) is effective and successfully managed if the roles are clear to both actors.

The perception of the school teacher is positive in relation to the participation in the workshop since she felt her contribution was positively embraced by both the student-teachers and the professor. The intervention of a school professional offers students a valuable input and the interviewees show they are fully aware of this relevance when they specify the rationale of their actions during the discussion phase.

The teacher also explains that student-teachers have offered her a different perspective on her class and made her notice behaviours and nuances that she hadn't considered, even when she watched her video by herself after the recording. She was, thus, able to compare her internal representation of the performance with the student-teachers' feedback.

She can't say if her professionalism has changed but she is self-confident that the opportunity to share her video with a group of practitioners enabled her to rethink some aspects of the design process and certainly made her acquire new reflection methodologies such as taking more notes during her class.

The university professor states an interest in making students visualize in the video the decisions made by the teacher and collectively reflect why and how she reached that decision.

The video makes students face different nuances of that relationship and can break the demagogic falsity of some claims, even if the student is put in a central role the teacher needs to take her decisions. In this process the teacher insists on justifying her choices while the university professor is interested in fostering the student-teachers 'participation in expressing themselves on the reasons behind those choices. The video should not give a "perfect" idea of what the teaching/learning process is to be useful, but reporting Star's words about the concept of "boundary object" "it could serve as the basis for conversation, for sharing data, for pointing to things—without actually demarcating any real territory" (2010, p. 608).

RESULTS

The adopted educational structure, as highlighted also in the interviews, "force" the three actors to activate a cognitive and emotional process that arise from the triangulation of their perspectives and by other factors that will here be deepened. The presence of a digital artifact in which the school teacher is a main actor makes her/him acquire a double role. On one hand he/she makes a defense of his/her conduct and analyzes the class with pupils as a group to safeguard it from external eyes. On the other hand, he/she feels part of the academic community and builds, in relation to university students, the same institutional and affective connection that he/she has with the school pupils. Comparing the workshop format with a traditional lecture also the professor, due to triangulation, plays the role of coordinator and mediator who modifies the attitude of the school teacher. If in the case of a traditional course the professor is the only person responsible and decides what to say and how ot should be told, in the workshop he has the role of a director, a coordinator and the communication flow cannot be managed directly by him. This role of coordinator opens up a tension between the process he is fostering toward the growth of the students and the attention to what school teachers say, the processes they activate, the personal dynamics they create and that, anyway, need to be respected and valorized.

The effect of triangulation for students is not different. The relationship student-professor fosters an attitude of acceptance and doesn't create incisive behavior. The triangulation, instead, creates the background for the creation of a more active role by students in which the wish to understand is connected to the need to ask questions and wonder how the school should be.

The effect of triangulation is the activation of an enactive approach in which the meaning comes from the cognitive and affective interaction that develop in the workshop. In the last two years the same videos were used and the same protocol to guide observation. Nevertheless, the different discussions that took place highlighted different aspects and set off various emotions.

One of the questions researchers (in this case the professor plays also the role of the researcher) asked themselves after developing the workshop for the third time with the same modalities and protocols was: why does the interaction with students (that is, non-expert actors) challenge the school teachers and the professor and activate their reflection processes? We need to add that one of the videos was also used as a means of *co-explicitation* between the professor and the school teachers. The *co-explicitation* process (Vinatier, 2011a) implies the presence of one or more researches and a school teacher and requires the following steps: one or more classes are recorded and often before and after those classes an interview with the teacher takes place in order to let him/her make it explicit the goals and the motivations of the choices made in class. After that the researcher analyses the video recordings and identifies significant elements to be discussed with the teacher, aspects that highlight the routines in the teacher's activity, events he/she manages, inputs coming from the students, the one valorized by the teachers and the ones that were not taken into consideration during the class. The researcher also analyses the effectiveness of the mediators, the class management and the interactions and tries to make a hypothesis about the teacher's motivations in his/her choices.

The step which follows implies the exchange between the researcher and the teacher. The researcher discusses the hypothesis with the teacher always recalling the video that was previously analyzed; the discussion lets the researcher reformulate the hypothesis made. The process concludes only when the two actors produce a shared interpretation of the process object of analysis.

The videos analysed with the students during the workshop were already object of a *co-explicitation* process (researcher-school teacher) and during the workshop the process enriched with the third actor, the students offering different results, even if the two processes were both significant and relevant. In the same way the discussions that took place were different. In the in-service training the debate focused on very specific issues of the didactical action, such as the mediators used, the typologies of tasks assigned to students, the management of the interaction. In the debate in which students were present, instead, different topics were addressed that were considered obvious by professionals, such as, for example, the power relation between the school teacher and the students. This difference can be connected to, or recall, the need of a recursive dialogue between goals and means required in the current training of professionals and that is fostered by the permeability between pre-service and in-service training.

The presence of students in the process of analysis could create the basis for questions that the professor considers fundamental, questions that challenge the general aims and roles of the school institution.

The presence of boundary objects (videos) and the triangulation of different actors foster bothcontinuity between pre service and in service training, also in terms of topic to be addressed.

The analysis of the video recordings made during the workshop (with the presence of the three actors, student, professor, school teacher) have shown a different behaviour by the school teacher, different from the one shown during the co-explicitation sessions with the professor/researcher (two actors, school teacher and professor/researcher). The same video was analysed, but in the co-explicitation session the discussion was mainly about the aspects connected to the problematic aspects in the daily routine of the school teacher and about possible alternative modalities of action. The choice of the mediators, of the strategies, the management of specific strategies and the procedures activated were the topics most addressed. Moreover, the behaviour of the school teacher showed the wish to discover and improve his/her professionalism. During the workshop, instead, more general aspects were highlighted, such as the power relation between the school teacher and the student in class and the opportunities given to pupils to speak out, the attention to their questions. The school teacher showed, more than once, a defensive posture. In the final interview the school teachers make it explicit two issues. In primis they have admitted that watching the videos with the perspectives of university students and their questions let them capture elements that were previously ignored, aspects that they had not taken into account, since they are the results of consolidated teaching choices. The second issue was connected to emotional involvement. The school teachers admitted that some questions asked by the university students were felt to be particularly sensitive and caused reaction of defence and, sometimes irritation.

As a general impression the school teachers were surprised by the generative power in the observations made by the students. A deeper analysis of the typologies of questions asked by the students let the researcher understand that that they were caused by the lack of experience in their initial professional path in the direction of becoming teachers.

The interviews made to students showed what they got from the interaction with the school teachers. Being students their attention was always focused on their learning process without having an adequate perception of the autonomous and indirect role of the teaching process. The words "transmit" and "acquire" well represent the transparency and the interpretation of learning as a process caused by external inputs and students easily identified the effects of the school teacher's interventions on their own learning process. The teaching process can be given a positive or negative role and its effects can be useful or useless. The uselessness can be attributed to the pedagogical/disciplinary inappropriateness of the teacher or to a low attention to the pupils' needs. If, instead, the perspective is the teacher's perspective the students understand that the teacher cannot always predict the effects of his/her actions, since they depend also and mainly on the postures of the pupils, and words such as "transposition" and "mediation" can describe this process better.

The workshop let students modify the perspectives with which they interpret the learning process and activated that metamorphosis from the student status to the teacher status being now able to capture the indirect and mediated role of teaching.

Most of the students' questions during the workshop and the discussion after watching the video were about the management of the atmosphere in class by the school teacher, the way he/she fostered the participation of the pupils, if and how the pupils' questions were accepted and how they were given value and used as inputs, maybe different from the ones initially planned by the teacher. Many observations were focussed on the management of the class. Some examples are the following sentences: "that child raised his hand all the time, but the teacher rarely gave him permission to speak", "the pupils' questions used by the teacher were only a few and the ones useful for the path he had planned, but some have also opened different paths, such the one about the water" ; " when there were divergent questions by the pupils, in some cases the teacher used a routine: some seconds of reflection, then he acted a devolution (pupils, what do you think?), and finally has synthesized"; "the posture of the pupils was different in the different phases of the class: when the teacher was speaking they paid attention, but when there was a discussion about issues raised by some peers the pupils were sitting in a less relaxed way having their body up straight".

Students also focused a lot on the aspects related to the values: how much did the teacher valorize his pupils? How much did the teacher pay attention to the pupils' observations and their behavior?

At the end of the course students needed to have an exam for the final evaluation and they were required to watch a 9 minute video. The professor got about 80 papers (Group A). The same video was shown to students of different universities of the same degree course asking them to comment (Group B). Students for other universities had studied the same disciplines and were enrolled in the same course year, but they didn't use the video in their classes. Students from Group A highlighted elements in the environment and in the path that were interconnected. For example, they highlighted the relation between the organization of the class (position of the desks and other objects) and the role of the teacher with activities and typologies of the interaction that took place. The students' observations of Group B reported more descriptive elements. They highlighted elements in the environment that were not relevant for the development of the teacher's action and the relationship between what was described and the specific didactical path was not always specified (Rossi et al. 2015).

A similar difference can be seen in the same students involved in the workshop of General Didactics between their first descriptions/narratives after watching a video in the first meeting of the workshop and their interpretations in the final step of the workshop. In the initial phase, in fact, they mostly produce lists of aspects they noticed, while in the final meetings they are able to find connection amongst elements/events: objectives, mediators, didactical strategies, interaction management.

ISSUES, CONTROVERSIES, AND PROBLEMS

One of the controversial aspects is related to the aim of the workshop. The training is meant as an opportunity to reach a common professional vision, but the paths followed by student-teachers, by the university professor and by the school teachers with their own perspectives are rather different. The challenge is to use the video as a "boundary object" (Star, 1988) to merge and make the different actors' background and experiences significant for all. Star refers to the notion of boundary object saying "like the blackboard, a boundary object sits in the middle of a group of actors with divergent viewpoints" (p. 46) and if we examine its three components, that is "the interpretive flexibility, the structure of informatic and work process needs and arrangements, and, finally, the dynamic between ill-structured and more tailored uses of the objects" (Star, 2010, p. 601) we can find how the use that has been made of the video in the workshop, object of the analysis, helps us in solving the controversy.

The collective vision of the class video recording is meant as a boundary object in the sense of the opportunity to have a shared place in which the different actors work together, using Star's words "something people act toward and with" (p. 603).

What student-teachers watch is "a form of work that is invisible to the whole group" (p. 607) and we can add, is somehow invisible to the supervisor and professor too. But the shared representation of what is happening in the video recorded class can acquire meaningfulness and, thus, be of undeniable usefulness for all actors.

The impact of the video on the effectiveness of the workshop is related to what we call the "didactical engineering" (Rossi & Pezzimenti, 2012), that is the rationale with which the professor and the supervisors choose the video clips and the way they decide to show them in order to foster student-teacher participation.

An additional critical aspect is the one related to the inclusion of the teacher-supervisor in the academic context. Even if the role of the supervisor is set by law in the graduate course for primary teacher training, the impact of such inclusion is not futile. The use of video recorded classes in which the supervisor is the actor is one of the means with which such inclusion can find a successful trajectory of collaborative work.

One of the difficulties encountered during the process is the double role of the professor who is, on one hand a reference point for students since he teaches the classes on the strategies to be adopted at school and, on the other hand, in the workshop, he puts himself as an object of analysis. The professor's availability in putting himself into discussion becomes, then, central for the success of the workshop.

A further difficulty is related to students. Asking a question is a way to exhibit yourself in front of the professor who will, also, "judge" you so it's relevant to create an atmosphere of mutual trust.

SOLUTIONS AND RECOMMENDATIONS

The years in which the workshop has been developed let the researchers identify some elements that can offer the opportunity to improve its functioning with a better quality of the processes activated.

The first issue to consider is an accurate preparation of the processes. In the month that precedes the beginning of the workshop the professor meets the school teachers to decide time and modalities. During those meetings the following aspects were addressed: theoretical approaches and details related to the attitude to have during the discussion sessions with students, aspects related to the didactical engineering, specifically the sequences of the different phases and the inputs to give to students.

A second issue, not to be underestimated, is the selection process of videos and the length of the video sequences to be shown. Technical quality is an obvious necessity considering that in a primary school class the voices of pupils can overlap and a background noise can be present. The choice to use *video-verité* is to be seen as the necessity to make the event and what cannot be predicted visible in the didactical action. This doesn't mean that there's no need to make an accurate selection of video sequences to be analysed. Even if the sequences are not meant as prescriptive modalities of behaviours, they need to show significant situations that can represent learning opportunities for students.

Concerning the length, in our experience, too short sequences don't let students catch the meaning of the path and identify pupils' and teacher's behaviours, in the same way it's difficult to catch a significant event in few seconds of recordings. At the same time too long sequences don't let students catch the connection between the general development of the class and specific attitudes. It happened that a long discussion was run after a sequence of just a few seconds of video. In a sequence the school teacher, for example, while progressing with his class has, at the same time, recalled the attention of the students simply by using his hands and a glance. This event was noticed and discussed by several students who observed how the teacher was able to manage two different languages and paths, the first about the disciplinary topic, and the second about the management of the class.

Following the experiences of the three years a good compromise seems to be a sequence of 6-12 minutes.

An additional key element is the alternation between the activities run by the professor and the ones developed by students by themselves. In the first phase the school teachers don't give indications, but analyze the video playing a reference role. Afterwards students work in small groups (3-5 people) to analyze the video themselves and each group contribution will then enrich the collective reflection. After working in groups we can have two options to progress with the workshop and the choice depends on the time available and on the need to make it consistent with the discussion: sometimes the group work continued with a higher number of participants (15-25 people) to share the different results from the first discussion in small groups and to finally join the whole class group (about 80 people); in other cases the small group work was followed directly with the discussion in the whole group class.

Finally, but not secondary, it's recommended to plan proper times for the whole process, 3 hours each meeting so that it's possible to conclude the process in the described discussion steps. A separation of the activities could produce some difficulties for students in keeping the inner consistence and attention on the discussion.

FUTURE RESEARCH DIRECTIONS

How to improve the workshop? How to foster the alternation and the continuity in a more articulated way?

The first direction is to have a wider set of videos to be used to be able to cover the different typologies of Teaching Learning Activities (Laurillard, 2014). Up till now the hardest difficulty met is taking ethical issues into account, mainly in relation to school students and their families.

A further step would be to select videos taking into account a better global consistence and by offering a vision of the class context and of the process in its totality. We are, in fact, thinking to also show students video interviews of the school teacher recorded soon before the workshop, that is before he/she clarifies objectives, epistemological nodes to face and the difficulties that he/she believes school students can encounter. It could also be interesting to have a post-workshop interview in which the meeting is analyzed with experts. Such a huge set of data require a major availability of time or the need to watch the videos (or some of them) before the seminar meeting among students and school teachers.

We are also experimenting with other *dispositifs*. In a workshop of the third year in 2015-2016 academic year a session will be developed in which students are required to design a work session to be developed in the primary school through the triangulation between school teachers, academic professors and students. The same designed session will be implemented in two parallel classes of the primary school and video recorded. Finally, the video recording will be discussed in the university course in a meeting in the presence of the three actors (school teachers, professor, students). The objective is to make students reflect on how the design process and the management of the didactical action are connected with the context and their specific problems, as well as the embodied knowledge and the general aim of the course. If professionalism is the skill to build operative solutions proper to the context, those processes will be relevant for training.

A further reflection is connected to research. What additional *dispositifs* could be used to foster a continuity between pre-service and in-service training? Besides the triangulation in the analysis of videos and the use of videos to show vicariant practices, we have already proposed alternation as a model and as a *dispositif* and the e-portfolio as artifact to be started in the pre-service training and to be continued in in-service training. The alternation practices such as the internships by students in schools, show many of the same characteristics present in the use of vicariant practices in class as the videos do. An example is the double flow of information and knowledge, from the school teacher to university students (the relations and the practices of teachers) and from university students to school (they present new models, they propose activities learnt in their studies and simulated during the workshops).

What additional ways?

Unfortunately, such processes are related just to workshop and internships. What about the lectures? How to create a more complex and invasive interaction between theories and didactical practices? The further step is certainly to see the *dispositifs* of alternation and continuity between pre-and in-service training. The need for lifelong learning is due to the impossibility to cover all the wide and complex apparatus of knowledge needed in the professional context within the pre-service training. This is true in most of the activities. The difficulty is not only caused by the width of the necessary knowledge background, but also by the necessity to direct that knowledge in relation to the context. It would even be impossible to foresee the evolution of a discipline.

CONCLUSION

The contribution states that a better continuity between pre-service and in-service training offers a better quality training and a more consistent approach with the goal of training teachers as professionals.

The workshop on didactics, in which the triangulation among the perspectives of the students, the school teachers and the professor is developed with the support of videos, demonstrated to be a valid *dispositif* to activate such triangulation. The advantages depend on the autonomous, but interwoven and enactive evolution of the three actors. The student starts his/her professional vision construction during the workshop and faces the dynamics the school teachers need to manage in the class. The professor can reorganize his/her knowledge, examine his/her practices from a distanced perspective and review the practices from the naive perspectives of the students. This process requires that concepts and visions considered crystalised and taken for granted in the work context, are put under discussion and are objects of a further reflection: the presence of students and their observations, apparently naive, let all actors focus on those concepts. Finally, the triangulation pushes the professor away from his/her frontal position and requires that he/she plays a coordinating role since he/she is no longer the only source of knowledge. The professor seems, then, to be required to reconstruct his/her theories starting from the practices, validating his/her knowledge in action.

The results obtained with students in the three years in which such procedure was activated confirm the validity of the *dispositif*.

As shown by the comparison with other training contexts in which videos are not used in didactics, the contexts in which a triangulation process among students, school teachers and professors take place in the use of videos, fosters a holistic and complex vision of the didactical action, a professional vision.

From the last year in Italy a recursive process that connects class practices to reflection on them has been adopted in the teacher training of newly enrolled teachers, that is, teachers in their first year of employment. Last year the process involved 28.000 teachers and the current year more than 80.000. In the previous years, newly employed teachers were required to follow training courses but in the last two years they are invited to develop some hours of classes with the presence of an expert teacher and then they are invited to reflect on this experience thanks to a set of guiding questions and documents uploaded in an e-portfolio. An immersive and distancing process is being developed, a process that implies the presence of an expert teacher, that is similar to the process described in the present article to train students, since it requires alternation, attention to and study of practices, specifically in the micro-activities, and the reflection on the them.

The alternation, the continuity between pre-service and in-service training and the recursivity between immersion and distancing between practices and reflection is at the centre of different training paths of the teacher (pre-service, induction and in-service) and the chance that a pattern is repeated in the three phases lets the teacher acquire the habitus of the teacher, becoming his/her operative posture.

The process, anyway, is neither easy nor automated. It requires going deeper in the interactions created by the triangulation and also requires a wide time interval to be developed. The sequences of activities which involve the use of the videos gain relevance in the triangulation and many of the described practices, specifically the one which requires the use of videos, need a specific attention to detail. An example is the process of triangulation in which listening skill, interpreting skill, and respect for the others are central. Similarly the attention to all verbal and non-verbal languages is central. In this last direction the video can provide a relevant support, even if it is the means of the process itself.

REFERENCES

Abell, S. K., & Cennamo, K. S. (2004). Videocases in elementary science teacher preparation. In J. Brophy (Ed.), *Using video in teacher education* (1st ed., pp. 103–129). Boston: Elsevier.

Altet, M. (2012). L'apporto dell'analisi plurale dalle pratiche didattiche alla co-formazione degli insegnanti. In P. C. Rivoltella & P. G. Rossi (Eds.), *L'Agire didattico* (pp. 291–311). Brescia: La Scuola.

Berten, A. (1999). *Dispositif, médiation, créativité: Petite généalogie*. Paris: CNRS Edtions.

Biggs, J. (1993). From theory to practice: A cognitive systems approach. *Higher Education Research & Development*, *12*(1), 73–85. doi:10.1080/0729436930120107

Blomberg, G., Sherin, M. G., Renkl, A., Glogger, I., & Seidel, T. (2014). Understanding Video as a Tool for Teacher Education: Investigating Instructional Strategies Integrating Video to Promote Reflection. *Instructional Science*, *42*(3), 443–463. doi:10.1007/s11251-013-9281-6

Carbonneau, M., & Hétu, J. C. (2006). Formazione pratica degli insegnanti e nascita di un'intelligenza professionale. In M. Altet, E. Charlier, L. Paquay, & P. Perrenoud (Eds), Formare gli insegnanti professionisti. Quali strategie? Quali competenze? (pp. 77-95). Roma: Armando editore.

Coffey, A. M. (2014). Using Video to Develop Skills in Reflection in Teacher Education Students. *Australian Journal of Teacher Education*, *39*(9), 86–97. doi:10.14221/ajte.2014v39n9.7

Damiano, E. (2013). *La mediazione didattica. Per una teoria dell'nsegnamento*. Milano: FrancoAngeli.

Desgagné, S. (1998). La position du chercheur en recherche collaborative: Illustration d'une démarche de médiation entre culture universitaire et culture scolaire. *Recherches Qualitatives*, *18*, 77–105.

Desgagné, S., & Larouche, H. (2010). Quand la collaboration de recherche sert la légitimation d'un savoir d'expérience. *Recherche en éducation. Hors Série.*, *1*, 7–18.

Entwistle, N., & Peterson, E. R. (2004). Conceptions of learning and knowledge in higher education: Relationships with study behaviour and influences of learning environments. *International Journal of Educational Research, 41*(6), 407–428. doi:10.1016/j.ijer.2005.08.009

Fenstermacher, G. D. (1990). Philosophy of Research on Teaching: Three Aspects. In M. C. Wittrock (Ed.), *Handbook of research on teaching. A project of the American Educational Research Association* (pp. 37–49). New York, London: Macmillan.

Gaudin, C., & Chaliès, S. (2015). Video viewing in teacher education and professional development: A literature review. *Educational Research Review, 16*, 41–67.

Goodwin, C. (1994). Professional vision. *American Anthropologist, 96*(3), 606–633. doi:10.1525/aa.1994.96.3.02a00100

Hancock, D. R., & Algozzine, B. (2006). *Doing Case Study Research*. New York: Teachers College Press.

Haynes, J.M., & MillerJ., E. (2015). Preparing pre-service primary school teachers to assess fundamental motor skills: Two skills and two approaches. *Physical Education and Sport Pedagogy, 20*(4), 397–408. doi:10.1080/17408989.2014.892064

Laurillard, D. (2014). *Insegnamento come scienza della progettazione*. Milano: FrancoAngeli.

Llinares, S., & Valls, J. (2009). The building of pre-service primary teachers' knowledge of mathematics teaching: Interaction and online video case studies. *Instructional Science, 37*(3), 247–271. doi:10.1007/s11251-007-9043-4

Lussi Borer, V., Durand, M., & Yvon, F. (2015). *Analyse du travail et formation dans les métiers de l'éducation*. Louvain la Neuve: De Boek.

Magnoler, P. (2009). I dispositivi didattici e l'online. In P. G. Rossi (Ed.), *Tecnologia e costruzione di mondi. Post-costruttivismo, linguaggi e ambienti di apprendimento* (pp. 206–254). Roma: Armando Editore.

Masats, D., & Dooly, M. (2011). Rethinking the use of video in teacher education: A holistic approach. *Teaching and Teacher Education, 27*(7), 1151–1162. doi:10.1016/j.tate.2011.04.004

McCormack, A. C. (2001). Investigating the Impact of an Internship on the Classroom Management Beliefs of Preservice Teachers. *Professional Educator, 23*(2), 11–22.

Pajares, M. F. (1992). Teachers' beliefs and educational research: Cleaning up a messy construct. *Review of Educational Research, 62*(1), 307–332. doi:10.3102/00346543062003307

Paquay, L., Altet, M., Charlier, E., & Perrenoud, Ph. (Dir.) (1996). Former des enseignants profession-nels. Quelles stratégies? Quelles compétences? Bruxelles: Editions De Boeck.

Rhine, S., & Bryant, J. (2007). Enhancing pre-service teachers' reflective practice with digital video-based dialogue. *Reflective Practice, 8*(3), 345–358. doi:10.1080/14623940701424884

Riley, C. (2009). Teacher quality v teaching quality: What's the difference? *Innovations, 8*, 6–9.

Rossi P.G., Fedeli L., Biondi S., Magnoler P., Bramucci A., & Lancioni C. (2015). The use of video recorded classes to develop teacher professionalism: the experimentation of a curriculum. *Journal of e-Learning and Knowledge Society, 11* (2), 111-127.

Rossi, P.G., Magnoler, P., Giannandrea, L., Mangione, G. R., Pettenati, M.C., & Rosa, A. (2015). Il teacher portfolio per la formazione dei neo-assunti. *Pedagogia Oggi, 2.*

Rossi, P. G., & Pezzimenti, L. (2012). La trasposizione didattica. In P. C. Rivoltella & P. G. Rossi (Eds.), *L'agire didattico. Manuale per l'insegnante* (pp. 167–183). Milano: La Scuola.

Santagata, R., & Stürmer K. (2014). Video educazione: nuovi scenari per la formazione degli insegnanti. *Form@are, 14* (2), 4-6.

Schuetze, H. G., & Sweet, R. (2003). *Integrating School and Workplace Learning in Canada: Principles and Practices of alternation Education and Training.* Montreal: McGill-Queen's University Press.

Seidel, T., Stürmer, K., Blomberg, G., Kobarg, M., & Schwindt, K. (2011). Teacher learning from analysis of videotaped classroom situations: Does it make a difference whether teachers observe their own teaching or that of others? *Teaching and Teacher Education, 27*(2), 259–267. doi:10.1016/j.tate.2010.08.009

Shanahan, L. E., & Tochelli, A. L. (2014). Examining the use of video study groups for developing literacy pedagogical content knowledge of critical elements of strategy instruction with elementary teachers. *Literacy Research and Instruction, 53*(1), 1–24. doi:10.1080/19388071.2013.827764

Sherin, M. G., Jacobs, V. R., & Philipp, R. A. (2011). *Mathematics teacher noticing: Seeing through teachers' eyes.* New York: Routledge.

Sherin, M. G., & van Es, E. (2009). Effects of video club participation on teachers' professional vision. *Journal of Teacher Education, 60*(1), 20–37. doi:10.1177/0022487108328155

Shön, D. A. (1993). *Il professionista riflessivo. Per una nuova epistemologia della pratica professionale.* Bari: Edizioni Dedalo.

Shulman, L. S. (2004). *The Wisdom of Practice: Essays on Teaching, Learning, and Learning to Teach.* San Francisco: Jossey-Bass.

Star, S. L. (1988). The structure of ill-structured solutions: Boundary objects and heterogeneous distributed problem solving. In M. Huhns & L. Gasser (Eds.), *Readings in distributed artificial intelligence* (Vol. II, pp. 37–54). Menlo Park, CA: Kaufman.

Star, S. L. (2010). This is Not a Boundary Object: Reflections on the Origin of a Concept. *Science, Technology & Human Values, 35*(5), 601–617. doi:10.1177/0162243910377624

Stokking, K., Leenders, F., de Jong, J., & van Tartwijk, J. (2003). From student to teacher: Reducing practice shock and early dropout in the teaching profession. *European Journal of Teacher Education, 26*(3), 329–350. doi:10.1080/0261976032000128175

van Es, E., & Sherin, M. G. (2002). Learning to notice: Scaffolding new teachers' interpretations of classroom interactions. *Journal of Technology and Teacher Education, 10*(4), 571–596.

van Es, E., & Sherin, M. G. (2008). Mathematics teachers' "learning to notice" in the context of a video club. *Teaching and Teacher Education*, *24*(2), 244–276. doi:10.1016/j.tate.2006.11.005

Vanhulle, S., Merhan, F., & Ronveaux, C. (2007). Du principe d'alternance aux alternances en formation des einsegnants et des adultes. In F. Merhan, C. Ronveaux, & S. Vanhulle (Eds.), *Alternances en formation* (pp. 7–45). Bruxelles: De Boeck.

Veyrunes, P. (2015). Configuration de l'activité collective en classe et culture du métier dans la formation des einsegnants. In V. Lussi Borer, M. Durand, & F. Yvon (Eds.), *Analyse du travail et formation dans les métiers de l'éducation* (pp. 33–48). Louvain la Neuve: De Boek.

Vinatier, I. (2011a). Comment penser la possibilité d' "apprendre des situations" pour des enseignants en formation: Une co-élaboration entre chercheur et praticiens? *Education Sciences & Society*, *2*(1), 97–113.

Vinatier, I. (2011b). La recherche collaborative: Enjeux et fondement théoriques. In J. Y. Robin & I. Vinatier (Eds.), Conseiller et accompagner. Un défi pour la formation des enseignants (pp. 45-60). Paris, France: L'Harmattan.

West, C. (2012). Developing reflective practitioners: Using video-cases in music teacher education. *Journal of Music Teacher Education*, *22*(2), 11–19. doi:10.1177/1057083712437041

KEY TERMS AND DEFINITIONS

Alternation: It is meant as a concept, that is, the recursivity between theory and practice, and as a *dispositif*, that is the immersion in contexts of practice and the distancing posture in study contexts in which you can reflect on practices and acquire new modalities.

Boundary Object: A concept that was firstly put forward by Susan Leigh Star in 1988 and, then, in 1989 the concept was described as follows in an article written in collaboration with Jim Griesemer "Boundary objects are objects which are both plastic enough to adapt to local needs and constraints of the several parties employing them, yet robust enough to maintain a common identity across sites. They are weakly structured in common use, and become strongly structured in individual-site use. They may be abstract or concrete. They have different meanings in different social worlds but their structure is common enough to more than one world to make them recognizable, a means of translation. The creation and management of boundary objects is key in developing and maintaining coherence across intersecting social worlds". A different view of boundary objects is the one by Etienne Wenger who focused on as boundary objects as entities that can link communities.

Co-Explicitation: Vinatier (2011) refers to process of co-explicitation when there's the activation of an opportunity of discussion among researchers and school teachers in analysing educational situations in school contexts. Researchers and teachers activate an exchange of perspectives in order to foster the reflection and the construction of the professional vision.

Dispositif: A word coming from the theoretical approach of Foucault. With this word we refer to a space-time and the affordance that it gives to all involved actors in such space-time. We thus use "dispositive" to mean both the structural aspect of the environment, the procedures that take place in there, and the behaviours of the actors. As an example, Foucault refers to school and prison as *dispositifs*. We, then, wish to highlight the constraints of the environment on human behaviour, and also the generativity and scaffolding that the environment can play in relation to personal and professional trajectories of the actors.

Professionalization: A process strictly connected with identity construction and development and results from the combination of two processes: *professionality* and *professionalism.* Professionality is meant as the process to acquire the due competencies required to practice a profession while professionalism as the construction of a social identity.

Triangulation: Usually related to research methodology and can affect the use of different data sources, different observers/researchers and methods of analysis. In this contribution authors refer to the involvement of different profiles (student, school teacher and university professor) in the teaching/learning path aimed at developing student-teacher professional vision.

Vicariant Practices: We refer to the concept set by Bandura and, in this contribution, we specifically refer to the importance for learners to observe videos of teaching/learning events in order to be able to catch relevant inputs for the development of their professional identity. This doesn't mean that the vicariant practice should replace the real practice in the context, but they can be used as a preliminary and in-service training to optimize the learning process.

ENDNOTES

1 *Dispositif* is a term coming from the theoretical approach of Foucault. With this word we refer to a space-time and the affordance that it gives to all involved actors in such space-time. We thus use "dispositive" to mean both the structural aspects of the environment, the procedures that take place in there, and the behaviours of the actors. As an example, Foucault refers to school and prison as *dispositifs*. We, then, wish to highlight the constraints of the environment on human behaviour, and, also, the generativity and scaffolding that the environment can play in relation to the personal and professional trajectories of the actors. (Berten, 1999; Damiano, 2013; Magnoler, 2009)

2 Collaborative research (*recherche collaborative*), as designated by francophone researchers implies the collaboration between university researchers and school staff taking into account the different competences of the actors in their contexts and practices. Specifically, the university researchers don't develop their research process on students and their teachers, but instead with their active collaboration. Three steps are identified to activate *a recherche collaborative* (Desgagné, 1998): contextualize the research within the theoretical framework, cooperate in the data gathering and analysis, and draw conclusions matching different viewpoints, or better, cultures.

3 As an example we suggest referring to the following website with video material about legal education, URL: http://legaledweb.com/blog/2014/11/11/qzrnjo448fezeifnlbf3xzzh0pbkad come materiali video per la legal education.

4 In the Italian system the "internship" implies two kinds of training opportunities for the student. The first is developed at a Primary School where, under the supervision of a school teacher, the student-teacher can acquire an experience directly in the context. In the second case the internship is developed at the University with the guide of a supervisor, a school teacher who is currently partly or fully working at the university, and coordinated by a university professor.

Chapter 3
Didactic Models and Professionalization of Teachers:
Research Approaches

Daniela Maccario
University of Torino, Italy

ABSTRACT

This chapter explores the possibility and potential of using video devices as recording instruments for didactic practices, within the context of the discussion of lines of analysis, aimed at the development of didactic models, as artefacts produced by pedagogic research in support of teaching processes and the professionalization of teachers. The main theoretical references are cited which analyse the validity of didactic models in teaching innovation processes and which point to possible new avenues for research in this field, with specific attention focused on practice-based approaches. Exploring and developing the potentiality of video research in line with directions specifically corresponding to the problems of analysis in the education field is clearly important. The same is discussed starting from an analysis of specific research experience.

INTRODUCTION

One of the main tasks of research in the pedagogical-didactic field involves the elaboration of knowledge in support of the professionalization of teachers and educators. With specific reference to applied research and research-development, the studies aimed at refining innovative methodologies, construction of didactic devices and materials and the definition of good practices represent a work direction that has to take into account the fact that professional training processes are particularly linked to an acquisition of the ability to analyse and compare practices, design and regulate action, and to reflect on one's own practices and those of others (Rossi, 2015). If one considers the paradigm of normativity and prescriptivity as definitively superseded, an analysis direction that seems to be coherent with these requirements is represented by the elaboration of didactic models as theoretical-practical artefacts that can offer actors contexts for operational principles and criteria, sustaining them in the processes of conceptualisation,

DOI: 10.4018/978-1-5225-0711-6.ch003

Copyright © 2017, IGI Global. Copying or distributing in print or electronic forms without written permission of IGI Global is prohibited.

analysis and reflection regarding their work, thereby promoting self-regulation. This is an option that implies recognition of professional practice as essential for any innovative proposal and the subject of study to be prioritized by research in that it constitutes a primary source of problems to be studied and tackled and a definitive criterion for discussing and evaluating the depth of knowledge acquisition and the solutions identified. *New Didactics Research- La Nuova Ricerca Didattica* (Damiano, 2006; Rivoltella & Rossi, 2012), an area in which the study presented in this chapter can be framed, when it focuses on the question of the most suitable research strategies for the elaboration of didactic models, is mainly committed to explication processes, analysis and discussion of the body of knowledge inherent in the professional practices of teachers, as an essential knowledge base in support of innovation processes and the improvement of teaching processes, within the context of a practice-theory-practice research strategy. According to this approach, the researcher does not aim at elaborating solutions for practice, starting from theories of a general character, but at valorising and developing, including thanks to conceptual outlines and explicatory hypotheses, made available by "contribution" disciplines (psychological, sociological etc.), proposals based on the practical knowledge which the operators have available as a result of their professional experience. This is essentially in relation to repeatedly recognised difficulties regarding knowledge of a general character in "covering the subject" directly and adequately, or in understanding and explaining teaching processes that aim at promoting learning processes from the point of view of the actors in situ and their need to take decisions "here and now", in conditions of relative uncertainty. This constitutes a research strategy that tends to implement processes involving 'theorization of practices starting from practices', in accordance with some essential stages: descriptive reconstruction of actions; distancing with analysis/interrogation of action modalities to test and interpret them; elaboration of hypotheses and operational principles starting from practice, in relation to development. The expected results of this type of research are first and foremost represented, as the basic outcome, by reconstruction of the phenomenology of the practices to the study, aimed at offering knowledge in the service of adequately informed designing and decision-making. These are descriptive outlines that refer to theoretical-conceptual systems and categories in which operators can recognise themselves, but which must also embrace features that can be potentially transferable, such as to render them intelligible and usable beyond their specific contexts, on the part of other actors working in the field, and also accessible to those who are not in the profession, or by researchers. A fundamental challenge posed by this research approach is represented by the creation and refinement of analysis systems that make it possible to embrace the development of professional action viewed from within, in accordance with approaches of a holistic and contextual character, which restore, as faithfully as possible, the dynamic complexity of actions and their meaning for the subjects. This represents a research logic that involves the participation of actors as sources of investigation, within a context of alliances to be constructed (Damiano, 2006; Hadji & Baillé, 1998) on the basis of agreed questions and objectives, and the use of specific observation devices, including videos and narrations which acquire strategic significance. Within the context of these factors, the chapter sets out the process and main results of research aimed at identifying modelization lines for innovative didactic practices, starting with the *Fenix Programme* (Coggi, 2009; 2015). This is a didactic artefact that is particularly focused on the need to support learning on the part of subjects with scholastic difficulties, constituted by an organized set of materials of a ludic-multimedia character, to be used in support training and reinforcement in the acquisition of knowledge, abilities, logic skills and motivational dispositions relative to basic curricula elements, in workshop settings, which provides relative autonomy of exploitation on the part of the student (within the context of courses having a mainly individual or small group character) and mediation facilitated by adults. Starting from the encouraging results obtained in experimentation under control conditions, previous research has substantially confirmed the possibility of valorising the Fenix programme, including in current didactic situations, in the ordinary management of teaching aimed at relatively large and heterogeneous class-groups. However, the study has highlighted the need to explore the main elements of a didactic mediation that is inevitably characterised by its own unique features relative to the operational lines originally set out by the Programme. As regards these presuppositions, the research path set out in this chapter seeks to identify and describe typical didactic dynamics, recursive action directions relative to the elaboration of guiding principles that are useful in diffusing the Fenix approach in support of classroom teaching in different scholastic contexts. Thanks to the intensive use of video recording devices, alongside further elements confirming the validity of the original didactic system, the research highlights a fertile and diversified didactic phenomenology, starting from which it seems possible to identify the initial lines of development for a *Fenix Didactic Model*.

PRACTICE-BASED RESEARCH-DEVELOPMENT

Elaboration of Didactic Models as the Task of Pedagogic Research

The utility of didactic models as research constructs constituted by formalized schema in support of teachers to think and act in practice is assumed as a hypothesis (Damiano, 2007). Moreover, it is felt the same can become the subject of explanation and analysis on the part of actors, in a process considered essential for encouraging professional growth. These are theoretical hypotheses that must embrace the procedurality of events which the operators in the field practice and control, exploitable in so far as they are identifiable by the actors as useful in representing their work (Cardarello, 2016), helping them to understand it in order to be able to improve it. Recognition of the situated and dynamic character of teaching processes and the professional nature of the work of teachers involves switching from the method concept to the didactic model. The idea of method, in general taken from knowledge acquired in scientific contexts related to the pedagogic sector, or starting from results of experimentations in the field or, again, from experience of the terrain, both individual and collective, or from operational implications and militant choices deriving from the espousal of education ideals, accentuates the procedural aspects of didactic action, in an approach that is tendentially prescriptive or recommendatory and, implicitly, recognises teaching practice as a body of application behaviours that can be regulated thanks to precise indications which are accorded general validity. Among the difficulties that can be attributed to this position, it is important to note the fact that a method, in its ideation and implementation, is not independent of its reference to specific education contexts and its evaluation cannot consist in the appreciation of its effects in absolute terms. The same method can have different effects relative to situations, the students it is intended for and the teachers and educators that use it (Bru, 2015). The affirmation of the model concept can be traced, essentially, to the recognition of a "knowledge of practices" or the value of knowledge processes linked to professional activity, different in nature from knowledge processes of a more generalising and abstract character. With reference to didactic practice and, in general, professional practice, interpretational hypotheses have been put forward that identify, in "modellizing" and "schematizing" processes, a crucial aspect of knowledge. The term "model" is used to indicate a general and schematic mental representation of a situation that permits the actor to imagine a certain number of variants of the same, thereby sustaining the simulation processes required for action (Damiano, 2007;

Van der Maren, 2014, 2003), analogous to the schema concept, understood as the organization of action that anticipates its goals, rules, possibilities of interference in situations, operational non-variants, and which makes it possible to reason and act relative to certain conditions (Vergnaud, 2011; Le Boterf, 2013). The didactic models, when appropriately validated in their adherence relative to problems and the intrinsic nature of teaching action, represent artefacts in support of mental modellizing implicated in practical choices, which encourage control of the same. In terms of Professional didactics (Pastré, 2007), one can say that the availability of scientifically based didactic models can represent a source of development of action models if it enriches the armoury of "cognitive models" available to teachers, as interpretational keys that can, relative to a comparison of dialogue with professional action, support the evolution of pragmatic schema already in use. Adopting a different approach, some have spoken about the acquisition of competence in teaching in terms of didactic patterns (Laurillard, 2012), whose development can be encouraged by the comparison with general principles which can take form through reflective processes. Didactic models would therefore represent useful devices in increasing the intelligibility of situations on the part of operators, with a heuristic function, supporting in situ reflection and decision-making. A didactic model can be understood as a "simplified representation of operational schemas to realise education actions" (Damiano, 1994, p.91). This is a construct that refers to the representation of the "action of teaching, in the distinct operations it comprises, relative to design-execution-reflection, and which explain the procedures and respective arguments that justify them" (Damiano, 2007, p.71). In this light, a didactic model must be accredited as a teaching theory that serves to optimise action, to produce situations and activate processes that can be potentially effective at lower cost, taking into account the limitations of the context. In general, a model includes a reference to the learning aims or goals it is intended to pursue, selects guide-criteria for the action, provides a body of indications that are useful for "professional activity", offering a simplified representation of didactic events with the intention of saying not "how you must act" but "how you can act", taking operational conditions into account.

Contextually-Based Research Approaches

Among the theoretical positions that constitute a reference for didactic research focused on the study of innovative programmes, models, didactic devices, in an English-speaking context, Design Based Research –DBR- constitutes an accredited approach for having highlighted, starting with the proposals of Brown and Collins (Brown, 1992; Collins, 1992), the need to take into account the situated character of learning and teaching processes, and to study education processes and the modalities for increasing their education contents in natural conditions (DBR Collective, 2003; Barab, & Squire, 2004; Sandoval & Bell, 2004; Anderson & Shattuck, 2012). The focus is concentrated on the applied aspect of research in the pedagogic field. This takes, as its privileged task, the elaboration of intervention projects that can support the action and choices of operators, in an attempt to overcome, on the one hand, the difficulties related to measurements, on a wide scale, of rigidly experimental methodologies, based on controlled analyses that tend, by their very nature, to validate the quality of new intervention modalities, de-contextualizing them, and, on the other hand, the difficulty faced by ethnographic-type studies in overcoming the descriptive and interpretive paradigm, in order to embrace the challenge of transformationality (Pellerey, 2005). This involves simultaneously pursuing two aims considered classics in research in the education field i.e. understanding how people can be placed in a condition that is conducive to learning productively in education contexts – particularly in scholastic ones – and to ideate strategies and courses that can offer better guarantees of effective learning. All of which involves a methodological system whose essential features consist in "combining, from a design point of view, the theoretical and practical needs of the education system via the prefiguring of interventions that embody assumptions of a theoretical nature, deriving from previous studies, and the precise verification of their validity in the concrete context of education practice" (Pellerey, 2005, p.725). The validity of the research consists in knowing how to refer to natural education conditions, thanks to results that can be effectively used to evaluate, communicate and increase the efficacy of practices in the context under study and hopefully in a range of other situations. Paraphrasing Brown (1992, p.143), the efficacy of an intervention, from a DBR point of view, can be traced back to its transferability in ordinary situations, with 'average' actors – teachers and students – relative to organizational, structural and realistic instruments. The identification and construction of interventions is a collaborative task assumed by researchers and operators, starting from a careful evaluation of operational contexts and their problems, taking into account the most significant literature in this area, the relevant theories and practices of other contexts, and aims to respond to specific problems or introduce improvements in particular practices (e.g. classroom management, evaluation modalities, use of education technologies etc.). The declared presupposition at the heart of the partneriat between researchers and operators is represented by a recognition of the difficulty, on the part of the latter, in reconciling their training and commitment in the field with the requirements of research, and the difficulty on the part of researchers in providing incisive interventions given their limited knowledge and understanding of the culture and objectives of education policies. The collaboration process affects the initial problem identification phase, the reconstruction of the theoretical context, the development of the intervention project and its construction, realisation, evaluation and the creation of theoretical and operational principles. The research projects are conceived to encourage the development of design principles, models or theorisations based on the problems of operators in education situations. The attention focused on theoretical comprehension is particularly present in the last phase of DBR research, as reflection concerning the production of design principles and operational solutions relative to the store of knowledge made available subsequent to experience in the field. The product of the research is constituted not by de-contextualised principles or by conceptual models to be considered valid for all contexts, but by theories that reflect the conditions in which they have been constructed, which have the function of supporting the comprehension and identification of adjustments to be introduced as improvements. However, unlike approaches based on research-action, DBR studies are developed not just to respond to local needs but to promote advances on a theoretical level with reference to problems regarding 'how' to teach and educate. This research strategy, open to multiple measurement methodologies/devices, inspired by classic data processing models and ethnography-inspired quantitative methods, has also been conceptualised as "interventionist ethnography" (Dede, 2005, p.6), through which research work explores typical education contexts, introducing projects influenced by theoretical considerations, since it seeks to gather implications for new theories relative to teaching, learning, scholarization (Pellerey, 2005, p.6) that have some general validity. Experts and researchers, who are particularly involved in the construction of design systems, are specifically tasked with recording time, commitment, unforeseens that characterise the creation and implementation of interventions, outcomes and operational implications that can be deduced on the basis of a return to theory. The same are documented such that the readers of research work can judge for themselves the appropriateness of realising a similar or improved intervention in other operational contexts. Although there is no lack of debate concerning the difficulties associated with the DBR approach, or the risk of system differentiations that undermine the effective unity of the approach in epistemological and strategic-methodological terms, for some, in terms of its evidential guarantee, it constitutes a key research tool, one that is considered promising since it has (re) prioritized the question of the significance and relevance of education research.

Towards an Ontological Change of Direction: Practice-Based Approaches

If within the context of the DBR approach one effectively notes the need for the coherence in research and its theorisations with education situations, considered as a "test bench" of their validity, other positions more directly require congruence relative to practice and education action, identified as a true object of study, giving rise to a de facto ontological change of direction. This is a prospect that is accompanied by the recognition of the professional character of teaching, in turn encourages research to embrace, as its mandate of choice, support for the professional activity and development of teachers, with specific attention focused on training. As a result, research paths are increasingly characterised by a 'practice-theory-practice' approach.

'Epistemological Rupture' and 'Clinical' Approach

With reference to problems associated with applied research and, more specifically, with development research, the position of Jean Marie Vander Maren (2015) is significant within the French-speaking world. With the progressive recovery of evidence deriving from French-speaking ergonomy and from the simplexity paradigm (Van der Maren, Yvon, 2009), he has recognised professional practices as a distinctive subject of study. Among the basic assumptions, there is a recognition that the problems to be tackled are related to "doing well in complex contexts using those resources available and with actors whose presence is non-negotiable [...] a complexity that involves the diversity of the dimensions at play in the delimitation of action possibilities: ethical, political, economic, material, contextual, social, psychological, cultural etc."(Van der Maren, 2015, p. 26). This constitutes contextualised research, in the sense that it has to take into account contexts in which solutions must be realised: opportunist because it is carried out in given conditions, with the resources available, for the most part relative to those opportunities that arise; ecological in that it tries to enrich or maintain the quality of relations between the actor, his partners and the operational context, without complicating them; eminently professionalizing, since it seeks to maintain or increase mastery, on the part of practitioner, over his professional gestures and increase control over those conditions relating to his actions (Van der Maren, 2015, p. 68). As regards research tasks, the essential focus concerns the problem of teachers in actively and consciously constructing their work, conceptualizing it and re-conceptualizing it, and having available didactic artefacts – "pedagogic objects" – that are useful in this sense, and which can be used not just locally and temporarily, but can constitute long term utilities, relative to their assumptions, principles and proven efficacy, as well as constituting logical-methodological instruments for the critical exercise of didactic and education modalities which at times rest on less than secure foundations. For researchers, this essentially involves finding strategies to operationalize ideas and theories that can effectively be at the service of the professional activity of teachers. A research field can be considered whose criterion of validity, rather than truth, is functionality, which implies the identification of practicable and incisive solutions, given a collection of priorities and restrictions. Such solutions must be satisfying, efficacious and efficient with respect to a range of values and customs (social and moral norms). In addition, it is important to consider that in the application field (e.g. human sciences, but not only), the situations are too complex to be analyzed and resolved by recourse to just one theory. To construct an object – practical or conceptual – which functions in reality, it is necessary to valorise different theories by accepting compromises. A functional object is by its nature eclectic and composite. Research can assume, in this way, a transdisciplinary or transtheoretical character, in the sense that practical application valorises different elements and theories, taking elements from both. Solutions can be generated from the combination of different elements, taken from different theories and practices, including in relation to the fact that functional practice transcends theories, characterised preeminently by cunning – craftiness – which makes it possible to arrive at, on a case by case basis, the most appropriate solutions. And not just that. The essential and distinctive point in this position consists in admitting, with Gaston Bachelard, an "epistemological rupture", one which means, in preliminary terms, standing at a certain distance from one's pre-conceptions and theoretical beliefs, and from already defined analyses, to embrace practice from a relatively 'de-centred' approach relative to the same. The insufficiency of a single contributory theory is very much a consideration when it comes to focusing on complex situations and epistemological problems that can generate theories which, valid in their several domains, are not so when used to ground teaching practices and education interventions because they have not been constructed in relation to the same. They therefore tend to neutralize a certain number of constitutive elements, ignoring them. The risk in such cases is that the researcher, directing his work on the basis of one or more theories, constructs fallacious research devices. The "verisimilitude" criterion, according to which theories must restore a representation of the object to which they refer – professional practices – demands control over the coherence of knowledge logics, the devices used and the nature of the data constructed. The traces of the activity of the subjects must testify to this activity, without any deformations due to inappropriate theoretical-conceptual categories and incongruent instrumentation. This in turn confirms the inappropriateness of approaches which tend to generate decontextualization and the artificial simplification of situations, due to an analysis that isolates their constitutive elements, to the advantage of interpretations that tend to be comprehensive and dynamic. In definitive terms, one is dealing with research that does not tend to elaborate solutions starting from theories but instead aims at valorising and developing the formulation of solutions which practitioners have available to them, starting with experience. Hence the applied function of the research is associated with a "clinical" approach that implies the participation of actors in the analysis of problems and in the identification of possible responses and solutions. One can therefore postulate an enquiry logic based on the theorization of practices in accordance with a cycle that starts with a description of the actions, standing at a certain distancing from the same, interrogates the same with questions aimed at identifying and explaining successes and failures, to construct, subsequently, action schema and hypotheses 'starting from and relative to practice'. With specific reference to research-development, which aims at the construction of models, prototypes and didactic objects, qualifying points comprise the analysis of needs or problems which must be resolved; the definition of expected results relative to the possibility of resolving the problems identified or responding to those needs which emerge (what must users of the constructed device be able to do? To which needs must it respond? What are the reference contexts and restrictions?); the analysis of scientific and professional literature in order to conceptualise or reconceptualise, in a hypothetic manner, the object-device, starting from the itemisation of those needs/problems which must be resolved; the refinement of the prototype-model via testing of a clinical character in the field, through "evaluation chains" aimed at recording the use that the subjects – teachers, students, teachers and students together – make of the device, followed by other tests, of a clinical or even experimental nature. The tests of a clinical character in the field are aimed, more than at measuring the final result, at reconstructing the process with specific attention paid to what the subject has or has not been able to realise, so as to enrich the comprehension of the problems/needs of users and to identify the modifications/integrations to be introduced to improve the device or the utility conditions. In other words, a clinical diagnosis, which is based on observation in situ regarding conduct and meanings recognised by the subject committed to the execution of a task, can be followed by further tests, with the same or with other subjects, according to different schema, aimed at checking the validity of the device.

Professional Action as a Subject of Analysis

Other research avenues have particularly focused on the need to identify categories that make it possible to explore and operationalize the work of actors in the situation, restoring its constitutive complexity, to make it explicit and interpretable in formalized terms. Didactic action is characterised, in general, in terms of inter-action, which can be observed in its contextual dynamicity with the remark of recursive dynamics relative to the manifest variability of the processes. These are positions that confirm the need for a research approach that involves the actors as witnesses to the execution of processes and their direction and who embrace congruent methodologies and detecting devices. According to the enactivist matrix hypotheses, which presuppose, essentially, a non determinist relation between subject and environment, such that the environment influences the subject relative to the sense that the latter attributes to it, and is in turn influenced, the action is understood as space-time in which subject and environment interact, articulating with each other and co-evolving (Rossi, 2011; Rossi, Prenna, Giannandrea, & Magnoler, 2013). The notion of actor-situation "structural coupling" is proposed, understood as "incarnate and incorporated totality", situated dynamically in a spatial, temporal, material, cultural and social context, in a permanent process of creation and attribution of meanings. The concept, relative to didactic action, and research that seeks to make it the subject of study, indicates that it is particularly interesting to note the reciprocal influence between the autopoietic systems of the teacher and the student – more than the direct action of one system on the other – before learning tasks (which involves, in addition to the cognitive sphere, a continuity between brain, mind, body, emotions). Inter-action that tends towards the conquest of reciprocal autonomy. To study didactic action, it is essential to equip oneself to understand the "regulation process, between scaffolding and fading, between power and autonomy, which is at the centre of education". Reference can also be made to the notion of "coactivity, to indicate that the analysis should be carried out on both units", teacher and student, highlighting the circularity between teaching and learning processes, in their "ambiguous autonomy"(Labate, Pezzimenti, & Rossi, 2013). Within the context of this approach, there also seems to be a valorisation of the heuristic significance of the paradigm of simplexity which, starting from, among other things, the distinction proposed by the ergonomy of the French language, between work prescribed and real activity, would make it possible to identify, in researching the teacher's professional action, units of analysis in terms of "typicalization". It is possible to identify, as a qualifying feature of the professional activity, the complexity-simplicity-simplicity dynamic i.e. the undertaking, on the part of the actor, of the relative complexity inherent in any task, problem, situation, according to a modality characterised by astuteness and elegance. Such simplicity would characterise the structural coupling – the exchanges – between actor and context, and would be supported by typicalization processes i.e. the search for similarities between the current situation and previous experiences, in the direction of forms of generalisation necessary for the action: "The actors isolate, in the continuum of their activity, certain events to which they attribute a meaning, which can be the subject of generalization through transformation into types, or into exemplary examples. The construction of knowledge for/within the action is not derived from the abstraction of logic properties, but from the constitution of types, that is operated in relation to the efficacy of the actions, through reinforcement or weakening of the previously created types, the construction by election of a case into a type, abduction, induction, systematic deduction processes etc." (Poizat, Salini, & Durand, 2013, p.107). From other epistemological perspectives, relative – essentially – to the recognition of a renewed centrality on the part of the student, as the 'reality' around which, in the didactic process, one constructs or should construct, it is possible to propose the valorisation of a conversational paradigm in order to conceptualize the action, confirming the significance, in the research, of the study of interactions in class (Pellerey, 2014). The student, the subject with his 'resistances', unexpected answers, his own world of meanings, represents the work reference which the teacher, starting from his own projects, intentions, action hypotheses, implements the moment he recognises the student as such. This is an action which, rather than being aimed directly at the student, is aimed by the teacher at himself, to try to construct the most suitable possibilities for interacting and helping the student, starting with those subjective and objective-instrumental resources that seem useful to him in achieving this goal. This is a complex process, one which arises from the dialogue between the teacher and his representations, intentions and actions, and the student, who may be more or less disposed to respond to them. The observation focus to be prioritized comprises exchanges between the teacher and students and between the latter to detect and understand what the teacher does in order to create a situation that is appropriate for promoting learning by the students through direct or indirect forms of communication. What counts is the conversational space which the teacher creates, with more or less systematically repeated interactions, in which he involves himself and the students, in order to encourage activities that make it possible to achieve the expected learning results. From an epistemological point of view i.e. one that is Piaget-constructionist in style, the conceptualization of didactic action as "medial action" (Damiano, 2013) recovers the specificity of the interaction between the teacher and student in the scholastic context as negotiated sharing of learning tasks around cultural objects, in a dynamic that structures and distinguishes the didactic action from other types of professional action. The proposal is positioned within a context that specifies the limits of the "deficit model" and normativeness, assigning to didactic research the task of indicating solutions to teachers in order to increase the efficacy of their interventions, in a directly applied mode, often with limited bases in terms of the knowledge of teaching constitutive processes (presumably, for this very reason, with modest impact on didactic practices). The road to travel down – relatively unexplored – is represented by the study of teaching as action in its concrete reality, for what it is, in order to know how and why teachers 'make things work', at least from their point of view, in a singular and contextual approach. The aim of the research is represented by 'what the teacher does relative to what the student does in order to learn cultural objects': "the task of the teacher is to carry out studies, set and vary their content and rhythm, make knowledge and methods available which he thinks that students are not able to provide for themselves, or obtain from the environment, on the assumption that only if students apply themselves can they generate learning by themselves" (Damiano, 2013, p.134). The medial character which qualifies the didactic action indicates that direct knowledge of the world – involving informal learning - is not primarily involved but, instead, an understanding of how others have described and explained it. The challenge for research is above all to succeed in bringing to light that crucible of activities which sees teachers and students committed, through a combination of mediators (active, analogue, iconic, symbolic), to processes that appropriate cultural contents, in a play of perspectives between the reality to be understood and its representation. This is a particularly uncertain and difficult process, in which the teacher, starting from his expectations, hypotheses and representations on how to teach, continually adjusts his intervention trajectories: "learning descriptions of the world with the mediation of experts is different from the way in which we learn something about the world when we act alone... students need help to be motivated and to learn since formal learning rewards the learner in the distant future, if one discounts the intrinsic reward of intellectual curiosity. Any person trying to learn something needs help in understanding how to manage the learning of concepts that are the product of other people's thoughts" (Damiamo, 2013, p.136). The 'professional routine' construct (Damiano 2006; 2013; 2014), as a possible analysis unit, is proposed due to its multidimensionality and the relative unpredictability of the teaching action, with the inclusion of intention and space-time dimensions that are constitutive of the same. The choice derives from the valorisation of constructs like that of 'scheme', in a Piaget sense, or 'habitus', in line with Bourdieu, and, nearer to home (in an articulated context of epistemological and methodological references derived from sociology, ethno-methodology, ergonomy and philosophy), the positions of Antony Giddens in particular who, in the process of routinization, recognises the aptitude of man for controlling his action through the attribution of rules which encourage efficacy and adaptation to circumstances. Routines are to be understood as sequences of operations characterised by high regularity, which make it possible to identify the distinctive features of didactic action. A routine can be considered as a sort of canvas, one that leaves margins of adaptations required to take the mutability of situations into account. Alongside a nucleus of actions that are repeated, a routine also constitutively provides for a certain degree of variability. Finally, it is felt that a routine can be the subject of observation since it is a condensation of what the processes of mutual interaction and adaptation teach actors. Taken together, routines should be "... recognised as a tendentially unitary structure that characterises teaching, made manifest through actions that correspond to the same" (Damiano, 2014, p.35). In point of fact, routines tend to aggregate together, organizing themselves in networks, like articulations that make it possible to realise an overall design that delineates a didactic activity. They associate together without any interruptions, a fact that encourages researchers to consider them as elements within an overall context that represents their meaning. Further study themes, for the most part Piaget-Cognitivist/Vygotskyano-Situationist in character, derived from professional didactics, work psychology, French language ergonomy and Schön's professional reflectivity paradigm, focusing in particular on teacher training problems, propose studying teaching from the point of view of the "action structures" or operational non-variants implied in professional actions in situ (Pastré, 2007; Vergnaud, 2011). This constitutes a way of self-regulating the action in relation to the specific features of a situation, described as "functional dynamics totality" or identifiable units of a subject's activity, which develop over a certain time frame, structuring themselves in relation to objectives and anticipations (the teacher makes certain choices in relation to certain objectives, expecting to obtain certain results), rules of action, inference possibilities in situ, identifiable in the unchanging organization of conduct for an entire class of situations. The concept of practice "organizer", albeit with interpretational polysemy problems, is proposed as a useful category in the operationalization and analysis of practice (Bru, Pastré, & Vinatier, 2007).

VIDEO AND STUDY OF DIDACTIC PRACTICES: A RESEARCH

The following sets out the system and main results of an empirical study which, in the context of the stated premises, makes it possible to make a number of considerations and indications relative to the possible paths of research-development in the didactic field in accordance with *contextually-practice-based* approaches, which recognise as research premises, the situated nature of the teaching processes and didactic action as the subject of study and, in the use of video-recording devices, a recording instrument whose use, relative to the reconstruction requirements of didactic processes from an internal approach, is still to be problematized. The 'ontological change in direction' and the epistemology in play offer new methodological challenges to didactic research in relation to a subject – the flow of action-with sense - that is particularly complex and relatively unexplored.

Problem, Objectives, and Research Approach

The study, based on the intensive adoption of video recording in natural conditions, aims to identify modelization lines for didactic practices in support of learning starting from the *Fenix Programme* (Coggi, 2009; 2015) with reference to primary school. The Programme comprises sequences of didactic activities based on the use of ludic type software, structured in accordance with curricular progression criteria, aiming at the reinforcement of cognitive and learning processes and support for motivation as factors militating against scholastic failure. The learning of mathematics and Italian language are identified as activity areas, as well as cognitive training relative to logic processes involved in the acquisition of basic disciplinary elements (e.g. development of critical thinking). The Programme is conceived as a scholastic support instrument for students with non-specific learning difficulties, in the context of individualized didactic courses based on activities carried out in the workshop with the mediation of a teacher-tutor.

Experiments carried out in the controlled conditions provided have confirmed the positive impact of the Programme on learning in curricular areas selected by 'slow' students (Coggi, 2009; 2015). A previous study has also substantially confirmed the possibility of 'curricularization' of the Programme in ordinary didactic conditions – relative to the primary school in Italy – in other words the possibility of using Fenix materials to support the learning of students in difficulty within the context of didactic paths aimed at the entire class-group, in ordinary didactic settings (Maccario, 2009). More specifically, the latter study sought to measure the features of didactic mediation in accordance with a participated research approach which, valorising 'practices knowledge' – experimenting teachers in situ – made it possible to reconstruct constitutive aspects of the didactic processes implemented. The research represented an initial effort in the unveiling of didactic practices which a systematic adoption of the Programme in natural conditions can generate, with the aim of studying the possibility of development in the direction of a 'Fenix Didactic Model'. The research availed itself of a set of instruments that was also chosen in accordance with a participatory logic, with the aim of increasing the validity of the observation process 'within' the processes to be studied. A phenomenology emerged, characterised by a training intentionality implicit in the adoption of the Programme by teachers, that was relatively extensive and articulated (consolidation of learning, motivational support, differentiation of didactics, introduction to multimedia languages in formal learning), with the identification of addressees of the intervention, not just among the most fragile students from a learning point of view, and an organization of work judged to be functional in accordance with two modalities: whole class, with articulation for pairs or small work groups – homogeneous or heterogeneous (including according to trajectories differentiated in line with training needs), or according to an alternation of didactic activities carried out with the support of Fenix material with ordinary didactic activities. In both cases an essential operational criterion was represented by the co-presence of two or more teachers in the management of the class-group. The Programme is mediated by teachers, both with respect to the choice of materials (supplementing the ordinary curriculum), to be calibrated relative to the learning needs of the children (as reinforcement and recovery or consolidation materials), and via the formulation of tasks or consignments, which regulate the start or progression of activities and offer stimuli relative to the type of exercise, rhythm and work modalities. Communication occurs in line with a differentiated logic, with an attitude expressing proximity and communicative reciprocity that seeks to guide the students in difficulty, encouraging the verbalization of learning to make it the subject of explicit and shared reflection, to activate forms of metacognitive reflection. Starting with the first 'sustainability verification' of the Programme in teaching in natural conditions and from the nuclei of actions measured, the research referred to below (PRIN 2012[1]) set itself, in accordance with an 'evaluative chains' logic, to re-submit the Programme to the terrain test, in contexts and with subjects in different operational conditions, with the aim of studying, in particular, the potentialities of the Fenix Programme in support of didactic action, considered in terms of inter-action, which originates between teacher and students committed to curricular learning mediated by the multimedial device, in line with recursive cycles or routines. The aim was to reconstruct elements of didactic modelization implicit in the teachers' practices, or 'practices' knowledge regarding 'how' it is possible to teach, valorising the resources made available by the Programme in the context of the actors, as an essential knowledge base for discussion of the possibilities of formalizing a Fenix Didactic Model in support of teaching action aimed at sustaining, in particular, cognitive and metacognitive processes at the heart of the acquisition of disciplinary contents, with an approach that customizes the interventions. This involved reconstructing the didactic processes in order to further enrich comprehension of the same in view of the definition of a didactic artefact – a work scheme – that was more in line with conditions on the ground.

Research Design and Observing Devices

The study was developed in accordance with a number of stages:

1. Formation of the research group (researchers, expert Fenix teachers) and identification of 'experimental' schools;
2. Validation in the research group of the problem and objectives;
3. Definition of the operational hypothesis and agreement on observation modalities;
4. Didactic interventions in the field;
5. Detention and constitution of the data base;
6. Elaboration and discussion.

We will carry out a short review of the methodological system to particularly problematize the use of video cameras within the context of the measurement device. The research strategy adopted is represented by case studies, in accordance with the strategy of multiple cases (Denzin & Lincoln, 2011; Miles, Huberman, & Saldaña 2014), instrumental to the research, chosen in compliance with an approach that makes it possible to carry out intensive observation, in accordance with relative variability criteria. More specifically, the didactic practices of three teachers were made the subject of observation[2]. These were teachers with decades of professional experience who, including in relation to the observed need to increase their patrimony of experience, following participation in the first phase of the research, decided, on a voluntary basis, to valorise the training acquired in the field, adopting the Fenix Programme in response to teaching personalization requirements in new and different class-contexts. The cases studied correspond to different operational options shared in the research group: a. use of the Programme in accordance with a relatively autonomous exploitation modality on the part of the students in the workshop situation, followed by a shared phase mediated by the teacher; b. use of the Programme in the workshop situation with the mediation of the teacher; c. proposal of Fenix activity in mixed form with 'ordinary' didactic activity in class. The options were shared in the research group, starting from the developments and results of the preliminary research, taking into account resources and contextual limitations. The research involved three schools in Piedmont, Italy (Cuneo province), in contexts involving small-medium size towns, with students from families characterised by average socio-cultural conditions, with a modest number of students per class judged by the teachers to experience difficulty in following the average rhythms of the class (3-5 students per class), in light of the overall learning results of the class-groups, to be reinforced in terms of learning and motivational autonomy as well as personal knowledge elaboration processes. The didactic interventions were carried out with systematic frequency for four months of the scholastic year. Observation of didactic practices was carried out on the basis of identification, by the actors, of observation units represented by interventions/lessons characterised by a launch, development and conclusion, making them identifiable and distinct from others, relative to their representativity for actors regarding teaching modes, valorising Fenix activities. The expectation was therefore to have a sample of significant professional activities for the actors and relatively defined, to be subject to intensive observation in order to identify recurrent action cycles or didactic routines. The use of video recordings with the camera in a fixed position represented an option that appeared to be not just advantageous, due to the possibility of returning to observed processes, conceding distancing space between observation and codification, thereby opening up the possibility of a more precise reconstruction of the phenomena, but appropriate for ensuring optimum observation validity since such positioning makes it possible to simultaneously take into account three essential polarities of both didactic action – teacher, students, contents – and learning, as well as their dynamic interactions. Technical limitations, but above all the features of the analysis units – the routines – nevertheless recommended a combined use of video together with other instruments (Vander Maren, 2014). The limited range of the visual field of the cameras, with the possibility of missing events outside the visual field, or losing in depth information, was overcome, where possible, by using more than one video device at the same time and, in all cases, by making field notes so as to reconstruct, as completely as possible, the dynamics of the events. However, the fundamental challenge posed by the adopted research approach was constituted by the possibility of obtaining a much more extensive representation of professional activity, including not just the "work carried out" but also the "work adopted" or taken in hand, which includes the meaning which the actors construct around their actions (Vander Maren, Yvon, 2009). In relation to the same actions, the meaning assigned can also change, including on the part of the same actor - elements that cannot be ignored when reconstructing the phenomenology of didactic action. As regards the research in question, attempts were made to obviate this type of difficulty by means of short explanations at the end of each observation unit (Vermesh, 2011), to permit the subject to return to the actions and, 'then and there', make their meaning explicit, and by means of two focus groups (one intermediary, one final), with these too video recorded, hypothesising that the inter-subjective comparison conditions could encourage both a certain critical distancing from the work carried out and the identification of implicit motives. A useful triangulation was de facto implemented. This was useful in compensating for the limits of the instrument which, however, still posed difficulties due to the fact that the "explained work" necessarily suffered from a posteriori rationalisations as well as social desirability bias, only partially contained within the collaborative approach between actors and researcher. The realisation of focus groups represented an attempt to also measure the "shared work" which, however, limited the possibility of narration in line with the spontaneous experience exchange modalities between peers – modalities which were not provided for by the research system, but potentially more valid modalities (Vander Maren, Yvon, 2009).

Some Results

Video recordings, relative to lessons, focus groups and audio-recording of explicitation discussions were transcribed and codified to be subject, as an integration, to analysis of their contents with the support of N-Vivo 10 software. The condensation into categories (Miles, Huberman, & Saldaña, 2014) is based on the unit of analysis represented by didactic routines or recurrent cycles of action, through which the teacher seeks to promote the activation of students, in view of the appropriation of cultural objects with the support of the Fenix Programme. The routines made it possible to identify features characterising the didactic models implicit in the practices of teachers, as a nucleus of knowledge – practical – to be developed, in view of the hypothesis definition, regarding a Fenix didactic model, with relatively general validity, transferable to other contexts (through analysis and formulation of explicatory hypotheses of the reconstructed phenomenology based on available theories). We set out below, by way of example, some results in terms of routines identified, aimed at acquiring discussion elements regarding the validity of the approach used, with specific reference to the modality of using the video-recording devices. The analysis of the cycles of recurrent action highlights three categories of routines-R: organizational R.; R referring to the development of learning sequences; conversational R. We briefly describe some routines of the second type, with the aim of emphasising – and discussing – the information potential of the devices adopted relative to the study of didactic action. A cycle of typically recurrent action in case a. (autonomous utilization of the Programme by students, following by sharing mediated by the teacher) is characterised by the sequence: 'immersion' – problematization – analysis and reconstruction of resolutory-transfer/mobilitation strategies to other tasks/situations. In this case, the teacher uses the Fenix Programme with reference to disciplinary knowledge already acquired by the students (e.g. calculation procedures and logics), mainly to experiment their possibility of use in different and new contexts, both ludic in character – those provided for by Fenix games – and referring to relatively more complex situations e.g. scholastic and other. The initial utilization phase for games occurs without mediation of the teacher (who limits himself to pre-selecting a certain number of games to offer the students), in pairs or small cooperative groups, with the aim of creating the conditions for comparison regarding both work organization strategies and resolutory strategies, thereby obtaining conditions which the teacher considers suitable for explicitation and sharing in the next activity phase, with the entire class. The second step involves, thanks to the mediation of the teacher, a problematizing return to the tasks carried out, in accordance with some phases, which imply, for each game explored, the analysis and verbalisation of consignment by each group; the comparison between groups, regarding the resolutory strategies adopted, with analysis of their efficiency-efficacy (recognition and analysis of any errors, identification of improvement possibilities…) and shared formalization in writing, for the most part through display using a map (on the blackboard or poster, at the discretion of the teacher); the formulation of hypotheses regarding possibilities of transfer to other situations, including with new developments. Again, with reference to case a., a partially different action cycle is structured around the 'immersion' – problematization – development of new learning – support for transfer sequence. In this case the teacher uses the Fenix Programme to construct new knowledge through an inductive course that valorises the ludic potential of Fenix activities. The initial games utilization phase occurs without the mediation of the teacher, who limits himself to pre-selecting a certain number of games to offer the students, who work in pairs or in small cooperative groups. Selection is carried out so as to permit the students to reactivate knowledge they already possess, developing it first in an intuitive form, thanks to the exchange between peers. The second phase, mediated by the teacher, who coordinates the work of the entire class, provides a problematizing return to tasks carried out, through analysis and verbalisation of the consignment by part of each group and comparison involving a discussion of resolutory strategies and obstacles faced, focusing on the new knowledge implicated. Thanks to a lesson carried out using a heuristic approach, the teacher systematizes and develops the students' intuitions and encourages the transfer to other tasks or situations, including via written formalization (on the blackboard). A different didactic cycle, which characterises case b., involves the use of Fenix games to develop and consolidate work strategies and, in general, a strategic attitude relative to scholastic work. In this case, the teacher selects games that permit the recovery/consolidation of previous acquisitions, proposing them in appropriate sequence to the students, who work in pairs or in small groups at their PC worksites. The teacher adopts a mediation role in encouraging verbalised comparison between students, supports and encourages individual and collective reasoning, guides the analysis of difficulties and errors and, in general, animates group activity. Without wishing to proceed further in an exposition of the study results, one can note – including in a comparative sense using results obtained from the first study, which adopted a different analysis approach and a different set of observation instruments – that the analysis of the video recordings of classroom activity, supplemented by videos of the focus group and the explicitations of teachers, made it possible to highlight the articulations of an operational structure which, albeit with differentiations in individual cases, indisputably highlight the added value of teacher mediation, starting from the work criteriology offered by the Programme. The teacher constructs inter-action processes with and between the students in a comparison with disciplinary contents, which make it possible not only to confirm the educational potential of the Fenix Programme, but to extend it, in the direction of a true teaching model, in support of didactic interventions for the development of problem posing and problem solving processes; consolidation and development of knowledge through the support of 'horizontal' (analogous tasks) and 'vertical' (complex tasks) transfer; development of diversified study and thought strategies; development of social skills and group work etc. Starting with the experience acquired, one clearly notes the information power of devices based on video research (Goldman, Pea, Barron, Derry, 2014), particularly in the opportunities they offer, making it possible to embrace phenomena whose complexity and dynamism easily escapes 'classic' measurement devices. Research in the field can particularly take advantage of this, including through further explorations concerning the possibilities of specific and precise valorisations, relative to problems and knowledge requirements.

Video-Research and Study of Didactic Practices: Problems and Prospects

The use of video recordings in the context of observation devices for didactic action, from the point of view of routines or recurrent action structures, can be placed in perspective, starting with the above-mentioned example, recovering the distinction between "action semantics" and "action intelligibility semantics" (Van der Maren, 2014; Barbier J.-M., 2000), polarities relative to which research in the didactic sector must apply a synthesis when it is committed to the construction of valid discursive traces of the object it is studying, in accordance with intelligibility approaches that make it possible to overcome the limits of knowledge encapsulated in the action and situation – and the discourses referring to them – to acquire significance of a general nature. One can compare a possible register, that of the words of the practitioners who talk about the action, strongly connected to and in line with the subject of the research, and therefore with 'high validity potential', with a more objectivising register that focuses on the discourses about the practices valorised by the research. In the first case one is dealing with discourses that tend to represent, but also to present to others, one's own actions, characterised by emotions; axiologically, from the link between the existing and what is desired; which are anchored in the situations but also characterised by meanings referring to other situations (exhibiting traces of typification), in a network or chain that expresses the execution of the action as a process; they are also discourses that are strongly based on operational images. One is dealing with discourses that are difficult to valorise, in a direct manner, in accordance with 'classic' research modalities, even when one accepts the paradigm of contextuality and action as a basis. The research tends, perforce, to represent the action by standing at a certain distance from it, with the use, on the part of teachers and the researcher – in accordance with participatory logic – of concepts to explain the same. Meanings of a univocal type are pursued, referring to the existing and excluding the desirable. One aims at establishing forms of relationships between elements and processes. A solution that combines the two discursive modalities, so as to obtain reconstructions of the object that are sufficiently congruent with its nature, but also adequately explicit and formalizable, can be recognised within the context of a "clinical" research approach (Van der Maren, 2014). We recommend preliminary observation of the action as it is executed in natural conditions, with measurement of primary traces, as video recordings can be, in order to encourage a return to the activity by the operators to obtain discursive explicitations that make it possible to reconstruct the meaning of the action in terms that can be compared in an intersubjective manner. The use of video recordings in the present research can be placed within the context of this approach to the extent in which the same, appropriately transcribed, represent the primary trace on which the researcher works, in a recovery of the meaning of the action through explicitation discussions and focus groups (in a research context in which the researcher assumes legitimation, including as a participant – in some way – in the problems and point of view of the operators). Improvement possibilities, in the direction of greater validity of measurements, or the possibility of obtaining a representation of the didactic action in which practices can be recognised, within the research's efforts to acquire sufficient intelligibility in the discourses it proposes, can be perceived in two directions. In one case, in close compliance with the discussed research process, in light of possible development, subjecting the reconstructions (derived from the videos with the integration of discussions and focus groups) to further validation by the teachers. A second route, alternative to that adopted, can move in the direction of a preliminary co-analysis of the videos among/ with the operators in the research group, with a process of direct comparison and the sharing of meanings, from which one can construct discursive traces to be subjected to analysis. Both prospects, at least with reference to Italy, pose feasibility problems, particularly with respect to the investment required of the teachers which, moreover, reconnects with a problem involving research carried out using a participatory approach i.e. the paradigm and approaches in discussion.

'NEW DIDACTICS RESEARCH,' RESEARCH DEVELOPMENT, AND VIDEO RESEARCH

The maturation of the 'paradigm' of the "New Didactics Research", understood as research that recognises, as its subject of study, professional action in the education field, with specific attention focused on didactic action in formal contexts – medial action – and, in this context, practice-based development research, is strongly conditioned by the refinement of devices adapted to embrace the complexity of the subject. The proposal of categories to operationalize practices focused on recursivity of inter-action cycles, placing front and centre the significance of devices that can restore primary traces of a subject and, in this context, a reflection on the possible directions of the video-research, in accordance with modalities increasingly less derived or significantly influenced by other social sciences and communication, and more precise relative to the nature of pedagogic knowledge, which recognises, among its tasks, that of describing, to understand them, education phenomena in accordance with an approach that supports the transformationality of processes (for the promotion of personal and social development pathways). In particular, the research-development context seeks to find a way to increase the validity of measurements, to counter the problems of abstraction and poor specificity in the research proposals, in order to promote improvement processes for practices. All of which takes us back to the possibility – and difficulty – of constructing the necessary 'alliances' between researchers and practitioners. A situation which exists within the transferability of the knowledge to be constructed, closely linked to the possibility and modes of formalizing didactic action. Here, of course, we also run the risk of falling back on description, which requires particular vigilance in maintaining the dialogue between practice and theory alive, in the direction of a construction of theories that are increasingly more practice-based.

CONCLUSION

The chapter has taken into consideration the use of video devices as recording instruments in the context of the discussion of research lines aimed at the development of didactic models based on the study of professional action. The approach explored implies overcoming the paradigm of prescriptivity and normativity, which has often proved to be lacking in precision relative to the transformativity of didactic practices – at least as regards expectations – due to an underestimation of the study of didactic processes de facto and the knowledge of practices as a crucial factor relative to innovation and improvement in teaching. Within this context, one of the applied research tasks in the education field – research development – is represented by the elaboration of didactic models, understood as a format that can assume artefacts or 'pedagogic objects' potentially able to sustain didactic innovation through the professional development of teachers. The research approaches and strategies which the literature indicates as most coherent with these requirements were discussed, noting the problematization linked to recognition of the contextual nature of education processes and teaching, while also pointing out the need for a true ontological change of direction, identifying didactic action as a privileged object of study and a departure point in the elaboration of didactic models, imposing on theory a more dialogue-orientated approach relative to practice. The hypothesis is gaining ground relative to the appropriateness of a 'clinical' approach which, thanks to the construction of alliances between actors and researchers, starts with practice, trying to explain its processes and meaning, analysing its problems and instances, to identify operational schema that make it possible to develop it. As part of this approach, the use of devices adapted to the construction of didactic action traces to make them available for analysis recognises that video devices and video research play a crucial role, in accordance with lines that know how to problematize the specific requirements of pedagogic research. Among these, the possibility of understanding the internal meaning – for the actors – of actions, in an approach embracing external meaning, constitutes a crucial advance.

REFERENCES

Anderson, T., & Shattuck, J. (2012). Design-Based reseach: A Decade of Progress in Education Research? *Educational Researcher*, *41*(1), 16–25. doi:10.3102/0013189X11428813

Barab, S., & Squire, K. (2004). Design-Based research: Putting a Stake in the Ground. *Journal of the Learning Sciences, 13*(1), 1–14. doi:10.1207/s15327809jls1301_1

Barbier, J.-M. (2000). Sémantique de l'action et sémantique de l'intelligibilité des l'action. In B. Maggi (Ed.), Manières de penser, manières d'agir en education et en formation. Paris, France: PUF (Presses Universitaires de France).

Brown, A. (1992). Design experiments; Theoretical and methodological challenges in creating complex interventions in classroom settings. *Journal of the Learning Sciences, 2*(2), 141–178. doi:10.1207/s15327809jls0202_2

Bru, M. (2015). Les méthodes en pédagogie. Paris, France: PUF (Presses Universitaires de France).

Bru M., Pastré P., & Vinatier (Eds.) (2007). Les organisateurs de l'activité enseignante. Perspectives croisées. In *Recherche et formation pour les professionnels de l'éducation*, 56. Paris, France: INRP (Institut National de Recherche Pédagogique).

Cardarello, R. (2016). Ricerca didattica: fare il punto. *Form@re, 3*(15), 1-10. Retrieved from http://fupress.com/formare

Coggi, C. (Ed.). (2009). *Potenziamento cognitivo e motivazionale dei bambini in difficoltà. Il Progetto Fenix*. Milano, Italia: Franco Angeli.

Coggi, C. (Ed.). (2015). *Favorire il successo a scuola. Il Progetto Fenix dall'infanzia alla secondaria*. Lecce, Italia: Pensa Multimedia.

Collins, A. (1992). Toward a design science of education. In E. Scanlon & T. O'Shea (Eds.), *New directions in educational technology* (pp. 15–22). New York: Springer-Verlag. doi:10.1007/978-3-642-77750-9_2

Collins, A., Joseph, D., & Bielaczyc, K. (2004). Design research: Theoretical and methodological issues. *Journal of the Learning Sciences, 13*(1), 15–42. doi:10.1207/s15327809jls1301_2

Damiano, E. (1994). *L'azione didattica. Per una teoria dell'insegnamento*. Roma, Italia: Armando.

Damiano, E. (2006). *La nuova alleanza. Temi, problemi, prospettive della Nuova Ricerca Didattica*. Brescia, Italia: La Scuola.

Damiano, E. (2007). *Il sapere dell'insegnare. Introduzione alla didattica per concetti con esercitazioni*. Milano, Italia: Franco Angeli.

Damiano, E. (2013). *La mediazione didattica. Per una teoria dell'insegnamento*. Milano, Italia: Franco Angeli.

Damiano, E. (2014). Epimeteo. Colui che, avendo fatto, pensa. Una ricerca nella prospettiva dell'attore. In C. Leneve, & F. Pascolini (Eds.), Nella Terra di Mezzo. Una ricerca sui Supervisori del Tirocinio (pp. 23-42).

Denzin, N., & Lincoln, Y. (2011). *The Sage Handbook of Qualitative Research*. Los Angeles, London, New Delhi, Singapore, Washington DC: Sage.

Design- Based Research Collective. (2003). Design- Based Research: An Emerging Paradigm for Educational Inquiry. *Educational Researcher*, *1*(32), 5–8.

Goldman, R., Pea, R., Barron, B., & Derry, S. (Eds.). (2014). *Video Research in the Learning Science*. New York, London: Routledge.

Haji, C., & Baillé, H. (Eds.). (1998). *Recherche et éducation. Vers une nouvelle alliance*. Bruxelles, Belgique: De Boeck.

Labate S, Pezzimenti L., & Rossi P.G. (2013). Oltre il costruttivismo. L'azione come spazio di mediazione. *Pedagogia e vita*, *71*, 71-95.

Laurillard, D. (2012). *Teaching as a Design Science. Building Pedagogical Patterns for Learning and Technology*. New York, N Y: Routledge.

Le Boterf, G. (2013). *Construire les compétences individuelles et collectives*. Paris, France: Eyrolles.

Maccario, D. (2009). Sostenibilità del Programma Fenix in situazioni didattiche correnti. In C. Coggi (Ed.), Potenziamento cognitivo e motivazionale dei bambini in difficoltà. Il Progetto Fenix (pp. 331-351). Milano, Italia: Franco Angeli.

Miles, M., Huberman, M., & Saldaña, J. (2014). *Qualitative Data Analysis. A methods Sourcebook*. Los Angeles, London, New Delhi, Singapore, Washington DC: Sage.

Pastré, P. (2007). Activité et apprentissage en didactique pfosessionnelle. In M. Fabre & M. Durand (Eds.), Les situations de formation entre savoir, problems et activité (pp. 102-123). Paris, France: L'Harmattan.

Pellerey, M. (2005). Verso una nuova metodologia di ricerca educativa: La Ricerca basata su progetti (Design-Based-Research). *Orientamenti Pedagogici*, *5*(52), 721–737.

Pellerey, M. (2014). La forza della realtà nell'agire educativo. *ECPSJournal*, *9*, 63–81.

Poizat, G., Salini, D., & Durand, M. (2013). Approche énactive de l'activité humaine, simplexité et conception de formations professionnelles. *Education Sciences &Society*, *4*(1), 97–112.

Rivoltella, P. C., & Rossi, P. G. (Eds.). (2012). *L'agire didattico.Manuale per l'insegnante*. Brescia, Italia: La Scuola.

Rossi, P. G. (2011). *Didattica enattiva. Complessità, teorie dell'azione, professionalità docente*. Milano, Italia: Franco Angeli.

Rossi P.G. (2015). Ripensare la ricerca educativa nell'ottica della professionalità docente e della generalizability. *Pedagogia Oggi*,(2), 49-64.

Rossi, P. G., Prenna, V., Giannandrea, L., & Magnoler, P. (2013). Enactivism and Didactics. Some Research Lines. *Education Sciences & Society*, *1*, 37–57.

Sandoval, A., & Bell, P. (2004). Design-Based research methods for Studying Leaning in Context: Introduction. *Educational Psychologist*, *39*(4), 199–201. doi:10.1207/s15326985ep3904_1

Van der Maren, J.-M. (2003). *La recherché appliqué en Pédagogie. Des modèles pour l'enseignement*. Bruxelles, Belgique: De Boeck.

Van der Maren, J.-M. (2014). *La recherché appliquée pour les professionnels. Éducation, (para)medical, travail social*. Bruxelles, Belgique: De Boeck.

Van der Maren J.-M, & Yvon F. (2009). L'analyse du travail entre parole et action. *Recherches qualitative*, 7, 42-63.

Vergnaud, G. (2011). Au fond de l'action, la conceptualization. In J.-M. Barbier (Ed.), Savoir Théoriques et savoir d'action (pp. 275-292). Paris, France: PUF (Presses Universitaires de France).

Vermesh, P. (2011). *L'entretien d'explicitation*. Paris, France: ESF.

KEY TERMS AND DEFINITIONS

Design Based Research-DBR: A research methodology that has been developed, starting with the proposals of A. Brown and A. Collins (1992), to communicate the need for pedagogical research which, in offering solutions to education and training problems, can take into account those contexts in which education practice is carried out, overcoming difficulties relative to measurements on a large scale, typical of experimental methodologies, which tend to propose general and decontextualized solutions, and those connected to descriptivity and interpretationality paradigms, regarding studies of an ethnographic character, which are less than entirely successful in offering directly transformative support for didactic practices. Advantages include the substantial renunciation of results generalization, thereby pursuing transcontextual transferability aims, using research approaches that are rigorous but willing to take on board the experiences of operators, together with the valorization of an articulated body of measurement instruments that are both quantitative and qualitative in character.

Didactic Action: The kind of action that sees both teacher-educator and student jointly involved in learning tasks. It is characterised in terms of inter-action i.e. the reciprocal influence of the same system on both parties, made possible and conditioned by mutual recognition relative to the tasks both parties carry out. With specific reference to formal learning contexts, the interaction is constructed around cultural objects – study disciplines – as condensates of reality representations, scientifically and socially validated, whose appropriation by the student is intended to encourage the progressive construction of his own representations of the world, pathways to comprehension and action that are increasingly more autonomous. Didactic action can be defined as action which the teacher executes to create material, organizational, symbolic, communicative and relational conditions relative to what the student is doing to learn cultural objects.

Participatory Research: Research strategies which, in general, embrace, as a presupposition, the need for convergence between theoretical and practical approaches in order to better understand human, social and education problems. In light of this, they promote general cooperation between researchers and operators/actors on the ground, starting with the definition of research objectives and questions. It is felt that the research process can advantage researchers to the extent that they gain access to original and internal approaches relative to the problems they explore and, therefore, can construct more comprehensive and precise knowledge relative to the phenomena they investigate. The actors, by participating in the research process, have an opportunity to 'take a step back', in cognitive terms, relative to professional routines and representations, thereby acquiring greater understanding of their work and the possibilities of self-regulating the same. As regards measurement methodologies, analysis and data interpretation, qualitative approaches are prioritized, albeit not exclusively. One of the main problems of participatory type research involves construction of the necessary 'alliances' between researchers and 'practitioners', subjects with different intentions, expectations, approaches and skills relative to research tasks and results.

Practical Knowledge: The kind of knowledge that is generated when exercising professional practices. It is the product of the need to know how to move in uncertain and complex situations, finding solutions that take into account one's own needs and those of others. It is not generated by reasoning processes of a linear type, which make a direct connection between aims and means, but by a knowledge of the situations in which one works, acquired through processes defined as "reflection-in action", reasonableness, mètis or astuteness etc. In the didactic field, these represent the main way to reconcile the structural antinomy that exists between the freedom of the student, which is achieved starting from a position of relative impotence, and the authority of the teacher, which is justified by its provisional character, intended to progressively decrease with the increasing autonomy of the student. Among its distinctive features, practical knowledge can be highly situated and contextualized. It is also socially characterized because, to a degree, it is the fruit of negotiation with others (community of practices, action addressees, reference organization). For the most part this is tacit and implicit, in that it is contained in the actor's action, in a general sense, without the latter having any (complete) awareness of the same.

Practice Based Research-PBR: A composite research approach, which has essentially been developed to tackle the problem of the limited impact of education research on teaching practices, particularly in relation to difficulties experienced by academic research in producing results that take the features of operational contexts into account, embracing education problems from a holistic and dynamic point of view, to generate practical indications in natural professional operating conditions. PBR seeks to produce research results which can benefit schools and generate effective changes. For this reason, it aims at the construction of theories based on practice. It provides for close interaction between researchers and professional in the field, including in accordance with non-linear developments. It assumes contextuality as a criterion for the design and development of knowledge and explicitation hypotheses. And it also provides for the integration of different theoretical contributions and various methodological approaches. As regards problems, it is important to note the tension, still unresolved, between the need to respond to requirements and standards of a scientific character and those of a pragmatic type.

Professional Routines: Action approaches, characterized by repetition, which are generated by processes involving the reciprocal interaction and adaptation of a subject relative to work conditions. They are the fruit of active construction on the part of the subject, deriving from the desire to control one's actions through the definition of rules which encourage their efficacy and adaptation to circumstances. A routine is characterized by a high level of regularity in its response to professional tasks, together with a degree of flexibility, which permits accommodation margins that are needed in order to take into account the relative mutability of operational conditions. In overall terms, professional routines constitute the essential structure of a professional activity.

Research-Development: From a pedagogical point of view, this is a field of research that focuses on the elaboration of innovative programmes, models and didactic materials in support of teacher activity. The aim of this type of research is essentially that of constructing theoretical-practical devices that make it possible for teachers and educators to overcome the limitations of didactic approaches which are largely intuitive and artisanal, characterised by a limited design component, offering instead work schema and criteria that are subject to validation in terms of scientific aspects, practicability and their potential training impact.

Video Research: Different ways videos can be valorized in education research: from the collection of videos to produce data on teaching and learning processes in formal contexts, aimed at encouraging the comprehension and design of training environments; to the realisation of videos on interactions in non-formal education contexts, as an instrument for the comprehension and promotion of learning processes; to surveys that concern the learning possibilities offered by videos, whose aim is to help researchers to design situations in which videos represent privileged training devices; to the production and use of video-cases, aimed at professional development, via sharing and comparison within the professional community. The main critical-discursive aspects include questions regarding the choice of audio-recording strategies, video selection criteria and the possibilities of data analysis starting with video recordings.

ENDNOTES

[1]   Project of national interest. Funding Ministry of University and Scientific Research (2012). National coordination: Prof. Gaetano Domenici- Roma Tre University. Local coordination: Prof. Cristina Coggi - University of Turin.

[2]   We thank the teachers: Stefania Cucco; Alessandra Bettonagli (Mondovì-CN - Direzione Didattica 1; Anna Maria Cornaglia (Fossano-CN - Direzione Didattica 1)

Chapter 4
Designing a Collaborative Video Learning Lab to Transform Teachers' Work Practices

Valérie Lussi Borer
University of Geneva, Switzerland

Alain Muller
University of Geneva, Switzerland

ABSTRACT

Video is increasingly used in professional development programs for teachers. Several studies have shown that the ability to notice and analyze pertinent classroom elements is the mark of an expert teacher, but little research has focused on how to use video to bring about real transformations in teachers' classroom activity. A research program was therefore developed to address this issue, drawing on Dewey's notion of collaborative inquiry and key concepts from work analysis. The research revealed three processes of professional development that video-artifacts can bring to the fore and enrich: mimetic engagement, the comparison and cross-fertilization between activities, and the deconstruction-reconstruction of activity. On the basis of these processes, the researchers designed a program called the Collaborative Video Learning Laboratory, which has yielded promising preliminary results for professional development. The advantages and challenges of this program are discussed and the new perspectives for professional development programs for teachers are presented.

INTRODUCTION

Teacher education and professional development (PD) have long been modeled on curriculum-based programs, with teachers attending classes on a regular basis to acquire new or updated knowledge about their profession. Yet these programs are increasingly being seen as unsatisfactory in bringing about transformations in professional practices, notably at a time when the schools are often pressed to adapt to rapidly changing social contexts (OECD, 2014). This observation is thus not new, but the dissatisfac-

DOI: 10.4018/978-1-5225-0711-6.ch004

Copyright © 2017, IGI Global. Copying or distributing in print or electronic forms without written permission of IGI Global is prohibited.

tion has become acute and educational policies are needed that can respond with new ways to improve PD in the schools. We believe that in this context a developmental approach holds promise.

A developmental approach to education presupposes the design of *ad hoc* programs that:

1. Support teachers as they develop professionally and not just as they acquire the knowledge needed to begin their practice[1],
2. Allow educators to function as facilitators rather than as transmitters of knowledge,
3. Flexible enough to allow the educational contents to be closely adapted to the professional obstacles or problems that the teachers themselves identify (Leblanc & Ria, 2014), and
4. Let the educational program unfold in various non-anticipable and negotiated timeframes (Durand, 2011).

This chapter describes why and how video-based education contributes to a developmental perspective. Video- and artifact-based programs are increasingly used for teacher education and PD for four main reasons:

1. Explosive growth in the technological potential of digital techniques,
2. Simpler use of video tools,
3. A clearer picture of the teaching practices that the reforms in educational policies and PD programs have targeted for change, and
4. The increasing conviction that training and actual professional practice must be more closely associated (Blomberg et al., 2013; Calandra & Rich, 2014; Gaudin & Chaliès, 2015; Janik & Seidel, 2009).

The use of video is nevertheless often limited, perhaps reductively, to:

1. Bringing authentic images of the real practices of teachers and students,
2. Illustrating the steps of good practice transmission,
3. Standardizing the practices to be used in the schools and classrooms in response to new reforms, and
4. Building a "prescriptive learning path to improve teacher professional competencies" (which was denounced in the introduction to this book).

As to the research on the effects of using video for teacher education and PD (Brouwer, 2011; Santagata & Guarino, 2011; Seidel & Stürmer, 2014), the studies indicate that video use promotes the development of teachers' cognitive and reflexive processes – particularly their ability to notice and interpret classroom events – but the evidence is scant that the improvement of these processes is actually correlated with changes in teaching practices. Some of the studies have focused specifically on transforming practices through the introduction of video clubs in the schools (Borko et al., 2008; Coles, 2013; van Es, 2012). These studies were able to show that video use by communities of practice encourages positive transformations, thereby underlining the need to examine how to create and sustain a professional community in which PD through video analysis is the collective goal, what type of school-based setting best promotes such a community (Brouwer, 2011; Gallimore et al., 2009), and what kinds of features will facilitate its development (van Es et al., 2014).

As this brief review of the literature shows, video-based education has garnered considerable research attention and it seems set to become a major international research topic, as there is still much to learn about:

1.   The effectiveness of the transformations in teaching practices during video-artifact-based programs,
2.   Teachers' activity *vis-a-vis* the videos and how this activity influences the development of their own classroom practices,
3.   The design of programs that can elicit and support PD, and
4.   How facilitators can design and implement video-based PD programs.

The authors' research has therefore been focused on exploring new video support modalities with peer involvement both to accompany teachers at the start of and throughout their careers and to provide opportunities for lifelong PD (Flandin, Leblanc & Muller, 2015). The preliminary findings about a video-based program called the Collaborative Video Learning Lab (CVLL) offer some intriguing directions for reflection (Lussi Borer & Muller, 2014a; Lussi Borer *et al.*, 2014).

The CVLL is presented in this chapter. First, the theoretical assumptions underlying the CVLL design are introduced; next is a description of how it functions and how it affects teachers' activity, based on observations of two kinds of CVLLs. The conclusion is a discussion of the results of this exploratory research and a presentation of the new perspectives for teachers' PD and future research opened by the CVLL.

THEORETICAL BACKGROUND AND ASSUMPTIONS ABOUT PROFESSIONAL DEVELOPMENT

To design the CVLL from a developmental perspective, the authors were inspired by concepts derived from Dewey's pragmatism (experience, reflexivity, and collaborative inquiry) and Francophone ergonomics (activity and real work).

Work Practices and Activity

In the CVLL, facilitators and teachers use the concept of "work activity," a holistic concept for capturing, understanding and transforming work practices. Human activity is defined as anything an actor is doing at a given moment while performing a social practice, and work activity as anything a worker is doing while performing a work task. Human activity can be characterized as:

1.   Dynamic, because it is endlessly being transformed;
2.   Situated, because it is rooted in an environment;
3.   Meaningful, because it produces personal and/or shared meaning;
4.   Having emotional and affective valence and involving subjective commitment; and
5.   A source of experience for the actors (Durand, 2011).

For Francophone ergonomics, there is always a gap between the prescribed task (mandatory work, the curriculum) and its actual performance (De Montmollin, 1974; Ombredane & Faverge, 1955). This gap is not necessarily due to a failing, such as a worker's incapacity to perform adequately: rather, workers have to interpret the established norms[2] within a context of continually changing situations so that they can ultimately complete the prescribed task. Education from a developmental perspective therefore must take as the central objects both the real work and the actor's constant reinterpretation of the norms (renormalization). This in no way suggests that institutional prescriptions and scientific and professional knowledge should be sidelined or discarded in the educational program. But it does mean that these prescriptions and knowledge should be dealt with not as such, but as *objects to be re-normalized* – that is, as rules which, being resources for acting, have to be experienced in action and, if necessary, revised in order to be viable (Lussi Borer & Muller, 2014a).

As Schwartz expressed it (2007), the activity of renormalization deals with more than prescribed work:

As the distinction between "prescribed work" and "real work" at the microscopic level suggests, debates about norms are an endless preoccupation of human activity: debates about norms, of which "prescribed work" may be one, versus trends toward renormalization, which is reflected at the microscopic level by "real work" or "actual work". (p. 131)

These norms are of various orders. Depending on the epistemological position, one could cite ethical rules, work rules, knowledge *in order to* teach, tacit knowledge, professional habitus, beliefs or representations, and so on, all conscious or unconscious, formal or informal, personal or collective, related to a subject or completely unspecific: all, in any case, driving the work at different levels. These norms are identifiable in daily work situations, directly because of their input to actions, objects, situations and events, and indirectly because they can be partially accessed via the experience of actors, who can thus express them. However, they are not easily identifiable and isolated because exogenous norms may be explicit (formalized in the workplace by texts, codes of ethics, etc.) or implicit (peer expectations, informal work culture) and they intersect with endogenous norms that are implicit (dispositions to act; Muller & Plazaola Giger, 2015) or explicit (personal norms developed through language) (Lussi Borer & Muller, 2014b).

WORK EXPERIENCE

Dewey (1938) assumed that human experience has the following characteristics:

1. It designates both the here-and-now experience associated with a practice and the capitalization of past experiences,
2. It borrows from past experiences and modifies the quality of future experiences,
3. It arises from a process that Dewey called the experiential continuum, and
4. It is a finalized social event that involves contacts and communications and within which an interaction between the actor and the environment continuously unfolds.

Based on these characteristics, Dewey provided a frame that gave meaning to human development as a continuity and an ongoing renewal of experience. In the same vein, Francophone ergonomists insist on the importance of taking work experience into account (Durand, 2011). All work activity transforms the real (it is productive) and transforms the actor who performs the work (it is constructive). Taking into account the constructive dimension is the aim of the CVLL: to understand the heart of work means to understand the transformations in the worker who performs that work.

To access the process of constructing experience, observing actors during work activity is fundamental but often insufficient. Therefore, it is often useful to ask the actors themselves to contribute to the analysis of their own work as they can contribute information that only they can give. This information concerns the covert (or non-observable) aspects of working such as decision-making, evaluations and judgments, thinking and analyses, emotions, intentions, mobilized knowledge, postural adjustments, etc. In the CVLL, experience is accessed during individual self-confrontation interviews (confronting actors with their own activity reveals the lived experience during this activity; Theureau, 2002), during which actors comment on their activity (i.e., that part that can be shown, mimed, told about and commented on in the right conditions) while watching a recording of their activity alongside a facilitator who questions them about the indices perceived in the situation and their concerns, intentions, expectations, emotions, and cognitions (Lussi Borer & Muller, 2014b).

Inquiry and Collaborative Inquiry

The concept of inquiry that Dewey proposed (1938) refers to the transformation of a situation (the interaction of actors with their environment) from one that is *indeterminate* (confusing, contradictory, vague) into one that is *problematic* (that poses a clearly identified problem) and ultimately into one that is *determinate* (or more viable). A situation is indeterminate when the actor-environment balance is in some way disrupted (e.g., the body feels hunger, an actor does not understand an event). But the imbalance should not be imputed to the actor: hunger is not a lack in the body but an imbalance in the subject-environment exchanges (the same for a lack of understanding). Inquiry is the reestablishment of the actor-environment balance by transforming the situation – as much for the environment as for the actor.

Inquiry refers to a concrete transformation within a given situation through close observation followed by the generation of ideas for possible solutions. Observation thus produces the ideas, which, if they are functional, will in turn bring to light new observable elements, and this process will continue until the situation becomes organized into a coherent whole. "Collecting" observations and suggesting ideas are interactive processes: ideas guide observation, which in turn suggests new ideas. As the initial ideas are often too vague to point to a solution, they need to be examined as ideas, having meaning within a system of meanings. This then is the start of the process of clarifying ideas, but working on meaning is not mere conceptual work, utterly detached from observation, because the clarification of ideas *brings to light* new facts.

This pragmatist conception of inquiry offers a "natural" developmental model that can be transferred to the design of education programs. This transfer is based on the hypothesis that a PD program can ultimately do nothing more than *support, accelerate, accompany*, and *structure* the developmental processes that are *already* at work in the PD endeavor. Defining a PD object thus must make sense to the trainees and be negotiated with them.

Individual and collective inquiries take place simultaneously in the CVLL, the objective being that the individual inquiries are enriched by the collective inquiry and *vice versa*. According to Dewey (1927), an inquiry becomes collaborative as soon as several actors work together to transform their respective situations. This assumes a process of inter-objectivation – that is, "the constitution of objects depending on the possibilities for agreement between several experiences" (Zask, 2004, p. 148). Although the participants may have specific experiences that differ, they nevertheless must come to agreement on a general and *common* "inquiry object" they will investigate both together and separately. In the CVLL, the inquiry is carried out principally by doing and by conceptualizing and elaborating the activity and experience together in the midst of interactions (principally through language) with others. Dewey connects experience and meaning to the concept of reflection:

Thought or reflection… is the discernment of the relation between what we try to do and what happens in consequence. No experience having a meaning is possible without some element of thought… Thinking, in other words, is the intentional endeavor to discover specific connections between something which we do and the consequences which result, so that the two become continuous. (1916, p. 170)

The CVLL is based on the postulate that actualizing these connections and putting them into words can be enriched by exchanges and collaborations with other actors who are implicated in the same process and are exploring the same inquiry object together. This enrichment occurs because in this context the individual systems of norms and connection-building are brought together and expressed, and the result is potentially a broadening of the participant's range of connections – and therefore possible meanings – linked with renormalization processes. Thus, other actors serve as mediators between a given actor and the actor's activity that is the object of common inquiry. The other participants are asked to put themselves in the inquiring actor's shoes by accessing their concerns, intentions, expectations, emotions, and cognitions and to offer alternative viewpoints that make the transformation in the actor's activity possible "from itself" as the realization of one's own potential that the differences among the actors reveal. In the CVLL, the inquiry that is encouraged is geared toward the development of "enriched reflection" in the actors. Reflection is accentuated by collaboration, in the sense that the personal processes of conceptualization and elaboration are enriched by these same processes being carried out by others.

Based on these theoretical assumptions, education design from a developmental perspective means encouraging and supporting the actors' "natural" process of inquiry and keeping the focus on the professional objects that have been collectively negotiated. These objects are investigated from traces of activity taken from real work. Real work includes the productive and observable dimensions of work activity and the more hidden constructive dimensions that concern the actor's constant interaction with the activity and his or her experience of this activity. The CVLL puts the focus on these constructive dimensions by encouraging the actors to think and verbalize with peers how they established connections between what they did in relation to what they intended to do and what this did to them in return. When actors verbalize to peers how they established these connections, they mobilize their systems of norms and give access to their construction of meanings, effectively moving the inquiry from an *indeterminate* situation to a *problematic* situation (even *determinate,* or the inquiry object may be modified).

Putting a program that is structured as an inquiry into effect is quite a complex task, for at least three reasons. It is complex because, first, the choice to analyze real work is a major change in that most of the conventional education designs (including for initial education) take into account only the prescribed work. Second, "ordinary" work activity gives an illusion of evidence or transparency because the ways of doing the work have been "naturalized" (we rarely think of how we tie our shoes). In this sense, ordinary activity is analogous to light, which we see as white although it is actually polychromatic. To see each of its colors, diffractive lenses have to be used and, to continue the analogy, this leads to the notion of designing educational artifacts. Also, the choice to analyze both observable activity and the way the actor experiences this activity means that the program must be designed to be sufficiently nonjudgmental, safe and benevolent so that the actors will risk putting their experience into words and sharing it with others. Last, bringing to light the norms that underlie activity and working on them is difficult because actors do not necessarily want to disrupt the balances they have already achieved only at a certain cost and as shown above, they are not always able to distinguish between what is part of their own norms as opposed to those of others (Lussi Borer & Muller, 2014b). To overcome these obstacles, the creation and use of video-artifacts are promising leads, as the authors will now show.

VIDEO-ARTIFACTS TO "AUGMENT" A PROFESSIONAL DEVELOPMENT PROGRAM

Video-artifacts are used in the CVLL to drive the inquiry. Artifacts, in this context, are the video clips resulting from processing: by editing, annotation, the configuration of successive extracts, and so on. These artifacts are used from a perspective inspired by the notion of "augmented reality," as a way to enrich the environment of the participants as they are analyze professional activity and thereby encourage and support their PD. The term augmented reality refers to its earliest definition as "the intersection between virtual and physical reality, where digital visuals are blended in to the real world to enhance our perceptions" (Cassella, 2009). To generate this enhancement, augmented reality uses a variety of media that are "superimposed" over real world objects in such a way that it changes how we experience the world. To design videos-artifacts from this perspective means first thinking about how to enrich the clips with systems of annotation, access to additional information or images, the expression of associated experiences, and the configuration of successive extracts. All of them should themselves be able to enrich actor-environment interactions and generate new formative experiences. To create and use these artifacts, the authors relied on three main processes that emerged from their research on video use in education programs and seemed to hold promise:

- Mimetism and fictional experience (act as if).
- Comparison and cross-fertilization between activities.
- Production of and navigation between different semiotic frames.

Mimetism and Fictional Experience (Act as If)

As noted by Flandin, Leblanc and Muller (2015), the phenomenological process that has been most documented by research is the *mimetic* process, which consists of linking an activity being viewed and the video-artifact user's activity in terms of the proximity between the two. Users experience the activity of another as if it were their own, which tends to spatially and temporally *immerse* them in the activity being viewed, to live it by *proxy* and to *replay* their own activity through a synchronization process, the creation of expectations, and anticipation.

This mimetic process can also be understood as connecting the relationship between the viewed activity and the user's activity from a dual point of view, both egocentric: I live what I see as if it were really me living it, and allocentric: I put myself in the other person's place. The shift from an egocentric to an allocentric point of view can open on to a third point of view, less tied to experience and more *analytical* or *decontextualized* (Leblanc & Ria, 2014).

This immersion in viewed activity may also be expressed as a *fictional experience* (Zaccai-Reyners, 2005) in which new possibles for one's own real activity emerge from the meaningful elements identified in the viewed activity, bringing to life a whole new scenario of *act as if*. The mimetic experience generated by video-artifacts provides experiential registers that are situated as globally analogous relationships rather than as homologous. Projecting oneself into closely related but not identical situations – into situations having a "family resemblance" to those personally encountered (that's *not* what I do, but it's *not not* what I do) – is a way to "bring to light" the "germinating" dimensions of the activity, which too close or too distant a proximity would not allow for. According to Zaccaï-Reyners, this fictional immersion creates "states of consciousness conducive to exploring possibles in a minor key" (2005, p. 17), and this allows the actor to project into other possible roles without putting professional identity at too great a risk.

In an augmented reality environment like the CVLL, video-artifacts are configured to:

1. Engage actors mimetically as they view their own recorded activity or that of other professionals performing similar tasks involving the inquiry object,
2. Disturb the actors' expected horizons (e.g., what would you do if you were in this teacher's shoes right now?), and
3. Try to bring together and allow connections between experiences (e.g., what direct or indirect personal experiences does this classroom episode bring to mind?).

Comparison and Cross-Fertilization Between Activities

The comparisons of viewed activities can be made at several levels. The following three emerged as most frequent in the authors' research findings.

The comparisons can be qualitative, expressing differences on the order to "what works" and "what doesn't" or "what works less well." Viewing a video-artifact can reveal a satisfaction or dissatisfaction that is *already there* (but tacit or unconscious) with one's own activity or it can reveal a new satisfaction or dissatisfaction that becomes apparent at the moment when the viewed activity is perceived as comparatively better or worse than one's own (Flandin, 2015). The process can be described as follows: actors view a filmed activity that reminds them of their own and (i) they are satisfied, which generates an attribution of meaning or even reinforcement of their activity as it is congruent with their system of norms (*determinate* situation) or (ii) they are dissatisfied, which generates a feeling of frustration and a sense of incoherence with their system of norms and thus an inquiry is begun (*indeterminate* situation) to identify where exactly the problem resides (*problematic* situation) to ultimately find ways to improve (Flandin & Ria, 2014).

Identifying the qualitative differences between activities often elicits a description of events or actions from the actors that *make* the difference. This thematization is particularly interesting because (i) it highlights the system of norms of the inquirers and (ii) it shows that the work of comparison is analytical: the inquirers first grasp the general qualities, then move in "for a closer look" to search for those elements that contribute to "what works" and "what doesn't work."

The comparison can ultimately become more general: the inquirers try to understand the differences between activities as a *set of events* or the principles that drive them.

In summary, the *comparison between activities* highlights the overall differences that make for success, the differences between ways of doing things, and the differences in norms that are expressed by the activities. The work of viewing, analyzing and comparing raises awareness of what might make a difference, even in the smallest detail, in similar situations.

Research shows that although comparison allows inquirers to notice the relevant components of the activity, it is often not enough to help them to find concrete ways to transform their own activity (Lussi Borer *et al.*, 2014). The authors' findings show that the move of comparison can be more helpful if the analysis is enriched with a second move that consists of noticing and then thematizing *what could have been different* in the unfolding activity. This second move helps the inquirers to notice the unrealized *possibles* in the analyzed activity. These identifications of *what would have been possible to do* allow inquirers to enter into *an activity that is unfolding*, rather than limiting the activity to its actual outcome. In this way, it helps inquirers to notice the moments of the activity when bifurcations would have been conceivable.

Comparison opens concrete directions for transformation when the thematization of the *possibles* resulting from activity analysis is cross-fertilized with another activity. When inquirers signify a *difference* perceived in a comparison between activities as making a *possible* for another activity, they construct a link between something already realized elsewhere and a *possible* in the activity under consideration. This cross-fertilized *possible* allows for the reconfiguration of the activity by giving it a propensity to develop in a different direction. It opens up paths of transformation that are all the more relevant in that they have already been tested in another configuration of activity. It then becomes possible to see and understand not only the qualities, action-events or principles that make the difference, but also where exactly in these qualities, action-events and principles the differences reside. This double move helps the inquirers to extract the promising *possible* from one analyzed activity and to suggest ways to implant and adapt/fit this *possible* to another activity in order to transform it, of course taking into account the "ecological equilibrium" of the interaction between the actor and his or her environment (experience, system of norms, intentions, etc.).

PRODUCTION OF AND NAVIGATION BETWEEN SEMIOTIC FRAMES

The authors' initial analyses grounded in Peirce's semiotics (1978) show the relationships that actors weave with an activity (whether their own or that of another) when they view it using video-artifacts (Lussi & Borer Muller, 2014a). These analyses indicate what happens when CVLL participants (teachers and facilitators) work individually or collectively with video-artifacts and provide facilitators with guides for orienting the nature of the interactions in the CVLL depending on the negotiated inquiry object. The relationships can be classified into two major categories of signs, each consisting of five levels:

The first level expresses the relationship to the viewed activity as:

1. **Simple Reaction:** Head shake, smile, etc.
2. **Event Description**: "The students quietly show up".
3. **Interpretation of the Activity**: "She looked at the student to signal that he needed to calm down".
4. **Explanation of the Activity**: "If the class is quiet it's because habits have been built".
5. **Evaluation of the Activity**: "It's good… it works".

The second level expresses the relationship of the viewed activity to another activity (often that of the one who is viewing) as:

1. **Description of one's own activity.**

2. **Mapping the Two Events:** "I too have really difficult classes".
3. **Mapping the Intentions:** "I also try to motivate the students".
4. **Contrasting the Two Activities:** "She lets the students enter as they want ... I say no... in my class they enter as a group".
5. **Evaluation of the Activity:** "putting the students in a line... for students at that age, it's not really relevant".

When an actor views a peer's filmed activity, a process seems to be set in motion of producing semiotic frames related to the activity being viewed and this activity as compared with one's own activity – and this type of comparison has the potential power to transform.

Our interest in this process is based on the following hypothesis: producing signs of different levels – that is, relationships differentiated in terms of *what is seen and heard and makes experience* – and weaving these differentiated relationships together produces a process of *deconstruction-reconstruction* of both the viewed activity and the viewer's activity. The CVLL is based on the educational effects of this process. Analysis has shown that teachers viewing filmed activity tend to produce *semiotic frames* by navigating through the various levels, with the result being that what is initially "said" at a certain level can later be modified after navigating through other levels. For example, teachers may shift from evaluation to description *via* the interpretation of an activity, and find that they have arrived at a new and different evaluation.

The initial research results have shown that when these productions and navigations between semiotic frames are articulated with mimetic processes, fictional experiences and comparison and cross-fertilization between activities, they generate renormalization processes that embody the formative impulse of the inquiry. This process of renormalization consists, according to Schwartz (2007), of reinterpreting not only norms coming from the environment, but also endogenous norms, in order to configure this environment as being one's own. In Dewey's language, it produces a new and determinate situation. This continuous work of renewing the rules to elaborate experience and the rules to follow in action enriches the inquiry. When the CVLL participants are able to see and use the different semiotic levels to talk about the viewed activity, the rules and norms that support the activity are revealed (e.g., *I do this because I have to ... I think it's good to... etc.*). Participants often struggle to distinguish between institutional expectations, colleagues' expectations and their own expectations. Viewing clips and the exchanges that ensue are ways to make the rules explicit, highlight the conflicts that several co-existing norms may generate, and thus open the way to arbitration.

CVLL INQUIRY-FOCUSED DESIGN: THREE STEPS

To prompt and support inquiries in the CVLL, three steps are needed to:

1. Determine the inquiry objects shared by the participants based on their real work activities,
2. Encourage them to participate in a collaborative inquiry about the object they have selected *via* video-artifacts, and
3. Support them as they try to transform their teaching practices.

Exploratory studies have shown that these steps promote activities and experiences likely to induce PD (Lussi, Ria, Durand & Muller, 2014).

To illustrate the implementation and operation of a CVLL, the authors present two examples that they have followed as researchers and facilitators. The first example comes from a CVLL set up in three primary pilot schools in the context of a partnership with a French region involved in the three-year Ministry of National Education Project "More Teachers Than Classes".[3] The second example comes from a CVLL set up in a secondary teacher induction program (Lussi Borer & Muller, 2014b).

Step 1: Co-Definition of the Shared Object of Inquiry

The first step in CVLL inquiry is the co-definition of an object by the designer-facilitators and the participants. Several constraints should be heeded:

1.   The object must come from real work,
2.   It must be possible to document traces of the activity,
3.   The object must make sense to all participants and thus truly represent one of their concerns,
4.   The concern must be linked to professional activity as a real "problem of the job" so that all participants are at least minimally interested in the collective inquiry, and
5.   The participants must all stand to gain from the inquiry in terms of PD, both individually and collectively.

The participants define a shared object of inquiry, or a learning object, by taking into account their concerns/intentions and then agree as well on how this object should manifest in the activity under analysis. As observed by Dewey (1916), PD objectives should not be defined from the "outside" as a reflection of institutional prescriptions: a part of them must be drawn from "inside" the activity in order to take into account and express its potentials for development. The "learning objects" (Durand, 2011) that are meaningful for the participants emerge when their concerns about the real work are collectively shared.

Illustration from a Primary In-School CVLL

In the CVLL of the three primary pilot schools, co-teaching was prescribed by the reforms, although the teachers were not accustomed to this type of teaching. The first inquiry object unanimously defined

Table 1. Description of the CVLLs' data analyzed

CVLL Set Up In	Primary In-School PD Programs	Secondary Teacher Induction Program
Timeframe	2013-2016 Three-year program	2012-2016 One-year program, every academic year
Location	France, Department of Haute-Savoie	Switzerland, University of Geneva
Schools/teachers involved	3 schools 28 primary in-service teachers	79 secondary teachers during their induction year
CVLL filmed sessions (1h30)	24 sessions (2 to 3 every year, per school)	39 sessions (2 per year, per group of 2 to 5 teachers)
Video data analyzed	24 x 1 hour 30 minutes: 36 hours	38 x 1 hour 30 minutes: 58 hours

by the three teaching teams was: *How should we teach when there are two teachers in the classroom? What does co-teaching mean? How do we share classroom space, time for speaking, lesson work and interventions (content matter and disciplinary) with students?* Once the object was defined, the teachers chose the traces of activity that they wanted to have recorded and how they wanted to document them with the facilitators: they chose both individually (self-confrontation interviews to express their experience) and collectively (video clips and filmed interviews viewed with the entire teaching team). The traces consisted of a lesson during which they shared intervening with the students, either in the first part of the lesson during the students' oral participation or in the second part in interventions during the students' individual work.

Step 2: Co-Analyzing the Shared Inquiry Object

The author's initial research based on Peirce's semiotics was an observation of how the teachers related to the video clips of activity, and the first results showed that the levels of their relationship to the activity were mostly "spontaneously" normative: those who viewed the activity judged it positively or negatively (Lussi Borer & Muller, 2014b). At this initial stage, judgment stopped the inquiry, made it impossible to enter into an analysis of the elements and events present in the viewed activity, and established a standard of assessment that encouraged a focus on "what is lacking in the activity" rather than "the potential already present in the activity." This "spontaneously" normative relationship was so common that the participants were not even aware of it or its impact on the inquiry. The first video-artifact created in the CVLL therefore aimed to help the participants to:

1. Become aware of this normative tendency;
2. Deconstruct and reconstruct the activity by navigating through the semiotic frames at different levels;
3. Consider work activity as a "process" resulting from an "operational compromise" between what was prescribed and the conditions for actually performing the work, with efficiency depending on both objective and subjective constraints; and
4. Focus their comments on the activity and not on people.

Illustration of a CVLL in a Secondary Teacher Induction Program

The "Viewing is first of all judging" artifact: The participants viewed a short video excerpt of a teaching activity Néopass@ction platform (Institut Francais de L'Education, 2016). The facilitators recorded and transcribed the comments and then provided a grid for analyzing the activity on three levels[4]:

- **Descriptive:** Reporting what one sees as "neutrally" as possible, with a simple set of facts and observed elements (e.g., the teacher is in front of the blackboard, she is asking the students to give examples). At this level, there may be different descriptions of the same situation, but there should not be conflicting descriptions;
- **Interpretative:** Reporting the protagonist's intentions in the situation viewed, what she wants to do, what her concerns are (e.g., the teacher wants to work from the students' examples because she thinks they will understand better this way). At this level, there may be conflicting interpretations;

- **Evaluative:** Assigning a value to the viewed activity (e.g., the teacher clearly validates or invalidates the students' examples). At this level, evaluation conflicts are common.

The facilitators then asked participants to read the transcribed comments and assign them to one of the three levels. They observed that about 80% of the comments were at least partly negative evaluations and therefore were at the level where most conflict occurs. They then viewed an excerpt of the self-confrontation interview of the teacher who had been filmed, as she expressed intentions, concerns, and feelings. This allowed them to confirm or discard their interpretations and to consider what the teacher had said she wanted to do alongside what was actually done. While using the "Viewing is first of all judging" artifact, the participants were able to transform the way they viewed a video and commented on it, and they became more aware of the levels as they navigated between them. This transformation is vital to ensure that the fundamental ethics underlying the collaborative inquiry in the CVLL are not merely expressed in the designer-facilitators' discourse, but are experienced and meaningful for the participants.

The goal of the CVLL is to prompt the participants to compare and identify *possible differences* in the analyzed activities so that they are able to cross-fertilize their own activity. The participants will do so if they are equipped with tools for the deconstruction and comparative analysis of activities and they are presented with activities close to their own so that they can compare and cross-fertilize the activities as they produce assessments and ideas/directions for transformation. By deconstructing and comparing activities, the participants conduct inquiries into what "makes" an activity as opposed to another. They become able to discern the possible bifurcations in the analyzed activity and the differences between two activities (their own and the viewed) or more. When conducting these inquiries, they make use of their personal systems of norms, thereby opening themselves up to the processes of renormalization.

A method for analyzing an activity similar to the one they just viewed in the artifact presented above was then introduced during the analyses of the participants' filmed activity.

The inquiry-focused protocol comprises the following stages:

1. The participants view a filmed activity that has a "family resemblance" to their own activities, based on the co-construction of the inquiry object.
2. The participants describe the objective elements of the classroom situation linked with the defined learning object step-by-step and with as much detail as possible (positions and postures of teacher and students, type and nature of interactions, teacher's actions, teaching content) (the teacher whose activity has been filmed listens without participating).
3. The participants propose interpretations of the intentions, expectations, knowledge, preoccupations, and emotions of the teacher being viewed (the teacher whose activity has been filmed listens without participating).
4. The teacher whose activity has been filmed then confirms or rejects the suggested interpretations in such a way that the other teachers understand more fully his or her experience during the recorded situation and are able to relate the observable facts to the situated intentions and preoccupations.
5. The participants then collectively assess the viability and/or the relevance of the analyzed activity regarding the chosen learning object and the ecology of the activity (taking into account the actor's experience, his or her environment including the students) by crossing their interpretations.
6. If the viability and/or the relevance is unsatisfactory, the inquirers suggest ideas for possible solutions to transform the analyzed activity concerning the learning object, making these suggestions as realistic and feasible as possible and compatible with the analyzed activity's ecology.

This protocol was designed to elicit the following effects in the participants. We describe them one by one, but most of time they occurred simultaneously and seemed to overlap:

1. Viewing the filmed activity provokes mimetic engagement in the participants and they experience the activity as if it were their own.

2. Describing the activity in minute detail means that the participants deconstruct it, and this leads them to come to agreement on what exactly the activity is, or is doing. For the inquirer whose activity is being analyzed, hearing it described by the others helps to gain some distance from it and take a more objective view of it.

3. By having to explain their interpretations of the filmed activity (e.g., when I see the teacher do this here, I think that she's trying to do that there), the participants bring alternative meanings as they share in the analysis of the activity (they are viewing someone else's activity from their own experience and personal systems of norms). They thereby identify differences between the filmed activity and their own and become aware of "what makes the difference" as they compare their interpretations with those of the other participants. For the inquirer whose activity is being analyzed, hearing this exchange helps to envisage interpretations of his or her activity other than the one already personally constructed. The filmed inquirer observes the others "experiencing his or her own activity" – an activity that can now suddenly be viewed "as if it belonged to someone else."

4. In this step, the filmed teacher's experience and personal system of norms take on even more sense for the other participants in relation to how far they have projected themselves into the activity and experienced it "as if it were their own." It is therefore not only the activity but also the experiences that accompany it that are shared and contrasted with others. In this way, the participants come to a deeper understanding of both the differences between experiences and "what exactly these differences are made up of."

5. In this step, the participants together assess "what the filmed inquirer was trying to do" and "what actually happened" in relation to the inquiry object and *via* their analysis of the activity. Renormalizations can be observed at this point: these might give rise to a new meaning and a new evaluation regarding "what the filmed inquirer was trying to do" or "what actually happened," depending on the "ecological" dimensions of the activity that are taken into account. If there is little or no difference between the two, the inquiry stops (the situation is *determinate*). If a gap exists, the inquiry is reconfigured or a new inquiry is started (identification of a new *indeterminate* situation).

6. If the inquiry continues, the participants are again asked to project themselves into the viewed activity as if they were the filmed teacher (i.e., I adopt the intentions, perceptions and values of the teacher whose activity is being inquired into in order to think about transforming his or her activity). Together they try to focus on bringing the potential already present in the work activity into action, and they do this by spotting the moments when this activity might have bifurcated, and extract propositions from their own activity (what they have experienced that could work in the same kind of classroom situation) and suggest *possibles* that are closer to the system of norms of the teacher whose activity is being analyzed.

Step 3: Accompanying the Trial to Transform the Shared Object of Inquiry

Different methods were designed for the CVLL to pursue the inquiry objects, organize the individual and collective analyses of the viewed teacher's activity, and propose and experience different types of transformation. As with the inquiry objects, the inquiry methods were negotiated with the CVLL participants and could evolve. During the inquiries, the authors observed that these methods helped them to shift from an *indeterminate* to a *problematic* situation, but that shifting to a *determinate* situation was more complex because, although ideas for transformation may have been identified, it was not always evident how to implement them and even when they could be implemented, the results did not always meet expectations (Lussi Borer *et al.*, 2014). Supporting attempts at transformation (moving from a *problematic* to a *determinate* situation) is thus a major step in the CVLL, in terms of observing and analyzing both what these attempts transform in work activity and what they generate as experience for the participants.

Illustration of a Primary Pilot School Operating with Co-Teaching: Methods put into Place over Two Years of an In-School CVLL

1. **Workshop to Define the Inquiry Object and the Inquiry Methods (Participants + Facilitators):** "How should we teach when there are two teachers in the classroom?"
2. **Video Recording of Teaching Sequences in Three Classes of the Same Grade and Self-Confrontation Interviews with All the Teachers (Facilitators):** The supernumerary teacher taught the same one-hour introductory lesson on multiplication, three times successively. Planned and organized by the three regular teachers and the supernumerary teacher, the lesson varied in each of the classes:
   a. The regular teachers ranged in how much they made the students participate in the example being given on the blackboard; and
   b. The supernumerary teacher in each case suggested to the regular teacher who would be taking over for the upcoming hour different ways to arrange and improve the lesson based on what had just occurred.
3. **Production of Video-Artifacts (Facilitators):** Compiling excerpts of the first five minutes of the lesson in the three classes, the *verbatim* from the self-confrontation interview of the supernumerary teacher, and the *verbatim* from the self-confrontation interviews of the three regular teachers of the three classes. The video-artifact was edited to encourage comparison of the unfolding lesson in the three classes, comparison of the experiences of the two teachers in each of the classes, and comparison of the experiences of the three regular teacher-supernumerary teacher dyads.
4. **Inquiry Workshop Based on the Video-Artifact / Redefinition of the Inquiry Object (Participants + Facilitators):** Collective viewing of the video-artifact generated:
   a. The identification of gestures and postures during co-teaching that had remained intuitive up to this point;
   b. Mimetic engagement in the classroom activity of another teacher rendered easier because each time the same lesson was filmed;
   c. Comparisons of the different ways to give the same lesson to different classes and the identification of which ways aroused greater student participation (cross-fertilization);

    d.   Dissatisfaction with the students' general participation and their understanding of the distributive property, which provoked a collective debate on how to reconfigure the lesson to get them more involved.

5.   **Transformation of the Inquiry Object:** "What are the pupils doing when there are two teachers in the classroom? Are they active/passive, waiting for one of the teachers?"

6.   **Films of Teaching Sequences in 2x2 Classes and Two Collective Confrontation Interviews[5] (Facilitators):** Films of the same lesson designed with the supernumerary teacher in 2x2 classes of the same grade.

7.   **Inquiry Workshop Based on the Video-Artifact:** With meaningful elements noticed by the participants during the collective confrontation interview; the facilitators had selected and assembled the corresponding film excerpts from the lesson. The video-artifact was designed to show both the similar dimensions in the lesson (each student's individual work at his or her desk) and the contrasting dimensions (teachers working with a small group of students while the other students work autonomously *versus* teachers moving around the classroom to respond to requests from students, some of whom waited with their hands raised).

8.   **Inquiry Workshop Based on the Video-Artifact (Participants + Facilitators):** Collective viewing of the video-artifact brought out:

    a.   The dissatisfaction with classroom situations in which the teachers were unable to respond to all the student requests, with many of them waiting long minutes (comparison);

    b.   The recognition that what the teachers saw, i.e., working with small groups without being called upon by the other students, who kept their heads down while working on their task, could also be done in their own classrooms (fictional projection);

    c.   The brainstorming of the dissatisfied teachers along with the others about how to put into place the practices that elicit autonomous work that they had just viewed and felt were "better" than in their own classrooms (extraction, importation and adaptation from something done in the viewed activity into their own);

    d.   A project to collect all the formats for sessions and activities that were used to prompt students' autonomous work in order to enrich the school's database (creation of a "conservatory of practices" for the school).

9.   **Film of the Teaching Sequences in Four Classes and Analysis of the Behavior of Target-Students (Facilitators):** Films of the lessons in which the methods for prompting autonomous work were experimented with and, in each class, films of two "strong" students and two "weak" students during autonomous work. Among these films were the films of the introductory lesson on multiplication modified after workshop 4.

10.   **Production of Video-Artifacts (Facilitators):** Selection and assembly of excerpts for close-up observation of students' activity during autonomous work and construction of a table to compare the time spent by the four students being observed in each class (2 strong students, 2 weaker ones).

11.   **Inquiry Workshop Based on the Video-Artifact/Transformation of the Inquiry Object (Participants + Facilitators):** Collective viewing of the video-artifact brought out:

    a.   Dissatisfaction related to inter-individual variations in the work of the students working on their own and a reconfiguration of the inquiry object (new *problematic situation*): "What can be done to ensure that the students working on their own are truly engaged in their work?"

    b.   Satisfaction with the film clips on the introductory lesson on multiplication after it was modified in workshop 4. According to the teachers, this satisfaction was corroborated by the evaluations of the students' work and the decision was made to stop the inquiry on this object because a viable and reproducible configuration for the following year had been found. We therefore observed the renormalization of this lesson, which changed from a teaching-through-dialogue style to one that was more constructivist, with the focus being on supporting students as they manipulated new material.

DISCUSSION AND FUTURE RESEARCH DIRECTIONS

The authors' exploratory research on the CVLL in different education contexts has yielded several results, some quite promising and others more challenging. Further systematic investigation is therefore needed.

Promising Elements Observed in the CVLL

- Defining the inquiry object on the basis on the teachers' concerns and using traces of their real work engages them in the PD program.
- The collective analysis of real activity *via* video-artifacts is a way to identify the differences in norms that are operating, which in turn helps to move the inquiry from an *indeterminate* situation to a *problematic* situation.
- The inquiry-focused protocol helps to identify the *possibles* that are present in an activity to cross-fertilize them with promising elements that have worked well elsewhere, which enriches the activities.
- In the *problematic* situation, collectively sketching out ideas and directions for transformation prompts "risk-taking" in the conception and implementation of innovative and ambitious teaching practices. The participants are more willing to try out new practices that they might not have dared on their own from the moment they have seen in the video excerpts of their colleagues that these practices actually work and these practices have become the inquiry object that is collectively shared and investigated by the team.
- Planning, organizing, carrying out and analyzing lessons with other teachers helps to exchange ideas not only on the prescribed work but also on the real work carried out in the classroom. By collectively sharing ideas about the satisfactory and unsatisfactory elements in the lessons being viewed, the teachers in the collaborative inquiry end up discussing their opinions about the norms and rules to follow for action. The inquiry is not carried out on the basis of disembodied subjective values, but rather on the basis of the shared observables of the object chosen for inquiry in relation to the intentions and experience of the filmed teachers. In this way, the process of *renormalization* emerges. The authors observed that conflicts of norms make potentially good inquiry objects as they represent the dilemmas specific to the teaching culture. Nevertheless, these conflicts cannot evolve without being brought back to the activity's operational dimensions, which function as:
  - Ways to analyze the expression of conflicting norms in the analyzed situation,
  - Directions for transformation (notably through another person's activity),
  - Spaces to practice the projected transformations, and
  - Spaces to validate the pertinence of transformed activity.
- As a support, the CVLL functions as a laboratory (a space where directions for transformation in classroom practice are suggested and explored), an observatory (recording and analyzing attempts

at transformation to determine what works/what works less well and how the participant experienced it), and a conservatory (collective identification and acknowledgment of "typical" activities or "rules of the job" about which all the participants show minimal agreement and which will form part of the teaching knowledge base, taking into account the local context). The functions are part of the iterative loop of the inquiry, which is continually reconfigured.

Challenges

- The inter-objective dimension of the inquiry, or the definition of inquiry objects that are both individually and collectively relevant, is a key phase that becomes increasingly complex as the numbers of participants rises and consensus-building becomes correspondingly difficult.
- The process of renormalization offers new perspectives to teachers for transforming their teaching practices, but it is not because these perspectives are attractive that the teachers will necessarily act, or that the manner of doing so will create positive experiences so that the transformed practice becomes a reference for the future.
- Training facilitators to run the CVLL is a major concern: for the moment, researchers have assumed this role, but ultimately PD leaders will need to be trained to take over for them. The competencies needed to support the participants are crucial, as van Es et al. showed (2014): facilitators must have:
  - A theoretical background in activity analysis,
  - Technological skills to use video and create the video-artifacts,
  - Didactic skills so that they can stage the inquiry objects from real work to PD program, and
  - Interpersonal skills to manage the communications between the participants.

Their moves as facilitators are decisive in setting the stage for a detailed analysis of the videos, as this analysis is dependent on each participant's contributing freely regarding descriptions, interpretations, and evaluations, all the while avoiding a break in the flow because of interpersonal conflicts about norms.

- Video-artifacts designed to "augment" the PD program must arouse satisfaction/dissatisfaction as a way to provoke inquiries and engage the participants, while avoiding the trap of traditional video use as a way to present the "good practices" that should be reproduced in the classroom, as prescribed by the facilitator or institution. The designer therefore has to "augment" the participants' environment by selecting, articulating and enriching the video excerpts. The artifacts have to provoke mimetic experiences, the comparison and cross-fertilization of activities so that transformations occur because projects with meaning have been built from the participants' own experience. In this way, the video-artifact configuration remains localized in time and space, which raises questions about the viability and generalization of this type of education program.

CONCLUSION

Building "augmented" environments for PD based on real work activity and participants' professional concerns rather than knowledge content signals a radical break with the usual design of PD programs.

Borrowing and articulating tools from work analysis and video-education are features of an innovative trend that has been gaining in prominence over the past fifteen years. This trend has remained marginal in teacher education and PD, although it is more widely recognized in adult education and the professional world under such names as "workplace learning" or "lab change" (Billet, 2001; Engeström et al., 1996). The research findings that led the authors to configure the CVLL as presented in this chapter will certainly need to be empirically confirmed, but they do strongly suggest the potential of video-artifacts to enrich collaborative inquiries and the analysis of work activity. Whether by mimetic process, or by comparisons and cross-fertilization, the experiences that were actualized or that aroused feelings of satisfaction or dissatisfaction generated inquiries from the CVLL participants. These inquiries evolved from situations in which the experience of satisfaction or dissatisfaction was implicit (*indeterminate* situation) toward situations in which this experience was put into words as a problem. From theses *problematized* situations, ecological solutions were sought to make the situations more viable (or *determinate*). In this step, the collected observations and suggested ideas were enriched by the video-artifacts, which made it possible to stop, go back in or fast-forward the time of the activity that was the object of inquiry. This back-and-forth in time ensured that critical elements that had been overlooked in the first viewing were picked up in later viewings because of the reciprocal enrichment between observations and generated ideas. Similarly, the navigation between semiotic frames with video support made it possible to restart the inquiry by returning to the description level when the participants' interpretations and evaluations differed too much. This also allowed individual processes of renormalization to function so that the participants were able to judge the viewed activity differently once they had navigated between the frames, identified elements that had remained unidentified up to that point, and put these elements into relation with their own experience and the experience of the actor in the filmed work activity. Through this process, it seems clear that using video-artifacts goes well beyond the introduction of authentic and complex images of teaching activity to education sessions or a support for reflection. By helping to "augment" the PD program so that analyzed activities can be observed through different lenses and cross-fertilized, video-artifacts provoke processes of renormalization in participants, and these processes are particularly promising for PD.

REFERENCES

Billett, S. (2001). *Learning in the workplace*. Sydney: Allen and Unwin.

Blomberg, G., Sherin, M. G., Renkl, A., Glogger, I., & Seidel, T. (2013). Understanding video as a tool for teacher education: Investigating instructional strategies integrating video to promote reflection. *Instructional Science*, *41*(3). doi:10.1007/s11251-013-9281-6

Borko, H., Jacobs, J., Eiteljorg, E., & Pittman, M. E. (2008). Video as a tool for fostering productive discussions in mathematics professional development. *Teaching and Teacher Education*, *24*(2), 417–436. doi:10.1016/j.tate.2006.11.012

Brouwer, N. (2011). Equipping Teachers Visually. Zoetermeer: Kennisnet. Retrieved from http://www.kennisnet.nl/onderzoek/alle-onderzoeken/equipping-teachers-visually/

Calandra, B., & Rich, P. J. (Eds.), (2014). *Digital video for teacher education: Research and practice*. NY: Routledge.

Cassella, D. (2009). *What is Augmented Reality (AR): Augmented Reality Defined, iPhone Augmented Reality Apps and Games and More.* Retrieved from http://www.digitaltrends.com/features/what-is-augmented-reality-iphone-apps-games-flash-yelp-android-ar-software-and-more/

Coles, A. (2013). Using video for professional development: The role of the discussion facilitator. *Journal of Mathematics Teacher Education, 16*(3), 165–184. doi:10.1007/s10857-012-9225-0

de Montmollin, M. (1981). *Le taylorisme à visage humain.* Paris: PUF.

Dewey, J. (1916). *Democracy and Education.* New York: The Macmillan Company.

Dewey, J. (1927). *The Public and Its Problems.* New York: Holt & Co.

Dewey, J. (1938). *Logic: The Theory of Inquiry.* New York: Holt & Co.

Durand, M. (2011). Self-constructed activity, work analysis, and occupational training: an approach to learning objects for adults. In P. Jarvis & M. Watts (Eds.), *The Routledge international handbook on learning* (pp. 37–45). London: Routledge.

Engeström, Y., Virkkunen, J., Helle, M., Pihlaja, J., & Poikela, R. (1996). The Change laboratory as a tool for transforming work. *Lifelong Learning in Europe, 1*(2), 10–17.

Flandin, S. (2015). *Analyse de l'activité d'enseignants stagiaires du second degré en situation de vidéoformation autonome: Contribution à un programme de recherche technologique en formation* [Unpublished doctoral dissertation]. Clermont-Ferrand: Université Blaise Pascal.

Flandin, S., Leblanc, S., & Muller, A. (2015). Vidéo-formation « orientée-activité »: quelles utilisations pour quels effets sur les enseignants? In V. Lussi Borer, M. Durand & F. Yvon (Eds.), Analyse du travail et formation dans les métiers de l'éducation (Raisons éducatives, pp. 179-198). Bruxelles: De Boeck.

Flandin, S., & Ria, L. (2014). Un programme technologique basé sur l'analyse de l'activité réelle des enseignants débutants au travail et en vidéoformation. *Activités (Vitry-sur-Seine), 11*(2), 172–187. doi:10.4000/activites.970

Gaudin, C., & Chaliès, S. (2015). Video viewing in teacher education and professional development: A literature review. *Educational Research Review, 16*, 41–67. doi:10.1016/j.edurev.2015.06.001

Institut Frances De L'Education. (2016) *Plateforme Néopass@ction.* Retrieved from http://neo.ens-lyon.fr/neo

Janík, T., & Seidel, T. (Eds.), *The power of video studies in investigating teaching and learning in the classroom.* Munich: Waxmann Publishing.

Leblanc, S., & Ria, L. (2014). Designing the *Néopass@ction* Platform Based on Modeling of Beginning Teachers' Activity. *Design and Technology Education, 19*(2), 40–51.

Lussi Borer, V., & Muller, A. (2014a). Quel apport/usage du « voir » pour le « faire » en formation des enseignants du secondaire. In L. Paquay, P. Perrenoud, M. Altet, J. Desjardins, & R. Etienne (Eds.), *Travail réel des enseignants et formation. Quelle référence au travail des enseignants dans les objectifs, les dispositifs et les pratiques?* (pp. 65–78). Bruxelles: De Boeck.

Lussi Borer, V., & Muller, A. (2014b). Exploiter le potentiel des processus de renormalisation en formation à l'enseignement. *Activités (Vitry-sur-Seine)*, *11*(2), 129–142. Retrieved from http://www.activites.org/v11n2/v11n2.pdf

Lussi Borer, V., Ria, L., Durand, M., & Muller, A. (2014). How Do Teachers Appropriate Learning Objects Through Critical Experiences? A Study of a Pilot In-School Collaborative Video Learning Lab. *Form@re, Open Journal per la formazione in rete, 14*(2), 63-74. Retrieved from http://www.fupress.net/index.php/formare/article/view/15137

Mollo, V., & Falzon, P. (2004). Auto- and Allo-confrontation as Tools for Reflective Activities. *Applied Ergonomics*, *35*(6), 531–540. doi:10.1016/j.apergo.2004.06.003 PMID:15374760

Muller, A., & Plazaola Giger, I. (Eds.). (2014). *Dispositions à agir, travail et formation*. Toulouse: Octarès.

Ombredane, A., & Faverge, J.-M. (1955). *L'analyse du travail*. Paris: PUF Organisation for Economic Co-operation and Development (OECD). (2014). *Education at a Glance 2014*. Retrieved from http://www.oecd.org/edu/Education-at-a-Glance-2014.pdf

Peirce, C. S. (1978). *Ecrits sur le signe*. Paris: Seuil.

Santagata, R., & Guarino, J. (2011). Using Video to Teach Future Teachers to Learn from Teaching. *ZDM The International Journal of Mathematics Education*, *43*(1), 133–145. doi:10.1007/s11858-010-0292-3

Schwartz, Y. (2007). Un bref aperçu de l'histoire du concept culturel d'activité. *Activités (Vitry-sur-Seine)*, *4*(2), 122–133. Retrieved from http://www.activites.org/v4n2/v4n2.pdf doi:10.4000/activites.1728

Seidel, T., & Stürmer, K. (2014). Modeling and measuring the structure of professional vision in pre-service teachers. *American Educational Research Journal*, *51*(4), 739–771. doi:10.3102/0002831214531321

Theureau, J. (2002). Self Confrontation Interview as a Component of an Empirical and Technological Research Programme. Retrieved from http://www.coursdaction.fr/06-English/2002-JT-C93ENG.pdf

van Es, E. A. (2012). Examining the development of a teacher learning community: The case of a video club. *Teaching and Teacher Education*, *28*(2), 182–192. doi:10.1016/j.tate.2011.09.005

van Es, E. A., Tunney, J., Goldsmith, L. T., & Seago, N. (2014). A framework for the facilitation of teachers' analysis of video. *Journal of Teacher Education*, *65*(4), 340–356. doi:10.1177/0022487114534266

Zaccaï-Reyners, N. (2005). Fiction et typification. Contribution à une approche théorique de la transmission de l'expérience. *Methodos*, *5*, 1–21. doi:10.4000/methodos.378

Zask, J. (2004). L'enquête sociale comme inter-objectivation. In B. Karsenti & L. Quéré (Eds.), *La croyance et l'enquête. Aux sources du pragmatisme* (pp. 141–163). Bruxelles: De Boeck.

ENDNOTES

[1]   *As many skills and pedagogies are best developed on the job, support should also be provided to teachers during the early stages of their careers, through induction and mentoring programs, and*

> *later on, by offering incentives and resources to participate in ongoing professional development activities* (OECD, 2014).

2   The authors define norms broadly as the rules to follow in action, whatever the "nature" (epistemic, axiological, etc.) or the "place" (institutional, informal collective, personal) of their production. According to Schwartz (2007), norms concern both scientific and technical knowledge in the form of equipment, procedures and instructions, as well as the organizational codes that are much more linked to the social aspects of work and networks of power, ownership and authority.

3   The partnership was with pilot schools in the Haute-Savoie, France. For two years, these schools had a supernumerary teacher as a resource assigned to a teaching team charged with collaborating to organize and optimize its input to classes in order to (i) improve student performances (6 to 8 years old) in French and mathematics (enhanced learning for disadvantaged students) and (ii) change pedagogical practices by getting teaching teams to innovate.

4   These three levels are what we call a "bifacial concept", in that they make it possible to link research concepts (10 levels in relation to activity) and concepts from the professional field.

5   In a collective confrontation (Mollo & Falzon, 2004), the participants together with the facilitators successively viewed films made in the first and then the second class.

Chapter 5

Observing to Understand, Understanding to Develop:
A Point of View of Professional Didactics on the Teaching Activity in Multilingual Context

Amélie Alletru
Université de Nantes, France

Grégory Munoz
Université de Nantes, France

ABSTRACT

Observing teaching-learning situations in order to better understand them, such was the OPEN project (Altet, Bru and Blanchard-Laville, 2012). This project has been transformed into the research federative structure of OPÉEN&ReForm (the passage from observation by research to observation for training being at stake). In this chapter, the resort to the video aiming at analyzing the activity is carried out according to an approach of professional didactics (Pastré, 2011; Vinatier, 2013) with the purpose to help the professionals in their development (Vinatier, 2013). The authors introduce the case study of a co-analysis approach of the video traces of a teacher activity, according to her point of view, in a collaborative research (Vinatier et al., 2012) in French Polynesia, what seems to constitute for her a potential situation of professional development (Mayen, 1999), in her authorizing herself to try out new ways to lead her teaching.

INTRODUCTION

Observing teaching-learning situations to understand them better, identify observation criteria which can become resources both in the service of teachers training and of their continuous professional development, that is the outline of the research federative structure *OPÉEN&ReForm: Observation of Educational and Teaching Practices, from Research to Training* which we participate in. One of the perspectives consists

DOI: 10.4018/978-1-5225-0711-6.ch005

Copyright © 2017, IGI Global. Copying or distributing in print or electronic forms without written permission of IGI Global is prohibited.

in enrolling collectives of professionals in forms of collaborative researches (Vinatier et al., 2012) and tracking their effects. Within the framework of the latter, the professionals by collaborating with the researchers in the sharp understanding of their activity are potentially in position to better understand their acting in order to be able to display it differently. But observing is not obvious and requires the resort to specific methodologies as to collect or analyze dimensions of the activity; relevant methodologies for the extension of the actor's power of action. The account for the activity theory which our modes of observation are grounded upon, is necessary if we want observation not to be limited to describe, but may also enable to explain, under certain methodological and theoretical conditions.

According to the point of view of professional didactics (Pastré, 2011; Vinatier, 2013) which we share with them, if with some experience, the professionals are often able to display relevant choices, adapted to the very situation, as well consistent with their professional values; on the other hand, they are not still able to explain choices prevailing in their decision-making, upstream or in the course of action. The research purpose is to help them doing it, but it can only be achieved by realizing analyses with and for the professionals themselves, that is in the service of the extension of their choices of action, and if they consider it necessary. From our point of view, it is out of point that the research works to conceive new prescriptions which would aim at being orders to act differently, just because they would be a matter of "best practice". For teaching practices are very diverse and are a matter of complex and varied contexts, as for example multilingual contexts prove it. The purpose of professional didactics is to accompany the professionals in the development of their power to act (Vinatier, 2009). This prospect, spread within the framework of collaborative researches (Vinatier et al., 2012), proposes a process of co-analysis of the video traces of the professional's actual activity, realized from his own point of view, by confronting him with the researcher analysis. This point is essential because it supposes a didactic approach by the researcher, whose goal is to convey his theoretical perspective, aiming to its appropriation by the professionals. It is a matter, indeed, of supplying the professionals with necessary resources so that they can fit the analysis process by and to themselves. Two purposes are aimed: at the level of the research, it is a matter of enabling the researcher to decipher the specificities of a professional activity, enrich his theoretical frame and make it didactizable; and at the level of the training, it is a question of enabling the professional to build a reflexive approach of the organization of his activity and of a part of the reasons founding it[2]. This approach means enabling the professional to have access to the implicit conceptualizations which he or she spreads in working situation (Vergnaud, 2007).

That is why it is a matter of observing to understand, to contribute to the power to act development of professionals. But how, and under what conditions? From a case study within the framework of a collaborative research in French Polynesia we try to understand how an analysis of the activity, from a confrontation of a first degree teacher with the video, can constitute for her a potential situation of professional development (Mayen, 1999), in the fact that she allows herself to try out new ways to lead her teaching.

A first part will introduce our epistemological position, in professional didactics, grounded upon a constructivist approach, according to which succeed is not enough to understand, but one also needs to adopt observation practices, as proposed by the research federative structure OPÉEN&ReForm. A second part will explain our frame of collaborative research and our case study methodology, as well as its context. The third part will provide some observation elements connected to the actor's point of view, and enabling to bring up the hypothesis of an evolution of schemas of action constituted in interaction with the pupils for one of the participating teachers in the study, by sketching her development from her initial positioning. A discussion relative to these first analyses enables us to provide in conclusion a new underlining hypothesis, once again, but in a revisited way, the highly interactionist nature of teaching activity.

BACKGROUND: OBSERVING TO UNDERSTAND

A Constructivist Approach

Since Piaget (1936), development is considered as an adaptation, being a matter of a form of invention in action, which allows the construction of operating cognitive resources to face the fluctuations in the reality. Piaget (1970, p. 12) was able to show that it is on the "progressive construction that the united elaboration of the subject and the objects depends ", proving a form of constructivism in which subject and object (in its wide meaning) are co-constructed in interaction. Between the subject and the objects in the world, invariant instruments of assimilation-accommodation constitute, as the experience of the subject goes along. That is why, Piaget (1970, p. 10) "sees in knowledge a continual construction". Vergnaud (1996, 2007) carries on this viewpoint by granting it however a less structural than situational basis. As a didactician, he puts in perspective the sometimes absolute Piagetian conclusions character to prefer a more partial version of the development, connected to the contents and to the situations faced by the subject. Vergnaud (1999) indicates besides that this development continues at the adult's. Works in professional didactics (Pastré, 2011) gave it examples, by the fact of being able to learn from situations, but according to the contents of the situations, and properties which the subjects build, in function of their intentionality (Vergnaud, 1996, 2007).

In agreement with Piaget (1936), Vergnaud (2007) sums up the notion of scheme, as an operating form of knowledge, to deconstruct it in its various components: purposes, sub-purposes and anticipations, sending back to the actor's intentionality and desire; action, information intaking and control rules: the generative part of the scheme which gives rise to as one goes along the activity course (process of action regulation); operating invariants (concepts-in-act and theorems-in-act): the epistemic part of the scheme (which introduces the conceptualization, the main function of which is to categorize the elements of the reality for the action, as a not always explicit system of concepts); inferences: the adaptive part of the scheme. So, the scheme is neither automatism nor simple application, but local adaptation and progressive adjustment. We indeed distinguish the purposes that the actor gives himself or herself (tackled in his or her speech) from the modalities enabling him or her to achieve them (observable in situation). The latter are rules of action based on operating invariants built during the daily or professional experience. If the subjects in particular the professionals are able to state the stages of their action, on the other hand it is difficult for them to clarify advisedly the principles considered as truths which they base on, to organize it. These operating invariants are a matter of properties and relations which they consider as the truths about the situations objects and phenomena within which the subjects interfere, but whose incorporated character of the action, from then on autonomous, makes them hardly explicit. Piaget (1974) showed that there is indeed a difference for the subject between making, with its success and failures, and understanding, with the explication of the reasons of success and failures. The dialectic between success and understanding is to be connected to the fact that there is an operating shape of knowledge which is first and which precisely is a matter of schemes built by the subjects during their action in situation (Pastré, 2011). From it is the professional didactics main proposition to learn from situations, with as a condition the cognitive analysis of the activity and the clarification of the mobilized schemas of action, either adapted or not in situation.

An Approach through Professional Didactics: Understanding in Order to Train

The aim of professional didactics is to develop a theoretical and methodological corpus and to design an approach of training favoring the professionals' power-in-action development (Rabardel, 2005; Clot, 2008). In this respect, professional didactics rejects prescriptive approaches, which would try to impose hypothetical "best practice" on the actors, considered generalizable in any contexts. Indeed, the professionals, confronted with particular contexts, were brought, during their experience, to build knowledge-in-act (Vergnaud, 1999, 2007). They so had the opportunity to feel by themselves forms of reasoning adapted or not to the specificities of the situations, the control of which they had to lead. This knowledge-en-act incorporated into their activity is not always explicit and summons up processes of awareness if they want to reach it, by the appeal to methodologies of analysis of the activity. It is for example the case for nursery tutors who have to accompany pupils in the construction of knowledge of action generally barely clarified neither in training in school, nor during the training courses in professional circles (Munoz & Boivin, 2016. This turns out all the truer in jobs involving human relationships, for which the situations demand to consider variability which prevent from "ready-to-wear answers". In these cases, it is important to realize a diagnosis of the situation, to know how, when and about what to act, at the same time upstream from the situation, but also in a permanent interactivity with it (Schön, 1994). For Pastré, it is from such diagnosis of situation that the professionals make adapted decisions and steer their activity as a consequence. That is why, in these open dynamic situations, such as Rogalski (2004) qualifies teaching-learning situations, the actors have to lean on the operating invariants which they consider as true, not in the absolute of a hypothetical transferability between situations, but in specific and contextualized situations, being possibly a matter of the same situations class (Vergnaud, 1990).

So, as Vergnaud indicates it (2008, p. 97), according to his epistemological perspective, "conceptualization intervenes in the action without being inevitably phrased". The passage from the operating shape of knowledge (in act) to a predicative form (put down in words) is a major stake, for school and for training, "provided that we do not forget that culture is made by situations, actions and practices, and not only by words and texts"; that is why Vergnaud invites to exceed Vygotski's point of view which "makes language the psychological instrument with which the subject acts on himself and is transformed", by taking interested in the other forms of the activity, not reducible in the linguistic activity, even internal; because according to him, "interiorization does not only deal with language, but also action, gestures, and perceptive processes by which subjects select relevant information for the action and adapt to the objects and to their properties". That is why we proceed to a multimodal approach also taking actions into account.

A Plural Analysis: Observing to Understand and to Train

To clarify the concepts-in-act subjacent in the actors' coordinated action, the resort to traces of the activity is essential to the analysis methodology of the activity in professional didactics. Resorting to observation of the activity as it takes place concretely, in professional situations and not only in the way of the prescriptions (Leplat, 1997) can enable actors to reach a part of understanding of what organizes their decision. But this reflexivity work, (Schön, 1994) is not obvious and demands observation methodologies. The latter enable to increase the understandibility of the situations, by bringing to emphasizing their multi-dimensionality, to understand better and document the activity, in particular that of teachers. This is what the research program *OPEN* proposes: *Observatory of Teaching Practices* (Altet, Bru & Blanchard-Laville, 2012; Numa-Bocage et al., 2014), stemming from the frame of plural analyses (Altet, 2002). "If in the OPEN network the definition of the practice adopted by the teams varies according to the theoretical referents, common elements of definition were retained: those who consider the practice as established by multiple dimensions, as a situated professional activity, led by issues, purposes, standards, that of a professional group, conveying a person's knowledge, processes and skills-in-acts in a professional situation" (Altet, 2003, p. 38). This point of view is summarized and achieved within the federative structure *OPÉEN&ReForm: Observation of Educational and Teaching Practices, from Research to Training*, but by turning more to actors' training and development. The use of video recording, to make up traces of the activity contributes to it.

METHODOLOGICAL FRAME: A CASE STUDY

Just as its others components, the intentional part of the scheme, which is one of the straightest apprehensible, is open to evolution. It is exactly what we shall try to exemplify here, through the case study of Maeva, a teacher participating in a collaborative research resorting to the video for the observation of the effective practice. We have adopted a qualitative and comprehensive case study approach (Creswell, 2007). In this same vein, we chose to present her in-depth portrait, because this particular practitioner explains her activity during several methodological steps: interviews, observations and self-confrontation interview. We shall at once make clear that our results would not long to be generalized, since they are due to a case study: in other words, they are deeply tied to the analysis of an only one professional activity. Nevertheless, the case of this teacher is indeed particularly interesting, as far as the purposes which she shows, as well as the modalities in her activity differ appreciably between two stages of the research (at the beginning then at mid-term). In an aim of contrastive analysis, we shall track evolutions in her teaching activity using:

1. The videos of two lessons shot nine months apart; and
2. Three interviews with the teacher (two - pre-and post-observation - stemming from the exploratory phase, and a self-confrontation interview led during the second phase).

We shall introduce in this part the methodology we used, as well as the context of this research led with five first degree teachers in French Polynesia[1], in Tahiti exactly. In the perspective opened by the ECOLPOM (Overseas Multilingual School: Evaluation of the origin languages teaching programs in diglossic context in primary school in New Caledonia, in French Polynesia and in Guiana [2009-2012]) and ReoC3 (*Reo mā'ohi* reinforced teaching in cycle 3 as prevention and fight against illiteracy in French Polynesia [2011-2014]) programs, our research is aimed at the observation of their effective practices. We try to track conceptualization by these teachers of Polynesian Languages and Culture (LCP) teaching situations. Eventually, our work will contribute on reflection led by the local actors on teachers' pre-service and in-service training in a multilingual perspective.

Research Methodology

Collaboration in the Research

We join a comprehensive approach of the activity. Indeed, so that training proposals are adapted to professionals' real needs, it is necessary to recognize, beyond institutional orders, the central place held by the activity representative situations and to characterize them. In this way, knowledge of the work requires the teachers' participation to the analysis and their contribution to the validation of the results. We thus favor the collaboration with them, which implies to build a space of communication in which words can be exchanged without any fear of judgment. This mode of collaboration asks for a particular vigilance as for the investigation relationship and for the explanation of the roles assigned to each, professional(s) and researcher, whose mutual skills combine for the analysis. We are willing to understand the phenomena by building the object of research by considering each of the teachers' representations on the same phenomena, in an iterative approach in which direct and indirect observation complement each other. We call indirect observation the consideration of the observations (in the wide sense) by the very actors, and their reconstruction.

The institutional context in which the teachers evolve implied a formal approach for authorization request to competent authorities to obtain permission to enter the ground. It was not possible to negotiate the demarcation of the study ground. On the basis of the criterion brought up by the researcher of five to six volunteer teachers susceptible to be interested, five of them were "selected" (*dixit* the LCP educational adviser of the district chosen by the inspector). The participation of these five teachers was thus made late, on the basis of a name by their immediate superior and with a minimal communication as for the contents of the project, impacting on the researcher-professional relationship and the construction of shared purposes. Besides, the presentation of the project to the five participants confirmed that the interest carried in their own perception constituted for them something new. From then on, the conditions of possibility of collaboration, within our goal, deserve to be questioned. It was thus necessary to establish a frame of collaboration enabling them to grasp the stakes linked to the importance of their speech to relevantly co-analyze their activity on one hand, and on the other hand, the interest which themselves might find in this cooperation, of a new shape for them. We shall add two spatiotemporal factors to the constraints pressing on the collaboration: on one hand the geographical estrangement implies the preservation of a (very long-) distance communication, a discontinuous presence of the researcher on the research ground and some emergency on the occasion of her short on-the-spot stays; and on the other hand, no time was institutionally planned for the teachers' participation in the research, which led them to use their personal or class time. Nevertheless, our exteriority situation was an opportunity to make our neutrality explicit in the institutional positioning, and our misunderstanding of the Tahitian language enabled to get rid of any possible suspicion of overhanging position. The introductory meetings aimed at clarifying the respective expertise complementarity in order to bring to a successful conclusion the co-analysis process: the professional is the expert of his/her own experience; the researcher proposes analysis processes and tools to reveal the deep forces.

The implementation of the research relationship thus based itself on several inescapable elements: the researcher's understanding of the teachers' evolvement context, the construction and strict respect for the communication frame, the insurance of the researcher independence towards the institutional authorities, her neutrality and her absence of judgment on the observed practices, the meeting of the interests of the participants, the construction of shared purposes, and the progressive emergence of questions. It is not enough to express those principles so that they become updated, but it is the researcher's responsibility (which watches to protect the methodological and ethical necessities) for gradually setting them up in-act in the relationship by transforming the extrinsic motivation aroused by the institutional command (perceptible in a disembodied speech on "best practice") into intrinsic motivation (locatable in a speech on the real-life experience): make the research collaboration an opportunity of enrichment for one, thanks to the opportunity to make one's real practice explicit, in one's successes and doubts, aspiration and dead ends. While sharing this intention, the methodological device was able to be co-constructed. The teachers' involvement in the research project being variable, it was necessary to create a negotiation space so that a device reached a consensus, ending in a schedule of individual meetings for interviews and observations in class on the basis of types of collectively determined lesson.

Phases of the Research and the Implication of the Teacher

Our research, fitted in an ethnographical approach, is made up of three phases resorting to video: an exploratory phase[2] orientated towards the apprehension of the context, the installation of the collaboration and the demarcation of the research object; a phase dedicated to the systematic analysis of five LCP teaching situations (a session by participant); and a phase devoted to the presentation of the results and their discussion with/by the participants (the feasibility of this third phase being for the moment submitted to constraints of material order).

Concerning the teacher whose evolution we shall introduce here, her commitment in the collaborative research deserves to be dealt with. Not having been warned by the educational adviser, she was not able to be free for the first collective meeting. The collaboration project was thus individually introduced to her, within the class, while her pupils were at work. The warm reception, gave less space for real exchanges than for a presentation by the researcher of the collaboration objectives and considered modalities. Maeva showed herself relatively distant (using the 'vous' form usually reserved for immediate superiors), little involved, asserting that she implemented a practice such as recommended. The dimension of a co-analysis of the effective practices beyond the prescription apparently seemed new and relatively misty to her. Nevertheless, the independence of the researcher towards the hierarchy and her ethical commitment to protect the participants aroused some surprise and a form of growing relief. Questioned about the profits which she considers concerning her participation into the research, she does not perceive any for herself and more readily mentions the necessity of supplying teachers with appropriate and affordable tools, going to the lines of practices "improvement" at a collective level for LCP teaching. At the end of that first meeting which concluded with setting up the calendar and exchanging the whereabouts, we felt the construction of a real collaboration would require a quite particular care to co-construct purposes to be shared. That feeling was confirmed by Maeva's absence, without her warning the researcher of it, on the day suited for observation and video recording, then by the difficulty getting again in touch with her to set up a new appointment. Nevertheless, she dedicated an important personal time for both pre-and post-observation interviews: 1h54 for the first one and 1h06 for the second one. On the reserve at the beginning, she little by little left a suited speech on "best practices" to open up without restraint by sharing her doubts, difficulties and sufferings. After the departure of the researcher, some remote exchanges enabled to keep contact on a very cordial mode.

Teacher's Progressive Confrontation with Her Own Activity

In certain contexts, the resort to cinematic traces of the activity is not a procedure to which teachers are used to, in order to analyze their own practice. This is exactly the case for the teachers we have collaborated with, which implied to adopt a progressive approach. During the three phases of the research, Maeva is formally confronted five times with her activity, which involves her in a different relationship to it, in a form of a powerful increasing of the co-analysis.

During the exploratory phase, two interviews, pre-and post-observation, lead her to express herself about her teaching activity. The first interview, semi-directive, is directed towards its declared practice. It aims at understanding her vision of the local teaching context and at having her express herself on her educational and didactic organization regarding LCP, in order to approach her representations. The second interview, following immediately lessons in French and in Tahitian observation and video recording, allows to better understand her linguistic profile, career and commitment in the project, and to progressively approach her practice. Indeed, the researcher shares her first observations on-the-spot, to which Maeva is asked to react by validating, invalidating or specifying these interpretations of the observed class supervision. The researcher observations offer a bend leading the teacher to take her own activity as object of reflection.

During the second phase (nine months later), a self-confrontation interview invites the teacher to comment on her activity by viewing the movie of her second observed session[3]. The support on video traces leads to consider effective practice in a finer grain, by giving meaning to the real-life experience. Following direct observation (without possibility of a deeper analysis by the researcher), it is a matter of enabling an authentic expression by Maeva on what leads her in lesson and directs her action, and of building together an understanding of the observed activity. The questioning of the researcher-observer is fed by a double concern:

1. To bring to the foreground what, in situation, is significant from the teacher's point of view, constitutes an event according to her, and what consequently, contributes to direct her activity;
2. To reveal elements enabling to understand the activity in a multimodal perspective.

The verbalizations thus obtained, coupled with activity traces, give access to the real of the activity, defined as "the possible and impossible activity" because "the man is full at every minute of unimplemented possibilities" (Clot, 1999/2006). So, "suspended, impeded or prevented activities, even counter-activities must be admitted in the analysis" because "it is indeed on that "collision point" between all possible and impossible activities of a subject that the action condenses around purposes to be achieved" (Clot, 1999/2006).

The last phase of the research is situated at the end of the exhaustive analysis of data by the researcher. During an individual interview, the researcher provides Maeva with her results, what she understands and the hypotheses she built, what establishes another mediation level to reach the real of the activity. Co-explanation made possible by the provision of the researcher's theoretical tools hires the discussion around her interpretations and more emphasizes the teacher's conceptualization of her activity. Co-analysis takes a new dimension during the ultimate stage which gathers the five teachers and the researcher for a collective allo-confrontation[4], which constitutes a sort of collective reflexive activity (an activity on the activity, led between peers in the presence of the researcher): that interview, because it confronts each one with another practice than one's, and enables the discussion thanks to the theoretical tools proposed by the researcher, leads to the explanation and to the development of the representations of the members of the group, and to the construction of shared knowledge (Mollo & Falzon, 2004). So, a comprehensive aim (for the researcher) coexists with a developmental perspective (for the teachers), where stemming from experience knowledge and stemming from research knowledge mutually fertilize (Vinatier & Morissette, 2015).

A Multimodal Analysis of the Activity

We inscribe our analysis in interaction ecology: any interaction is situated and cannot be reduced to only its linguistic components. Mondada (2012) specifies that "the choice of the linguistic resources is profoundly connected with the management not only of the embodied interaction between the participants, but more radically still by the ecology of their action, constituted by the physical, intentional and material properties, made relevant by them. It invites to integrate into the linguistic description at the same time the emergent temporality of the action, the corporeity of the interaction - itself supplied with with multiple and muddled temporalities - and the characteristics of the ecology of the activity - themselves appearing in a contingent way and profoundly indexical". The ecology of the interaction is characterized by an emic approach which considers language as radically incorporated and indexed to the context. That embodied vision of language in interaction leads, in the analysis of their (inter)activity, to take into account the diverse resources which the actors[5] seize: gestuality, looks, facial mimes, body postures, movements, spatial arrangements and artifacts manipulation (Mondada, 2008). In this way, our linguistic misunderstanding of Tahitian leads us to be sensitive to the "speaking body" play (Jorro, 2007): professional act conceals a cultural dimension, gesture carrying a symbolic, significant dimension, aiming at the pupil's construction of study gestures, themselves interpreting in their turn these forms of expression mediatized by the body (whose one of the properties is its plasticity[6]). Gestures perform a socialization function.

From then on, we can seize the play of bodies, postures, movements as significant of the class functioning, considered as a cultural community sharing a symbolic system of values, exchanges and powers according to the Brunerian proposal (Munoz, Minassian & Vinatier, 2012). It is a matter for us of understanding what takes place in the teaching-learning lessons when we look not at the knowledge but at the functioning of a class in a given culture, not to compromise the analysis by mobilizing a sole *a priori* explanatory factor of cultural order, in an essentialist tendency (Bazin, 2008). The observation of Maeva's effective practice, in an interactionist perspective, leads us to ask a set of questions: what are these gestures? What regularities can we observe? What variations can we track? How do they articulate with the actors' words? [7]

Resort to video is justified in an aim of multimodal analysis. Within the framework of our contribution, we shall present the evolution of the purposes as well as the rules of action to try sometimes to reconstruct the operating invariants which lead the teacher's activity, leaning on observation data and discursive data from the interviews (pre-and post-observation made during the exploratory phase and during the self-confrontation interview of the second phase). To document the effective practice into a multimodal viewpoint, we carried out in an iterative way to the progressive construction of indicators enabling us to track the interactive dynamics characterizing every lesson. Coupling videos viewing and interview data is indeed necessary to clarify the meaning of the observed gestures, and not reduce the observation to the only behavioral data. Triangulation as a validation procedure is particularly important given our paradigm of reference and given our methodological choices of the observational approach.

Roundtrips between observable data and teacher's verbalizations thus enable the elaboration of a key for reading the effective practice. Validation of the data collected through this ethnographic observation is subjected to a specific care: presently, both researchers have shared their own analysis of the coupled data in order to stabilize any concordance between their results. Moreover, the teacher is necessarily implicated in the validation of the results (during the last phase of the research) and her own interpretation contributes to co-construct the results. The specificity of the methodological choices within our perspective is that no indicator can be predetermined neither generalizable, what can be considered by some as a weakness in terms of validity of the results and of transfer into teachers' training. Indeed, we assume that position in the way that the situated feature of concerted decision between researcher and practitioner is the very foundation of our ethnographic approach.

We can therefore highlight both weaknesses and strengths of our methodological choices. On one hand, a case study cannot lay claim to an over generalization of its results depending on the specificity of ethnographic validity, which thus questions their very sustainability in terms of transfer towards training programs. The effort to co-construct and share valuable indicators necessarily implies that no certainty can be granted concerning the success of such an enterprise: the results are strongly linked to the activity of one practitioner. On a pragmatic level, its technical device, institutional constraints and need in time are actually demanding. On the other hand, we claim a highly epistemic and ethic relevance: the concern for the point of view of one teacher on his own activity is inescapable in our mind (he has the right to the last word in the end). Leaning on situated action, sizing as resources the very tracks of the activity is for us a strongly consistent way to acceed to conceptualization in action. Both pragmatic and theoretical knowledge would emerge from that kind of research.

For the analysis dealt with within this chapter, we adopted the flowing encoding (Table 1.) which, by centering on the teacher's activity, takes into account the actors to whom, her words, gestures (by favoring pointing gestures) or looks are addressed.

Table 1. Adopted encoding for multimodal analysis

Encoding	
Actors	Maeva: teacher P: pupil Ps: pupils
Used language	*French speech* *Tahitian speech, among which: "///"*
(Gesture indications)	• Lc: looks at the whole class • Lp: looks at a pupil • Lps: looks at pupils • Lb: looks at her book • Lslide: looks at a slide on the blackboard • Pp: points at a pupil • Pslide: points at a slide • Ghand: gestures with her hand • Mime: mime • +: simultaneously

A Context in Tension

The context of this research led on the Tahitian ground deserves to be quickly described in the sense that it presents some characteristics susceptible to enlighten the understanding of the teacher's effective practice.

Education and Training Context

Aiming at reducing the massive academic failure in the country[8], the top-down administrative and educational piloting is led by the pupils' results, and the teachers are *de facto* associated to this issue. They put on the collective dynamics impulsed by a teacher made alive and/or motivated in a field, which on one hand is individually lived as a heavy load to be carried, and what on the other hand, position the working collective as an essential cog of a school, even a sector efficiency. Particularly regarding Polynesian Languages and Culture, the training system seems unsuitable and is regularly incriminated by researchers, whatever their reference scientific horizons are[9]. Training actions, aiming at the distribution of "best practice", show themselves modelizing and little reflexive. Difficulties lived on the ground by teachers and their real training needs are only little taken into account and the training process conception is mainly centered on the analysis of type-lessons as well as on tools and turnkey resources distribution. Teachers are rarely in situation to analyze their own practice. In the training courses (individual or collective) we were able to observe, trainers indeed assume this role: they encourage practice elements they judge "good" and track down those who deserve to evolve, according to them, before prescribing a "better" way of proceeding. Consequently, expressing oneself as capable subject (Rabardel & Pastré, 2005) on one's own practice, taking it for an analysis object in an aim of professional development, is an unrecognized exercise for teachers.

Prescribed Objectives

Teaching LCP is an obligation to which Maeva submits. Indeed, the primary school teaching programs (2012) indicate that 2h30 a week must be actually dedicated to this teaching domain (2h40 in nursery school) to:

1. Contribute to the pupils' linguistic development (practicing, beside the control of French, a Polynesian language, sanctioned at the end of primary schooling by level A1 of the Common European Framework of Reference for Languages, but "in consideration of pupils' knowledge and known linguistic and cultural skills");
2. Participate in the individual and citizen training (local heritage valuation and linguistic and cultural transmission); and
3. Contribute to pupils' success at school. The actual hourly volume (which can be raised up to 5 hours a week, according to schools) has to appear on the timetable, by favoring daily sessions from 30 till 35 minutes.

Communication and culture languages, the Polynesian languages are officially considered on the plan school as teaching languages. The LCP programs, developed in reference to the CECR, set reasons adduced for every cycle of primary schooling and favor an actional approach (acquisition of the language based on tasks fulfillment) and are organized into five linguistic activities: understanding, reacting and speaking in interaction, understanding in the oral, continuously speaking, reading, writing. A specific appendix for the LCP program declines every linguistic activity in the form of a table indicating examples of interventions, proposing formulations in Polynesian language, and specifying the associated cultural, lexical, grammatical and phonological skills. The cultural and lexical skills are then resumed into three chapters (family and social environment, natural, historic, geographical and economic environment, intellectual and artistic environment). Finally, the phonological, grammatical and syntactical skills are clarified.

From nursery school, it is recommended to lead learning in a coordinated management: simultaneous development of the same linguistic skills in French and in the other languages, comparative approach of the languages, their tones and their graphic correspondences. Oral expression and understanding are favored in nursery school until the familiarization with the principle of the correspondence between oral and written practices. Then in a parallel to lexical enrichment, the written skill is introduced into a more important way in the second cycle, that of the "fundamental learnings" (progressive learning of reading and writing in *reo* and first initiation into grammar and spelling following the Tahitian Academy standards). Finally, in the third cycle, that of the "further improvements", the written skill mastery is strengthened by learning a second written code, that of the *Maohi Protestant Church*. At the end of primary school, both codes must be mastered.

The prescription is thus explicit since 2012 with the programs and specific appendix writing. Concerning LCP teaching, textbooks are still deficient at the time of our research. Resources[10] are gradually made available by digital way by the trainers' teams, mainly stemming from the work made during the teachers training courses. It is up to each teacher to approach their sector educational advisers to get them Our observations showed that teachers are taken into a form of tension between an applicationnist approach to which they are submitted (see above) to which they can be tempted to adhere without other way of questioning, and the discretionary activity which is expected from them regarding operational declension of the LCP prescriptions. Our interviews with various local actors show that teachers regret the lack of available useful (and easy of appropriation) resources, while trainers assure that these are accessible and in sufficient number.

ANALYSIS: EVOLUTION OF THE INTERACTION MODALITIES

To show the evolution of the teacher's interaction modalities with her pupils[11], we chose to expose in parallel, first of all, the main characteristics of each of both lessons in the form of synopsis (Table 2.), supported by the introduction of every lesson's respective scenes by using photos (Figure 1 and Figure 2), then the systematic analysis of the first five minutes of each of both lessons, to bring out coordination of action forms or scheme of interaction, showing the evolution of the teacher's physical involvement between both lessons. From these elements, we shall sketch hypotheses as for the teacher's conceptualizations in action, regarding her progressive commitment in the collaborative research.

Synopsis

Figures 1 and 2 show the scene both sessions.

Table 2. Synopsis of both observed sessions

Lesson 1 Year 5 – Year 6 Reading Comprehension of a Heritage Text (Legend) 35 Minutes	Lesson 2 Year 3 Reading Comprehension of a Heritage Text (Youth Literature Album) 30 Minutes

Spatial device (Figure 1):
• Desks are ordered in rows aligned in front of the blackboard
• Maeva sits at her desk, facing her pupils
Lesson opening
• In French, reminder of the working methods: read the text and underline the not understood words (1 min. 30)
• A pupil hands out the text printed on sheets; the teacher moves to give a text to the researcher and show her collection of legends (1 min. 45)
Text reading
• Collective reading of the title and title words translation (45 sec.)
• Silent individual reading of the text, while Maeva is leafing through a dictionary (3 min. 50)
• Reading aloud paragraphs of the text by 6 voluntary pupils appointed by Maeva; occasional help by Maeva; some pupils go out to and back from the toilet (5 min. 30)
Text comprehension
• Maeva explains and translates the text last paragraph by (1 min.)
• In French, Maeva gives the order to underline misunderstood words; pupils comply while Maeva goes through a dictionary (2 min.)
• Pupils indicate the words which they underlined; Maeva sets collective understanding questions; pupils spontaneously answer by short sentences either individually or collectively, and Maeva completes by explanations, other questions and translations, reads some passages. Exchanges take place in both languages (18 min.)
Lesson closure
• Maeva congratulates the pupils, the pupils tidy up their school materials (15 sec.)
	Spatial device (Figure 2):
	• Pupils sit at their desks arranged in an arc in front of blackboard
	• Maeva stands in front of them, next to the blackboard on which slides are displayed
	Lesson opening
	• Greetings (15 sec.)
	• Expression of the week day (45 sec.)
	• Announcement: reading of an album seen in year 2 (10 sec.)
	Album reading
	• Slide of the front cover:
	  o Title reading by several appointed pupils (1 min. 15)
	  o Comprehension: spontaneous expression by pupils, collective questioning and individual questions to some pupils (1 min. 20)
	• Picture 2/2 bis/2 ter (6 min.15):
	  o Description of the picture without any text (1 min. 45)
	  o Progressive display of the text: reading then comprehension (4 min. 30)
	• Picture 3/3 bis/3 ter: same methods with writing of words on the blackboard and occasional use of French to translate, question and explain (3 min.)
	• Picture 4/4 bis/4 ter: same methods with Maeva miming and occasional use of French (5 min.)
	• Picture 5/5 bis/5 ter: same methods with Maeva miming and occasional use of French (3 min.)
	Role playing
	• Picture 1 without any text: designation of pupils by Maeva (2 min.)
	• Picture 2: *idem* (1 min.)
	• Picture 3: *idem* (1 min.)
	• Picture 4: *idem* (1 min.)
	Lesson closure
	• Maeva congratulates the pupils; switches the slide show off; asks pupils if they liked, what they learnt, how to say it in French (1 min.)
	• Maeva displays the front cover slide and asks pupils de transform the text by shifting the characters (1 min.)
	• Maeva switches the slide show off; thanks the pupils; sings twice with them a gesture song and congratulates them (1 min. 30)

Figure 1. Photography presenting the scene of the class in lesson 1 "4ᵗʰ and 5ᵗʰ years of primary school: legend"

Figure 2. Photography presenting the scene of the class in lesson 2 "2nd year of primary school: album"

Multimodal Analysis of the First Five Minutes

Our research orientation in an interactionnist perspective tries to track "the sense" of the professional's physical involvement in teaching situations, in particular its part in the interaction with her pupil in LCP lessons.

All in all, this comparative table of the teacher's action modes during the first five minutes of both observed lessons (Table 3.) shows globally a more important interactive density within the second lesson with regard to the first one. It also shows, in lesson 1 a quasi-monopole of speech by Maeva, with regard to a more well-balanced distribution of speech, besides more fluid, in lesson 2. Continuous interactions are more important, involving pupils and teacher in a dynamics of dialogical exchanges, about which the teacher is satisfied with its "active" character during the self-confrontation interview: "somewhere, I was satisfied, because it was euh, it was active."

A first quantitative tracking (Table 4.) allows contrasting strongly its physical involvement in both sessions. Indicators relative to looks and pointing are selected here.

It is important to specify also that the choice of the referent varies: it is individual in lesson 1, because each pupil works in front of his or her sheet while it is collective in lesson 2, which favors the convergence of looks and also justifies pointing slides.

A Different Action Organization for Two Subclasses of Situation

It seems with regard to these first five minutes, that beyond the different dynamics of involvement the teacher requests from her pupils, it is possible by the analysis, to bring to the foreground a continuation of coordinated actions, often repeated, about which we can make the hypothesis that it is a matter of a "scheme of interactivity with the pupils", that we could consider in this case specifically situated as a "scheme of interactivity centered on a shared referent to build", and about which we can think that she leads the construction by selecting elements of centration on parts of the pictures or by questioning on the one hand; and by choosing people she calls out, on the other hand.

This scheme gradually forms, and is specific to the didactic context proposed by the teacher, in connection with the transactional object of the interaction situation (Vinatier, 2013, p. 69), the legend or the displayed youth literature album; but also with the exchanges modes that are actualized in the interaction which she spreads in situation with the pupils.

Table 3. Multimodal analysis of the first five minutes of both observed lessons

Lesson 1 **Year 5 – Year 6** **Reading Comprehension of a Heritage Text (Legend)**	**Lesson 2** **Year 3** **Reading Comprehension of a Heritage Text** **(Youth Literature Album)**
2'02: (Maeva sits at her desk, facing Ps sitting at their table. Ps are silent) 2'05: Maeva (Lc): « *So, this morning, we're going to see a text in reo*» 2'06: P: « *Shhh* » 2'09: Maeva: « *As usual, you hand the text out, and then?* » 2'13: Ps: « *We write* » 2'15: Maeva (Lc): « *a reading... and after?* » 2'16: P: « *We underline words we don't undersand* » 2'19: Maeva: « *That's it. So we'll try to do a little bit more of reo this morning, a little bit more in reo, right?* » 2'30: (Maeva holds the photocopies of the legend text out to a P who stands up to take and hand them out to the other Ps. She stands up and brings a photocopy to the observer. She walks back to her desk, sits down, takes her legends collection, walks to the rear of the classroom to present it to the observer, then walks back with her collection to sit to her desk, waiting for P to end the handing out) (Lp)	(Ps sit at their desk arranged in an arc in front of blackboard, Maeva stands in front of them, next to the blackboard) 0'50: Maeva: « *Today, we're going to see a story...* » 1'02: Maeva (leans over her computer): « *... that you probably have already seen in year 2* » (Lslide, displays the front cover picture and title) 1'10: (stands up straight, Lslide, steps back) 1'12: Ps: *Read the title aloud* 1'13: Maeva: (Lc + Pslide) *Asks a question* 1'18: Ps *answer all together* 1'19: Maeva: « *Hand raised* » (raises her hand, Ps raise their hand), *calls a P* (Lp) 1'21: P: *Reads the title with mispronunciation* 1'26: Maeva: (listens to P, steps towards the blackboard + Lslide, Pslide) *repeats the sentence with the same mispronunciation?* (Lp) 1'28: Ps: (some Ps raise their hand) *Read the title in a correct way* 1'30: Maeva (steps towards Ps + Pp, Ps shut up) *Calls P* (Lp, Lslide, Lp) 1'33: P: *reads, partly correcting himself* (Maeva Lslide) 1'35: Maeva: (Lc) « *It is not ///, it is ///* » (Lslide, Lp) 1'38: Ps: *Repeat* 1'39: Maeva: (Lp) *Repeats.* (Pp + Pslide, Pslide). *Asks a question* (Lc) 1'43: P2: « *///* » 1'44: Maeva: (Pp2 + Lp2) *Talks to her in a low voice* 1'46: P: *Mumbles the title* 1'47: Maeva: (Lp, arms along her body) *Pronounce* words P comes up against (Lslide, Lp) to help him. « *Very good* » (Pps) « *Who wants to help him?* » (P3 raises her hand, Maeva Pp3)
4'15: Maeva (Lc) *collectively asks pupils for the title* 4'20: (4 Ps rise their hand up) Maeva *appeals to a P by naming him* 4'24: P *reads the title* 4'2: Maeva (Lc): *repeats the title* and *collectively asks for the meaning of one of the title words* 4'30: Ps: *half low voice answers by Ps* 4'33: Maeva *asks once more* 4'35: Ps: « *death* » 4'36: Maeva: « *the death* », then *collectively asks the meaning of another word in the title* 4'37: Ps: « *the tree* » 4'39: Maeva (Lc): « *Te tumu?* » (no answer from Ps) (Ghand) « *///?* » 4'43: Ps: « *euh...* » 4'44: Maeva (Lc): « *Tumu? ////?* This is the...? » 4'46: P: « *the cause* » 4'47: Maeva (Lc) « *That's it.* » (Ghand) « *This is the cause or the reason.* » (Lp) « *///?* » 4'57: P: *(inaudible)* 4'59: (Ps silently read the text, Maeva Lb, thumbs through it)	2'00: P3: *Reads a word* (Maeva Lslide, then Lp) 2'03: P: *Reads the title* 2'08: Maeva: (Lp) *Repeats.* « *Repeat* » (Lc) 2'09: Ps: *Repeat* 2'11: Maeva: *Repeats* (Pps, Lslide) 2'12: Ps: *Repeat* 2'14: Maeva: (Lc) *Reads the text by parts* 2'15: Ps: *Repeat by parts* 2'19: Maeva (Lp4 + Pp4) *Asks him to repeat* 2'21: P4: *Repeat* 2'24: Maeva: (Lslide) « *Very good* ». (Steps towards the blackboard, Lslide + Pslide) *Asks a question* (steps towards Ps, Lc) 2'29: P: *Starts an answer* then stops 2'32: Maeva: (Pp) *Calls P?* (Pslide) *Asks a question* 2'41: Ps et P5: *Answer* 2'42: Maeva: (Turns around towards her left, Pp5, Lslide, Pslide + Lc) *Asks a question* 2'45: Ps: *Answer* 2'46: Maeva: (Lc, steps towards Ps) « *Yes* ». *Asks a question. Starts to answer* (Pp2) 2'53: P2: *Partly answers* 2'54: Maeva: *Repeats the whole answer* (Lslide + Pslide). *Asks a question* (Pslide + Lc, put her hand on the slide, steps towards Ps, steps back, Pslide + Lc, Pp)

Continued on next page

Table 3. continued

Lesson 1 Year 5 – Year 6 Reading Comprehension of a Heritage Text (Legend)	Lesson 2 Year 3 Reading Comprehension of a Heritage Text (Youth Literature Album)
5'40: (Maeva *asks a P in a half loud voice to fetch her the dictionary which is at the rear of the classroom.* P stands up to fetch her the dictionary. Maeva Lb, Lc, leafs through her book, Lc)	3'11: Ps: *Answer* 3'12: Maeva (Lslide) *Asks a question* (steps towards the blackboard + Lslide, Pslide + Lc) 3'15: Maeva + Ps: *Answer* simultaneously 3'17: Maeva (Pslide + Lc): « *It's the little boy who asks ''Hey, Mum, what are you doing?''* ». (Lp + Pp) « *Repeat* » 3'26: P: *tries to answer* shyly 3'28: Maeva: (Pslide + Rp) « /// » (Pslide) 3'36: P: *Shyly reads the title*, Maeva *starts words* (Lp), P *repeats* 3'45: Maeva: « *Very good* ». (Pslide, Lc) « /// » (leans over her computer, displays a second picture without any text, steps back towards the blackboard, Lslide, Pslide) *Asks a question* (Ghand, Lc, Ps are silent). *Asks a question* (Pslide, Lc)
8'10: Some pupils walk in the corridor. Maeva stands up to close the classroom door)	4'04: P: *Answers* (Maeva Lp, steps towards Ps) 4'06: Ps: *Answer* (Maeva steps back towards the blackboard, Pslide) 4'10: Maeva: (Pslide + Lc) *Asks a question* 4'13: Ps: *Answer* (Maeva Pp nodding her approval) 4'16: Maeva: *Starts a sentence* (Pslide + Lc) 4'20: P: *Ends the sentence by a word* (Maeva Lp) 4'22: Maeva: *Repeats the word.* (P another p) « *Repeats. Come on, P name* » (Lp, Lslide). *Asks a question* (Lp) 4'29: P3: *Answers* 4'30: Maeva: (Lp3, Lp) « *Come on!* » (Mimes P with her hands in front of her mouth) « *Remove your hands* ». (*Repeats some parts of the sentence*, Lp, her arms along her body) 4'39: P: *Repeats the sentence* 4'48: Maeva: « *Very good* ». (P another P, Lp) « *Océane, ///* » (steps towards Ps + Lp). « *Repeat* ». (Steps back + Lp) 4'53: P: *Repeats the sentence* (Maeva Lp + nods) 4'59: Maeva: *Repeats the sentence* (Lp)
	5'02: P: *Ends the sentence* 5'03: Maeva: (Lc) *Repeats the beginning of the sentence* 5'06: Ps: *End the sentence* 5'07: Maeva: (Lc) *Ends the sentence with them.* (Lslide, Pslide) *Asks a question* (her arms along her body). (Lp) « *Sullivan !* » (silence) 5'17: Ps: 2 Ps *answer the question* 5'18: Maeva (steps towards the blackboard, Lslide + Pslide). *Asks a question* (steps towards Ps) 5'22: P: *Answer* 5'24: Maeva: (Lc) *Asks a question* 5'26: Ps: « *No...* » 5'28: Maeva: (Nods her approval) « *Yes* » (Pp) 5'29: Ps: *Answer* 5'30: Maeva: (Nods, Lslide, Lc) *Ends the sentence.* (Leans over her computer, displays a text on the picture, steps back) *Asks a question* (Ps read aloud, Maeva Pslide + Lc), *starts a question* (Lc, let Ps read, Lslide + her hands in her pockets, Lc + her hands in her pockets, Lslide) 5'55

Table 4. Quantitative comparison of some action modes between both lessons

	Lesson 1	**Lesson 2**
Lc: looks at the whole class	10	24
Lp: looks at a pupil	2	28
Lb: looks at her book	2	/
Lslide: looks at a slide on the blackboard	/	23
- Pp: points at a pupil - Pps: points at pupils	0 0	12 2
Pslide: points at a slide	/	22
Ghand: gestures with her hand	2	1

If such a scheme is difficult to identify within lesson 1, given that diverse modalities of interaction are deployed by the teacher; a "singular way of involving in the exchanges" (Vinatier, 2013, p. 137) establishes and remains, even strengthens during lesson 2. This scheme is characterized by a double alternation: an alternation of pointing at a pupil to invite him to participate and in pointing the reference image on one hand; and an alternation of look oscillating between the questioned pupil and the displayed picture, sometimes supported by a still posture, in the position of answer request, either by liveliness gestures or words addressed to one or several questioned pupils.

For instance, in the beginning of lesson 2, from 3 min. 50:

The teacher bends towards her computer to change slide and has a scene of everyday life appear (a mother in a cooking kitchen, up in front of a pan on the fire, and behind her a seated child) at which the teacher points (3'59), by alternating pointing at the characters and look in the direction of the pupils who answer her, while adopting a more fixed position arm swinging along the body (4'03), awaiting answer from the pupils. She welds then her finger towards the pan of the displayed image (4'08), to refocus on a more precise object, and listen to the answers. Then, she turns on her right-hand side and points at a pupil (4'15), then at the slide, then at another pupil, who pronounces a word (4'22), by pointing again at the image while looking towards the pupil (4'28), by saying "come on" to encourage him; while pointing the fingers at him (4'32), she helps him by pronouncing with him, while adopting again the posture with the swinging arms along her body, which could be interpreted, as a form of physical micro-disengagement to better make way for the pupil's words (4'43). Then, she points at another pupil (5 '47).

This scheme is actualized on many occasions during the whole lesson, but with all the nuances its adaptive part constitutes; it modulates according to the micro-circumstances of the situation. For example, we find that "scheme of interactivity centered on a shared referent to build", with nevertheless some specific reorientations, at every change of slide, as this extract arising later in the lesson gives evidence:

17'40: change of slide: new scene: the teacher points at a pupil and points then, on the image, at a particular character (7'47) with her arms swinging along her body in a waiting state, slightly nodding to better help the pupil to express a sentence (17'54). Then, she points at another character on the picture and turns towards other pupils (18'03), calling them out by saying "what's the word in Tahitian?", while slightly turning on the other side, while pointing at another pupil at the rear of the classroom, who answers, then another one (18'16), then another one (18'18), while supporting his sentence, then turns again to the other side, by pointing at other pupils (18'24), by putting her arms down as to wait for an answer, or by supporting her words expressed simultaneously to certain pupils by supporting them by waving her hand (18'31), putting herself in position to lower her arms as to wait for answers, which she obtains while sketching a gesture in direction of the image (18'35), then by pointing at a pupil at the front (18'39).

This scheme seems relative to the purpose to have pupils participate in the interaction, with several sub-objectives: either to make them express words or sentences from the everyday life scene displayed picture, either to induce them to answer questions about the presented scene; either, sometimes, to make them read the sentences which accompany the picture stemming from the album. This purpose is going to change into a new purpose of even more dialogical interactivity, which Maeva tells this way during the self-confrontation interview: "yes, there, I really went out of ... of my lesson in itself", and which she complexifies accordingly, in the course of interaction: "there that comes, that comes smoothly" ; "I say to myself that they are able to build, there, at this moment" ; "I increase a little the difficulty" ; "I saw that ... some of them managed to recite, to say the sentence, thus I said to myself: "go, well, we are going to introduce the dialogue all the same "!").

She thus experiments for the first time new modalities ("it is the first time we do a... a text"), "to diversify", by taking a risk: "there, I set off on eh! (Laughter)"; while specifying to the researcher: "and it was the right moment, because you were coming"; "I didn't very well what it would produce"; "it is risked"; "when I prepared last night euh, I told myself" into which adventure am I launching?" (Laughter)". Her satisfaction as for the result of the lesson leads her to look from now on "to complicate even more". As the lesson goes along, Maeva realizes that her pupils show more capacities than what she estimated: "I've all the same had what I wanted. Here we are. And even more"; "I noticed that... they understood, damn it all"; "I didn't expect that"; "you see, with regard to their level, I was a little... I underestimated them"; "I saw that, hum they were capable to, to read, to say with the intonation"; while specifying that she feels an intense satisfaction: "I realize that... it really enthralled them".

Maeva feels at the end of lesson the spontaneous need to thank her pupils. She even improvises a song for that purpose: "yes, that deserves well, euh... that they sing the song they like". Contrary to all expectations from her, this lesson of an unpublished kind for her pupils involves her in a new dynamics of LCP teaching which she considers more carrier: "I dash […] (Laughter). It makes or breaks! (Laughter) […] It passed. Thus as a result, hum... I'll go on!". At the end of this lesson, she will even project herself to the following one.

More globally, how to explain the difference of activity between both sessions? If both lessons are of the same class of situation connected to the objective of "reading comprehension of a local heritage text", it seems that we can infer for the professional two situations subclasses bound to her pupils' class level: 4th year and 5th year of primary school during lesson 1 and 2nd year of primary school during lesson 2; to which she adapts herself taking into account the nature of the artifacts she brings up, but not only. If in the lesson 1, she also requires the intervention of the pupils, it seems undeniable that her physical involvement largely differs from the second observed lesson. A part of the answer to this question seems relative to her relationship to LCP teaching.

Maeva's Relationship to LCP Teaching

Maeva presents a dysharmonic linguistic profile: she thinks that she better controls Tahitian than French, but possesses a better metalinguistic control of the latter, which is her favorite language in the daily use. As a consequence, she considers herself deprived on the didactic field for the *reo* teaching and to make it a teaching language, she regrets the lack of Tahitian drafted tools for grammar teaching and structural sentences analysis. Indeed, the existing documents propose a didactic support mainly drafted in French, which makes her translate them then into Tahitian. This task seems difficult to her because the Tahitian Academy dictionary only offers the translation from Tahitian into French and only a part for the translation from French into Tahitian (from A to D). According to her, "they tell us what to do, but they don't tell us how to do it". When she revisits her pre-service training[12], she remembers a very low hourly volume dedicated to LCP and contents of which were mainly aimed at the oral and written understanding of literary texts.

Her relationship to Tahitian language is ambivalent. She is a native speaker since Tahitian was used within her family, beside French. Then in her teens, she "rejects" this language for the benefit of French (the death of her grandfather was the opportunity not to have to speak Tahitian in her family any longer). As a teacher, she was again reluctantly confronted with Tahitian, since for two years, she had to teach it at the rate of 5 hours a week in nursery school, what she found "very hard" at the beginning. When we met her at the beginning of the research, Maeva had unwillingly participated on the previous two years (she qualifies herself as "designated volunteer") to the ReoC3 program in which she had in charge 3rd year then 4th year pupils, who had extensively learnt LCP since nursery school (5 hours a week within the framework of the program ECOLPOM) and whom ease in Tahitian was obvious from her point of view. It was in spite of her the opportunity "to re-weave links with Tahitian language", feeling "less refusal now", even if there also, she found the experience "very hard", because asking for a consequent personal investment for preparation and implementation of the activities in class. By means of this experiment, she perceived the cultural and patrimonial issue of Polynesian languages and culture transmission, but shows herself reluctant in regard to their establishment as a school subject and doubts about the educational interest in the strengthening of LCP for learning. Within the framework of her participation to the program, she was able to benefit from two annual training weeks (dispensed in French in her great disappointment) massively directed to the creation by the teachers of resources and activities for the class. She also deplores a too weak metalinguistic equipment in Tahitian and the absence of working time with the sector trainers at times institutionally planned for that purpose. Strongly disappointed with the absence of gratitude to the teachers on behalf of the educational authorities, she chose to leave the device without sharing the tools she had been able to develop.

At the moment of the exploratory phase, Maeva is teaching in 4th and 5th years of primary school (level which she says preferring because "they have more knowledge") with pupils having attended an ordinary course, without any strengthened LCP teaching, what was a shock for her ("then there, I took myself a slap!") with regard to their very low mastering of Tahitian which seems for them "as a foreign language". It was impossible to her with this public to propose a teaching with which she had become reconciled little by little, leaving her totally deprived ("I had to stop making as before. Then, there, it was impossible!"). Her meeting with these pupils, about whom she was under "the impression that they laugh" at her when she expresses herself in Tahitian, profoundly destabilized her and caused a very big loss of motivation as for LCP teaching ("Since I have to do it, therefore I do it").

Her lack of motivation is also fed by her positioning within the school. Put aside since she is another school headmaster's daughter, she feels she is "perceived as a spy". Upon her arrival, she asked about relative to LCP projects before realizing they did not exist and that this teaching was little practiced (what her pupils Tahitian level evaluation confirmed to her), except by another teacher practicing in another level than hers. Furthermore, collective work within this important size school is made difficult by disagreements between teachers' teams. She consequently gave up trying to impulse a collective dynamics relative to LCP. Maeva is thus an isolated and suffering teacher, who asks for her transfer for the year after and only teaches LCP because she is forced to it.

Her didactic and pedagogical choices reflect her posture. While 2h30 a week in LCP teaching are officially expected, she only teaches three times 30 minutes at the most. Among obstacles met to plan her teaching, she mentions her difficulty to complexify learning and letting her pupils enter the Tahitian literary dimension, herself better mastering a form of usual language. She proposes "very school like" exercises and repetitive activities centered on "simple texts" chosen as for their semantic contents, favors the work on reading skills (decoding, written understanding and oralisation), written transcriptions (dictations) and only works through coordinated management for a lesson a month, incriminating the low metalinguistic competence of her pupils. The written understanding is part of the unique objective of the yearly programming which counts very few variations, because "it takes time to accustom the pupils". Although she estimates that exclusive expression in Tahitian during a LCP lesson can be beneficial, she explains that her "pupils disconnect very quickly in *reo*" and "get tired fast", what brings her to resort in a very frequent way to explanations in French to "motivate them" and keep their attention (she shows herself sensitive to a possible "blocking of the pupils" towards *reo*). She rarely elaborates projects, which would ask her "some more work".

CONCLUSION: UNDERSTANDING TO DEVELOP

On one hand, this work of compared analysis of two teaching-learning situations for a same teacher nine month apart enables to characterize the development of her forms to act; on the other hand, it also enables to see a form of not yet spread interactivity which encourages us to propose several hypotheses.

We can move forward a first micro-genetic hypothesis connected to a shape of interactive reciprocity, about what we saw that she gradually formed during lesson 2. Indeed, with regard to the first elements of this lesson analysis, it would seem that her power to act redeployment establishes in interaction with the one that she esteems at her pupil's. This aspect sends back to a didacticians' well-known axiom according to which the didactic situation is a "cooperative paradoxical and conditional game", where "the teacher wins by authorizing"; "the teacher wins if and only if the pupil wins, but provided that the pupil plays reasonably *proprio motu*, "of his own movement", of himself" (Sensevy, 2008, p. 44). Yet, in our study, this mandate is not straightaway given, but is built during the interactive activity. Indeed, it is by enabling her pupils to be able "to play the game" otherwise, to spread differently their power to act, by proposing them, gradually during the ongoing lesson, more complex tasks, that the teacher becomes aware of their more widened possibilities of action. What gives her the opportunity to further involve, by trying stabs the effects of which she perceives, with a certain enjoyment moreover, considered positive, which she announces to her pupils, by thanking them. In this respect, we had put forward besides the neighboring hypothesis that the trainer's creativity as for the conception of their training devices would be all the more developed as it would enable a more opened creativity from the point of view of the learners whom they address (Villeret et al., 2014).

A second more macro-genetic hypothesis is a matter of a professional development form at Maeva's. Beyond an effective practice evolution, it seems to us that we can indeed speak for this case study of subject development. Indeed, we utter the hypothesis that the teacher was able to operate an "instrumental genesis" (Rabardel, 2005) thanks to a conjunction of factors. In the first place, it is obvious to notice how, even though she considers negatively the prescription proposals, in particular, within the experimental program in which she participated, she can appropriate, but in her own way, and for herself, the artifacts that the program had permitted her to build, but without neither using them nor sharing them. While mobilizing in situation these artifacts, to make them instruments in the service of new educational proposals she bends her own project of action. Secondly, it is maybe the classes level change intervened between two moments of observation, that enabled her to consider a new subclass of LCP written language comprehension situation, specific to youngest pupils level (2nd year of primary school instead of 4th year and 5th year of primary school), inviting her to invent a new form of more shared action, because at the same time common to the whole class, by means of the video screening, and at the same time more supported, by the pictures, allowing until interaction dialogic forms, contrasted in regard to an individual and more exclusively bookish activity, in the case of the lesson relative to the legend.

This double series of factors (contextual but also inherent to the subject) is reminiscent of both kinds of invariants highlighted by Vinatier (2009): situational invariants and subject invariants, which seem to combine in the evolution identified by our study. It is a set of choices by Maeva herself which were able to preside over the onset of this change of interaction form, in connection with her positioning and values, gradually bent. Would she have found in her, in interaction with the contextual factors, to express a felt potentiality, from then on become actualizable?

But beyond this factors conjunction, which enabled new perspectives for action to actualize at this teacher's, we can detect an interesting concomitance. Indeed, let us notice that it also coincides with a moment of stronger involvement in the collaborative research on behalf of the teacher, reserved, as we saw her as for the beginning. Does not she say it herself, when she implies she will be able to authorize herself to experiment a new modality with her pupils: "and it was the right moment, because you were coming"? If it is difficult to surely assert that the observation of her activity enabled to constitute a "potential situation of development" (Mayen, 1999), in any case, it is important to pledge that the continuation of the research will otherwise enable, if not to de-imbricate all the factors, at least to forward consider the role of observation.

In the long term, to go further, it would be a matter of reflecting about manners to didactize the observation modalities in order to make them transferable into training, to even more, contribute to the development of the practitioners' power to act. If our methodological device choices do not constitute a limit in terms of research modalities, we can however wonder how this observational approach can be led to teachers' training, and, according to the variability of the contexts, on which institutional, epistemic and pragmatic conditions?

REFERENCES

Altet, M. (2002). Une démarche de recherche sur la pratique enseignante: L'analyse plurielle. *Revue Française de Pédagogie*, *138*(1), 85–93. doi:10.3406/rfp.2002.2866

Altet, M. (2003). Caractériser, expliquer et comprendre les pratiques enseignantes pour aussi contribuer à leur évaluation. *Les Dossiers des Sciences de l'Education, 10*, 31–43.

Altet, M., Bru, M. & Blanchard-Laville, C. (2012). *Observer les pratiques enseignantes: pour quels enjeux ?* Paris: L'Harmattan.

Bazin, J. (2008). *Des clous dans la Joconde. L'anthropologie autrement.* Toulouse: Anacharsis.

Clot, Y. (1999/2006). *La fonction psychologique du travail. 5ème édition corrigée.* Paris: PUF.

Clot, Y. (2008). *Travail et pouvoir d'agir.* Paris: PUF.

Creswell, J. W. (2007). *Qualitative inquiry and research design: Choosing among five approaches.* Thousand Oaks, CA: Sage.

Leplat, J. (1997). *Regard sur l'activité en situation de travail - Contribution à la psychologie ergonomique.* Paris: PUF.

Mayen, P. (1999). Les situations potentielles de développement. *Education permanente*, 139, 65-86.

Mollo, V., & Falzon, P. (2004). Auto- and allo-confrontation as tools for reflective activities. *Applied Ergonomics, 35*(6), 531–540. doi:10.1016/j.apergo.2004.06.003 PMID:15374760

Mondada, L. (2008). « Production du savoir et interactions multimodales – Une étude de la modélisation spatiale comme activité pratique située et incarnée », *Revue d'anthropologie des connaissances,* 2(2), 219-266.

Mondada, L. (2012), « Organisation multimodale de la parole-en-interaction: pratiques incarnées d'introduction des référents », *Langue française,* 175, 129-147.

Munoz, G. & Boivin, S. (2016). Accompagner les tuteurs à expliciter leur connaissance-en-acte. *Education permanente*, 206, 109-117.

Munoz, G., Minassian, L., & Vinatier, I. (2012). An analyzing of co-piloting in the teaching-learning process: a case study of science class debate. *WORK: A Journal of Prevention, Assessment, & Rehabilitation* (Special issue on Ergonomic Work Analysis and Training), 41, 187-194. http://iospress.metapress.com/content/l1683274520015h1/

Numa-Bocage, L., Marcel, J.-F., & Chaussecourte, P. (Eds.), (2014). L'observation des pratiques enseignantes, *Recherches en Éducation*, 19. Retrieved from http://www.recherches-en-education.net/IMG/pdf/REE-no19.pdf

Pastré, P. (2011). *La didactique professionnelle. Approche anthropologique du développement chez les adultes.* Paris: PUF.

Piaget, J. & al. (1926). *La représentation du monde chez l'enfant.* Paris: F. Alcan

Piaget, J. (1936). *La naissance de l'intelligence chez l'enfant.* Paris, Neuchâtel: Delachaux & Niestlé.

Piaget, J. (1970). *L'épistémologie génétique.* Paris: PUF.

Piaget, J. (1974). *Réussir et comprendre.* Paris: PUF.

Rabardel, P. (2005). Instrument, activité et développement du pouvoir d'agir. In P. Lorino & R. Teulier (Eds.), *Entre connaissance et organisation: l'activité collective* (pp. 251–265). Paris: La Découverte.

Rabardel, P., & Pastré, P. (2005). *Modèles du sujet pour la conception.* Toulouse: Octarès.

Rogalski, J. (2003). Y a-t-il un pilote dans la classe. *Recherches en didactique des mathématiques, 23*(3), 343–388.

Salaün, M. (2010). *A l'épreuve de l'autochtonie. Penser la décolonisation de l'école. Une comparaison France/Etats-Unis (Nouvelle-Calédonie/Hawaï).* Dossier d'Habilitation à Diriger des Recherches sous la direction d'Elisabeth Bautier, Université Paris 8 Saint-Denis.

Salaün, M. (2011). *Renforcer l'enseignement des langues et cultures polynésiennes à l'école élémentaire. Contribution à l'évaluation de l'expérimentation ECOLPOM en Polynésie Française: aspects sociolinguistiques, Rapport de recherche.* ANR.

Schön, D. (1994). *Le praticien réflexif: à la recherche du savoir caché dans l'agir professionnel.* Montréal: Les éditions logiques.

Sensevy, G. (2008). Le travail du professeur pour la théorie de l'action conjointe en didactique, *Recherche et formation,* 57, 39-50. Retrieved from http://rechercheformation.revues.org/822

Theureau, J. (2004). *Le cours d'action: Méthode élémentaire.* Toulouse: Octarès.

Theureau, J. (2006). *Le cours d'action: Méthode développée.* Toulouse: Octarès.

Vergnaud, G. (1990). La théorie des champs conceptuels. *Recherche en didactique des Mathématiques, 10*(2-3), 133–170.

Vergnaud, G. (1996). Au fond de l'action, la conceptualisation. In J. M. Barbier (Ed.), *Savoirs théoriques et savoirs d'action* (pp. 275–292). Paris: PUF.

Vergnaud, G. (1999). Le développement cognitif de l'adulte. In P. Carré & P. Caspar (Eds.), *Traité des sciences et des techniques de la formation* (pp. 103–126). Paris: Dunod.

Vergnaud, G. (2007). Représentation et activité: deux concepts associés. *Recherche en éducation,* 4, 9-22, http://www.recherches-en-education.net/IMG/pdf/REE-no4.pdf

Vergnaud, G. (2008). Culture et conceptualisation, *Carrefours de l'éducation,* 26, 83-98.

Villeret, O., Munoz, G., & Boivin, S. (2014). Quelle créativité dans la conception de dispositifs de formation basés sur l'analyse de l'activité? Paper presented at the Colloque HEP (haute école pédagogique): *Créativité et apprentissage: un tandem à ré-inventer?* Lausanne, Vaud, 15 & 16 mai.

Vinatier, I. (2009). *Pour une didactique professionnelle de l'enseignement.* Rennes: PUR.

Vinatier, I. (2013). *Le travail enseignant. Une approche par la didactique professionnelle.* Bruxelles: De Boeck.

Vinatier, I., Fillietaz, L. & Kahn, S. (Coord.). (2012). Enjeux, forme et rôle des processus collaboratif entre chercheurs et professionnels de la formation: pour quelle efficacité? *Travail et apprentissage,* 9.

Vinatier I., Morrissette J. (2015). Les recherches collaboratives: enjeux et perspectives. *Carrefours de l'éducation*, 39, 137-170.

ENDNOTES

[1]   Let us remind that French is the official language (and thus language of schooling) of the country which is characterized by a very important glottodiversity, in particular of Polynesian languages (*reo mā'ohi*). Five main languages, as well as their variants, are spoken. Tahitian is the Polynesian mainly spoken language and constitute, with French, a lingua franca also used in the linguistic areas consisting of the other archipelagoes.

[2]   Information collected during the exploratory phase proceeds of a hybrid device, constituted of moments formally dedicated to data collection (semi-directive interviews, professional and institutional documents communication, direct observation of lessons in class, training initiatives), as well as of informal moments giving more widely access to the actors' "life". The analysis of some and others' positioning of is this completed by a participating observation.

[3]   Having determined together with the teacher's class situations likely to be the object of a thorough analysis, we filmed for each of them a lesson in Tahitian. The participants' lack of availability led us to give up joint identification of representative situations of their activity. Instead, we identified what is problematic in situation and determined with them lessons during which these difficulties were at the heart of their activity.

[4]   Extracts of each teacher's lessons are selected by the researcher to be collectively viewed. The choice of extracts is based on their representative character of each one's activity (objectives, rules of action, ways of acting) and on the expression of their particular conceptualization (appearance of organizing principles, principles considered as truths, values).

[5]   "By "multimodal resources" we thus send back to all forms -including linguistic- and to all the details which the participants summon up to make the interaction understandable, resources they turn towards in practices of understanding, interpretation, even real time analysis of the current interaction, immediately incorporated into the action which they produce" (Mondada, 2008).

[6]   According to Jorro (2007), "the teacher's speaking body is thus the vector of process of semiotization". The "body movements which mobilize non-verbal dimensions and linguistic practices constitute "essential expressions" interpreted by the pupils".

[7]   This questioning opens an access to the understanding of the activity at a "micro" level (the contrastive analysis of the effective practice of five teachers in situation). The consideration of the other data in our ownership enables us to investigate two other levels, the object of which the present contribution is not): at a level "meso", we question the meaning they endow their LCP teaching activity, with their difficulties and their resources; at a "macro" level, we try to identify their school teaching conceptions in the specific context of French Polynesia. By investigating those various levels, the ambition is to reach, thanks to the teachers' participation, their conceptualization of the LCP teaching situations (their organizing principles) in connection with the cultural dimension peculiar to the community formed by the class on the Tahitian ground. The tracking of possible tensions at the intra-individual, interpersonal and transverse levels (relationship to knowledge, language, culture, school disciplines, school purposes, learning, education, writing, oral ...), which

express a type of necessity of the cultural at school, can lead to spot characteristic dimensions of LCP teaching.

[8] The lack of linguistic mastery in Polynesian and French languages by the pupils (combined with very great socioeconomic difficulties of the population) is moved forward as an explanatory factor of the academic failure. The country thus challenged itself to gradually evolve from a situation of undergone diglossia towards a more harmonious bilingualism. The linguistic question is then set out as a keystone for the enterprise success in a triple objective: political, patrimonial and educational (Salaün, 2010, 2011).

[9] Are pointed in this respect: structural breaks between university, pre- and in-service trainings due to the institutional subdivision; an insufficiency of the means assigned by the ministry to implement a institutionally shown priority; a frequent renewal of the supervision structures within the Head office of Education and Teachings, leading to a reduction and to an instability of LCP specialists trainers teams; unsuitable training contents and their low hourly volume. As a result, from this, a self-training necessity and a consequent personal investment based on teacher's voluntary service, their voluntary work off school time, as well as their own equipment and supports financing in sufficient amount for their class.

[10] Mainly proposals for youth literature albums pedagogical exploitation, translations of these albums in various Polynesian languages, resources for declamatory art teaching. In 2015 the first Tahitian textbook for the 5th year of primary school level is diffused.

[11] Let us give some additional information concerning the class context. Even if the classrooms differ from one group to the other, the material conditions are roughly identical, in terms of space and resources. Working conditions are globally comfortable, revealing no particular specificities linked to the local context: approximately 20 pupils, each of them seated at his table, the classroom is provided with walls, a blackboard, a desk for the teacher, a video-projector, books and various classical tools and resources…

[12] After four years of supply posts (without any pre-service training), Maeva succeeds in the competitive entry examination. She spends her first year training on the ground, then benefits from a theoretical training the year after. Six years have passed by since then, during which she taught in nursery school during three years, then in primary school in this new school for the third consecutive year.

Chapter 6

Learning to Unpack Standards–Based Mathematics Teaching through Video–Based Group Conversations

Rossella Santagata
University of California, Irvine, USA

Janette Jovel
Independent Researcher, USA

Cathery Yeh
Chapman University, USA

ABSTRACT

Research that focuses on understanding pre-service teachers' learning processes as they engage in video-based activities is still limited. This study investigates pre-service teachers' group conversations around videos of mathematics teaching. Conversations of two groups attending a ten-week video-based course introducing standards-based instruction were videotaped, transcribed, and analyzed. Pre-service teachers' discussions included elements of an analysis framework used to guide their viewing: mathematics content, analysis of teaching and of student thinking and learning, and suggestions for instructional improvement. Analyses became more elaborated over the duration of the course. In addition, pre-service teachers discussed standards-based mathematics teaching by increasingly valorizing its characteristics. Findings highlighted important dimensions for working with video in teacher collaborative settings: the purpose, viewing lens, group dynamics, and facilitator role.

INTRODUCTION

Digital video is gaining attention as a tool for teacher learning. Advocates of a practice-based approach to teacher preparation have found in the use of digital video a series of important affordances. Video recordings of teaching can be viewed multiple times, allowing for decomposition of complex practices into smaller components that can be articulated, unpacked and studied, thus facilitating novice teachers'

DOI: 10.4018/978-1-5225-0711-6.ch006

Copyright © 2017, IGI Global. Copying or distributing in print or electronic forms without written permission of IGI Global is prohibited.

learning (Hatch & Grossman, 2009). Video is also used to develop beginning teachers' abilities to attend to the details of student thinking (Santagata, Zannoni, & Stigler, 2007; Santagata & Guarino, 2011; Sherin & van Es, 2002), to analyze the effects of teaching on students' learning (Santagata & Angelici, 2010), and to develop self-reflection abilities (Davis, 2006; Lee, 2005). The positive effects of video use in teacher preparation have been documented by studies that have investigated pre-service teacher (PST) development of various abilities and dispositions, such as noticing skills (Star & Strickland, 2008, van Es & Sherin, 2002), analysis and reflection abilities (Santagata & Guarino, 2011; Stockero, 2008) and knowledge of equitable practices (Park, 2008; McDuffie, et al., 2013). Research that focuses on understanding PSTs' learning process as it is facilitated by video-based activities is instead still limited. Attention needs to be given not only to outcomes measured at the end of PSTs' learning experiences, but also to their learning processes as evidenced by the content of their collaborative discussions around videos and how these change through the course of learning experiences (LeFevre, 2004). These investigations can provide both a theory of technology-enhanced teacher learning and practical implications for the design of teacher preparation interventions.

This study contributes to closing the gap in this research area. It is part of a larger project that investigates the impact of a video-enhanced teacher education course designed to encourage specific dispositions, knowledge, and practices for teaching mathematics for understanding and for learning from mathematics teaching.

BACKGROUND

In the United States new curriculum standards for the teaching and learning of mathematics were recently introduced (National Governors Association for Best Practices, 2010). The Common Core Standards for Mathematics present an ambitious vision for high-quality mathematics instruction and include Mathematical Practice Standards that support the development of students' understanding of central mathematical ideas (as delineated by the Mathematical Content Standards). This vision of mathematics instruction proposes, for example, that students develop conceptual understanding of core mathematical ideas as well as procedural fluency in a range of domains. Additionally, students should construct increasingly sophisticated forms of mathematical argumentation as well as critique the reasoning of others, learn to communicate their reasoning effectively using multiple representations, and make connections between different representations. Student thinking and mathematical learning practices clearly play a fundamental role in this vision.

The course studied here was designed to prepare teachers for a standards-based approach to mathematics teaching. Designed as a supplement to math methods instruction, this required 10-week course met once a week for a total of approximately 25 hours and focused on analysis of student thinking and learning and discussions of instructional effectiveness. It used a framework, the Lesson Analysis Framework (Santagata, Zannoni, & Stigler, 2007; Santagata & Guarino, 2010) to guide PST analysis of videos of classroom teaching. This framework is intended to develop routines to systematically observe, analyze, and reflect on classroom instruction, specifically as it pertains to student mathematics thinking and the interrelation between pedagogical decisions and student learning.

Through this process of analysis pre-service teachers also develop new knowledge about students' mathematical understandings, questioning strategies that open windows into student thinking, mathematical tasks that push students' reasoning as well as knowledge of teaching methods and discourse moves that are not as effective. In other words, a systematic reflection on the effects of their practices on students' learning provides opportunities for teachers themselves to learn from their daily work in the classroom and improve their competence on the job (Yeh & Santagata, 2015).

The framework consists of a series of key questions:

1. What are the main student learning goals of this instructional episode?
2. Did the students make progress toward the learning goals? What evidence do we have that students made progress? What evidence do we have that students did not make progress? What evidence are we missing?
3. Which instructional strategies supported students' progress toward the learning goals and which did not? Finally,
4. What alternative strategies could the teacher use? How might one expect these strategies to impact students' progress toward the lesson learning goals? If any evidence of student learning is missing, how could the teacher collect such evidence?

Pre-service teachers were introduced to the framework at the beginning of the course and subsequently applied it to several videos. Course sessions focused on different questions and unpacked the subskills necessary to complete a detailed and elaborated analysis. Video was used throughout the course to aid this process. Sometime PSTs were asked to view interviews of children solving mathematics problems and to attend to the details of their thinking. Other times, they watched key segments of a lesson and discussed its effectiveness in light of the learning goals and as evidenced by student learning; yet other times, they searched over the internet for videos of instructional practices that are aligned with practices advocated by the Common Core Standards. In other words, video was used to slow down the teaching process and facilitate structured analysis guided by the framework and group discussions of teaching and learning (for details on types of video and viewing tasks that were used in the course, see Santagata & Guarino, 2011).

Video was used not as a model of teaching to adhere to, but rather as a representation of teaching that can elicit discussion. The assumption here is that simply showing a model of teaching that teacher educators consider effective does not automatically translate in teachers adopting that approach. Teachers need to understand the principles at the basis of approaches that are research based, but not common in classrooms so they can appropriate them and own them. Learning to teach is not about acquiring a set of teaching strategies or skills; it is about developing flexible competence and professional judgment. Through the consideration of the specific student learning goal(s) a teacher would like to focus on during a given lesson, the teacher will identify tasks and activities that her prior experience indicated as successful. Alternatively, a teacher might test a task and/or activity s/he learned during teacher preparation or in a professional development program and carefully monitor its effects on students' progress towards the specific lesson learning goal. In this sense, video is not used to *train* teachers, rather it is used to develop teachers' *professional judgment* (Cochran-Smith & Zeichner, 2010).

The impact of this course focused on analysis of practice was investigated through a pre and post-test study of pre-service teachers' abilities to reflect on a videotaped lesson taught by another teacher and through analyses of the quality of their instruction and self-reflection (as illustrated in video clips of their teaching and accompanying commentaries they submitted as part of the required teacher performance assessment designed to measure the teaching standards for California student teachers). Results from these studies revealed that pre-service teachers learned to attend to the details of student thinking and to discuss instructional practices that elicited and built on student thinking. In addition, they learned to implement these practices in their own lessons and to use evidence of student learning to discuss effective and problematic aspects of their own teaching. These findings thus supported the use of video guided by structured analysis of practice to develop teachers' professional judgment. Teachers in fact were able to reflect on evidence of student learning to assess the effectiveness of their instructional choices and to plan for next steps. Two prior publications summarize these outcomes (Santagata & Guarino, 2011; Yeh & Santagata, 2015).

MAIN FOCUS OF THE CHAPTER

We view learning to teach as a socialization process that occurs within particular sociocultural contexts. PSTs engage with teacher educators, mentor teachers, their peers, and artifacts and tools of the profession to become part of a community of practice (Lave & Wenger, 1991). This socialization process also involves the development of a professional identity that is defined over time through interactions with others (Wenger, 1998). In this chapter, we zoom in and focus on a particular socialization setting: discussions among peers. This focus will also allow us to better understand the pre-post learning outcomes reported in prior publications and summarized above. Specifically, in this chapter we examine pre-service teachers' participation in group discussions in response to the video-based activities described above to explore PSTs' meaning making processes and development of new understandings. We analyze the progression of their discussions through the duration of the ten-week course attending to whether these changed over time.

PSTs' interactions with the course instructor and with each other around video followed a general sequence represented in Figure 1. Sometimes this process was repeated a few times during a course session. The focus of our investigation is the second step, pre-service teachers' analyses of teaching and learning.

Figure 1. Sequence of activities that structured interactions around video

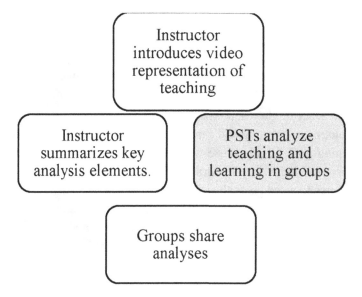

The following research questions are addressed:

1. What is the focus of pre-service teachers' video-elicited discussions? Do pre-service teachers attend to the elements of the framework used to guide their analyses of teaching? What else do they discuss?
2. Do pre-service teachers' discussions change over time and if they do, in what ways?

METHODS: PARTICIPANTS AND CODING PROCESS

Participants were two groups of five pre-service teachers each enrolled in a one-year post-bachelor elementary teacher preparation program at a large research university. The two groups were randomly selected from the six groups attending the course. Groups were formed based on performance on a lesson analysis task completed at the beginning of the course and were intentionally heterogeneous in terms of analysis abilities. Each group was comprised of four female and one male pre-service teacher. The project resources did not allow us to study the conversations of all groups attending the course. However, by including two randomly-chosen groups we were able to see whether certain conversations were peculiar to one group or whether they occurred across the two groups. Participants attended the three-hour course once a week for ten weeks. The course was taught by an instructor who split her time teaching at an elementary school and lecturing for teacher preparation courses. All course lectures and both groups' discussions were videotaped and transcribed.

To investigate systematically the themes that pre-service teachers discussed during the course, we began by separating the transcript into topic segments. Every time pre-service teachers' conversations switched topic, a new segment was identified (Jacobs & Morita, 2002). For example, if participants were discussing a particular teacher-student interaction in a video they just watched then moved on to discuss the mathematics at the core of the lesson, a new topic segment was identified.

Coding categories were created by reviewing the videos and transcripts several times and by adopting both a top-down and bottom-up analysis process (Strauss & Corbin, 1998). Conversation themes that were identified reflected both the analysis tasks assigned by the instructor and other prevailing themes that emerged spontaneously from the participants' discussions. The analysis revealed that pre-service teachers followed the tasks' prompts and discussed themes relevant to the analysis framework introduced in the course. Each topic segment was thus categorized to capture these themes according to the following categories of focus:

1. Mathematics content,
2. Analysis of teaching strategies,
3. Analysis of student thinking and learning, and
4. Suggestions for instructional improvement (see Table 1 for a description of each theme and sample comments).

In most cases, participants discussed more than one theme in each topic segment. In other words, it happened often that participants discussed the teacher's practices in the video in conjunction with the mathematical ideas that students in the video were supposed to learn, or they discussed math content while also analyzing student thinking, and so on. Because we were interested in documenting the sub-

Table 1. Coding categories and excerpts of sample conversations

Theme and Levels of Elaboration	Example
Mathematics Content	
Descriptive: Math content is mentioned, but it is limited to the content already referred to in the representation of teaching being analyzed.	"The teacher should talk to them- if 2/4 would fill up this other half, does that mean 2/4 equals ½?"
Elaborated: Math content is integral to the analysis and pre-service teachers draw from mathematical knowledge beyond the content included in the representation of teaching being analyzed.	"The teacher needs to change her vocabulary. She says take away instead of subtract. We learned in [education] 327 that when you say that, it is incorrect because in higher math you do take away from zero, so this might confuse the child in later math"
Analysis of Teaching Strategies	
Descriptive: Pre service teachers describe the teacher's actions with no or limited elaboration	"She told them that changing their mind is okay too during the discussion. She just wants to figure out why they're coming to a specific answer."
Elaborated: Pre service teachers comment on teachers' actions by referring to principles of effective teaching and/or evidence of student thinking/learning present in the representation of teaching being analyzed.	"The teacher had the students write out the problem, use the manipulative and the number line and the students saw it in different ways and got it, instead of just giving them the circle then they would know it's out of a whole and do it that way"
Analysis of Student Learning	
Descriptive: Pre service teachers describe students' actions with no or limited elaboration	"The kids have to kind of struggle through it and figure it out themselves like so we can actually see which ones understand"
Elaborated: Pre service teachers comment on students' actions by inferring understanding of mathematical idea or knowledge of mathematical procedures.	"The girl, she put everything on one line. It seemed like they didn't know how to connect the number sentences that they were working with... with the manipulative and how to show them visually."
Suggestions for Instructional Improvement	
Descriptive: Pre service teachers suggest instructional improvements with no further elaboration.	"She should encourage more abstract thought. It's like you said very visual and I think it's really easy."
Elaborated: Pre service teachers suggest instructional improvements and provide explicit rationale for choices based on principles of effective teaching or by discussing potential impact on student learning.	"That didn't make sense. I thought when they were talking they could incorporate the significance of folding the paper and dividing fractions. She could have said like dividing in 1/2 each time to make that concept a little more clear. Like 1/4 is 1/2 of this half and 1/8 is 1/2 of that. Then the kids would see it, you know"
Standards-Based Math	
Challenging: Pre service teachers challenge the merit and feasibility of standards-based math teaching, by discussing issues of time constraint, student ability, lack of specific directions for students, and their ability as novices to teach that way.	"She didn't teach anything, she leaves them off to their own work and just kind of stares at them working on the problem. No instructions or steps; they just do what they want to do with it."
Embracing: Pre-service teachers highlight weaknesses of traditional teaching or highlight effective features of standards-based math teaching by referring to principles discussed in class.	"What she did... it was good. You can give them a triangle and ask them how would you make a rectangle from this? And see if they can make a connection between triangles and rectangles. Now they can start thinking in terms of half the area of a rectangle is the area of a triangle"

stance of all their conversations, for each topic segment we marked all the themes that were discussed. We then calculated for each theme the percentage of topic segments in which it was discussed to see whether certain themes were more prevalent than others.

When coding topic segments, we also noticed that different levels of sophistication were reflected in the conversations. Thus, every time a theme was discussed, a score was assigned based on the following: When conversations tended to give an account of what happened in the video, they were coded as "descriptive"; when they included comments that went beyond what was observed in the video and showed an effort to make sense of teaching and learning, they were coded as "elaborated." To document changes in the level of sophistication, we then averaged the percentages of elaborated segments for each theme during the first five weeks and during the last five weeks of the course. Based on prior studies we conducted (Santagata, Zannoni, & Stigler, 2007) and on the broader literature on PSTs' abilities to analyze teaching (Star & Strickland, 2008; Stockero, 2008) we had some expectations about participants' analysis processes. We expected that at the beginning of the course, most of their conversations would be limited to a description of what they saw in the videos. We also expected that conversations would change over time. As mentioned above, the post-data we collected on their ability to analyze a videotaped lesson showed an increased ability to interpret instructional events and reflect on their effectiveness. We were thus interested in seeing whether group discussions among peers contributed to the development of these analyses abilities.

Finally, based on differences emerging from the conversations themselves, each topic segment was also coded in terms of pre-service teachers' dispositions towards standards-based math teaching. Two categories captured two distinct dispositions:

1. **"Challenging":** When participants challenged the merit and feasibility of standards-based math teaching, by discussing issues of time constraints, student ability, lack of specific directions for students, and their ability as novices to teach that way; or
2. **"Embracing":** When participants highlighted weaknesses of traditional teaching or effective features of standards-based math teaching by discussing the positive effects on student learning.

In this case, we did not have any predictions that these conversations would occur. As we will discuss later, this dimension of socialization into a particular approach to mathematics teaching resulted to be very prominent in participants' conversations.

Again, to trace changes in groups' conversations over time, results are reported by comparing average percentages of topic segments that either challenged or embraced standards-based math teaching during the first five and last five weeks of the course. Analyses of the conversations were performed separately for each group to see whether group differences existed. Coding categories and excerpts of sample comments during pre-service teachers' conversations are included in Table 1.

FINDINGS

A total of 170 topic segments were identified for group 1 and of 224 for group 2. For both groups, the number of segments were fewer during the first 5 weeks of the course than the second 5 weeks (i.e., group 1: 71 and 99; group 2: 88 and 136). To some extent, pre-service teachers discussed all elements targeted by the analysis framework (i.e., math, teaching, student learning, and suggestions for improvement) indicating that the course activities elicited the intended themes of discussion. Although some differences were observed between groups in the percentage of topic segments in which each theme was discussed, these were not substantial. For brevity, we thus decided to report percentages as averages between the two groups. The two groups discussed the mathematics content of the teaching episodes represented in the video on average in 42.5% topic segments; they analyzed the teaching strategies observed in the video on average in 58% topic segments; they analyzed student thinking and learning on average in 39% topic segments; and finally, they proposed suggestions for improvement on average in 50% of topic segments.

Conversations changed over time in terms of their level of sophistication and similarly for both groups, with one exception that will be discussed below. The reader should refer back to Table 1 for definitions and sample comments that illustrate descriptive versus elaborated comments. For the themes of math content, analysis of teaching strategies, and analysis of student thinking and learning, the percentage of elaborated conversations increased over time (averages of the two groups are reported in Figure 2). For the segments in which mathematics content was discussed, the percentage of conversations that extended beyond the mathematics ideas not directly talked about in the video increased from 28% of topic segments that discussed math content to 65%. For the segments that included analysis of teaching, conversations that went beyond description and discussed the effectiveness of teaching approaches or strategies increased from 27% of topic segments that discussed teaching to 56%. For the segments that included analysis of student thinking and learning, conversations that went beyond description and included inferences about student understanding of mathematical ideas or knowledge of mathematics procedures increased from 26% of topic segments that discussed student thinking to 55%. For the segments that included suggestions for instructional improvements, the two groups behaved differently. In the first group, the percentage of segments in which instructional improvements were suggested and justified by drawing on principles of standards-based teaching and/or its potential impact on student learning increased from 23% of topic segment that included suggestions to 35%. The second group, on the contrary, proposed elaborated suggestions in 46% of topic segments that included suggestions during the first 5 weeks of the course and in 21% of topic segments during the second 5 weeks. Results are summarized in Figure 2.

Finally, throughout the ten-week course, pre-service teachers' co–constructed images of standards-based mathematics teaching either by challenging its instructional aspects or by embracing them. This theme was discussed by the two groups on average in 80% topic segments during the first part of the

Figure 2. Percentage of topic segments during the first 5 and last 5 weeks of the course coded as elaborated

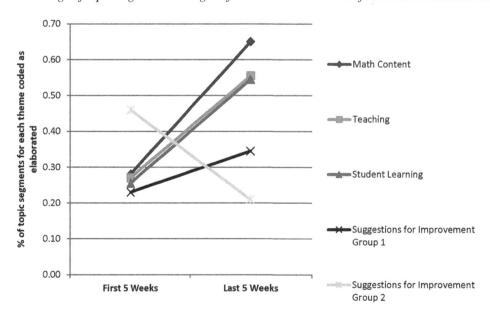

course and in 86% topic segments during the second part of the course. Table 2 reports the percentages of topic segments in which standards-based math teaching was discussed that were coded as challenging or embracing during the first and second part of the course. Percentages show a clear reverse pattern. Over time, participants developed a more positive disposition towards standards-aligned teaching.

DISCUSSION AND SIGNIFICANCE

Findings support the structuring of pre-service teachers' analyses in groups. Participants' conversations focused on the elements of teaching targeted by the analysis framework introduced in the course and the quality of their conversations improved over time by becoming more elaborated. Although this was one of the multiple settings in which PSTs might have learned to analyze teaching (whole-class discussions and conversations with their mentor teachers might have been others settings that have contributed to their learning), the findings suggest that peer discussions indeed contributed to the development of the learning outcomes that we have documented in prior publications. We thus conclude that peer discussions guided by structured questions can be productive settings in which PSTs learn to analyze teaching.

Although an important focus of the course was attention to student thinking and learning, this theme was the least frequently discussed by the PSTs. Perhaps this indicates that at this stage of their careers, pre-service teachers' attention is naturally still more focused on the teacher's actions. Or perhaps, the prompts that were used in the course to guide pre-service teachers' analyses and the instructor's feedback need to be reviewed to elicit more student-focused discussions. This is supported by previous research that has found that prior to professional development teacher-focused observations are very common and only structured and repeated experiences that provide opportunities to dissect student thinking slowly move teachers to student-centered observations (Stockero, 2008; van Es & Sherin, 2008). On the other hand, both their comments on teaching strategies and on student thinking and learning became more sophisticated over the duration of the course, indicating that the video-enhanced discussions facilitated their learning process. To note is that the sophistication of their comments improved the most for the math content theme, indicating that participants were able to connect the mathematics they were learning in the methods course to the content of the course studied here.

While the two groups behaved similarly for most aspects we investigated, the second group's suggestions for improvement were of better quality during the first than the last part of the course. Further transcript analyses are necessary to better understand how the group dynamics influenced this process.

The most surprising finding was the extent to which participants spontaneously and explicitly discussed the strengths and challenges of standards-based math teaching, co-constructing through their group conversations images of mathematics teaching practices still unfamiliar to them. This provides

Table 2. Average percentage of topics segments in which standards-based math teaching was discussed that were coded as challenging versus embracing

	Challenging Reform-Based Math Teaching	Embracing Reform-Based Math Teaching
First 5 Weeks	66%	34%
Last 5 Weeks	24%	76%

evidence of the importance of pre-service teachers' existing views about mathematics teaching and learning most likely formed during their past schooling experiences and sometimes reinforced in their fieldwork placements. These views serve as lenses through which they initially interpret the content and experiences of the courses they attend. Others have discussed teacher beliefs as influencing ways teachers' perceive the experiences provided to them and as driving their decision making processes (Philipp, 2007). It seems fundamental to provide video images of standards-based practices and a safe space for pre-service teachers to make sense of them through confrontations with peers and instructors. It is through these conversations that their views are challenged and valorized and new understandings are formed. This finding highlights the role that peer interactions may have in socializing future teachers into the profession and in developing a sense of belonging in a community of practice that shares particular views about teaching and learning.

This study provides some light on PST's development and progression in the acquisition of dispositions, knowledge and practices for analyzing mathematics teaching in response to video-based activities. An important aspect of PSTs' learning that was left out from this investigation relates to the guidance and feedback that the instructor gave after each video-based activity. Our future analyses will focus on the instructor's facilitation moves to identify their role in moving participants' learning process forward and possible places where this could be improved.

CONCLUSION

This study documented pre-service teachers' group conversations around videos of mathematics teaching. In addition to the findings reported above, this research highlighted four important dimensions of working with video in teacher collaborative settings that teacher educators might want to consider as they design similar learning experiences.

First, a clear vision of the role of video needs to be made explicit. Because video is only a representation of practice, it can be used for different purposes. Video is a tool that can facilitate different goals for teacher learning. In this project, it was used to bring into the teacher preparation program concrete and shared images of teaching that could be discussed and problematized. Video thus served as a text that needs to be unpacked.

Second, because video of teaching tends to be perceptually complex and many lenses can be adopted as teachers' review images, it is important to adopt frameworks that guide teacher viewing. These can be structured as a series of activities teachers are asked to engage in as they interact with video. In this project, the viewing framework included a series of questions for pre-service teachers to consider. A key research question for the project was to document participants' conversations to see whether the questions elicited the desired type and level of analysis.

Third, when working in collaborative settings, frameworks provide a structure for teacher viewing, but the group dynamics may also shape the work teachers do around video and their learning outcomes. This project provided evidence that pre-service group conversations can be productive. Pre-service teachers' analyses of teaching in fact increased in sophistication over time. Since on average teachers' individual ability to analyze teaching as documented in prior studies improved from the beginning to the end of the course, we can hypothesize that peer conversations were one of the contributing factors to this improvement.

Finally, unless teacher learning is structured within a distal learning environment that is guided by artifacts only, the teacher educator plays a fundamental role in shaping the video-enhanced teacher learning experience (van Es, Tunney, Goldsmith, & Seago, 2014). This is not an aspect to which this project has so far attended, but it is certainly a direction for future research.

REFERENCES

Brophy, J. (2004). *Using video in teacher education*. New York, NY: Elsevier.

Cochran-Smith, M., & Zeichner, K. M. (Eds.). (2010). *Studying teacher education: The report of the AERA panel on research and teacher education*. New York, NY: Routledge.

Davis, E. (2006). Characterizing productive reflection among preservice elementary teachers: Seeing what matters. *Teaching and Teacher Education*, *22*(3), 281–301. doi:10.1016/j.tate.2005.11.005

Ghousseini, H., & Sleep, L. (2011). Making practice studyable. *ZDM Mathematics Education*, *43*(1), 147–160. doi:10.1007/s11858-010-0280-7

Hatch, T., & Grossman, P. (2009). Learning to look beyond the boundaries of representation. *Journal of Teacher Education*, *60*(1), 70–85. doi:10.1177/0022487108328533

Jacobs, J., & Morita, E. (2002). Japanese and American teachers' evaluations of videotaped mathematics lessons. *Journal for Research in Mathematics Education*, *33*(3), 154–175. doi:10.2307/749723

Lave, J., & Wenger, E. (1991). *Situated learning: Legitimate peripheral participation*. Cambridge, UK: Cambridge University Press. doi:10.1017/CBO9780511815355

Lee (2005). Understanding and assessing preservice teachers' reflective thinking. *Teaching and Teacher Education, 21*, 699-715.

LeFevre, D. M. (2004). Designing for teacher learning: Video-based curriculum design. In J. Brophy (Ed.), *Using video in teacher education* (pp. 235–258). New York, NY: Elsevier.

McDuffie, A. R., Foote, M. Q., Bolson, C., Turner, E. E., Aguirre, J. M., Bartell, T. G., & Land, T. et al. (2014). Using video analysis to support prospective K-8 teachers' noticing of students' multiple mathematical knowledge bases. *Journal of Mathematics Teacher Education*, *17*(3), 245–270. doi:10.1007/s10857-013-9257-0

National Governors Association Center for Best Practices, Council of Chief State School Officers. (2010). *Common Core State Standards (Mathematics)*. Washington, DC: National Governors Association Center for Best Practices.

Park, J. (2008). Preparing secondary mathematics teachers in urban schools: Using video to develop understanding of equity-based discourse and classroom norms. University of California, Los Angeles.

Philipp, R. A. (2007). Mathematics teachers' beliefs and affect. In F. K. Lester (Ed.), Second handbook of research on mathematics teaching and learning (pp. 257-315). National Council of Teachers of Mathematics. Charlotte, NC: Information Age Publishing.

Santagata, R., & Angelici, G. (2010). Studying the impact of the *Lesson Analysis Framework* on pre-service teachers' ability to reflect on videos of classroom teaching. *Journal of Teacher Education*, *61*(4), 339–349. doi:10.1177/0022487110369555

Santagata, R., & Guarino, J. (2011). Using video to teach future teachers to learn from teaching. *ZDM. The International Journal of Mathematics Education*, *43*(1), 133–145.

Santagata, R., & Yeh, C. (2014). Learning to teach mathematics and to analyze teaching effectiveness: Evidence from a video-and practice-based approach. *Journal of Mathematics Teacher Education*, *17*(6), 491–514. doi:10.1007/s10857-013-9263-2

Santagata, R., Zannoni, C., & Stigler, J. W. (2007). The role of lesson analysis in pre-service teacher education: An empirical investigation of teacher learning from a virtual video-based field experience. *Journal of Mathematics Teacher Education*, *10*(2), 123–140. doi:10.1007/s10857-007-9029-9

Sherin, M. G. (2004). New perspectives on the role of video in teacher education. In J. Brophy (Eds.), Using video in teacher education (pp. 1-27). New York: Emerald.

Star, J. R., & Strickland, S. K. (2008). Learning to observe: Using video to improve preservice mathematics teachers' ability to notice. *Journal of Mathematics Teacher Education*, *11*(2), 107–125. doi:10.1007/s10857-007-9063-7

Stockero, S. L. (2008). Using a video-based curriculum to develop a reflective stance in prospective mathematics teachers. *Journal of Mathematics Teacher Education*, *11*(5), 373–394. doi:10.1007/s10857-008-9079-7

Strauss, A., & Corbin, J. (1998). *Basics of qualitative research. Techniques and procedures for developing grounded theory*. Thousand Oaks, CA: Sage Publications.

van Es, E. A., & Sherin, M. G. (2002). Learning to notice: Scaffolding new teachers' interpretations of classroom interactions. *Journal of Technology and Teacher Education*, *10*(4), 571–596.

van Es, E. A., & Sherin, M. G. (2008). Mathematics teachers' "learning to notice" in the context of a video club. *Teaching and Teacher Education*, *24*(2), 244–276. doi:10.1016/j.tate.2006.11.005

van Es, E. A., Tunney, J., Goldsmith, L., & Seago, N. (2014). A framework for the facilitation of teachers' analysis of video. *Journal of Teacher Education*, *64*(4), 340–356. doi:10.1177/0022487114534266

Wenger, E. (1998). *Communities of Practice: Learning, Meaning, and Identity*. Cambridge, UK: Cambridge University Press. doi:10.1017/CBO9780511803932

Yeh, C., & Santagata, R. (2015). Pre-Service Teachers' Learning to Generate Evidence-Based Hypotheses about the Impact of Mathematics Teaching on Learning. *Journal of Teacher Education*, *66*(1), 21–34. doi:10.1177/0022487114549470

KEY TERMS AND DEFINITIONS

Coding: A data analysis process through which similar types of things are grouped together into categories.

Facilitator: A person that guides a group of learners through a series of collaborative activities and discussions.

Framework: A basic structure underlying a process, a concept, or a theory.

Pre-Service Teachers: Students in a teacher preparation program that are studying to become teachers.

Professional Growth: The development of a person's knowledge and skills for carrying out a specific profession.

Standards-Based Instruction: Classroom teaching that adheres to pre-defined curriculum standards.

Topic Segments: Segments of talk defined by a particular topic of discussion.

Chapter 7
The Use of Videos in the Training of Math Teachers:
Formative Assessment in Math Teaching and Learning

Giorgio Bolondi
*Alma Mater Studiorum Università di Bologna,
Italy*

Alessandro Gimigliano
*Alma Mater Studiorum Università di Bologna,
Italy*

Federica Ferretti
*Alma Mater Studiorum Università di Bologna,
Italy*

Stefania Lovece
*Alma Mater Studiorum Università di Bologna,
Italy*

Ira Vannini
Alma Mater Studiorum Università di Bologna, Italy

ABSTRACT

The purpose of this chapter is to present a systematic observational research on the math teachers' assessment practices in the classroom. This research is a specific phase of an international project (FAMT&L - Comenius Multilateral Project) and it is aimed to promote the use of formative assessment in teaching mathematics to students aged from 11 to 16. The observational study is carried out by a plan of systematic observations of teachers' behaviour in the classroom with the help of video recording. Thanks to a specific tool of video analysis (a structured grid), developed using indications from international literature and experiences of teacher training in the five Partner countries involved (Italy, France, Holland, Switzerland and Cyprus), we managed to gather many different indicators on good and bad practices for the formative assessment of mathematics teachers. Furthermore, the analysed video will be used in in-service teacher training courses in order to promote a correct use of formative assessment and to improve achievements in learning mathematics.

DOI: 10.4018/978-1-5225-0711-6.ch007

Copyright © 2017, IGI Global. Copying or distributing in print or electronic forms without written permission of IGI Global is prohibited.

FRAMEWORK ON FORMATIVE ASSESSMENT IN MATHEMATICS TEACHING AND LEARNING[1]

Assessment in classroom has always been a key tool in order to promote, or to hinder, democratic values at school. An education system that does promote quality and equity for the learning achievements of its students, uses assessment as a key element to qualify the action of teaching in a democratic way, both at the beginning and during the process of teaching-learning; moreover it will consider the differences among the students and their possible learning difficulties as opportunities to make the teaching actions flexible in order to reach goals of quality for all (Vertecchi, 1976; Grandi, 1977; Weeden, Winter, & Broadfoot, 2002).

As we can read in Crahay and Issaieva (2013), it has to be a kind of assessment which adheres to a principle of equality of achievements (Bloom, 1968; Black & Wiliam, 1998; Guskey, 2005), hence to an idea of "fairness" in teaching, by offering more to whom possesses less.

This need of fairness in achieving the competences for citizenship (OECD, 2012; 2015; Eurydice, 2012) is more evident in every education system when considering basic competences and at high and junior high school level, before the completion of the compulsory cycle of studies. In particular, relevant problems appear in the field of math teaching, with important gaps in the conduct of the specific teaching-learning processes.

ASSESSING MATHS LEARNING: A DIDACTIC AND A SOCIAL PROBLEM

In Italian school practice, the assessment of Mathematical learning has been and in fact is yet traditionally oriented to a summative function, performed by means of written open tests (only recently the use of multiple choice tests is increasing) and oral-at-the-blackboard interrogations. Hence, is focuses primarily on students' *products* (results of calculations, presentations of proofs, …). On the other hand, formative assessment, as it will be detailed below, requires being careful mainly of students' *processes*. In this sense, we may say that in Italy math teachers have no formative assessment tradition, and in fact there is no systematic presence of it in pre-service training, and it is sporadic also in in-service training.

It must be noted that assessment, in math, has a crucial role in determining students' beliefs and attitudes, which in turn influence students' achievements (Di Martino & Zan, 2002; Bolondi & Ferretti, 2015). Therefore recovering a formative dimension for assessment is a strategic goal for maths teacher and it may became a fundamental tool for switching all the didactic focus from the contents (the mathematical objects) to the actors (the students).

Maths activity in the classroom involves many components: discourses, technologies, visual representations; it is performed through explorations, work on specific tasks, explanations. Formative assessment takes place in this complexity of actions. Then it is important to train teachers to observe significant elements of this complexity, and for this purpose video analysis is a natural tool.

As examples of situations that are worthwhile to analyse, we may list:

- Administration of a written task, with discussion about it (the content, the form);
- Administration of a written task, with explanation of the objectives of the activity;
- Administration of a written task with the explicitness of the evaluation criteria;
- Individual interview with the use of tools of observation and interaction;

- Self-assessment, written or oral;
- Classroom time devoted to peer assessment with shared criteria (for instance, Group A evaluates and discusses the tasks of a student of Group B, better with no crossing);
- Classroom discussion about the feedback of written test of formative assessment;
- Interaction among the class, the teacher and the student interviewed during an individual interview;
- Discussion groups in the class about a problem;
- Discussion in a group on the feedback of a task performed by the group;
- Discussion at the end of a task;
- Students' or group's reports of a performed task to the class;
- Return of a corrected task, with explanation of strengths and weakness points of the student.

Formative Assessment: A Support to Promote the Processes of Teaching-Learning

Since its origins (Scriven, 1967; Vertecchi, 1976), the main function attributed to formative assessment (FA) has been to use it as a regulator tool for teaching and learning.

Referring to the current international scientific debate on this issue, we can say that formative assessment is characterized specifically as an assessment *for* learning (Weeden, Winter, & Broadfoot, 2002; Allal & Laveault, 2009). This means that it has to be an assessment which is functional to backing up and promoting learning; it is embedded in the teaching-learning process in a dynamic way, modifying the teaching actions by following the needs of the students. The aim will never be just to attribute marks, or to make a résumé on the abilities of a student; formative assessment helps a teacher to gather information, to improve and make her/his teaching more effective.

Thus, when a teacher uses formative assessment, s/he is implementing two fundamental actions (Vertecchi, 1976):

- A diagnostic analysis of the achievements (knowledge, abilities) that the student is acquiring and which meta-cognitive strategies the student is following;
- Reconstructing the teaching routes by following the student's needs and differentiating times and methods of the didactic process.

Thanks to this diagnostic function, formative assessment analyses the learning situations and can give information in order to take coherent and effective decisions. It focuses on the "errors" of the student and of the teacher, by considering them as resources for designing and re-designing interventions in view of the teaching goals.

This kind of assessment which has to be implemented *continuously* during the teaching process requires a high level of professionalization of the teacher. Such as a coach in the training of an athlete or a team (Bennet, 2010; 2015) who proposes activities and tasks to the trainees (as a trial for their abilities), detects and immediately corrects their errors (by discussing with the trainees about them), understands the specific needs and gives formative feedback.

As every assessment procedure (Gattullo, 1967), also FA is characterized by three steps (Gitomer & Zisk, 2015, p.3):

- An initial step of cognitive representation of which data we want to collect ("what we are trying to measure");
- A step of specific gathering of data, by empiric observation ("how we collect evidence");
- The interpretation of the data ("how we make sense of the evidence").

Collecting evidence is an unavoidable phase (Ruiz-Primo & Furtak, 2004), inasmuch as it characterizes FA as a specifically evaluative action, either if it is formally or informally done (informally as in the course of a teacher's day-to-day activities) (Bell & Cowie, 2001; Duschl, 2003; Shavelson et al., 2002). Without a willing gathering of evidence we would not be doing FA, but just a teaching activity.

The next step, data interpretation, is equally important. Doing summative assessment this step would end in the attribution of marks or of a judgment, doing FA any judgment is suspended. It is formative feedback that must take place in this moment, instead: the teacher's answer to the needs/requirements of the student. Researches show that feedback – together with FA – is the crucial element, which contributes, in a statistically significant way, to improve the results in the students' learning (Hattie & Timperley, 2007; Hattie, 2009; 2012; Huelser & Metcalfe, 2012).

For this reason, the teacher's practices in class are particularly important, both in the moment when data about the students' achievements are gathered and analysed, and when interpreting the data, elaborating hypotheses about the kind of mistakes the students do and implementing feedback actions to help them in the critical steps in their apprehension. All this is really fundamental in the teaching of mathematics.

The feedback activity is a complex set of actions by the teacher, not easily described by a set of rules or given operations; for this reason, research in this field are particularly relevant and stringent: it is necessary, in fact, to clear up, in detail, which are the most effective conducts that the teacher has to implement in classes activities when facing a "stumbling" student.

Via the feedback, the teacher should manage to make the student's errors explicit, and make them valuable as an asset in the learning process; in the meanwhile, the teacher has to sustain the students' motivation to learn and to mobilize all their meta-cognitive strategies in order to overcome the obstacles. Here the didactic mediation is substantial; the teacher must use several and differentiated didactic tools, give additional explanations, sustain the students' aloud reasoning (Weeden, Winter, Broadfoot, 2002; Bennet, 2010; Doabler et al., 2014).

Several researches about teachers' behaviour highlight that they agree about the fundamental role of FA for the quality of teaching, nevertheless – in their practice – they follow more often summative assessment praxis. Also, in spite of the fact that they use FA in their ongoing activities, they may use superficial tests, propose mechanical answers, or give a feedback that is too generic (Looney, 2011, p.10). In fact, they seem not to be prepared to interpret the evidence they have about their students' learning and often they attribute to external reasons the impossibility to implement FA (too many students in their classes, too large curricula to teach, organizational difficulties in their schools) (OECD, 2005).

The Importance of the Classroom Observation of Teachers' FA Practices to Improve Their Professionalism

The experience in the schools shows that FA is not a natural habit for the teachers and there is a need to improve the teachers' practices of FA.

In order to achieve this, it is essential to acquire a deep knowledge of what happens in class during assessment activities, so to pinpoint "good" and "bad" practices and to plan effective paths for teachers training and staff development.

To better understand the object of the detecting phase of the research, it can be useful make explicit what we mean with "good and bad practices" in FA.

We consider a "good" practice of formative assessment a practice which actually gives a feed-forward to the teacher and the students, providing an improvement of the teaching-learning processes in progress. For instance, in line with our theoretical framework, it is a good practice if the teacher, while presenting a task that will be formally evaluated, shares the criteria of assessments with the students. Moreover, we consider a "good" practice if, during the administration of a task, the teacher gives enough time so that every student can work on the test/task and monitors the good use of time and if, during the assessment, the teacher records facts and observations related to students' behaviour.

In our framework it is stressed the importance of peer and self-assessment as formative forms of assessment; so, for example, we consider a good practice when the teacher interacts with the peer and self-assessment process of the students.

Therefore, on the other hand, for us, these are examples of what we consider practices not suitable for a really formative assessment: teachers that don't share the aim and the object of the assessment, that don't keep care if the students actually understand the tasks and don't accept students' observations, that bound their feedback only to numerical marks.

Furthermore, teachers should assure a relaxing relation mood in classroom and don't generate anxiety and any situations of competition among student.

At last, we assume that the formative assessment must generate feedback on the teaching and learning processes, so it is important that teachers use also the summative results in order to create an occasion of formative assessment: in this way, for example, the use of errors found in summative assessments can become a tool for a "good" practice of formative assessment.

Thus the FAMT&L project is aimed to analyse specifically the assessment behaviour of the teachers and this is why having videos of the activity in class and analysing them is a very important tool.

The systematic observation of the behaviour of teachers in their classes dates back to work of Skinner and Bandura about teaching models and programmed instruction; it is from here that also the use of videos starts, above all with the strategy of *microteaching*, tuned up in 1963 by two researcher – K. Romney e D. Allen – at Stanford University (Allen, 1967).

Up to these days, many researches show that *microteaching* (Calvani et al., 2011) is quite effective and, more in general, so it is the observation of the teacher in class, with video analysis (of their own and other colleagues' practices) in order to promote teachers' changing of behaviours and to increase their professionalization (Rossi et al. 2015), and this also in the specific case of the teaching of mathematics (Casabianca et al., 2013; Walkowiak et al., 2014;). In particular, these strategies realize a tight link between theory and praxis, yield to a "view from outside" of the teacher with respect to themselves and to reconsidering what they did through a "reply" of their activity, via the recorded video sequences (Altet, Charlier, Paquay, & Perrenoud, 2006). All this:

- Allows a deeper reflection by the teachers on their own pratices and is a better answer to their needs of formation (Meyer, 2012; Ertmer, Conklin, & Lewandowski, 2002; Mottet, 1997);
- Guides any teacher to identify improvement strategies (much more than what the mere analysis of their students' results could do) (Kane et al. 2011).

This perspective is adopted by the researchers in the US (and Anglo-Saxon countries in general) (Guernsey & Ochshorn, 2011), and in particular by the major American professional associations (see the *New Teacher Project*; the *New America Foundation*, the *TeachStone*), but also by the research in Francophone countries about assessment and self-assessment of teachers (cf.. Laveault & Pasquay 2009; Paquay et al. 2010).

Thus also in the complex area of studies on FA, video-analysis strategies could give a valid contribute to act efficiently for the renovation in class assessment practices.

Research carried out by Kane et al. (2011) has attempted to explore the connections between the teaching practices of teachers and the student performances. It is precisely from these studies that the need for specific observational procedures emerges, in order to focus on the actions of the teachers in classroom, in particular on assessment practices. This is important both in the early phase of collecting information on students' learning, and in the specific phase in which the teacher is engaged in *formative feedback* to the student.

Observation in classroom aims to detect the assessment strategies used by the teachers during the teaching-learning process:

- How the teacher conveys tasks and criteria for the assessment to the students;
- How the teacher presents and hands out the assessment tests;
- How the teacher gathers information in class about students' learning;
- How the teacher corrects the valuation tests and the relative mistakes;
- How the teacher conveys a formative feedback to the students.

Via such observations it is possible to ponder about which are the good practices and which are not in FA; the analysis and the reflection with the teachers will help to achieve effective actions in teacher training.

Therefore, the training for teacher's in-service that was designed for the project FAMT&L uses the procedures of observation in the classroom as a tool to support the teacher professionalism, by sustaining the teachers in specific situations, in order to design and to improve their FA practices.

The FAMT&L Project and Its Phases

The project of research, which this chapter refers to, is the LLP Comenius Project "FAMT&L - Formative Assessment in Mathematics for Teaching and Learning" and it has as its main object the use of formative assessment in the process of teaching-learning and the role it assumes in particular didactic practices of mathematics teachers at the middle level of school (students aged from 11 to 16).

The five member partners involved in the project are the Alma Mater Studiorum University of Bologna in Italy, the University of Applied Sciences and Arts of Southern Switzerland, the University of Cergy-Pontoise in France, the University of Cyprus, and the Netherlands' Hogeschool Inholland.

Research is based on a descriptive design, with the use of observational studies and surveys in order to understand analytically math teachers' beliefs and practices and to detect training needs that require courses aimed at promoting a correct use of methodologies and tools to conduct correct formative assessment activities.

The phases of the work designed to achieve the objectives, consisted in:

- Survey on the beliefs and practices of students and teachers of mathematics about the evaluation of learning in the classroom;
- The design and the implementation of a web repository for teacher training, to support the adoption of a proper use of formative assessment in situations of teaching and learning of mathematics;
- The development of a training model for mathematics teachers;
- The subsequent testing and validation of the same.

Thus, the analysis started with the administration of questionnaires to teachers and students of each Partner's Country to gather information about beliefs and practices on assessment.

Furthermore, during the first phase (exploratory study), we conducted some case studies, with the help of video recording, to develop and try out an observational tool (a structured grid) to analyse assessment practices in the classroom.

At present, in the second phase, we are carrying out a systematic observation study on a larger sample of video sequences of teachers in the five Partner countries involved (Italy, Switzerland, France, and Holland).

A specific tool (a structured grid described in the next paragraph) has been defined for such analysis; by using indications from international literature and experiences of in-service training, we managed to gather many different indicators on good and bad practices for the formative assessment of mathematics teachers.

Via video-analysis, and the use of the observation grid, research pinpoints the habits of teachers about gathering information on the students' learning process, about correcting errors and using feedback to support learning.

With the videos collected about formative assessment situations, researcher will create a web-repository and design a teacher training program based on the use of such repository.

The project of the pilot training model started with the analysis of the results of a qualitative investigation about the beliefs and practices of mathematics teachers (in particular about the assessment in classroom), compared with the beliefs of their students.

In this work we will focus on the process of gathering and analysis of videos made in class, and then on the creation of a repository which will has to be able to include those and other didactic material to be used in training courses which will aim to promote FA in the practices of in service math teachers.

The videos collected for the web repository consist in recordings of real class situations, when mathematics teachers of the associated schools were performing assessment practices.

Examples of "interesting" situations that were considered are: the submission of a proof to students, the conduction of a written, oral or practical task, the correction of an assigned task (in group, individual or in pairs), the reflection on the mistakes that were made in a test; the teacher's formative feedback during the work on an individual exercise, etc.

From these "long" recordings a number of short video-sequences were obtained. The short sequences will be the main training tool for the platform implemented for the training pilot course and will be analysed through systematic observations, so as to detect the presence or absence of indicators of behaviour which we defined in detail.

The tool that was built for the analysis of the video-sequences constitute a coding scheme that allows a meta-dating of each sequence, and a more specific micro-analysis, which can be used for individual or group interpretations with trainee teachers.

In the next sections we will consider the operations of observing and analysing the videos we gathered by using a tool that was specifically created and tuned for this aim. This analysis allows archiving and metadata analysing of the micro-sequences and also led to a system of annotating the videos facilitating their storing in a web repository. These systematic processes should give an easy way to find specific materials in the repository, and also to integrate them into "pilot" training courses which should be a guide to promote a correct use of FA as a tool to improve the teaching of math.

In fact, this was the idea that guided the recording-analysis of the videos: to be able to use the analysed video-sequences as part of training courses for in service teachers. Such courses are aimed to the acquisition of specific skills in the use of formative assessment as an element that improves the quality of teaching.

In line with what emerges from the debate on teacher training, we can notice that the observation by the teachers of their own practices would allow them to change their behaviour by themselves and encourage processes of reconsideration on assessment and teaching.

A TOOL FOR OBSERVATION OF TEACHERS' ASSESSMENT PRACTICES AND VIDEO ANALYSIS

The correlation between the research on teachers' beliefs and the first phase of the observational research allowed to understand what kind of misconceptions the teachers have about formative assessment in the classroom.

What is shown is a common penchant towards the use of traditional practices of summative assessment and a difficulty in perceiving formative assessment as an useful tool to improve teaching and learning.

The difficulties in conceiving the efficacy of formative assessment have also been found while watching the video analysis of the first cases in consideration.

Many of the natural situations of mathematics teaching in the classroom, analysed through videos, point out an use of assessment with the following characteristics:

- It is specifically aimed at summative assessment, in order to give marks;
- It is not rigorous. The cases observed in natural environment show gaps in the "measuring" learning and an incorrect use of feedback to the student (labelling);
- It is poor at recording analytically the learning difficulties of each student.

The first results highlighted by the systematic observation of the videos allow us to understand the features of "bad" and "good" practices for formative assessment and to design specific interventions for teachers training.

Clearly, in order to get valuable information for our research, we had to build a tool for observation and analysis which could also be used to analyse the videos taped in class and for the archiving and categorizing of video sequences that can actually be used in future training courses.

Every video we got gets equipped with metadata which allow its categorizing and a sequent descriptive analysis (caring for correlations) that will help us define the profiles of assessment practices in the classroom.

Thus the grid we used has been structured with many levels. At the first level we find the data apt to "identify" the video files, so to allow a first archiving: Video's identification code; Country; Language;

Type: audio/video (length, format); Creation date; Author; School level target; Number of pupils in classroom, Presence of students with particular educational needs.

At the next level we use categories which allow to get deeper in a qualitative analysis as much as we consider many variables which get into play in such a specific and complex process as assessment is.

From an environmental perspective (Bronfenbrenner, 1979), this observation grid allows us to gather different indicators on assessment practices of mathematics teachers, grouped in five macro-categories:

1. Mathematics' contents (contents and capabilities which are the object of the teaching)
2. Time of assessment (before, during or after a specific learning activity)
3. Setting of assessment (with all the students in the classroom, with groups of students or with each individual student)
4. Kind of tools for data gathering of students' skills (written tests, oral exams, behavioural observation, etc.)
5. Phases of formative assessment (presentation of the assessment activity; gathering of information; correcting errors; feedback). (presentation of the assessment activity; gathering of information; correcting errors; feedback)

In the first category we consider information on the mathematics contents which are the teaching subject for each lesson/situation. With a view on the complexity of the teaching-learning process, clearly activities in this category cannot just be considered as contents in mathematical knowledge (*maths objects*), but we had to widen our horizon in order to take into account the abilities and skills that the students put into play in the learning *process*. Thus, we adopted a two-dimensional frame contents/capabilities, a scheme based on the OECD-Pisa approach (OECD-Pisa, 2013). For contents: Numbers; Spaces and shape; Uncertainty and data; Relations and functions. For capabilities: Communication; Mathematizing; Representation; Reasoning and Argumentation; Devising strategies for problem solving; Using symbolic, Formal and technical language and operations; Using mathematical tools.

The second category (time) is useful in order to allocate where the (formative) assessment activity takes place in the longer time of the whole lesson. The setting (third) category considers the context of the formative assessment. This is needed since both categories, time and space/context (where we consider also the predisposition of the class group), are variables which can condition the didactic process and, if pedagogically planned and sufficiently suited to the specific learning situation, can have a very positive role in facilitating the apprehension.

The tools that the teachers use in their assessment activity are very important too (the fourth category is dedicated to them); in fact, in order to guarantee a correct and rigorous valuation, the teachers must use tools that are suitable and functional to gather data on what the students have learned.

The last category is perhaps the most interesting and the most characterizing for our tool/grid because it gathers several kinds of behaviours and actions which will be considered as indicators to be observed in the different phases of the assessment procedure.

This grid has been revised in time and it is still subject to "additions", above all additions to the list of observable indicators. In fact, the researchers were able to complete and validate it via the systematic use of it in video-analysis, hence in observing specific actions and behaviours of teachers and students in class, during processes of assessment.

This tool has been proved to be very useful and also well implemented. It has been integrated in the online repository which contains short analysed extracts from the videos, so it makes easy the analysis itself and the metadata to insert in the videos, which can be found using single "words" of the grid as research and gathering criteria.

The repository (which will be better described in the next section) can at this time be accessed only by the researchers working with our project, because they are working to analyse videos and upload them on the present platform. As soon as the number of videos and other material will be adequate in order to be a valuable support for formative activities dedicated to teachers of several countries, the repository will become public.

Videos for Teacher Training on Assessment: Web Repository and E-Learning Platform

The grid described above has been set up specifically for micro-sequences (short videos) so to have a valuable tool for observation and analysis. To identify the observable indicators is a complex activity which has engaged all the partners in several attempts and working hypotheses and which produced a list of descriptions of situations which cannot be exhaustive since it is not possible to foresee all the meaningful possible situations that can happen in class. Hence there are blanks of the grid which have been left "open" for future comments and notes.

The University of Cergy-Pontoise (Paris) has been working video-analysis for years, hence their specific expertise and their hardware and software tools have been a very valuable support for our work. With their indications as a starting point, we carried out a research and a study of the most well-known software systems (both free and not) that are available for the analysis of human behaviour with the help of video recording (for example The Observer XT by Noldus Information Technology, or iCoda, only for Apple computers, and the free software Transana and Anvil).

Within the limits of our money resources and with the specific needs of our project, we realized a specific system for FAMT&L, which took its inspiration from the several software we have examined. Such system is a real repository which allows, on one hand, to gather the videos which have been endowed of metadata and analysed into a sort of on line catalogue which allows to easily search and find the archived material using different criteria of searching. This way of organizing with metadata appears to be very functional also to gather quantitative data for statistics elaborations, to a macro-level, since it allows to find the total number of videos containing a particular value of some indicator.

On the other hand, this on line system permits also to get an easier visualization of the video sequences, of the categories used to label them and of the behaviour indicators that can be observed in the video itself.

The videos which have been gathered and analysed using this grid are systematically archived in the repository which has been designed for the web and implemented in order to be inserted in training programs specifically directed to in-service Math teachers (but it can also be used in pre-service training situations). We considered school grades corresponding to ages 10-16.

In order to allow the systematic use of the videos and of the other materials in pilot courses for the training of in-service teachers from the several countries in the project, we realized also a platform (Espace) which will permit to supply formative routes both on line and in person. At the beginning, such pilot courses will be tested in every country with in-service teachers and they will have a common model, to which the different materials (in different languages) will be adapted. Our perspective is though that those materials and courses could be adapted more specifically to different contexts and also be used in forming the future teachers.

In the learning environment (e-learning platform), different types of tools for teachers will be available: examples of learning contexts, video situations of mathematics teaching, assessment tools, training courses, etc.

All these educational materials can be used to promote a proper use of formative assessment in the teaching-learning situations; this platform will be the support for the training of mathematics teachers associated with the project.

The training program is based both on teaching general knowledge related to the field of didactic design and assessment practices, and on specific knowledge of mathematics education, with particular regard to formative and summative assessment, and assessment *for* learning. In fact, we think that it is the appropriate use of a correct FA methods and techniques is a key element to make the teaching of Mathematics more effective and innovative.

CONCLUSION: THE VIDEOS IN THE TEACHER TRAINING, BETWEEN THEORY AND PRACTICE

In the last years the teachers' professionalism is a subject of debate and international research (Perrenoud, 2002; Anderson, 2004; Darling-Hammond & Bransford, 2007; Koster & Dengerink, 2008; European Commission, 2002, 2003, 2005, 2012; OECD, 2005; UNESCO, 2005); and this research has been central in the matter of teacher training, as a strategic factor to improve the national educational systems (see Richardson & Placier, 2002; Darling-Hammond, 2006; Darling-Hammond et al., 2007; Coggi, 2014).

In particular, a good part of the scientific debate about teachers training activities seems to focus on a fundamental "crux" given by the relationship between theory and praxis, between knowledge and competences, i.e. by the research of how to form the teachers in such a way to get that the information they gain will really develop into new behaviours and competences that will enter into play in their everyday teaching practices.

In this line of thought, it is particularly relevant the concept of *recursivity* between theory and praxis, meaning an alternation between distinct (but at the same time interrelated) steps in a specific learning process (Atlet, 2003) which are able to translate theoretic knowledge and methodology into an *action* and also, at the same time, reflection on the action itself, a reflection that, in turn, becomes new knowledge, and so forth. There are several different contributes to this debate, based on interdisciplinary studies (in Pedagogy, Psychology, in Neuroscience) as the ones of Evidence Based Learning[2], which offered a quite structured setting of knowledge about the most effective teaching methods, or as the most specific investigations aimed to point out the crucial factors in teaching behaviours in order to valuate and promote their efficacy, see the Gates Foundation's study (2013) or the work by international projects such as PISA, TIMMS, PIRLS (Pearson, 2012).

Many of those studies seem to validate the idea that a fundamental step for the professionalization of teachers is the identification of the most suitable ways to *conceptualize* their explicit practices in teaching (Rossi, 2014) by means of recursive processes, integrated and interdependent among them (Seidel and Stürmer, 2014), as are observation, comprehension, anticipation or prediction (Rivoltella, 2014) of what happens and can happen after a specific action.

From here several indications stem about the most effective methodologies to promote the co-presence of theory and praxis in the teachers training (both in-service or pre-service). Such are the practices of laboratory activities and/or traineeship (Betti et al., 2014) and many techniques that can be based on the use of specific support tools, as, in particular, the videos.

Usually the training activities which are based on the use of videos are defined *"video education"*, an expression which covers an ample range of teaching experiences, starting with the first movies in the last century, to the use of television and analogue supports (VHS) and then to digital (CD/DVD) and telematic ones (PC and multimedia) to end up with the Internet and the so-called Web 2.0 (O'Reilly, 2005).

The presence of videos in training activities for teachers is more and more common, with several modalities in their use (Masats and Dooly, 2011):

- As both an object and a tool for observation and analysis, to show a subject to the teachers (we speak of *video-viewing*, in this case);
- As an example or display, when the video shows the practices and the behaviour of experienced teachers in specific situations (*video modelling*);
- As a record of the teachers themselves, which is shared with the others, making it an occasion of comparison and debate with collegues or with a trainer (*video coaching*).

These modalities open several implications. The videos' content can be quite different: a teacher records her/him-self, use recording of colleagues or other experts, focus on specific didactic practices or behaviours, attitudes, interactions. Moreover, the videos can be presented as an example of everyday teaching activity (Carbonneau & Hétu, 2006; Clarke et al., 2008), or as a "best practice" which rarely could be directly observed, or as a specific experience or experimentation (Santagata & Guarino, 2011). Also the length of the proposed videosequences can vary, from very short excerpts to longer and complex sequences.

Several studies, anyway, confirm the effectiveness of video-based interventions in the training of teachers: videos become a tool which is able to integrate and support, via the visual activity, the direct observation and the learning of good teaching practices of which, otherwise, there could only be a description, oral or written (Santagata, Zannoni, & Stigler, 2007).

In the last years the didactic technique of *microteaching* has gained much credit; actually it is a technique that dates back to the experiences in the '60-'70's by K. Romney and D. Allen at Stanford University. Allen himself defines (1975) microteaching as a method which consists mainly in having the trainee teacher to present to a small group of students a short time teaching session, concentrated on a specific subject. The short session is monitored from trainers which use videorecording as main tool. This will allow the supervisors of the microteaching session to show to the trainees, via the analysis of the teaching sequence, which abilities will help them to solve the problem in their teaching practice end the errors they can do in their activities. Such an analysis can promote and facilitate a reflexion on what is done in the class, which contributes to an improvement of the teaching practices. This attention to the reflexivity as an attitude of the teachers to analyse and think over about their own practices, is essential to get an educational success (Dewey, 1961), and is what allows us to speak of the teachers as *reflective practitioners* (Schön, 2006; Damiano, 2007), and of a professional knowledge of their own (Calvani, Bonaiuti, & Andreocci, 2011).

Thus it is impossible not to see how effective the use of videos can be in the teachers training, but it is also important that this use take place within a well structured educational path, characterized by:

- A clear and thought over choice of the learning objectives that one wants to achieve with the trainees teachers (Blomberg et al., 2013; Seidel et al., 2011; Rossi, 2015);
- The production or selection of the videos best suited to the defined objectives;
- A good support and guide to the vision, comprehension and analysis of the video;
- Elaborating suitable tools for evaluation, appropriate to the objectives (Calvani et al, 2014).

Following these ideas, the FAMT&L project is aimed now at the elaboration of a pilot model of a course for mathematics teachers that can be followed in part as a distance course and in part in person. Such a course should integrate and use the analysis of videos made in class with teachers involved in the project with different modalities, but all oriented to the achievement of specific formative targets.

As we have already said, the idea that guided the recording-analysis of the videos was to be able to use the analysed video-sequences as part of training courses for in service teachers that can acquire specific skills in the use of formative assessment as an element that improves the quality of teaching.

In line with the debate on teacher training, the observation of teaching practices by themselves would allow changes in their behaviour and encourage processes of reconsideration on assessment and teaching.

In fact, the pilot course that will be developed will seek to use the video sequences analysed in order to promote critical thinking of teachers in training.

The model of the course will be tested and its efficiency verified with mall group of mathematics teachers in the several partner countries, so that it can be proposed as a model to be adopted also in other activities, both for in-service or pre-service teachers.

In the repository will take place videos and other materials which could be used in several different activities:

- Activities of self-training, for expert teachers;
- More "formal" activities, where teachers are guided using analysed videoes to promote development of assessment skills;
- Activities in which the teachers may decide to be filmed to start a process of critical reflection on their teaching and evaluation methods so to be able to improve themselves.

Currently, the international research team is analysing the videos in the partner countries. The elements that are emerging are particularly interesting and underline the importance of observation in the classroom as a means for increasing the teacher professionalism.

REFERENCES

Allal, L., & Laveault, D. (2009). Assessment for learning. Evaluation-soutien d'apprentissage. *Mésure et Evaluation en Education, 32*(2), 99–104.

Allen, D. W. (1967). *Micro-teaching. A description*. San Francisco: Stanford University Press.

Altet, M., Charlier, E., Paquay, L., & Perrenoud, P. (Eds.), (2006). Formare gli insegnanti professionisti. Quali strategie? Quali competenze? Roma: Armando.

Anderson, L. W. (2004). *Increasing teacher effectiveness* (2nd ed.). Paris: UNESCO – IIEP.

Atelet, M. (2003), *La ricerca sulle pratiche di insegnamento*. Brescia: La scuola.

Bell, B., & Cowie, B. (2001). The characteristics of formative assessment in science education. *Science Education*, *85*(5), 536–553. doi:10.1002/sce.1022

Bennet, R.E. (2010). Cognitively based assessment of, for, an das learning. A preliminary theory of action for summative and formative assessment. *Measurement; Interdisciplinary Research and Perspectives*, 8, 70-91.

Bennet, R. E. (2015). The changing nature of educational assessment, *Review of Research in Education*. *AERA*, *39*, 370–407.

Betti, M., Ciani, A., Lovece, S., & Tartufoli, L. (2014). Developing planning and evaluation skills using laboratory's teaching. *Italian Journal of Educational Research,* *7*(13), 29-48. Retrieved from http://ojs.pensamultimedia.it/index.php/sird/article/view/1093

Black, P., & Wiliam, D. (1998). Assessment and classroom learning. *Assessment in Education: Principles, Policy & Practice*, *5*(1), 7–74. doi:10.1080/0969595980050102

Blomberg, G., Renkl, A., Gamoran Sherin, M., Borko, H., & Seidel T. (2013), Five research based heuristic for using video in pre-service teacher education. *Journal for educational research online, 5*(1), 90-114.

Bloom, B. S. (1968). Learning for mastery. *Evaluation Comment*, *1*(2), 1–12.

Bolondi, G., Ferretti, F. (2015), Pratiche didattiche, convinzioni e motivazioni degli studenti in matematica: uno studio di caso basato sul framework.

Calvani, A. (2012). *For evidence-based education. Theoretical analysis on international methodological effective teaching and inclusive*. Trento: Erickson.

Calvani, A., Bonaiuti, G., & Andreocci, B. (2011). Il microteaching rinascerà a nuova vita? Video annotazione e sviluppo della riflessività del docente. *Italian Journal of Educational Research*, *4*(6), 29–42.

Calvani, A., Menichetti, L., Michelett, S., & Moricca, C. (2014). Innovare la formazione: Il ruolo della videoeducazione per lo sviluppo dei nuovi educatori. *Italian. The Journal of Educational Research*, *7*(13), 69–84.

Carbonneau, M., & Hétu, J. C. (2006). Formazione pratica degli insegnanti e nascita di un'intelligenza professionale. In M. Altet, E. Charlier, L. Paquay, & P. Perrenoud (Eds.), Formare gli insegnanti professionisti. Quali strategie? Quali competenze? (pp. 77-95). Roma: Armando. .

Casabianca, J. M., McCaffrey, D. F., Gitomer, D. H., Bell, C. A., Hamre, B. K., & Pianta, R. C. (2013). Effect of observation mode on measures of secondary mathematics teaching. *Educational and Psychological Measurement*, *73*(5), 757–783. doi:10.1177/0013164413486987

Clarke, D. J., Mesiti, C., O'Keefe, C., Xu, L. H., Jablonka, E., Mok, I. A. C., & Shimizu, Y. (2008). Addressing the challenge of legitimate international comparisons of classroom practice. *International Journal of Educational Research*, *46*(5), 280–293. doi:10.1016/j.ijer.2007.10.009

Coggi, C. (2014). Verso un'Università delle Competenze. In A. M. Notti (Ed.), *A scuola di valutazione*. Lecce: Pensa Multimedia.

Crahay, M., & Issaieva, E. (2013). Conceptions de l'évaluation et principes de justice chez des enseignants primaires en Fédération Wallonie-Bruxelles. *Paper presented at ADMEE 2013 - Evaluation et autoévaluation. Quels espaces de formation?,* Fribourg. Retrieved from http://www.admee2013.ch/ADMEE-2013/7_files/Crahay-Issaieva-Marbaise-ADMEE-2013.pdf

Damiano, E. (Ed.). (2007). *Il mentore. Manuale di tirocinio per insegnanti in formazione.* Milano: Franco Angeli.

Darling-Hammond, L. (2006). Constructing 21st-Century Teacher Education. *Journal of Teacher Education, 57*(3), 300–314. doi:10.1177/0022487105285962

Darling-Hammond, L., & Bransford, J. (Eds.). (2007). *Preparing Teachers for a Changing World: What Teachers Should Learn and Be Able to Do.* New York: John Wiley & Sons.

Dewey, J. (1961). *Come pensiamo: una riformulazione del rapporto fra il pensiero riflessivo e l'educazione. (Trad. It. A. Guccione).* Firenze: LaNuova Italia.

Di Martino, P., & Zan, R. (2002, April 4-8). An attempt to describe a `negative' attitude toward mathematics. In P. Di Martino (Ed.), *Current State of Research on Mathematical Beliefs XI,Proceedings of the MAVI-XI European Workshop,* Pisa.

Doabler, C. T., Nelson, N. J., Kosty, D. B., Fien, H., Baker, S. K., Smolkowski, K., & Clarke, B. (2014). Examining teachers' use of Evidence-Based practices during core Mathematics instruction. *Assessment for Effective Intervention, 39*(2), 99–111. doi:10.1177/1534508413511848

Duschl, R. A. (2003). Assessment of inquiry. In J.M. Atkin, J.E. Coffey (Eds.). Everyday assessment in the science classroom (41-59). Washington, DC: National Science Teachers Association Press.

Ertmer, P. A., Conklin, D., & Lewandowski, J. (2002). *Using exemplary models to increase preservice teachers' ideas and confidence for technology integration. Proceedings of.* American Educational Research.

European Commission. Directorate-General for Education and Culture; Eurydice, information network on education in Europe (2002). *Key topics in education in Europe, Volume 3. The Teaching profession in Europe: profile, trends and concerns. Report II: Supply and demand. General lower secondary education.* Brussels: Eurydice.

European Commission, Directorate-General for Education and Culture. Eurydice, the information network on education in Europe (2003). The Teaching profession in Europe: profile, trends and concerns. Report III: Working conditions and pay. General lower secondary education. Brussels: Eurydice.

Eurydice (2012). *Developing key competences at school in Europe: Challenges and opportunities for Policy.* Brussels: Education, Audiovisual and Culture Executive Agency. Retrieved from http://www.indire.it/lucabas/lkmw_file/eurydice/key_competences_finale_EN.pdf

Gattullo, M. (1967). *Didattica e docimologia.* Roma: Armando.

Gitomer, D. H., & Zisk, R. C. (2015). Knowing what teachers know, *Review of Research in Education. AERA, 39,* 1–53.

Grandi, G. (1977). *Misurazione e valutazione.* Firenze: La Nuova Italia.

Guernsey, L., & Ochshorn, S. (2011). *Watching teachers works. Using observation tools to promote effective teaching in the early years and early grades. Education policy program.* New America Foundation.

Guskey, T. R. (2005, April 11-15). Formative classroom assessment and Benjamin S. Bloom: Theory, research and implications. *Paper presented at the Annual Meeting of the AERA (American Educational Research Association)*, Montreal, Canada. Retrieved from http://files.eric.ed.gov/fulltext/ED490412.pdf

Hattie, J. (2009). *Visible learning. A synthesis of over 800 meta-analysis relating to achievement.* London, New York: Routledge.

Hattie, J., & Tymperley, H. (2007). The power of feedback. *Review of Educational Research, 77*(1), 81–112. doi:10.3102/003465430298487

Huelser, B. J., & Metcalfe, J. (2012). Making related errors facilitates learning, but learners do not know it. *Memory & Cognition, 40*(4), 514–527. doi:10.3758/s13421-011-0167-z PMID:22161209

Kane, T., Taylor, E. S., Tyler, J. H., & Wooten, A. L. (2011). Identifying effective classroom practices using student achievement data. *The Journal of Human Resources, 46*(3), 587–613. doi:10.3368/jhr.46.3.587

Koster, B., & Dengerink, J. J. (2008). Professional standards for teacher educators: How to deal with complexity ownership and function experience from the Netherlands. *European Journal of Teacher Education, 31*(2), 135–149. doi:10.1080/02619760802000115

Laveault, D., & Paquay, L. (Eds.). (2009). L'évaluation en salle de classes: des politiques aux pratiques. Mesure et évaluation en éducation en éducation, 32 (3).

Looney, J. W. (2011). *Integrating formative and summative assessment: progress toward a seamless system?* OECD Education Working Paper 58. OECD Publishing.

Masats, D., & Dooly, M. (2011). Rethinking the use of video in teacher education: A holistic approach. *Teaching and Teacher Education, 27*(7), 1151–1162. doi:10.1016/j.tate.2011.04.004

Meyer, F. (2012). Les vidéos d'exemples de pratique pour susciter le changement. *Revue internationale de pédagogie de l'enseignement supérieur, 28*(2), 1-19.

Mottet, G. (1997). La vidéo, outil de constrction des compétences professionelles des einsegnants. In G.Mottet (Ed.). La vidéo-formation. Autres regards, autres pratiques (pp. 21-36). Paris: L'Harmanattan.

O'Reilly, T. (2005). *What is web 2.0? Design patterns and business models for the next generation of software.* Retrieved from http://www.oreilly.com/pub/a/web2/archive/what-is-web-20.html

OECD. (2005). OECD Annual report 2005. Retrieved from http://www.oecd.org/about/34711139.pdf

OECD. (2012). Education at a Glance 2012: OECD indicators. Retrieved from http://www.oecd.org/edu/EAG%202012_e-book_EN_200912.pdf

OECD. (2012). *PISA 2012* Retrieved from http://www.oecd.org/pisa/keyfindings/pisa-2012-results.htm)

OECD. (2013). *PISA 2012 Assessment and Analytical Framework, PISA.* OECD Publishing.

OECD. (2015). *Mathematics performance (PISA) (indicators)* Retrieved from https://data.oecd.org/pisa/mathematics-performance-pisa.htm

OECD. (2015). *OECD Skills Outlook 2015: youth, skills and employability*. Retrieved from http://www.oecd-library.org/docserver/download/8714011e.pdf?expires=1443443835&id=id&accname=ocid1952 06&checksum=F738E31FEDCCBB3F972B655C3800656B

Paquay, L., Van Nieuwenhoven, C., & Wouters, P. (Dir.) (2010). L'évaluation, levier du développement professionnel? Bruxelles: De Boeck-Université.

Pearson (2012), *The Learning Courve, Lessons in Country. Report Performance in Education*. Retrieved from http://media.pearsonitalia.it/0.698971_1399648396.pdf

Perrenoud, P. (2002). Dieci competenze per insegnare. Roma: Anicia. (Originale ed.: Perrenoud, P.) (1999). Dix nouvelles compétences pour enseigner. Paris: ESF.

Richardson, V., & Placier, P. (2002). Teacher change. In V. Richardson (Ed.), *Handbook of research on teaching* (4th ed.). Washington, DC: American Educational Research Association.

Rivoltella, P. C. (2014). *La previsione*. Brescia: La Scuola.

Rossi, P. G. (2014). Le tecnologie digitali per la progettazione didattica. *Journal Of Educational, Cultural Psychological Studies*, 2014, 113–133.

Rossi P.G. et al. (2015), The use of video recorded classes to develop teacher professionalism: the experimentation of a curriculum. *Je-LKS – Journal of e-Learning and Knowledge Society, 11* (2), 111-127.

Ruiz-Primo, M. A., & Furtak, E. M. (2004). Informal formative assessment of students' Understanding of scientific inquiry. CSE – Center for the Study of Evaluation – Report 639, Los Angeles, CA.

Santagata, R., & Guarino, J. (2011). Using the video to teach future teachers to learn from teaching. *ZDM. The international Journal of Mathematics Education, 43*(1), 133-145.

Santagata, R., Zannoni, C., & Stigler, J. W. (2007). The role of lesson analysis in preservice teacher education: An empirical investigation of teacher learning from a virtual based field experience. *Journal of Mathematics Teacher Education, 10*(2), 123–140. doi:10.1007/s10857-007-9029-9

Schön, D. A. (2006, trad. It.). Il professionista riflessivo: per una nuova epistemologia della pratica professionale. Bari: Deedalo.

Scriven, M. (1967). The metodology of evaluation. In R. E. Tyler, R. M. Gagnè, & M. Scriven (Eds.), *Perspecive of corriculum evaluation*. Chicago: AERA Monograph Series in Education.

Seidel, T., & Stürmer, K. (2014). Modeling and Measuring the Structure of Professional Vision in Pre-service Teachers. *American Educational Research Journal, 51*(4), 739–771. doi:10.3102/0002831214531321

Seidel, T., Stürmer, K., Blomberg, G., Kobarg, M., & Schwindt, K. (2011). Teacher learnign from analysis of videotaped classroom situations: Does it make a difference wether teachers observe their own teaching or that of others? *Teaching and Teacher Education, 27*(2), 259–267. doi:10.1016/j.tate.2010.08.009

Shavelson, R. J., Black, P., Wiliam, D., & Coffey, J. (2003, January). On aligning summative and formative functions in the design of large-scale assessment system. *Paper presented at theNational Research Council's workshop on Assessment in Support of Instruction and Learning.*

UNESCO. International Institute for Educational Planning (2005) *Education reforms and teachers' unions: avenues for action*. Paris. Retrieved from http://unesdoc.unesco.org/images/0014/001410/141028e.pdf

Vertecchi, B. (1976). *Valutazione formativa*. Torino: Loescher.

Walkowiak, T. A., Berry, R. Q., Meyer, J. P., Rimm-Kaufman, S. E., & Ottmar, E. R. (2014). Introducing an observational measure of standards-based mathematics teaching practices: *Evidence of validity and score reliability. Educational Studies in Mathematics*, *85*(1), 109–128. doi:10.1007/s10649-013-9499-x

Weeden, P., Winter, J., & Broadfoot, P. (2002). *Assessment. What's in it for schools. London: Routledge. Trad. It. Scalera, V. (2009). Valutazione per l'apprendimento nella scuola. Strategie per incrementare la qualità dell'offerta formativa*. Trento: Erickson. doi:10.4324/9780203468920

ENDNOTES

[1]   The chapter has been designed and shared in all its parts by all the five authors. In particular, The 1st and the 2nd § are by Giorgio Bolondi, the 3rd § and the 4th § by Ira Vannini, the 5th § by Federica Ferretti, the 6th, 7th, 8th § by Stefania Lovece.

[2]   The Evidence-based Learning (EBE) is an approach that, through comparative investigation methods (meta-analysis, systematic reviews, best evidence synthesis) tends to take stock of what is known about the effectiveness of teaching ("what works in what circumstances"). A critical synthesis of the results dell'EBE and convergences between these findings and some of the more relevant Instructional Design is presented by A. Calvani (2012) in "For evidence-based education. Theoretical analysis on international methodological effective teaching and inclusive "(Trento: Erickson).

Chapter 8
Videos in Teacher Training

Patrizia Magnoler
Università degli Studi di Macerata, Italy

Maila Pentucci
Università degli Studi di Macerata, Italy

ABSTRACT

What role has video analysis today in activating, supporting and guiding this professional development process? In this chapter, we will try to provide some answers and open up research paths that can provide suggestions for redirecting training and joint-training processes. The use of video-analysis as a tool for self-comparison was found to be vital; it was however decided to not give it an exclusive role, but include it as part of a more complex training device. The interest of the study was aimed at understanding action, in its planning, the contextualised situation, a review of the action and perception of oneself before and after the intervention. The research in question is based on a holistic case study that was selected for its representative nature within the group of teachers in the research-training, and can therefore be defined as an "emblematic case".

INTRODUCTION

Identifying a new kind of teacher means reflecting on the most frequently used methods in training. Modelling, prescriptive indications, occasions when the transmission of knowledge prevails, are no longer adequate for supporting the change that can lead a teacher towards intentional, aware, professional action in relation to the context and changes that this requires. The aim of training becomes more complex, it goes from "training" to the idea of "professional training", not just teaching techniques and strategies, but skills that allow you to make decisions "independently, based on learning theories with systematic reflection on the teaching process. The teachers are no longer seen as passive subjects; to the contrary, they are active agents, professionals in their work" (Santagata, 2012, p. 59).

This therefore mean adopting professional development as the aim of training, with all the implications of the central nature of action (Barbier & Durand, 2003), of theoretical-practical connection (Zeichner & Cochran-Smith, 2005) that allows transformation of all *outil* (material or conceptual) in instruments,

DOI: 10.4018/978-1-5225-0711-6.ch008

Copyright © 2017, IGI Global. Copying or distributing in print or electronic forms without written permission of IGI Global is prohibited.

found in gestures and in thinking the action (Rabardel, 1995), to give rise to *Formats Pédagogiques* that characterize the action of the teacher (Veyrunes, Imbert, & San Martin, 2014).

What role has video analysis had and have today in activating, supporting and guiding this professional development process? In this paper, we will try to provide some answers and open up research paths that can provide suggestions for redirecting training and joint-training processes.

FROM MICRO TEACHING TO ENACTIVE DEVICES

The Micro-Teaching (M-T) model devised at Stanford in 1963 by a team of trainers (Acheson, Allen, Bush, Clark, Cooper, Fortune and Ryan) provided for some steps in methods and aims that in time generated other training models that use video-filming in the classroom to allow teaching to be investigated.

The main problem came from having to overcome the gap between theoretical training and the "class test". In fact, training as an intervention was placed in the induction and pre-service phase. This goal, according to M-T, could be pursued by acquiring pedagogic skills (Allen & Ryan, 1969), via obligatory phases, "plan, teach, observe, re-plan, re-teach and re-observe"; in which the analysis by the subject observing his/her own actions, supported by experts and colleagues, allowed him/her to see which conduct to change and to start up substitute learning (Bandura, Ross, & Ross, 1961). The expected result was to acquire an increasingly expert method that complied with quality standards considered to be acceptable by the professional community and by research, a sort of modelling that could be aided by imitating processes (Bartley, 1969), by identifying one's own starting point and next target to be achieved through reaching increasingly difficult levels[1]. Different trajectories and themes that characterize the use of video for the initial and in-service teacher training emerge from the above mentioned observations. First, the transition from observation of the others' action to observation of his/her own action. Second, the exchange activated by observation of the video: between peers (novices), between novices and experts, between experts (Ria, 2015).

Already Aubertine (1967), Borg (1968) and Ward (1970) had begun this transition to in-service training, currently widely used for professional training in various fields, for example, for health (Poizat, Bailly, Seferdjeli, & Goudeaux, 2015) or artisan-industrial (Magnoler, Pacquola, & Tescaro, 2014). This process is aimed at different goals over time.

For example, in pre-service, there is currently emphasis on describing, understanding and identifying the pedagogical though (Seidel & Stürmer, 2014) and the regulation in action (Altet, 2012), or on noting the critical situations (Lussi Borer & Muller, 2014).

In service, it is the capacity to gather significant elements from within the classroom situation (Sherin & van Es, 2002) or in the students' analysis of reasoning and learning (as in the case of the Video Clubs. Van Es & Sherin, 2010), that are often missed during teacher-pupil interaction during the lesson (van Es & Sherin, 2008; Lewis, Perry, & Hurd, 2009). The problems of learning can be discovered by comparing several points of view (Kazemi & Hubbard, 2008), something that would otherwise be more complex if it was just one teacher analysing his/her own video (Tochon, 2007). The use of video for in-service training is also central in the *Analyse Plurielle* model, by Vinatier and Altet (2008), applied to video sequences to trace the development of the epistemological, pragmatic and relational issues involved in every teaching situation.

Another aspect of M-T looked at is the expansion of the concept of teaching to phases prior to and following classroom activity. The analysis is not limited to the action, but extends to the thought that precedes the action, to the habitus (Griffiths, MacLeod, & McIntyre, 1977; Bourdieu, 1980; Perrenoud, 2006) and the post-action reflections in order to reconstruct the thought in the action.

In this direction, studies of *Didactique Professionnelle* (Pastré, Mayen, & Vergnaud, 2006) are emblematic: these focus on the patterns that underlie the action (Vergnaud, 1996) to understanding the conceptual structure of the action (Pastré, 2011) and the organizers (Clanet, 2007; Vinatier & Pastré, 2007) that characterise the teacher's action, which allow them to address several situations while maintaining consistency of action.

Knowing *les théoremes en acte* (Vinatier, 2009) that influence the decisions in a situation is an important resource for training to understand which elements to focus the intervention on in order to allow the subject to be more capable of self-regulating his/her own work and to activate a real transforming learning process (Mezirow, 2000).

A longitudinal view of the action is taken that, in the *Cours d'action* (Theureau, 2006, 2009) brings about the realisation of *pre-reflechive* knowledge[2] and a post-action, analysis on two levels: the first aimed at recovering visible factors in the video and the second in reconstructing the "reasoning in the action", to find out how the relationship between context and subject has been established enactively. The enactive perspective, that forms the background from which the *Cours d'action* has been generated, refuses any determining cause/effect relationship between teaching and learning and eliminates any possibility of modeling to arrive at a standard expected, to concentrate on how each subject reprocesses his/her own interaction mode with the context, within typical situations (*situation thypique*) that characterise the work (Leblanc, Ria, Dieumegard, Serres, & Durand, 2008)

This type of research requires increasingly sophisticated techniques to support analysis of event, creating real protocols that are necessary for carrying out *Autoconfrontation simple* sessions and *Autoconfrontation croisée* sessions[3].

Modelling to acquire skills that will allow good practice is the topic of discussion. There are two different evolutions: to identify the factors, on the basis of experimental validation, to be applied in teaching (Evidence Based Education, Hattie, 2009) or to activate a participatory research between teachers and between researchers and teachers, finding optimal solutions in context.

Also in this case there are important differences. The current Lesson Study model (Yoshida, 1999; Stigler & Hiebert, 1999) aims to identify the structure of a lesson, by confronting teachers, that can be helpful to students' learning. Attention is not on the teacher's actions. But on the internal validity of the lesson itself, for how it has been planned: there is therefore a return to the causal principle between lesson and its modelling effect.

In another direction, the *Recherche Participative* perspective (Anadon, 2007) looks at the relationship between research and training above all, focused on the teacher's action. The tendency to change and innovation that permeates the *Vidéo-exploration* (Mottet, 1997), *Recherche-action* (Barbier, 2007) and *Recherche-intervention* models (Cappelletti, 2010), has brought about thought on the fact that in the 1990s they led to the creation of the *Recherche Collaborative* model (Desgagné; 1997; Bednarz, 2013; Morrisette, 2015) that sees co-research as the opportunity for real change in shared practice among teachers and researchers. This does not entail building practice or principle models for training purposes, but to understand how knowledge constructed through researching practice can be used to understand better how teachers act in situ[4].

Gathering the above-stated training models shows a cross-the-board matter: how to choose the video to be analysed? The analysis proposed by Santagata (2012) is aimed above all at identifying the purposes for which a type of video is chosen. Each selection must be made in relation to the goals (improving educational transfer? Developing the skills of observation and analysis? Understanding how to develop students' learning?), the types of video (long or short), choosing which lessons (participants or unknown teachers' videos, considered to be efficient or simply typical) and which type of support to use for observation. The researcher from the University of California created a Lesson Analysis Framework that guides observation on both teaching and on learning, comparing the teachers' and students' actions, as already found in the *Analyse de Pratiques* and the *Analyse plurielle*.

A topic that re-emerges to some extent within the various models is that of evaluation: how to evaluate the capacity to analyse one's own or others' action (Santagata & Guarino, 2011)? How to evaluate professional development that occurred thanks to training? This problem is complex, as it is a change that takes place over time and highlights a transformation of the deepest structures, permanent ones that effectively show a transforming and generating learning. The concept of professional development, in French environments, is described according to two dynamics that are connected with each other:

1. The development of individual and collective skills (Barbier, Chaix, & Demailly, 1994) in an interdependent way as the "culture of the job" has a strong influence on building meanings by the subject (Jorro, 2010).
2. Identity transformation that begins when the subject recognises himself in his own actions, allocated a *pouvoir d'agir* to himself that is also recognised by others. Identity is dynamic and is articulated through phases of identification and differentiation (Lipianski, 1992; Dubar, 1998; Tap, 1998) that give rise to the differences in each teacher within the professional community (difference between "*style*" and "*genre*", Clot, 2008). Therefore, how can we see, in a learning environment, the traces that allow us to understand whether and how a subject evolves in terms of skill and identity construction?

This short synthesis shows the topics that permeate training for teachers and that can be summed up as follows: the relation between theory and practice, via the principle of alternation and relative devices, the centrality of action for the professionalisation process, the presence of identifiable levels, (in pre-service and in-service) to aid self-planning and evaluation (self-evaluation, co-evaluation, hetero-evaluation), the presence of set goals to succeed in tracking the efficacy of training, the need to work on visible elements, the relation between subject and group, with regard to constructing a professional culture.

The differences also emerge that are partly found in the criticisms of M-T: the difference between modelling and structural pairing (Maturana & Varela, 1987), between selecting isolated fragments and complexity in teaching, between self-regulation and hetero-evaluation, between artificial training contexts and real contexts, between contextualisation and generalisation, between observation of others' and/or own practices.

DATA COLLECTION

The research has been realized within the RAIN project (Ricerca Azione sulle Indicazioni Nazionali), started at the end of 2013 and funded by the Ministry of Education, University and Research (MIUR) as part of the "Accompanying Measurements to National Indications" (CM 22 dated 26 August 2013). The project will run for three years, and will end at the end of the 2015/2016 academic year. It was conceived with the aim of setting up a detailed path of *Recherche Collaborative* (Lenoir, 2012) that includes cooperation between theory and practice around the subject of the study taken from educational practice: each of the subjects involved uses and recognises the other's skills to co-construct new knowledge aimed at the scientific community that has effects in terms of utility in the school community (Dubet, 1994: criterion of *Double Vraisemblance*).

It provides for collaboration between the Department of Educational Science at the University of Macerata (Italy) and a network of seven schools in the same province. The subject focus in this path is Geo-history; the use of a subject point of view allowed reification of the theoretical concepts and practical thoughts, into a form of institutionalised knowledge with a given value in a school environment.

The aim of the project is to activate virtuous paths of reflection about their own practices among teachers in training, in order to experiment significant changes in their daily teaching practices and thus allow for professional development in terms of skills and perceptions of themselves.

The video-analysis as a tool for reflection on practice and as a means to encourage and detect change was used by a small group of seven teachers, all volunteers, who were willing to start a path of self-analysis supported by interviews, both before and after the video-recordings of lessons in the classroom, during history and geography lessons. The sample was identified through self-candidacy by the teachers, with whom a training contract was shared that had been negotiated with the researchers. The required implication, in fact, was the provision of cognitive and emotive resources, permission to intrude in a learning environment that is already structured and consolidated, a discussion on one's conduct and thoughts compared to the professional persona that could only be allowed through willingness and full motivation in the subjects involved.

The use of video-analysis as a tool for self-comparison was found to be vital; it was however decided to not give it an exclusive role, but include it as part of a more complex training device.

The interest of the study was aimed at understanding action, in its planning (and therefore the teachers' conceptions that guide such choices), the contextualised situation (implementation of the planned activity and regulation when in action), a review of the action and perception of oneself before and after the formative intervention.

the video analysis has taken center stage for two investigation's reasons: examine the action in its complexity; understand what originates and justifies action, according to the mind of the teacher. Interviews were also prepared and performed to support and optimize the video viewing, in order to allow a reconstruction of the meanings associated with the observed activities.

A complex sequence of data collection was then drawn up, that was repeated three times in each of the two school years on all teachers in the small group.

The phases of the study were as follows:

1. *Entretien D'explicitation* (**Vermersch, 1991**): Used as an ice-breaker for the entire process, in terms of familiarisation among the subjects involved and the interviewed subject and the methods and subjects involved in the path.
2. **Semi-Structured Interview:** Aimed at gathering the project stages (starting with and adding to the elements that already emerged during the preparatory interview). Each video-recording in the classroom was preceded by an interview, carried out using the teacher's preparation material or outlines of the lesson plan. The reporting on the preparation was accompanied by reformulation and new questions (Vermersch, 1994), trying to gain an explanation of the goals, the choices made in terms of methodology and epistemology, and the forecasts of development of the action.

3. **Filming in the Classroom:** The video recording was filmed by one of the researchers during a history or geo-history lesson, agreeing such times with the teacher. The duration of the video is in line with the lesson and filming was between 1 and 2 hours. The length of the video, from which shorter episodes are taken, but which are still all analysable, makes this survey method different from typical procedures of Video Clubs, that only takes pieces of limited parts of the lesson (Santagata, 2012).

Two cameras were used, one fixed that filmed all the classroom for all the time, and a mobile one, used to focus on some aspects considered to be important by the researcher, or to offer a dual view in certain moments.

4. **Video Analysis:** The researchers and the teacher selected fragments of video on which confronted according to various criteria: representativeness compared to the practices of the teacher (e.g. the way to introduce a topic), problem situations (e.g. the students did not understand), didactic or educational problems.
5. **Semi-Structured Interview with Pupils/Students:** The questions asked at the end of the lesson were structured on indicators that looked back at the conceptualisations that emerged from the previous interview with the teacher, to understand if the goals set by the teacher were recognised by the children.
6. **Written Report on the Reflections Made at the End of the Entire Path:** Only some teachers, the ones most loyal to the path, considered it useful to let us have short written thoughts after seeing the materials. Although they are not structured, the reports have been found to be a very important tool for understanding the perception of change by the teacher and the usefulness of using the video for training in individual cases.

The goal of the research was to collect relevant data to answer to the following questions: the video analysis can (and how) to help the teacher to be aware of their action and then implement significant changes in their teaching practices? Subsequently, can the teacher increase the awareness of his/her professional development?

STUDY DESIGN AND ANALYSIS

The research we are speaking about is based on a holistic case study that was selected for its representative nature within the group of teachers in the research-training, and can therefore be defined as an "emblematic case". Its characteristics make it so that it aids a transfer of elements found to the analysis of other cases via an analogising process. It is therefore an intensive case study (Yin, 1984) aimed at the subsequent realisation of a comparative case study that can be extended to the remaining members of the group of teachers. The survey, carried out over two years, is a longitudinal one, and aims to describe and understand the complex structure of relationships that identify and characterise the case in itself, in its unique, unrepeatable specific nature, that can help to cast light on more general matters connected with the concept of professional development.

With regard to understanding the effects of training, the case study has an explorational purpose, thus defined by Roberto Trinchero (2002):

... describing the effects (visible and less visible), in real contexts, of specific educational interventions and studying the situations in which a specific educational intervention causes or does not cause the desired effects. (Trinchero, 2002, p. 84)

The data was collected using triangulation of methods (semi-structured interviews before the lesson, video footage to track the action, analysis from the video) and analysed using a triangulation of researchers (at least two researchers with different expertise and different theoretical frameworks of reference). A database of data and materials was drawn up (transcribed interviews, videos of lessons, documents written by a single teacher) that allowed the empirical basis of the study to be inspected.

The material analysis procedures were organised into the following phases and methods:

1. **Material Analysis by the Researchers:** The gathered data was analysed separately by the three members of the research team at first, and was then compared. The data was selected: from inside the text of interviews, the fragments that allowed understanding of the teachers' principles, logic and processes that brought them to their decisions; the parts of the video that could be more significant for detecting consistency with what was planned previously, regulation in action (the changes made to what was planned in relation to the events in context), the emerging difficulties (obstacles in learning by students, non-continuity in the phases of the lesson as conducted by the teachers). These selections were then compared and the most important parts considered jointly for supporting the analysis were chosen.

2. **The *Analyse Plurielle* Model (Vinatier & Altet, 2008):** Used for the analysis, it allows a comparison of the researchers' different points of view; in this case they were an expert in teaching methodology, an expert in Geo-history and an expert in action analysis.

3. At the same time, the teacher involved was watching his/her own video-recording and transcript of interviews that were given to him/her, as foreseen in the training contract. The viewing of materials was not binding to being able to access the next step, however, i.e. the confrontation with the researchers. The teacher could find traces (parts of the text, parts of the video) that he/she wanted to talk about with the researchers.

4. *Co-Explicitation* (Vinatier, 2009): Between researchers and teachers, in order to conceptualise the learning situation in a shared manner, using objective tracks shown to the teachers or presented by them. The confrontation brings to light the underlying values of the practice and the "discussion" of implicit professional knowledge (Faingold, 2011).

RESULTS

The longitudinal path, the multiple data collected and multifocality of investigation's points of view have provided an interpretation by the method of crystallization (Janesick, 2000); This has allowed us to investigate and understand the observed object, the Teaching-Learning process, in depth, in its complexity and in in its different faces (Maree & Van der Westhuizen, 2009).

It was caught, in fact, in its dinamicity thanks to the relatively long time of the investigation focussed on the only teacher and thanks to the regularity of the monitoring process on the action through the use of videos.

Finding the project and teaching practices of teacher P. can be considered as a transferable process relating to three dimensions:

- The characteristics of the teacher can be largely generalised (age, years of experience, subject taught, type of school, sharing of professional culture, motivation for own training, continuity in working with the same class); consequently, the process can be started with other teacher.
- The validation of the results it was possible with the data collection multiple method and with the plural visions to detect the change in both the teacher's practice and in thought. In this way the assumptions deduced in similar contexts can be generalized.
- The accompaniment, in time, becomes a true "alliance" (Damiano, 2006), supported by the exchange between theory and practice in the survey. The path of cooperation and sharing between researchers and teachers can be an effective research model.

The diachronic comparison, both in the design practices and in the taught practices and the recrossing of the path in a longitudinal way, let us find some answers to questions that guided the research, highlighting a progressive change in the action and in the process of rethinking the action made by the observed teacher.

To systematise the traces of change over the teacher's entire cycle, Shulman's Pedagogical Reasoning and Action model (1987) was used; The phases are shown in Table 1.

In fact, the deepness, the duration and the multifocality of the analysis needed a decomposition and an organization of the analysed practices and postures in precise moments that Shulman classifies as

Table 1. A model of pedagogical reasoning and action

Comprehension		Of purposes, subject matter structures, ideas within and outside the discipline.
Transformation	Preparation	Critical interpretation and analysis of texts, structuring and segmenting, development of a curricular repertoire, and clarification of purposes.
	Representation	Use of a representational repertoire which includes analogies, metaphora, examples, demonstrations, explanations and so forth.
	Selection	Choice from among and instructional repertoire which includes modes of teaching, organizing, managing and arranging.
	Adaptation and Tailoring to Student Characteristics	Consideration of conceptions, preconceptions, misconceptions, and difficulties, language, culture, and motivations, social class, gender, age, ability, aptitude, interests, self-concepts, and attention.
Instruction		Management, presentations, interactions, group work, discipline, humor, questioning, and other aspects of active teaching, discovery or inquiry instruction, and the observable forms of classroom teaching.
Evaluation		• Checking for student understanding during interactive teaching. • Testing student understanding at the end of lessons or units. • Evaluating one's own performance, and adjusting for experiences.
Reflection		Reviewing, reconstructing, reenacting and critically analyzing one's own and the class's performance, and grounding explanations in evidence.
New Comprehensions		• Of purposes, subject matter, students, teaching and self. • Consolidation of new understandings, and learnings from experiences.

Shulman, 1987, p. 15.

steps present in the didactical action; this is considered as a "text", meant as a segment of the community's knowledge and of the personal teacher's knowledge that converge in the didactical transposition.

We can find elements of change in every phase within the model, confirming the perception of transformation and progress already identifiable in the overall vision of collected data.

CHANGES IN PRACTICES

Comprehension

This is the pre-teaching moment, when the teacher's thoughts and conceptions are summed up compared to the cultural subject being referred to. P. begins his/her path with the idea of taught history linked to the transposition made by the manual being used.

In the film dated January 25, 2014, a lesson on the origin of the earth is shown. The idea is taken from the textbook being used (Fortunato & Girotti, 2009); the teacher sets up a learning setting that involves the dramatisation of several excerpts: four people representing science, religion, legend and myth becomes the voices of the respective theories regarding the origin of the Earth. (0'00''–18'05''). An a-historical or extra-historical conception emerges from the operations asked of the children (from 23'20"), reduced to a series of theories on which a simple opinion must be given, in spite of the complex nature that it poses, regarding historical skills.

In P's thoughts there is a problematic epistemological knowledge; the given scale of values and the dogma seems to be hetero-directed by a professional culture rather than by a thorough knowledge of the matter.

When the researcher asked him/her to explain why it was considered suitable to begin teaching about the history of the earth without man, rather than the history of man on earth (Christian, 2011), P. answered *that is how the book begins* (*co-explicitation* dated mar., 3, 2014).

The problem detected in the context of Geo-history is comparable with the low efficiency of learning design: it closely linked with the schoolbook and don't build a situated device in Teaching-Learning process.

Viewing the first videos and the shared reflections with the researchers compared to the problems found in the transposition had an effect on his/her idea of the subject and convinced him/her about the need to have a deeper knowledge of method and epistemology. This is one element of awareness that was gained following training. In fact, after almost two years from the start of the path, P. writes:

I must study! Because in order to think of a rich, complex, motivating learning environment, I must also have thorough knowledge of the subject to help me. If I don't have that, it is also difficult to make an issue of the mis-knowledge that textbooks that we use often contain. (Report on sept., 3, 2015)

We can also see a new view of history and the teaching of history:

... I had never thought so deeply about the time, space indicators, about the concept of time in its deepest meaning....

… it makes you think [the research] about things that otherwise you wouldn't think about (…) it made me understand what I was doing. Because it was just routine for me. This too. Such deep reflection just doesn't happen. (Co-explicitation dated jun., 23, 2015)

Transformation

The changes that emerge from the video recordings of lessons mainly concern the aspects of representation and selection, within the transformation phase.

The changes that took place in P's representational repertory can be seen by comparing the video from the first year and that from the second year.

A micro-routine for activating pupils is clear at the beginning of the path: asking them to give an opinion or inquisitiveness on the subject addressed. The children's answers are normally noted by the teacher.

Because when we talk about hypothesis, I say: What do you think that means? And so each child gives his/her hypothesis and I mark them up on the board. (Interview from jan., 13, 2014)

In the second video recording, this process is repeated three times (March 5, 2014, Part I, 5'52"; 9'32"; 28'41").

Collecting the relative answers requires a long part of the lesson (about twenty minutes) but the purpose is not clear. In fact, they will no longer be filmed in the activity, which continues with readings and the collective construction of a map.

This set of questions asked by the pupils has no cognitive purpose, however, also because the teachers asks questions that encourage the processing of opinions, preferences, points of view, personal interests and have a mainly emotive value. They are needed to involve and motivate, they are part of the setting of the lesson.

The move from emotive to cognitive is the element that defines the change shown in the pupil activation process. While not completely abandoning his/her way of communicating, the teacher continues to note the remarks from each pupil, but uses them as a project basis for his/her own lessons.

In the video recording on February 2, 2015, the teacher begins the lesson by returning to the observations made previously by two pupils:

C. asked me, remind me C… if other populations were in the same situation while the Egyptians had this type of agricultural development. I didn't give an answer, I said: this is a problem, we need to go back and look at that. Then while I was testing F., he spoke about maize and S. answered: you are maybe getting confused because my grandfather said that maize came to Europe after the discovery of America. Before that it was only in Mesoamerica.

So what did I think? Let's try and solve these two problems together today. (1'05"-2'50")

The available time for speaking left for the children this time has no relational or motivating role, but is essential in the teaching and learning process.

The teacher structured the lesson, selected materials and set tasks starting from the two questions that had remained unanswered, as he/she declares in the interview about planning on February 2, 2015.

The change that the teacher shows in the selection processes, in particular in the teaching mediators offered, is closely connected with the questions asked by the pupils.

In this case too, he/she moves from a choice made due to an emotive or creative reason, to choices connected with the learning goals, from the planned paths.

The turning point, also confirmed by the teacher's words (*co-explicitation* dated jun., 23, 2015) can be seen in the videoed lesson from April 3, 2014. On this occasion, P. accepts a suggestion made by the researcher about the possible use of multimedia animation in class regarding the population of the earth, to build the sense of space-time simultaneity and to dismantle the stereotype of the successive nature of events, that can be found in most books used in schools.

Multimedia cartoon validated by the authorities, the Bradshaw Foundation, that works on research for mapping the human genome, moves P's teaching practice to different cognitive operations, that are outside the teacher's own routines. The most obvious change is in the central nature of lesson management, self-allocated up to this moment and now fully shared with the mediator chosen, that supports processes and steps that are not usual for P. The lesson begins with immediately showing the cartoon, dismantling a rule of action that was precious for her at a motivation level (involving the children in a conversation before proposing the content):

P.: *I have said that previously, when we began to study history, we sat down, we told the story, we read, looked at documents. Is that right? This morning we are going to do it differently and we are going to watch a film. (video dated April 3, 2014, part I, 1'36")*

The routines re-emerge at the end of the film, when the teachers give instruction:

P.: *I'm going to get some sheets because I want to hear what you have to say. What do you think? Shall we have a chat after watching this video? (part II, 5'55")*

A change can be seen here too: In fact, during the discussion with the pupils, P. stops to give them the key to reading the dynamic elements found in the mediators, according to a perspective of time and space (from 18'00") She realises a change has taken place also in the children's posture, which reflects the change in action and accepts the mobilising of simultaneity, outside the truly historical context:

P.: *I wanted to say something really lovely: a child has said something very interesting to me. He asked me whether today, at the same time as us, somewhere else, in other spaces in the world, is everybody doing what we are doing? Does everyone like l do? (Co-explicitation dated May 5, 2014)*

Education

By education, we mean managing learning and teaching, including all aspects of the mediation used: presentations, interaction, teamwork, questions, discoveries.

At this level, changes emerge regarding two aspects, linked in particular to the interactions between teacher and pupils: how much the teacher speaks during the lesson and the regulation carried out, in particular regarding the questions asked of the children.

This central position in talking in the lesson is seen as a problem by the teacher from when she sees the first video.

A quantitative measurement provides the answer to this perception: in the first lesson, excluding the 18 minutes dedicated to dramatisation, the teacher speaks for almost all the remaining 40 minutes of the lesson, even when asking for the children's opinions. In action, she doesn't just ask the question, but repeats it, supports each child's answer, reprocesses and explains the various answers. Alongside the oral report, she also copies the children's words onto a sheet.

It is difficult to understand the different communication purposes that the teacher applies to the segments of the lesson in this dimension. It is not always possible to extrapolate the moment of providing or asking from the speech, when what has already been said is confirmed, the simple addressing the pupils, the explanation of the subject.

In spite of immediately becoming aware of this invasive mode, the teacher does not know how to limit it. The change, in terms of quantity and quality of "what is said" can only be seen in the video of the second year.

In the first video recording (Feb., 25, 2015) the teacher's presence is still predominant. However, both the tone of voice, lower and less excited, and the articulation of the first part of the lesson show a considerable change in attitude. This time it is possible to distinguish the stages of the lesson, that can be traced back to a precise series of cognitive operations that the pupils must carry out (1'33"-14'40")

This is a speech that is organised better, is cognitively relevant, supported by efficient mediators, selected according to pre-set goals. It can be maintained that this change occurred not so much when the teacher realised the problem but when she began to structure her lesson plans in a more organic way, preparing a full device, with precise times based on specific aspects of knowledge and skills to be developed.

Another change, connected with the reduction in the teacher's presence and also probably due to the changed planning process used, is regulation of action. This is a difficult element to note by observing the video, as it concerns the continuous re-interpretation of the context by the teacher immersed in it (Rossi, 2011).

P. changes her regulation in the procedure with regard to the questions asked to the class. Previously, P tended to repeat the question until she got the answer she expected and had already pre-formulated, sometimes suggesting the start, or talking over the pupils' answers (Video from January 25, 2014, 27'21"; 30'00." Video from mar., 5, 2014, part I, 4'34"). These closed questions were necessary for her to continue the talk aimed at the pre-set result, also when harming the real participation of pupils. (Altet, 1994)

Seeing herself in action showed up this conduct and made the teacher (very attentive to the extent of interaction with the children) realise that the space of action set aside for them was actually not real, limited by her guidance (Magnoler & Iobbi, 2015).

In this way, she was able in time to combat this pattern with another (Perrenoud, 2001), enacted through intentional regulation.

Researcher: *you are reducing your interventions, leaving more space for them to talk*
P.: *yes Before it was non-stop, it was only me talking. Children slowly have to get used to being left.*
[…]
Researcher: *they need less reassurance, to say what you want to hear.*
P.: *that still happens to me I think that isn't the answer I expected but I think and say that it's ok anyway. I limit myself (Co-explicitation dated September 22, 2015)*

As Altet (2001) underlines, the action is carried out in a dynamic of wanting to let the pupils speak and progressing the debate: P. must solve the situation immediately learning to be present but separate from the pupils at the same time.

The video training acted to facilitate awareness building in this case, not as video-modelling (Masats & Dooly, 2011), to change the teacher's conduct to a prescribed paradigm. P. has used a new outline through reflecting on her own practice and questioning it, helped by a cognitive view of the view and the help of the researchers.

Evaluation

The evaluation part of P. teaching method started from the second start. The teacher often spoke to the researchers about her reluctance regarding overly judging evaluation processes, that in her mind affect collaboration and harmony that she tries to include in her classes.

The teacher prefers to observe the children's behaviour in activity, rather than setting rigid checking and evaluation tools (interview on February 10, 2015).

In this context, it is not possible to detect changes in P.'s practice but only the increasing presence of the problem of evaluation of skills that P is showing more frequently, as a current problem.

Reflection

Reflection on one's own actions is the final purposes of the whole training project: it is professionalising skill, considered to be vital in the collaborative research process. Critical reconfiguration of teaching paths and thought structures in teachers is the goal.

On reflection, P says, during the final *co-explicitation*, at the end of the second year (June 23, 2015):

... I had never thought so deeply in my whole life... in my career or life - what I can do, who I can be - or from an epistemological point of view, of my knowledge. Therefore, I have truly begun again."

This skill of reviewing and rethinking that P. can now enact has developed along the way, not hetero-directed by the researchers through their verbal suggestions or instructions. It is a natural result of the path walked with the teacher, trying to reveal her deepest thoughts through interaction and new ideas. In this way, P. has progressively taken on her new stance in confrontations within her working mode, defining herself (*I have truly begun again*) as a thinking professional (Schön, 1983).

Acquiring the skill of self-analysis changes what P. sees in the video and the way in which she underlines and explains what she notes. An alignment takes place between practical and theoretical over time, in identifying the video sequences that are considered most significant, and in thinking back to things, the concepts leading action, the language used and the theoretical references.

This change in reflection and self-analysis also changes the teacher's perception of herself, that bears witness to this total transformation in her habitus, seen during *co-explicitation*.

The video analysis, rather than providing evidence to support this, is a tool and means itself through which change takes place and becomes, in a path that provides for deconstruction of previous conceptions, a path of research and reflection about oneself, and one's actions, to then redefine one's own professional figure compared to the context you act in.

Researcher: *For example: you seem to have changed perception that you have of yourself as a teacher.*

P.: *well, if I'm honest, I was much more sure of myself before! Did you think the contrary?*

[…]

P.: *I'm worried now, I was about to say so before: I am very worried, this year (...)*

Researcher: *what are you worried about?*

P.: *I', frightened of everything! Everything means... What should I study before and then teach, but also how, as it is true that it can't be a fairytale or be banal, but the children are still so young...*

The impact of the training has therefore also caused some negative elements, it would seem: P. as a teacher with many years' experience, considered positively in her working context by several people that she interacts with, loses her confidence that such attribution of value had provided her with.

Reviewing and analysing herself in action dismantles a number of routines, that confirmed her being a "good teacher" as she uses facilitating aids in her teaching. The video affects the efficacy of many of her plans, she knows she has to rethink and restructure, plan long paths in an orderly mode. She says of herself: *"I am looking for..."*, not saying what, but showing that she has taken on another of the essential dimensions of a professional teacher, that of research.

She can't dip into repertoires that, when questioned on the video, now show their limits, compared to the new needs that the teacher herself has developed, thanks to her reflection. She is now aware that transformation is not a destination, but a constant stance in her new professional position.

P. is in a dynamic situation, in fieri: after overcoming the "unfreezing" step (Lewin, 1951), when she dismantled barriers and the typical inertia of the community's culture, she is in an intermediate phase which is perceived as destabilising and temporary in which the change is occurring: the previous reference point was destructured, but the new one is not yet well defined. The third year of video analysis and guiding actions will be directed to identifying the presence of refreezing, that is the strengthening of the new acquisitions that can give back the self confidence that P. had before strating the process.

The most obvious change is the one she explains regarding her role in the school community that she is part of.

Researcher: *as a professional gain, has there been any?*

P.: *oh yes, a lot! Another thing I often do is to share it with a colleague. Before I didn't. Confidence makes you act alone, now I don't, I try to share, to discuss, to search together, to think together and this is another aspect that has improved this path.*

P. has overcome the dimension of solitude, of autonomy and self-referencing where expert teachers often complain about when they have been in the same school for a long time. She has realised, learning it during the training, that confrontation with others is useful to strengthen the two new dimensions that were spoken of before, reflection and research.

She also makes more progress, as the path taken in her group of peers gives her a new air of authority, that is a reference point:

Researcher: *was has changed now?*

P.: *I don't know. Perhaps we have involved more people. Before it was F. and me, and we provided our experience, as if you trained us and then they wanted the recipe: tell us, show us how you did it. I didn't understand what we had done and how this experience had changed me... This year, I don't* *know, we have involved more people. ...the whole school is involved, then we started talking, about our experience, and then they took the matter to the other complexes. It is as if everyone took part in the change.*

She accepted the need for change that she can now see in her school and has tried to spread the reflections that have made her change too.

CONCLUSION

Research on this specific case study identifies some elements that can be the basis for analogising, for the analysis of other teachers with the same research path or who in the future can use tracks in their own actions and perceive their own professional identity. Compared to the change in teaching practice, evidence should be collected that allows focus on how teachers:

- Are reviewing their own knowledge on subjects, in which direction and why (comprehension);
- Change their routines and why; transforms "current theorems" (Vergnaud, 1996, Vinatier 2009) that are the foundation for decisions before and during action; make decisions when organising their learning mediation (transformation);
- Regulate actions in situ depending on the evidence that emerges from the video analysis (instruction);
- Identify problems and place them at the centre of a personal survey (reflection);
- Reposition themselves compared to their expertise as perceived previously.

Also, with regard to the perception of themselves, it is useful to reconstruct the path leading to a more mature professional nature, full of tendencies to improve skills and also to replan in a dimension that goes beyond the classroom, beyond personal details, to contribute to the teaching profession's culture.

One essential aspect is the longitudinal analysis that provides an image of thorough change, no longer reversible, not generated by external impositions of innovation, that often do not modify the depth behind actions, do not affect the deeper dimensions of the subject's professional and personal self (Flandin & Ria, 2012).

Training has progressively left room for co-training, a co-research among experts and peers, but in Italy perhaps, the direction being traced in the teachers' professional world nationally (Law 107/2015) is co-training among peers with different levels of expertise. Video analysis, in a broader context of reflection on the practices, through sources that document the action in different languages and from different points of view, can become a professional skill of senior teachers. New digital tools for capturing classroom video make the teacher protagonist of the entire process, from self-capture to analysis, individual, mutual, and collective (van Es., Stockero, Sherin, Van Zoest, & Dyer, 2015). Senior teachers can propose some of the expertise acquired in the co-research between theories and practices. This could implement the creation of real communities of practice, for self-training through reflection on actions and could support the processes of growth in professional culture in single communities and school organisations.

REFERENCES

Allen, D., & Ryan, K. (1969). *Microteaching reading*. Boston, MA: Addison Wesley.

Altet, M. (1994). *La formation professionnelle des enseignants*. Paris: PUF.

Altet, M. (2001). Les Compétences de l'enseignant-professionnel: entre savoirs, schèmes d'action et adaptation, le savoir analyser. In L. Paquay, M. Altet, E. Charlier, & P. Perrenoud (Eds.), Former des enseignants professionnels. Quelles stratégies? Quelles compétences? (pp. 27-40). Bruxelles: de Boeck.

Altet, M. (2012). L'apporto dell'analisi plurale dalle pratiche didattiche alla co-formazione degli insegnanti. In P. C. Rivoltella & P. G. Rossi (Eds.), *L'agire didattico. Manuale per l'insegnante* (pp. 291–311). Brescia: La Scuola.

Anadon, M. (2007). *La recherche participative*. Québec: Presse de l'Université du Québec.

Aubertine, H. E. (1967). Use of Microteaching in Training Supervising Teachers. *High School Journal*, *51*, 99–106.

Bandura, A., Ross, D., & Ross, S. (1961). Transmission of Aggression through imitation of aggressive models. *Journal of Abnormal and Social Psychology*, *63*(3), 575–582. doi:10.1037/h0045925 PMID:13864605

Barbier, J.M., Chaix, M.L., & Demailly, L. (1994). Recherche et développement professionnel. *Recherche et formation, 17*, 1-175.

Barbier, J. M., & Durand, M. (2003). L'analyse de l'activité: Enjeux de recherche et de professionnalisation. *Recherche et Formation*, *42*, 5–6.

Barbier, R. (2007). *La recherche-action*. Paris: Anthropos.

Bartley, D. E. (1969). Microteaching: Rationale procedures and application to foreign language. *Audiovisual Language Journal*, *7*(3), 139–144.

Bednarz, N. (2013). *Recherche collaborative et pratique enseignante*. Paris: L'Harmattan.

Borg, W. R. (1968). *The Minicourse: Rationales and Uses in the In-Service Education of Teachers*. Berkley, CA: Far West Laboratory for Educational Research and Development.

Bourdieu, P. (1980). *Le sens pratique*. Paris: Les Editions de Minuit.

Cappelletti, L. (2010). La recherche-intervention: quels usages en contrôle de gestion? Crises et nouvelles problématiques de la Valeur, HAL. Retrieved from https://halshs.archives-ouvertes.fr/hal-00481090/document

Christian, D. (2011). *Maps of Time. An Introduction to Big History. With a New Preface*. Berkley, CA: University of California Press.

Clanet, J. (2007). Un organisateur des pratiques d'enseignement: les interactions maitre élève(s). *Recherche et éducation, 56*, 47-66.

Clot, Y. (1999). *La fonction psychologique du travail*. Paris: Presses Universitaires de France.

Clot, Y. (2005). L'autoconfrontation croisée en analyse du travail: l'apport de la théorie bakhtinienne du dialogue. In L. Filliettaz & J.P. Bronckart (Eds.), L'analyse des actions et des discours en situation de travail. Concepts, méthodes et applications (pp. 37-55). Louvain, CH: Peeters.

Clot, Y. (2008). *Travaille et pouvoir agir*. Paris: Presses Universitaires de France.

Clot, Y., Faïta, D., Fernandes, G., & Scheller, L. (2001). Entretiens en auto-confrontation croisée: Une méthode en clinique de l'activité. *Education Permanente*, *146*(1), 17–25.

Damiano, E. (2006). *La Nuova Alleanza. Temi, problemi e prospettive della nuova ricerca didattica*. Brescia: La Scuola.

Desgagné, S. (1997). Le concept de recherche collaborative: L'idée d'un rapprochement entre chercheurs universitaires et praticiens enseignant. *Revue des Sciences de l'Education*, *2*(2), 371–393. doi:10.7202/031921ar

Dubar, C. (1998). *La socialisation. Construction des identités sociales et professionnelles*. Paris: Colin.

Dubet, F. (1994). *La sociologie de l'expérience*. Paris: Éditions du Seuil.

Faingold, N. (2011). Explicitation des pratiques, décryptage du sens. In C. Barbier, M. Hatano, & G. Le Meur (Eds.), Approches pour l'analyse des activités (pp. 111-155). Paris: L'Harmattan.

Flandin, S., & Ria, L. (2012). Vidéoformation des enseignants: apports de la didactique professionnelle. In *2ème Colloque International de Didactique Professionnelle*. Retrieved from http://didactiqueprofessionnelle.ning.com/page/colloque-2012-nantes

Fortunato, F., & Girotti, G. (2009). *Il tempo dei draghi. Per la terza classe elementare*. Milano: Minerva Italica.

Griffiths, R., MacLeod, G., & McIntyre, D. (1977). Effects of Supervisory Strategies in Microteaching on Students' Attitudes and Skill Acquisition. In D. McIntyre, G. MacLeod, & R. Griffiths (Eds.), *Investigations of Microteaching* (pp. 131–141). London: Croom Helm.

Hattie, J. A. C. (2009). *Visible learning: A synthesis of 800+ meta-analyses on achievement*. Abingdon, UK: Routledge.

Janesick, V. (2000). The choreography of qualitative research design: Minuets, improvisations, and crystallization. In N. K. Denzin & Y. S. Lincoln (Eds.), *Handbook of qualitative research* (pp. 66–81). Thousand Oaks, CA: Sage Publications.

Jorro, A. (2010). Le développement professionnel des acteurs: une nouvelle fonction de l'évaluation? In L. Paquay, C. Von Nieuwenhoven, & P. Wouters (Eds.), *L'évaluation, levier du développement professionnel?* (pp. 251–264). Bruxelles: De Boeck.

Kazemi, E., & Hubbard, A. (2008). New directions for the design and study of professional development attending to the coevolution of teachers' participation across contexts. *Journal of Teacher Education*, *59*(5), 428–441. doi:10.1177/0022487108324330

Leblanc, S., Ria, L., Dieumegard, G., Serres, G., & Durand, M. (2008). Concevoir des dispositifs de formation professionnelle des enseignants à partir de l'analyse de l'activité dans une approche enactive. *Activités (Vitry-sur-Seine)*, *5*(1), 58–78. doi:10.4000/activites.1941

Legge 107 (2015). Riforma del sistema nazionale di istruzione e formazione e delega per il riordino delle disposizioni legislative vigenti. *Gazzetta Ufficiale della Repubblica Italiana, S.G., 162*.

Lenoir, Y. (2012). La recherche collaborative entre recherche-action et recherche-partenariale: spécificités et implications pour la recherche en éducation. *Travaille et apprentissage, 9*, 13-39.

Lewin, K. (1951). *Field Theory in Social Science*. New York: Harper and Row.

Lewis, C. C., Perry, R. R., & Hurd, J. (2009). Improving mathematics instruction through lesson study: A theoretical model and North American case. *Journal of Mathematics Teacher Education*, *12*(4), 285–304. doi:10.1007/s10857-009-9102-7

Lipiansky, E. M. (1992). *Identité et communication*. Paris: PUF.

Lussi Borer, V., & Muller, A., (2014). Connaître l'activité des eneseignants en formation sur la plateforme Néopass@ction. *Recherche et formation, 75*, 65-80.

Magnoler, P., & Iobbi, V. (2015). L'insegnamento agito. *Giornale italiano della ricerca educativa, 14*, 127-139.

Magnoler, P., Pacquola, M.C., & Tescaro, M. (2014), Knowledge in action for training. *Formazione, lavoro, persona, 12*, 1-13.

Maree, K., & Van Der Westhuizen, C. (2009). *Head start in designing research proposals in the social sciences*. Cape Town: Juta and Company Ltd.

Masats, D., & Dooly, M. (2011). Rethinking the use of video in teacher education: A holistic approach. *Teaching and Teacher Education*, *27*(7), 1151–1162. doi:10.1016/j.tate.2011.04.004

Maturana, H. R., & Varela, F. J. (1987). *The tree of knowledge: The biological roots of human understanding*. New Science Library/Shambhala Publications.

Mezirow, J. (2000). *Learning as Transformation: Critical Perspectives on a Theory in Progress*. San Francisco, CA: Jossey-Bass Publishers.

MIUR. (2013). Avvio delle misure di accompagnamento delle Indicazioni nazionali 2012. Primi adempimenti e scadenze, Circolare Ministeriale n. 22. Retrieved from http://www.indicazioninazionali.it/documenti_Indicazioni_nazionali/CM_22_2013_Misure_Accompagnamento_IN.pdf

MIUR. (2014). Misure di accompagnamento per l'attuazione delle Indicazioni Nazionali per il curricolo (DM 254/2012) e per il rafforzamento delle conoscenze e delle competenze degli alunni (DM. 762/2014). Prosecuzione e avvio di nuove iniziative formative. Anno scolastico 2014-2015.Circolare Ministeriale n. 49. Retrieved fromhttp://www.indicazioninazionali.it/documenti_Indicazioni_nazionali/CM_49_19-11-2014.pdf

Morrisette, J. (2015). Une analyse interactionniste de la complémentarité des positions de savoir en recherche collaborative. *Carrefour*, *39*(1), 103–118. doi:10.3917/cdle.039.0103

Mottet, G. (1997). *La vidéo-formation. Autres regards, autres pratiques.* Paris: L'Harmattan.

Oppenheimer, S. (2003). [Interactive Map]. *Journey of mankind. The peopling of the world.* Retrieved from http://www.bradshawfoundation.com/journey/

Pastré, P. (2011). *La didactique professionnelle.* Paris: PUF. doi:10.3917/puf.faber.2011.01

Pastré, P., Mayen, P., & Vergnaud, G. (2006). La didactique professionnelle. *Revue Française de Pédagogie, 154,* 144–198.

Perrenoud, P. (2001). Le travail sur l'habitus dans laformation des enseignants. Analyse des pratiques et prise de conscience. In L. Paquay, M. Altet, E. Charlier, & Ph., Perrenoud, (Eds.), Former des enseignants professionnels. Quelles stratégies? Quelles compétences? (pp. 181-208). Bruxelles: de Boeck.

Poizat, G., Bailly, M. C., Seferdjeli, L., & Goudeaux, A. (2015). Analyse du travail et conception dans le cadre de recherches technologiques en formation: illustration sur le terrain de la radiologie médicale. In V. L. Bore, M. Durand, & F. Yvon (Eds.), *Analyse du travail et formation dans les métiers de l'éducation* (pp. 71–91). Louvain La Neuve: De Boeck.

Rabardel, P. (1995). *Les hommes et les technologies; approche cognitive des instruments contemporains.* Paris: Collins.

Ria, L. (2015). Former les enseignants au 21ème siècle. Volume 1: établissement formateur et vidéo-formation. Bruxelles: De Boeck.

Rossi, P. G. (2011). *Didattica enattiva. Complessità, teorie dell'azione, professionalità docente.* Milano: Franco Angeli.

Santagata, R. (2012). Un modello per l'utilizzo del video nella formazione professionale degli insegnanti. *Form@re-Open Journal per la formazione in rete, 12*(79), 58-63.

Santagata, R., & Guarino, J. (2011). Using video to teach future teachers to learn from teaching. *ZDM Mathematics Education, 43*(1), 133–145. doi:10.1007/s11858-010-0292-3

Schön, D. A. (1983). *The reflective practitioner: How professionals think in action.* New York, NY: Basic books.

Seidel, T., & Stürmer, K. (2014). Modeling and Measuring the Structure of Professional Vision in Preservice Teachers. *American Educational Research Journal, 4*(4), 739–777. doi:10.3102/0002831214531321

Sherin, M. G., & Van Es, E. A. (2002). Using video to support teachers' ability to interpret classroom interactions. *Society for Information Technology & Teacher Education International Conference, 2002*(1), 2532-2536.

Shulman, L. (1987). Knowledge and teaching: Foundations of the new reform. *Harvard Educational Review, 1*(1), 1–22. doi:10.17763/haer.57.1.j463w79r56455411

Stigler, J. W., & Hiebert, J. (1999). *The teaching gap: Best ideas from the world's teachers for improving education in the classroom.* New York, NY: Free Press.

Tap, P. Marquer sa différence, in J.C. Ruano-Borbalan (Ed.), L'identité: l'individu, le groupe, la société (pp. 65-68). Auxerre: Sciences Humaines.

Theureau, J. (2006). *Le cours d'action: méthode développée*. Toulouse: Octares.

Theureau, J. (2009). *Le cours d'action: méthode réfléchie*. Toulouse: Octares.

Tochon, F. (2007). From video cases to video pedagogy: a framework for video feedback and reflection in pedagogical research praxis. In R. Goldman, R. Pea, B. Barron, & S. J. Derry (Eds.), *Video research in the learning sciences* (pp. 53–65). Mahwah, NJ: Routledge.

Trinchero, R. (2002). *Manuale di ricerca educativa*. Milano: Franco Angeli.

Van Es, E. A., & Sherin, M. G. (2008). Mathematics teachers' "learning to notice" in the context of a video club. *Teaching and Teacher Education, 24*(2), 244–276. doi:10.1016/j.tate.2006.11.005

Van Es, E. A., & Sherin, M. G. (2010). The influence of video clubs on teachers' thinking and practice. *Journal of Mathematics Teacher Education, 13*(2), 155–176. doi:10.1007/s10857-009-9130-3

Van Es, E. A., Stockero, S. L., Sherin, M. G., Van Zoest, L. R., & Dyer, E. (2015). Making the Most of Teacher Self-Captured Video. *Mathematics teacher educator, 1*(4), 6-19.

Vergnaud, G. (1996). Au fond de l'action. La conceptualisation. In J. M. Barbier (Ed.), *Savoirs théoriques et savoires d'action*. Paris: PUF.

Vermersch, P. (1991). L'entretien d'explicitation. *Les cahiers de beaumont, 52 bis 53*, 63-70.

Vermersch, P. (1994). *L'entretien d'explicitation en formation initiale et en formation continue*. Paris: ESF.

Veyrunes, P., Imbert, P., San Martin, J. (2014). L'appropriation d'un format pédagogique: l'exemple du contrat de travail individuel à l'école primaire. *Éducation et didactique, 8*(3), 81-94.

Vinatier, I. (2009). *Pour une didactique professionnelle del'enseignement*. Rennes: PUR.

Vinatier, I., & Altet, M. (Eds.), (2008). *Analyser et comprendre la pratique enseignante*. Rennes: PUR.

Vinatier, I., & Pastré, P. (2007). Organisateurs de la pratique et/ou de l'activité enseignante. *Recherche et éducation, 56*, 95-108.

Von Cranach, M. (1982). *Goal-directed action*. London: Academic Press.

Ward, B. E. (1970). A Survey of Microteaching in NCATE-Accredited Secondary Education Programs. Washington, D.C.: Office of Education (DHEW).

Yin, R. K. (1984). *Case study research: Design and methods*. Beverly Hills, CA: Sage Publication.

Yoshida, M. (1999). *Lesson study: an enthnographic investigation of school-based teacher development in Japan* [Unpublished doctoral dissertation]. University of Chicago, IL.

Zeichner, K. M., & Cochran-Smith, M. (2005). *Studying teacher education: The report of the AERA panel on research and teacher education*. Mahwah, NJ: Lawrence Erlbaum Associates.

KEY TERMS AND DEFINITIONS

Analyse de Pratiques (Analysis of Practices): Training device that uses traces of practices transcribed, recorded in audio or video. The subject involved and the peer group analyze these traces. The analysis is accompanied by a trainer that encourages reflection and thoroughness.

Analyse Plurielle (Plural Analysis): Methodology for the analysis of a sequence of teaching processed by different experts (education, communication, discipline). It builds a systematic vision of teaching. It provides an overview of the methodological, epistemological, relational, pragmatic perspectives.

Co-Explicitation (Joint Explication): Comparison device between the researchers and teachers. It brings out the conceptualizations and the thinking underlying the teaching practices. It aims to lead the teacher from a thought in action to a deep consciousness of activity.

Double Vraisemblance (Double Verisimilitude): Indicates the account attributed to the result of research conducted between researchers and teachers. Interpretation and reorganization of data, produce a good result for the teachers, to manage the action: for the researcher, to feed the knowledge of the academic community.

Habitus: System of stable requirements (but not unchangeable) that develops in the socialization process experienced by each individual within a community. The habitus allows to adjust the action in relation to the context and to anticipate the sense of situations.

Outil (Tool): The word is used to identify material artifacts or concepts that allow the subject to act and condition the mode of action. The *outil* (tool) becomes an *instrument* (instrument) when it is fully internalized by the subject. It becomes transparent: it is not a gesture or a process thought intentionally, but is now a constituent part of action.

Professionalization: Development process that changes the person involved at the level of self-knowledge in action. It makes the action more effective and theoretical reference points become more founded.

Recherche Collaborative (Collaborative Research): Research model designed to teachers training. The theorists and the teachers cooperate in all phases of the process. The result is a knowledge thath changes the practice of the school community and renews the research results.

ENDNOTES

[1]   One aspect of M-T is the strict nature of the principle it aspires to (reducing a complex educational situation into segments that can develop pedagogic skills) associated with flexibility in operating methods used to proceed with identifying and handling the said segments.

[2]   The experience born of the prestructural pairing of subject and action (Theureau, 2009)

[3]   The Autoconfrontation is an analysis method of human activity that consists of placing the subject who has acted in front of the video-recording that traces his/her action so that he can analyse it and comment on it with the support of the trainer/researcher. Introduced by Von Cranach (1982) it was later taken up again by French ergonomic studies and used by Theureau in reconstructing the *Cours d'action.*

The *Autoconfrontation Croisée* (Clot, 1999; 2005; 2008; Clot, Fäita, Fernandez, & Scheller, 2001) comprises individual and collective reflection on working activity. It helps to compare the conceptions, different ways with which to fulfil a task.

4   There will be a conference in 2016 organised by OPEEN ReForm on the relationship between research and training, to focus on the current state of the relationship between observation for training,
retrived october, 10, 2015 on http://www.opeenreform.univ-nantes.fr/76446603/0/fiche___pagelibre/

.

Chapter 9

The Use of Video Recording in the Study and Conceptualization of the Didactic Transposition Process: A Case Study

Ljuba Pezzimenti
University of Macerata, Italy

ABSTRACT

This research is born of a dual interest: on one hand in the concept of didactic transposition, i.e., "the work done to manufacture a teaching object out of an object of knowledge," (Chevallard, 1985, p. 39), and on the other hand, for studying practical research and training methods for teachers, based on observation and on the study of teaching practices. This paper describes a case study in which several filmed lessons of a primary school teacher have been analysed by the author using a model to study didactic transposition that was developed following an advanced theoretical study. By then combining the video films with interviews between the researcher and teacher, the results of lesson analysis were provided to the teacher in order to raise his awareness of some of the characteristic aspects of the way in he performed the didactic transposition for the subject of history. The training aim is followed by a research aim, i.e., "assessment" by the researcher of the training or educational route achieved by the teacher. This assessment is the linchpin of this paper.

INTRODUCTION

This paper begins with an advanced theoretical study on the concept of didactic transposition, i.e., the job of transforming a body of knowledge, adapting it for a public that is not particularly expert. Following this advance study, a model was created to decode and boost understanding of didactic transposition. The model served as a framework with which to study video recordings of some lessons taught by

DOI: 10.4018/978-1-5225-0711-6.ch009

Copyright © 2017, IGI Global. Copying or distributing in print or electronic forms without written permission of IGI Global is prohibited.

primary school teachers, in order to add to their professional skills. This aim for professional expertise has been pursued by using *entretiens de co-explicitation* (ECE), i.e., interviews in which the researcher and teacher work together to conceptualize the actions, with objective indications as a starting point - in this case, video films (Vinatier, 2009, 2010; Altet, 2012, p. 305). The training objective is followed by a research aim: assessment of training by the researcher.

The development of the research is as follows.

Background: after providing an outline of the concept of didactic transposition[1], the model used to examine the constructed didactic transposition is set out, considering the aspects of the transposition process most often repeated in the theories of the authors being examined. As will be seen, this model features four perspectives or logics, each one reified by indicators. The following section explains the concepts for analysing practices and *entretien de co-explicitation*, highlighting the role that video filming can have for teacher training purposes.

The main focus of the chapter describes the author's case study of a primary school teacher. The teacher accepted to be filmed during some of his history lessons; the aim of the recordings was to study the didactic transposition process conducted by the teacher. The study was performed based on the concept of didactic device (Rossi & Toppano, 2009; Damiano, 2013) and the abovementioned model. Once the lessons had been studied by the researcher, a report was submitted to the teacher during one of the co-clarifying interviews (ECE). This was for two reasons. On one hand, because educational practice is more than the teacher's way of doing things; it is also about "the procedures for doing them" (Altet 2003, 2012), including skills and knowledge, but also aims, purposes and choices (Altet, 2012), and therefore, studying these practices for the purposes of de-codifying the transposition process could not be limited to applying the model and researcher's interpretation, dialogue with the teacher was needed to make it as complete and objective as possible. And on the other hand, to promote the teacher's professional expertise by raising awareness of the some of the aspects of his/her way of transposing the specific subject.

If the training aim was pursued through reading and study – by the teacher – of the transcripts from co-clarifying interviews, then the research aim, i.e., training assessment, was pursued through the researcher's analysis of the teacher's interpretation.

The aim of this research is therefore to focus on the way in which training through video films and co-clarifying interviews can lead to a real raising of the individual's awareness of different aspects of his/her teaching methods.

BACKGROUND

Didactic Transposition

The term didactic transposition was coined by Y. Chevallard in the mid-80s, and it is used to refer to the work of restructuring "intelligent knowledge", the knowledge produced by scientific communities for the purpose of adapting it to a public of non-experts, thereby turning it into taught and then learned knowledge. The subject of didactic transposition has been discussed from different perspectives by various authors. For a study of the authors and the perspectives forming the basis of the concept, please see Rossi, P.G., and Pezzimenti, L. (2012). Since the ongoing transposition process coincides with the activity of mediation or mediated action, as discussed by Elio Damiano in his latest work (2013); please refer to this for more information on the concept.

Reconstructing the thoughts of authors who have dealt with didactic transposition has led the author to summarise for each of them the aspects that he/she feels are characteristic of the transposition process: for example, maintaining ties between "aware knowledge" and taught knowledge (principle of epistemological vigilance); dependence of the content to be taught on the values in which the teacher believes; the idea of the way in which students learn, etc.

After analysing the different authors, all of the aspects that characterises the process of didactic transposition for each one are listed. Elements that for at least two authors represent didactic transposition, provided the logic for a model used to study this process.

Based on this model, the knowledge transposition process takes place according to four perspectives, moulded together. One such perspective is epistemological, i.e., during the knowledge transformation process, the teacher must never lose sight of the epistemological foundation of the subjects or concepts they are teaching (Chevallard, 1985). Transposed knowledge needs to maintain a link with the method, language, and fundamental and more general concepts of their subject.

A second perspective concerns values. The knowledge being taught inevitably involves values: first and foremost, ministerial programmes are drawn up based on the values of the society of the time. However, the value criteria for knowledge also depend on the personality of the teacher, who not only believes in the principles governing choice from a point of view of content or teaching, but who also transposes his or her own set of values through behaviour or in other words, *manner* (Fenstermacher, 1986).

A third viewpoint is that of didactic engineering: knowledge is transposed in class through methods and strategies (frontal lessons, dialogue lessons, discussions, clinical interview, brainstorming, group work, simulation, etc.), with didactic (active, iconic, analogue and symbolic) mediators, tools (traditional and interactive or multimedia boards, calculators, etc.), in specific areas (classrooms, gyms, gardens, etc.) and at set times, assigning specific tasks, using a set form of communication (specific examples, metaphors, discussion-opening questions, etc.).

The fourth and final perspective is what we refer to as learning or in other words, the teacher, preparing the knowledge to be taught, must have a clear idea of the psychological, physical, and cognitive development age of the students so as to adapt content to suit.

Indicators have been identified for each didactic transposition perspective or logic to guide the researcher in the study of the filmed teaching situations. These are:

- **Epistemological Logic:** Based on the subject being considered, there are elements forming its framework and derived from its epistemology. They are:
  ◦ The research methodology for the subject, also including validation criteria;
  ◦ More general concepts or epistemological nuclei of the subject;
  ◦ Specific language.
- **Value/Moral Logic:** Values enter schools first and foremost through educational aims, which are the specific dimension in which the values and culture of a society are implemented within the school. They are in fact the subject of the premises for ministerial programmes and they define the idea of citizen that society has in a given place and time, as well as the direction in which the school needs to move. During daily teaching activities, the teacher also voices values through:
  ◦ Didactic and content choices (mediators, structured learning situations, content);
  ◦ Judgement and opinions during explanations, discussions, and conceptualisation;
  ◦ "Manner" (Fenstermacher, 1986), or in other words, behaviour and attitude towards students during teaching activities;

- ◦ verbal communication, which is a transversal dimension of learning content.
- **Didactic Engineering Logic:** "Didactic engineering" is an expression coined by Guy Brousseau (1998) to describe the method used by a teacher to transpose knowledge content in class. The elements belonging to this logic are therefore:
  - ◦ Didactic mediators[2], often supported by technology;
  - ◦ **Didactic Procedures (or Didactic or Methodological Formats) and Assessment:** These identify the type of lesson that the teacher uses, depending on the type of interaction s/he decides to establish with his or her students (Laurillard, 2012; Calvani 2009);
  - ◦ Tasks, deliveries that the type of lesson or activity involves;
  - ◦ Strategies, or teaching tools, such as reading a story or using a situation as a starting point for a discussion;
  - ◦ Organisational conditions, as referred to by Marguerite Altet (2003). These concern the organisation of time, area, groups of students - essential elements of a teaching device.

When transposing knowledge, verbal communication plays an essential role; the elements that are a part of this are:

- Words or "narrative organisational ideas" used by the teacher to communicate concepts (Altet, 2003);
- Analogies, metaphors, examples, and demonstrations used by the teacher to explain concepts (Shulman, 1987). These must be adapted to the linguistic code used by the students;
- Deliveries, opening questions for a discussion, but also questions to guide a discussion.
  - ◦ **Logic of Learning:** The elements belonging to this area of interpretation concern the cognitive psychology of students, i.e., the model that represents their way of learning for the teacher, which cannot omit:
- The stages of psychomotor and cognitive development theorised by Piaget, with regard to which the teacher defines content, concepts, and subjects that s/he considers pupils will be able to understand and learn.
- According to Bruner, any concept can be understood at any age if a suitable means of communication is found for the age and subjects in question. Bruner states that school education should follow "natural" learning methods (active, iconic, and symbolic).
- The idea of the way in which students learn and how they can learn at a given age is linked to the difficulties they may encounter with regard to their ingenuous representation at that given age with regard to the content to be learned. The concept of "anchorage ideas" developed by Ausubel (1978) refers to knowledge that learners already possess about a subject and to which they connect the new content being learned.

The Purpose of Video Recording within the Analysis of Practices and the Co-Clarifying Interview (Entretien De Co-Explicitation)

Video footage has different purposes in a training environment. Santagata and Guarino (2011) sum up three of these, referring specifically to pre-service training: to foster elaborate reflection on the teaching process; to focus attention of trainees on the way in which students thinks; to help trainees to learn class practices according to the most recent guidelines. In French education too, video is mainly used to develop the analysis capabilities and training methods that are based on analysing and reflecting on practice experiences[3] and is known as analysis of practices. The idea at the basis of this method is that the teachers acquire their professional knowledge on the job, during their experience. The professional expertise of the teacher is therefore built on the development of a "meta-skill": "being able to analyse" (Altet, 1994; Altet, 2006, p. 41). To acquire this meta-skill, the teacher, with the aid of an expert tutor, must take a step back from his or her practice, reflecting on it and analysing it through "knowledge-based tools" constructed from research (Altet, 2006, p. 42). There are many ways to trace the action to be considered: written and oral narration (Mortari, 2009), audio recordings, video recordings. Video recordings doubtless provide the most objective material for the activity. Philippe Perrenoud calls video a "rugged test" but however, "due to the image …more effective than any speech when it comes to awareness, for example, of communication dilemmas." (2006, p. 195). What video makes possible more than any other tool is that which Gérard Mottet – initiator of video training experiences in France, together with Nadine Faingold – calls a dimension of "collectivisation" (1996, p. 30). Originally, this dimension took the shape of a constructed network between the *écoles normales* in which each *team* of trainers participated in permanent discussion of training practices. Subsequently, the "community dimension" became "a methodological reason" (Mottet, 1996, p. 31), both in terms of the different skills that this type of training calls to the fore, and for the possibility for trainees to share and collectively analyse practices. For Mottet, the mediation of the group "in prolonging the objectification started by the video, triggers the socialisation of the act of teaching" (1996, p. 31).

Marie Cécile Wagner stresses the way in which the video is an interesting tool in the construction of reflective practices as it allows "deferred, repeated self-observation" (2006, p. 165) stimulating reflection both individually and of the group. In fact, the video becomes "a unique reference for a remote consideration of the process brought into play" (Wagner & Paquay, 2006, p. 165).

For Sherin and others, video has the potential to provide a means of studying and developing the professional vision. Teacher's professional vision is the "ability to notice and interpret significant interactions in a classroom or classroom events relevant for student learning" (Sherin, 2001; Sherin, 2007; Sherin, Russ, Sherin, & Colestock, 2008; van Es & Sherin, 2008). Video allow teachers to look, retrospectively, excerpts of their own teaching or the teaching of colleagues and reflect on which events they consider relevant and why. For this purpose, researchers organize "video clubs" (Shering & Han, 2004; Sherin, 2007).

In this research, the possibility given by video to capture, block, and watch the action again and again, has allowed the author to make an analysis using the above model as her framework. The possibility to socialise and collectively study the filmed practices has been used within a training method that brings together the researcher's analysis with interviews with the teacher. This is the *entretien de co-explicitation* or co-clarifying interview (ECE). This means was developed by Isabelle Vinatier, *Maître de conférences* HDR in Educational Sciences at the University of Nantes.

The theoretical framework of reference for this instrument is that of "conceptualising within the action," (Vergnaud, 1990) and professional didactics (Pastré, 1997). Within professional teaching environments, reflection on one's self in action is central above all to the identification of the action frameworks that define one's *habitus* (Bordieu, 2005), i.e., which implicitly affect the behaviour and choices of the professional, mainly when s/he needs to make "urgent" decisions (Perrenoud, 2006, p. 182). The end of the interview is therefore the "conceptualisation of one's own professional practices" or rather, the "reconfiguration of the sense of the activity beginning with its traces (video recordings or transcriptions of verbal interactions), supported by the constituent elements of the framework: finding purposes, action rules, collecting information and control from the perspective of content considered to be in tension with the inter-subjective challenges inherent to every interaction situation" (Vinatier, 2010, p. 113).

Vinatier stresses how what she calls an *entretien* has nothing to do with the better-known *entretien d'explicitation* (Vermesh, 1994). The difference lies in the approach. In the *entretien d'explicitation* an external interviewer tries to conduct the professional towards evoking his or her situation through the description of a succession of "elementary actions" that the subject implements to achieve his or her aim and which regard just one aspect of the global experience (Vermesh, 1994, p. 41). In the *entretien de co-explicitation* first of all, no mention is made of "evocation", which is based on memory, but rather on conceptualisation, starting with the study of the objective traces of the activity. These are traces of the teacher's activities recorded to video or transcriptions of verbal exchanges between teacher and students during the filmed situations. The interviewer is also not an external subject but the researcher, who plays a significant role in the conceptualisation process that the professional needs to undertake.

In an interview in 1996, transcribed and translated by François Tochon, American education philosopher, Gary Fenstermacher, talks about a device that is very similar to the *entretien de co-explicitation* and which he calls the *entretien d'élucidation*. This interview, which he conducted with the teacher, aimed to reconstruct "practical subjects", i.e., the "motives for the actions of this teacher", the reasons pushing him or her to act in a given manner (Fenstermacher, 1996). For Fenstermacher, practical subjects have a moral basis and this needed to be probed in interviews. Essentially, the interviews proceeded as follows: the researcher made between 6 and 20 hours of recordings of classroom events, mainly filming the teacher. Then he or she made a copy of the whole recording for the teacher, but only for reasons of transparency. The researcher then viewed the whole recording, seeking to isolate "incidents" that in his or her opinion could be used for "debate" (Fenstermacher, 1996, p. 618). These were "incidents rich with meaning" (ibid.) that could be brought together into 25 to 45 minutes of recording that the teacher then viewed in order to discuss them. While researcher and teacher watched the video together, the researcher would ask the teacher questions. This shared viewing and discussion was also recorded to video. When the teacher began to reconstruct a practical argument through reflection, the researcher tried to ask more general questions about the coherence of the argument, giving the teacher a summary (written) of the discussion up to that moment. If the teacher agreed with the summary, this was used to commence a moral reconstruction of the action, always through questions.

The ECE devised by Vinatier aims to construct a professional identity through the interaction of researcher and teacher (Vinatier, 2009; 2010). Vinatier's method of proceeding within this device is as follows: an initial stage consisting of the development of an interview with the researcher and teacher, or the researcher- teacher -group (Vinatier, 2011) in order to understand[4] the teacher's actions, not to judge them. This occurs by setting out theoretical research and pragmatic knowledge frameworks, of experience, and therefore, by sharing knowledge, which allows neither of the two stakeholders to be above the other. Vinatier stresses that the elements for starting the conversation ("ouvreurs") are: 1) subjective tracks of work situations (filmed activities or transcriptions of verbal interaction), 2) analysis of the activities supplied by the researcher (retrieval of structuration of the situation, significant verbal occurrences, epistemic, pragmatic and relational aspects). The second stage of the co-clarifying device concerns analysis of the interview (also recorded to video and transcribed[5]) by the researcher for the purposes on one hand, of bringing out the conceptualisation of the action, and on the other, to examine the interaction dynamic between the researcher and teacher [6]. The result of this second analysis is to assess the subjects' investment in the conversation, measured through their taking the floor, the "speaking volume", and the "speaking position" of every interlocutor (Vinatier, 2010, p.116-117). Both types of interview analysis aim to define that which R. Samurçay and P. Rabardel call "constructive activity and productive activity" (2004); the former concerns the transformation of reality by the person, the latter the transformation of the person through their activities. Vinatier stresses that within the framework of the ECE, the aim is the performance of constructive activity.

The author of the contribution, partly shaping the above instrument to suit requirements, analysed the *entretiens* focusing on bringing out the conceptualisation elements of the action.

MAIN FOCUS OF THE CHAPTER

This paper is the result of a study involving three primary school teachers, each teaching history to a year 4 class. The teachers were asked for permission to film them during some of their lessons in order to capture and fix the process of their knowledge transposition in class (didactic transposition in progress) and to then discuss the recorded material together – researcher (the author of this paper) and teacher. This would serve to study and understand the specific nature of the transposition process, also for the purpose of professional enrichment. For reasons of space, only the experience of one of the three teachers has been included.

The teacher (who we will call B.) is aged between 40 and 50. B. qualified from a state Art School and after working for over 10 years in a firm as a graphic designer, he decided to leave his secure, well-paid job to follow his ambition: teaching. B. chose to get back in the game as a student too, and he registered for an Education Sciences degree at the Education Science Faculty of the University of Macerata. It is here that the author of this paper met him and asked him to take part in this research.

Of course the sample is not neutral: B. is a teacher who has accepted to try new things and to question himself, consenting to being filmed as well as to watching himself in action in order to reflect, together with the author, on his practices. We might call him a "convenience sample" (Maubant et al, 2005).

B's class is made up as follows: 19 pupils with similar backgrounds.

The films of the teacher covered a total of 10 hours, meaning 5 lessons, each two hours long.

The method used was that of the case study (Mortari, 2007) using "electronic observation" (Dupin de Saint-André, Montésinos-Gelet, & Morin, 2010, p. 167), i.e., video recordings of the teacher's practices. As well as video recordings, an initial interview was made as well as some *entretiens de co-explicitation*. The different stages of the study were: data collection, data analysis, co-clarifying interviews, analysis of the interviews, and dual formalisation of interviews. All in all, the experiment lasted 6 months.

- **Data Collection:**
  - **Interview:** The collection of data commenced with an interview with the teacher (Table 1) in order to understand, on one hand, his own idea of the meaning of history and the purpose of his teachings, and on the other, the way in which he planned a history lesson. Planning is in fact an integral part of the transposition process[7]. From a formal viewpoint, the interview was semi-structured, i.e., although there was a fixed outline, it could be varied based on the subject's answers.
  - **Video Recordings:** The second means of data collection were the video recordings of the teacher's lessons. Each film lasted two hours. The author-researcher made the films in two ways: either placing a fixed video camera at the back of the classroom, or using a mobile video camera to zoom in on some details or situations. Since the researcher was interested

in uncovering objective traces of the didactic transposition process, in agreement with the teacher, it was decided to record lessons in which different activities were performed and where the teacher's role was prominent. For example, lessons based exclusively on group work were not included.

- **Data Analysis:** To process the data, the author analysed the "observed" or "observable" data (Philippot & Niclot, 2009, p. 3) as well as the content, starting with the transcription of the interview, of some of the episodes from the video films, and the *entretiens de co-explicitation* which were also recorded to video. In practice, the analysis took the following route:

    - The author transcribed and analysed the initial interview in the light of the criteria defining the educational philosophy of a teacher (Seldin, 2004; Shulman, 1987). These are: conception of teaching and learning, didactic choices and the values guiding them, and the way in which taught subjects are conceived. These elements generally influence lesson planning. Additionally, the aspects defining educational philosophy adhere mainly to the logic of the model used to study didactic transposition. The interview allowed the author to capture the aspects of the "stated".

    - The films were watched in order to identify and describe the didactic devices put in place by the teacher. Didactic devices are understood as spatial-temporal organisation constructions for precise contexts and purposes. Within this organisation, the stakeholders (teacher and pupils) have roles in which there are activities to be performed using specific devices (Rossi & Toppano, 2009). In this study, the description of didactic devices consists of indicating the times and actions of the teacher and the actions of the students. The analysis of devices that were given names based on the activities performed within their framework, allowed the author to have a clearer picture of the teacher's work during the different lessons. It was possible to identify the devices most repeatedly employed in the filmed lessons as a whole.

    - Some episodes were then chosen for four different devices. "An episode consists of several exchanges about a subject or an action; it is the unit of communication strength" (Altet, 2003, p. 68).

    - The episodes were studied analysing verbal and non-verbal communication, didactic mediators and spatio-temporal organisation.

        - Verbal and non-verbal communication are intended as the way in which the teacher questions students, the room to talk that the teacher gives them, the explanations s/he provides, the questions s/he asks, remarks and examples s/he makes, as well as deliveries, concepts and gestures. Starting from a transcription of verbal interaction during episodes, an "interpretive analysis" was made of content (Van der Maren, 2006, p. 78) inferring the indicators of the different logic employed (Table 2).

        - There are four types of mediator: items, images situations and symbols. These make up both the transcribed and observation material. The researcher has used them to infer aspects linked to logic.

The framework for the episode analysis is ultimately the model for didactic transposition study (Table 2)

- **Data Analysis Results:**
    - **Interview:** A summary of the results from the initial interview is provided in Table 3.

- ◦ **Films:** An initial analysis of film material was used to identify the devices brought into play by the teacher. These are summarised in Table 4 (devices that are repeated have been highlighted using the same colour). A description of the devices from one lesson is included. Each device has been described by clarifying the time of use, the teacher's actions, and the students' actions (Table 5). The devices most used in the lessons taught by B. were:
  - ▪ Observation and explanation of images.
  - ▪ Reading from the text book.
  - ▪ Recovery of subjects from previous lessons.
  - ▪ Questions.

These episodes were then analysed by the author. During the experiment, some episodes contained in four of the identified devices were studied. Each episode was analysed transcribing the verbal interaction and studying this discursive material, as well as the material that could be observed using the logic of the model described in the background. An analysis is provided of extracts from episodes belonging to the device of "observing the standard of Ur on the interactive board". This analysis begins with a transcription of verbal interaction[8].

1. *Cl: Oh, lovely!*
2. *B: This way we can enlarge it and see better how it is made. Do you see? Do you remember anything we read about what it is? Who can tell me something about it?*
3. *Student: It's a flag.*
4. *B: Where was it found?*
5. *Student: In a tomb*
6. *B: Well, let's read a bit. Look up here (B. reads from the board) It is called a standard because it looks like a flag. We don't know what it was used for and there are some inlaid figures in precious materials. Do you know what 'inlaid 'means?*
7. *Francesco: Sculpted?*
8. *B: Hmmm, nooo, OK, inlaid... means that from the surface ... let's give you a simple example: it's as if I dug a hole and then filled it up again with a different material. I've inlaid it and... You can often see it on furniture; on credenzas or tables, which are flat but they have these designs created with different types of wood and these form a picture or a design. Have you ever noticed them? Yes or no?*
9. *Student: Yes*
10. *B: So, pay attention now. (reads) On one side, there are war scenes. On the other, there is a peaceful scene. Now, I'm going to ask you a question: who do you think is telling this story? The winners or the losers?*
11. *Student: The losers.*
12. *Student: The winners.*
13. *B: Put your hand up before you answer. Alex.*
14. *Alex: The winners.*
15. *B: Hmmm. You?*
16. *Francesco: The winners.*
17. *B: You?*
18. *Student: The losers.*

19. *B: The losers. What do you all think?*

Didactic mediation occurs using the interactive board, which projects the image of the standard, plus a text. Therefore, we have one iconic and one symbolic mediator. The practice of inlaying is accurately explained by B. at point 8, using art-specific terminology (as well as inlay and inlaying, B. uses the word inlaid). The digression about inlaying, starting with observation of the image and reading the text logically connects didactic engineering and epistemological logic, this latter, however, concerning art and not history.

The teacher's attitude is one of openness, welcoming all suggestions without trying to influence any answers (11-19). At line 19 the teacher asks the opinion of the majority; this again seems to show his adhesion to democratic principles and values (value logic).

The results of the data analysis were shown to the teacher during the *entretiens de co-explicitation*. During these interviews, the teacher and researcher first watched the video sequence previously analysed by the researcher. After the teacher had clarified his impressions, the researcher submitted an analysis for feedback, asking for the reasons behind certain didactic choices or for some of the behaviour. This usually led to a discussion.

All in all there were four co-clarifying interviews: the first to reflect on the results from the analysis of the interview; the second to discuss and reason on the devices brought into play by the teacher and identified by the researcher; the other two to discuss together what the researcher had identified as the devices repeated most frequently.

The *interviews*, video films and transcriptions were interpreted twice. The first time, directly by the teacher; he extrapolated various characteristic features of his teaching methods, which he then formalised. The second time, indirectly by the researcher, who researched and shed light on the formalization of the teacher, and indirectly during each ECE, pointed out words and expressions indicating a new awareness, or passages in which a conceptualisation of the action emerged. Essentially, after the training and its formalisation by the teacher, the researcher returned to this latter to analyse the aspects that represented a real new awareness for the teacher and one that could provide value and significance to the process. In this spiral reading, where the teacher analysed the interviews, the researcher analysed the teacher, and the research aim is added to that of training.

The next section looks at the results of the researcher's interpretation.

ISSUES, CONTROVERSIES, PROBLEMS

First ECE

An initial *entretien* took place to discuss the information emerging from the initial interview.

The teacher's attention was focused in particular on one aspect: the fact that no idea of history and its significance had emerged and that the discourse had shifted from the importance to the function of this discipline. Observation led him to reflect on the possible causes of this "gap" and the answer he gave is in the fact that he is the main class teacher. This is positive on one hand: on an affective and relational level, it offers the opportunity for him to be a strong, stable reference; on a teaching level, it allows him to integrate content, activity, and methods, creating interdisciplinary plans. On the other hand, however, he is unable to look at all subjects in sufficient depth. The reason for this was also traced back by the teacher to the fact that he indicated the text book as one of the central elements to his teaching. He also stated that he finds it a valid means to reconstruct the continuing theme that helps a child to re-order ideas, above all when having to study alone. However, he did stress the need for a well-structured text and of teachers making informed choices when it comes to using this tool.

Further acquired awareness through reflection on the interview involved the aims of teaching history. Specifically, the teacher realised that he had not mentioned how the teaching of this subject can influence the development of a sense of responsibility within citizens with regard to a shared heritage, although in his teaching, he often orientates his activities in this direction. The conclusion he drew is that perhaps he was doing so without the right degree of awareness.

As far as concerns the other elements from the interview, with regard to the idea of teaching-learning, the value dimension of history and teaching in general, and the didactic dimension, the teacher agreed with the findings, taking the opportunity to develop them further, and making use of authoritative, expert references. This occurred when stressing the importance of student motivation and emotional involvement for the purpose of learning, and in noting the prominence of the narration, use of irony, etc.

Second ECE

During the second co-clarifying interview, the researcher showed the teacher the diagram of devices identified during his five lessons. The researcher's aim was first of all to instil a dialogue with the teacher concerning the division made: "I don't know if you would rather call this device 'text book reading' or, as I thought, 'observation of the picture and reading/explanation'".

The first professional gain was in terms of awareness, i.e., he stated his realisation, for the first time, of aspects that characterise his classroom activity.

For the first time I was able to focus on that which Rossi calls the "granular level" and be more aware of the aspects that are characteristic of my classroom activity. I had the impression of looking at a full-colour image through a magnifying glass and perceiving, its essential components according to the principles of subtractive synthesis: granules or better still, coloured dots in yellow, cyan, magenta and black. Of course, when we look at an image with the naked eye, the dots seem to disappear, since they are not perceived individually, but absorbed into an overall view. If I were to use a metaphor, with no claims to entering the laws at the base of colour perception, my didactic devices seemed to me to be like larger dots forming an image.

The teacher stated that for the first time, he clearly understood the concept of device and its importance in the planning stages.

Since I've have been teaching, I have only ever heard talk about tools and text books, without anyone stopping to say which devices to use (there still isn't enough awareness of their use or relevant planning); in fact, they are never mentioned during the planning stages.

On the other hand, the teacher realised that although he did not know about devices, he was using them on a daily basis in his lessons. His encounter with expert knowledge allowed him to give a name to and conceptualise his experience, and when one gives a name to things, they are "born" and become clearer to the mind. At this juncture, it seems that what Maturana and Varela call 'structural coupling'

(1980, 1987) has occurred, i.e., a cognitive process that is actuated thanks to a meeting, but which is put in place independently, without one system acting directly on the other (Damiano, 2009).

From a planning viewpoint, the teacher is aware of the fact that each device has an aim and how the f-v-p [objective-variable-course] model (Rossi & Toppano, 2009), up to this point, studied in theory, underlies every device and is useful for planning and envisaging the course to be taken in class.

What the teacher acquired concerns the planning aspect of his teaching activities and this troubled him, leading him to think more deeply about what he does in the classroom, why he does it in a particular fashion, how he plans it with colleagues and on the bases of which ideas. His conclusion is that planning

… is limited to identifying the content to be taught, the underlying educational aims, targets and skills to be achieved. We agree together on the guidelines and plan the activities of the different lessons. The script is almost never expressed; it is like some cloudy sketch in the minds of individual teachers and only takes shape when the action is performed

This latter aspect for the teacher may be positive in part, as it leaves room to change an action based on student reaction. However, the script needs to be negotiated.

The teacher explained the difficulty in putting these reflections into practice since they "smash convictions and certainties, bringing out a strange feeling of incompetence"; in spite of this, he was encouraged to continue to think about the action in order to identify the motives behind the devices put into play:

- Image observation to arouse curiosity and interest;
- Preliminary conversation to arouse curiosity, activate motivation and interest, and identify students' knowledge of the subject;
- Conversation during or after the course as an incentive for dialogue and negotiating the meanings of what has been learned;
- Text book reading to provide information and ideas to think about;
- Frontal lesson to look deeper at subjects and clear up any doubts;
- Role playing as first-hand experience, learning through the body;
- Retrieval of subjects to sum up and consolidate content;
- Tests in dialogue form to boost the organisation and structuring of ideas and to involve the class group actively during oral exposure of contents.

The teacher's reflections continued for the purpose of identifying actions and strategies to arouse interest in learning and pursue the main purpose of his teaching, i.e., to "foster the development of students and provide them with learning and growth opportunities in terms of responsibility and autonomy."

Third and Fourth ECE

During the third and fourth interview, the researcher drew the teacher's attention to the devices most repeated in his lessons. The first is that of "image observation and explanation". Reflecting on his activities of didactic mediation, starting with the researcher's analysis, the teacher agreed that iconic support plays a central role here. Encouraged by the researcher to express the reasons for this, he stated that he considers images able to quickly convey feelings, emotions and knowledge, to create an immediate emotional involvement and introduce children to the context of the theme they are dealing with. For the teacher, images arouse curiosity and this is why he also uses them in Italian language lessons, to promote independent writing.

Regarding the device of "observing and explaining the standard of Ur", where the stated aim is to extrapolate information from observing a source, the researcher pointed out to the teacher how his attention was more focused on the perception of the image as an art work than as an historical source. The teacher realised what the researcher was pointing out and admitted his digression regarding inlaying techniques and the characteristics of the materials used to make the relic, using specific terms from the art world. In short, the epistemology at the base of his discourse seemed to be more about art than history.

His attitude was similar when looking at a bas-relief in the text book. In this case too, the starting point of an image and source was to serve as information about the culture of the Sumerians. After reading the caption and briefly looking at the image, the teacher went to the board and with detailed sketches, pointed out the differences between low relief, high relief and in the round. After completing this explanation, instead of continuing to look at the image, he passed straight on to reading the text. Information was therefore acquired but not reconstructed. Both teacher and researcher's thoughts on this aspect of knowledge mediation led them to reason that this action depended on the influence of the teacher's art training on his teaching[9]. This acquisition is accompanied by another that the researcher put to the teacher, summing up and reflecting his thoughts: if at times the epistemological aim seems not to be satisfied in the reconstruction of information based on sources, there is another, to date implicit for the teacher, which is that of making students understand how art has always been a favoured channel of expression for humankind.

Moreover, in spite of frequent shifts in focus from the epistemology of history to art, the teacher stated that he realised thanks to films and analysis, that he gives weight to the methodological aspect of history:

Analysing the episodes, some interesting elements emerge that emphasise and capture some aspects of my professional activity. First of all, that I do not neglect – as I thought – the methodological aspect of history; for example, during activities, I often stress the importance of sources, whether written, iconic or material.

And also, specifically, referring to the device of "image observation in the text book",

... in this activity (involving questions that lead to observation and connecting the text to the image) it can be seen that there is an aim to make pupils aware of an important methodological aspect of historical research: the reconstruction of information starting from a source.

Watching the device of "observing and explaining the standard of Ur" allowed the teacher to realise an aspect of his teaching that amazed him:

Watching the film, I am amazed by the fact that I only showed the side representing the war scene and neglected the peace scene on the other side completely. And yet, every day, I take the opportunity in class to stress peace as an essential value for civilised society. In this case, analysing the peace scene would also have served to explain the class inequality of the Sumerians and how women were excluded from social life. I think that my choice was influenced by the time variable. I think that the perception of time, together with the fear of not being able to cover all of the envisaged content is a common factor for many teachers and this inevitably affects teaching activities.

The video places the teacher's certainties about his didactic mediation in discussion and above all, the reasons why this follows a given method. It seems that a variable - in this case, time - can affect the action more than ethical beliefs.

The positive nature of the co-clarifying device lies in the possibility given to the teacher, through the researcher's prompts, to justify his choices and behaviour. One such example has already been given. On two other occasions, also within the same device, the teacher reflected on the communication method used. He justified the transmissivity characterising his artistic explanation of the standard, stating that his aim in this circumstance was to "convey the specific lexicon of art", while he criticised the questions he asked the students to help them reconstruct information starting with an image.

Looking at the episode again, I get the impression that I didn't make the most of the opportunities to "look at history by reading an image." I noticed that I asked the students some tautological questions: "Why is the king bigger?" or "Why did they show a musical instrument in the hands of one of the figures?" I didn't realise this while the lesson was going on and only now do I realise that a teacher should never ask questions that already contain an answer

This observation led the teacher to stress an important aspect of didactic communication and transposition in general, i.e., the process of problematisation of knowledge. The researcher pointed out to the teacher that the students were in any case interested in the image shown and the conversation that arose: they continued to ask questions and wanted to intervene. The teacher agreed with the researcher that this allowed them both to specify the first gain in terms of knowledge and didactic engineering: that the iconic mediator (images) is the mediator favoured by the teacher.

Reviewing and reflecting on the device of "giving the information extrapolated in groups back to the class," the researcher pointed out to the teacher how all of the pictures represented different aspects of ancient civilisation that he had constructed with his pupils were mainly figurative; the text part was reserved exclusively to the name of the indicator and the name of the civilisation that was the central focus. The space given to different indicators is filled with drawings and images cut from papers and this once again shows the importance that the teacher gives to iconic support, even unconsciously.

Also with regard to the pictures of civilisations, the researcher pointed out to the teacher an aspect that is inherent to the epistemology of the subject, i.e., that this tool (the picture of the civilisations) allows an approach to the concept of civilisation by carrying out the first of the necessary cognitive operations needed to construct historical knowledge: thematisation (Mattozzi, 2005). This was a pleasant discovery for the teacher:

I must admit that I was not fully aware of this since, as I already said, I have never attended a course in teaching history and nor have I studied the subject in depth. In the past I read articles and that is why I decided to approach our study of the great civilisations using pictures.

From the viewpoint of didactic communication used within this device, the teacher showed his prevalent orientation towards listening and intervening only for the purpose of mirroring, i.e., to specify, sum up and if necessary, ask for explanations using stimulus questions. He said that the aim of this open attitude is to promote autonomy within his students. He was also pleased to find a good atmosphere within the class, with students appearing interested and taking an active part in conversations. The teacher said that he walks between desks during this type of activity to show his closeness, to give support and encouraging smiles. Establishing a good relationship with his students is very important to him and he repeated this when he saw, within the device "observing the standard on the interactive board" "gestures that tend to reduce the natural distance put in place by the asymmetrical relationship between teacher and student, […] and in facial expressions, a communicative smile that conveys a sense of complicity with learners".

Returning to mediators, the teacher also considered analogue mediators to have a good deal of potential. This element emerges reflecting on another device: barter simulation. The researcher and teacher agreed on the importance, for understanding and learning, of hands-on experience and then returning to reflect on that experience. The teacher stressed how "pretending" involves and motivates students.

When reflecting after stimulation, the communication exchanges led to a situation in which it was possible to identify ethical aspects, specifically with the pupils' requests to express their opinion of allocating something to those who were unable to barter, and in taking final decisions as a majority. The researcher pointed out to the teacher how his attitude on the one hand conveyed democratic values (the teacher also made explicit references to democracy when asking the opinions of students) and on the other, expressed the attention of each member of the class and therefore, the value of each individual. The teacher was pleased to hear this and said that in fact, he is a firm believer in democracy, which he tries to transpose whenever the occasion arises.

Usually I involve them in all of the events concerning class activities and decisions are taken following a majority vote. I think this is a good way to convey and interiorise the type of behaviour suited to our future "democratic citizens," who will be freely and independently able to make choices, taking on board the requests of others.

With regard to the attention to the wellbeing and satisfaction of all pupils, after expressing his pleasure at this observation, the teacher referred to an expert source to stress the importance of the attitudes adopted by teachers in class, since these will form learners' future behaviour

With regard to value logic, I am pleased to hear your remarks when you stress my attitude as an expression of the value I place on the whole class without exception. And when you say my "manner", to coin a term used by Fenstermacher (1986), demonstrates two character virtues that can help to form the personalities of pupils: generosity and attention to the wellness of everyone. A teacher's behaviour transmits values and therefore, to make sure that pupils behave in a certain way, the teacher needs to behave in the way he would like them to do. I think this is an essential aspect and one that all teachers need to think about in order to focus more on all of the attitudes that they often, implicitly and involuntarily, adopt in class.

This section was concluded stating the problems encountered in the implementation of the experience described and mainly inherent to the use of video.

1. Initial distrust by the teacher of the video film. During the one of the interviews, the teacher mentioned that when he had heard video recordings and analysis of practices mentioned for the first time, he had said to himself that he would never have been willing to participate in such "treatment", mainly because of fear of judgement from academics.

    a. *I can remember three elements that made me uneasy: a sense of inadequacy, a lack of familiarity with the researcher and the idea that my statements would be recorded […] I think that the emotional aspect was not completely irrelevant. Initially I went through this experience with the same feelings as a student going into an exam. I was unconsciously waiting for a value judgement that of course never came; that was definitely not the aim of the research.*

2.   Lack of spontaneous behaviour due to the presence of the video camera. The external observer, complete with video camera, is not neutral (Beaugrand, 1988). During the interviews, the teacher mentioned more than once that the presence of the video camera probably inhibited some of his behaviour.

    a.   *Although I firmly believe in the value of humour and irony ... seeing the video of my lessons, I was surprised that I did not pick up on many episodes where the communication was ironic, which usually I do. I wondered about this aspect and I asked myself if I was perhaps put off by the presence of the video camera and by a fear of looking less than serious and professional.*

    b.   *The tone is calm and the modulation is doubtless inhibited by the presence of the video camera. I usually love to play about with my voice, changing my tone to arouse curiosity, emphasise, problematize and play down elements.*

    c.   *Usually, during activities, I walk about between the desks even more; to show my "closeness", give my support to those who need it, and to give out some encouraging smiles. In this case too, the camera must have put me off.*

3.   The analysis is like the researcher's interpretation, although in this case, it begins with an objective tracing of the action[10].

SOLUTIONS AND RECOMMENDATIONS

The possible solutions to the problems listed above are:

1.   Establishing a relationship of trust, respect and honesty between the researcher and the teacher, convincing and reassuring the latter that the purpose of analysing his practices is not a value judgement. From the words of the teacher at the end of the experience, it seems that this type of relationship was created.

The attitude of L. (researcher) was in any case very discreet, welcoming and extremely patient. In the workplace she showed herself to be a person of great human depth. Her attitude was mainly focused on listening, sharing and collaboration so as to create the right space to allow me to analyse, reflect, describe and capture thoughts, feelings, sensations, perplexities, emotions and gradually become more aware of my teaching style.

The author's opinion is that humanity and attention to relations are the first elements to look after in experiences such as this one, where the identity and professionalism of the teacher are involved.

2.   Duration of the video filming experience for a longer amount of time; i.e., it is thought that there should be at least 5 filming sessions, each lasting a couple of hours, at a distance of 1-2 days from one another. In this way, the teachers and pupils will become used to the camera and pay it less and less attention. It is also easier to highlight routines and recursive behaviour modes in this way.

3.   Dialogue between researcher-teacher within interviews such as the ones described and/or triangula-
     tion of data, i.e., data analysis by more than one researcher. At the end, shared interpretation and
     highlighting of shared elements.

CONCLUSION

The use of video in this study first of all allowed the researcher to try out the theoretical model, through
delayed analysis of real didactic transposition situations.

The use of the *entretien de co-explicitation* as a device to foster professionalisation based on reflection
and beginning with objectively tracing actions, has allowed the researcher to compare, together with the
teacher, her own analysis of the teacher's transposition process. This comparison and shared discussion
have led researcher and teacher to identify some of the teacher's routines, of which this latter was either
partially or completely unaware.

First of all, the teacher becomes aware of the more characteristic actions in his teaching method;
thanks to analysis of these actions, scanning the devices brought into play. Coming into contact with
the concept of devices enlightens the teacher with regard to a planning method that, in his opinion, is
not used in school. In this method, the different elements (aims, objectives, tools, activities, etc.) need
to be coherently connected in a context.

From an epistemological viewpoint of historical knowledge, the teacher has acquired the following: 1) being orientated towards a specific aim, to make the extent of artistic heritage understood as a
communications channel for people of all periods and therefore, a means of finding out about the past.
2) Focusing on the main methodological aspect of history: reconstruction of information commencing
with observation of sources (mainly iconographic). 3) Performing that which is, from the epistemological viewpoint of history, the first operation needed for research and study in this field: thematisation.

From a didactic engineering viewpoint, what the teacher has mainly acquired has involved the following:

1.   Use of the icon as a privileged mediator due to its impact, as it intrigues and engages;
2.   The ability to create didactic communication that can create a climate of faith and participation
     (connection with value logic);
3.   The sometimes insufficient activity of knowledge problematisation.

With regard to ethical logic, there are gains in terms of:

1.   Ability to create a positive atmosphere, thanks to a communications model based on listening and
     trust (connection with the logic of didactic engineering);
2.   The importance given to the value of democracy;
3.   The good deal of attention to personal behaviour, since this will form student behaviour.

This experience has allowed the author to ascertain how the co-clarification model enables the
occurrence of a "transformation" in the teacher[11], due to a meeting of research-based knowledge and
experience-based knowledge (Vinatier, 2009; 2010). This transformation is not so much a change in the
teacher's action as the ability to give a name, a theoretical framework, to their professional behaviour.
This type of transformation, which depends on the person, although it stems from a meeting with another

person and boosts the power of action of both, is known as structural coupling (Maturana & Varela, 1987; Damiano, 2009).

From a methodological viewpoint, it has emerged that the success of interviews depends on there being a climate of trust between the researcher and the teacher, and on conceptualisation being the result of instigation, reflection and discussion.

Ultimately, spiral interpretation of the path[12] shows real gains in terms of knowledge concerning personal teaching methods, which then gives a sense and value to professionalisation processes based on reflecting on one's own actions, starting with the objective traces provided by the video.

REFERENCES

Altet, M. (1994). *La formation professionnelle des enseignants*. Paris: PUF.

Altet, M. (1996). Les dispositifs d'analyse des pratiques pédagogiques en formation d'enseignants: une démarche d'articulation pratique-théorie-pratique. In C. Blanchard-Laville & D. Fablet (Eds.), L'analyse des pratiques professionnelles, (pp. 11-26). L'Harmattan: Paris.

Altet, M. (2003). *La ricerca sulle pratiche d'insegnamento in Francia*. Brescia: La Scuola.

Altet, M. (2006). Le competenze dell'insegnante-professionista: saperi, schemi d'azione, adattamenti ed analisi. In Altet M., Charlier E., Paquay L., Perrenoud P. (Eds.), Formare gli insegnanti professionisti. Quali strategie? Quali competenze? (pp. 31-44). Roma: Armando.

Altet, M. (2012). L'apporto dell'analisi plurale dalle pratiche didattiche alla co-formazione degli insegnanti. In P.C. Rivoltella, P.G. Rossi (Eds.), L'agire didattico. Manuale per l'insegnante, (pp. 291-312). Brescia: La scuola.

Ausbel, D. (1978). *Educazione e processi cognitivi: guida psicologica per gli insegnanti*. Milano: Franco Angeli.

Beaugrand, J. (1988). Observation directe du comportement, in M. Robert (Ed.), Fondements et étapes de la recherche scientifique en psychologie (pp. 277-310). Saint-Hyacinthe: Edisem.

Bourdieu, P. (2005). *Il senso pratico*. Roma: Armando.

Brousseau, G. (1998). *Théorie des Situations Didactiques*. Grenoble: La pensée sauvage.

Bruner, J. S. (1999). *Verso una teoria dell'istruzione*. Roma: Armando.

Calvani, A. (2013). *Principi dell'istruzione e strategie per insegnare. Criteri per una didattica efficace*. Roma: Carocci.

Chevallard, Y. (1985). *La transposition didactique. Du savoir enseignant au savoir enseigné*. Grenoble: La Pensée Sauvage.

Damiano, E. (2013). *La mediazione didattica. Per una teoria dell'insegnamento*. Milano: Franco Angeli.

Damiano, I. (2009). *Unità in dialogo. Un nuovo stile per la conoscenza*. Milano: Bruno Mondadori.

Dupin de Saint-Andre, M., Montesinos-Gelet, I., Morin, M.-F. (2010). Avantages et limites des approches méthodologiques utilisées pour étudier les pratiques enseignantes, *Nouveaux cahiers de la recherche en éducation*, 13(2), 159-176.

Fenstermacher, G. (1986). Philosophy of research on teaching: Three aspects. In M. C. Wittrock (Ed.), *Handbook of research on teaching* (pp. 37–49). New York, NY: Macmillan.

Kerbrat-Orecchioni, C. (1990). *Les interactions verbales* (Vol. 1). Paris: Armand Colin.

Laurillard, D. (2012). *Teaching as a Design Science: Building Pedagogical Patterns for Learning and Technology*. New York, NY: Routledge.

Mattozzi, I. (2005). *Un curricolo per la storia*. Bologna: Cappelli Editore.

Maturana, H. R., & Varela, F. G. (1980). *Autopoiesis and Cognition*. Dordrecht: Reidel. doi:10.1007/978-94-009-8947-4

Maturana, H. R., & Varela, F. J. (1987). *L'albero della conoscenza*. Milano: Garzanti.

Maubant, P., Lenoir, Y., Routhier, S., Auraujo Oliveira, A., Lisee, V., & Hassni, N., 2005, L'analyse des pratiques d'enseignement: le recours à la vidéoscopie, *Les dossiers des sciences de l'éducation*, 14, 61-93.

Mortari, L. (2007). *Cultura della ricerca e pedagogia*. Roma: Carocci.

Mortari, L. (2009). *Ricercare e riflettere. La formazione del docente professionista*. Roma: Carocci.

Mottet, G. (1996). Du voir au faire. Le trajet de la vidéo-formation, *Recherche et formation*, 23, 29-54.

Paquay, L., & Wagner, M.-C. (2006). Competenze professionali privilegiate negli stage in video-formazione. In Altet M., Charlier E., Paquay L., Perrenoud P. (Eds.), Formare gli insegnanti professionisti. Quali strategie? Quali competenze? (149-174). Roma: Armando.

Pastré, P. (1997), Didactique professionnelle et développement, *Psychologie française*, 42(1), 89-100.

Perrenoud, P. (2006). Il lavoro sull'habitus nella formazione degli insegnanti. Analisi delle pratiche e presa di coscienza. In Altet M., Charlier E., Paquay L., Perrenoud P. (Eds.), Formare gli insegnanti professionisti. Quali strategie? Quali competenze? (175-200). Roma: Armando.

Philippot, T., & Niclot, D. (2009). La professionnalité des enseignants de l'école primaire en France: une démarche qualitative. In Actes du 2ème colloque international francophone sur les méthodes qualitative. Lille.

Rossi, P. G., & Pezzimenti, L. (2012). La trasposizione didattica In P.C. Rivoltella, P.G. Rossi (Eds.), L'agire didattico. Manuale per l'insegnante (pp. 167-184). Brescia: La scuola.

Rossi, P. G., & Toppano, E. (2009). *Progettare nella società della conoscenza*. Roma: Carocci.

Samurçay, R., & Rabardel, P. (2004). Modèles pour l'analyse de l'activité et des compétences. In R. Samurçay & P. Pastré (Eds.), *Recherches et pratiques en didactique professionnelle*. Toulouse: Octarès.

Santagata, R., & Guarino, J. (2011). Using video to teach future teachers to learn from teaching. *ZDM Mathematics Education*, 43(1), 133–145. doi:10.1007/s11858-010-0292-3

Seldin, P. (2004). *The Teacher Portfolio*. Bolton, MA: Anker Publishing.

Sherin, M. G. (2001). Developing a professional vision of classroom events. In T. Wood, B. S. Nelson, & J. Warfield (Eds.), *Beyond classical pedagogy: Teaching elementary school mathematics* (pp. 75–93). Hillsdale, NJ: Erlbaum.

Sherin, M. G. (2007). The development of teachers' professional vision in video clubs. In R. Goldman, R. Pea, B. Barron, & S. Derry (Eds.), *R. Goldman, R. Pea, B. Barron, & S. Derry, Video research in the learning sciences* (pp. 383–395). Hillsdale, NJ: Erlbaum.

Sherin, M. G., & Han, S. (2004). Teacher learning in the context of a video club. *Teaching and Teacher Education*, *20*(2), 163–183. doi:10.1016/j.tate.2003.08.001

Sherin, M. G., Russ, R. S., Sherin, B. L., & Colestock, A. (2008). Professional Vision in Action: An Exploratory Study. *Teaching Education*, *17*(2), 27–46.

Shulman, S. L. (1987). Knowledge and Teaching: Foundations of the New Reform. *Harvard Educational Review*, *57*(1), 1–21. doi:10.17763/haer.57.1.j463w79r56455411

Van der Maren, J.-M. (2006), Les recherches qualitatives: des critères variés de qualité en fonction des types de recherche. In L. Paquay, M. Crahay, J.-M. De Ketele (Eds.), L'analyse qualitative en éducation. Des pratique de recherche aux critères de qualité, (69-84). Bruxelles: De Boeck.

van Es, E. A., & Sherin, M. G. (2008). Mathematics teachers "learning to notice" in the context of a video club. *Teaching and Teacher Education*, *24*(2), 244–276. doi:10.1016/j.tate.2006.11.005

Vergnaud, G. (1990). La Théorie des champs conceptuels. *Recherches en Didactique des Mathématiques*, *10*, 2–3, 134–169.

Vermersch, P. (1994). *L'entretien d'explicitation en formation initiale et en formation continue*. Paris: ESF.

Vinatier, I. (2009). *Pour une didactique professionnelle de l'enseignement*. Rennes: PUR.

Vinatier, I. (2010). L'entretien de co-explicitation entre chercheur et enseignants: une voie d'émergence et d'expression du "sujet capable". *Recherches en éducation*, 1, 111-130.

KEY TERMS AND DEFINITIONS

Conceptualisation of Actions: Reconstruction of the sense of the action.

Didactic Action: Teaching activities.

Didactic Mediation: Teaching conceived as the structuring of an environment in which the pupil can enter into a relationship with the fields of knowledge and learn them actively. It is the opposite of transmission.

Didactic Transposition: The work of restructuring knowledge so that students can understand and learn it.

Entretiens de Co-Explicitation: Interviews between the researcher and the teacher, based on objective traces of an action, for the purpose of reflecting on it and constructing the teacher's professional identity.

Reflexivity: The ability to distance oneself from one's own actions in order to study and conceptualise them.

Study of Practices: Training method based on watching and group discussion of own videotaped lessons.

Teacher Practice: The teacher's method, understood as his or her personal method of transferring knowledge and of managing a class, but also the total of knowledge and skills required to teach.

ENDNOTES

[1]   For an even larger picture of the study of this concept, see Rossi, P.G., & Pezzimenti, L (2012). Didactic transposition in P.C. Rivoltella, P.G. Rossi (Eds.), *L'agire didattico. Manuale per l'insegnante*, (pp. 167-184). La scuola: Brescia.

[2]   For a detailed look at didactic mediators, see Damiano, E. (2013). *La mediazione didattica. Per una teoria dell'insegnamento*. Milano: Franco Angeli.

[3]   A teaching practice is "the way of being a teacher" as well as "the procedures to follow" (Altet 2003, 2012)

[4]   I.e. to reconfigure it conceptually

[5]   The *entretien* is analysed by splitting it into episodes. Each episode corresponds to the identification of a subject (Vinatier, 2010, p. 115).

[6]   The theoretical, interactional approach used by Vinatier is the one developed by C. Kebrat-Orecchioni (1990).

[7]   . French didacts and educational theorists see didactic transposition as the planning stage preceding the action.

[8]   KEY: B = teacher; student = student who cannot be identified in the recording; Cl. = class, when the students' voices overlap and it is not possible to see where they come from; […] = omitted parts of the text.

[9]   The teacher has an art high school diploma and worked as a textile graphic designer for ten years.

[10]   "The researcher observes a class situation conceived and implemented by someone else; s/he collects information […], records it […] but also sees actions for which s/he does not understand the reason. From this comes the question of the meaning s/he can give to what s/he sees." (Niclot, 2009, p. 5).

[11]   A process of change also occurs within the researcher.

[12]   The teacher interpreted and studied the co-clarifying interviews; the researcher studied the teacher's interpretation.

APPENDIX

Table 1. Initial interview

What is the history for you? What is the specificity of this subject?
How do you give information to your students in order to avoid that they will accept such information like an absolute truth?
What's/are the formative purpose/s of history?
For you, what are the fundamental thematic nucleuses of history that should be addressed in your class?
How do you give sense to the history during the lesson? How do you make significant the history teaching for students?
Do you think that what makes the history significant for students coincides with the educational purpose of history?
Usually how do you design a history lesson? Where do you start?
How do you choose the contents/topics?
How do you document yourself?
In your opinion, which are the limits and potential of your way to organise lessons and, in general, to "do" history at school?

The framework for the episode analysis is ultimately the model for didactic transposition study.

Table 2. Framework for episode analysis

Logics	Indicators
1. Epistemological logic 2. Value/moral logic 3. Didactic engineering logic 4. Logic of learning	1. More general concepts or epistemological nuclei of the subject; 1. Specific language; 2. Didactic and content choices (mediators, structured learning situations, content); 2. Judgement and opinions during explanations, discussions, and conceptualisation; 2. "Manner": Behaviour and attitude towards students during teaching activities; 3. Didactic mediators, often supported by technology; 3. Didactic procedures (or didactic or methodological formats) and assessment: Type of lesson; 3. Tasks, deliveries that the type of lesson or activity involves; 3. Strategies, or teaching tools, such as reading a story or using a situation as a starting point for a discussion; 3. Organisational conditions: Organisation of time, area, groups of students - essential elements of a teaching device. 3. Words or "narrative organisational ideas" used by the teacher to communicate concepts; 3. Analogies, metaphors, examples, and demonstrations used by the teacher to explain concepts; 3. Deliveries, opening questions for a discussion, but also questions to guide a discussion; 4. Consideration of the stages of psychomotor and cognitive development and the "natural" learning methods (active, iconic, and symbolic); 4. The students ingenuous representations.

Table 3. Interview analysis summary

Teaching-Learning Idea	Value Dimension and Aims	Didactic Dimension (Strategies, Methods)	Essence of History and Teacher's Relationship with Historical Knowledge	Philosophy and Epistemology of History
• Learning implies emotional involvement; this can be obtained through awareness of what is going to be done; the teacher relates his own personal experiences; gradualness; knowledge itself. • Outline of a constructivist perspective of learning.	• Purpose of history: development of critical ability • through perception of the relevant viewpoints, awareness of the conventional nature of some terms, ideas, and information. Aims of teaching in general: • to approach life situations with philosophy and irony; to question self, starting with the input that study can give • Value point of view: • the non-absoluteness of values but at the same time, the existence of values that remain constant and which are transmitted.	• Dialogue (discussion-conversation) and the use of texts as central elements in teaching; providing • many examples; using humour and "speaking with metaphors"; talking about personal experience. • Planning. • Considering: o Aims, o Materials, o Class needs. • The teacher uses many sources and materials in his preparation.	• History is knowledge of origins to direct the future. • Relationship with knowledge: • for B. history was absolute truth, there were absolute values.	

Table 4. Study of devices

Lesson 05_11_'10	Lesson 12_11_'10	Lesson 19_11_'10	Lesson 26_11_'10	Lesson 28_01_'11
Recovery of subjects from previous lessons	Explanation of how the lesson will be carried out and recovery of subjects from previous lessons	Looking at and explaining the standard of Ur as projected on an interactive board (and reading of the descriptions and captions. Participatory explanations	Return of group work	Test on Egyptian civilisation
Reading of text book. Looking at and explaining the pictures in the text book with reading of the captions and Participatory explanations	Simulation of the ancient practice of barter	Colouring and completion activities using photocopies of the standard of Ur		Looking at a conceptualised map of Egyptian civilisation on the interactive board.
	Guided reflection activities on the simulated bartering	Group work: reading and identification of the most important information		
	Simulation of the practice of tax collection			
	Guided reflection activities on the simulated tax collection			
	Reading of text book and Participatory explanation			
	Written comprehension questions about the ziggurat			

Table 5. Description of devices used in the lesson on 19_11_2010

20': Looking at the Standard of Ur on the Interactive Board and Participatory Explanation	
Teacher	**Students**
• Reads a description of the standard in the projected text. • Provides a more detailed explanation with more information. • Asks questions needing reflection ("What do you think?", "Why?"). • Invites students to note down information.	• Look. • Listen. • Begin to complete the photocopy of the standard with the information they have on the interactive board. • Answer the questions. • Intervene spontaneously and ask questions.
22': Colouring and Completion of the Photocopy of the Standard of Ur with the Colours and Information Shown on the Interactive Board	
Teacher	**Students**
• Cuts out the sheets for successive activities. • Answers questions from the students while they colour. • Asks more questions.	• Colour the photocopy observing the standard on the interactive board. Ask questions spontaneously about what has been seen and said.
15': Group Work: Reading of a short Text from a Different Book than the Text Book and Identification of the Most Important Information to Refer to Classmates	
Teacher	**Students**
• Splits pupils into groups of 3 and gives each group two or three pages, selected and photocopied from different texts on subjects regarding Sumerian society (homes, discoveries …). • Gives indications about what to do. • Passes among groups to help pupils to highlight the main information.	• Read. • Discuss the information to be underlined

Chapter 10
Video–Analysis and Self–Assessment in Teaching Work

Loredana Perla
Università degli Studi di Bari, Italy

Nunzia Schiavone
Università degli Studi di Bari, Italy

ABSTRACT

Video-research, which represents a multi-methodological practice and an interdisciplinary study area, responds to various knowledge problems created by the complexity of the didactic phenomena to be investigated, and proposes instruments and technologies that have a very high potential about phenomena description, reproduction and comprehension, not only for researchers but also for teachers themselves who are the protagonists of those phenomena. Starting by these preliminary remarks, this chapter will be focused on the introduction of the preliminary results of a video-research itinerary achieved by the DidaSco group (School Didactics) throughout a project itinerary that involved six infant, primary and secondary (first degree only) schools in Bari and its province, working on History didactics intermediary processes. In the meantime, in this chapter a particular attention will be paid to the introduction of a video analysis form which was realized by the authors.

INTRODUCTION

Can teachers' professionalism be assessed? If so, which tools should be used? What theoretical frameworks should be considered?

This paper[1] aims at providing a potential answer to the important issues raised in Italy after the ratification of the Regulation on the National Education Assessment System (Italian Republic Presidential Decree 80/2013), even though these questions have been involving the educational scientific community for almost a century. Art. 6 of the Decree associates the assessment procedure of school institutions with actions that may enhance the role of schools in self-assessment procedures, thus recognising the primary role of this kind of actions. No assessment procedures can be scientifically recognised if they are not included in self-assessment and quality-based methodologies (Perla, 2004). The same criteria

DOI: 10.4018/978-1-5225-0711-6.ch010

Copyright © 2017, IGI Global. Copying or distributing in print or electronic forms without written permission of IGI Global is prohibited.

were established by the European Commission in the Recommendation of the European Parliament and the European Council (February 12, 2001) on the assessment of quality in teaching; this document introduced some guidelines on assessment and self-assessment procedures in the school system, recommending Member States to support effective systems for quality assessment by means of self-assessment methods[2]. In Italy, the Regulation of the National Education Assessment System has been ratified twelve years after the EU recommendation. It affirmed the relevance of the connection between self-assessment and external evaluation, and the resulting relationship between self-assessment and enhancement of quality in school systems[3].

It should be reminded that the in last two decades the assessment of teachers' conduct has been increasingly taken into consideration, as the interest for teachers' evaluation increased. The initial and ongoing teachers' training quality has been recognised as a key factor by institutions like OECD, UNESCO and the European Commission, which have carried out broad research (EC 2005; 2012; OECD, 2005; 2013a, Dordit, 2011). Among the research on teachers' assessment (like *Teaching and Learning International Survey, TALIS*[4]), in 2009 OECD carried out a research to analyse assessment policies and practices for schools, students, teachers (OECD, 2013b).

At present, in Italy the issue of teachers' assessment is part of the political, scientific and professional debate. There is a transition from a period in which teachers' assessment was missing towards a delicate stage in which some methodologies are even superficial and intrusive (Previtali, 2012). The risk for polarisation is a serious issue. Assessing teachers' actions is not a mere certification, and it has to consider the practical point of view in research (Perla, 2010). Enhancement processes in schools cannot be triggered without the active co-participation of the professional community in the actions and projects that aim at assessing teachers' actions. This implies the pressing achievement of theoretical-methodological frameworks that consider the specific, professional features of Italian teachers and can be consistent in identifying assessment criteria to evaluate teachers' actions, including their relating and effective tasks.

In this paper we would try to support an argumentation: assessing teachers' actions is the same side of the identical question, that is the achievement of a system that could ensure and direct towards teachers' lifelong training; a system that could rely on scientifically valid tools that could trigger a "triangulation" of different points of view (teachers, researchers, students) on the same element. One of these innovative tools is represented by video-analysis, as described in a following section.

If innovative training is considered the starting point for teachers' professional enhancement, an effective assessment process can be carried out. This choice is intentional, and it is connected with an independent decision made by each school, being only partially managed by external agents. It should start from the promotion of recognised training for career-oriented aims (as hinted by the Italian Decree 107, July 13, 2015), with scientific grounds (therefore it should be carried out in partnership with Universities and/or research institutions) and aimed at the differentiation of teachers' professional profiles.

Training is a "strategic lever" for assessment procedures, and it should be a system action within which meritocracy is awarded and teachers' professional careers are supported. Only in this way assessment actions could stimulate the "hunger" for professional enhancement, thus having comebacks in terms of productivity in ordinary education practices. The system should be organised following the steps shown in Figure 1.

Training is a way to enhance teachers' competence, and a spur for innovation. In turn, innovation is meaningful if it is seen in relation to teachers' training needs and not as a formal adaptation to the normative framework. The internalisation of an innovative process can only spring from the experience-based research, the knowledge of experience, the analysis of one's actions. Innovation is included in four

Figure 1. Steps for assessment procedures

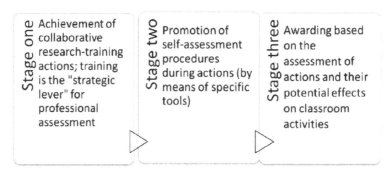

strategic aims mentioned in the Programme "Education and Training 2020 - ET 2020" ratified in the concluding remarks of the European Council in May 12, 2009 and part of a strategic plan for European cooperation in training and education; innovation is one of the "duties" of the education systems that "monitors the smooth functioning of the knowledge-based triangle represented by education/research/ innovation".

TEACHERS' SELF-ASSESSMENT FOR PROFESSIONAL DEVELOPMENT

It is a well-known fact that almost all teaching staff think that taking part in training or (individual or group) research activities is the most influencing feature in the development of the professional quality in their job (Talis, 2013). Earliest research on education assessment in the 1920s aimed at finding predictive variables which could lead up to effective teaching methods in order to suggest adequate modalities for teachers' recruitment; product-related variables were also considered according to which students' results represent the most reliable marker to assess education effectiveness[5]. Therefore, there is the need to find out the best requisites for educators based on the recurring features and on the results achieved by excellent students[6]. In this branch of research, the main focus was on teachers rather than on their actions in terms of personal and professional judgement. There was also an underlying reason of "control" in order to carry out a preliminary selection or to identify excellence or inadequacy rather than enhancing teachers' professional performance. In those models there was an external perspective - researchers or recruitment institutions - without a direct involvement of teachers in the assessment process.

As these assumptions were overturned, the main assessment focus reverted on teaching processes and on the actual behaviours held by teachers and students in their class activities. Teaching actions were becoming a specific assessment marker within an evaluation perspective which aimed at involving teachers in their professional actions (Damiano, 1993). The preliminary results achieved by assessment-based research dealt with the creation of several "teaching analysis systems" (Dussault et al., 1976; Ballanti, 1975, 1979, 1980) in the 1940s and were based on the behaviourist paradigm. As Dussault puts it, this is defined as "a tool in order to observe, denominate, classify, assess and interpret different observable phenomena in school environments" (Dussault et al., 1947, p. 49). Irrespective of the differences in the theoretical planning and operational equipment, these approaches aimed at developing models of "professional self-assessment" that let researchers describe their own teaching method in order to enhance it.

On the other hand, assessment procedures for the professional development of teachers, usually an internal procedure within schools and not controlled at a national level, refer to a training-related assessment that helps teachers to reflect and to learn by identifying both strong and weak points of teaching and providing them with feedbacks in order to enhance educational practices (Pellegrini, 2014). We are fully convinced that in order to develop a project on school assessment it is important to consider the most important element that makes the difference and qualifies school activities, that is teachers' professional competence, the latter being developed during one's whole professional career as it allows a lifelong enhancement. From this perspective, concrete results would follow. In a perspective of professional development, considering ongoing training as the main focus in teachers' assessment means analysing their training-related implications (Damiano, 2005, Previtali, 2012); this means that evaluation is a device for educational mediation (Damiano, 2013) that is needed to shift from a skilled experience to a pondered experience in order to acquire the so called "meta-professionalism" that should qualify the role of teachers (Schon, 1993). In the background there is a vision of training as a reflection on professional practices (Altet, Vinatier, 2008; Altet, 1999, 2006, 2008; Damiano, 2006; Perla, 2010, 2011, 2012) and teachers' supervision (Sergiovanni, Starrat, 2003) that need observable procedures and tools that distance from experience. The topic of teachers' self-assessment is closely related to the "referentiality process" of professional competence (Coulet, 2007, 2010, Samurcay, Rabardel, 2004; Perrenoud, 1999, Perla, 2011) which, starting from the analysis of teachers' activities, aims at defining teachers' professional competence in a four-point scheme (organisation of activities): operational invariants, inferences, action rules, anticipations (Vergnaud, 1990). All these elements aim towards a "production-related activity". From a theoretical point of view, in this paper we focused our attention on the self-training, follow-up "tools" that make teachers independent in different stages such as the phenomenology description and the multi-dimensional analysis of educational practices. The second part of this paper is dedicated to the analysis of the correlation between self-assessment and professional development, as well as the investigation of a specific tool for analysis and reflection of educational practices in a self-assessment perspective.

VIDEO-ANALYSIS AS A SELF-ASSESSMENT TOOL FOR TEACHERS

Video-analysis has been representing a field with a strong tradition. The early attempts of this methodology, called *microteaching*, took place at Stanford University (Allen, 1966); then, video contents were used to enhance *teacher effectiveness* (Orme, 1966) and lately they have been used for teachers' initial and ongoing training (Blomberg, Stürmer & Seidel, 2011; Santagata, Guarino, 2011; Seidel, Stürmer, 2014). Video techniques are versatile methodologies and they may be used in several training and research studies with different aims: a) learning practices; b) the enhancement of teachers' disciplinary knowledge, observation, a personal vision of one's professional career, peer comparison, documentation of results and educational processes. Video contents may be also used to analyse and meditate on some specific contexts and actions: video footage, if analysed together with researchers, may represent a valuable starting point to favour both explicit and auto-assessment processes[7]. In this sense, it has to be underlined that video-analysis as a multi-methodology practice and an interdisciplinary field of study (Goldman, Pea, Barron, Derry 2007) is useful to provide an answer to complex educational phenomena, as well as it provides tools and technologies with a high potential of description and understanding of different phenomena. Both researchers and teachers may benefit from this methodology. Videos, indeed, stimulate the metacognitive and the reflective dimensions on educational practices. In this perspective, during the observation of the different stages of the training protocol of video analysis, there are some variables to be considered:

- *Finalisation variables, which consider educational aims (socialisation, metacognition);*
- *Technical variables, that is the "professional actions" and all designing, assessment, organisation features;*
- *Communicative variablesconveyed by verbal and non-verbal codes;*
- *Contextualisation variables connected with the so called "school culture";*
- *Relational variables, including all educational practices: guiding, care, personalisation, listening.*

There are also other students' variables which can be analysed by means of questions focused on students' learning and on questions dealing with progresses and/or regressions that can be identified during video analyses. Each of these variables can be analysed through observation protocols which can enhance teachers' educational strategies (Rossi-Rivoltella, 2011). Our research only focused on the variables involving teachers' actions. Let us see them in detail.

RESEARCH PLANNING

The project "La storia e la scuola. Senso e metodi di un insegnamento" (*History and school. Meanings and methods of teaching*) is an analysis of teaching practices of History in primary and secondary schools supported by the Faculty of Educational Sciences, Psychology & Communication, University of Bari "Aldo Moro" and the DidaSco (DidatticheScolastiche, *School teaching*) research project coordinated by Professor Loredana Perla, in cooperation with USR Puglia (Apulian Regional School Office) and the Labor school network.

The project involved 22 History teachers working in six schools in Bari and its district[8] and focused on the analysis of teaching practices of History. The project aimed at focusing on the central role of mediation processes (Damiano, 2013) in History teaching and on the curricular actions implied by these mediation processes of this discipline (Brusa, 1991,1993).

This research-training project had several aims. Here are the most relevant ones:

- To explain teachers' implicit knowledge, beliefs and representations dealing with the process of History teaching and learning;
- To make teachers aware of the reasons of the choices guided by textbooks;
- To deduce some elements that could build a vertical curriculum to be used in the primary education level and in Italian comprehensive schools;
- To implement a professionalisation process that can be used in the primary education level.

The project implies a three-year duration. The methodological protocol considers some specific actions to be carried out each year.

In the first year (2013-14) the protocol is split in four stages.

In the first stage, a co-analysis of textbooks has been carried out. The research achieved a deep analysis of the textbooks used by the teachers involved in the project.

In the second stage, a video recording of a History class has been carried out. Then, the video was edited and uploaded on a dedicated platform.

In the third stage a triangular video-analysis between researchers and teachers has been carried out. In this stage teachers watched the video and filled in an *analysis form*, a self-assessment tool created by this research group in order to make teachers independent in the different stages of the phenomenological description of the educational processes in school environments; then, after viewing the video an interview has been made (Altet, 2006; Altet, Vinatier, 2008). The aim of this stage was to allow teachers to describe and analyse the multi-dimensional nature of educational practices in school environments with researchers.

In the final stage a CSSL test has been carried out. By adopting a social community methodology, teachers could share articles and reviews, could launch a question & answer system and could upload non-structured educational contents (texts, slideshows, pdf files, pictures, videos, tests) via iPaper. The online platform can be accessed only by means of personal user credentials; the platform has the following four main sections:

- **Board:** It is a general section in which all participants can read news, notices or important communications by project coordinators and course supervisors.
- **Activities:** In this section there are some synchronous & asynchronous communication tools in order to let participants interact with tutors and coordinators and between them easily and effectively. The designed tools are a chatroom, a discussion forum and interviews to teachers. The latter will be analysed in detail hereafter.
- **Experts:** In this section the training documentation will be provided.
- **Participating Schools:** In this section each school has some personal folders for teachers who will upload and share their training documentation.

The platform allowed teachers to refresh educational practices in History teaching starting from the shared development of documentation and educational resources in a shared learning environment.

In the second year (2014-2015) a training activity has been carried out. Here, educational and subject-specific contents have been introduced; in the final year of the study (2015-2016) the analysis protocol used in the first year will be used again in order to find any possible difference in the educational methods (Rivoltella, Rossi 2012).

In detail, training activities for the second year have been divided into two sessions: the first, called "Laboratori del tempo presente" had a two-fold aim: promoting a critical reflection on the use of historical sources that could be used in History teaching contexts, and guiding teachers in the development of *competence units*[9] by means of guidelines provided by the research group. The second session, called "Identità Italiana and curricolo di storia" aims at developing a vertical curriculum[10] starting from the key concept of *Italian identity*. The course structure has been developed in cooperation by teachers and the research group starting from the identification of the idea of antinomy (part-whole; centre-periphery; unity-division, etc.) and the selection of contents and/or core contents dealing with History-based knowledge.

As for the analysis device is concerned, together with 22 teachers involved in 6 schools, this device could lead to a systematic analysis of History teaching/learning processes in order to identify the most important features in process itself and to analyse them so that they could spark new knowledge that can be used in future contexts (Sherin, 2007; van Es and Sherin, 2002)[11]. In detail, by means of this tool teachers were guided towards an integrated analysis of the three educational elements (Damiano, 2013):

- **Teachers:** Teachers' actions are difficult to be analysed. Teachers' aim could be easy to be defined - make sure students learn - but there is an underlying knowledge, many skills and competences that teachers should master in order to perform their duties effectively. For instance, they have to know the subject matter the teach, the educational strategies that ease both the general and specific learning of that subject matter, some representations that could clarify some difficult notions, students' cognitive and emotive level, their level of understanding according to their school level, the curriculum of the subject matter they teach, the textbook they use and some useful teaching software (see Santagata, 2010);
- **Students:** Starting from a specific analysis of students' learning processes, teachers can emphasise those representations that may ease learning processes, the way through which students understand some mathematical notions, their difficulties and their common mistakes, and the educational strategies that can be effective for some school levels.
- The subject matter analysed in both the general features and the specific methods.

The video analysis form called *Mediazione & Storia* (M&S, *Mediation and History*) was created in order to identify the mediation processes (Damiano, 2013) in History teaching and in the related education organisers. The dimensions implied in the functioning of the mediation processes considered in the form were classified according to 5 macro-areas: Area 1a - Space/Time classroom organisation; Area 1b - Classroom structure; Area 2 - Educational relation; Area 3 - Mediation processes; Area 4 - Educational inclusion; Area 5 - Students' actions. Each macro-area has been split into *markers* and *description items* of the actions to be observed (see Figure 2).

Figure 2. Checklist index: Video - analysis form

A Teachers' actions - History teaching	B Students' actions - History learning
Area 1a -*Classroom organisation (time/space)* Markers • *Management of teachers' spaces* • *Management of students' spaces* • *Management of teachers' time* • *Management of students' time* **Area 1b** - *Classroom structure* Markers • *Desk placement* • *Tools/materials use and placement* **Area 2** - *Educational relation* Markers • *Classroom atmosphere* • *Behavioural rules* • *Communication* • *Body attitude* **Area 3** - *Mediation processes* Markers • *Management of experience/discipline* • *Mediation interventions for learning processes* • *Educational mediators* • *Educational relations teacher-student* **Area 4** – *Educational inclusion* Markers • *Management of classroom activities* • *Inclusive methodologies* • *Inclusive values* • *Inclusive-oriented time* • *Inclusive-oriented space*	**Area 5** - *Students' actions* Markers • *Classroom relations* • *Students' involvement* • *Students' answers*

In detail, the video-analysis form *Mediation and History (M&S)* is made up of three sections to be filled before, during and after the analysis, respectively.

1. **Section I:** Information about the teacher, the class to be recorded, the period of the analysis.
2. **Section II:** It includes the video-analysis checklist. The checklist is used to mark the frequency of the actions included in the list. It is made up of two parts:
   a. **Teachers' Actions:** History teaching,
   b. **Students' Actions:** History learning.
3. **Section III:** here teachers' comments and any comment arisen during the analysis are included.

As an example, area 3 - "Mediation processes" from the checklist "Video-analysis form - teachers' actions" is here included (see Figure 3).

Figure 3. Area 3: Mediation processes

Area 3 - *Mediation* processes								
Markers		Description element	Analysis Intervals					
			1	2	3	4	5	6
Mediation processes	M. Management of experience/discipline	M.1 The teacher tells their students the aim of the lesson and tells them what they are going to learn						
		M.2 The teacher tells the aims linked with the strengthening of acquired knowledge						
		M.3 The teacher asks questions aimed at looking for students' opinions and previous knowledge about the topic indicated						
		M.4 The teacher shares the content of the lesson (**descriptive lesson**)						
		M.5 The teacher shows schema or he/she writes keywords on the blackboard during the lesson						
		M.7 The teacher starts his/her lesson by asking questions in order to trigger a debate (**conversational lesson**)						
		M.8 The teacher includes reading activities						
		M.9 The teacher asks for students' intervention in order to compare the hypotheses advanced from the reading activity						
		M. 10 The teacher creates tests in order to instil the acquired knowledge						
		M.11 The teacher shows practical and motivated learning contents by means of projects, research activities, problem-solving (**operative lesson**).						
		M. 12 The teacher explains the aims of the assigned tasks during the lesson						
	N. Mediation interventions for learning processes	N. 1 The teacher gives students a task included in the textbook dealing with the topic taught						
		N. 2 The teacher suggests students to carry out a research on the Internet in order to complete the contents of the lesson (**individual task**)						
		N.3 The teacher tells students to read a passage from the textbook (**individual task**)						
		N.4 The teacher hands out materials and gives students some guidelines for a class test (**individual task**)						
		N. 5 The teacher organises a poster by creating groups and by giving them a specific task (**group task**)						
		N. 6 The teacher assigns a task and tells students to work in pairs (**pair task**)						
	O. Educational mediators	O.1 The teacher uses active mediators during the lesson						
		O.2 The teacher uses icon-based mediators during the lesson						
		O.3 The teacher uses symbol-based mediators during the lesson						
		O.4 The teacher uses diverse mediators during the lesson						
	P. Educational relations teacher-student	P.1 The teacher tells students to pay attention						
		P.2 The teacher tells students to report any doubts						
		P. 3 The teacher tells students to prepare some questions						
		P. 4 The teacher tells students to wait one's turn						
		P. 5 The teacher tells students to be active part in group activities						
		P. 6 The teacher tells students to care for the educational materials						
		P. 7 The teacher tells students to accept failures						
		P. 8 The teacher tells students to involve themselves in the tasks assigned in order to balance their limits						
		P. 9 The teacher helps students in stimulating their potential						
Frequency of actions		M. Management of experience/discipline						
		N. Mediation interventions for learning processes						
		O. Educational mediators						
		P. Educational relations teacher-student						

Results from the analysis form are a useful reference in order to enhance the teachers' professional level. Here, only some of the results from *Area 3 - Mediation processes* will be outlined.

DATA ANALYSIS

The area dealing with the educational mediation offered an interesting framework about several aspects that involve History teaching & learning processes: the management of experience or disciplines (see Figure 4), the mediation interventions for learning processes used during lessons (see Figure 5), the typologies of educational mediators used during a History class (see Figure 6) and the quality of the relationship teacher-student (see Figure 7).

The data are showed by means of charts created by gathering information obtained from the teachers involved in the research project. In each chart, with different colours, there are the time intervals that make up a lesson (time interval 1 - T1; time interval 2 - T2; time interval 3 - T3; time interval 4 - T4; time interval 5 - T5; time interval 6 - T6). The time interval used in order to verify if an action is carried out is 5 minutes (30 minutes overall).

In each chart there are the description elements for each analysis area, with percentages found for each time interval. Percentages for each description element refer to the frequency of actions found by each teacher involved.

Here is some detailed information found during the research.

The first element deals with the lesson models conceived by teachers.

- **Debate-Based Class:** The frequency of this action is scattered though it is high in the first time interval (58% time interval T1) and tends then to decrease considerably up to reach 0% in the final time interval.
- **Descriptive Lesson:** In which the core activity is represented by the direct exposition by the teacher. The frequency of this action is very homogeneous in the different time intervals (23% T1, 23% T2, 12% T3, 8% T4, 12% T5, 8% T6).
- **Operative Lesson:** Based by the sharing of practical and motivated contents by means of projects, research activities, problem-solving. For this action percentages in each time interval are low. (8% T1, 12% T2, 15% T3, 8% T4, 15% T5, 8% T6).

The second element deals with the modes through which teachers organise and share aims and contents of the lesson. Teachers tell their students the aim of the lesson and tells them what they are going to learn. The frequency of this action is very high in the first time interval (46% T1) and tends to decrease in the following time intervals. Higher percentages are found for the description element "teachers ask questions aimed at looking for students' opinions and previous knowledge about the topic indicated". Teachers tend to recall aims linked with the strengthening of acquired knowledge. Nevertheless, this action is not constant during the lesson: the highest percentages are found in T1(46%) and T4 (12%).

The third element deals with the modes through which teachers share the teaching contents, that is the mediation interventions for learning activities. There is a very high percentage for the description elements "the teacher hands out materials and gives students some guidelines for a class test" (27% in T1) and "The teacher gives students a task included in the textbook dealing with the topic taught" (14%

Figure 4. Chart: management of experience/discipline

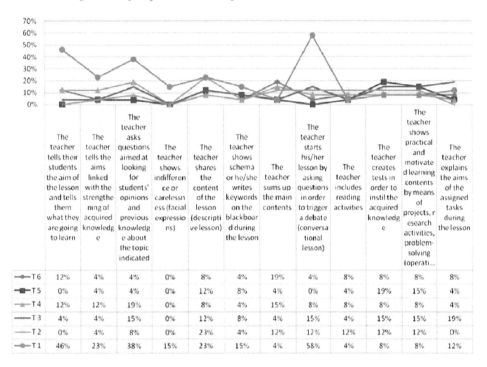

	The teacher tells their students the aim of the lesson and tells them what they are going to learn	The teacher tells the aims linked with the strengthening of acquired knowledge	The teacher asks questions aimed at looking for students' opinions and previous knowledge about the topic indicated	The teacher shows indifference or carelessness (facial expressions)	The teacher shares the content of the lesson (descriptive lesson)	The teacher shows schema or he/she writes keywords on the blackboard during the lesson	The teacher sums up the main contents	The teacher starts his/her lesson by asking questions in order to trigger a debate (conversational lesson)	The teacher includes reading activities	The teacher creates tests in order to instil the acquired knowledge	The teacher shows practical and motivated learning contents by means of projects, research activities, problem-solving (operati...	The teacher explains the aims of the assigned tasks during the lesson
T 6	12%	4%	4%	0%	8%	4%	19%	4%	8%	8%	8%	8%
T 5	0%	4%	4%	0%	12%	8%	4%	0%	4%	19%	15%	4%
T 4	12%	12%	19%	0%	8%	4%	15%	8%	8%	8%	8%	4%
T 3	4%	4%	15%	0%	12%	8%	4%	15%	4%	15%	15%	19%
T 2	0%	4%	8%	0%	23%	4%	12%	12%	12%	12%	12%	0%
T 1	46%	23%	38%	15%	23%	15%	4%	58%	4%	8%	8%	12%

Figure 5. Chart: mediation interventions for learning processes

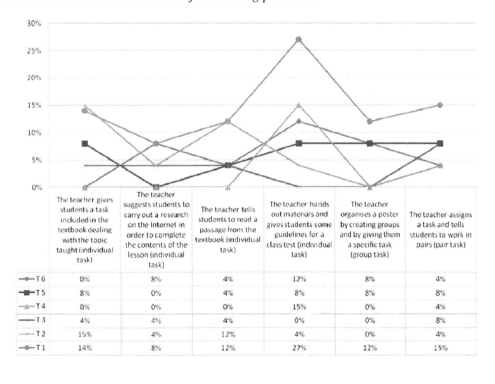

	The teacher gives students a task included in the textbook dealing with the topic taught (individual task)	The teacher suggests students to carry out a research on the Internet in order to complete the contents of the lesson (individual task)	The teacher tells students to read a passage from the textbook (individual task)	The teacher hands out materials and gives students some guidelines for a class test (individual task)	The teacher organises a poster by creating groups and by giving them a specific task (group task)	The teacher assigns a task and tells students to work in pairs (pair task)
T 6	0%	8%	4%	12%	8%	4%
T 5	8%	0%	4%	8%	8%	8%
T 4	0%	0%	0%	15%	0%	4%
T 3	4%	4%	4%	0%	0%	8%
T 2	15%	4%	12%	4%	0%	4%
T 1	14%	8%	12%	27%	12%	15%

Figure 6. Chart: educational mediators

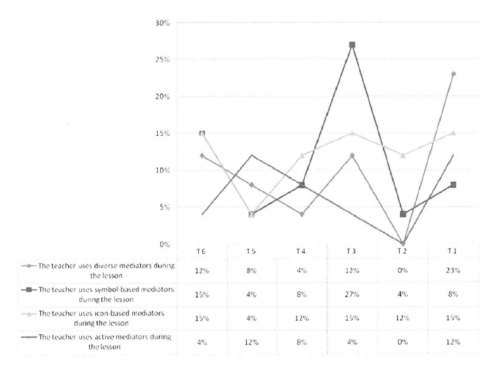

Figure 7. Chart: educational relations teacher-student

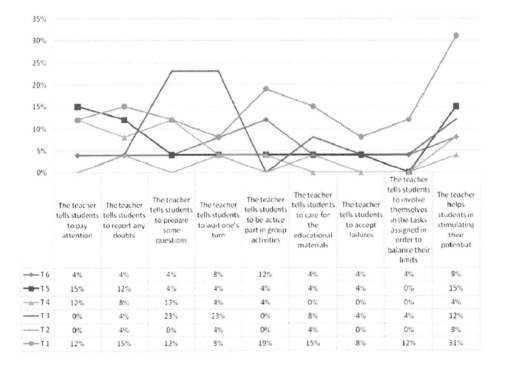

in T1). What is more, a low percentage of teachers tells his/her students "to carry out a research on the Internet in order to complete the contents of the lesson" (8% in T1 and T6).

The form also suggested that individual tasks predominate, thus reducing the possibility to create an active, cooperative and community environment for learning processes. This trend is confirmed by comparing percentages in the following description items:

- "The teacher gives students a task included in the textbook dealing with the topic taught" (14% T1, 15% T2, 4% T3, 0% T4, 8% T5, 0% T6).
- "The teacher tells students to read a passage from the textbook" (12% T1, 12% T2, 4% T3, 0% T4, 4% T5, 4% T6).
- "The teacher hands out materials and gives students some guidelines for a class test" (27% T1, 4% T2, 0% T3, 15% T4, 8% T5, 12% T6).

The fourth element deals with the types of mediators that teachers use in order to share the contents of a lesson. The analysis shows that the most used mediators are symbols such as letters, numbers and other symbols in order to represent variables and the resulting relations (8% T1, 4% T2, 27% T3, 8% T4, 4% T5, 15% T6) and icon-based mediators (pictures, maps, scale models, or films, videotapes, dynamic pictures) (15% T1, 12% T2, 15% T3, 12% T4, 4% T5, 15% T6). These description items are scattered quite homogeneously in each time interval.

Lower percentages are found for the description item "The teacher uses active mediators during the lesson" (12% T1, 0% T2, 4% T3, 8% T4, 12% T5, 4% T6). These data show that in History teaching direct experience is not used as a mediator to "transform and shift" structured knowledge in knowledge to be taught. Higher percentages are also found for the description item "The teacher uses diverse mediators during the lesson" (23% T1, 0% T2, 12% T3, 4% T4, 8% T5, 12% T6).

The fifth element deals with the modes through which the relationship teacher-student is developed. For the description item "The teacher tells students to report any doubts" the highest percentages are only found in T1 (15%) and T5 (12%); in the remaining time intervals percentages are considerably lower. In the description item "The teacher tells students to prepare some questions" the highest percentage is found in one-time interval (23% T3). Low percentages are also found in the following description items:

- "The teacher tells students to pay attention" (12% T1, 0% T2, 0% T3, 12% T4, 15% T5, 14% T6).
- "The teacher tells students to wait one's turn" (8% T1, 4% T2, 23% T3, 4% T4, 4% T5, 8% T6).
- "The teacher tells students to be active part in group activities" (19% T1, 0% T2, 0% T3, 4% T4, 4% T5, 12% T6).
- "The teacher tells students to pay attention" (15% T1, 4% T2, 8% T3, 0% T4, 4% T5, 4% T6).

Low percentages are found in the description items:

- "The teacher tells students to accept failures" (8% T1, 0% T2, 4% T3, 0% T4, 4% T5, 4% T6).
- "The teacher tells students to to involve themselves in the tasks assigned in order to balance their limits" (12% T1, 0% T2, 4% T3, 0% T4, 0% T5, 4% T6).

Finally, as for the description item "The teacher helps students in stimulating their potential" the highest percentages have been found, but only in some time intervals (31% T1; 12% T3, 15% T5).

PRELIMINARY RESULTS

Summarising the answers obtained from the *Mediation processes* area, the result is consistent with the principles explained in the literature dealing with *ongoing* educational transposition processes in teaching practices (Chevallard,1985; Bruner, 1978; Develey, 1995; Astolfi, 1997; Damiano, 2004, 2013): the adaptation of disciplinary contents to educational cognitive structures needs a deep reorganisation of knowledge-related structures.

The first marker in the area we analysed deals with the "organisation of experience and/or the subject". In this area the most recurrent answer is: "the teacher tells students about the aim of a lesson and suggests them what they are going to learn" (46% in time interval T1), "the teacher tells the aims associated with the strengthening of acquired competences" (23% in time interval T1). The teacher asks questions aimed at looking for opinions and pre-acquired knowledge about the suggested topic" (38% in time interval T1). Nevertheless, there is a high frequency ratio only in the first time interval; this clearly compromises the possibility to promote *significant learning* forms that would rather need the implementation of a constant methodological & educational "structure". Analysing the results dealing with the types of lessons carried out by the teachers involved, it should be noted that 58% of them stated that they have *dialogue-based* and *question-based* classes (Perla, 2011). The frequency of this action is scattered though it is high in the first time interval and tends then to decrease considerably up to reach 0% in the final time interval. This result underlines the fact that only in the first stage of classes teachers stimulate the confrontation and sharing of hypotheses starting from the topic of the class itself. This implies that "teachers explain the content of his/her lesson", as the relevance of this marker suggests. An *explanation-based* model is then mostly applied. What is more, two results proved to be surprising. The first deals with the integration of technologies within History teaching: a very low ratio of teachers declared they ask students to "search on the Internet in order to complement the contents of the lesson with additional information". The second one deals with the organisational decisions adopted by teachers in the creation of the educational setting: though in the latest years some national and international research showed that group-based teaching methods proved to be useful as students foster the learning process with one another, the analysis showed that the most recurrent method is individual, thus reducing the possibility to create a common environment in which an active and collaborative learning process can be triggered.

CONCLUDING REMARKS: TOWARDS A REFLECTIVE SELF-ASSESSMENT OF HISTORY TEACHING-LEARNING PROCESSES

These results within a reflective and self-assessment setting allowed the analysis of teachers' educational practices in a real environment and prepared the second stage of this research & training project (Perla, 2011; Magnoler, 2012).

In detail, the professional self-assessment tool tested in this research allowed teachers to express their educational action in concrete form, and this is a requisite needed in order to set up a systematic reflection activity. In this sense, the reflective activity stimulated in the teachers by means of the above-mentioned tool aimed at guiding teachers to reconsider their actions critically, stimulating the development and the strengthening of their professional actions.

As underlined by Dewey, in order to develop knowledge from experience it is needed to reflect over the events; there is also the need for a close contact with the events themselves, together with a keen interest and a mind involvement in situations (Dewey, 1986, p. 200). In other words, *knowledge arisen from experience* is not the simple consequence of taking part in an experience context, but it implies the intervention of reflective practices, that is to be thoughtfully present in an experience (Mortari, 2000). As Edgar Morin puts it, *"the legitimate need of knowledge, no matter who or how, should be the following: there is no knowledge without knowing knowledge"* (Morin, 1989, p. 41).

What are the "effects" of reflective self-assessment procedures, or those arising from the tool tested in this research? Surely the ability to identify some enhancement areas underneath teaching processes - in this case History teaching - starting from the critical issues identified in the research.

The areas here described deal with the mediation processes analysed in the previous sections:

- **Strengthening Meta-Cognition and Critical Reworking:** As indicated in the analysis, classroom communication is not oriented towards a (meta)cognitive behaviour by students; they are not always guided to recognise the *skills* needed to carry out learning tasks or encouraged in choosing adequate *operative strategies.*

- **Providing School Knowledge with a Reasonable Value:** Developing a disciplinary knowledge, that is the specific knowledge of a discipline, does not only mean acquiring the core notions through which any other specific knowledge can be interpreted, but also the *involvement in the process that allows knowledge to be developed* (Bruner, 1999, p. 114). In order to provide knowledge with a reasonable value, problems and questions should also be taken into account (Fabre, 1999, 2009, 2011).

- **Supporting the Relationship Between Shared Knowledge and Disciplinary Epistemology:** In this process an important role is represented by teachers' epistemology-based responsibility towards the notion to be taught; this relationship depends on the relationship between teachers and the discipline they teach (Chevallard,1985; Bruner, 1978; Develey, 1995; 1992Astolfi,1997; Martinard, 2001, 1986, Rézeau, 2004, Avanzini, 1996; Vigotskji,1990; Damiano, 2004, 2013, Martini, 2005, 2001, 2000).

- **Enabling Competence-Based Teaching within History Teaching:** In History teaching direct experience is not used as a mediator to "transform and shift" structured knowledge in knowledge to be taught. Therefore, competence-based teaching should be taken into consideration, as it is based on fostering students' operational abilities, no matter their school level.

- **Regaining the Narrative Dimension of History Teaching:** Setting a narrative-based education (Demetrio, 2013, Biffi, 2014) means achieving an educational practice in which a comparison with the same experience of personal, voluntary, aware and meaningful human actions is carried out, no matter what is taught and the methods used.

By means of a self-assessment tool, this research let teachers develop a permanent reflective attitude of their school actions, of the management of the mediation process among people who learn, disciplinary contents, methodologies, strategies and tools adopted in order to *develop enhancement* plans.

What is more, the project developed some interesting perspectives in order to implement a documentary culture in schools, which is not based on bureaucratic-administrative principles but it is aimed at supporting self-assessment processes. In this sense, it is important to underline that self-analysis and self-assessment procedures imply the renewal of teachers' professional competence, in particular the documentary competence (Schiavone 2015, *in press*). For this reason, there is the need to develop specific methodological tools that can support teachers in self-assessment actions. We hope this research could identify some guidelines and could offer a useful contribution in order to foster research on self-assessment models for the professional development of teacher staff.

REFERENCES

Allen, D. W. (1966). Micro-teaching is a scaled down teaching encounter in class size and class time. *High School Journal*, *49*(8), 355–362.

Altet, M. (2002). L'analyse plurielle de la pratique enseignante, une démarche de Recherche. *Revue Française de Pédagogie*, *138*, 85–93. doi:10.3406/rfp.2002.2866

Altet, M. (2006). Le competenze dell'insegnante-professionista: saperi, schemi di azione, adattamenti ed analisi. In L. Paquay, E. Charlier, Ph. Perrenoud (Eds.), Formare gli insegnanti professionisti. Quali strategie? Quali competenze? (pp. 31-44). Roma: Armando.

Altet, M., & Vinatier, I. (2008). *Analyser et comprendre la pratique enseignante*. Rennes: Presses Universitaires de Rennes.

Astolfi, J. P. (1997). Du "tout" didactique au "plus" didactique. *Revue Française de Pédagogie*, *129*(1), 67–73. doi:10.3406/rfp.1997.1157

Ballanti, G. (1975). *Il comportamento dell'insegnante*. Roma: Armando.

Ballanti, G. (1979). *Analisi e modificazione del comportamento dell'insegnante*. Teramo: Giunti &Lisciani.

Ballanti, G. (1980). La formazione professionale dell'insegnante (partiamo da zero). Il primo obiettivo professionale:la competenza minima insegnante. *Psicologia e Scuola*, *I*, 34–38.

Blomberg, G., Stürmer, K., & Seidel, T. (2011). How pre-service teachers observe teaching on video: Effects of viewers' teaching subjects and the subject of the video. *Teaching and Teacher Education*, *27*(7), 1131–1140. doi:10.1016/j.tate.2011.04.008

Bruner, J. S. (1978). *Dopo Dewey. Il processo di apprendimento nelle due culture*. Roma: Armando.

Bruner, J. S. (1999). *Verso una teoria dell'istruzione*. Roma: Armando.

Brusa, A. (1991). *Il manuale di storia*. Firenze: La Nuova Italia.

Brusa, A. (1993). *La programmazione di storia*. Firenze: La Nuova Italia.

Chevallard, Y. (1985). *La transposition didactique. Du savoir enseignant au savoir enseigné*. Grenoble: La Pensée Sauvage.

Coulet, J. C. (2007). Le concept de schème dans la description et l'analyse des compétencesprofessionn elles:formalisation des pratiques, variabilité des conduits et régulation de l'activité. In *M.Merri, Activité humaine et conceptualisation. Question à Gérard Vergnaud* (pp. 297–306). Toulouse: PUM.

Coulet, J. C. (2010). La "referéntialisation" des compétences à l'école, conceptions et mises en œuvre. in Les référentiels en formation: enjeux, légitimité, contenu et usage, Recherche & Formation, 64, 47-62.

Damiano, E. (1993). *L'azione didattica. Per una teoria dell'insegnamento*. Roma: Armando.

Damiano, E. (2004). *Insegnare i concetti. Un approccio epistemologico alla ricerca didattica*. Roma: Armando Editore.

Damiano, E. (2006). *La Nuova Alleanza*. Brescia: La Scuola Editrice.

Damiano, E. (2013). *La mediazione didattica. Per una teoria dell'insegnamento*. Milano: FrancoAngeli.

Develay, M. (1995). *Savoirs scolaires et didactique des disciplines*. Issy-les-Moulineaux: ESF Editeur.

Dewey, J. (1933). *How we Think. A Restatement of the Relation of Reflective Thinking to the Educative Process*. Boston: Heath.

Dordit, L. (2011). *Modelli di reclutamento, formazione, sviluppo e valutazione degli insegnanti. Breve rassegnainternazionale*. Trento: IPRASE.

Durand, M. (2011). Self-constructed activity, work analysis, and occupational training: an approach to learning objects for adults. In P. Jarvis & M. Watts (Eds.), *The Routledge international handbook on learning* (pp. 37–45). London: Routledge.

Dussault, G., Leclerc, M., Brunellem, J., & Turcotte, C. (1976). *L'analisi dell'insegnamento*. Roma: Armando Editore.

EC. EuropeanCommission. (2005). *Common Europeanprinciples for teachercompetences and qualifications*.

EC. EuropeanCommission. (2012). Ripensare l'istruzione. Retrieved from http://europa.eu/rapid/press-release_IP-12-1233_it.htm

Fabre, M. (1999). *Situations-problèmes et savoir scolaire*. Paris: PUF.

Fabre, M. (2009). *Philosophie et pédagogie du problème*. Paris: EditionsVrin.

Goldman, R., Pea, R., Barron, B., & Derry, J. S. (2009). *Videoricerca nei contesti di apprendimento. Teorie e metodi*. Milano: Raffaello Cortina Editore.

Leblanc, S. (2014). Vidéoformation et transformations de l'activitéprofessionnelle. *Activités (Vitry-sur-Seine)*, *11*(2), 143–171. http://www.activites.org/v11n2/v11n2.pdf

Lewis, C., Perry, R., & Murata, A. (2006). How should research contribute to instructional improvement: The case of lesson study. *Educational Researcher*, *35*(3), 3–14. doi:10.3102/0013189X035003003

Magnoler, P. (2012). *Ricerca e formazione. La professionalizzazione degli insegnanti*. Lecce: Pensa Multimedia.

Martinand, J.-L. (1989). Pratiques de référence, transposition didactique et savoirs professionnels en sciences et techniques. *Les Sciences de l'Education pour l'Ere Nouvelle*, *1-2*, 23–35.

Martinand, J. L. (2001). Pratiques de référence et problématique de la référence curriculaire. In A. Terrisse (Ed.), *Didactique des disciplines. Les références au savoir* (pp. 179–224). Bruxelles: De Boeck Université.

Martini, B. (2001). *Didattiche disciplinari. Aspetti teorici e metodologici*. Bologna: Pitagora.

Martini, B. (2006). *Formare ai saperi. Per una pedagogia della conoscenza*. Milano: FrancoAngeli.

Martini, B. (2011). *Pedagogia dei saperi. Problemi, luoghi e pratiche per l'educazione*. Milano: FrancoAngeli.

Morin, E. (1986). *La methode, 3: La connaissance de la connaissance*. Paris: ÉditionSeuil.

OECD. Organization for Economic Co-operation and Development. (2005). Teachers matter. Attracting, developing and retaining effective teachers. Paris: OECD Publishing. Retrieved from http://www.oecd.org/education/school/34990905.pdf

OECD. Organization for Economic Co-operation and Development. (2012). Teaching practices and pedagogical innovation: evidence from TALIS. Paris: OECD Publishing. Retrieved from http://www.oecd.org/education/school/TalisCeri%202012%20(tppi)--Ebook.pdf

Orme, M. (1966). *The effects of modeling and feedback variables on the acquisition of a complex teaching strategy [Unpublished doctoral dissertation]*. Stanford, California: Stanford University.

Pellegrini, M. (2014). La valutazione degli insegnanti nell'area OECD. *Form@re, Open Journal per la formazione in rete*, 4(14), 105-117.

Perla, L. (2010). *Didattica dell'implicito. Ciò che l'insegnante non sa*. Brescia: La Scuola.

Perla, L. (2011). *L'eccellenza in cattedra. Dal saper insegnare alla conoscenza dell'insegnamento*. Milano: FrancoAngeli.

Perla, L. (2012). *Scrittura e tirocinio universitario. Una ricerca sulla documentazione*. Milano: FrancoAngeli.

Perla, L. (Ed.). (2014). *I nuovi Licei alla prova delle competenze. Guida alla progettazione nel biennio*. Lecce: Pensa Multimedia.

Perrenoud, P. (1999). *Dix nouvelles compétences pour enseigner: invitation au voyage*. Paris: ESF.

Previtali, D. (2012). *Come valutare i docenti?* Brescia: La Scuola.

Rézeau, J. (2004), *Médiatisation et médiation pédagogique dans un environnement multimédia - Le cas de l'apprentissage de l'anglais en Histoire de l'art à l'université* [Thèse de doctorat]. Université Victor Segalen Bordeaux 2.

Rivoltella, P. C., & Rossi, P. G. (Eds.), (2012). *L'agiredidattico. Manualedell'insegnamento*. Brescia: La Scuola.

Samurçay, R., & Rabardel, P. (2004). Modèles pour l'analyse de l'activité et des compétences, propositions. In R. Samurçay & P. Pastré (Eds.), *Recherches en didactique professionnelle* (pp. 163–180). Toulouse: Octarés.

Santagata, R., & Angelici, G. (2010). Studying the Impact of the Lesson Analysis Framework on Pre-service Teachers' Abilities to Reflect on Videos of Classroom Teaching. *Journal of Teacher Education*, *61*(4), 339–349. doi:10.1177/0022487110369555

Sergiovanni, T. J., & Starratt, R. J. (2007). *Supervision: A redefinition* (8th ed.). New York: McGraw Hill.

Talis (2013). Results: An International Perspective on Teaching and Learning, OECD from http://www.oecd.org/edu/school/talis.htm

Verganud, G. (1990). La théorie des champs conceptuels. In Recherche en didactique des mathématiques, 10(2-3), 133-170.

KEY TERMS AND DEFINITIONS

Educational Evaluation: The evaluation process of characterizing and appraising some aspects of an educational process. Educational institutions usually require evaluation data to demonstrate effectiveness to funders and other stakeholders, and to provide a measure of performance for marketing purposes.

Educational Mediation: The set of interventions that teachers carry out in order to train cognitive frameworks by means of disciplinary structures; they are represented with praxis-, icon-, symbol-based codes consistent with the evolution stages of the learner(s).

Professional Development: The achievement of useful knowledge, attitudes, behaviours and competences during one's professional career that can enhance and innovate educational practices.

Professional Self-Assessment: A training-oriented assessment that helps teachers in the identification of both strong and weak points in their actions, and to provide feedbacks useful to enhance educational practices.

Research-Training: A kind of applied research protocol that deals with educators' and teachers' specific issues. Thanks to this kind of research, teachers could analyse their own practices and can assess suitable strategies in order to enhance their educational actions and the related performance of their students.

Self-Reflection Tool: A tool aimed at supporting teacher staff in the phenomenological description and multi-dimensional analysis of educational practices. A self-reflection tool supports teachers in explicating values, beliefs, certainties, education practice-related knowledge that influence the contents taught and have comebacks on students' training and education.

Video-Analysis: Multi-methodology practice and an interdisciplinary field of study is useful to provide an answer to complex educational phenomena, as well as it provides tools and technologies with a high potential of description and understanding of different phenomena. Videos stimulate the metacognitive and the reflective dimensions on educational practices.

ENDNOTES

[1]   This chapter is the result of a shared project. L. Perla wrote the Introduction and paragraphs 1, 2, 3. N. Schiavone wrote paragraphs 4, 5, 6.

2   For further reference see: Recommendation of the European Parliament and of the Council of 12 February 2001 on quality evaluation in school education - Official Journal L 60/51.

3   With the ratification of D.P.R 80/2013 (Italian Republic Presidential Decree), that is the National Education Assessment System Guidelines, INVALSI (the Italian National Institute for Education and Training Assessment) provides schools with assessment-related tools (art 3, par. d).

4   For further details about TALIS research see OECD website: http://www.oecd.org/edu/school/talis.htm and MIUR (Italian Department for Education and Research): http://hubmiur.pubblica.istruzione.it/web/ministero/talis

5   The approach refers to process-product research. See also Bennet, 1981.

6   As for the principle of excellence see Perla, 2011.

7   In this framework, Tochon F.V. developed some interesting results. See Tochon F.V. (2009), Dai video-casi alla video-pedagogia. Una cornice teorica per il video-feedback e la riflessione con i video nella pratica di ricerca pedagogica. In Goldman, R., Pea R., Barron, B., Derry S.J. (Eds). Video-ricerca nei contesti di apprendimento. Teorie e metodi, Milano: Cortina. See also Perla L., Schiavone N. (2013). Quels dispositifs de documentation de l'implicite dans la formation des enseignants? In Atti del Secondo Convegno Internazionale IDEKI 2013 (in press).

8   Teachers involved in the research work in pre-schools, primary and secondary schools.

9   It is the scheduling unit aimed at achieving a specific training aim and one or more related competences.

10   A vertical curriculum is the development of a set of educational actions designed with increasing complexity, from pre-schools to secondary schools.

11   This knowledge may refer to strategies for History teaching that are effective for students' learning and that may be used in the following classes.

Chapter 11
Films, Multiliteracies, and Experiences About Fruition, Analysis, and Production in Education:
The Lumière Minute and the Episodes of Situated Learning

Monica Fantin
Federal University at Santa Catarina, Brazil

ABSTRACT

This paper discusses the relationship between cinema and education based on opportunities for the frui-tion, analysis and production of video in educational contexts. To do so, it locates different approaches to cinema in schools and analyzes the importance of principles and proposals for working with audiovisual materials in the education of teachers and students. Based on the media-education perspective and on multiliteracies, the paper addresses aspects of an experience with audiovisual production in the initial education of teachers, with students in at a teacher's college, based on the Lumière Minute proposal and the Situated Learning Episodes methodology. Finally, the paper indicates some challenges and possibilities for working with video in education.

INTRODUCTION

The different subjective exchanges that film offers are key to its relationship with education. The interaction of students and teachers with film put into play multiple world views, cultural practices and possibilities for being in the world. This takes place not only because diversity is an important part of people's lives, but also because the contemporary world is permeated by dissensions, conflicts, tensions, challenges and new forms of organizing life. Given this presumption, the starting point for the discussion between

DOI: 10.4018/978-1-5225-0711-6.ch011

Copyright © 2017, IGI Global. Copying or distributing in print or electronic forms without written permission of IGI Global is prohibited.

cinema and education in this paper refers to the various possibilities for approaching video in schools, which involve appreciation, analysis and production. By expanding the dimensions of the audiovisual experience in the context of literacy, this paper discusses the relationship between the various languages from the multiliteracies and new literacies perspectives, to give potential to educational practices for video production in schools as opportunities for belonging and participation in the digital culture. In this sense, the text presents an experience with audiovisual production undertaken with students of initial education at a teacher's college, which sought to stimulate a discussion about the pioneers of cinematographic production with the activity known as the Lumière Minute, in articulation with the Situated Learning Episodes methodology, seeking a productive dialog between the formal and informal learnings of students mediated by the integration of mobile digital devices in education. Finally, the text discusses some dilemmas and challenges for working with the possibilities and limits of video in education.

APPROACHES TO FILM IN SCHOOLS: FRUITION, ANALYSIS, AND PRODUCTION

The diversity of proposals for working with cinema and audiovisual materials in schools can be analyzed from different perspectives, including those that are presented in this book. This chapter is based on the media-education perspective.

Media-education implies the adoption of a critical and creative posture of communicative, expressive and relational capacities for ethically and aesthetically evaluating what is being offered by the media, to significantly interact with its productions and to produce media as well. Its critical, methodological and expressive perspectives question school mediations, given that education for the medias is not limited to the different media and their instrumental aspects, because media is culture and is located in an arena of production of meanings beyond their instrumental character.

In the relationship between cinema and media-education, the ethical and aesthetic dimensions are related to a discussion about what touches us in a film, in the sense of Barthes' (1984) idea of *punctum*, which refers to an aesthetic experience activated during the fruition. Without proposing rules or an analytical model Sorlin (1997) defined this experience based on a mental state, an attitude of opening aimed at the force of expression in the construction of an aesthetic route that he affirms is formed by *intuition* (the initial moment of perception), by *judgement/taste* (perception based on a given socio-cultural context linked to an idea of beauty) and by *opinion* (an interpretive moment, the posteriori evaluation).

An aesthetic experience is triggered in the encounter with the film, without being limited to it, based on different forms of appropriation: of ludic-evasive fruition as well as an educational appreciation that goes beyond "spontaneous" fruition and involves an intentionality concerning the different dimensions of knowledge (narration, critical analysis, interpretation and production).

In the book *L'hipothèse Cinemà*, Bergalla (2002) discusses how schools can be places for encounters with "art cinema," because films considered to be works of art allow students to confront a form of alterity to which they would not have access in another space. The author begins with the hypothesis that schools should work with art films, and distinguishes the experience of teaching and initiation in relation to cinema. For Bergalla, the act of teaching implies transmitting a knowledge that exists and in the field of art there is no previously existing understanding or knowledge, which he affirms presents the process of initiation. Initiations begin first with the experience of the person who watches the film, and in this case, the teacher and her experience with the film, because it is more a question of attitude and posture than of knowledge.

Based on this understanding, Bergalla (2002) mentions some pedagogical principles about how to address cinema with children, young people and teachers. In relation to *art films* the artistic quality of the film should be unquestionable: "is this film a work of art or not?" And in the understanding of *film as culture* he believes that young people see film as consumption and entertainment and thus the presentation of film in school should create another space for this experience, showing other repertoires and constructing relations between them with a critical spirit. In addition, the experience should maintain the amazement, surprise and wonder, if not, the work is closer to communication and not to art, according to the author.

Other scholars who emphasize the construction of this aesthetic experience in an educational context argue that cinema in schools can be understood as a combination of various social practices, and an instrument of diffusion of the cultural heritage of humanity and document of the study of history (Rivoltella, 2005). In this way, the cultural practice of watching films is a socializing practice that allows different encounters: of people with people in different contexts of exhibition, of people with themselves, of people with the film narratives, of people with the cultural diversity present in the representations that the films offer, of people with a wide variety of imaginaries, etc. In these encounters between identities and imaginaries, the spaces of local and or universal recognition can create other forms of understanding and cinematographic and cultural belonging.

By presenting the customs and ways of life of various social groups, films also present the cultural heritage of humanity and some films are similar to other products of science, art and literature (Rivoltella, 2005). In addition to being a *symbolic environment* of different generations, cinema allows sharing a wide variety of social meanings and to the degree that it contributes to cultural transmission, it is also a cultural fact (Fantin, 2009).

By highlighting the educational relevance of using audiovisual materials in school, Rivoltella (2005) locates the *cultural* validity (recognizing cinema as a cultural expression particular to our time, together with art and literature and their aesthetic and critical judgments); *alphabetic or instrumental validity* (comprising the learning of the grammar and syntax of audiovisual or cinematographic language, in relation to both consumption and production); and *cognitive* validity (describing the cinema as a space for historic research aimed at contemporary political and social reality). These aspects can be joined with a *psychological* validity (exploring identifications and projections of feelings through interaction with the cinematographic narratives and their processes of signification); an *aesthetic* validity (understanding moments of pleasure and displeasure in the contexts of fruition of the audiovisual that provoke emotion and wonder in the construction of other forms of seeing and representing the world); and a *social* validity (constructing spaces that make the practice of watching films a collective event that allows various dialogs and interactions (Fantin, 2011). It is possible to expand this list by also including *ethical* validity (discussing the values that the narratives offer and the ideological aspects of the film) and *political* validity (affirming the sense of citizenship, of public policies for the production, distribution and exhibition of audiovisual materials, the need for audiovisual education in the schools, and the right to access quality audiovisual productions in schools and movie theaters).

From this perspective, audiovisual materials in schools, in the context of the broader relationship between film and media-education, can be seen as instruments through which education is conducted and as thematic objects of educational intervention through reading, interpretation, analysis and production of audiovisual materials. These aspects have been worked with by various authors including: Jacquinot

(1999) who situates the dimensions of film as a support for and object of study; Eugeni (1999) who describes the forms of social knowledge of cinema, highlighting both the object as knowledge and the instrument as competencies; Rivoltella (2005) who emphasizes the possibility of "educating for film" and "educating with film"; and by Reia-Batista (1995) who highlights the pedagogical dimension of the filmic and cinematographic phenomenon as an acquisition of knowledge and of critical reflection both of recent culture and of the marks that we have long left in "images and sound interlinked in various forms" (p.1).

For all these reasons, from the media-education perspective (Rivoltella, 2005; Fantin, 2006; Tufte & Christensen, 2009) the use of cinema reaffirms the presence of audiovisual materials in schools as part of human education in society today, as an artistic and aesthetic experience and as a global communicative phenomenon that is present in contemporary cultural practices.

Media-education can function as a cultural and educational tool in the practical-reflexive training and professional development of media-education teachers. As a cultural tool, it provides an opportunity to reflect on the didactics used to develop the competence of teachers, given that their work must be in tune with the new languages of the media and youth, and with educational functions and social responsibilities. As Rivotella (2014) emphasizes, the constant redefinitions of media-education from the perspective of citizenship lead it beyond critical thinking and reading. The dynamic nature of media-education "reflects the connection between children, youth and the communication media - during leisure time in educational institutions – and develops on the tense border between media-education practices, empiric knowledge and theories" (Tufte & Christensen, 2009, p.102). If young students today are considered to have innovative media practices, they often lack greater cultural understanding of the repertoires coming from the media and tools needed to interpret the scenery of filmic and media culture. It is these abilities and competencies that media-education teachers have the responsibility to provide, and this reveals the need for media-education and for the professional competencies that are relevant in this field. If they possess these competencies, media-educators can act, as Rossi proposes (2013, p.34); like a film director or screenwriter who provides the environment and sketch of the issue, or like an actor who acts and flexibly interprets the text offered. For Rossi, these roles require different competencies and attitudes, which in our view approximate the competencies requested of the media-educator (Rivoltella, 2005; Morcelini & Rivoltella 2007).

Fruition

The moment of fruition of films in school is related both to the right to access to culture and to the concept of aesthetic participation, understood as "an awakening of meaning no less than creativity and intelligence, and is also aware of possibility" (Sorlin, 1997, p.44) and according to the author, that which constitutes its particular quality. By asking about aesthetic participation in videos, the author understands that films and television programs instruct, distract, inform and also hide, and that their artistic value is not evident and is not the *a priori* reason for their diffusion. Frequently, their value leaves spectators and specialists indifferent, considering they must plunge into a work to capture what is original about it. For Sorlin, recognizing the aesthetic strength of a film involves retaking the path of the work, in finding pleasure upon exploring the various elements that are combined in the whole.

This condition is constructed based on the contact with film at the moment of fruition. The more opportunities are offered for interactions with various works, the more conditions for recognition there are. Given that aesthetic participation is constructed in the encounter with film, it is important to consider the conditions of these encounters, because taste also expresses a sense of belonging. Although taste, ways of dressing, living and having fun are some signs of distinction, they are not absolute, because they are determined by the sociocultural context, and in a society in which diversity is a value, this can be relativized in a more plural perspective.

In the same way, the construction of the aesthetic opinion understood as an interpretation of the work is also immersed in this context of relations. To express an aesthetic opinion in the moment of fruition, the value of the group interferes in the construction of taste – and this concept is useful for understanding the meaning that the environment surrounding the school provides and the aesthetic models that construct the cultural capital of the students and teachers.

By considering that aesthetic participation is stimulated by each person's sensibility, this can be expressed in each gesture provoked by audiovisual production that expands the ways of seeing. For Sorlin, this experience involves time and space, in a relationship of continuity and inference that transcends the work, and the beauty of this route is that each spectator, as inattentive or secure as they are in their approximation, allows themselves to become involved in that which the film does not always make explicit. Film, with its history, meanings and language seeks, in the first place, a passionate and co-involving illusion of immediacy through its colors, forms, movements and sounds. Nevertheless, in this process of aesthetic participation, the spectator can be taken by a mysterious force and experience a sensation of distancing in relation to that which is proposed.

Emotion and pleasure are also preliminary and necessary conditions for aesthetic participation, because the spectators touched by the qualities of the film can allow themselves to be seduced by the involvement aroused at this moment. But the aesthetic apprehension also involves disturbances and discomforts and this tangling of sensations can remain in the spectators and become transformed. When the desire arises to repeat the experience "only" for the pleasure provoked or to recompose the route to capture it better, the impressions produced can go beyond, in the direction of analysis and knowledge. This appropriation is manifest in a form of interpretation, opinion and possible (re)creation, a fruit of ambiguity and of the dynamics of the aesthetic route that also involves the identification and negation of the spectator. Colors, tones, lights, gestures and histories oscillate between that which the film refers to and the impression that it raises, and often acquires its own life, developing, modifying, completing and contradicting itself in each person's imagination. "The work of art is a challenge and a provocation for the intelligence, and stimulates pleasure and emotion, awaking in the spectator the conviction that it is possible, or even necessary to not be limited to first impressions and - to the contrary - place oneself more deeply in relation to it" (Sorlin, 1997, p.59).

In this way, the aesthetic experience created by the fruition of films in educational contexts, in schools or in movie theaters, is a condition for any work with film in education. This relates to the film repertoires that enter in play, beginning with experiences of appreciation. From the media-education perspective, the appreciation of films in school can also help create spaces of alterity and authorship to assure the rights of children and youth in relation to the media: that is the right to protection, provision and participation, which implies discussing the criteria of choice and suitability of the films in school (Fantin, 2015).

In this sense, the choice of films for exhibition in school can be based on some presumptions that support the proposals for appreciation and fruition of films, such as:

1.   Expanding the cultural repertoire by assuring the presentation of films that depict a diversity of sociocultural contexts, languages, values ethics and aesthetics.

2. Understanding that any film can be educational, depending on the relationship that is established with it, even considering "inherent qualities" that certain films have.
3. Considering the levels of development and knowledge that students have (children and youth): their interest, capacities and preferences related to cultural capital, the conditions of living childhood/ youth, to real and potential capacities, age, gender, class, ethnicities, etc.
4. Reaffirming the degree of opening and uncertainty that films have, to allow various interpretations.

Thus, the fruition of films in school and their mediations can allow the possibility for interpretation understood as creative dialog and understanding permeated by emotion and complex power relations, as Ferrès (2013) reminds us when discussing the power of the screens, of emotions and of media education in the interlinking of neuroscience, media-education, media-communication and art.

Films in Debate

Understood as one of the possibilities that is often used in pedagogical practices, the debate about films in educational contexts can be proposed in different manners, depending on the teacher's intentions. From an operative perspective, as methodological indications linked to media-educational aspects mentioned previously, Rivoltella (2008) highlights at least 3 possibilities that can be articulated among each other and that refer to the meaning of the discussion that film can promote:

1. **Speaking About the Film:** Concerns the perspective of pre-textual reading, which at times involves an illustrative function that becomes a pretext for introducing problematics or seeking confirmation of something in the images worked with.
2. **Speaking of the Film:** Implies a textual perspective, which goes beyond a content and illustrative oriented logic, because the film becomes a cultural object to be deconstructed and reconstructed, not to authorize paths of arbitrary and subjective reading, but to develop criticisms based on the materiality of the filmic text.
3. **Choosing What to Focus on in the Discussion:** If the choice emphasizes the *watching,* emphasize attention on the aesthetic structures of the film and its style; speak about the director, his or her choices, the singularity of the film in the context of his or her body of work, or that is, take an approach similar to that of a film critic. If the choice is to emphasize *knowing*, emphasize the filmic approach by paying attention to the significant structure of the film, the devices of the codes, the narrative functioning (what story is told, how, what are the editing choices). If the choice emphasizes *believing* the attention refers to an approach that emphasizes the ethical and existential dimension of the film.

The promotion of a significant discussion about the film can be undertaken based on an emphasis with three lines of focus and their related competencies, which can be summarized in this way (Rivoltella, 2008, pp.246-247):

1. The linguistic-expressive focus promotes competencies related to *knowing how to see,* and emphasizes the grammatical and syntactical aspect that concerns the elements: photography (lighting, contrast, composition); color (natural, balanced, symbolic value, effects); field and planes (typology

and uses); angles and inclinations in the use of the camera (present, hidden); editing (types and rhythms) and the audio sphere (voices, noises, music).

2. The narrative-thematic focus activates competencies of *knowing how to understand* and emphasizes aspects about the contents of the film and its forms of retelling, and involves: the narrative structure of the film (the main scenes, moments, the plot developments); characters (their characteristics, relations of reciprocities and function in the script); the content (the recurring themes, problematics and symbolic functioning).

3. The ethical and value-oriented focus promotes competencies of *knowing how to evaluate* and is related to the ideological aspect of the film that implies evaluations about: the aesthetic dignity of the film (the artistic quality, whether the story is developed well), the problematics at stake (how the film addresses the theme), the impact on the viewer (the director's ethical commitment).

It is desirable for the teacher to have command and or experience with these foci with a certain facility to be able to promote certain competencies in the student viewers. This perspective establishes a support that allows working better with the possibilities of film and the use of audiovisual materials in schools, particularly in activities related to the debate and analysis of films.

Film Analysis

The activities promoted by the discussion of films can be deepened in proposals for film analyses, which historically have marked various proposals concerning film and education since the 1950s when film analysis was born. At that time, the French journal *Cahiers do Cinema* created space for film directors to write and publish articles and essays about their own films. Based on memories, notes taken during screenings, watching a film various times, observing the reactions of viewers, the tools of analysis become more sophisticated, particularly with the support of semiotics, and the development of various types of equipment (such as videocassettes and later DVDs that allowed stopping the image, returning to a scene and rewatching the film a number of times), which gradually organized a more specialized knowledge that is better articulated and has a stronger methodological foundation.

The analysis of films today can be understood as approaches that recur to different methodologies, and involve a quite useful controversy about its meanings and implications. This discussion will not be deepened at this time, for a more complete look specialized literature can be consulted (Casetti and Di Chio, 2004; Aumont, 1995; Stam, 2003; Mosconi, 2005).

As a pedagogical possibility, some aspects of film analysis in educational contexts and their principal steps stand out, recognizing the complexity involved and the difficulty in making viable this type of activity in classrooms. Etymologically, to analyze means to "dissolve." In the most common sense, to analyze something implies reducing its complexity and decomposing it into more simple elements. This is what is done when one analyzes a text, and after an initial reading seeks to understand its parts to then (re)articulate the sense of the whole. In this process, its organizational parts are decomposed and the text is recomposed in search of a general interpretation. Something similar occurs with filmic text or with the analysis of films and involves two moments.

First, decomposition involves a pre-analysis that occurs when one watches a complete film, and perhaps more than once. Together with this, paratextual elements are sought to help understand the film (interviews with the director, actors and film critics) as preliminary tasks. At a second moment, the linear decomposition of the film involves the reconstruction of its narrative, the identification of the main parts, interesting sequences or scenes that can be transcribed and noted as a decoupage. These are tasks that allow a deeper decomposition, with the description of the operation of the iconic, linguistic and editing codes and an analysis of the characters.

The elements that emerge from these moments are necessary for recomposing the text, which can be reconstructed in various forms: identifying the central theme (the main relation that it addresses) describing its internal articulations (how it was introduced, what was the perspective, what opening or closing it offered), verify how these aspects function in the plane of meanings (such as questions of plot and characters that operate on an anthropological, philosophical or existential plane triggering emotions that reflect on the meaning of life in general).

Some scholars affirm that analysis can "destroy" the meaning of a film, while others believe analysis enriches and makes the aesthetic experience more sophisticated (Stam, 2003). In educational contexts, the meaning of the film analysis will depend on the educational intentionality and on the adaptation possible to school activities.

Audiovisual Production

Another possibility mentioned about audiovisuals in the school is its sense of production, which in most cases is articulated with the possibilities mentioned above. Previous works have discussed proposals for the educational routes and didactic itineraries about using film in schools for children (Fantin, 2006, 2011) and in initial teacher education (Fantin, 2009, 2014).

In initial teacher education, some experiences with audiovisual production can be mentioned in the context of different classes that have been offered in the teacher's college at the Federal University at Santa Catarina, Brazil,[1] whose proposals are based on media-education concepts. One of these will be presented in detail in this article. The objectives involve constructing interdisciplinary and transversal routes that in the specific curriculum of each discipline would expand the concept of student agency: as film viewers, to stimulate the sense of analysis, interpretation and audiovisual production as experiences of fruition, aesthetic participation, authorship and signification.

From this perspective, the educational mediation is based on the ideas of media-education, making education *with* the media (using films in contexts of fruition), *about* the media (conducting critical readings through films analysis) and *through* the media (producing audiovisuals). The activities conducted involve moments of knowing, doing and reflecting on audiovisuals as an experience of Initiation and Teaching and their relationship with other languages (the plastic arts, theater, music, literature, photography) and technologies, in which the didactic intervention is based on the fruition of films, on the understanding of their instrumental character and as object of knowledge, of various readings and analyses, as well as the opportunity for material production.

The themes of the productions, the search for the interest and or choice of the "subject" to be addressed is always based on something linked to the experience of each student and or their motivations and curiosities. It is based on this relationship that the subject emerges and can become interesting. This is the source of the vast possibilities for audiovisual production, beyond "curricular contents."

Some moments and practices can be highlighted that are based on didactic routes developed in teacher education through means of *audiovisual production workshops* (Fantin, 2009, pp. 24-30) and can be summarized as follows:

1. **Contextualization of the Presumptions and Objectives of Media-Education:** A brief reflection on the opportunities for media-education in school to anchor the context of audiovisual production by students.
2. **Elaboration of the Screenplay and Definition of the Theme to be Filmed:** Justification and summary-synthesis of the screenplay or argument of the film locating the objectives and information about what, when, where, how.
3. **Choosing the Narrative Genre to be Used:** Study of the audiovisual language, of the formats and filmic-textual structures: documentary, advertising, interview, video-clip, animation and the specificities of fictional works: drama, romance, comedy, suspense, adventure, etc. considering the convergence and hybrid nature of the genre to choose the best form of "telling the story".
4. **Research:** Study and preparation about the content to be worked with.
5. **Pre-Production:** Planning of the recording, the available resources, equipment, inside and outside spaces, scenery, costumes and definition of tasks: "who does what".
6. **Production:** Editing and finishing involving the choice of scenes, graphic and visual effects, subtitles, audio, vignette, authorship, credits, support and making of.
7. **Promotion:** Exhibition and evaluation of the material produced with the authors and the group to socialize the experience.

This proposal highlights that it is important that teachers want to learn about the filmic and cinematographic universe and that their education contemplates the mediations necessary to do so, which also relates to audiovisual literacy, which relates to the meaning of *multiliteracies* and is part of teacher education.

AUDIOVISUAL AND MULTILITERACIES

To ask what it means to be literate today implies recognizing the increasing immersion in the plurality of languages and various types of representation that require competencies beyond the reading and writing of words. Today, the reading of the world and of the word involves written, artistic, audiovisual, media and digital production in the context of multiliteracies (Cope & Kalantzis, 2000), media literacy (Buckingham, 2005), informational literacy (Rivoltella, 2008) and the new literacies (Lankshear & Knobel, 2011; Jenkins, 2006; Fantin, 2011a).

The new literacies do not refer only to the shifts from the electronic to the digital era but to going beyond it, because the construction of knowledge in the digital culture involves the convergence of technologies and of different languages (written, plastic, musical, audiovisual, digital), their codes, their supports, their specificities as well as their different meanings in social practices. Moreover, the participative culture requests various competencies and abilities that require new literacies and at times change the focus from individual expressions to collaborative work and that in network (Jenkins, 2009). These learning processes are complex and involve concepts and dimensions that interlink in the multiliteracy and new literacies perspectives.

The concept of multiliteracies expands the traditional concept of literacy by relating different languages and meta-languages in the complex processes of production of meanings that are articulated between the linguistic, visual, audio, gestural, spatial and multimodal designs (Cope and Kalantzis 2000). Articulated to that perspective, the authors highlight the Pedagogy Literacies, which involve 4 components: situated practice; open learning; a critical approach and a transformative practice. The multiliteracies perspective considers that the growing variety of forms of texts associated to the Information and Communication Technologies and the multi-medias involve a competent understanding of the forms of representation that are becoming increasingly more significant in the global communication environment, such as the relations between the linguistic, visual, audio, gestural spatial and multimodal designs (Cope & Kalantzis, 2000). This concept necessarily implies a sense of critical reflection and approach.

In this sense, when thinking of film in school it is essential to discuss the perspective of working critically with the multiple languages, understood as a repertoire of correlated capacities. In this process, the multiliteracies interlink art, science, narrative and play as fundamental languages in which it is possible to express and communicate feelings, ideas and experiences of a wide variety of forms: oral, written, plastic, corporal, musical, electronic, audiovisual and digital.

The challenge is to work with the idea of new literacies that concern the "complex interfaces between linguistics, anthropology and epistemology to examine the relations between social practices, cosmovisions, orality and literacy" (Lankshear & Knobel, 2011, p.26) in the context of the multiliteracies as a condition for being able to conduct a significant work with cinema and audiovisual materials in schools. To do so, once again it is essential to appropriate the audiovisual codes and produce meanings based on the filmic narrative; identify and recognize the elements of the visible sphere (light, color, planes; movement of character and of cameras; scenography; special effects; writing, editing) and from the audio sphere (sounds, actors' lines, dialogs; noises, music) as competencies needed for audiovisual understanding and expression alongside the other languages. This can be redimensioned in the articulation between Designed – Designing- Redesign proposed in the multiliteracies approach and by the Situated Learning Episodes (EAS) (Rivoltella, 2013) methodology.

In this framework, the work with video can also be understood through its role as an iconic mediator, given that contributes to the didactic of the image. Among the didactic mediators proposed by Damiano (2013), the iconic mediators are characterized by the use of figuration, and more than working with language that "reconstructs reality through a sophisticated code and offers representations that despite the similarity with things – maintain a vague unavoidable sense and require special training, both for reading and for writing" (p.178). Thus, working with images teaches educators to see a scheme as a model similar to reality, not as reality or the truth, in a format that may be close to or distant from reality, the author maintains.

AN EXPERIENCE WITH THE *LUMIÈRE MINUTE* AND *SITUATED LEARNING EPISODES (SLE)* IN INITIAL TEACHER EDUCATION

The experience with audiovisual production in initial teacher education that is presented below is located in the context of a class in Film, Childhood and Education given in the teacher's college at the Federal University at Santa Catarina. The objectives of the discipline, concern a: Reflecting on the artistic-cultural dimensions of the relationship between cinema, childhood and education; b: analyzing the representations of childhood and children in film; c: identifying aspects of the analysis of films and their possibilities in school and d: discussing themes of childhood and of education *based on* and *with* films. As a methodology, the class articulates theoretical studies with practical experience, seeking an approximation with the Situated Learning Episodes proposal by engaging students in the reading and discussion of texts; a cycle of film exhibitions in different contexts of fruition; the analysis of films about childhood and education; interviews with children, filmmakers and or directors; and video production workshops. In these workshops, an effort was made to combine the SLE methodology (Rivoltella, 2013) with the Lumière Minute (Bergalla, 2002) proposals.

The SLE methodology is based on 4 key ideas: teaching as design, learning by doing, flipped teaching and neurodidactics, which can be summarized as follows (Rivoltella, 2015, pp.14-17):

1. **Teaching as Design:** This involves the dimensions of the organizational idea and planning, of the aesthetic of form or style, and of the contents of culture. That is, it understands that teachers are architects of education, an idea that is based on the book *Teaching as a Desjgn Science,* by Laurilard (2012). It envisions teaching as a linguistic work in which teachers act with multiple languages in the context of the sociocultural life in which students are inserted, based on the idea of design proposed by Cope and Kalantzis (2000). It also encompasses the idea of didactics as a montage of cultural objects inspired by the dialectic between disassembly and assembly of Francastel (as cited 2005 in Rivoltella, 2015, p.15).

2. **Learning by Doing:** This involves two perspectives: one, which understands laboratory work as a didactic device and method that acts as analogical and active mediators (Damiano, 2013), beyond the reference to the space or classroom. Its foundations are in the principles of the active school, particularly in Dewey (2004) and Freinet (2002). Its other perspective considers thinking as habits of action, inspired by the epistemology of Peirce (as cited in Rivoltella, 2015, p.15), for whom the function of thinking is to produce actions.

3. **Flipped Teaching:** This means to invert the logic according to which traditional didactics organize the teaching mode through class presentations by teachers (teaching at school) and students' home-work (learning at home). The idea of flipped teaching inverts this sequence so that students are first asked to search for information about the theme of the class at home (learning at home) and in the classroom they discuss and share their understanding and doubts through activities that involve the application of these contents (learning at school). The idea of the flipped lesson is inspired by Freinet's (2002) a posteriori lesson and is now widely diffused in various countries through the work of Mazur (1997), Cecchinato (2014) and others. The dialogical perspective proposed by Freire (2000) in the 1960s in the context of his pedagogy should also be highlighted.

4. **The Intersection between Neurosciences and Didactics:** This involves three aspects. The first concerns the simplexity paradigm proposed by Berthoz (2012) and aims to understand how living organisms face complexity and develop intermediary mechanisms that instead of simplifying things can reduce the complexity developed as a function of mediation in the selection and search for information, making the EAS a simplex mechanism. The second involves the body-mind-brain system that is at the foundation of learning, redimensioning its fundamental modalities by resignifying the role of repetition, imitation and experience.

The SLE methodology is organized on a structure in which each class involves three elements that can be synthesized as follows:

1. A preliminary moment, constituted of a conceptual table or of a situation-stimulus (using a video, image, experience, document, socialized statement) that is a preparatory activity for the students;

2.   An operative moment that involves a micro-activity of production in which the students are asked to resolve a problem or produce a content about the situation-stimulus;

3.   A restructuring moment, which consists in a debriefing about what happened in the previous moments and a return about the processes activated and the concepts that emerge to sustain the reflection and gain awareness of the processes undertaken and their results, to establish aspects that deserve to be highlighted (Rivoltella, 2013, pp. 52-53).

Table 1 shows a synthesis that situates the moments and actions of teachers and students and learning strategies.

In this proposal, the elements are organically articulated – the preliminary moment solicits the preparation of an activity to be later shared with the group in an operative moment, which will be reflected on at the time of systematization – and necessarily involves the contexts of informal and formal learnings. The stimulus is based on an individual choice motivated by experience and when shared, discussed, systematized and reflected on in the group makes viable the passage from the implicit to the explicit, articulating informal and formal learnings. It should be emphasized that this methodology is inspired by the idea of micro-learning (Pachler, 2007), in the *a posteriori* lesson proposed by Freinet since the 1940s, and in the Flipped Lesson (Mazur, 2007), and is based on the theory of Simplexity (Berthoz, 2012) and on neuro-didactics (Rivoltella, 2012).

It is important to emphasize that in the EAS/SLE structure, video is usually used in the preparatory phase to assist in the fruition and analysis of films. Nevertheless, this phase can also be articulated with the production of audiovisual texts in the operational phase, depending on the time that is available in the planning of activities.

In turn, the Lumière Minute, inspired by the L'Hipothèse Cinemà of Bergala (2002), calls for an activity of video production that can revive a bit of film history in the first films made by the Lumière brothers.

As the name suggests, the Lumière Minute is an activity that engages students in the production of a one-minute video based on 5 rules: 1) the video will have one minute of continuous action with no cuts; 2) it will depict a scene/action from daily life; 3) use a fixed camera; 4) have no colors; 5) and no synchronized audio (the instrumental sound accompaniment is added during the editing). This is an exercise of approximation with audiovisuals that involves discovering new points of view about a theme to be determined. The experience plays with the choices of direction, research, scenery, framing, light

Table 1. EAS methodological framework

Steps	Teacher's Actions	Student's Actions	Learning Strategy
Preparation	• Gives homeworks • Makes a conceptual framework • Shares it with the students • Gives inputs • Gives an assignment	• Does homeworks • Hears, reads and understands	Problem solving
Activity	• Sets activities' times • Manages students' work	Builds and shares products	Learning by doing
Debriefing	• Assesses • Discusses misconceptions • Defines concepts	• Analyses schoolmates products • Discusse with them • Reflects on products and processes	Reflective Learning

Rivoltella, 2015, p.84.

and mise-en-scène, and questions chance, the construction of the scene and a look at reality based on a fragment, and allows an approximation with film production.

In this way, in a didactic route that involves theoretical studies, discussions, moments of fruition and analysis of films, the proposal for video production intends to expand the repertoire of students, given that the majority already produce audiovisuals and share their productions on networks, but do not always reflect on what they produce and share.

The workshop in an SLE format has the special participation of a former student,[2] and was conducted in a meeting of three class hours. In the *preparatory moment* (an initial activity organized by the teacher), there was an exhibition that sought to contextualize film history, by presenting a type of a condensed history from the first attempts at capturing images in movement until today. The so-called pre-cinema was presented as well as optical toys and the most rudimentary equipment passing to the most modern and contemporary devices that enchant us with the possibilities of post-cinema. With the use of images, miniatures, optical toys, a flip book and video-stimuli to awaken students' interest and motivation, clips were shown of classic scenes by George Meliès and the Lumière brothers, instigating curiosity about these productions realized more than 100 years ago.

During the *operative moment* (an activity of student production) it was suggested that the group conduct an experience with the Lumière Minute about an theme of their choice, and the daily life or routine at the university was chosen to see what each student perceived and how they reveal the different scenarios following the 5 rules (tell the story in 60 continuous seconds and without cuts, depicting scenes from daily life with a fixed camera, without color and without direct sound, with the sound track and instrumental sound added during editing, with the credits). The activity sought an approximation with the experience of the pioneers in cinema, seeking to "reproduce" – recognizing the different circumstances – the conditions of the experience of this art form as it was conducted in the first films, but with the use of current technologies, including mobile technologies for capturing images. After all, if the students could do this, they could make "any film" later, as in fact some already do, but without understanding the peculiarities of the history of film. The proposal was to provide an initiation that could later be applied to any context with children and youth of any age.

The group was divided into pairs of students, and each made a plan in a brief script, chose the scenes and captured the images with the use of personal cell phones and smart phones. Then, the editing was performed to include an instrumental sound track and the credits. At this time, it was necessary to clarify and reinforce the procedures according to the editing programs known by the group and the processes for exporting images, creating projects, finalization and transformation of the projects into videos saved in files. Once this was done, the videos produced were exhibited and socialized in the group, which watched, commented and offered various observations, comparing the different choices made in relation to the same proposal.

Then, still in the operative moment, another proposal was worked on: to narrate the routine of a university class in 12 ten-second takes without cuts. This activity requested a new perspective on university life, and in teams of 4 students, each group would film a moment of the academic routine. Based on the sketch of a collective script, which was prepared to help organize the idea that each group would film, the exercise was conducted of shooting 12 ten-second takes without cuts with the use of a cell phone or smart phone, exporting the material for editing on a laptop, creating the project, which was saved to then export the video.

Finally, the *restructuring moment* (the moment for synthesis), discussed the narratives that appeared about that daily educational life and the different perspectives on the spaces and times of the university, about the students' routines and other aspects of the cinematographic language. In the two audiovisual production activities, the highlight on the sound track was evident. Therefore, some concepts were presented about the rise of the film documentary compared with the facility of audiovisual production today, which is made possible with the access to mobile digital devices. There was also discussion about the forms of sharing these productions, the question of use and authorization of images, and if the sharing of the videos would be restricted to the group or done on an open network. Given the ludic-academic character of the "micro-documentaries," it was decided that they would be posted on the class's virtual environment, on the moodle platform.

Some statements and comments made by the students express their evaluations of the class-workshop with an SLE and Lumière Minute: "it was great," "it made me want to learn more, it was a trip from the time of cinema to reach the computer," "it motivated me to learn more about the video-editing programs and the possibility to do this with the children," "it was a great inspiration," "I think, what most called attention was the importance of the lighting, the angles, I could have gotten better and after we watched it, it made me want to cut and edit again, but that was the idea, right?" "for me, this activity removed my fear of editing, I did not know how to work with this program and now I saw that it's not that difficult," "I liked the work in group and everyone's cooperation."

The singularity of this experience with audiovisual production among students in initial teacher education, offered in the workshop in the class Film, Childhood and Education, can be analyzed from a few angles. It illustrates some of the aspects mentioned in this article and various possibilities for working with cinema in the education of teachers in a significant, ludic and authorial manner.

We emphasize that in the continuity of the discipline, other SLEs were proposed involving production of scripts for children, stop-motion workshops and others activities linked to the diversity of cinematographic productions in education.

DILEMMAS AND CHALLENGES OF VIDEO IN EDUCATION

Given what was discussed above, it is important to highlight that regardless of the approaches and possibilities for the use of audiovisuals in schools, some care and details can make a difference in the experience with film, based on the cinematographic-educational mediation. These include the importance of:

1. First asking what film represents and means for you (as a teacher) and what it can represent and mean for your students;
2. Keeping in mind some criteria of choice and the suitability of the film to be exhibited or worked with in educational contexts, particularly with children and youth, to assure their rights to protection, provision and participation in relation to the media;
3. Contextualizing the work and provoking certain curiosities before exhibition;
4. Preparing the encounter with the film, mentioning that which is essential for promoting the encounter and stimulating curiosity;
5. After the film, reserving a space for an individual moment that allows thinking of one's experience and memory of the film, and try to recall the story and the important elements of the film; then create the collective moment, a space for sharing the first impressions;

6.   In the moments of film analysis, it is important to be careful to not steer the possible interpretations, because the film offers no single truth nor only one way of seeing, but in the interlinking of the spectators' truths and modes of seeing a common objective reality can be identified and discussed;

7.   In the proposals for audiovisual production, seek the authorship of the group from the perspective of a significant learning process that does not only consider the final product but that problematizes the routes and processes, expanding the cultural repertories and the possibilities for mediation.

In addition to the cares, principles and dilemmas already discussed, we elect some challenges for the use of film and audiovisuals in school:

1.   The question of the repertoire and of the construction of the taste of teachers and students and their negotiations. The challenge is to not use film only for the transmission of knowledge, because the artistic quality of film can always be discussed based on the aesthetic experience.

2.   The choice between "film art" and "commercial film" and the tension between art-culture-entertainment-consumption. The challenge is to expand the understanding of "film as culture," "film as art," "film as consumption," because if film today creates a realm of consumption for many children and youth, the mediation can present other possibilities, make articulations among them and stimulate critical thinking so that they can re-interpret and construct other relations.

3.   The specificities between the experiences of teaching x initiating. When working with film and education, one challenge is to identify the differences between "teaching and initiating" and understand that in this proposal the meaning of teaching goes beyond transmission and involves exchanges of knowledge present in the teaching-learning process, and that the meaning of initiation comes first from the experience of those who watch the film. Thus, in the teaching-initiating process, teachers and students begin from their experiences with film as a condition for studying, teaching and learning about film.

4.   To go beyond the sense of "teaching" film. The challenge is not to think of the creation of a "film school," but of schools as places for educating *about, with* and *through* film and all its nuances and possibilities.

Finally, the use of audiovisual materials in professional education can affirm this space as one imbued with life, discovery, and a socialization of experiences and learnings that can educate students and teachers who become better clarified about themselves, film and the world today, and in the past and future. In this process, the SLE is a very powerful and vigorous didactic proposal that allows articulating multiliteracies and mobile learning devices in audiovisual production with the specificity of the Lumière Minute exercise. Given the possibilities discussed in this text, if "there are two secrets in film and one is not revealed," we see that video in education can narrate and invent many stories and perhaps reveal many other secrets.

REFERENCES

Aumont, J. (1995). *A Estética do filme*. Campinas: Papirus.

Barthes, R. (1984). *A câmara clara*. Rio de Janeiro: Nova Fronteira.

Bergala, A. (2002). *L'hypothèse cinema*. Paris: Cahiers du Cinema.

Bergala, A. (2011). A presença do cinema no contexto escolar. *Paper presented atSecond Meeting Cinema and Education*, São Paulo.

Berthoz, A. (2011). *La Semplesssità*. Torino: Codice.

Buckingham, D., Grahame, J., & Sefton-green, J. (1995). *Making Media: practical production in media education*. London: English & Media Centre.

Casetti, F., & Di Chio, F. (2004). *Analisi del film. 14*. Milano: Bompiani.

Cecchinato, G. (2014). Flipped classroom: innovare la scuola con te tecnoloige digitali. In TD Tecnologie Didattiche, 22 (1), 1-20.

Cope, B., & Kalantzis, M. (Eds.). (2000). *Multiliteracies: literacy learning and the design of social futures*. New York: Routledge.

Damiano, E. (2013). *Didattica come teoria della mediazione*. Milano: Franco Angeli.

Dewey, J. (2004). *Esperienza e Educazione*. Milano: Nuova Italia.

Fantin, M. (2011). *Crianças, Cinema e Educação: além do arco-íris*. São Paulo: Annablume.

Fantin, M. (2011a). Beyond Babel: Multiliteracies in digital culture. *International Journal of Digital Literacy and Digital Competence*, 2(1), 1–6. doi:10.4018/jdldc.2011010101

Fantin, M. (2014). Audiovisual na escola: abordagens e possibilidades. In M. C. S. Barbosa & M. A. Santos (Eds.), *Escritos de alfabetização audiovisual* (pp. 47–67). Porto Alegre: Libretos.

Fantin, M. (2015). Novos paradigmas da didática e a proposta metodológica dos Episódios de Aprendizagem Situada, EAS. *Educação & Realidade*, 40(2), 443-464. Retrieved from http://seer.ufrgs.br/index.php/educacaoerealidade/article/view/46056

Ferres, J. (2014). *Las pantallas y el cérebro emocional*. Barcelona: Gedisa.

Freinet, C. (2002). *La Scuola del Fare*. Bergamo: Junior.

Freire, P. (2000). *Pedagogia da Indignação: cartas pedagógicas e outros escritos. São Paulo: Editora Unesp. Eugeni, R (1999). Film, sapere, società: per un'analisi sociosemiotica del testo cinematografico*. Milano: Vita e Pensiero.

Jacquinot, G., & Leblanc, G. (1999). *Appunti per una lettura del cinema e della televisione*. Napoli: Editoriale Scientifica.

Jenkins, H. (2006). *Confronting the Challenges of Participatory Culture:Media Education for the 21st Century*. MacArthur Foundation.

Lankshear, C., & Knobel, M. (2011). Nuevos Alfabetismos (3rd ed.). Madrid: Morata.

Laurilard, D. (2002). *Rethinking University Teaching*. London: Routledge. doi:10.4324/9780203304846

Mazur, E. (1997). Peer Instruction: Getting Students to think in Class. In Edward F. Redish & John S. Rigden (Eds), The Changing Role of Physics Departments in Modern Universities (pp. 981-988). New York: Woodbury.

Morcelini, M., & Rivoltella, P. C. (2007). La sapienza do comunicare: dieci anni di media education in Italia ed Europa.Trento: Erickson.

Pachler, N. (Ed.). *Mobile Learning. Towards a Research Agend*. Retrieved from <http://www.wlecentre. ac.uk/cms/files/occasionalpapers/mobilelearning_pachler_2007.pdf>

Reia-Batista, V. (1995). Pedagogia da Comunicação, Cinema e Ensino. In *Educación y Medios de Comunicación en el Contexto Iberoamericano*. La Rabida: Universidade Internacional de Andalucia.

Rivoltella, P. C. (2005). Il cinema luogo di educazione, tra sacuola ed extra-escuola. In Malavasi, P., Polenghi, S. & Rivoltella, P.C (Eds), Cinema, pratiche formative, educazione. (pp. 67-88). Milano:Vita e Pensiero.

Rivoltella, P. C. (2008). Usare el cinema in scuola. In P. Ardizone & P.C. Rivoltella (Eds), Media e tecnologie per la didattica. Milano: V&P.

Rivoltella, P. C. (2012). *Neurodidattica. Insegnare al Cervello che Apprende*. Milano: Raffaello Cortina Editore.

Rivoltella, P. C. (2013). *Fare Didattica con gli EAS. Episodi di Apprendimento Situati*. Brescia: La Scuola.

Rivoltella, P. C. (2014). Episodes of Situated Learning. A New Way to Teaching and Learning. *Research on Education and Media*, 6(2), 79-87. Retrieved fromhttp://ojs.pensamultimedia.it/index.php/rem_en/ article/view/1070/1040

Rivoltella, P. C. (2015). *Didattica inclusiva con gli EAS*. Brescia: La Scuola.

Rossi, P. G. (2013). *Didattica enattiva: complessità, teorie dell'azzione, professionalità docente*. Milano: Franco Angeli.

Sorlin, P. (1997). *Estetiche dell'audiovisivo*. Firenze: La Nuova Itália.

Stam, R. (2003). *Introdução à teoria do cinema*. Campinas: Papirus.

Tufte, B., & Christensen, O. (2009). Midia-educação entre teoria e prática. *Perspectiva*, 7(1), 97–18.

Xavier, I. (Ed.), (2003). A experiência do cinema: antologia. Rio de Janeiro: Graal: Embrafilme.

KEY TERMS AND DEFINITIONS

Aesthetic Participation: Experience of sensibility and intuition that is triggered in the interaction with the wide variety of objects of culture.

Cinematographic-Educational Mediation: Ethical and aesthetic mediation to all cultural, artistic and cinematographic production that is within the reach of children, youth and teachers in the educational context.

Lumière Minute: Proposal for an activity for the production of a one-minute continuous video, without cuts, about a daily scene, with no color or sound.

Media-Education: The opportunity to work pedagogically with media to conduct education with, about and through the medias and technologies articulating the critical, instrumental and productive perspectives.

Multiliteracies: A concept that expands the traditional concept of literacy relating different languages and meta-languages in the processes of production of meanings to articulate linguistic, visual, audio, gestural, spatial and multimodal designs.

New Literacies: Literacy practices that involve immersion in digital culture considering linguistic, anthropological, epistemological and pedagogical interfaces, based on a convergence of technologies, different languages, their codes, supports and specificities in social practices.

Situated Learning Episodes: Methodological proposal for working with the integration of mobile devices with didactics based on the flipped lesson and micro-learning.

ENDNOTES

[1]   Such as the following classes taught by the author: Teaching Practice in the Early Years (2007 - 2010), Education and Communication (2012 and 2013) and Cinema, Childhood and Education (2012, 2013, 2014 e 2015).

[2]   Alessandra Collaço da Silva conducted a master's study about cinema and education under the author's supervision.

Chapter 12
Video and Its Incorporation into Social Networking Sites for Teacher Training

Juan De Pablos-Pons
University of Seville, Spain

Pilar Colás-Bravo
University of Seville, Spain

Teresa González-Ramírez
University of Seville, Spain

Jesús Conde-Jiménez
University of Seville, Spain

Salvador Reyes-de-Cózar
University of Seville, Spain

José Antonio Contreras-Rosado
University of Seville, Spain

ABSTRACT

This chapter is proposed with the primary aim of analysing the massive incorporation of the video in social networking sites, as a narrative resource support in those platforms. At the same time, and more specifically, it aims to show how they are able to be used in teacher training, since social networking sites appear as enhancing the use of video possibilities in open teacher training. However, in the educational field are shown as an aspect that still needs to explore and deepen this line of research. First, this chapter presents the phenomenon of the incorporation of video into social networking sites. Second, we present a systematization of the research work on the pedagogical value of videos and social networking sites in teacher training. This new scenario favours knowledge democratization and involves a reformulation of teacher training models and professional identity.

INTRODUCTION

This chapter looks into the role that video has played in teaching and its integration as a narrative resource in social networking sites. It concludes by looking at its applications in the field of teacher training.

Specifically, its development deals with the following aspects:

1. Contributions of research with regard to the pedagogical vale and use of social networking sites;

DOI: 10.4018/978-1-5225-0711-6.ch012

Copyright © 2017, IGI Global. Copying or distributing in print or electronic forms without written permission of IGI Global is prohibited.

2.   Results of the Research on the use of videos as a resource for teaching/learning; and
3.   Status of the issue on pedagogical applications of videos for teacher training.

The analysis of the research results in these lines of work constitutes the basis to identify future lines of research and educational intervention supported on videos incorporated into social networking sites.

The classical mass media, such as television, commercial cinemas or printed newspapers are gradually being replaced by new digital media and new ways of accessing this information and entertainment. This is also changing how these contents are produced and presented to users. Changes in the uses and preferences of social networking sites are continuous, with one of the latest tendencies being the incorporation of digital video as a communication tool.

In the last years, mass media have experienced a great evolution linked to the development of digital technologies. This phenomenon has changed users' habits, moving "live" television consumption to "deferred" and "on demand" through a multiple screens (computers, tablets, smart phones, etc.). Viewers, especially young people, are moving from being passive recipients, to become producers-consumers (prosumers). The great entertainment monopoly that open-television was, is giving way to digital media, largely because of social networking sites.

The presence and use of television and, subsequently, video as a training resource comes from far and is based on the incorporation of portable and familiar formats that permitted to extend its use (Maurice et al., 1983). Modalities such as the micro-teaching started in the '60s at the University of Stanford. Currently, the so-called MOOCs or "Massive Open Online Courses" play a key role in the development of this university, including the use of video in different ways. Developments like Social Gaming, which includes videos to achieve goals, are being implemented in the online universe of Stanford and other prestigious universities.

Video currently represents a substantial part of the interactions which create globally shared information. Internet video platforms are mushrooming, with television channels, online television aggregators, social networking sites (My Space, FaceBook, Tuenti, Instagram), video sharing portals (YouTube, BlipTV, Google videos), blogs, microblogs, videoblogs, all posting their video content. The transposition of television to cyberspace has important narrative repercussions. By definition, television always has a certain territorial coverage and a temporal articulation, scheduling, consisting of the succession of programs over time. Television overcomes spatial limitation, becoming ubiquitous and it may be fragmented over time (Díaz, 2009).

Regarding social networking sites and their impact, it is evident that they are an important stage in the development and use of the Internet, and therefore they have been the subjects of a growing research in the last years, even if their historical trajectory as a resource is relatively recent (Colás-Bravo, González-Ramírez & De Pablos-Pons, 2013).

BACKGROUND

Incorporation of Video into Social Networking Sites: Data and Figures

The insertion of video into social networking sites started in the world of marketing and advertising. Nowadays they are a mass phenomenon, in which Internet users load and spread multiple contents through the network, through videos, which are easy to handle, within the context of information society. Emerging within this reality are concepts such as trending topics or going viral to express the mass impact of topics, contents and/or network videos, quantified in the numbers of visits received by Internet users. As Alcocer (2014) points out, it was Twitter's purchase of Vine that started this phenomenon, as it was this platform that allowed users to record a six second video and then post it. Users can also view videos made by other people, and collect the most popular and successful videos and offer the latest trends using hashtags.

BlogInZenith (2014) remarks that Vine was by far the fastest growing network in 2013 (over 403% increase). Its restricted video length appeals to both users and brand names. It currently has more than 40 million users, and it has the advantage that its videos can be shared on Twitter or Tumblr and integrated easily on a blog or website. The phenomenon of YouTube, a web site to share videos, created in 2005 by three former employees of PayPal, and acquired by Google Inc. one year later, constitutes another relevant precedent. This successful platform, together with others such as Vine and Instagram, has contributed to the development of the use of video online (BlogInZenith, 2014). Figure 1 illustrates the growth we have mentioned.

Once it had become clear how successful Twitter had been with this new format, Facebook, the social networking site *par excellence*, used first of all Instagram, so that, in addition to the publication of images, it could publish short videos. This has led to the emergence of other platforms and/or applications with similar characteristics such as Socialcam, Viddy, Cinemagram or Tout, but they have not managed to achieve such a large influence as Facebook and Twitter. Figure 2 shows the number of videos shared by users on social networking sites in 2014.

Videos in Social Networking Sites/Platforms Aimed at Education

Proof of education's commitment to the use of video lies in the emergence of an increasing number of platforms dedicated specifically to the dissemination and consumption of educational videos. The

Figure 1. Growth of social networking sites including videos in 2013
GlobalWebIndex; cit. in BlogInZenith, 2014.

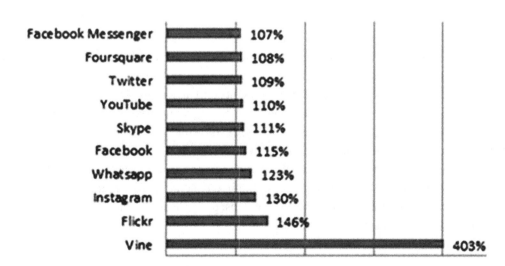

Figure 2. Videos shared on social networking sites in 2014
Socialbakers 2014; cit. in James, 2015.

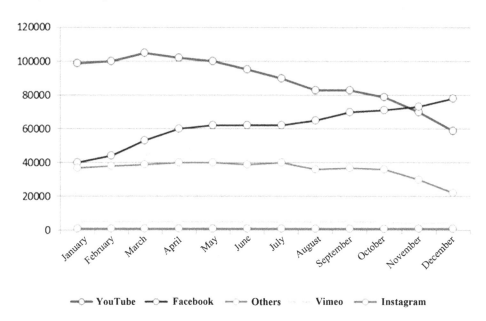

growing number and proliferation of these initiatives has been supported by some of the world's most prestigious universities.

Universities such as Stanford, Harvard, Massachusetts Institute of Technology (MIT), Yale, Princeton or Berkley, amongst others, are spearheading the creation of their own educational videos and disseminating them via specific digital platforms aimed at an audience which is growing continuously and becoming increasingly selective. This turn towards the unification of teaching materials centralized in the same area (site), with free access, enables better organization and classification of material and a segmentation of the potential audience (students or teachers) and of the contents (primary, secondary, university education, academic, etc.). Table 1 lists some of the most important academic portals and the modalities of videos included.

In relation to the pedagogical use of video on these education specific social platforms, YoutubeEDU is a resource bank similar to a matrix network that organizes videos and resources of an educational nature in different models and subjects under the same overall interface. In contrast, BigThink opts for self-production and the format of short talks given by experts. In the case of Education for All, apart from its educational videos, it offers programs of contents and an extensive bibliography as in the case of language courses that come with text books, audio CDs, etc. Academic Earth works in a similar way to YoutubeEDU, in that it stores multi-subject videos from different sources, but with the difference that they are chosen individually to ensure the quality of their contents. This network is an example of the synchrony of video platforms with other social networking sites such as Facebook and Twitter. Lastly, ForaTV forms part of the university setting with its main characteristic being the use of iTuneU as the main format for storing conferences, presentations, videos, podcasts, etc. which can be played on devices which are compatible with that technology.

Table 1. Description of the use of educational video in specific education networks

Educational Social Platforms	Modalities of Pedagogical Videos Included
YoutubeEDU	The result of a voluntary project, the objective of this portal is to collect and improve access and visibility of the many educational videos on this site. With thousands of videos including lectures, debates, interviews, etc. and with subjects ranging from IT to law, via biology, literature or philosophy, its creators are counting on a significant increase in contents as more and more universities and institutions sign up.
Big Think	This defines itself as "a global forum connecting people and ideas". Its collaborators include the Nobel Prize winner Paul Krugman or the North-American poet laureate Billy Collins.
Education for All	Apart from educational videos this portal offers teaching materials and recommended lectures to complete the learning experience. Proof of this is the financial market course given by Prof. Robert Schiller, of Yale University; the course also offers copies of exams, the answers and discussion forums for visitors.
Academic Earth	Founded by Richard Ludlow, a Yale graduate, the aim of this portal is to "give everyone on earth access to a world-class education". With the collaboration of many of the most prestigious academics in the US, it includes material from the universities of Harvard, MIT, Princeton, Stanford, Yale and Berkley amongst others.
Fora.TV	This education portal offers videos of conferences, think tanks and events of the collaborating universities. The aim of its founders was to make it possible for anyone interested to be able to enjoy and share contents however and wherever they want, without physically attending these events. Using iTunesU technology, the portal has more than 150,000 documents including conferences, presentations, videos, lectures and podcasts available for iPods.

Besides the differences existing among the different educational websites, we can identify four potential audience profiles common for all of them. First, there are adults with intellectual curiosity (lifelong learning) looking for contents to enrich their knowledge about specific subjects. The second profile identified would be those students from secondary or university education that use teaching materials as a training complement or as a research tool for papers or training projects. In the third place there are those professionals, in general, who improve their work competences or update their knowledge through the video lessons offered. And in the fourth place, teaching professionals, specifically, who use teaching materials of these websites as educational resources for their own training.

SCIENTIFIC BASIS TO ASSESS THE EDUCATIONAL POTENTIAL OF SOCIAL NETWORKING VIDEOS IN TEACHER TRAINING

Analysing and assessing the use of social networking sites for teacher training involved a scientific tour through different previous lines of research. They provide important scientific grounds to assess such educational potential. In this sense, we have identified three lines of research, that constitute the content of the following sections:

1. Research works on the pedagogical use and value of social networking sites.
2. Research works on the use of videos as a resource for teaching/learning.
3. Research works on the use of videos for teacher training.

The information obtained from these three fields will allow us to lay the scientific foundations both of present applications and of future pedagogical projections.

Research Works on the Pedagogical Use and Value of Social Networking Sites

According to Lim and Ismail (2010), after the arrival and boom of Web 2.0 tools, educators started to look for technological tools to experiment their application potential to improve teaching and learning processes. The popularity of social networking sites (such as MySpace, Facebook, Cyworld & Bebo) turned them into a focus of pedagogical interest (Boyd & Ellison, 2007). It started an entire line of research aimed at assessing the impact of the potential of such social networking sites, especially Facebook, applied to education. Quickly, a critical trend appeared at the same time questioning the high expectations attributed to social networking sites applied to education (Madge, Meek, Wellens & Hooley, 2009; Duffy, 2011; Friesen & Lowe, 2012; Manca & Ranieri, 2013). Specifically, Friesen & Lowe (2012) questioned the suitability of social media for education regarding their valuable potential on collective learning (Siemens, 2005). According to these authors, the social networking sites cannot separate themselves from the commercial obligation that characterizes them. In such a way that they would be saying that commercial social media have an influence over online learning models, imbuing them with their characteristics (Selwyn, 2009), and we should consider its suitability. Authors Manca & Ranieri (2013), in a critical review of the literature about Facebook as a learning environment, concluded that, besides its great popularity as the social network par excellence, Facebook's educational value cannot be completely determined and research results are contradictory, as some of them highlight its pedagogical strengths whereas other results are completely opposite. We present below some conclusions of the research works regarding the potential applications of social networking sites to education, showing this dualism in the results.

Before starting, we should point out that most of the existing studies on social networking sites are related to higher education (Baran, 2010; Ismail, 2010; Cain & Policastri, 2011; Duffy, 2011; Ellison, Steinfield & Lampe, 2011; Hew, 2011; Allen, 2012; Çoklar, 2012; LaRue, 2012), and secondary education (Fewkes & McCabe, 2012).

Some of the advantages and benefits of using the social networking sites for educational purposes are:

1. **Popularity and Expansion:** According to Madge, Meek, Wellens & Hooley (2009) more than 95% of British university students are regularly using social networking sites. Therefore, we are talking about a tool that students already know; certain effective learning processes naturally fit in Facebook, simply because of its popularity (Allen, 2012). This fact also supported by the existence of an open and reflective attitude by students to use Facebook in their training processes (Roblyer, McDaniel, Webb, Herman & Witty, 2010).

2. **Increase of Interactive Possibilities:** There are multiple studies that have concluded that the use of social networking sites facilitates interaction and communication (Ellison, Steinfield & Lampe, 2011; Allen, 2012; Çoklar, 2012), as well as the creation of practical learning communities (DiVall, & Kirwin, 2012). Thus, social networking sites offer a divergent and convergent learning environment depending on their interests. On the other hand, the presentation of contemporary topics and thoughts through the media link students with real-world problems and needs (Cain & Policastri, 2011). Likewise, according to Lim & Ismail (2010), students have a positive perception in Facebook of information spreading, as it encourages interest, motivation and interaction opportunities. According to these authors, Facebook has the potential to attract students to take part in significant academic conversations. Roblyer, McDaniel, Webb, Herman, & Witty (2010) also

highlight that the social networking sites strengthen educational communication and collaboration between teachers and students, both vertically and horizontally.

3. **Barrier Breaking:** Another value observed is the breakdown of space-time barriers (Cain & Policastri, 2011), which allows working in an asynchronic and synchronic manner, both online and offline (Boyd & Ellison, 2007).

4. **Change of the Roles of Educational Agents:** Teacher turns into a facilitator and a guide and students turn into active agents, content producers and support elements (LaRue, 2012), profiles of educational agents common to constructivism.

5. **Influence in Academic Performance:** According to Rouis, Limayem & Salehi-Sangari (2011), with regard to the impact of the use of Facebook in the students' academic achievements, the self-regulation offered by social networking sites affects the improvement of academic achievements.

6. **Identity Construction:** Some scientific results point out that social networking sites promote the formation of the individuals' personal and professional identity, making them stronger and more heterogeneous and divergent (Ellison, Steinfield & Lampe, 2011).

7. **Socio-Emotional Strengthening and Social Capital Exploitation:** This is another incipient line, with a great educational interest. Some researchers (Ellison, Steinfield & Lampe, 2011) have exposed the creation of social and emotional bonds generated in the communicative processes among students who share interests. Goodband, Solomon, Samuels, Lawson & Bhakta (2012) show how social networking sites promote support among students, strengthening their ability for confrontation and reducing anxiety before problematic situations. According to Ismail (2010), social networking sites, besides providing a learning environment, are also an assistance-support platform for students in their adaptation to cultural diversity.

In short, increasing learning contexts, updating and immediacy, the ability to hybridize multiple and divergent interaction possibilities, etc., are evidences of the possible applications of social networking sites to teacher training.

However, there is another scientific trend that questions the benefits of the educational applications of social networking sites. Allen (2012) argues that the reasons that support them is the fact that Facebook challenges traditional educational ideas, as well as the relations between teachers and students, together with the little grounding of the use of social networking sites in education.

Some of the most alarming arguments about the doubts about the benefits of the application of social networking sites in education highlight first the diffusion of the traditional limits between formal and non-formal education (Allen, 2012). According to the author, students intend to keep a separation between their daily life and the specific aspects of student life; apparently, there is an imbalance in the implementation of the networks in formal education. Thus, there are many studies that point out that students generally accept Facebook as a social technology instead of a formal teaching tool (Selwyn & Grant, 2009; Usluel & Mazman, 2009; Baran, 2010). Even if students accept it as a teaching tool (Roblyer, McDaniel, Webb, Herman & Witty, 2010), apparently in practice there are some tensions between its formal and informal uses in education (Madge, Meek, Wellens & Hooley, 2009). Hew (2011) warns about the risk for students' privacy of using social networking sites.

Some critics highlight those that consider that social networking sites may generate distractions, reducing, as a result, the time devoted to study by students (Kirschner & Karpinski, 2010; Fewkes & McCabe, 2012).

In addition, Lim and Ismail (2010) have also warned about the quantity and quality of information, which may give rise to control problems due to excessive and/or repetitive information (Çoklar, 2012). On the other hand, Hutchens & Hayes (2012) have proved that the excessive use of the social network may give rise to a negative perception of teachers' credibility by students.

Finally, Hew (2011) suggests that social networking sites, specifically Facebook, up to now, have a very poor educational use. Their main application is directed to social communication.

However, some recent research works carried out in the university environment in order to explore the possibilities of the social network Facebook in teachers' initial training (Colás-Bravo, Conde-Jiménez & Martín-Gutiérrez, 2015) reveal how this new scenario promotes a more active role of the students with their learning process, as well as more autonomy and responsibility in decision-making; one example is emotional feedback and communicative interaction. These aspects promote a significant use of the social and intellectual capital of all the educational agents. These results coincide with other research works that analyse the role of social networking sites as generators of social capital and/or social welfare (Ellison, Steinfield & Lampe, 2011; Goodband, Solomon, Samuels, Lawson & Bhakta, 2012). These results coincide with the potential aspects attributed by scientific literature to social networking sites.

The scientific outlook describes leads us to conclude about the need of increasing the research and experimentation of the educational value of social networking sites.

Research Works on the Use of Videos as a Resource for Teaching/Learning

The use of television and video with educational purposes has experienced a boom since 1980, coinciding with the increase and development of more flexible and accessible technological tools, as well as cost reduction in the creation of audio-visual contents and materials (Carver & MacKay, 1986; Montgomerie, 1987). The ability of video to capture the complexity and wealth of reality, with all its shades, together with the cultural evolution dominated by audio-visual elements, have turned it progressively into a key element of teaching-learning processes (Beauregard, Rousseau, & Mustafa, 2015; Koc, Peker, & Osmanoglu, 2009; Zhang, Lundeberg, Koehler, & Eberhardt, 2011).

Nowadays, learning techniques based on video are more and more varied and extended (Giannakos, Chorianopoulos, & Chrisochoides, 2015). Likewise, students can enjoy and gain access to these contents through more and more platforms (YouTube, Facebook, Wikis, etc.) and devices (TV, desktop, Smart phone, Tablets, etc.), which provide them with an unprecedented opportunity to date to interact, exchange, create and share information (Giannakos, Chorianopoulos, & Chrisochoides, 2015; Siemens, 2011). According to Giannakos, Chorianopoulos & Chrisochoides (2015), traditional lessons cannot keep pursuing the only purpose of spreading information, as students can recover it through innumerable virtual platforms. At present, the once innovative video lectures (teaching material based on video whose goal is recording and distributing class lessons through the internet (Brecht, 2012)), are making way for the creation of new, more developed methodologies such as inverted or flipped classroom (innovative class structure that takes content exposition out of the classroom through the use of technology, leaving activities and practical tasks to work on them in class (Strayer, 2007), SPOC, etc. (Fox, 2013).

Blended-learning makes the most of present technologies, especially video, to take classes from classrooms to the outside, providing both students and teachers with time in class to devote it to other teaching-learning processes (Roehl, 2012). However, according to Fox (2013), these resources must be used in order to complement the processes developed in class and not as substitutes, in order to upgrade teaching processes, students' performance, specialization and engagement (Fernandez, Simo & Sallan,

2009; Giannakos, Chorianopoulos & Chrisochoides, 2015; Hürst & Waizenegger, 2006; Mitra, Lewin-Jones, Barrett & Williamson, 2010).

Recent research works on students' experiences in the use of video as an educational tool say that students seemed really receptive with this methodology and showed a very satisfactory response (Veeramani & Bradley, 2008; Woo et al., 2008; see Shephard, 2003 for a summary of case studies from 2002), and that they preferred the use of video to classic academic texts (Chan, 2010), showing a special interest for those videos that included human elements and sense of humour (Harrison, 2015; Hibbert, 2014). Other research works (Cooke et al., 2012; Dey, Burn, & Gerdes, 2009) suggest that students do not want to replace face-to-face classes, but that they think that audio-visual materials are an ideal complement for their training, supporting them to go over tests, review lesson and go in depth into the subject (Cooke, et al., 2012; Dey, 2008, Harrison, 2015).

Besides those mentioned above, at present, according to scientific literature, we might find a wide range of examples of use of videos in the educational field, both inside and outside the classroom (Kolås, Munkvold & Nordseth, 2012):

1. **Inside the Classroom:** We can find uses such as watching movies or videos about a specific subject (Torgersen, 1998), active movie watching (Newby et al., 2006), recording the teacher's interactions in class (Axberg et al, 2006), creation and recording of in-house videos generated by students or teachers (Lambert, 2009; Høiland & Wølner, 2007; Olsen & Wølner, 2003) and use of video mobile technologies under the "low effort" approach (Kolås et al, 2012).
2. **Outside the Classroom:** The video can be used to go in depth, study and review specific subjects, as well as part of the aforementioned inverted classroom methodology (Bennett et al., 2011; Kolås, el al., 2012).

However, after the boom of online training, more and more present in syllabus and different training modalities, many authors have laid on the table some of the possible disadvantages of these modalities (Conrad, 2015). According to this author, students may often feel disconnected both from the materials they have to use and from their teachers and classmates. This inevitably leads to students with low engagement rates (Kahn, 2014), low performance (Pascarella, Seifert & Blaich, 2010) and high withdrawal rates (Yasmin, 2013). However, according to Conrad (2015), video can develop a sense of belonging to a community among students, as, even in a virtual way, they can see real people, which may give rise to a sense of loyalty (fans, followers, etc.). In turn, this sense of belonging to a community may foster emotional and intellectual links, both with teachers and with other online classmates.

Systematization of the Different Types of Educational Videos

In an effort to summarize or categorize the different types of educational videos, authors Kolås, Munkvold & Nordseth (2012) have established two general classifications that respond to two different criteria: time and nature. According to time, videos are divided as synchronic and asynchronic. When we talk about synchronic learning we mean the educational practice performed through technological tools that offer real-time interactions inside the classroom, such as surveys, instant messages, conferences, chat, etc. (Huang & Hsiao, 2012; Hatsell & Yuen 2006; Lonie & Andrews 2009), whereas when we talk about asynchronic learning, we refer to interactions spread out in time, such as a virtual platform in which teachers may encourage debates and activities to which students respond during a specific period of time (Moore & Kearsley, 2012; Zingaro & Oztok, 2012).

Regarding nature, the authors have established the following groups: conferences/virtual classrooms and CBT: Computer-Based Training.

1. **Conferences:** They offer an online synchronic platform for educational practice. Tools like audio, video, chat and shared desktop provide teachers with a wide set of resources to use them in class (Ellingson & Notbohm 2012; Lonii & Andrews, 2009).
2. **Virtual Classrooms:** Both virtual classrooms and lectures have turned into key terms for distance learning (Volette, Venable, Gose & Huang, 2010). Nowadays, video transmission is essential for any higher education institution and students have a good opinion of online teaching, considering it more effective than traditional lessons, thanks to their permanent interaction and the variety of activities they offer (Hartsell & Yuen, 2006; Fernández, Balsera, Huerta & Montequin 2012).
3. **Computer-Based Training (CBT):** Any device connected to the Internet can gain access to online educational contents. Certain studies, such as those carried out by Dubrowsky & Xeroulis (2005) or Tan, Tan & Wettasinghe (2011), apparently confirm that this kind of computer-based training is achieving positive rates of success both from the viewpoint of students and teachers. According to the authors, even if video was considered as a complementary resource or equal to other teaching methods, the results confirmed that students had improved their acquisition and retention of new knowledge.

Speaking of Computer-Based Training (CBT), it is worth analysing a special kind of video, originated by technological evolution (Denis, 2014): we are talking about video podcasts. The research works on the use of video podcasts in education started on the year 2002, making reference to audiographs, video streaming (Foertsch, Moses, Strikwerda & Litzkow, 2002; Loomes et al., 2002; Green et al., 2003; and Shephard, 2003) and Internet broadcasting (Reynolds & Mason, 2002).

Between 2000-2005, high-speed connections were relatively uncommon (Smith, 2010) and therefore podcasts were quite limited due to download time. At a later time, between 2006-2010, access to high-speed Internet rapidly increased at homes and schools (Smith, 2010), as the research works on the use of podcasts grew.

Authors Heilesen (2010), Hew (2009) and McGarr (2009) prepared three bibliographical reviews on the use of podcasts. Hew (2009) observed that students were prone to listen to podcasts at home rather than in mobile devices and that its main benefit was to review materials missed or poorly understood in class. McGarr (2009) identified three main uses of podcasts: lectures, support material and creative use. Finally, Heilsen (2010) came to the conclusion that, even if emotional and cognitive attitudes were positive, podcast-based learning was limited.

There are different kinds of categories according to the different ways in which first video podcasts appeared. Kay (2012) proposed a widely accepted classification from year 2005, based on four variables: purpose, segmentation, pedagogical strategy and academic focus.

1. **Purpose:** It groups four kinds of video podcasts: lecture-based (Heilesen, 2010), enhanced (Holbrook & Dupont, 2010), supplementary (McGarr, 2009) and worked examples (Crippen & Earl, 2004). Lecture-based podcasts are recordings of lectures that students can review anywhere or any time. Enhanced podcasts is a video footage of Power-Point slides, presented with an audio explanation.

Supplementary podcasts are focused on the teaching-learning process through summaries of class lessons, textbook chapters and additional material that may broaden or deepen student understanding. Finally, worked examples provide video explanations of specific problems, often in the area of mathematics or science.

2. **Segmentation:** Segmented video podcasts are broken up into smaller chunks that can be searched and viewed according to the needs of the user (Zhang, Zhou, Briggs & Nunamaker, 2006).

3. **Pedagogical Strategy:** It is another way of identifying podcasts through three distinct teaching approaches (receptive viewing, problem solving and created video podcasts).

4. **Academic Focus:** It consists in the categorization of video podcasts through two academic foci: practical and conceptual. Those that targeted practical skills are short in length or segmented, whereas conceptual podcasts are relatively long and may be segmented.

This tour through the variety of video formats and applications to teaching/learning generated by technological development and WEB2.0 takes us to consider the need of preparing meta-analysis and systematizations useful to orient possible pedagogical applications in teacher training.

Research Works on the Use of Videos for Teacher Training

The educational value of video for teacher training has a wide consensus among researchers (Brophy 2004; Darling-Hammond 2006; Goldman et al., 2007; Blomberg et al., 2014). It has many potential benefits as a tool for teacher training: it transmits the complexity and subtlety of teaching in real time, conserving the richness and immediacy which other types of resources cannot provide; it builds bridges between theory and practice, illustrating particular theories, etc.

Initially, video's use with teacher training was linked to the concept of micro-teaching and from that it has developed to current pedagogical models such as the flipped classroom in which video is omnipresent. This change has had a strong impact on how to focus teacher training. Beforehand teachers received training in the transversal teaching competencies they had to learn before putting them into practice; the viewing of video and continuing training guaranteed success in training. In the flipped classroom model the use of video is linked to a given learning goal that teacher wants to explore in a context of specific learning. With this last approach, teachers cede control of learning to students; thus the training of teachers must be oriented towards enabling them to create multimedia spaces with specific goals and an individual focus which connects with students' needs.

In this development, it is also clear that there has been little research into the specific pedagogical approaches that underlie the use of video as a tool for teacher training. A review of the research works carried out on this subject in the last years has allowed us to categorize the uses of video regarding different pedagogical goals: a) Promoting reflective teaching practice, b) Observing teaching practice, c) Self-evaluation of practice and d) encouraging teachers' learning potential through video. The results of these works allow us to observe the pedagogical potential of video for teacher training from different approaches and analysis methodologies.

Uses of Video to Promote Reflective Practices

The works carried out by Ellis, McFadden, Anwar and Roehrig, (2015), Blomberg et al. (2014), Hamilton, (2012) and McCullagh, (2012) are focused in analysing the role of video to *promote trainee teachers' reflection on their own practice.* One of the main conclusions of this study was that there are important differences in how experienced and novel teachers interpret the reality of the classroom and how video can help to improve students' reflexive capacity. Experienced teachers classify learning situations with a high level of abstraction while the analysis of trainee teachers is more descriptive and superficial. On the basis of these findings, researchers conceptualize the reflective skills of teachers on different levels of analysis (Sabers, Cuching & Berliner, 1991; Borko & Livingston, 1989; Evertson & Green, 1986; van Es, 2009; van Es & Sherin, 2002), identifying three levels:

1. Describe, identify and differentiate between the events observed without making any value judgment about what is observed.
2. Make a reflective assessment of the events observed bearing in mind the consequences for the learning of the student incorporating value judgments.
3. Connect the observation of the facts to previous professional knowledge and categorize them according to the main aspects of the teaching-learning process in order to make inferences about what has occurred.

On the first level, the use of video has a merely descriptive or superficial function of the observed reality, in the second it is interpretative and in the third it is inferential or prospective. These studies conclude that learning to think productively through video during the initial training of teachers can give a strong indication of how these teachers will teach their students in the future (Kersting et al., 2010; van Es & Sherin, 2002).

In this line, the work carried out by Ellis, McFadden, Anwar, & Roehrig, (2015) uses video as a social context with technological potential to promote interaction among colleagues and the feedback of one's own practice. The type of discourse generated in that interaction space is subject of analysis. The results obtained show that trainee teachers have to develop a critical discourse about their teaching activity to develop an "analytical mind" (Sherin, 2004) and learn to define the bridge between theory and practice through a reflective practice among peers, so that training improvements become a reality. From another analysis approach, the study conducted by Santagata, Zannoni & Stigler (2007) with two groups of trainee teachers looked into the role played by video as a tool for the development of teachers' professional judgment. Over a relatively short period of time, two groups of teachers on a training program with video improved their ability to analyse teaching by moving from mere descriptions of what they saw to an analysis focusing on the effects of the teachers' actions on their students' learning.

Speaking of methodology, the self-ethnographic work carried out by Hamilton (2012) concluded that video can be used to study and question one's own teaching; taking as a reference the analysis of his recordings in three analysis categories: positioning, teaching (students' commitment, classroom dynamics, students' interaction, teacher-student dialog, etc.) and one's own practice.

Speaking of theory, the research work carried out by McCullagh (2012) uses video starting from the assumptions of the sociocultural theory as a tool to stimulate teachers' close development area, promoting that teachers may gain a higher control of their progress within a social constructivist approach applied to professional development.

In short, we could say that the use of video in teacher education programs has moved on from being a way of showing future teachers specific behaviours they have to imitate, to being a tool for the development of teachers' professional judgment. In other words, when trainee teachers are given the chance to observe learning situations through video they become more reflexive and make a more complex analysis of the learning context, which in turn facilitates the internalization of educational processes.

Uses of Video to Observe Teaching Practice

Another teaching modality in which video appears as a key tool is the observation of the educational practice performed to analyse it later and, therefore, improve such action. In this sense, we may highlight the research works by Baecher and McCormack (2015) or Taylor, Ling, Ming & Hui (2013), who base their studies on observation as the start of subsequent strategies, such as sharing experiences with colleagues or identifying aspects to improve after watching their own teaching practice.

Baecher, McCormack and Kung (2014) used video so that teachers could watch and analyse their practice, with the appropriate later interaction. This is, the use of video increased teachers' interventions regarding lesson analysis. Specifically, video becomes a tool to increase participation and collaboration in conversations directed to observe teaching practice.

We know that the students' learning results depend to a great extent on teachers' quality and this, in turn, on the training quality received during teacher training. The fact that a teacher can separate, split and analyse his educational practices, as well as his structures by watching recordings, allows him to continue learning, feedback, transform and improve his daily teaching practice. Taylor, Ling, Ming & Hui (2013) start from this premise and highlight that watching video recordings on pedagogical classroom practices allows to characterize this practice and identify effective teaching behaviours, tools or strategies. In this sense, these videos can also record, to analyse and transform it later, teachers' movements in the classroom as well as their interaction with students.

Other Noted Uses in Teacher Training

Besides one's own thoughts on the practice carried out or the visualization around the observation of teaching practice, video appears as a tool for different uses for teacher training. In this sense, the research works carried out show two key uses: practice self-assessment and as a tool to encourage teachers' learning potential.

In this sense, Christ, Arya and Chiu (2014) propose video as an element to promote debate and discussion. This research work uses video as a tool to start debate and promote discussion among persons who are training as teachers. The results of this study suggest that the method used is effective for teacher training. This information is relevant, considering that debates based on videos are at its peak.

Another aspect to be considered in this sense would be the possibilities of the use of videos to self-assess teaching practice. Numerous scientific contributions consider video as an essential support for the teaching process, especially as a pedagogical tool for teachers under training who intend to improve their learning. In this sense, according to Linston (2015), video may play functions or uses to prepare, produce, study or show experiences that provide teachers with knowledge. The fact that a teacher under training can be recorded as he imparts his lesson and that he can watch it later allows him to analyse in detail his weaknesses and strengths, learning to question, improve, change, transfer and transform his teaching model, strategies, tools, discourse and, in short, his pedagogical practice in the classroom in the meanwhile.

Table 2 summarizes the uses of video oriented to teaching training and the dimensions subject to analysis in each of the works consulted.

Table 2. Research on the use of video for teacher training

Uses of Video	Measures Subject to Analysis	Authors
Promoting reflective practice	Interaction and reflection	Ellis, McFadden, Anwar, & Roehrig, 2015
	Developing analytical mentality	Sherin, 2004
	Changes in teaching actions	Santagata, Zannoni & Stigler, 2007
	Studying and questioning one's own teaching	Hamilton, 2012
	Close development area	McCullagh, 2012
Observation of teaching practice	Subsequent interaction	Baecher & McCormack, 2015
	Movement and interaction	Taylor, Ling, Ming & Hui, 2013
Interaction development	Debate and discussion	Christ, Arya & Chiu (2014)
Self-assessment of practice	Identifying strengths and weaknesses Questioning practice Transferability Discourse on practice Transformation ability	Linston (2015)

The public availability of videos in social networking sites opens a new perspective for teacher training still unexplored, but with an enormous potential to transform traditional approaches of teacher training. Before an individualist Concepcion of training, social networking sites facilitate the development of training processes linked to the collaborative construction and management of knowledge.

Issues, Controversies, Problems

As we have discussed above, there is an important documentary and scientific grounding from the application of to teacher training. The incorporation of social networking sites to training also has more and more studies in favour of the possibilities of their educational potential. The inclusion of videos to social networking sites opens a new space for scientific exploration applied to their potential to enrich teacher-training processes. But, in turn, these technologies are fostering conceptual changes and promoting other training models. Therefore, in the educational field, according to Veletsianos & Navarrete (2012), the use of social networking sites has been assessed by numerous researchers on Educational Technology as a tool to have an influence and transform traditional training systems, both due to their technical characteristics and to their ability to boost educational innovations, as social networking sites facilitate the use of participative pedagogies and a more active learning. On the other hand, Barcelos & Batista (2013) highlight the social function played by the use of social networking sites as a training instrument.

In spite of the educational value of the videos available in social networking sites, we cannot say that it is always positive, as we must consider numerous variables to guarantee a valuable use of them For example, sometimes we cannot obtain the results expected due to the lack of an educational design or the narrative ambiguity, among other aspects. On the other hand, the success of these applications is also conditioned by the criteria of the trainer for their selection and educational use. Therefore, in this kind of problems, the model of teacher that we intend to train is a key criterion to assess the potential of these technologies, as well as the selection of the resources that we may find in them. In this sense, we may point out the importance of integrating these subjects in teachers' initial training and in the programs for the updating of exercising teachers, linking it to a command of technological competences, both regarding the creation and the assessment of online videos according to pedagogical criteria.

SOLUTIONS AND RECOMMENDATIONS

Given this new reality, teacher training has moved away from models of technical rationality to become a "social practice" in which ICTs constitute "cultural artifacts" (intellectual resources) which acquire meaning and value when applied to teaching activity in a context of specific learning.

This technological-pedagogical mediation between the tools in a social setting (network) with a specific training objective requires a thorough analysis of all its pedagogical components. The teacher has to learn to dialog with the resources, be aware of their potential to be able to fit them to variable training objectives: motivation towards learning, exemplification of models, generation of reflexive processes, awareness raising about an educational reality, etc. These resources employed in different learning contexts generate different educational processes and results. The pedagogical criteria that, at a teacher level, are used to select the resource (video) form part of a decision-making process that also affects the achievement of the training objective resources (video) belong to a decision-making process that also affects the achievement of the training goal.

A study performed by Del Moral & Villalustre (2012) concludes that trainee teachers point to three basic educational applications to social networking sites: a communication tool, a channel for transmitting information and a medium for socialization. As for how they would use them in their teaching activities, 38.5% of them agreed that they were useful as a means for publicizing activities and events of the class and school; while 33% saw them as an ideal media for encouraging communication among students and between them and teachers. Some 17.5% stated that they would use them to organize tasks (calendar and distribution), a marginal 6.5% indicated that they would use them to perform a variety of teaching activities (debates, asking for opinions about different issues, etc.), other purposes (4.5%) included applications linked to cooperation and collaboration between students, or to plan visits, excursions and after-school activities.

In the same line, a study published by Area (2008) on the potential of teaching networks in the internet applied to continual teachers' training, underlines among others the following:

1. Socially spreading the professional identity of teachers as a group.
2. Possibility of establishing a fluent and synchronic communication of teachers on their activity.
3. Sharing and exchanging materials and resources prepared individually.
4. Generating documents and/or materials through a collaborative process.
5. Collaborative management of knowledge.
6. Creation of news boards/channels of common interest for the group of teachers.

Therefore, these technical resources offer the opportunity of changing from a model of individual teacher training to an online cooperative learning model. Over the course of their professional career, teachers need instrumental, professional and emotional back up. The visualization of educational processes in a virtual environment situates the social group of teachers as the referent and generator of social capital. Through video, one can also motivate, involve and encourage the processes of self-construction of professional identity, ultimately favouring the virtual use of the network and the digital social inclusion of teachers.

FUTURE RESEARCH DIRECTIONS

The application of video incorporated into social networking sites to teacher training involves transforming and reinforcing certain directions. Specifically, one of the most powerful and relevant lines is that of teaching professionals' development. In this direction, online videos become research instruments able to generate professional knowledge, both conceptual and practical. These are some of the potential lines of work:

- *Online video as an instrument for learning and generation of professional knowledge based on a critical reflection on video practices.* In this sense, video creation becomes a means to analyse practices and compare the educational theories implicit in them, as well as to generate shared debates with teaching communities and, this way, to build a shared professional approach and reinforce professional identity. Online video also allows putting teaching practices into context, making it possible to analyse specific places and circumstances in which certain practices become valuable. Therefore, they generate learning potentially translatable to other places and cases that may increase the background of professional knowledge. Another aspect of interest corresponds with the recording of best teaching practices, which become reference models to redirect educational praxis. These materials may also illustrate new practices in teachers' initial training, stimulating thinking about strategies that may become confirmed. Therefore, interacting with videos shared in social networking sites is a valuable incentive for discussing, reflecting and testing new ideas.

The possibility for teachers of creating and editing videos is valuable in different aspects; on the one hand, it enriches educational productions that illustrate praxis and, on the other hand, there are multiple perspectives on a certain phenomenon, fostering critical analysis and reflection on practice.

- *Online video as a research instrument.* The observation of videos that depict real-life learning situations constitutes a valuable material to propose explanatory hypothesis of learning processes, as well as to build and refine pedagogical theories, both on educational practices and on teacher training processes. Online distribution and, therefore, the availability of numerous resources of this kind, become important references in order to prepare, refine and compare theories on educational praxis. This way the teacher-researcher approach becomes true, a teaching model defended in the present initial and permanent training plans for teachers. An essential aspect of this training model lies in the interrelation between theory and practice.

The videos available in social networking sites may offer information on theories according to four formulas:

1. Videos represent a part, aspect or viewpoint of a theory.

2. Videos use a theory to provide educators with a new direction for reflection, action and significant dialog.
3. The reconstruction of a theory to respond to the needs and problems of a specific context.
4. Providing educators with different approaches and standards to evaluate their practice, fostering in turn the creation of other possible alternatives.

Finally, we may mention the potential of *online video as an instrument for personal self-development.* Continual professional development, understood as the reinforcement of professional and pedagogical practice during teachers' career, is a key aspect. Belonging to learning networks or communities is very useful for this purpose (Holmes, 2014). Online videos offer numerous incentives for self-learning, besides promoting sharing and comparing personal proposals.

The approaches identified above open new lines of research that deserve to be explored in the near future. Looking forward, the uses we mentioned above and the possibilities offered by video for the education of teachers become more varied and diversified in social networking sites: the social network becomes an "authentic scenario". The fact of sharing, collaborating and interacting in a network on the use of video as a tool for education gives the use of social networking sites a relatively unexplored facet, helping in turn for the training of teachers to benefit from the synergy that the video-network binomial may provide. However, few studies have specifically tackled the use of video in social networking sites for teacher education. International scientific production has focused mainly on identifying why certain population groups use the networks, following a psychological line of work concentrating on different uses of individuals, their motivations and construction of network identity. In parallel, there is another more social line of research investigating the concepts of social capital and social compensation as basic referents for explaining the benefits that the use of social networking sites may provide to its users.

The results obtained in these studies (Colás-Bravo, González-Ramírez & De Pablos-Pons, 2013) allow us to propose certain ideas about how we can go about tracing in a not too distant future the use of video on social networking sites as a tool for educating teachers and the benefits that this could reap. To do this, we are going to take as a reference the concept of social capital, social compensation and teachers' emotional wellbeing. Social capital can be understood as the resources integrated in the social structure, to which individuals have access and which they mobilize in intentional actions (Lin, 1999). Specifically, Greenhow & Burton (2011) look at the potential use of social networking sites for the education of social capital. The fact that video is currently the most widely used resource on social networking sites makes the Internet itself an educational resource bank. On the same level, the guaranteed access to these resources contributes to the development of a social structure (learning communities) in which teachers can communicate, interact and share videos to guide their professional development. The interaction is privileged by the tool (video) thereby contributing to the creation of shared discourses about their interests, motivations and technological competencies. This flow of interactions produces positive feedback for teachers' emotional wellbeing and emphasizes group achievements (social compensation).

CONCLUSION

Throughout these pages, we have showed the growth experienced in the last years by the use of social networking sites. The evolution in the use of video in the scientific and educational field has promoted the democratization of knowledge from its inclusion in the social networking sites. This development show the leading role acquired by virtual spaces in nowadays society. These possibilities have acquired new forms through online video, with more and more users; and social networking sites are responsible for this phenomenon, as they play a very important role in their spreading.

Therefore, social networking sites and video converge nowadays, opening new opportunities for educational systems and specifically for teacher training. There is an important research flow to analyse educational applications of social networking sites and numerous works that analyse the role of video in teacher training. However, there are not many research works that analyse the use of video as a training tool through social networking sites. Therefore, convergence between video and social networking sites as an instrument for teacher training appears as an emerging research line.

From a prospective approach, the incorporation of video into social networking sites as an instrument for teacher training makes possible the creation of repositories at the service of virtual learning communities. Social networking sites have an enormous potential, but there are few empirical research works that analyse the impact in learning of the communication and interaction of social networking sites (De Haro, 2009; Cheung, Chio & Lee, 2011; Junco, Heiberger & Loken, 2011). The fact of sharing, collaborating and interacting online about the use of video as a training tool, measures the use of social networking sites in an unexplored facet, promoting in turn benefits for teacher training from the synergy fostered by the video-social network binomial. This new scenario has important consequences in teacher training models and in the development of a new teaching professional culture adapted to these requirements.

REFERENCES

Alcocer, A. (2014). *El auge de los vídeos móviles en las redes sociales.* Retrieved from http://www.societicbusinessonline.com/2014/07/22/el-auge-de-los-videos-moviles-en-las-redes-sociales/

Allen, M. (2012). An Education in Facebook. *Digital Culture & Education, 4*(3), 213–225.

Area, M. (2008). Las redes sociales en internet como espacios para la formación del profesorado. *Razón y palabra, 13*(63), 1-12.

Axberg, U., Hansson, K., Broberg, A. G., & Wirtberg, I. (2006). The Development of a Systemic School-Based Intervention: MarteMeo and Coordination Meetings. *Family Process, 45*(3), 375–389. doi:10.1111/j.1545-5300.2006.00177.x PMID:16984077

Baecher, L., & McCormack, B. (2015). The impact of video review on supervisory conferencing. *Language and Education, 29*(2), 153–173. doi:10.1080/09500782.2014.992905

Baecher, L. H., McCormack, B., & Kung, S. C. (2014). Supervisor use of video as a tool in teacher reflection. *The Electronic Journal for English as a Second Language, 18*(3). Retrieved from http://www.tesl-ej.org/wordpress/issues/volume18/ej71/ej71a5/

Baran, B. (2010). Facebook as a formal instructional environment. *British Journal of Educational Technology, 41*(6), 146–149. doi:10.1111/j.1467-8535.2010.01115.x

Barcelos, G. T., & Batista, S. C. F. (2013). Use of Social Networks in teacher training programs: A case study. *International Journal on New Trends in Education and Their Implications, 4*(1), 1–14.

Bennett, B., Spencer, D., Bergmann, J., Cockrum, T., Musallam, R., Sams, A., & Overmyer, J. et al. (2011). *The flipped class manifest*. New York, NY: The Daily Rift.

BlogInZenith. (2014). *Instagram y Vine, ¿responsables del auge del vídeo en las redes sociales?* Retrieved from http://blogginzenith.zenithmedia .es/el-video-online-crece-en-las-redes-sociales-vine-e-instagram-protagonistas/

Blomberg, G., Gamoran, M., Renkl, A., Glogger, I., & Seidel, T. (2014). Understanding video as a tool for teacher education: Investigating instructional strategies to promote reflection. *Instructional Science*, *42*(3), 443–463. doi:10.1007/s11251-013-9281-6

Borko, H., & Livingston, C. (1989). Cognition and improvisation: Differences in mathematics instruction by expert and novice teachers. *American Educational Research Journal*, *26*(4), 473–498. doi:10.3102/00028312026004473

Boyd, D., & Ellison, N. (2007). Social network sites: Definition, history, and scholarship. *Journal of Computer-Mediated Communication*, *13*(1), 210–230. doi:10.1111/j.1083-6101.2007.00393.x

Brecht, H. (2012). Learning from online video lectures. *Journal of Information Technology Education: Innovations in Practice*, *11*(1), 227–250.

Brophy, J. E. (Ed.), (2004). *Using video in teacher education*. Amsterdam, Netherlands: Elsevier.

Cain, J., & Policastri, A. (2011). Using Facebook as an informal learning environment. *American Journal of Pharmaceutical Education*, *75*(10), 1–8. doi:10.5688/ajpe7510207 PMID:22345726

Carver, J., & MacKay, R. C. (1986). Interactive Television Brings University Classes to the Home and Workplace. *Canadian Journal of Educational Communication*, *15*(1), 19–28.

Chan, Y. M. (2010). Video instructions as support for beyond classroom learning. *Procedia: Social and Behavioral Sciences*, *9*, 1313–1318. doi:10.1016/j.sbspro.2010.12.326

Cheung, C. M. K., Chiu, P., & Lee, M. K. O. (2011). Online social networking sites: Why do students use Facebook? *Computers in Human Behavior*, *27*(4), 1337–1343. doi:10.1016/j.chb.2010.07.028

Christ, T., Arya, P., & Chiu, M. (2014). Teachers' reports of learning and application to pedagogy based on engagement in collaborative peer video analysis. *Teaching Education*, *25*(4), 349–374. doi:10.1080/10476210.2014.920001

Çoklar, A. N. (2012). Evaluations of students on Facebook as an educational environment. *Turkish Online Journal of Qualitative Inquiry*, *3*(2), 42–53.

Colás-Bravo, P., Conde-Jiménez, J., & Martín-Gutiérrez, A. (2015). Social Networking Sites in Higher Education: Educational use of social and intellectual capital. *Revista Interuniversitaria de Formación del Profesorado (RIFOP)*, *83*(29.2), 105-116.

Colás-Bravo, P., González-Ramírez, T., & De Pablos-Pons, J. (2013). Young people and social networks: Motivations and preferred uses. *Comunicar*, *40*(20), 15–23. doi:10.3916/C40-2013-02-01

Conrad, O. (2015). *Community of Inquiry and Video in Higher Education Engaging Students Online* [Doctoral dissertation]. California State University, Fullerton.

Cooke, M., Watson, B., Blacklock, E., Mansah, M., Howard, M., Johnston, A., & Murfield, J. et al. (2012). Lecture capture: First year student nurses' experiences of a web based lecture technology. *The Australian Journal of Advanced Nursing*, *29*(3), 14–21.

Crippen, K. J., & Earl, B. L. (2004). Considering the efficacy of web-based worked examples in introductory chemistry. *Journal of Computers in Mathematics and Science Teaching*, *23*(2), 151–167.

Darling-Hammond, L. (2006). Assessing teacher education: The usefulness of multiple measures for assessing program outcomes. *Journal of Teacher Education*, *57*(2), 120–138. doi:10.1177/0022487105283796

De Haro, J. J. (2009). Las redes sociales aplicadas a la práctica docente. *Didáctica. Innovación y Multimedia DIM*, *13*, 1–8.

Del Moral Pérez, E., & Villalustre Martínez, L. (2012). Presencia de los futuros maestros en las redes sociales y perspectivas de uso educativo. *RELATEC. Revista Latinoamericana de Tecnología Educativa*, *11*(1), 41–51.

Dey, E. L., Burn, H. E., & Gerdes, D. (2009). Bringing the classroom to the web: Effects of using new technologies to capture and deliver lectures. *Research in Higher Education*, *50*(4), 377–393. doi:10.1007/s11162-009-9124-0

Díaz, R. (2009). Video in cyberspace: Usage and language. *Comunicar*, *33*(17), 63–71. doi:10.3916/c33-2009-02-006

DiVall, M. V., & Kirwin, J. L. (2012). Using Facebook to facilitate course-related discussion between students and faculty members. *American Journal of Pharmaceutical Education*, *76*(2), 1–5. doi:10.5688/ajpe76232 PMID:22438604

Dubrowski, A., & Xeroulis, G. (2005). Computer-based Video Instructions for Acquisition of Technical Skills. *Journal of Visual Communication in Medicine*, *28*(4), 150–155. doi:10.1080/01405110500518622 PMID:16503567

Duffy, P. (2011). Facebook or Faceblock: Cautionary tales exploring the rise of social networking within tertiary education. In M. J. W. Lee & C. McLoughlin (Eds.), *Web 2.0-base E-learning: Applying social informatics for tertiary teaching* (pp. 284–300). Hershey, PA, USA: IGI Global. doi:10.4018/978-1-60566-294-7.ch015

Ellingson, D. A., & Notbohm, M. (2012). Synchronous Distance Education: Using Web Conferencing In An MBA Accounting Course. *American Journal of Business Education*, *5*(5), 555–562.

Ellis, J., McFadden, J., Anwar, T., & Roehrig, G. (2015). Investigating the social interactions of beginning teachers using a video annotation tool. *Contemporary Issues in Technology & Teacher Education*, *15*(3), 404–421.

Ellison, N. B., Steinfield, C., & Lampe, C. (2011). Connection strategies: Social capital implications of Facebook-enabled communication practices. *New Media & Society*, *13*(6), 873–892. doi:10.1177/1461444810385389

Evertson, C., & Green, J. L. (1986). Observation as inquiry & method. In M. C. Wittrock (Ed.), *Handbook of research on teaching* (pp. 162–213). New York: Macmillan.

Fernández, V., Simo, P., & Sallan, J. M. (2009). Podcasting: A new technological tool to facilitate good practice in higher education. *Computers & Education, 53*(2), 385–392. doi:10.1016/j.compedu.2009.02.014

Fewkes, A. M., & McCabe, M. (2012). Facebook: Learning tool or distraction? *Journal of Digital Learning in Teacher Education, 28*(3), 92–98. doi:10.1080/21532974.2012.10784686

Foertsch, J., Moses, G. A., Strikwerda, J. C., & Litzkow, M. J. (2002). Reversing the lecture/homework paradigm using eTeach web-based streaming video software. *The Journal of Engineering Education, 91*(3), 267–274. doi:10.1002/j.2168-9830.2002.tb00703.x

Fox, A. (2013). From MOOCs to SPOCs. *Communications of the ACM, 56*(12), 2013, 38-40.

Friesen, N., & Lowe, S. (2012). The questionable promise of social media for education connective learning and the commercial imperative. *Journal of Computer Assisted Learning, 28*(3), 183–194. doi:10.1111/j.1365-2729.2011.00426.x

Giannakos, M. N., Chorianopoulos, K., & Chrisochoides, N. (2015). Making sense of video analytics: Lessons learned from clickstream interactions, attitudes, and learning outcome in a video-assisted course. *The International Review of Research in Open and Distributed Learning, 16*(1), 260–283.

Goldman, R., Pea, R., Barron, B., & Denny, S. J. (2007). *Video research in the learning sciences.* Mahwah, NJ: Erlbaum.

Goodband, J. H., Solomon, Y., Samuels, P. C., Lawson, D., & Bhakta, R. (2012). Limits and potentials of social networking in academia: Case study of the evolution of a mathematics Facebook community. *Learning, Media and Technology, 37*(3), 236–252. doi:10.1080/17439884.2011.587435

Green, S., Voegeli, D., Harrison, M., Phillips, J., Knowles, J., Weaver, M., & Shephard, K. (2003). Evaluating the use of streaming video to support student learning in a first-year life sciences course for student nurses. *Nurse Education Today Journal, 23*(4), 255–261. doi:10.1016/S0260-6917(03)00014-5 PMID:12727092

Greenhow, C., & Burton, L. (2011). Help from my "Friends" Social Capital in the Social Networks Site of Low-Income Students. *Journal of Educational Computing Research, 45*(2), 223–245. doi:10.2190/EC.45.2.f

Hamilton, E. (2012). Video as a Metaphorical Eye: Images of Positionality, Pedagogy, and Practice. *College Teaching, 60*(1), 10–16. doi:10.1080/87567555.2011.604803

Harrison, D. J. (2015). Assessing experiences with online educational videos: Converting multiple constructed responses to quantifiable data. *The International Review of Research in Open and Distributed Learning, 16*(1), 168–192.

Hartsell, T., & Yuen, S. (2006). Video Streaming in Online Learning. *AACE Journal, 14*(1), 31–43.

Heilesen, S. B. (2010). What is the academic efficacy of podcasting? *Computers & Education, 55*(3), 1063–1068. doi:10.1016/j.compedu.2010.05.002

Hew, K. F. (2009). Use of audio podcast in K-12 and higher education: A review of research topics and methodologies. *Educational Technology Research and Development*, *57*(3), 333–357. doi:10.1007/s11423-008-9108-3

Hew, K. F. (2011). Students' and teachers' use of Facebook. *Computers in Human Behavior*, *27*(2), 662–676. doi:10.1016/j.chb.2010.11.020

Hibbert, M. C. (2014). What Makes an Online Instructional Video Compelling? *Educause Review Online*. Retrieved from http://er.educause.edu/articles/2014/4/what-makes-an-online-instructional-video-compelling

Høiland, T. & Wølner, T.A. (2007). Fra digital ferdighettilkompetanse – om didaktikk for arbeid med digitalemedieriskolen. Oslo: Gyldendal akademisk.

Holbrook, J., & Dupont, C. (2010). Making the decision to provide enhanced podcasts to post-secondary science students. *Journal of Science Education and Technology*, *20*(1), 233–245.

Holmes, E. (2014). *El bienestar de los docentes. Guía para controlar el estrés y sentirse bien personal y profesionalmente*. Madrid: Narcea S.A. de Ediciones.

Huang, X., & Hsiao, E.-L. (2012). Synchronous and Asynchronous Communication in an Online Environment: Faculty Experiences and Perceptions. *The Quarterly Review of Distance Education*, *13*(1), 15–30.

Hutchens, J. S., & Hayes, T. (2014). In your Facebook: Examining Facebook usage as misbehavior on perceived teacher credibility. *Education and Information Technologies*, *19*(1), 5–20. doi:10.1007/s10639-012-9201-4

Ismail, S. (2010). International students' acceptance on using social networking site to support learning activities. *International Journal for the Advancement of Science & Arts*, *1*(2), 81–90.

Junco, R., Heiberger, G., & Loken, E. (2011). The effect of Twitter on college student engagement and grades. *Journal of Computer Assisted Learning*, *27*(2), 119–132. doi:10.1111/j.1365-2729.2010.00387.x

Kahn, P. E. (2014). Theorising student engagement in higher education. *British Educational Research Journal*, *40*(6), 1005–1018. doi:10.1002/berj.3121

Kay, R. H. (2012). Exploring the use of video podcasts in education: A comprehensive review of the literature. *Computers in Human Behavior*, *28*(3), 820–831. doi:10.1016/j.chb.2012.01.011

Kersting, N., Givvin, K. B., Sotelo, F. L., & Stigler, J. W. (2010). Teachers' analyses of classroom video predict student learning of mathematics: Further explorations of a novel measure of teacher knowledge. *Journal of Teacher Education*, *61*(2), 172–181. doi:10.1177/0022487109347875

Kirschner, P. A., & Karpinski, A. C. (2010). Facebook and academic performance. *Computers in Human Behavior*, *26*(6), 1237–1245. doi:10.1016/j.chb.2010.03.024

Koc, Y., Peker, D., & Osmanoglu, A. (2009). Supporting teacher professional development through online video case study discussions: An assemblage of preservice and in service teachers and the case teacher. *Teaching and Teacher Education*, *25*(8), 1158–1168. doi:10.1016/j.tate.2009.02.020

Kolås, L., Munkvold, R., & Nordseth, H. (2012). Evaluation and categorization of educational videos. In T. Bastiaens & G. Marks (Eds.), *Proceedings of E-Learn: World Conference on E-Learning in Corporate, Government, Healthcare, and Higher Education 2012* (pp. 648-657). Chesapeake, VA: Association for the Advancement of Computing in Education (AACE).

Lambert, J. (2009). *Digital storytelling: capturing lives, creating community.* Berkeley, CA: Digital Diner Press.

LaRue, E. M. (2012). Using Facebook as course management software: A case study. *Teaching and Learning in Nursing, 7*(17), 17–22. doi:10.1016/j.teln.2011.07.004

Lavolette, E., Venable, M. A., Gose, E., & Huang, E. (2010). Comparing Synchronous Virtual Classrooms: Student, Instructor and Course Designer Perspectives. *TechTrends, 54*(5), 54–61. doi:10.1007/s11528-010-0437-9

Lim, T., & Ismail, J. T. (2010). The use of Facebook for online discussions among distance learners. *Turkish Online Journal of Distance Education, 11*(4), 72–81.

Lin, N. (1999). Social networks and status attainment. *Annual Review of Sociology, 25*(1), 467–487. doi:10.1146/annurev.soc.25.1.467

Linston, M. (2015). The use of video analysis and the Knowledge Quartetin mathematics teacher education programmes. *International Journal of Mathematical Education in Science and Technology, 46*(1), 1–12. doi:10.1080/0020739X.2014.941423

Lonie, A.-L., & Andrews, T. (2009). Creating a Rich Learning Environment for Remote Post-Graduate Leaners. *Education in Rural Australia, 19*(1), 3–13.

Loomes, M., Shafarenko, A., & Loomes, M. (2002). Teaching mathematical explanation through audiographic technology. *Computers & Education, 38*(1– 3), 137–149

Madge, C., Meek, J., Wellens, J., & Hooley, T. (2009). Facebook, social integration and informal learning at university: 'It is more for socialising and talking to friends about work than for actually doing work'. *Learning, Media and Technology, 34*(2), 141–155. doi:10.1080/17439880902923606

Manca, S., & Ranieri, M. (2013). Is it a tool suitable for learning? A critical review of the literature on Facebook as a technology-enhanced learning environment. *Journal of Computer Assisted Learning, 29*(6), 487–504. doi:10.1111/jcal.12007

Maurice, M., Lowy, P., Girod, C., Irlande, J., Kempf, A., Moreau, M., & Zaidman, C. et al. (1983). *El video en la enseñanza.* Barcelona, Spain: Planeta.

McCullagh, J. F. (2012). How can video supported reflection enhance teachers' professional development? *Cultural Studies of Science Education, 7*(1), 137–152. doi:10.1007/s11422-012-9396-0

McGarr, O. (2009). A review of podcasting in higher education: Its influence on the traditional lecture. *Australasian Journal of Educational Technology, 25*(3), 309–321. doi:10.14742/ajet.1136

Mitra, B., Lewin-Jones, J., Barrett, H., & Williamson, S. (2010). The use of video to enable deep learning. *Research in Post-Compulsory Education, 15*(4), 405–414. doi:10.1080/13596748.2010.526802

Montgomerie, T. C. (1987). Facilitating "Extended Campus" graduate education through electronic communication. *Canadian Journal of Educational Communication, 16*(3), 239–256.

Moore, M., & Kearsley, G. (2012). *Distance Education: A Systems View of Online Learning.* Belmont, CA: Wadsworth, Cengage Learning.

Newby, T. J. et al.. (2006). *Educational technology for teaching and learning* (3rd ed.). Englewood Cliffs, NJ: Pearson Merrill Prentice Hall.

Olsen, K. R., & Wølner, T. A. (2003). *Storyline for ungdomstrinnet.* Oslo: Universitetsforlaget.

Pascarella, E. T., Seifert, T. A., & Blaich, C. (2010). How effective are the NSSE benchmarks in predicting important educational outcomes? *Change: The Magazine of Higher Learning, 42*(1), 16–22. doi:10.1080/00091380903449060

Reynolds, P. A., & Mason, R. (2002). On-line video media for continuing professional development in dentistry. *Computers & Education, 39*(1), 65–97. doi:10.1016/S0360-1315(02)00026-X

Roblyer, M. D., McDaniel, M., Webb, M., Herman, J., & Witty, J. V. (2010). Findings on Facebook in higher education: A comparison of college faculty and student uses and perceptions of social networking sites. *The Internet and Higher Education, 13*(3), 134–140. doi:10.1016/j.iheduc.2010.03.002

Roehl, T. (2012). Disassembling the classroom–an ethnographic approach to the materiality of education. *Ethnography and Education, 7*(1), 109–126. doi:10.1080/17457823.2012.661591

Rouis, S., Limayem, M., & Salehi-Sangari, E. (2011). Impact of Facebook Usage on Students' Academic Achievement: Role of Self-Regulation and Trust. *Electronic Journal of Research in Educational Psychology, 9*(3), 961–994.

Rudd, D. P. II, & Rudd, D. P. (2014). The value of video in online instruction. *Journal of Instructional Pedagogies, 13*(1), 1–7.

Sabers, D., Cushing, K., & Berliner, D. (1991). Differences among teachers in a task characterized by simultaneity, multidimensionality and immediacy. *American Educational Research Journal, 28*(1), 63–88.

Santagata, R., Zannoni, C., & Stigler, J. (2007). The role of lesson analysis in pre-service teacher education: An empirical investigation of teacher learning from a virtual video-based field experience. *Journal of Mathematics Teacher Education, 10*(2), 123–140. doi:10.1007/s10857-007-9029-9

Selwyn, N. (2009). Faceworking: Exploring students' education-related use of Facebook. *Learning, Media and Technology, 34*(2), 157–174. doi:10.1080/17439880902923622

Selwyn, N., & Grant, L. (2009). Researching the realities of social software use—an introduction. *Learning, Media and Technology, 34*(2), 79–86. doi:10.1080/17439880902921907

Shephard, K. (2003). Questioning, promoting and evaluating the use of streaming video to support student learning. *British Journal of Educational Technology, 34*(3), 295–308. doi:10.1111/1467-8535.00328

Sherin, M. G. (2004). New perspectives on the role of video in teacher education. In J. Brophy (Ed.), *Using video in teacher education* (pp. 1–27). Amsterdam: Elsevier.

Siemens, G. (2005). Connectivism: A learning theory for the digital age. *International Journal of Instructional Technology and Distance Learning*, *2*(1). Retrieved from http://www.itdl.org/Journal/Jan_05/article01.htm

Siemens, G. (2011). *Learning analytics: foundation for informed change in Higher Education*. Retrieved from http://www.slideshare.net/gsiemens/learning-analytics-educause

Smith, A. (2010). Home broadband. *Pew Internet & American Life Project*. Retrieved from http://www.pewinternet.org/topics/broadband/

Strayer, J. F. (2007). *The effects of the classroom flip on the learning environment: A comparison of learning activity in a traditional classroom and a flip classroom that used an intelligent tutoring system*. The Ohio State University. Retrieved from http://etd.ohiolink.edu/send-pdf.cgi/Strayer%20Jeremy.pdf?osu1189523914

Tan, A. L., Tan, S. C., & Wettasinghe, C. M. (2011). Learning to be a science teacher: Reflections and lessons from video-based instruction. *Australasian Journal of Educational Technology*, *27*(3), 446–462. doi:10.14742/ajet.954

Taylor, P., Ling, E., Ming, K., & Hui, C. (2013). Making learning visible in initial teacher education: A pedagogical characterisation scheme. *Educational Research for Policy and Practice*, *12*(3), 193–209. doi:10.1007/s10671-012-9140-2

Torgersen, G. E. (1998). *Læring med IT – Teoriogmetode for undervisning med informasjons- ogkommunikasjonsteknologi*. Oslo: Opplysningsfilm.

Usluel, Y. K., & Mazman, S. G. (2009). Adoption of Web 2.0 tools in distance education. *Procedia: Social and Behavioral Sciences*, *1*(1), 818–823. doi:10.1016/j.sbspro.2009.01.146

van Es, E. A. (2009). Participants' roles in the context of a video club. *Journal of the Learning Sciences*, *18*(1), 100–137. doi:10.1080/10508400802581668

van Es, E. A., & Sherin, M. G. (2002). Learning to notice: Scaffolding new teachers' interpretations of classroom interactions. *Journal of Technology and Teacher Education*, *10*(4), 571–595.

Veeramani, R., & Bradley, S. (2008). *Insights regarding undergraduate preference for lecture capture*. Madison, WI: University of Wisconsin-Madison.

Veletsianos, G., & Navarrete, C. C. (2012). Online social networks as formal learning environments: learner experiences and activities. *The international Review of Research in Open and Distributed Learning, 13*(1). Retrieved from www.irrodl.org/index.php /irrodl/article/view/1078/2077

Woo, K., Gosper, M., McNeill, M., Preston, G., Green, D., & Phillips, R. (2008). Web-based lecture technologies: Blurring the boundaries between face-to-face and distance learning. *ALT-J Research in Learning Technology*, *16*(2), 81–93. doi:10.1080/09687760802315895

Yasmin, D. (2013). Application of the classification tree model in predicting learner dropout behaviour in open and distance learning. *Distance Education*, *34*(2), 218–231. doi:10.1080/01587919.2013.793642

Zhang, D., Zhou, L., Briggs, R. O., & Nunamaker, J. F. Jr. (2006). Instructional video in e-learning: Assessing the impact of interactive video on learning effectiveness. *Information & Management*, *43*(1), 15–27. doi:10.1016/j.im.2005.01.004

Zhang, M., Lundeberg, M., Koehler, M. J., & Eberhardt, J. (2011). Understanding affordances and challenges of three types of video for teacher professional development. *Teaching and Teacher Education*, *27*(2), 454–462. doi:10.1016/j.tate.2010.09.015

Zingaro, D., & Oztok, M. (2012). Interaction in an Asynchronous Online Course: A Synthesis of Quantitative Predictors. *Journal of Asynchronous Learning Networks*, *4*(16), 12.

KEY TERMS AND DEFINITIONS

Digital Video: Digital video recording, shared and stored in online format, that can be viewed, commented and/or disseminated through Internet (blogs, social networking sites or other websites) by users.

Educational Social Platforms: Digital platforms dedicated specifically to the dissemination and consumption of educational videos.

Educational Video: Video recording made with a didactic intent, and those which, despite not having been developed for educational purposes, may be appropriate for teacher intervention.

ICT: Acronym for Information and Communication Technologies, which refer to various media, channels and resources that provide a specific way of access and manage information.

Podcast-Based Learning: A special type of recording, within the Computer-Based Training (CBT), which refers to audios, audio graphs, video streaming and Internet Broadcasting; and whose main advantages are the ability to be played asynchronous, low production costs and easy distribution.

Social Network: Social structure composed of a group of people who are related according to a centre of interest (professional, leisure, family, friendship, etc.).

Social Networking Site: Internet sites consist of groups of people who share common interests or activities; which allow them to communicate and exchange information between them.

Teacher Training: Set of actions, which are derived from the implementation of educational policies, aimed at generating processes of decision making about teaching, to meet a specific demand or teaching objective, responding to certain educational situations.

Web 2.0: All those websites that facilitate information sharing, interoperability, user-centred design and collaboration on the World Wide Web. A Web 2.0 site allows users to interact and collaborate with each other as creators of user-generated content in a virtual community.

Chapter 13
Videos as Tools of Expertise-Based Training (XBT) for the Professional Development of Teachers:
XBT Videos for Teacher Development

Hatice Sancar-Tokmak
Mersin University, Turkey

ABSTRACT

Teachers are the main foundations of the education system, and their professional development during their working life is vital in ensuring the success of any attempts to change that system. It is for this reason that in-service training is high on the agenda of most countries, although previous studies have shown that teachers are unable to transfer the knowledge they gain through in-service training to in-class activities, as more long-lasting help is required. One way in which teachers can be provided help in this regard is through the use of technology in line with a strong instructional design theory. This chapter aims to address this issue by showing how videos can be used in the professional development of teachers as part of an expertise-based training (XBT) program. The chapter is compiled in seven main parts: 1) Introduction 2) Background 3) Main Focus of the Chapter 5) Solutions and Recommendations 6) Future Research Directions, and finally, 7) Conclusions.

INTRODUCTION

According to Meskill, Mossop, DiAngelo and Pasquale (2002), adapting curricula, classroom design dynamics, teaching approaches and teaching with technologies constitute some of the more complex processes that teachers must work through. Similarly, Grossman, Hammerness and McDonald (2009) advocate that teaching is very complex practice. Avalos (2011) relates this complex process to professional development, and suggests that the requirements of professional development include: "…cognitive and

DOI: 10.4018/978-1-5225-0711-6.ch013

Copyright © 2017, IGI Global. Copying or distributing in print or electronic forms without written permission of IGI Global is prohibited.

emotional involvement of teachers individually and collectively, the capacity and willingness to examine where each one stands in terms of convictions and beliefs and the perusal and enactment of appropriate alternatives for improvement or change" (p. 10). Darling-Hammond and Richardson (2009) claim that professional development may prove to be more effective if focused on teaching practice and reflection, while Stürmer, Könings, and Seidel (2013) emphasize the importance of providing professional vision, which is the characteristics of experienced teachers. Sherin and van Es (2009) describe professional vision as the ability of noticing and interpreting important classroom interactions by stating the role of expertise in teaching. Avalos (2011) highlights the many research studies investigating the use of videos to this end, providing opportunities for teachers to observe real classroom practices and reflect what they have learned within a professional development program. Similarly, Barab, MaKinster and Scheckler (2003) state that an effective professional development environment cannot exist without a community of practitioners with responsibilities in the building and maintenance of their environment and the sharing of experiences. They go on to claim that during their professional development program, one medium that they use to allow teachers to observe, discuss and reflect on a pedagogical theory is video (Barab, *et al.*, 2003). Moreover, Sherin and van Es (2009) state that "we believe that far too little is known about how video supports teacher learning, particularly given its extensive use in teacher education and professional development." (p.20) That said, the level of contribution of technology to the effectiveness of instruction depends mainly on how instructors, accepted as the main foundations of the education system, integrate them into classroom activities. Mishra and Koehler (2006) state that the reason behind any lack of success in the use of technology in education stems mainly from researchers who focus on the technology itself rather than how it is used by the instructors. For this reason, many scholars of educational technology, such as Ertmer (1999), Jonassen (1995), Januszewski and Molenda (2008), Merill (1983), and Reiguluth and Stein (1983), focus on how technology can contribute to the effectiveness of instruction, and put forward theories, instructional design models or carry out researches to this end.

The literature presented here emphasizes that teaching practice, reflection, professional vision, and expertise in teaching are the concepts which should be center of teachers' continuing professional development programs, and videos are tools may serve for this purpose if they are used in line with a strong theoretical instructional approach. Expertise-based training (XBT) is an instructional design theory which may be used to develop expertise of professionals through videos including expert examples. Moreover, in-service training is one of the most important ways of helping teachers update their knowledge and competencies according to the changing needs of society over time, and for the development of new knowledge and communication with colleagues (Conco, 2004). Previous literature has shown that the effectiveness of in-service training is questionable, in that it often fails to bring the expected results (Conco, 2004; Gönen & Kocakaya 2006; Kaya, Çepni & Küçük, 2004; Ozer, 2004; Saiti & Saitis, 2006) due, for example, to the teaching methods used (Kaya, Çepni & Küçük, 2004), the insufficient time allocated for training or the lack of follow-up help (Schiffer, 2008).

Contributing to the above literature, this chapter aims to explain how videos, in line with XBT can be used to provide long-lasting support in the professional development of teachers, with particularly emphasis on how videos can be designed and used as part of an XBT professional development program.

BACKGROUND

Theoretical Background: Expertise-Based Training (XBT)

Fadde (2009a) states that modern information-processing theories related to expertise are based on studies in which the performances of expert and less-expert chess players were compared in different tasks. There have been many studies in a variety of different fields on expertise and the differences between experts and novices, and according to Ward, Suss and Basevitch (2009), instructional strategies can be extracted from these studies for the development of skills. Fadde (2009b) has proposed XBT as an instructional design theory based on the creation of instructional strategies formed in expertise research to hasten the development of advanced learners into experts. The most important issues addressed in this part may be the definition of instructional strategies and the manner and technologies used in the presentation of these strategies to learners.

Studies by both experts and novices have emphasized the importance of deliberate practice, described by Fadde and Klein (2010) as practice under the direction of a coach, as a strategy in the development of expertise. Ward *et al.* (2009) state that deliberate practice makes a difference in the success of sportsmen and women, based on their summary of studies of the sporting profession. However, Fadde and Klein (2010) and Ward *et al.* (2009) also claim that deliberate practice differs from profession to profession. In the sporting or music fields, becoming a perfect performer requires practice under the direction of a coach, while in teaching, Fadde and Klein (2010) suggest that deliberate practice may be provided through four different approaches, being estimation, experimentation, extrapolation and explanation. These exercises provide "an awareness of resources and the time needed to complete a task; learning from the results of an action, taking lessons from the actions of others, and concluding with a result for reflective explanation" (Fadde & Klein, 2010 as cited in Sancar-Tokmak, 2013 p. 132).

Previous literature provides examples of how an expert-novice research approach can be followed for the development of instructional strategies. Fadde (2010) used videos including where experts look for picking up predictive information to train sportsmen and women. Video clips showing the actions of experts were masked to show where experts look to pick up predictive information. The results of Fadde's study showed that training may improve perceptual-cognitive skills through video-occlusion training. Ifenthaler (2009) presented expert representations to the participants of a study by way of a concept map program known as HIMATT using three feedback models. He found that the direct presentation of expert representation as a feedback model did not help participants, and suggested that simulation environments including direct expert representation would be of help to the participants (Ifenthaler, 2009). In a study evaluating educational software that involved 43 pre-service mathematics teacher and three experts, Sancar-Tokmak and Incikabi (2012) presented case examples containing expert strategies to an XBT group of pre-service math teachers in an, while a second group in the study was not provided with the case examples. All of the participants evaluated the same educational software using a Software Evaluation checklist, and the results showed that the XBT group rated the educational software more closely to the experts than those using traditional methods.

In short, XBT is an instructional theory that has potential to develop expertise among people from different professions. Although the term XBT is not used in most research studies, there have been many studies aiming to enhance the expertise of professionals through the provision of expert examples. Also, included in this chapter is a specific discussion of the issue of expertise development in teaching through the presentation of expert teachers' videos.

Expertise in Teaching and Teachers' Professional Development

Expertise in teaching is one of the most important concerns of many countries. As Darling-Hammond (2000) states, the success of students is heavily reliant on the expertise of the teachers in teaching, and teachers who have received good teacher education are more successful than those who have not. There have been many studies, such as those of Draper, O'Brien and Christie (2004) and Orungbemi (2009),that attempt to describe how a teacher education program should provide the necessary knowledge and skills to pre-service teachers; however, does becoming a teacher mean that everything is done to provide teachers with expertise in teaching? It has been said in previous literature that the training required by teachers to gain expertise in teaching continues throughout their professional lives. Berliner (2001) states that one of the problems related to teacher expertise is that it is seen to increase over time, and also as advocated by Lee and Finger (2010) schools which are named "digital schools", who are responsible for providing their members with up-to-date information and technological skills. This means that the never-ending professional development of teachers should be high on the agenda of countries, in that, as stated by Ertmer (1999), Mishra and Koehler (2006), and Usta and Korkmaz (2010), teachers constitute the main foundation of education systems.

Sancar-Tokmak (2013) states that expertise in teaching may be also related with self-efficacy beliefs. Similarly, Gibson and Dembo (1984) advocate that if teachers realize that their teaching is encouraging student learning and that they are teaching well, they will probably enhance the students' academic achievements. Bandura (1997) states that the context and results of actions are two factors that affect perceived self-efficacy, and from this perspective. Moreover, Borko, Koellner, Jacobs and Seago (2011) highlight the different components of teaching expertise, *"One important component of teaching expertise is the ability to observe and interpret classroom events as a lesson unfolds, and to make instructional decisions based on those interpretations."* (p. 185). A study by Sancar-Tokmak and Karakus (2011), on the other hand, showed that during their teaching practice, novice Information Communication Technology (ICT) pre-service teachers came across many situations of which they had not been made aware, and faced difficulties in applying teaching strategies learned during the Teacher Education program to in-class activities. Moreover, in their summary of research studies, Meskill *et al.* (2002), identified differences between novice and expert teachers in terms of moment-to-moment decision making, lesson plans and the implementation of these plans, the ability to shift content, understanding the awareness of learners, the number and quality of the instructional strategies on their agenda, and their macro and micro planning decisions. Related to this point, some questions can be raised, such as "How can we help teachers become aware of these situations and develop teaching strategies that include expertise for teachers throughout their professional life?" or, "Can we benefit form technologies for that purpose", and if answer to this question is yes, "Which technologies can we use?"

To address these questions, scholars such as Avalos (2011), Barab *et al.* (2003), Borko, Jacobs, Eiteljorg and Pittman (2008), Borko *et al.* (2011), Darling-Hammond and Richardson (2009) and Robinson (2008) suggest providing an environment in which teachers can practice what they have learned through instruction, and then to discuss, reflect upon and observe the teaching practices of others, mentioning the potential of using videos for these purposes. Accordingly, this chapter it is focused on the use of videos in the professional development of teachers, especially in the provision of expertise in teaching.

Video as a Tool for Teachers' Professional Development and XBT

There have been many research studies and theoretical papers examining why and how videos may be used in teacher development programs. Videos are also linked with professional vision and expertise in teaching concepts by researchers as Stürmer *et al.* (2013), Sherin and van Es (2009), and Grossman *et al.* (2009). In this part of the chapter, five research studies analyzing the use of videos are presented, and while it should be noted that little emphasis is given to the uses of expert video in the professional development of trainee teachers in the reviewed literature, the five research studies all provide information about how expertise and professional vision may be provided through videos.

The first reviewed study was conducted by O'Sullivan (2002), who applied action research methods during an in-service Education and Training (INSET) program for three years. In this research, O'Sullivan (2002) investigated the reflective skills development of unqualified and underqualified primary school teachers in Namibia during training. In the study, O'Sullivan used videos and classroom observation in the development of the teachers' reflective skills and involvement, although after noticing that they were passive during training, she decided to use a semi-structured observation form that included factual and reflective questions (O'Sullivan, 2002). O'Sullivan (2002) concluded that this approach was much more successful in the development of reflective skills and involvement, and proposed a "structured reflection" approach.

Borko *et al.* (2008) examined the use of classroom videos to encourage productive discussions about teaching/learning and creating and maintaining a learning community in a two-year professional development project. Participating in the study were 16 mathematics teachers who, during the project, solved problems and developed lesson plans, and then implemented their lesson plans in the classroom using video recordings (Borko *et al.*, 2008). In the following stage, they discussed their teaching with their colleagues, which Borko *et al.* (2008) described as "productive", in that, thanks to video, the "….teachers talked in a more focused, in-depth, and analytical manner about specific issues related to teaching and learning the selected mathematical problems." (Borko et al., 2008)

Barab *et al.* (2003) conducted a research study into the design and evaluation of a web-based professional development system called the Inquiry Learning Forum (ILF), aimed at supporting a community of practice (CoP) of in-service and pre-service mathematics and science teachers. In the study they used teachers' classroom videos to create, reflect, share and improve teaching practices, defining six dualities, being Designed/Emergent, Participation and Reification, Local/Global, Identification/Negotiability, Online/Face-to-Face, and Diversity/Coherence (Barab *et al.*, 2003). They concluded that all of these dualities should be balanced from the inside rather than the outside, and videos provided trainees looking from inside.

Stürmer *et al.* (2013) conducted a research study aiming to investigate the effect of three university-based courses on pre-service teachers' acquisition of declarative knowledge and professional vision which were aspects of expertise. In one of these university-based courses, the groups of pre-service teachers watched and interpreted the videotaped excerpts of classroom situations (Stürmer et al., 2013). Then, they answered questions about three qualitatively different levels of knowledge-based reasoning (description, explanation, and prediction) drawn from expert researches, and the findings showed that pre-service teachers in video course had significantly outperformed their peers in other courses (Stürmer et al., 2013). Moreover, Stürmer et al. (2013) found that their prediction scores were higher than description scores, that these meant they had learned to predict classroom events for students learning rather than just describe those events.

In Sancar-Tokmak's (2013) study, videos were used to present expert teaching in a real classroom environment to novice pre-service science teachers. During the study, the participants watched the expert videos and discussed with the teaching strategies used by the experts with the other participants (Sancar-Tokmak, 2013). In the following stage, they conducted micro teaching assignments, the results of which showed the participants use of the experts' strategies during their micro teaching sessions. (Sancar-Tokmak, 2013)

The four research studies including the use of videos for teacher development provide some important lessons for practitioners:

1. The use of video in a real classroom setting is important in making the trainees aware of the challenges and problems they may face during teaching practice. For that reason, videos prepared in line with XBT may include real classrooms practice of experts.
2. Discussion and reflection should be encouraged with additional materials, such as reflective questions. For that reason, an educator who designs a teacher development program according to XBT supported with videos, should also use additional materials to provide opportunities for reflections. Dr. Davis' use of videos for reflection is a good example in the research study of Grossman, Compton, Igra, Ronfeldt, Shahan, and Williamson (2009).
3. Dialogue between the trainees about their own teaching practices should be encouraged to allow them to learn from one another. For that reason, an educator who would design a video-based XBT teacher development program should also allow dialogue between trainees, as well, provide the trainees opportunities for more than one time.
4. Improvement in practice requires additional follow-up and in-service training.

MAIN FOCUS OF THE CHAPTER[1]

Video is a tool that can be used for professional development in different ways. The studies of Fadde (2010) and Sancar-Tokmak (2013) reveal how such tools can be used as part of XBT for the development of expertise. While using videos for the purpose of professional development among teachers, factors related to the teaching profession, expertise, XBT and the capabilities/limitations of video should be taken into consideration. In this part of the chapter, the factors that may affect the success of using videos in the professional development of teachers are explained in line with related literature. With this in mind, two steps, being the preparation of videos and strategies for their use, are taken as reference.

Issues, Controversies, Problems

As Mishra and Koehler (2006) state, the educational technology field is littered with many failed attempts to utilize technology in the attainment of teaching goals. They advocate that those producing educational technologies should attribute much more importance to the use of technology than the technology itself, although the capabilities and limitations of the technologies should be known (Mishra & Koehler, 2006). Specifically for the case of videos, Seago (2004) puts forward similar ideas, pointing out that "… they [the videos] do not in and of themselves produce learning – it is how they are used to promote specific learning goals that can allow for the opportunity to learn" (p.263). Advocated by Sherin and van Es

(2009), very little is known about how video supports teacher learning. Moreover, Stürmer *et al.* (2013) state "Teachers' decisions about how to support students' learning processes can have crucial effects on instructional outcomes. These decisions are informed by teachers' professional vision…" (p.468). The professional vision is introduced as the characteristics of experienced teachers by Stürmer *et al.* (2013) and Sherin and van Es (2009). However, in the literature, there are few research studies and theoretical papers which focus on how the videos, described as extensively used tools for teachers' development by Sherin and van Es (2009), can be used to develop teachers' expertise on a specific skill in line with a strong instructional theory. For that reason, the focus of this chapter, how the videos may be prepared and used to develop inexperienced teachers' teaching expertise in line with an instructional theory, XBT, proposed by Fadde (2009). The following part of the chapter includes recommendations about the use and preparation of XBT videos.

SOLUTIONS AND RECOMMENDATIONS

In this part of the chapter, suggestions of how videos can be prepared in line with XBT and how they may be used are presented. Previous literature contains only limited studies into the use of videos as part of XBT, making it necessary to give some suggestions about the use and preparation of XBT videos. This section is compiled under two subheadings, being the preparation of videos for the professional development of teachers in line with XBT, and the use of videos prepared in line with XBT for such professional teacher development.

Preparation of Videos for the Professional Development of Teachers in Line with XBT

Videos prepared for the professional development of teachers in line with XBT should be prepared taking into account a number of factors related to XBT, the teaching profession and the capabilities/limitations of videos. Videos prepared in line with XBT may include input from an expert teacher or real classroom teaching provided by such a teacher. As stated at the beginning of the chapter, XBT is based on strategies taken from expertise literature, and for this reason, expert teachers should be informed about expertise strategies related to the content presented to the trainee teachers. This part of the chapter continues with an explanation of important issues to be addressed in the preparation of videos, which are as follows:

Content of Videos

Videos should include content related to the topics and intended goals of the training, which may, for example, be related to classroom management, technology integration, teaching methods, etc. The videos included in the expert teachers' real classroom teaching sessions included all of these elements, although videos may be prepared focusing on one specific topic. Stürmer *et al.* (2013) advocate the development of the ability to observe and interpret classroom situations are strongly knowledge-guided process. Moreover, videos may include interviews with experts on related issues at the end of the videos, during which they reflect upon their teaching methods. Providing a clear explanation of their methods and the applied teaching strategies can be beneficial for trainees.

For example, an expert video may be prepared for foreign language teachers with the topic of training being the integration of technology. The training goals are to provide trainee teachers with an awareness of the technologies they may integrate into their teaching, and examples may be given of how expert teachers integrate these technologies into their methods. One expert video may show how an expert foreign language teacher integrates educational computer games into their teaching. In such a video, an expert English teacher may teach, for example, the singular–plural topic to 6th-grade students with the support of educational computer games. After showing teaching methods, the video may include interviews with the expert teacher or with the students who attended the lesson on applied instructional design. In this regard, trainee teachers who are seeking to develop technology integration skills are provided with examples of appropriate technologies and are shown how these technologies are integrated into instruction. Moreover, the interview section provides reflection on why/how the expert teacher(s) make such decisions and strategies, which may provide trainee teachers with a clear explanation of the actions of the expert teacher(s) during teaching.

Expert Teacher/Teachers in Videos

Previous literature contains discussions about who can be called expert. Some studies suggest that the duration of work in a profession indicates expertise, while others claim that this is not indicative of expertise, claiming instead that the experience and ability to address different situations when doing a job should be the criteria for expertise. In summary, defining who is an expert in a profession is no easy task. Maybe an important strategy to be followed when defining expertise is to use both advised criteria: first, looking at the number of years that a teacher has been teaching, and then observing them during teaching to see how well s/he uses strategies for the target audience. Quiñones, Ford and Teachout (1995) found in their meta-analysis study that there is an estimated relation between job performance and experience, and the amount had one of highest correlations with measures of job performance After defining a teacher as an expert on his/her profession, it is time to record videos of his/her teaching on a specific topic.

Capabilities and Limitations of Videos

Videos allow people to visualize a situation/event that took place in the past. Previous literature contains many commentaries on the capabilities and limitations of technological tools and their effect on learning in the Instructional Technology field. There is a common understanding that it is not the technology being used that is the key to productive learning, but how we use it during instruction, although the capabilities and limitations of a technology should be known to ensure the best integration decision. For example, a technology that visualizes the situation/event is required to show trainee teachers what happened in class during an event and how an expert teacher deals with it. Imagine a student coming late to class, causing all other students to lose concentration How an expert teacher regains the students' attention is a key lesson for trainee teachers, and visualizing this situation is important in this case. In this regard, there are two ways of providing this experience:

1. Being in the room when the situation emerges; and
2. Watching an expert videos from the time.

This example provides clues about the capabilities and limitations of videos. On the capabilities side:

1. Trainee teachers can visualize a situation or event from the past;
2. They can observe the situation or event again and again; and
3. They can stop and start the situation or event at any time.

As for the limitations:

1. There is no opportunity for interaction (The watchers cannot speak, ask questions or raise their opinions about the situation or events with the people in the videos);
2. Videos can be recorded using special technologies that contain cameras, such as mobile phones, video cameras and webcams.
3. Videos can be watched using special technologies that contain cameras such as mobile phones, video cameras and webcams.

It is important that these capabilities and limitations are understood if technologies are to be used successfully during instruction. If the instructor wants a tool that is more interactive, videos may not be the best alternative, or the instructor should find a way to compensate for the interactivity problem, for example, by stopping and starting videos at any time to ask questions to the trainees or to discuss the situation or event being observed on the video. In summary, it is necessary to keep in mind that although the key factor in the use of a technology is its integration (methods applied during instruction), all capabilities and limitations should be known when making decisions related to its integration.

Use of Videos Prepared in Line with XBT for the Professional Development of Teachers

Desimone (2009) proposes a conceptual framework for studying the effects of professional development on teachers and students learning and defines the core features of professional development as content focus, active learning, coherence, duration, collective participation. In this part of the chapter, different options for the integration of videos in XBT with regard to face-to-face and web-based approaches are presented to provide an inside for instructional designers of the teacher professional development programs on how these core features can be provided while using videos in line with XBT. Face-to-face and web-based training require different instructional designs to ensure their success (Sancar Tokmak, Baturay & Fadde, 2013), given their different natures. The differences between the two may be clarified for the reader with the definition of web-based training provided by Barron (1998), "Web-delivered instruction (commonly referred to as Web-based Training or WBT) includes courseware in which instruction, interactions and feedback are delivered via the Web" (p.356). In face-to-face instruction, on the other hand, learning and teaching occurs in same place, while in web-based training, the learners and instructors are in different places and interact through the Internet. Following on from this, the following section of the chapter is compiled under two sub-headings: *Use of Videos in Training Offered Face to Face* and *Use of Videos in Training Offered Web-based*. As explained previously, as the aim of this chapter is to provide long-lasting help to teachers through videos prepared in line with XBT.

Use of Videos in Training Offered Face-to-Face

The use of videos in follow-up applications may help teachers remember what they learned during in-service training, and can also furnish them with up-to-date information and give them the chance to witness the best practices of real experts. As trainee teachers have undertaken previous in-service training, the videos may serve to remind them of what they learned at an earlier date. Taking this into account, video presentations may provide an introduction to in-service training at the beginning, or they may be reached by trainee teachers after completed a tutorial having in-service training content. In all these cases, attempts are made to enhance the use of knowledge gained during in-service training with videos prepared in line with XBT. Moreover, these videos may serve in the self-assessment of teachers to identify what the trainee teachers remember or whether they use knowledge in their in-class activities. For example, a trainee teacher may be asked which methods they prefer to use after observing the expert teachers' classroom conditions on video, or whether they face the same situations during their in-class activities, and what methods they used.

In summary, as a tool for follow up of in-service training, videos created in line with XBT may allow trainee teachers to check what they have learned, or to assess their level of knowledge and the use of knowledge during in-class activities. The main objective in this approach is create enthusiasm among teachers related to the use of in-service training. Accordingly, videos prepared in line with XBT may be provided to trainee teachers at predefined intervals, accompanied by a guide or a small book included in the in-service training materials.

Use of Videos in Training Offered Web-based

Web-based training is a form of distance education that according to Barron (1998) is referred to by many terms, such as Web-based training, web-based instruction, web-based learning or Internet-based, although all refer to the same approach. The history of the provision of instruction in which the learner and instructor are not in the same location started with letters, and then moved on to other media for the delivery of instruction in line with the changes in technologies (Cagiltay, Graham, Lim, Craner, & Duffy, 2001). Nowadays, the development of Internet technologies has allowed instruction to be delivered over distances through web-based technologies (Ozonur, 2013). The specific focus of this chapter is web-based training. Berge (1998) and Barron (1998) provided principles for instructional designers for the design of web-based training. Barron's (1998) principles are:

1. Conducting a thorough media analysis;
2. Updating information constantly;
3. The web's suitability for a widely dispersed audience;
4. The use of audio and video in content sparingly;
5. Using such communication media as e-mail and chats for students;
6. Placing course objectives first and foremost;
7. Analyzing the target audience;
8. Making the interaction meaningful;
9. Others as design issues and using hyperlinks, graphics and web-page numbers.

Berge (1998) categorizes the principles under Pedagogical, Social, and Technological/Support headings, and puts forward the following principles:

- **Pedagogical Principles:**
  - Compiling a list of purposes of planned activities, levels and types of interactivity and feedback;
  - Defining the levels of teacher, student or group control, as well as guided teacher control; and
  - Density of content should be less if synchronous communication heavily used in the web-based educational learning environment.
- **The Social Principles:**
  - Creating an environment of cooperation and trust among the students and the instructor; and
  - Using both synchronous and asynchronous communication tools in teaching and learning.
- **The Technical/Support Principles:**
  - Being aware of that web supports multiple media forms;
  - Using a technological minimalism principle; and
  - Providing technical support to both students and instructors.

The principles put forward by Barron (1998) and Berge (1998) differ, although both are focused on the instructional strategies rather than the tools or technology behind the web-based training. This part of the chapter will be focused on instructional decisions rather than technologies. However, videos use purposes and the strategies may be used in line with instructional design decisions are explained. An important issue related to the use of videos prepared in line with XBT in web-based training is that it should never ignore the purposes of training, although videos can be a tool for ensuring these purposes. The principles behind the use of videos are as follows:

- Define the objectives of the training;
- Analyze the target audience;
- Define which materials and media will be used during training;
- Define synchronous and asynchronous communication tools and strategies;
- Enhance collaboration between trainees;
- Use videos of XBT to support training objectives with different purposes: at the beginning and during training, to provide an opportunity for discussion and to reflect on complex topics; while at the end of the training, the learners' knowledge can be assessed;
- Define the density of the use of video and other media during training;
- Using design principles found on websites for adoption into web-based training.

In web-based training, the instructor may benefit from the expert videos during the training in several ways, including reflection on the topic of the training and discussing the topic through the videos; while at the end of the training, the videos may be used by the learners to reflect on what they have learned, to assess their level of knowledge and to realize the decisions made by the experts. The use of videos prepared in line with XBT is summarized in the Table 1 with important questions that the instructional designers should ask themselves during web-based training and face to face ones.

Table 1. Use of videos in line with XBT in face to face and web-based training

Questions Asked for Expert Video Use	Type of Training	
	Follow-Up of Face to Face Training	**Web-Based Training**
When	At the end of the in-service training	• At the beginning • During the training • At the end of the training
Why	• Remembering the topic offered in the training • Realizing best practice related with the training topic • Reflecting on what they learned • Discussing the topic through the videos • Assessing self-learning	• Reflecting on the topic of the training • Discussing the topic through the videos • Realizing the decisions made by the experts • Assessing the knowledge,
How	After the in-service training offered face to face through CDROM, or different means as e-mail, web, YouTube, discussion boards, and blogs.	As a part of the web-based training with various synchronous and asynchronous means as e-mail, discussion boards, video/teleconferencing, chat messaging, and blogs.
Examples	• Trainee teachers may be provided expert videos through CDROMs. Trainee teachers watch the videos and discuss the expert teachers' instruction in the videos via a discussion boards. • Trainee teachers may be provided expert videos on YouTube and wanted to answer some questions via e-mail about what they learned during in-service training.	• During the web-based training, trainee teachers may be requested to discuss the instruction designed by expert in the video via chat messaging. • At the end of the topic offered in web-based training, trainee teachers may be provided an expert video on YouTube and wanted to answer some questions by using an online testing software to assess the trainee teachers' knowledge.

In summary, in this chapter the main focus is the preparation and use of videos in XBT, with the aim of providing teachers with long-lasting assistance during their professional lives, especially after in-service training, or to support them with long-term training offered through the Internet.

FUTURE RESEARCH DIRECTIONS

In the future, teacher development will continue to draw the attention of researchers, educators and educational policies as changes in society, technology and student profiles continue to force changes in the education system. In this respect, change leads to professional development, and although the requirement for the professional development of teachers will not change, it is safe to assume that the strategies, means and tools will change. Past research has shown that the preference for online training will grow in line with the growing number of teachers who need professional development, economic concerns and advances in technology (Ozer, 2004). Whether provided face-to-face or online, videos will continue to find use in the in-service training of teachers for the reason best explained by Sherin (2004): "Video allows one to enter the world of the classroom without having to be in the position of teaching in-the-moment" (p. 13). Moreover, in the future, research will more focus more on the use of video rather than video itself, as advocated by Seago (2004)

XBT and expert videos have potential to attract the attention of the research community, and to provide expertise in teaching, although it is believed that this trend will be applied with real classroom teaching. In other words, in addition to the use of expert videos that allow trainee teachers to reflect on what they have learned, and to share and discuss in-class teaching, in-service training programs will include a practical element in which the trainee teachers apply what they have learned in their own classes.

Research into professional development among teachers may be designed to investigate follow-up application of teacher development program, and may attempt to answer the specific questions "Do teachers use what they learn during their in-class teaching after the in-service training?", "Does it affect the academic achievement of students?" in the future, when the videos may again be used for that purpose. For example, teachers may videotape their classroom teaching methods, after which experts can assess their level of expertise in the application of in-service training as a follow-up study. Further studies into the use of expert videos for the professional development of teachers may be designed using different research methodologies from those adopted in this case, being either empirical, or a mix of both.

CONCLUSION

In this part of the chapter, important points related to expertise in teaching, and the use and preparation of expert videos for teacher professional development in XBT are summarized:

- Videos are tools with the potential to support the education of teachers during in-service training.
- To what extent videos support in-service training depends on how they are used.
- Research has shown that videos are beneficial also in the construction of a community of practice (Barab *et al.*, 2003; Borko *et al.*, 2008).
- Additional materials (for example, observation forms including reflective questions) may be required if trainee teachers are to reflect and discuss the teaching methods in videos (O'Sullivan, 2002).
- XBT is an instructional theoretical approach that may be of benefit when using and preparing videos for the professional development of teachers.
- Although the use of expert videos is a key approach to fulfilling the intended goals of in-service training, their capabilities and limitations should be understood by the trainers.
- While preparing expert videos, the expertise of the teachers in videos should be verified by authorities or external expert reviewers.
- The content of expert videos should be in parallel with the training topics.
- Extensive use of expert videos should be avoided during in-service training.
- It should be kept in mind that the type of training (face-to-face, web-based, online or blended) may require a change in the use of expert videos.
- It is vital that the in-service training objectives are given primary importance, after which it can be decided whether or not expert videos can help achieve these objectives.

REFERENCES

Avalos, B. (2011). Teacher professional development in Teaching and Teacher Education over ten years. *Teaching and Teacher Education*, 27(1), 10–20. doi:10.1016/j.tate.2010.08.007

Bandura, A. (1997). *Self-efficacy: The exercise of control*. New York: Freeman.

Barab, S. A., MaKinster, J. G., & Scheckler, R. (2003). Designing system dualities: Characterizing a web-supported professional development community. *The Information Society*, *19*(3), 237–256. doi:10.1080/01972240309466

Barron, A. (1998). Designing Web-based training. *British Journal of Educational Technology*, *29*(4), 355–370. doi:10.1111/1467-8535.00081

Berge, Z. (1998). Guiding principles in web-based instructional design. *Educational Media International*, *35*(2), 72–76. doi:10.1080/0952398980350203

Berliner, D. C. (2001). Learning about and learning from expert teachers. *International Journal of Educational Research*, *35*(5), 463–482. doi:10.1016/S0883-0355(02)00004-6

Borko, H., Jacobs, J., Eiteljorg, E., & Pittman, M. E. (2008). Video as a tool for fostering productive discussions in mathematics professional development. *Teaching and Teacher Education*, *24*(2), 417–436. doi:10.1016/j.tate.2006.11.012

Borko, H., Koellner, K., Jacobs, J., & Seago, N. (2011). Using video representations of teaching in practice-based professional development programs. *ZDM*, *43*(1), 175–187. doi:10.1007/s11858-010-0302-5

Cagiltay, K., Graham, C. R., Lim, B.-R., Craner, J., & Duffy, T. M. (2001). The seven principles of good practice: A practical approach to evaluating online courses. *Hacettepe University Journal of Education*, *20*, 40–50.

Conco, Z. P. (2006). How effective is in-service training for teachers in rural school contexts? [Master Thesis]. University of Pretoria: Pretoria, Republic of South Africa.

Darling-Hammond, L. (2000). How teacher education matters. *Journal of Teacher Education*, *51*(3), 166–173. doi:10.1177/0022487100051003002

Darling-Hammond, L., & Richardson, N. (2009). Research review/teacher learning: What matters. *Educational Leadership*, *66*(5), 46–53.

Desimone, L. M. (2009). Improving impact studies of teachers' professional development: Toward better conceptualizations and measures. *Educational Researcher*, *38*(3), 181–199. doi:10.3102/0013189X08331140

Draper, J., O'brien, J., & Christie, F. (2004). First Impressions: The new teacher induction arrangements in Scotland. *Journal of In-service Education*, *30*(2), 201–224. doi:10.1080/13674580100200316

Ertmer, P. A. (1999). Addressing first- and second-order barriers to change: Strategies for technology integration. *Educational Technology Research and Development*, *47*(4), 47–61. doi:10.1007/BF02299597

Fadde, P. J. (2009a). Instructional design for advanced learners: Training recognition skills to hasten expertise. *Educational Technology Research and Development*, *57*(3), 359–376. doi:10.1007/s11423-007-9046-5

Fadde, P. J. (2009b). Expertise-based training: Getting more learners over the bar in less time. *Technology, Instruction. Cognition and Learning*, *7*(4), 171–197.

Fadde, P. J. (2010). Look 'ma, no hands: part-task training of perceptual-cognitive skills to accelerate psychomotor expertise. Proceedings of the Interservice / Industry Training, Simulation & Education Conference (I/ITSEC) (Vol. 1). National Training Systems Association.

Fadde, P. J., & Klein, G. A. (2010). Deliberate performance: Accelerating expertise in natural settings. *International Society for Performance Improvement, 49*(9), 5–14. doi:10.1002/pfi.20175

Gibson, S., & Dembo, M. H. (1984). Teacher efficacy: A construct validation. *Journal of Educational Psychology, 76*(4), 569–582. doi:10.1037/0022-0663.76.4.569

Gönen, S., & Kocakaya, S. (2006). Fizik öğretmenlerinin hizmet içi eğitimler üzerine görüşlerinin değerlendirilmesi. *Pamukkale Üniversitesi Eğitim Fakültesi Dergisi, 19*(19), 37–44.

Grossman, P., Compton, C., Igra, D., Ronfeldt, M., Shahan, E., & Williamson, P. (2009). Teaching practice: A cross-professional perspective. *Teachers College Record, 111*(9), 2055–2100.

Grossman, P., Hammerness, K., & McDonald, M. (2009). Redefining teaching, re-imagining teacher education. *Teachers and Teaching. Theory into Practice, 15*(2), 273–289.

Ifenthaler, D. (2009). Model-based feedback for improving expertise and expert performance. *Technology, Instruction. Cognition and Learning, 7*(2), 83–101.

Januszewski, A., & Molenda, M. (Eds.), (2008). *Educational Technology: A definition with commentary.* New York & London: Lawrence Erlbaum Associates

Jonassen, D. H. (1995). Computers as cognitive tools: Learning with technology, not from technology. *Journal of Computing in Higher Education, 6*(2), 40–73. doi:10.1007/BF02941038

Kaya, A., Çepni, S., & Küçük, M. (2004). Fizik öğretmenlerinin laboratuarlara yönelik hizmet içi ihtiyaçları için bir program geliştirme çalışması. *Kastamonu Eğitim Dergisi, 12*(1), 41–56.

Lee, M., & Finger, G. (2010). *Developing a networked school community: A guide to realising the vision.* Victoria, Australia: ACER Press.

Merrill, M. D. (1983). Component display theory. In C. Reigeluth (Ed.), *Instructional Design Theories and Models.* Hillsdale, NJ: Erlbaum Associates.

Meskill, C., Mossop, J., DiAngelo, S., & Pasquale, R. K. (2002). Expert and novice teachers talking technology: Precepts, concepts, and misconcepts. *Language Learning & Technology, 6*(3), 46–57.

Mishra, P., & Koehler, M. (2006). Technological pedagogical content knowledge: A framework for teacher knowledge. *Teachers College Record, 108*(6), 1017–1054.

O'Sullivan, M. C. (2002). Action research and the transfer of reflective approaches to in-service education and training (INSET) for unqualified and underqualified primary teachers in Namibia. *Teaching and Teacher Education, 18*(5), 523–539. doi:10.1016/S0742-051X(02)00014-8

Orungbemi, O. (2009). Awareness and use of teaching skills among primary school social studies teachers. *Sustainable Human Development Review, 1*(3), 127–138.

Ozer, B. (2004). In-service training of teachers in Turkey at the beginning of the 2000s. *Journal of In-service Education*, *30*(1), 89–100. doi:10.1080/13674580400200301

Ozonur, M. (2013). Sanal gerçeklik ortamı olarak ikincil yaşam (second life) uygulamalarının tasarlanması ve bu uygulamaların internet tabanlı uzaktan eğitim öğrencilerinin öğrenmeleri üzerindeki etkilerinin farklı değişkenler açısından incelenmesi [The design of Second Life applications as virtual world and examining the effects of these applications on the learning of the students attending internet-based distance education in terms of different variables] [Doctorate Thesis]. Mersin University: Mersin, Turkey.

Quiñones, M. A., Ford, J. K., & Teachout, M. S. (1995). The relationship between work experience and job performance: A conceptual and meta-analytic review. *Personnel Psychology*, *48*(4), 887–910. doi:10.1111/j.1744-6570.1995.tb01785.x

Reigeluth, C., & Stein, F. (1983). The elaboration theory of instruction. In C. Reigeluth (Ed.), *Instructional Design Theories and Models*. Hillsdale, NJ: Erlbaum Associates.

Robinson, B. (2008). Using Distance Education and ICT to Improve Access, Equity and the Quality in Rural Teachers' Professional Development in Western China. *International Review of Research in Open and Distance Learning*, *9*(1), 1–17.

Saiti, A., & Saitis, C. (2006). In-service training for teachers who work in full-day schools. Evidence from Greece 1. *European Journal of Teacher Education*, *29*(4), 455–470. doi:10.1080/02619760600944779

Sancar-Tokmak, H. (2013). Effects of Video-Supported Expertise-Based Training (XBT) on Preservice Science Teachers' Self-Efficacy Beliefs. *Eurasia Journal of Mathematics. Science & Technology Education*, *9*(2), 89–99. doi:10.12973/eurasia.2013.924a

Sancar-Tokmak, H., Baturay, H. M., & Fadde, P. (2013). Applying the context, input, process, product evaluation model for evaluation, research, and redesign of an online master's program. *The International Review of Research in Open and Distributed Learning*, *14*(3), 273–293.

Sancar Tokmak, H., & Incikabi, L. (2012). Understanding expertise-based training effects on the software evaluation process of Mathematics Education teachers. *Educational Media International Journal*, *49*(4), 277–288. doi:10.1080/09523987.2012.741198

Sancar-Tokmak, H., & Karakus, T. (2011). A Case Study on Contribution of Initial Teacher Training to Teaching Practice. *Contemporary Educational Technology Journal*, *2*(4), 319–332.

Schifter, C. (2008). *Infusing technology into the classroom: Continuous practice improvement*. Hershey: Information Science Pub. doi:10.4018/978-1-59904-765-2

Seago, N. (2004). Using video as an object of inquiry for mathematics teaching and learning. In J. Brophy (Ed.), *Using video in teacher education* (pp. 259–286). Oxford: Elsevier.

Sherin, M. G. (2004). New perspectives on the role of video in teacher education. In J. Brophy (eds), Using video in teacher education (pp.1-27). New Yok: Elsevier.

Sherin, M. G., & van Es, E. A. (2009). Effects of video club participation on teachers' professional vision. *Journal of Teacher Education*, *60*(1), 20–37. doi:10.1177/0022487108328155

Stürmer, K., Könings, K. D., & Seidel, T. (2013). Declarative knowledge and professional vision in teacher education: Effect of courses in teaching and learning. *The British Journal of Educational Psychology*, *83*(3), 467–483. doi:10.1111/j.2044-8279.2012.02075.x PMID:23822532

Usta, E., & Korkmaz, O. (2010). Öğretmen adaylarının bilgisayar yeterlikleri ve teknoloji kullanımına ilişkin algıları ile öğretmenlik mesleğine yonelik tutumları[Pre-service teachers' computer competencies, perception of technology use and attitudes toward teaching career]. *Uluslararası Insan Bilimleri Dergisi*, *7*(1), 1335–1349.

Ward, P., Suss, J., & Basevitch, I. (2009). Expertise and expert performance-based training (ExPerT) in complex domains. *Technology, Instruction. Cognition and Learning*, *7*(2), 121–145.

KEY TERMS AND DEFINITIONS

Expert: "The performer no longer relies on an analytical principle (rule, guideline, maxim) to connect her/his understanding of the situation to an appropriate action" (Benner, p.131).

Expertise-Based Training: XBT is an instructional theory proposed by Fadde (2009). This theory is based on drawing expert strategies from novice-expert literature to use for develop skills of advanced learners'.

Instructional Design Theories: "An instructional design theory is a theory that offers explicit guidance on how to better help people learn and develop" (Reigeluth, 1999).

Life Long Learning: Klamma et al. (2007) describe lifelong learning as "Learning is not restricted to the classroom and to formal learning inside learning institutions, it an activity which happens throughout life, at work, play, and home" (p.72).

Novice: "Beginners have no experience with the situations in which they are expected to perform tasks." (Benner, p.128)

Professional Vision: Sherin and van Es (2009) describe professional vision as the ability of noticing and interpreting important classroom interactions.

TPACK (Technological Pedagogical Content Knowledge): TPACK is a framework proposed by Mishra and Koehler (2005) mainly focuses on teachers' technology integration skills.

Chapter 14

Video as a Means to an End:
Problems and Techniques Associated with Using Video in Teacher Training

Beverly B. Ray
Idaho State University, USA

Angiline Powell
University of Memphis, USA

ABSTRACT

Having teachers who can demonstrate and document teaching effectiveness, ethical behavior, professional obligations, and willingness to embrace continuous learning is important to for the well-being of the field. Video serves as a viable means of addressing these concerns. In particular, use of video in teacher training promotes a disposition for reflection on and documentation of emerging practice. It also serves to document transfer of classroom based knowledge into teaching even as it provides a tool for the documentation of growth across time. The chapter provides an outline of best practices in the use of video in teacher training, focusing on problems and techniques of video production that support quality recording and production of videos in class and in the field. Various categories of video appropriate for use in Teacher Training programs are addressed and examples of use are provided. Directions for getting started are provided along with a process for implementation using both hard and soft scaffolding.

INTRODUCTION

Teacher trainers assume an obligation to the teachers we prepare to assist them to develop high level practices (Grossman, Hammerness, & McDonald, 2009), including such skills as noticing learning and how it occurs and systematically reflecting on and learning from the process of teaching and learning. However, pre-service and other novice teachers can experience difficulties acquiring these high level skills and translating them into effective practice (Grossman, Hammerness, & McDonald, 2009; Watson, Blakeley, & Abbot, 1998). This disconnect, compounded by other pivotal challenges faced by pre-service and other novice teachers, can be seen in research documenting high attrition rates, in some countries,

DOI: 10.4018/978-1-5225-0711-6.ch014

Copyright © 2017, IGI Global. Copying or distributing in print or electronic forms without written permission of IGI Global is prohibited.

including the United States, during the teacher induction years (Darling-Hammond, 2003; Moore Johnson, & The Project on the Next Generation of Teachers, 2004; Shen, 2003). Yet this disconnect between course work and the development of high level practices, many of which are hard to "integrate" without actually experiencing and reflecting on them beforehand, can be addressed via the use of video as tool for noticing and reflecting on practice (Santagata & Guarino, 2011). The ability to stop, rewind, and review multiple times when using video empowers pre-service and other novice teachers to carefully study, reflect on, and learn from video recorded classroom interactions (Brophy, 2004). Furthermore, the review of the literature concerning video use aligned with reform efforts in teacher education falls into three broad categories of use:

1.   Supporting efforts to transform existing beliefs and ideas,
2.   Supporting efforts to acquire pedagogical content knowledge, and
3.   Supporting efforts to develop deep pedagogical understanding.

Self-reflection on the meaningfulness of the teaching experience coupled with opportunities to model desire practices are supported by the literature as is using video to assist in the transformation of beliefs about teaching. In order to support this process, pre-service and other novice teachers need exemplars that can serve as models of effective practice (Wang &Hartley, 2003). Little work is found in the literature, however, on how-to capture quality video.

Having teachers capable of demonstrating and documenting teaching effectiveness, ethical behavior, professional obligations, and a willingness to embrace continuous learning is important for the well-being of the field. Video serves as a viable means of documenting this effort. In particular, use of video in teacher training programs or as a part of professional development programs promotes a disposition for reflection on and documentation of the novice's emerging practice. It also serves to document transfer of classroom based knowledge into teaching even as it provides a tool for documenting and reflecting on growth across time. However, before any of this can occur, pre-service and other novice teachers, along with their instructors or instructional coaches, need the process of video production scaffolded for them. Scaffolding the experience is critical to assuring successful use and integration of video into teacher training or professional development programs. Consequently, this chapter outlines best practices in the use of video, focusing on getting started with video and conquering common problems and mastering key techniques of video production that result in quality recordings in class and in the field. Those interested in using video to support teaching effectiveness, including pre-service and other novice teachers, instructional coaches, and other teacher trainers, will find outlined here specific directions for getting started.

TWO BROAD TYPES OF VIDEO WITH APPLICATIONS FOR TEACHER TRAINING

In general, there are two broad types of video that have applications within teacher training and professional development programs—instructor (expert) produced and novice (e.g., pre-service or other novice teacher) produced videos.

Expert Video

Expert video is used to demonstrate, or model, high level practices for pre-service or other novice teachers in a flexible context that allows them, individually or collectively, to parse out specific skills (Santagata & Guarino, 2011; Sun & van Es, 2015; van Es & Sherin, 2010), such as the scaffolding of knowledge acquisition or how expert teachers adapt their questioning to fit the emergent needs of individual students or to steer students away from conceptual misunderstandings.

Use of expert videos assists pre-service and other novice teachers to notice effective practice within a flexible context that allows them to view either a segment or a whole recorded session as many times as needed for them to notice, reflect on, and propose strategies for integrating exemplars into their own emerging practices. The opportunities to carefully scrutinize expert methods and strategies frame by frame and to watch as many times as needed to discern effective practice as modeled by expert teachers make these videos valuable additions to both per-service teacher training and in-service professional development programs.

Novice Video

Use of novice video is particularly effective when seeking to document emerging, or evolving, practice in the field. It is also useful as a form of rehearsal, when the delivery of content or pedagogical knowledge, skills, and, even, dispositions has not yet been mastered. Novice produced videos also can be used to document and self-reflect on successes and challenges occurring during a previously self-recorded teaching experience. Reviewing their video recordings allows pre-service and other novice teachers to learn from successes and failures. Review also allows them the opportunity to identify points of clarity and opportunities to clearly articulate what they did well and/or what they might have done differently to successfully resolve a challenging situation that impacted learning.

Additionally, video recorded in the field serves to promote key attributes of meaningful learning, including problem solving and discovery learning (Larson & Keiper, 2012). In particular, reflective video projects promote self-directed investigations into the very issues and problems that often confronted by pre-service and other novice educators. Creating, reviewing, and reflecting on their teaching videos allows pre-service and other novice teachers to think like the very professionals they seek to become even. It also provides them concrete examples from their own practice of issues they were able to resolve for themselves, enhancing their teaching self-efficacy. While doing so, pre-service and other novice teachers are afforded an opportunity to engage in processes of questioning, analyzing, drawing conclusions, and making recommendations for self (or peer) improvement or for taking appropriate action, again mirroring the work of expert teachers (Gallagher, Sher, Stepien, & Workman, 1995).

In this manner, novice produced videos function as a method of inquiry acting as a catalyst for awareness, self-efficacy and agency, including the confidence to propose solutions to solve specific classroom problems. And when shared with experts (i.e., instructors, instructional coaches, cooperating teachers, or other experts), valid judgements about progress toward formative and summative teaching goals can be made along with concrete recommendations for improvement. In addition to their usefulness for pre-service and novice teachers, these videos also provide experts opportunities to observe and comment on the day-to-day interactions occurring between pre-service and other novice teachers and students.

Rehearsal

Use of novice produced videos can be used to promote rehearsal of content as well as the use of appropriate instructional methods of learning. Review of self-recorded informal, or practice, videos allows pre-service and other novice teachers opportunities to revise their instructional approach in an environment that removes the costs of failure from the experience. Use also promotes reflection on action and active adaptation of planned procedures in advance of real world classroom implementation. Additionally, peer review coupled with instructor feedback, can improved teaching self-efficacy in advance of implementation. In summary, video rehearsal promotes nuanced reflection about teaching even as it functions as preparation for teaching.

IMPLEMENTING VIDEO IN TEACHER TRAINING AND OTHER EDUCATIONAL SETTINGS

The following implementations strategies are offered to spark the readers' thinking about how to use video in the teacher training and professional development courses they teach. Strategies are organized in descending order based on the complexity involved in implementing each type.

One Take Videos

One take, or one shot, videos allow experts or novices to use smartphones or tablets to quickly record a reflective observation about a lesson either in the moment (in action) or shortly after action. This type of video also allows users to capture critical moments of learning---or misunderstanding---as they occur. Whether recorded by the novice or the expert, the novice can later reflect on and learn from what was documented in the lesson. Because little or no editing (or snipping) of video is required for this type of video production, it is an effective use of video in teacher training and professional development settings. Additional, the small file sizes allow for their inclusion as artifacts in electronic or other professional portfolios. Small file size makes it possible to upload and share them using private course learning platforms (i.e., *Blackboard*™ or *Moodle*™) or public social media sites, such as a course *YouTube* channel, *Instagram*™, *Twitter*™, or *Facebook*™. Flexible, mobile apps available for use on smartphones and/or tablets, such as those offered by *Blackboard*™, *Tergity*™, *YouTube*™ or *Instagram*™, further enhance sharing of what was observed.

Video Slide Shows

Use of programs, such as *Animoto*™ or *Office Mix for PowerPoint*™, can assist pre-service and other novice teachers to animate still images of students' learning into a montage of images, which can include a music track or a simple reflective voice over. This type of video can document step-by-step progress through a lesson. Coupled with a reflective voice over provided by the pre-service or novice teacher, this type can be a simple and effective way of introducing video into instructional or professional development settings. Moreover, this type of video be used to model, in a step-by-step manner, critical implementation processes, such as classroom management strategies or, for example, how to teach latitude and longitude effectively to 7th graders.

Vox Pox (Voice of the People)

Use of Vox Pox allows pre-service and novice teachers to interview or ask questions summary questions of a number of learners (or others). Using this approach, novices can query learners to get their perspective on what was learned during a lesson or activity. Responses can be used as reflection prompts or to assess learning and make adjustments to address misconceptions documented in the (exit) video. Vo Pox responses also can be edited into a montage of learner responses that demonstrate understanding. When used this way, Vox Pox serves as a video exit pass for learners where they report what they learned that day. Once recorded. the pre-service or novice teacher views the video, reflects on learning, and adjust future instruction as needed. However, used Vox Pox can be used to promote reflection and to adapt future instruction.

Rehearsal/Modeling Videos

This video type is used to promote rehearsal of content or skills. Review of informal or practice self-recorded videos allows pre-service and other novice teachers opportunities for self-critique and self-reflection about what is effective and what may not be as effective before engaging in real world instruction. Rehearsal, in this context, allows the novice to apply knowledge or understanding, see what works at different stages, and then assess and revise a presentation to better promote learning (Adams, 2004). Use of rehearsal videos removes or mitigates the costs of failure in action. Use of peer review further enhances value. This type of video can also provide opportunities to carefully observe and learn techniques modeled by experts (or peers), providing opportunities for deep consideration, or imitation and reflection.

Screencasts

Screencasting promotes more teacher centric methods of instruction, such as lecture, model, or demonstration. Videos produced by Khan Academy demonstrate the value of this category for learning. Screencasts, created by experts or peers, can be used as planning tools or to introduce or model/demonstrate a particular skill, problem solving strategy or process used or to teach foundational or conceptual knowledge in advance of an in-person session (e.g., Flipped Classroom). Screencasts can also function as a form of rehearsal when they are used to walk through and review a lesson in advance of actual implementation. The primary goal of this type of video is to make teacher centric instruction more visual. It can also be used as a tool to provide learners opportunities for peer teaching or to demonstrate their understanding of what they have learned. Examples of popular screencasting applications include *Screencast'O'Matic™* and *Office Mix for PowerPoint™. Blackboard™ Collaborate™, Kaltura™* and *Camtasia™* also fall into this category.

Documentary Style

Documentary, or news report style, video is more complex than those outlined previously. However, it remains useful when used by pre-service and other novice teachers to document growth across time. It is particularly useful for telling a story; In this case, a story about teaching and learning. Creating the story involves more steps and, thus, more instructional time. It also requires the use of more complex hardware and software, such as inexpensive camcorder and tripod, a wireless microphone, and video snipping or editing software. Use of a wireless microphone assures mobility without a loss of sound quality. Use of video editing or snipping programs allows the pre-service or novice teacher to splice together evidence recorded at different points in time. Getting started with this method, one simply sets up and turns on the camcorder and then turns it off at the end of the lesson. However, other consideration come in to play if this type of video project is to be successful implement. We discuss those consideration and how to scaffold the experience in the next section.

USING NOVICE VIDEOS: SCAFFOLDING THE EXPERIENCE

Once decisions are made about which type(s) of video will be used to support learning, varied issues related to the effective use of video must be addressed. The following section outlines potential issues impacting implementation and provides guidance designed to assist pre-service and other novice teachers to overcome those issues. Using the documentary method as an example, this section demonstrate a scaffolded process that can help assure success. Firstly, given what we know about the effective use of video as a learning tool, learning using video should be scaffolded in order to assure that the intended learning occurs (Hall, Stark, Hilgers, & Chang, 2004; Kline, Stewart, & Murphy, 2006). Scaffolding the academic experience of viewing expert videos or creating novice videos is critical to the successful integration of video into teacher training and professional development programs as is addressing the purposes for using video at the beginning of a course (or before a specific lesson) or workshop. Likewise, participant buy-in is necessary and critical to the successful use of video in teacher training and professional development settings. Without that buy-in, the risk of failure is high (Holbrook, & Dupont, 2011). NOTE: This process of scaffolding the experience and assuring participant buy-in also informs the effective use of the other types of video outline above.

Planning the Project

As a first step in scaffolding the experience when using either expert or novice videos, consider these key questions:

- How much instructional time is available?
- What informational resources and technologies, including media tools such as cameras and tripods, are available for use?
- How much prior knowledge about video recording is exists within the group?
- What external help is available from the institution?
- What is the simplest type of video that can be used to assure success even as it supports targeted learning goals?

Hardware and Software Considerations

A number of options are available for creating videos, but when time and motivation to continue using video are considerations, use the simplest method available. For example, when creating expert videos, voicing over a slideshow type of presentation using *Office Mix for PowerPoint™* may be the most viable and effetctive option for busy instructors or instructional coaches. Since most teacher trainers, instructional coaches, pre-service and other novice teachers are familiar with *PowerPoint*, the need to learn the program is mitigated as is the need for technical support (Coulter & Ray, 2009). Additionally, using presentation software (or a screencasting app) enables the incorporation of previous written guiding notes even as it positively reflects concepts of universal design (Center for Universal Design, 2008) thus better meeting the needs of diverse learners. Finally, any computer with access to presentation software or app and a high-speed internet connection can be used to quickly and effectively create and publish videos (i.e., screencasts).

Camcorders and Wireless Microphones

Use of an inexpensive camcorder and tripod, rather than a smartphone or tablet, remains the simplest method of recording *quality* videos that can be used over and over. Use of a wireless microphone assures mobility in a classroom setting without a loss of sound quality. Using this method, one simply sets up and turns on the camcorder and wireless mic and then turns them off at the end of the lesson or session. NOTE: Many wireless (Bluetooth) or other microphones can be used with smartphones and tablets as well.

Smartphones and Tablets

While neither produce the same quality of audio or video as a traditional video camcorder and wireless microphone, both have potential uses in teacher training programs, particular when used to capture one shot or vox pox videos that might not be captured any other way. In fact, many instructors, instructional coaches, and pre-service and other novice teachers use these devices regularly in their personal lives. Consequently, the learning curve for their educational use is removed or greatly diminished given the simple functionality of apps such as *Explain Everything™* and the high quality build-in video recording apps that come with the *iPhone™, iPad™, Android™,* and other devices.

Video Snipping

Editing video, is a complex skill, that can require an investment of time and money to master, but snipping out sections of video requires far less time or effort. Snipping (or clipping) videos, as opposed to learning and using video editing programs, makes for a viable course assignment for pre-service students. Free phone and tablet apps, such as *Mpgstream Clip™*, available for *Windows™* or *Mac™* users, provide pre-service and other novice teachers the ability to quickly snip out and use a segment from a longer video recording. Once snipped, that segment can be quickly shared using a learning platform, email, or a social media site, including a course *YouTube™* channel. A snipped video can also, if needed, be further edited using another, more advanced editing program.

Editing Video

In order to make the highest quality video products, video editing software is essential. If using *Macs*™, users need to learn how to use a program such as *iMovie*. With PC computers, *Windows Movie Maker*™ remains a good free choice. When using *Chromebooks*™, *WeVideo*™ is a viable option. More complex editing, if or when needed, can be accomplished using the educational version of *Adobe Premier*™ or, the much easier to use, *Adobe Premiere Elements*™. However, the need for editing video really only applies to formal videos that need to be viewed formally outside of a course or workshop, such as at international or national conferences or institutional web sites or social media sites.

Tegrity, Camtasia, or Other Video Programs Contained with Learning Platforms

Tergity and/or *Camtasia*, video product commonly used with the Blackboard Learning Platform, are used by online instructors to produce documentary style video lessons. Most learning platforms come with some type of video program that can be repurposed for traditional classroom use. Once released in Blackboard, most students can learn the software quickly, particularly since most university technology resources centers provide PDF and/or video tutorials for *Tegrity* or other video programs aligned with their learning systems. However, this application ties instruction to the desktop of the laptop or tablet used for recording.

Instructional Approach

In addition to considering whether and to what extent expert or novice video production will be implemented, instructors and instructional coaches, should also consider whether videos will employ an inquiry or expository approach. Table 1 outlines the basic differences between these two approaches.

Developing Guiding Questions

Next, consider whether guiding questions (or specific or narrow topics) will be provided or whether the pre-service or other novice teachers will be asked to develop their own guideline questions for use in the project. Either way an overarching, provocative, or compelling (i.e., guiding) question serves to set the parameters of the project. They should also motivate pre-service or other novice teachers to begin work on the project even as they guide the project toward a successful conclusion (Jacobs 1997; Swan & Hofer, 2014). Once one or more questions are identified, consider the following points:

Table 1. Approaches to documentary video production in teacher training programs

Inquiry (Best)	Expository Report (Good Starting Place)
• Ask guiding/compelling questions • Research and collect evidence, including video evidence • Syntheses of evidence to draw a conclusion • Storyboard an outline that will present a perspective or position (argument) and draw conclusions (to sway the viewer). The video serves to answer an agreed upon guiding question	Facts, names, sequence or timeline of events as they occur in the classroom. The video documents knowledge of teaching and learning and informs others about teaching efficacy.

Source: Swan & Hofer (2014).

- Does the question represent an important issue or concern for practice?
- Is the questions open ended enough to allow for multiple responses?
- Does the questions represent a reasonable amount of content or other learning?
- Will the question maintain value across the project?
- Is the question appropriate given what is known or given available resources?
- Is the question challenging (i.e.., developmentally appropriate)?

Evidence Collection

As a next step in the process, pre-service or other novice teachers gather evidence to build a case for their emerging teaching effectiveness. They do this by recording their teaching and then selecting quality evidence that supports a thesis or provides an answer to their guiding question(s). Types of evidence might include: teaching events, one on one interactions with leaners, lesson plans or other textual evidence; data tables; images; interviews with experts, learners, or others who can provide insight on the topic; video clips; music; reputable Internet web sites; etc. (Bruner, 1961; Joyce, Weil, & Calhoun, 2014).

Interim Assessment

Also critical across a larger video projects is the process of stopping to assess learning and progress at designated points. Use of formative assessments of the progress videos, including review of selected teaching exemplars, allows pre-service and other novice teachers to know that they are proceeding in a manner that will be successful and that will allow the finalized project to truly show their best teaching efforts. It also can offer assurances that the contents of the finalized project will perform well on any assessment rubric used for summative assessment. NOTE: Various video assessments rubrics can be found online and adapted to meet the needs of specific projects.

Modeling Video Production

Modeling, where the instructor or instructional coach creates a similar video in step with those created by pre-service or other novice teachers can be an effective method of identifying problems and troubleshooting solutions that reflect those faced by pre-service and novice teachers during the project. The modeling process can result in a video that demonstrates for students step-by-step what to include in their own video projects (Swan & Hofee, 2014).

Graphical Organizers as Scaffolds

Across the various stages of the project, graphical organizers can serve to scaffold the project. These are particularly important when assigning video project for the first time and/or when assigning more complex types of projects for pre-service and other novice teachers to complete (Brush & Saye, 2002). Examples of useful organizers include pre-formatted 3x5 or electronic index cards, storyboards, scripting guides, and other organizers that can be used to sort or store evidence or sources of evidence. Organizers that provide daily or periodic formal checks of notes and sources help move the project forward as well.

Scripting

Most field or clinical settings do not allow for the use of scripts or storyboards. However, all settings allow for the use of rehearsal on the part of pre-service or other novice teacher and for the use of modeling on the part of expert teachers. And since video provides a viable option for both actions, use of scripts particularly for model or demonstration videos remains important. Scripts can range from detailed text based narratives that an instructor reads, or uses to voice over a pre-recorded classroom scene to ones that simply outline key steps in a lesson (e.g., an outline of the procedures section of a formal lesson plan). However, used, scripts promote direction and clarity even as they reduce the need for video editing. These script can be recycled as written transcripts that can be used to locate key information or review specific information as many times as needed for understanding to occur (Ray & Powell, 2014).

Recording extemporaneously (verses recording using a guiding script) promotes rehearsal along with mindful consideration of the most important concept, which leads to more effective video instruction, particular for expert video products. Indeed, speaking without guiding prompts can require multiple attempts at recording before a cohesive narrative is achieved consuming valuable time. Furthermore, scripted presentations tend to contain fewer verbal fillers (i.e., "ums" or "ah's") (Coulter & Ray, 2009). As such, informal outlining and/or detailed scripting of a video project remains a useful step in the process of video production.

Scripting is accomplished when pre-service or other novice teachers outline what they want to say about their teaching exemplars (i.e., evidence). Scripts assist them to decide in what order to present their evidence in the video. Scripting can be considered the storytelling stage of video production, where pre-service or other novice teachers write, edit, and rehearse a narrative that can be used to voice over the visuals used in the video. Again, writing out the script saves time later, cutting down on the need for multiple recordings and/or the need to learn (or use) video editing software (Ray & Powell, 2014). Examples of video scripts and templates that can serve as exemplars are available online. NOTE: Each line or paragraph in the script can be separated out to identify natural pauses. Scripts can be printed out using a larger font to make reading the text easier (Swan & Hofer, 2014).

Storyboarding

Storyboarding is another useful approach to video production, particularly when creating more complex video products. A critical first steps in the storyboarding process involves organizing images and/or video clips in sequential order. All images used should support the central argument or thesis of the video. Once selected they need to be balanced across the video to match the tone of the video and to support its visual appeal (Swan & Hofer, 2014).

About Copyright

Care should be taken to double check that all images, whether moving or still, are properly cited to their sources. Care should also be taken to assure that videos, whether expert or novice products, conform to United States or other international copyright laws. For example, in the United States educational users may use up to 30 seconds or 10%, whichever is less, of any copyright protected video in their video projects? Any further use is a violation of U.S. Copyright law.

Rather than worrying about copyright, however, direct pre-service and other novice videographers to create their own videos for use in the project, or require them to use only videos and images found using the search page located on the Creative Commons (CC) (see http://www.creativecommons.org) website. CC is an excellent source of public domain video and images that can be edited or used 'as is' in expert and novice video project.

Interim Assessment

Before moving into video production, instructors and instructional coaches should assess the previous steps to identify potential issues related to script development, storyboard development and image selection.

Video Production Tips

Once all logistical concerns addressed above are resolved, it is time to think about how to produce a high quality video product. Early in the project (i.e., before this stage) identify what hardware and/or software will be used and determine what information (e.g., tutorials) are needed to assure success. Be sure to use *Google*™ or *Bing*™ to find quality app or software tutorials and then provide links to them. Scaffolding the process of learning how to use required or recommended software or apps is important, particularly when using new or complex software programs. Often it can be appropriate to allow those with advanced technology skills to identify and select their own software or apps to use on personal laptops, tablets, and/or smart phones. However, narrowing down, or limiting the choices, can be effective as well.

Keep in mind that the video production stage can be as simple or as complex as needed. The following sections are offered for those ready for a more complex approach to video production. However, keeping things simple is never automatically a bad choice for busy educators, particularly when video is being used for the first time. Therefore, it is recommended that the reader refer to the following sections as needed across time and across video projects.

Selecting Appropriate Camera Angles and Shots

When using one or more cameras, many different camera shots can be used, but three key shots angles are used by the news broadcast news industry and by video documentarians. Those are the head shot/close up, long shot/establishing shot, and medium shot. Each can serve a useful role when used in classroom and field settings.

Full Body Shots

Television sets and most monitors still cannot reproduce fine details from a full body shot. Also, when watching the news or informational videos people prefer to look at other people's faces (Ascher & Pincus, 2013; Stockman, 2011). Therefore, full body shots have limited applications in many settings. However, for educational users in classroom, laboratory or other field settings, full body shots are a viable option. Consider using of this type of shot when the goal is to record multiple interactions with learners across the entire learning environment.

Head Shots

When filming a head shot only it is very important to include the entire face right down to the shoulders. The main objective here is to avoid having a floating or "disembodied" head in your view finder, as most viewers find this disturbing, and therefore distracting to the actual purpose of the video recording (Ascher & Pincus, 2013; Stockman, 2011). Consider using a head shot when the purpose of the goal is informational or reflective. Head shots are particularly effective when used in expert videos and when recording reflective statements about teaching that do not require any other video evidence.

Wide (or Long) Shots

Wide (or long) shots help viewers get a sense of "place." Most television broadcasts begin with a long shot to establish a sense of place before moving in to a closer head shot of the speaker. When used as an establishing shot, a long shot requires more than one cameras and/or use of video editing software to move from the wide shot to close shot (Stockman, 2011). However, when the goal is to video everything going on in a classroom or when a lot of movement is expected across the recording experience, using a wide shots removes or diminishes the need for both video editing and the use of more than one cameras. Consider using a wide shot whenever recording the entire learning environment is desired. But keep in mind that wide shots will record everything, including things that might later become distracts to the central goal for the recording. So observe the learning environment and make careful decisions about where to place the camera beforehand.

Medium Shots

A medium shot is a waist-up shot of a person. Medium shots help place a subject in context. They are particularly useful for recording video of people who gesture a lot or who are using a whiteboard to teach or demonstrate a concept. To shoot a medium shot, frame the subject in the view finder using the area between the waist line and the knees as your bottom point. Be sure to either declutter or dim the background area behind the person as that helps to cut down on visual distractions for the viewer. When filming medium shots, avoid extreme close ups or use of high and low angle shots. Keep in mind that "zooming" in or out while recording video is a bad idea for everyone except expert videographers. Also, when recording video, avoid headroom at the top of the shot. Too much headroom makes a shots look off-balance. (Ascher & Pincus, 2013; Stockman, 2011).

Conquering Sound

Sound is perhaps the most important element of video production. This is because most viewers are willing to tolerate, or watch, low resolution video. However, very few are willing to listen to a video containing low quality audio sound (Stockman, 2011). The more complex the video project the more careful attention must be paid to sound. Investing in high quality microphones assists in the production of high quality sound. As does, careful consideration of the placement of microphones, either on the person or in the classroom. In general, a wireless microphone clipped onto the teacher should rest roughly 14 centimeters below the chin.

Consideration should be given to the type of clothing worn as well. Clothes that rustle or that lack a secure place near the neck line to clip on a microphone create audio problems that could have been easily be avoided with a better sartorial choice. As does placing a microphone near a cluster of chatting children.

When recording simple, reflective videos, finding a quiet place to record can make all the differences. Also, when recording in an office, consider posting a "do not disrupt" or "on air" notice on a closed and locked door. Adding to the notice both the start and end time for recording can be useful as well.

Conquering Light

When recording video, focus on getting the right kind of light. There are two broad types of light, hard light and soft light. Hard light comes from a single source and thus produces sharp or "hard" shadows. A good example of hard light is sunlight. Conversely, soft light comes from a large but diffused source. Shadows casts by soft light are less defined or invisible. Some examples of soft light are the fluorescent and other lights found in most classroom settings and the light that exists outside on a cloudy day.

Keep in mind also, that every light source has a unique color. For instance, candles produce reddish light, sunlight produces a rich blue light, fluorescent lights produce a sickly green light, and incandescent light bulbs produce an orange light. Remember, the human eye compensates for these colors, but most cameras do not. Therefore, it is important to figure out ways to reduce the negative impact of these colors on the final video project. As an example, when recording in a classroom or office lite by fluorescents, first try recording without those lights turned on. If that is not an option, bring in other light by adjusting curtains or blinds to flood the room with an offsetting blue light. Also, consider supplementing classroom or office light sources using office lamps or inexpensive, portable spot lights (Ascher & Pincus, 2013; Stockman, 2011). Play around with placement of these alternative light sources until the room's light is improved and the greenish cast is neutralized.

A Basic Fix for Most Lighting Problems

Playing around with alternative light sources can be somewhat effective. But in order to really fix a lighting issue, three light sources are required. These lights can be set up in such a way as to make the main subject look more three-dimensional. The three main light sources needed are called key light, fill light, and back light. First consider key light. This is the brightest light in the set. The key light is positioned at eye level roughly 45 degrees left or right of the video's main subject. Next, the fill light is set directly opposite the key light using the same angel and elevation. Key and fill are the most important elements to good lighting. Finally, a back light is set directly behind or slight off center the main subject (Stockman, 2011).

Lamps or small portable spotlights can be used to create the three main light sources, if professional lighting is not an option. Whenever possible, any fluorescent lights in the area should be turned off to neutralize the impact of their greenish tint on the video recording (Ascher & Pincus, 2013; Stockman, 2011). Also, while the fluorescent light's flicker is not visible to the human eye, the pulsing light can mess up a video recording. Turning them off solves this problem as well. Whenever fluorescent cannot be turned off, try adding a soft light source, if possible, to fill in shadows and reduce the green cast of fluorescent bulbs. If nothing else works, try bouncing light off the classroom or office ceiling using white poster boards (Stockman, 2011). Another thing to consider is when to use outside light. For example, when shooting in a faculty office or instructional classroom, remove or reduce sunlight by closing, partially closing, or lowering shades or curtains.

Moving Beyond the Classroom

On occasion instructors, instructional coaches, and preservice and other novice teachers, need to shoot video outdoors. When shooting outdoors, these basic tips can improve video quality: add artificial light to fill out shadows, move into a shaded area to take advantage of more balanced light, and avoid shooting directly into the sun.

Snipping or Editing Videos

It is possible to create quality videos without employing complex video editing software. To do so, however, the pre-planning steps outlined earlier in this chapter are critical. In particular, scripting and storyboarding help to reduce---or remove---the need for video editing (Ray & Powell, 2014). However, the need for snipping may remain. If so, consider having students snip, or clip, videos to remove awkward beginnings or endings. Apps such as, *MPG Stream Clip*™ (Windows and Apple) or *Video Trim and Cut*™ (iPhone and iPad) are free, user friendly snipping options.

Keep in mind, also, that if tablet or smart phone are used to record video, it might be easier to edit the project using free, downloadable tablet or smart phone apps. However, when using traditional digital cameras, camcorders, or some smart phones, the need to transfer video files to a computer first may remain necessary. Transfer from these devices to the computer is often accomplished using a device's unique video cable. Newer equipment, including most smartphones, allow for cloud transfer instead. Whenever there is uncertainty about how to get video off a particular device and onto a computer, a quick *Google*™ or *Bing*™ search can help find necessary directions.

Editing Videos

If preferred, video editing programs, such as *Windows Live Movie Maker* ™ or *iMovie*™, can be used. Both come free with most computers. *Adobe Premiere*™, available inexpensively as an educational purchase, or *Adobe Premiere Elements*™ can also be used to expand the video editing skill set for those ready to tackle complex video editing tasks. Beyond these choices, however, the complexity of the software likely will take away from the goals for most educational video projects. Once a decision is made about what editor to use, a quick internet search will reveal a number of useful software tutorials.

Sharing the Video

A next step in achieving mastery of video for learning involves publishing or sharing completed videos. Placing them on a local server that can be useful. *Tegrity*™, if available, does a good job with this process. Downloading and viewing *Tegrity* ™v ideos is facilitated by a user friendly app that allows users to view videos on laptops, smartphones, and tablets. The downside to this method, however, is that many educational institutions still have limited server space and are reluctant to allocate space for extensive publication of videos, particularly student videos. However, many free or inexpensive social media or cloud hosting services, such as *Box*™, *Dropbox*™, or *Google Drive*™, are available for use.

YouTube™ Channels

YouTube™ channels function as free video storage and organization pages. These channels can be password protected, invitation only sites or, if preferred, they can be set for public viewing. Either choice provides control over current or future access to what, once graded, might be viewed as private or proprietary videos in some settings. Also, since *YouTube*™ channels can be password protected, many of the copyright issues associated with university and other educational servers can be avoided.

Other Considerations

Other practical suggestions to assure success include editing and/or compressing videos to reduce file size which then facilitates faster downloads, saving video files using other versions or file types, and, in some isolated cases, burning the videos to DVD. However, burning to DVD is no longer a useful or time saving activity for most teacher training programs---except in geographic areas where internet access remains problematic.

Extending Learning

Learning can be extended in a variety of ways. For example, consider hosting a viewing party for the class or professional development participants. Invite others to attend and share in the viewing experience. Provide simple snacks and encourage dressing up for the viewing party. Have others use smart phones to interviews presenters before and after viewing regarding the goals of video project. These short videos can then be used, potentially, to document reflection on what was learned across the experience either by the videographer or a viewer.

Peer review of video using an instructor or instructional coach provided evaluation rubric is another way to extend learning. Less formally, use of brief written or oral feedback about one another's videos can be required.

Summative Assessment

As a final assessment of the video project, it is useful to consider and assess the overall impact of the learning documented in the video. For example, does the evidence contained in the video adequately support a central thesis or argument? Does the evidence serve as a powerful visual statement that effectively interprets the argument for the viewer?

Careful reflection on the project whether via a quick one shot video or a more complex documentary video assists preservice and other novice teacher and their instructors to determine what was learned from the experience. It also allows the instructor or instructional coach to reflect on what went well across the project along with what needs to be adapted before implementing the video project again.

USING EXPERT VIDEOS: SCAFFOLDING THE EXPERIENCE

Use of viewing guide containing information about what the learner should do (i.e., hardware and software tutorials) or look for while viewing an assigned video (pre, interim, and post viewing) are critical to scaffolding an experience that promote meaningful learning with video. Ideally, viewing guides should prepare the learner not only for the contents of the video, but also notify them of what information or reflections they should bring with them into the classroom setting (e.g. discussion topics) and how that information is important to the goals of the individual lesson, lecture, and/or the goals of the course. Viewing guides should also inform students about how much time they are expected to spend viewing and reflecting on assigned videos. Instead of simply having students view and take self-directed notes from a pre-recorded lectures, teacher trainers should include learner centered tasks to complete before, during, and after viewing demonstration videos. Pre-service teachers should not ever have to guess what to look for in a video. Instead, they should be provided with an overview of what particular element, such as deep questioning, is demonstrated or modeled for them in the video (Ray & Powell, 2014).

KWHL Viewing Guide

When time is a premium, the construction of structured viewing guides may not be possible. In such cases, a simple KWHL can play a useful role in structuring a video assignment for the viewer. Using the KWHL, viewers begin by writing down what they know about the topic and what they want to learn about the topic in advance of viewing the assigned video. Next, students reflect on how they will learn, which includes the assigned video. These steps can be accomplished inside or outside of class. Once completed, students next view the video, again either inside or outside of class (e.g., using the Flipped Classroom approach) before completing the final section of the organizers, what was learned (Pitler, Hubbell, & Kuhn, 2012).

It is also important to realize that some pre-service teachers may attempt to circumvent the content of required videos and attempt instead to acquire via other means the information contained within the video. Others might choose to not view assigned videos assuming that their contents will be made apparent during seminars, class discussions, and/or lecture sessions. To reduce this issue to successful implementation of video in teacher training programs, instructors should set aside time at the beginning of the course (or specific class or seminar) to discuss the importance of viewing and reflecting on the videos to the successful completion of the class. Having students sign a statement acknowledging their responsibilities when accessing and viewing the assigned videos may prove useful (Coulter & Ray, 2009).

CONCLUSION

As teacher trainers, instructional coaches, and professional development leaders, we must model an authentic process of video use and production for our students if that practice is to become standardized within practice. Allowing pre-service and other novice teachers to learn from and reflect on their practice or that of others using video helps them develop—and hone--the very knowledge, skills, and dispositions that they need to succeed as teachers. But first, they will need help addressing the problems and issues that arise when using video in class.

Video can be appropriately used as a tool for teacher training and professional development. We note however, that use of video for video's sake alone, is never appropriate. Therefore, we offer a way of thinking about the use of video and a way of doing, or implementing that use, that can provide guidance to those considering requiring video projects for the first time. The ways of doing highlighted in this chapter are reflective of western educational theory and an emerging research base supporting the use of video to improve teaching self-efficacy.

It is expected that this chapter will assist teacher trainers, instructional coaches, and professional development leaders to create positive learning environments were video can be used to support learning even as those settings serve as models of best practices for video use.

The audience for this chapter includes pre-service teacher trainers and other educators tasked with the responsibility of assure that pre-service and other novice teachers succeed. Interest in the chapter is also shaped nationally, and internationally, by an emerging examination of whether and to what extend video can be used to improve instructional self-efficacy. Interest among public constituencies, including policy makers, may extend the reach of the proposed chapter beyond that of educators working with pre-service and other novice teachers. Furthermore, as today's technology savvy youth move into the teacher workforce, it becomes more likely that technologies, such as digital video, will be embraced as thinking, learning and training tools.

REFERENCES

Adams, K. (2004). Modeling success: Enhancing international postgraduate research students' self-efficacy for research seminar presentations. *Higher Education Research & Development, 23*(2), 115–130. doi:10.1080/0729436042000206618

Ascher, S., & Pincus, E. (2013). *The filmmaker's hand book: A comprehensive guide for the digital age.* New York, NY: Plume.

Brophy, J. (Ed.). (2004). *Using video in teacher education.* Boston, MA: Elsevier.

Bruner, J. (1961). The act of discovery. *Harvard Educational Review, 31*(1), 21–32.

Brush, T. A., & Saye, J. W. (2002). A summary of research exploring hard and soft scaffolding for teachers and students using a multimedia supported learning environment. *Journal of Interactive Online Learning, 1*(2), 1–12. Retrieved from http://www.ncolr.org/jiol/issues/pdf/1.2.3.pdf

Coulter, G., & Ray, B. (2009). Teacher candidates' perspectives on the efficacy of webcasts as online supplemental instruction in traditional education courses. *Proceedings of the World Conference on E-Learning in Corporate, Government, Healthcare, and Higher Education* (pp. 2475-2475).

Darling-Hammond, L. (2003). Keeping good teachers. *Educational Leadership, 60*(8), 6–13.

Darling-Hammond, L., & Bransford, J. (Eds.), (2005). *Preparing Teachers for a Changing World: What Teachers Should Learn and Be Able to Do. National Academy of Education, Committee on Teacher Education.* San Francisco: Jossey Bass.

Gallagher, S. A., Sher, B. T., Stepien, W. J., & Workman, D. (1995). Implementing problem based learning. *School Science and Mathematics*, *95*(3), 136–146. doi:10.1111/j.1949-8594.1995.tb15748.x

Grossman, P., Hammerness, K., & McDonald, M. (2009). Redefining teaching, re-imagining teacher education. *Teachers and Teaching: Theory and Practice.*, *15*(2), 273–289. doi:10.1080/13540600902875340

Hall, R. H., Stark, S., Hilgers, M., & Chang, P. (2004). A comparison of scaffolding media in learning systems for teaching web development. *Proceedings of the AACE E-LearnConference* (pp. 1906-1913). Retrieved from http://dl.aace.org/16707

Holbrook, J., & Dupont, C. (2011). Making the decision to provide enhanced podcasts to post secondary science students. *Journal of Science Education and Technology*, *20*(3), 233–245. doi:10.1007/s10956-010-9248-1

Jacobs, H. H. (1997). *Mapping the big picture*. Alexandria, VA: Association for Supervision and Curriculum Development.

Joyce, B., Weil, M., & Calhoun, E. (2014). *Models of Teaching* (9th ed.). New York, NY: Pearson Education.

Kagan, D. (1992). Professional growth among pre-service and beginning teachers. *Review of Educational Research*, *62*(2), 129–169. doi:10.3102/00346543062002129

Kline, S., Stewart, K., & Murphy, M. (2006). Media literacy in the risk society: Toward a risk reduction strategy. *Canadian Journal of Education*, *29*(1), 131–153. doi:10.2307/20054150

Larson, B. E., & Keiper, T. A. (2012). *Instructional strategies for middle and high school*. London: Routledge.

Moore Johnson, S.The Project on the Next Generation of Teachers. (2004). *Finders and keepers: Helping new teachers survive and thrive in our schools*. San Francisco: Jossey Bass.

Pitler, H., Hubbell, E., & Kuhn, M. (2012). *Using technology with classroom instruction that works* (2nd ed.). Alexandria, VA: ASCD.

Ray, B. B., & Powell, A. (2014). Preparing to teach with Flipped Classroom in teacher preparation programs. In J. Keengwe, G. Onchwari, & J. Oigara (Eds.), *Promoting active learning through the Flipped Classroom model*. Hershey, PA: IGI Global. doi:10.4018/978-1-4666-4987-3.ch001

Santagata, R., & Guarino, J. (2011). Using video to teach future teachers to learning from teaching. *ZDM Mathematics Education*, *43*(1), 133–145. doi:10.1007/s11858-010-0292-3

Shen, J. (2003). New teachers' certification status and attrition pattern. A survival analysis using The Baccalaureate and Beyond Longitudinal Study 1993–97. *Paper presented at theAERA annual meeting*, Chicago, IL.

Stockman, S. (2011). *How to shoot video that doesn't suck*. New York, NY: Workman Publishing Co.

Sun, J., & van Es, E. A. (2015). An exploratory study of the influence that analyzing teaching has on pre-service teachers' classroom practice. *Journal of Teacher Education*, *66*(3), 201–214. doi:10.1177/0022487115574103

Swan, K., & Hofer, M. (2014). *And Action! Directing documentaries in the social studies classroom.* Lanham, MA: Rowman & Littlefield.

van Es, E. A., & Sherin, M. G. (2010). The influence of video clubs on teachers' thinking and practice. *Journal of Mathematics Teacher Education, 13*(2), 155–176. doi:10.1007/s10857-009-9130-3

Wang, J., & Hartley, K. (2003). Video technology as a support for teacher education reform. *Journal of Technology and Teacher Education, 11*(1), 105–138.

Watson, D., Blakeley, B., & Abbott, C. (1998). Researching the use of communication technologies in teacher education. *Computers & Education, 10*(1-2), 15–21. doi:10.1016/S0360-1315(97)00074-2

Compilation of References

Abell, S. K., & Cennamo, K. S. (2004). Videocases in elementary science teacher preparation. In J. Brophy (Ed.), *Using video in teacher education* (1st ed., pp. 103–129). Boston: Elsevier.

Adams, K. (2004). Modeling success: Enhancing international postgraduate research students' self-efficacy for research seminar presentations. *Higher Education Research & Development, 23*(2), 115–130. doi:10.1080/0729436042000206618

Alcocer, A. (2014). E*l auge de los vídeos móviles en las redes sociales*. Retrieved from http://www.societicbusinessonline. com/2014/07/22/el-auge-de-los-videos-moviles-en-las-redes-sociales/

Allal, L., & Laveault, D. (2009). Assessment for learning. Evaluation-soutien d'apprentissage. *Mésure et Evaluation en Education, 32*(2), 99–104.

Allen, D. W. (1966). Micro-teaching is a scaled down teaching encounter in class size and class time. *High School Journal, 49*(8), 355–362.

Allen, D. W. (1967). *Micro-teaching. A description*. San Francisco: Stanford University Press.

Allen, D., & Ryan, K. (1969). *Microteaching reading*. Boston, MA: Addison Wesley.

Allen, M. (2012). An Education in Facebook. *Digital Culture & Education, 4*(3), 213–225.

Altet, M. (1996). Les dispositifs d'analyse des pratiques pédagogiques en formation d'enseignants: une démarche d'articulation pratique-théorie-pratique. In C. Blanchard-Laville & D. Fablet (Eds.), L'analyse des pratiques profession-nelles, (pp. 11-26). L'Harmattan: Paris.

Altet, M. (2001). Les Compétences de l'enseignant-professionnel: entre savoirs, schèmes d'action et adaptation, le savoir analyser. In L. Paquay, M. Altet, E. Charlier, & P. Perrenoud (Eds.), Former des enseignants professionnels. Quelles stratégies? Quelles compétences? (pp. 27-40). Bruxelles: de Boeck.

Altet, M. (2006). Le competenze dell'insegnante-professionista: saperi, schemi d'azione, adattamenti ed analisi. In Altet M., Charlier E., Paquay L., Perrenoud P. (Eds.), Formare gli insegnanti professionisti. Quali strategie? Quali competenze? (pp. 31-44). Roma: Armando.

Altet, M. (2006). Le competenze dell'insegnante-professionista: saperi, schemi di azione, adattamenti ed analisi. In L. Paquay, E. Charlier, Ph. Perrenoud (Eds.), Formare gli insegnanti professionisti. Quali strategie? Quali competenze? (pp. 31-44). Roma: Armando.

Altet, M. (2012). L'apporto dell'analisi plurale dalle pratiche didattiche alla co-formazione degli insegnanti. In P.C. Rivoltella, P.G. Rossi (Eds.), L'agire didattico. Manuale per l'insegnante, (pp. 291-312). Brescia: La scuola.

Altet, M., Bru, M. & Blanchard-Laville, C. (2012). *Observer les pratiques enseignantes: pour quels enjeux ?* Paris: L'Harmattan.

Altet, M., Charlier, E., Paquay, L., & Perrenoud, P. (Eds.), (2006). Formare gli insegnanti professionisti. Quali strategie? Quali competenze? Roma: Armando.

Altet, M. (1994). *La formation professionnelle des enseignants*. Paris: PUF.

Altet, M. (2002). Une démarche de recherche sur la pratique enseignante: L'analyse plurielle. *Revue Française de Pédagogie, 138*(1), 85–93. doi:10.3406/rfp.2002.2866

Altet, M. (2003). Caractériser, expliquer et comprendre les pratiques enseignantes pour aussi contribuer à leur évaluation. *Les Dossiers des Sciences de l'Education, 10*, 31–43.

Altet, M. (2003). *La ricerca sulle pratiche d'insegnamento in Francia*. Brescia: La Scuola.

Altet, M. (2012). L'apporto dell'analisi plurale dalle pratiche didattiche alla co-formazione degli insegnanti. In P. C. Rivoltella & P. G. Rossi (Eds.), *L'Agire didattico* (pp. 291–311). Brescia: La Scuola.

Altet, M. (2012). L'apporto dell'analisi plurale dalle pratiche didattiche alla co-formazione degli insegnanti. In P. C. Rivoltella & P. G. Rossi (Eds.), *L'agire didattico. Manuale per l'insegnante* (pp. 291–311). Brescia: La Scuola.

Anadon, M. (2007). *La recherche participative*. Québec: Presse de l'Université du Québec.

Anderson, L. W. (2004). *Increasing teacher effectiveness* (2nd ed.). Paris: UNESCO – IIEP.

Anderson, T., & Shattuck, J. (2012). Design-Based reseach: A Decade of Progress in Education Research? *Educational Researcher, 41*(1), 16–25. doi:10.3102/0013189X11428813

Anne, M. (2014). Using video to develop skills in reflection in teacher education students. *Australian Journal of Teacher Education, 39*(9), 6.

Area, M. (2008). Las redes sociales en internet como espacios para la formación del profesorado. *Razón y palabra, 13*(63), 1-12.

Areglado, N. (1999). I became convinced. *Journal of Staff Development, 20*(1), 35–37.

Ascher, S., & Pincus, E. (2013). *The filmmaker's hand book: A comprehensive guide for the digital age*. New York, NY: Plume.

Astolfi, J. P. (1997). Du "tout" didactique au "plus" didactique. *Revue Française de Pédagogie, 129*(1), 67–73. doi:10.3406/rfp.1997.1157

Atelet, M. (2003), *La ricerca sulle pratiche di insegnamento*. Brescia: La scuola.

Atkins, S. (1998). Best practice: Preservice teachers' perceptions of videodisc vs. videotape of classroom practices in a methods course. *Journal of Technology and Teacher Education, 6*, 51–59.

Aubertine, H. E. (1967). Use of Microteaching in Training Supervising Teachers. *High School Journal, 51*, 99–106.

Aumont, J. (1995). *A Estética do filme*. Campinas: Papirus.

Ausbel, D. (1978). *Educazione e processi cognitivi: guida psicologica per gli insegnanti*. Milano: Franco Angeli.

Avalos, B. (2011). Teacher professional development in Teaching and Teacher Education over ten years. *Teaching and Teacher Education, 27*(1), 10–20. doi:10.1016/j.tate.2010.08.007

Axberg, U., Hansson, K., Broberg, A. G., & Wirtberg, I. (2006). The Development of a Systemic School-Based Intervention: MarteMeo and Coordination Meetings. *Family Process*, *45*(3), 375–389. doi:10.1111/j.1545-5300.2006.00177.x PMID:16984077

Baecher, L. H., McCormack, B., & Kung, S. C. (2014). Supervisor use of video as a tool in teacher reflection. *The Electronic Journal for English as a Second Language, 18*(3). Retrieved from http://www.tesl-ej.org/wordpress/issues/volume18/ej71/ej71a5/

Baecher, L., & Kung, S. C. (2011). Jumpstarting Novice Teachers' Ability to Analyze Classroom Video: Affordances of an Online Workshop. *Journal of Digital Learning in Teacher Education*, *28*(1), 16–26. doi:10.1080/21532974.2011.10784676

Baecher, L., & McCormack, B. (2015). The impact of video review on supervisory conferencing. *Language and Education*, *29*(2), 153–173. doi:10.1080/09500782.2014.992905

Ballanti, G. (1975). *Il comportamento dell'insegnante*. Roma: Armando.

Ballanti, G. (1979). *Analisi e modificazione del comportamento dell'insegnante*. Teramo: Giunti &Lisciani.

Ballanti, G. (1980). La formazione professionale dell'insegnante (partiamo da zero). Il primo obiettivo professionale:la competenza minima insegnante. *Psicologia e Scuola, I*, 34–38.

Bandura, A. (1997). *Self-efficacy: The exercise of control*. New York: Freeman.

Bandura, A., Ross, D., & Ross, S. (1961). Transmission of Aggression through imitation of aggressive models. *Journal of Abnormal and Social Psychology*, *63*(3), 575–582. doi:10.1037/h0045925 PMID:13864605

Barab, S. A., MaKinster, J. G., & Scheckler, R. (2003). Designing system dualities: Characterizing a web-supported professional development community. *The Information Society*, *19*(3), 237–256. doi:10.1080/01972240309466

Barab, S., & Squire, K. (2004). Design-Based research: Putting a Stake in the Ground. *Journal of the Learning Sciences*, *13*(1), 1–14. doi:10.1207/s15327809jls1301_1

Baran, B. (2010). Facebook as a formal instructional environment. *British Journal of Educational Technology*, *41*(6), 146–149. doi:10.1111/j.1467-8535.2010.01115.x

Barbier, J.-M. (2000). Sémantique de l'action et sémantique de l'intelligibilité des l'action. In B. Maggi (Ed.), Manières de penser, manières d'agir en education et en formation. Paris, France: PUF (Presses Universitaires de France).

Barbier, J.M., Chaix, M.L., & Demailly, L. (1994). Recherche et développement professionnel. *Recherche et formation, 17*, 1-175.

Barbier, J. M., & Durand, M. (2003). L'analyse de l'activité: Enjeux de recherche et de professionnalisation. *Recherche et Formation*, *42*, 5–6.

Barbier, R. (2007). *La recherche-action*. Paris: Anthropos.

Barcelos, G. T., & Batista, S. C. F. (2013). Use of Social Networks in teacher training programs: A case study. *International Journal on New Trends in Education and Their Implications*, *4*(1), 1–14.

Barron, A. (1998). Designing Web-based training. *British Journal of Educational Technology, 29*(4), 355–370. doi:10.1111/1467-8535.00081

Barthes, R. (1984). *A câmara clara*. Rio de Janeiro: Nova Fronteira.

Bartley, D. E. (1969). Microteaching: Rationale procedures and application to foreign language. *Audiovisual Language Journal, 7*(3), 139–144.

Bazin, J. (2008). *Des clous dans la Joconde. L'anthropologie autrement.* Toulouse: Anacharsis.

Beaugrand, J. (1988). Observation directe du comportement, in M. Robert (Ed.), Fondements et étapes de la recherche scientifique en psychologie (pp. 277-310). Saint-Hyacinthe: Edisem.

Bednarz, N. (2013). *Recherche collaborative et pratique enseignante.* Paris: L'Harmattan.

Bell, B., & Cowie, B. (2001). The characteristics of formative assessment in science education. *Science Education, 85*(5), 536–553. doi:10.1002/sce.1022

Bennet, R.E. (2010). Cognitively based assessment of, for, an das learning. A preliminary theory of action for summative and formative assessment. *Measurement; Interdisciplinary Research and Perspectives, 8*, 70-91.

Bennet, R. E. (2015). The changing nature of educational assessment, *Review of Research in Education. AERA, 39*, 370–407.

Bennett, B., Spencer, D., Bergmann, J., Cockrum, T., Musallam, R., Sams, A., & Overmyer, J. et al. (2011). *The flipped class manifest.* New York, NY: The Daily Rift.

Bergala, A. (2011). A presença do cinema no contexto escolar. *Paper presented at Second Meeting Cinema and Education*, São Paulo.

Bergala, A. (2002). *L'hypothèse cinema.* Paris: Cahiers du Cinema.

Berge, Z. (1998). Guiding principles in web-based instructional design. *Educational Media International, 35*(2), 72–76. doi:10.1080/0952398980350203

Bergman, D. (2015). Comparing the Effects of Classroom Audio-Recording and Video-Recording on Preservice Teachers' Reflection of Practice. *Teacher Educator, 50*(2), 127–144. doi:10.1080/08878730.2015.1010054

Berliner, D. C. (1983). Developing conceptions of classroom environments: Some light on the T in classroom studies of ATI. *Educational Psychologist, 18*(1), 1–13. doi:10.1080/00461528309529256

Berliner, D. C. (2001). Learning about and learning from expert teachers. *International Journal of Educational Research, 35*(5), 463–482. doi:10.1016/S0883-0355(02)00004-6

Berten, A. (1999). *Dispositif, médiation, créativité: Petite généalogie.* Paris: CNRS Edtions.

Berthoz, A. (2011). *La Semplesssità.* Torino: Codice.

Betti, M., Ciani, A., Lovece, S., & Tartufoli, L. (2014). Developing planning and evaluation skills using laboratory's teaching. *Italian Journal of Educational Research, 7*(13), 29-48. Retrieved from http://ojs.pensamultimedia.it/index.php/sird/article/view/1093

Biggs, J. (1993). From theory to practice: A cognitive systems approach. *Higher Education Research & Development, 12*(1), 73–85. doi:10.1080/0729436930120107

Billett, S. (2001). *Learning in the workplace.* Sydney: Allen and Unwin.

Black, P., & Wiliam, D. (1998). Assessment and classroom learning. *Assessment in Education: Principles, Policy & Practice, 5*(1), 7–74. doi:10.1080/0969595980050102

Bliss, T., & Reynolds, A. (2004). Quality visions and focused imagination. In J. Brophy (Ed.), *Using video in teacher education* (pp. 29–52). Oxford, UK: Elsevier.

BlogInZenith. (2014). *Instagram y Vine, ¿responsables del auge del vídeo en las redes sociales?* Retrieved from http://blogginzenith.zenithmedia .es/el-video-online-crece-en-las-redes-sociales-vine-e-instagram-protagonistas/

Blomberg, G., Renkl, A., Gamoran Sherin, M., Borko, H., & Seidel T. (2013), Five research based heuristic for using video in pre-service teacher education. *Journal for educational research online, 5*(1), 90-114.

Blomberg, G., Sherin, M. G., Renkl, A., Glogger, I., & Seidel, T. (2014). Understanding Video as a Tool for Teacher Education: Investigating Instructional Strategies Integrating Video to Promote Reflection. *Instructional Science, 42*(3), 443–463. doi:10.1007/s11251-013-9281-6

Blomberg, G., Stürmer, K., & Seidel, T. (2011). How pre-service teachers observe teaching on video: Effects of viewers' teaching subjects and the subject of the video. *Teaching and Teacher Education, 27*(7), 1131–1140. doi:10.1016/j.tate.2011.04.008

Bloom, B. S. (1968). Learning for mastery. *Evaluation Comment, 1*(2), 1–12.

Bolondi, G., Ferretti, F. (2015), Pratiche didattiche, convinzioni e motivazioni degli studenti in matematica: uno studio di caso basato sul framework.

Borg, W. R. (1968). *The Minicourse: Rationales and Uses in the In-Service Education of Teachers.* Berkley, CA: Far West Laboratory for Educational Research and Development.

Borko, H. (2004). Professional development and teacher learning: Mapping the terrain. *Educational Researcher, 33*(8), 3–15. doi:10.3102/0013189X033008003

Borko, H., Jacobs, J. K., Eiteljorg, E., & Pittman, M. E. (2008). Video as a tool for fostering productive discussions in mathematics professional development. *Teaching and Teacher Education, 24*(2), 417–436. doi:10.1016/j.tate.2006.11.012

Borko, H., Koellner, K., & Jacobs, J. (2014). Examining novice teacher leaders' facilitation of mathematics professional development. *The Journal of Mathematical Behavior, 33*, 149–167. doi:10.1016/j.jmathb.2013.11.003

Borko, H., Koellner, K., Jacobs, J., & Seago, N. (2011). Using video representations of teaching in practice-based professional development programs. *ZDM, 43*(1), 175–187. doi:10.1007/s11858-010-0302-5

Borko, H., & Livingston, C. (1989). Cognition and improvisation: Differences in mathematics instruction by expert and novice teachers. *American Educational Research Journal, 26*(4), 473–498. doi:10.3102/00028312026004473

Bourdieu, P. (1980). *Le sens pratique.* Paris: Les Editions de Minuit.

Bourdieu, P. (2005). *Il senso pratico.* Roma: Armando.

Boyd, D., & Ellison, N. (2007). Social network sites: Definition, history, and scholarship. *Journal of Computer-Mediated Communication, 13*(1), 210–230. doi:10.1111/j.1083-6101.2007.00393.x

Brecht, H. (2012). Learning from online video lectures. *Journal of Information Technology Education: Innovations in Practice, 11*(1), 227–250.

Brophy, J. (2004). *Using video in teacher education.* Amsterdam, Netherlands: Elsevier.

Brousseau, G. (1998). *Théorie des Situations Didactiques.* Grenoble: La pensée sauvage.

Brouwer, N. (2011). Equipping Teachers Visually. Zoetermeer: Kennisnet. Retrieved from http://www.kennisnet.nl/onderzoek/alle-onderzoeken/equipping-teachers-visually/

Brown, A. (1992). Design experiments; Theoretical and methodological challenges in creating complex interventions in classroom settings. *Journal of the Learning Sciences, 2*(2), 141–178. doi:10.1207/s15327809jls0202_2

Brown, K. W., & Ryan, R. M. (2003). The benefits of being present: Mindfulness and its role in psychological well-being. *Journal of Personality and Social Psychology, 84*(4), 822–848. doi:10.1037/0022-3514.84.4.822 PMID:12703651

Bru M., Pastré P., & Vinatier (Eds.) (2007). Les organisateurs de l'activité enseignante. Perspectives croisées. In *Recherche et formation pour les professionnels de l'éducation*, 56. Paris, France: INRP (Institut National de Recherche Pédagogique).

Bru, M. (2015). Les méthodes en pédagogie. Paris, France: PUF (Presses Universitaires de France).

Bruce, D. L., & Chiu, M. M. (2015). Composing With New Technology Teacher Reflections on Learning Digital Video. *Journal of Teacher Education, 66*(3), 272–287. doi:10.1177/0022487115574291

Bruner, J. (1961). The act of discovery. *Harvard Educational Review, 31*(1), 21–32.

Bruner, J. S. (1978). *Dopo Dewey. Il processo di apprendimento nelle due culture*. Roma: Armando.

Bruner, J. S. (1999). *Verso una teoria dell'istruzione*. Roma: Armando.

Brusa, A. (1991). *Il manuale di storia*. Firenze: La Nuova Italia.

Brusa, A. (1993). *La programmazione di storia*. Firenze: La Nuova Italia.

Brush, T. A., & Saye, J. W. (2002). A summary of research exploring hard and soft scaffolding for teachers and students using a multimedia supported learning environment. *Journal of Interactive Online Learning, 1*(2), 1–12. Retrieved from http://www.ncolr.org/jiol/issues/pdf/1.2.3.pdf

Buckingham, D., Grahame, J., & Sefton-green, J. (1995). *Making Media: practical production in media education*. London: English & Media Centre.

Cagiltay, K., Graham, C. R., Lim, B.-R., Craner, J., & Duffy, T. M. (2001). The seven principles of good practice: A practical approach to evaluating online courses. *Hacettepe University Journal of Education, 20*, 40–50.

Cain, J., & Policastri, A. (2011). Using Facebook as an informal learning environment. *American Journal of Pharmaceutical Education, 75*(10), 1–8. doi:10.5688/ajpe7510207 PMID:22345726

Calandra, B., & Rich, P. J. (Eds.), (2014). *Digital video for teacher education: Research and practice*. NY: Routledge.

Calvani, A. (2012). *For evidence-based education. Theoretical analysis on international methodological effective teaching and inclusive*. Trento: Erickson.

Calvani, A. (2013). *Principi dell'istruzione e strategie per insegnare. Criteri per una didattica efficace*. Roma: Carocci.

Calvani, A., Biagioli, R., Maltinti, C., Menichetti, L., & Micheletta, S. (2013). Formarsi nei media: Nuovi scenari per la formazione dei maestri in una società digitale. *Formazione, Lavoro. Persona, 3*(8), 1–2.

Calvani, A., Bonaiuti, G., & Andreocci, B. (2011). Il microteaching rinascerà a nuova vita? Video annotazione e sviluppo della riflessività del docente. *Italian Journal of Educational Research, 4*(6), 29–42.

Calvani, A., Menichetti, L., Michelett, S., & Moricca, C. (2014). Innovare la formazione: Il ruolo della videoeducazione per lo sviluppo dei nuovi educatori. *Italian. The Journal of Educational Research, 7*(13), 69–84.

Cappelletti, L. (2010). La recherche-intervention: quels usages en contrôle de gestion? Crises et nouvelles problématiques de la Valeur, HAL. Retrieved from https://halshs.archives-ouvertes.fr/hal-00481090/document

Carbonneau, M., & Hétu, J. C. (2006). Formazione pratica degli insegnanti e nascita di un'intelligenza professionale. In M. Altet, E. Charlier, L. Paquay, & P. Perrenoud (Eds), Formare gli insegnanti professionisti. Quali strategie? Quali competenze? (pp. 77-95). Roma: Armando editore.

Carbonneau, M., & Hétu, J. C. (2006). Formazione pratica degli insegnanti e nascita di un'intelligenza professionale. In M. Altet, E. Charlier, L. Paquay, & P. Perrenoud (Eds.), Formare gli insegnanti professionisti. Quali strategie? Quali competenze? (pp. 77-95). Roma: Armando. .

Carbonneau, M., & Hétu, J. C. (2006). Formazione pratica degli insegnanti e nascita di un'intelligenza professionale. In M. Altet, E. Charlier, L. Paquay, & P. Perrenoud (Eds.), *Formare gli insegnanti professionisti. Quali strategie? Quali competenze? Armando editore* (pp. 77–95). Roma.

Cardarello, R. (2016). Ricerca didattica: fare il punto. *Form@re, 3*(15), 1-10. Retrieved from http://fupress.com/formare

Carter, K., Sabers, D., Cushing, K., Pinnegar, P., & Berliner, D. C. (1987). Processing and using information about students: A study of expert, novice and postulant teachers. *Teaching and Teacher Education, 3*(2), 147–157. doi:10.1016/0742-051X(87)90015-1

Carver, J., & MacKay, R. C. (1986). Interactive Television Brings University Classes to the Home and Workplace. *Canadian Journal of Educational Communication, 15*(1), 19–28.

Casabianca, J. M., McCaffrey, D. F., Gitomer, D. H., Bell, C. A., Hamre, B. K., & Pianta, R. C. (2013). Effect of observation mode on measures of secondary mathematics teaching. *Educational and Psychological Measurement, 73*(5), 757–783. doi:10.1177/0013164413486987

Casetti, F., & Di Chio, F. (2004). *Analisi del film. 14.* Milano: Bompiani.

Cassella, D. (2009). *What is Augmented Reality (AR): Augmented Reality Defined, iPhone Augmented Reality Apps and Games and More.* Retrieved from http://www.digitaltrends.com/features/what-is-augmented-reality-iphone-apps-games-flash-yelp-android-ar-software-and-more/

Cecchinato, G. (2014). Flipped classroom: innovare la scuola con te tecnoloige digitali. In TD Tecnologie Didattiche, 22 (1), 1-20.

Chan, Y. M. (2010). Video instructions as support for beyond classroom learning. *Procedia: Social and Behavioral Sciences, 9*, 1313–1318. doi:10.1016/j.sbspro.2010.12.326

Cheung, C. M. K., Chiu, P., & Lee, M. K. O. (2011). Online social networking sites: Why do students use Facebook? *Computers in Human Behavior, 27*(4), 1337–1343. doi:10.1016/j.chb.2010.07.028

Chevallard, Y. (1985). *La transposition didactique. Du savoir enseignant au savoir enseigné.* Grenoble: La Pensée Sauvage.

Christian, D. (2011). *Maps of Time. An Introduction to Big History. With a New Preface.* Berkley, CA: University of California Press.

Christ, T., Arya, P., & Chiu, M. (2014). Teachers' reports of learning and application to pedagogy based on engagement in collaborative peer video analysis. *Teaching Education, 25*(4), 349–374. doi:10.1080/10476210.2014.920001

Clanet, J. (2007). Un organisateur des pratiques d'enseignement: les interactions maitre élève(s). *Recherche et éducation, 56*, 47-66.

Clarke, D. J., Mesiti, C., O'Keefe, C., Xu, L. H., Jablonka, E., Mok, I. A. C., & Shimizu, Y. (2008). Addressing the challenge of legitimate international comparisons of classroom practice. *International Journal of Educational Research, 46*(5), 280–293. doi:10.1016/j.ijer.2007.10.009

Clot, Y. (2005). L'autoconfrontation croisée en analyse du travail: l'apport de la théorie bakhtinienne du dialogue. In L. Filliettaz & J.P. Bronckart (Eds.), L'analyse des actions et des discours en situation de travail. Concepts, méthodes et applications (pp. 37-55). Louvain, CH: Peeters.

Clot, Y. (1999). *La fonction psychologique du travail.* Paris: Presses Universitaires de France.

Clot, Y. (1999/2006). *La fonction psychologique du travail. 5ème édition corrigée.* Paris: PUF.

Clot, Y. (2008). *Travail et pouvoir d'agir.* Paris: PUF.

Clot, Y. (2008). *Travaille et pouvoir agir.* Paris: Presses Universitaires de France.

Clot, Y., Faïta, D., Fernandes, G., & Scheller, L. (2001). Entretiens en auto-confrontation croisée: Une méthode en clinique de l'activité. *Education Permanente, 146*(1), 17–25.

Cochran-Smith, M., & Zeichner, K. M. (Eds.). (2010). *Studying teacher education: The report of the AERA panel on research and teacher education.* New York, NY: Routledge.

Coffey, A. M. (2014). Using Video to Develop Skills in Reflection in Teacher Education Students. *Australian Journal of Teacher Education, 39*(9), 86–97. doi:10.14221/ajte.2014v39n9.7

Coggi, C. (2014). Verso un'Università delle Competenze. In A. M. Notti (Ed.), *A scuola di valutazione.* Lecce: Pensa Multimedia.

Coggi, C. (Ed.). (2009). *Potenziamento cognitivo e motivazionale dei bambini in difficoltà. Il Progetto Fenix.* Milano, Italia: Franco Angeli.

Coggi, C. (Ed.). (2015). *Favorire il successo a scuola. Il Progetto Fenix dall'infanzia alla secondaria.* Lecce, Italia: Pensa Multimedia.

Çoklar, A. N. (2012). Evaluations of students on Facebook as an educational environment. *Turkish Online Journal of Qualitative Inquiry, 3*(2), 42–53.

Colás-Bravo, P., Conde-Jiménez, J., & Martín-Gutiérrez, A. (2015). Social Networking Sites in Higher Education: Educational use of social and intellectual capital. *Revista Interuniversitaria de Formación del Profesorado (RIFOP), 83*(29.2), 105-116.

Colás-Bravo, P., González-Ramírez, T., & De Pablos-Pons, J. (2013). Young people and social networks: Motivations and preferred uses. *Comunicar, 40*(20), 15–23. doi:10.3916/C40-2013-02-01

Coles, A. (2013). Using video for professional development: The role of the discussion facilitator. *Journal of Mathematics Teacher Education, 16*(3), 165–184. doi:10.1007/s10857-012-9225-0

Collins, A. (1992). Toward a design science of education. In E. Scanlon & T. O'Shea (Eds.), *New directions in educational technology* (pp. 15–22). New York: Springer-Verlag. doi:10.1007/978-3-642-77750-9_2

Collins, A., Joseph, D., & Bielaczyc, K. (2004). Design research: Theoretical and methodological issues. *Journal of the Learning Sciences, 13*(1), 15–42. doi:10.1207/s15327809jls1301_2

Conco, Z. P. (2006). How effective is in-service training for teachers in rural school contexts? [Master Thesis]. University of Pretoria: Pretoria, Republic of South Africa.

Conrad, O. (2015). *Community of Inquiry and Video in Higher Education Engaging Students Online* [Doctoral dissertation]. California State University, Fullerton.

Cooke, M., Watson, B., Blacklock, E., Mansah, M., Howard, M., Johnston, A., & Murfield, J. et al. (2012). Lecture capture: First year student nurses' experiences of a web based lecture technology. *The Australian Journal of Advanced Nursing, 29*(3), 14–21.

Cope, B., & Kalantzis, M. (Eds.). (2000). *Multiliteracies: literacy learning and the design of social futures*. New York: Routledge.

Coulet, J. C. (2010). La "référéntialisation" des compétences à l'école, conceptions et mises en œuvre. in Les référentiels en formation: enjeux, légitimité, contenu et usage, Recherche & Formation, 64, 47-62.

Coulet, J. C. (2007). Le concept de schème dans la description et l'analyse des compétencesprofessionnelles:formalisat ion des pratiques, variabilité des conduits et régulation de l'activité. In *M.Merri, Activité humaine et conceptualisation. Question à Gérard Vergnaud* (pp. 297–306). Toulouse: PUM.

Coulter, G., & Ray, B. (2009). Teacher candidates' perspectives on the efficacy of webcasts as online supplemental instruction in traditional education courses. *Proceedings of the World Conference on E-Learning in Corporate, Government, Healthcare, and Higher Education* (pp. 2475-2475).

Coyle, D. (2004). Redefining Classroom Boundaries: Learning to Teach Using New Technologies. *Canadian Journal of Educational Administration and Policy*, 32.

Crahay, M., & Issaieva, E. (2013). Conceptions de l'évaluation et principes de justice chez des enseignants primaires en Fédération Wallonie-Bruxelles. *Paper presented at ADMEE 2013 - Evaluation et autoévaluation. Quels espaces de formation?*, Fribourg. Retrieved from http://www.admee2013.ch/ADMEE-2013/7_files/Crahay-Issaieva-Marbaise-ADMEE-2013.pdf

Creswell, J. W. (2007). *Qualitative inquiry and research design: Choosing among five approaches*. Thousand Oaks, CA: Sage.

Crippen, K. J., & Earl, B. L. (2004). Considering the efficacy of web-based worked examples in introductory chemistry. *Journal of Computers in Mathematics and Science Teaching*, *23*(2), 151–167.

Damiano, E. (2014). Epimeteo. Colui che, avendo fatto, pensa. Una ricerca nella prospettiva dell'attore. In C. Leneve, & F. Pascolini (Eds.), Nella Terra di Mezzo. Una ricerca sui Supervisori del Tirocinio (pp. 23-42).

Damiano, E. (1994). *L'azione didattica. Per una teoria dell'insegnamento*. Roma, Italia: Armando.

Damiano, E. (2004). *Insegnare i concetti. Un approccio epistemologico alla ricerca didattica*. Roma: Armando Editore.

Damiano, E. (2006). *La Nuova Alleanza*. Brescia: La Scuola Editrice.

Damiano, E. (2006). *La Nuova Alleanza. Temi, problemi e prospettive della nuova ricerca didattica*. Brescia: La Scuola.

Damiano, E. (2006). *La nuova alleanza. Temi, problemi, prospettive della Nuova Ricerca Didattica*. Brescia, Italia: La Scuola.

Damiano, E. (2007). *Il sapere dell'insegnare. Introduzione alla didattica per concetti con esercitazioni*. Milano, Italia: Franco Angeli.

Damiano, E. (2013). *Didattica come teoria della mediazione*. Milano: Franco Angeli.

Damiano, E. (2013). *La mediazione didattica. Per una teoria dell'insegnamento*. Milano, Italia: Franco Angeli.

Damiano, E. (2013). *La mediazione didattica. Per una teoria dell'nsegnamento*. Milano: FrancoAngeli.

Damiano, E. (Ed.). (2007). *Il mentore. Manuale di tirocinio per insegnanti in formazione*. Milano: Franco Angeli.

Damiano, L. (2009). *Unità in dialogo. Un nuovo stile per la conoscenza*. Milano: Bruno Mondadori.

Darling-Hammond, L. (2000). How teacher education matters. *Journal of Teacher Education*, *51*(3), 166–173. doi:10.1177/0022487100051003002

Darling-Hammond, L. (2003). Keeping good teachers. *Educational Leadership*, *60*(8), 6–13.

Darling-Hammond, L. (2006). Assessing teacher education: The usefulness of multiple measures for assessing program outcomes. *Journal of Teacher Education*, *57*(2), 120–138. doi:10.1177/0022487105283796

Darling-Hammond, L. (2006). Constructing 21st-Century Teacher Education. *Journal of Teacher Education*, *57*(3), 300–314. doi:10.1177/0022487105285962

Darling-Hammond, L. (2010). Teacher education and the American future. *Journal of Teacher Education*, *61*(1–2), 35–47. doi:10.1177/0022487109348024

Darling-Hammond, L., & Bransford, J. (Eds.), (2005). *Preparing Teachers for a Changing World: What Teachers Should Learn and Be Able to Do. National Academy of Education, Committee on Teacher Education*. San Francisco: Jossey Bass.

Darling-Hammond, L., & Bransford, J. (Eds.). (2007). *Preparing Teachers for a Changing World: What Teachers Should Learn and Be Able to Do*. New York: John Wiley & Sons.

Darling-Hammond, L., & Richardson, N. (2009). Research review/teacher learning: What matters. *Educational Leadership*, *66*(5), 46–53.

Davis, E. (2006). Characterizing productive reflection among preservice elementary teachers: Seeing what matters. *Teaching and Teacher Education*, *22*(3), 281–301. doi:10.1016/j.tate.2005.11.005

De Haro, J. J. (2009). Las redes sociales aplicadas a la práctica docente. *Didáctica. Innovación y Multimedia DIM*, *13*, 1–8.

de Montmollin, M. (1981). *Le taylorisme à visage humain*. Paris: PUF.

Del Moral Pérez, E., & Villalustre Martínez, L. (2012). Presencia de los futuros maestros en las redes sociales y perspectivas de uso educativo. *RELATEC. Revista Latinoamericana de Tecnología Educativa*, *11*(1), 41–51.

Denzin, N., & Lincoln, Y. (2011). *The Sage Handbook of Qualitative Research*. Los Angeles, London, New Delhi, Singapore, Washington DC: Sage.

Desgagné, S. (1997). Le concept de recherche collaborative: L'idée d'un rapprochement entre chercheurs universitaires et praticiens enseignant. *Revue des Sciences de l'Education*, *2*(2), 371–393. doi:10.7202/031921ar

Desgagné, S. (1998). La position du chercheur en recherche collaborative: Illustration d'une démarche de médiation entre culture universitaire et culture scolaire. *Recherches Qualitatives*, *18*, 77–105.

Desgagné, S., & Larouche, H. (2010). Quand la collaboration de recherche sert la légitimation d'un savoir d'expérience. *Recherche en éducation. Hors Série.*, *1*, 7–18.

Design- Based Research Collective. (2003). Design- Based Research: An Emerging Paradigm for Educational Inquiry. *Educational Researcher*, *1*(32), 5–8.

Desimone, L. M. (2009). Improving impact studies of teachers' professional development: Toward better conceptualizations and measures. *Educational Researcher*, *38*(3), 181–199. doi:10.3102/0013189X08331140

Develay, M. (1995). *Savoirs scolaires et didactique des disciplines*. Issy-les-Moulineaux: ESF Editeur.

Dewey, J. (1916). *Democracy and Education*. New York: The Macmillan Company.

Dewey, J. (1927). *The Public and Its Problems*. New York: Holt & Co.

Dewey, J. (1933). *How we Think. A Restatement of the Relation of Reflective Thinking to the Educative Process*. Boston: Heath.

Dewey, J. (1938). *Logic: The Theory of Inquiry*. New York: Holt & Co.

Dewey, J. (1961). *Come pensiamo: una riformulazione del rapporto fra il pensiero riflessivo e l'educazione. (Trad. It. A. Guccione)*. Firenze: LaNuova Italia.

Dewey, J. (2004). *Esperienza e Educazione*. Milano: Nuova Italia.

Dey, E. L., Burn, H. E., & Gerdes, D. (2009). Bringing the classroom to the web: Effects of using new technologies to capture and deliver lectures. *Research in Higher Education, 50*(4), 377–393. doi:10.1007/s11162-009-9124-0

Di Martino, P., & Zan, R. (2002, April 4-8). An attempt to describe a `negative' attitude toward mathematics. In P. Di Martino (Ed.), *Current State of Research on Mathematical Beliefs XI, Proceedings of the MAVI-XI European Workshop*, Pisa.

Díaz, R. (2009). Video in cyberspace: Usage and language. *Comunicar, 33*(17), 63–71. doi:10.3916/c33-2009-02-006

DiVall, M. V., & Kirwin, J. L. (2012). Using Facebook to facilitate course-related discussion between students and faculty members. *American Journal of Pharmaceutical Education, 76*(2), 1–5. doi:10.5688/ajpe76232 PMID:22438604

Doabler, C. T., Nelson, N. J., Kosty, D. B., Fien, H., Baker, S. K., Smolkowski, K., & Clarke, B. (2014). Examining teachers' use of Evidence-Based practices during core Mathematics instruction. *Assessment for Effective Intervention, 39*(2), 99–111. doi:10.1177/1534508413511848

Dobie, T. E., & Anderson, E. R. (2015). Interaction in teacher communities: Three forms teachers use to express contrasting ideas in video clubs. *Teaching and Teacher Education, 47*, 230–240. doi:10.1016/j.tate.2015.01.003

Dordit, L. (2011). *Modelli di reclutamento, formazione, sviluppo e valutazione degli insegnanti. Breve rassegna internazionale*. Trento: IPRASE.

Draper, J., O'brien, J., & Christie, F. (2004). First Impressions: The new teacher induction arrangements in Scotland. *Journal of In-service Education, 30*(2), 201–224. doi:10.1080/13674580100200316

Dubar, C. (1998). *La socialisation. Construction des identités sociales et professionnelles*. Paris: Colin.

Dubet, F. (1994). *La sociologie de l'expérience*. Paris: Éditions du Seuil.

Dubrowski, A., & Xeroulis, G. (2005). Computer-based Video Instructions for Acquisition of Technical Skills. *Journal of Visual Communication in Medicine, 28*(4), 150–155. doi:10.1080/01405110500518622 PMID:16503567

Duffy, P. (2011). Facebook or Faceblock: Cautionary tales exploring the rise of social networking within tertiary education. In M. J. W. Lee & C. McLoughlin (Eds.), *Web 2.0-base E-learning: Applying social informatics for tertiary teaching* (pp. 284–300). Hershey, PA, USA: IGI Global. doi:10.4018/978-1-60566-294-7.ch015

Dupin de Saint-Andre, M., Montesinos-Gelet, I., Morin, M.-F. (2010). Avantages et limites des approches méthodologiques utilisées pour étudier les pratiques enseignantes, *Nouveaux cahiers de la recherche en éducation, 13*(2), 159-176.

Durand, M. (2011). Self-constructed activity, work analysis, and occupational training: an approach to learning objects for adults. In P. Jarvis & M. Watts (Eds.), *The Routledge international handbook on learning* (pp. 37–45). London: Routledge.

Duschl, R. A. (2003). Assessment of inquiry. In J.M. Atkin, J.E. Coffey (Eds.). Everyday assessment in the science classroom (41-59). Washington, DC: National Science Teachers Association Press.

Dussault, G., Leclerc, M., Brunellem, J., & Turcotte, C. (1976). *L'analisi dell'insegnamento*. Roma: Armando Editore.

EC. EuropeanCommission. (2005). *Common Europeanprinciples for teachercompetences and qualifications.*

EC. EuropeanCommission. (2012). Ripensare l'istruzione. Retrieved from http://europa.eu/rapid/press-release_IP-12-1233_it.htm

Egger, M., Juni, P., Bartlett, C., Holenstein, F., & Sterne, J. (2003). How important are comprehensive literature searches and the assessment of trial quality in systematic reviews? Empirical study. *Health technology assessment (Winchester, England)*, *7*(1), 1–82. PMID:12583822

Ellingson, D. A., & Notbohm, M. (2012). Synchronous Distance Education: Using Web Conferencing In An MBA Accounting Course. *American Journal of Business Education*, *5*(5), 555–562.

Elliott, J. (2001). Making evidence-based practice educational. *British Educational Research Journal*, *27*(5), 555–574. doi:10.1080/01411920120095735

Ellis, J., McFadden, J., Anwar, T., & Roehrig, G. (2015). Investigating the social interactions of beginning teachers using a video annotation tool. *Contemporary Issues in Technology & Teacher Education*, *15*(3), 404–421.

Ellison, N. B., Steinfield, C., & Lampe, C. (2011). Connection strategies: Social capital implications of Facebook-enabled communication practices. *New Media & Society*, *13*(6), 873–892. doi:10.1177/1461444810385389

Engeström, Y., Virkkunen, J., Helle, M., Pihlaja, J., & Poikela, R. (1996). The Change laboratory as a tool for transforming work. *Lifelong Learning in Europe*, *1*(2), 10–17.

Entwistle, N., & Peterson, E. R. (2004). Conceptions of learning and knowledge in higher education: Relationships with study behaviour and influences of learning environments. *International Journal of Educational Research*, *41*(6), 407–428. doi:10.1016/j.ijer.2005.08.009

Eraut, M. (2000). Non-formal learning and tacit knowledge in professional work. *The British Journal of Educational Psychology*, *70*(1), 113–136. doi:10.1348/000709900158001 PMID:10765570

Ertmer, P. A. (1999). Addressing first- and second-order barriers to change: Strategies for technology integration. *Educational Technology Research and Development*, *47*(4), 47–61. doi:10.1007/BF02299597

Ertmer, P. A., Conklin, D., & Lewandowski, J. (2002). *Using exemplary models to increase preservice teachers' ideas and confidence for technology integration. Proceedings of.* American Educational Research.

Estabrooks, C. A., Field, P. A., & Morse, J. M. (1994). Aggregating qualitative findings: An approach to theory development. *Qualitative Health Research*, *4*(4), 503–511. doi:10.1177/104973239400400410

European Commission, Directorate-General for Education and Culture. Eurydice, the information network on education in Europe (2003). The Teaching profession in Europe: profile, trends and concerns. Report III: Working conditions and pay. General lower secondary education. Brussels: Eurydice.

European Commission. Directorate-General for Education and Culture; Eurydice, information network on education in Europe (2002). *Key topics in education in Europe, Volume 3. The Teaching profession in Europe: profile, trends and concerns. Report II: Supply and demand. General lower secondary education.* Brussels: Eurydice.

Eurydice (2012). *Developing key competences at school in Europe: Challenges and opportunities for Policy.* Brussels: Education, Audiovisual and Culture Executive Agency. Retrieved from http://www.indire.it/lucabas/lkmw_file/eurydice/key_competences_finale_EN.pdf

Evertson, C., & Green, J. L. (1986). Observation as inquiry & method. In M. C. Wittrock (Ed.), *Handbook of research on teaching* (pp. 162–213). New York: Macmillan.

Fabre, M. (1999). *Situations-problèmes et savoir scolaire*. Paris: PUF.

Fabre, M. (2009). *Philosophie et pédagogie du problème*. Paris: EditionsVrin.

Fadde, P. J. (2010). Look 'ma, no hands: part-task training of perceptual-cognitive skills to accelerate psychomotor expertise. Proceedings of the Interservice / Industry Training, Simulation & Education Conference (I/ITSEC) (Vol. 1). National Training Systems Association.

Fadde, P. J. (2009a). Instructional design for advanced learners: Training recognition skills to hasten expertise. *Educational Technology Research and Development*, *57*(3), 359–376. doi:10.1007/s11423-007-9046-5

Fadde, P. J. (2009b). Expertise-based training: Getting more learners over the bar in less time. *Technology, Instruction. Cognition and Learning*, *7*(4), 171–197.

Fadde, P. J., & Klein, G. A. (2010). Deliberate performance: Accelerating expertise in natural settings. *International Society for Performance Improvement*, *49*(9), 5–14. doi:10.1002/pfi.20175

Faingold, N. (2011). Explicitation des pratiques, décryptage du sens. In C. Barbier, M. Hatano, & G. Le Meur (Eds.), Approches pour l'analyse des activités (pp. 111-155). Paris: L'Harmattan.

Fantin, M. (2015). Novos paradigmas da didática e a proposta metodológica dos Episódios de Aprendizagem Situada, EAS. *Educação & Realidade*, *40*(2), 443-464. Retrieved from http://seer.ufrgs.br/index.php/educacaoerealidade/article/view/46056

Fantin, M. (2011). *Crianças, Cinema e Educação: além do arco-íris*. São Paulo: Annablume.

Fantin, M. (2011a). Beyond Babel: Multiliteracies in digital culture. *International Journal of Digital Literacy and Digital Competence*, *2*(1), 1–6. doi:10.4018/jdldc.2011010101

Fantin, M. (2014). Audiovisual na escola: abordagens e possibilidades. In M. C. S. Barbosa & M. A. Santos (Eds.), *Escritos de alfabetização audiovisual* (pp. 47–67). Porto Alegre: Libretos.

Fenstermacher, G. (1986). Philosophy of research on teaching: Three aspects. In M. C. Wittrock (Ed.), *Handbook of research on teaching* (pp. 37–49). New York, NY: Macmillan.

Fenstermacher, G. D. (1990). Philosophy of Research on Teaching: Three Aspects. In M. C. Wittrock (Ed.), *Handbook of research on teaching. A project of the American Educational Research Association* (pp. 37–49). New York, London: Macmillan.

Fernández, V., Simo, P., & Sallan, J. M. (2009). Podcasting: A new technological tool to facilitate good practice in higher education. *Computers & Education*, *53*(2), 385–392. doi:10.1016/j.compedu.2009.02.014

Ferres, J. (2014). *Las pantallas y el cérebro emocional*. Barcelona: Gedisa.

Fewkes, A. M., & McCabe, M. (2012). Facebook: Learning tool or distraction? *Journal of Digital Learning in Teacher Education*, *28*(3), 92–98. doi:10.1080/21532974.2012.10784686

Flandin, S. (2015). *Analyse de l'activité d'enseignants stagiaires du second degré en situation de vidéoformation autonome: Contribution à un programme de recherche technologique en formation* [Unpublished doctoral dissertation]. Clermont-Ferrand: Université Blaise Pascal.

Flandin, S., & Ria, L. (2012). Vidéoformation des enseignants: apports de la didactique professionnelle. In *2ème Colloque International de Didactique Professionnelle*. Retrieved from http://didactiqueprofessionnelle.ning.com/page/colloque-2012-nantes

Flandin, S., Leblanc, S., & Muller, A. (2015). Vidéo-formation « orientée-activité »: quelles utilisations pour quels effets sur les enseignants? In V. Lussi Borer, M. Durand & F. Yvon (Eds.), Analyse du travail et formation dans les métiers de l'éducation (Raisons éducatives, pp. 179-198). Bruxelles: De Boeck.

Flandin, S., & Ria, L. (2014). Un programme technologique basé sur l'analyse de l'activité réelle des enseignants débutants au travail et en vidéoformation. *Activités (Vitry-sur-Seine), 11*(2), 172–187. doi:10.4000/activites.970

Foertsch, J., Moses, G. A., Strikwerda, J. C., & Litzkow, M. J. (2002). Reversing the lecture/homework paradigm using eTeach web-based streaming video software. *The Journal of Engineering Education, 91*(3), 267–274. doi:10.1002/j.2168-9830.2002.tb00703.x

Fortunato, F., & Girotti, G. (2009). *Il tempo dei draghi. Per la terza classe elementare.* Milano: Minerva Italica.

Fox, A. (2013). From MOOCs to SPOCs. *Communications of the ACM, 56*(12), 2013, 38-40.

Freinet, C. (2002). *La Scuola del Fare.* Bergamo: Junior.

Freire, P. (2000). *Pedagogia da Indignação: cartas pedagógicas e outros escritos. São Paulo: Editora Unesp. Eugeni, R (1999). Film, sapere, società: per un'analisi sociosemiotica del testo cinematografico.* Milano: Vita e Pensiero.

Friel, S., & Carboni, L. (2000). Using video-based pedagogy in an elementary mathematics methods course. *School Science and Mathematics, 100*(3), 118–127. doi:10.1111/j.1949-8594.2000.tb17247.x

Friesen, N., & Lowe, S. (2012). The questionable promise of social media for education connective learning and the commercial imperative. *Journal of Computer Assisted Learning, 28*(3), 183–194. doi:10.1111/j.1365-2729.2011.00426.x

Gallagher, S. A., Sher, B. T., Stepien, W. J., & Workman, D. (1995). Implementing problem based learning. *School Science and Mathematics, 95*(3), 136–146. doi:10.1111/j.1949-8594.1995.tb15748.x

Gattullo, M. (1967). *Didattica e docimologia.* Roma: Armando.

Gaudin, C., & Chaliès, S. (2015). Video viewing in teacher education and professional development: A literature review. *Educational Research Review, 16*, 41–67. doi:10.1016/j.edurev.2015.06.001

Ghousseini, H., & Sleep, L. (2011). Making practice studyable. *ZDM Mathematics Education, 43*(1), 147–160. doi:10.1007/s11858-010-0280-7

Giannakos, M. N., Chorianopoulos, K., & Chrisochoides, N. (2015). Making sense of video analytics: Lessons learned from clickstream interactions, attitudes, and learning outcome in a video-assisted course. *The International Review of Research in Open and Distributed Learning, 16*(1), 260–283.

Gibson, S., & Dembo, M. H. (1984). Teacher efficacy: A construct validation. *Journal of Educational Psychology, 76*(4), 569–582. doi:10.1037/0022-0663.76.4.569

Gitomer, D. H., & Zisk, R. C. (2015). Knowing what teachers know, *Review of Research in Education. AERA, 39*, 1–53.

Goldman, R., Pea, R., Barron, B., & Denny, S. J. (Eds.). (2007). *Video research in the learning sciences.* Mahwah, NJ: Lawrence Erlbaum.

Goldman, R., Pea, R., Barron, B., & Derry, J. S. (2009). *Videoricerca nei contesti di apprendimento. Teorie e metodi.* Milano: Raffaello Cortina Editore.

Goldman, R., Pea, R., Barron, B., & Derry, S. (Eds.). (2014). *Video Research in the Learning Science.* New York, London: Routledge.

Gönen, S., & Kocakaya, S. (2006). Fizik öğretmenlerinin hizmet içi eğitimler üzerine görüşlerinin değerlendirilmesi. *Pamukkale Üniversitesi Eğitim Fakültesi Dergisi, 19*(19), 37–44.

Goodband, J. H., Solomon, Y., Samuels, P. C., Lawson, D., & Bhakta, R. (2012). Limits and potentials of social networking in academia: Case study of the evolution of a mathematics Facebook community. *Learning, Media and Technology, 37*(3), 236–252. doi:10.1080/17439884.2011.587435

Goodwin, C. (1994). Professional vision. *American Anthropologist, 96*(3), 606–633. doi:10.1525/aa.1994.96.3.02a00100

Gough, D. (2007). Weight of evidence: A framework for the appraisal of the quality and relevance of evidence. *Research Papers in Education, 22*(2), 213–228. doi:10.1080/02671520701296189

Gough, D., & Elbourne, D. (2002). Systematic research synthesis to inform policy, practice and democratic debate. *Social Policy and Society, 1*(3), 225–236. doi:10.1017/S147474640200307X

Grandi, G. (1977). *Misurazione e valutazione*. Firenze: La Nuova Italia.

Greenhow, C., & Burton, L. (2011). Help from my "Friends" Social Capital in the Social Networks Site of Low-Income Students. *Journal of Educational Computing Research, 45*(2), 223–245. doi:10.2190/EC.45.2.f

Green, S., Voegeli, D., Harrison, M., Phillips, J., Knowles, J., Weaver, M., & Shephard, K. (2003). Evaluating the use of streaming video to support student learning in a first-year life sciences course for student nurses. *Nurse Education Today Journal, 23*(4), 255–261. doi:10.1016/S0260-6917(03)00014-5 PMID:12727092

Griffiths, R., MacLeod, G., & McIntyre, D. (1977). Effects of Supervisory Strategies in Microteaching on Students' Attitudes and Skill Acquisition. In D. McIntyre, G. MacLeod, & R. Griffiths (Eds.), *Investigations of Microteaching* (pp. 131–141). London: Croom Helm.

Gröschner, A., Seidel, T., Kiemer, K., & Pehmer, A. K. (2014). Through the lens of teacher professional development components: the 'Dialogic Video Cycle' as an innovative program to foster classroom dialogue. *Professional Development in Education*.

Grossman, P., Compton, C., Igra, D., Ronfeldt, M., Shahan, E., & Williamson, P. W. (2009). Teaching practice: A cross-professional perspective. *Teachers College Record, 111*(9), 2055–2100.

Grossman, P., Hammerness, K., & McDonald, M. (2009). Redefining teaching, re-imagining teacher education. *Teachers and Teaching. Theory into Practice, 15*(2), 273–289.

Grossman, P., Hammerness, K., & McDonald, M. (2009). Redefining teaching, re-imagining teacher education. *Teachers and Teaching: Theory and Practice., 15*(2), 273–289. doi:10.1080/13540600902875340

Gruber, H. (2001). Acquisition of expertise. In J. Smelser & P. B. Baltes (Eds.), *International encyclopedia of the social and behavioral sciences* (pp. 5145–5150). Amsterdam: Elsevier. doi:10.1016/B0-08-043076-7/02371-8

Guernsey, L., & Ochshorn, S. (2011). *Watching teachers works. Using observation tools to promote effective teaching in the early years and early grades. Education policy program*. New America Foundation.

Guskey, T. R. (2005, April 11-15). Formative classroom assessment and Benjamin S. Bloom: Theory, research and implications. *Paper presented at the Annual Meeting of the AERA (American Educational Research Association)*, Montreal, Canada. Retrieved from http://files.eric.ed.gov/fulltext/ED490412.pdf

Haji, C., & Baillé, H. (Eds.). (1998). *Recherche et éducation. Vers une nouvelle alliance*. Bruxelles, Belgique: De Boeck.

Hall, R. H., Stark, S., Hilgers, M., & Chang, P. (2004). A comparison of scaffolding media in learning systems for teaching web development. *Proceedings of the AACE E-LearnConference* (pp. 1906-1913). Retrieved from http://dl.aace.org/16707

Hamilton, E. (2012). Video as a Metaphorical Eye: Images of Positionality, Pedagogy, and Practice. *College Teaching*, *60*(1), 10–16. doi:10.1080/87567555.2011.604803

Hancock, D. R., & Algozzine, B. (2006). *Doing Case Study Research*. New York: Teachers College Press.

Harden, A., & Thomas, J. (2005). Methodological issues in combining diverse study types in systematic reviews. *International Journal of Social Research Methodology*, *8*(3), 257–271. doi:10.1080/13645570500155078

Harford, J., & MacRuairc, G. (2008). Engaging student teachers in meaningful reflective practice. *Teaching and Teacher Education*, *24*(7), 1884–1892. doi:10.1016/j.tate.2008.02.010

Harlin, E. M. (2014). Watching oneself teach–long-term effects of teachers' reflections on their video-recorded teaching. *Technology, Pedagogy and Education*, *23*(4), 507–521. doi:10.1080/1475939X.2013.822413

Harrison, D. J. (2015). Assessing experiences with online educational videos: Converting multiple constructed responses to quantifiable data. *The International Review of Research in Open and Distributed Learning*, *16*(1), 168–192.

Hartsell, T., & Yuen, S. (2006). Video Streaming in Online Learning. *AACE Journal*, *14*(1), 31–43.

Hatch, T., & Grossman, P. (2009). Learning to look beyond the boundaries of representation. *Journal of Teacher Education*, *60*(1), 70–85. doi:10.1177/0022487108328533

Hattie, J. (2009). *Visible learning. A synthesis of over 800 meta-analysis relating to achievement*. London, New York: Routledge.

Hattie, J. (2009). *Visible learning: A synthesis of over 800 meta-analyses relating to achievement*. New York: Routledge.

Hattie, J. A. C. (2009). *Visible learning: A synthesis of 800+ meta-analyses on achievement*. Abingdon, UK: Routledge.

Hattie, J., & Tymperley, H. (2007). The power of feedback. *Review of Educational Research*, *77*(1), 81–112. doi:10.3102/003465430298487

Haynes, J.M., & MillerJ., E. (2015). Preparing pre-service primary school teachers to assess fundamental motor skills: Two skills and two approaches. *Physical Education and Sport Pedagogy*, *20*(4), 397–408. doi:10.1080/17408989.2014.892064

Heilesen, S. B. (2010). What is the academic efficacy of podcasting? *Computers & Education*, *55*(3), 1063–1068. doi:10.1016/j.compedu.2010.05.002

Hew, K. F. (2009). Use of audio podcast in K-12 and higher education: A review of research topics and methodologies. *Educational Technology Research and Development*, *57*(3), 333–357. doi:10.1007/s11423-008-9108-3

Hew, K. F. (2011). Students' and teachers' use of Facebook. *Computers in Human Behavior*, *27*(2), 662–676. doi:10.1016/j.chb.2010.11.020

Hibbert, M. C. (2014). What Makes an Online Instructional Video Compelling? *Educause Review Online*. Retrieved from http://er.educause.edu/articles/2014/4/what-makes-an-online-instructional-video-compelling

Hiebert, J., Gallimore, R., & Stigler, J. W. (2002). A knowledge base for the teaching profession: What would it look like and how can we get one? *Educational Researcher*, *31*(5), 3–15. doi:10.3102/0013189X031005003

Høiland, T. & Wølner, T.A. (2007). Fra digital ferdighettilkompetanse – om didaktikk for arbeid med digitalemedieriskolen. Oslo: Gyldendal akademisk.

Holbrook, J., & Dupont, C. (2010). Making the decision to provide enhanced podcasts to post-secondary science students. *Journal of Science Education and Technology*, *20*(1), 233–245.

Holbrook, J., & Dupont, C. (2011). Making the decision to provide enhanced podcasts to post secondary science students. *Journal of Science Education and Technology, 20*(3), 233–245. doi:10.1007/s10956-010-9248-1

Holmes, E. (2014). *El bienestar de los docentes. Guía para controlar el estrés y sentirse bien personal y profesionalmente.* Madrid: Narcea S.A. de Ediciones.

Huang, X., & Hsiao, E.-L. (2012). Synchronous and Asynchronous Communication in an Online Environment: Faculty Experiences and Perceptions. *The Quarterly Review of Distance Education, 13*(1), 15–30.

Huelser, B. J., & Metcalfe, J. (2012). Making related errors facilitates learning, but learners do not know it. *Memory & Cognition, 40*(4), 514–527. doi:10.3758/s13421-011-0167-z PMID:22161209

Hutchens, J. S., & Hayes, T. (2014). In your Facebook: Examining Facebook usage as misbehavior on perceived teacher credibility. *Education and Information Technologies, 19*(1), 5–20. doi:10.1007/s10639-012-9201-4

Ifenthaler, D. (2009). Model-based feedback for improving expertise and expert performance. *Technology, Instruction. Cognition and Learning, 7*(2), 83–101.

Institut Frances De L'Education. (2016) *Plateforme Néopass@ction.* Retrieved from http://neo.ens-lyon.fr/neo

Ismail, S. (2010). International students' acceptance on using social networking site to support learning activities. *International Journal for the Advancement of Science & Arts, 1*(2), 81–90.

Jacobs, H. H. (1997). *Mapping the big picture.* Alexandria, VA: Association for Supervision and Curriculum Development.

Jacobs, J., & Morita, E. (2002). Japanese and American teachers' evaluations of videotaped mathematics lessons. *Journal for Research in Mathematics Education, 33*(3), 154–175. doi:10.2307/749723

Jacquinot, G., & Leblanc, G. (1999). *Appunti per una lettura del cinema e della televisione.* Napoli: Editoriale Scientifica.

Janesick, V. (2000). The choreography of qualitative research design: Minuets, improvisations, and crystallization. In N. K. Denzin & Y. S. Lincoln (Eds.), *Handbook of qualitative research* (pp. 66–81). Thousand Oaks, CA: Sage Publications.

Janík, T., & Seidel, T. (Eds.), *The power of video studies in investigating teaching and learning in the classroom.* Munich: Waxmann Publishing.

Januszewski, A., & Molenda, M. (Eds.), (2008). *Educational Technology: A definition with commentary.* New York & London: Lawrence Erlbaum Associates

Jenkins, H. (2006). *Confronting the Challenges of Participatory Culture:Media Education for the 21st Century.* MacArthur Foundation.

Jennings, P. A., & Greenberg, M. (2009). The prosocial classroom: Teacher social and emotional competence in relation to child and classroom outcomes. *Review of Educational Research, 79*(1), 491–525. doi:10.3102/0034654308325693

Jonassen, D. H. (1995). Computers as cognitive tools: Learning with technology, not from technology. *Journal of Computing in Higher Education, 6*(2), 40–73. doi:10.1007/BF02941038

Jorro, A. (2010). Le développement professionnel des acteurs: une nouvelle fonction de l'évaluation? In L. Paquay, C. Von Nieuwenhoven, & P. Wouters (Eds.), *L'évaluation, levier du développement professionnel?* (pp. 251–264). Bruxelles: De Boeck.

Joyce, B., Weil, M., & Calhoun, E. (2014). *Models of Teaching* (9th ed.). New York, NY: Pearson Education.

Junco, R., Heiberger, G., & Loken, E. (2011). The effect of Twitter on college student engagement and grades. *Journal of Computer Assisted Learning, 27*(2), 119–132. doi:10.1111/j.1365-2729.2010.00387.x

Kagan, D. (1992). Professional growth among pre-service and beginning teachers. *Review of Educational Research*, *62*(2), 129–169. doi:10.3102/00346543062002129

Kahn, P. E. (2014). Theorising student engagement in higher education. *British Educational Research Journal*, *40*(6), 1005–1018. doi:10.1002/berj.3121

Kane, T., Taylor, E. S., Tyler, J. H., & Wooten, A. L. (2011). Identifying effective classroom practices using student achievement data. *The Journal of Human Resources*, *46*(3), 587–613. doi:10.3368/jhr.46.3.587

Kaya, A., Çepni, S., & Küçük, M. (2004). Fizik öğretmenlerinin laboratuarlara yönelik hizmet içi ihtiyaçları için bir program geliştirme çalışması. *Kastamonu Eğitim Dergisi*, *12*(1), 41–56.

Kay, R. H. (2012). Exploring the use of video podcasts in education: A comprehensive review of the literature. *Computers in Human Behavior*, *28*(3), 820–831. doi:10.1016/j.chb.2012.01.011

Kazemi, E., Franke, M., & Lampert, M. (2009). Developing pedagogies in teacher education to support novice teachers' ability to enact ambitious instruction. In *Crossing divides: Proceedings of the 32nd annual conference of the Mathematics Education Research Group of Australasia* (Vol. 1, pp. 12-30).

Kazemi, E., & Hubbard, A. (2008). New directions for the design and study of professional development attending to the coevolution of teachers' participation across contexts. *Journal of Teacher Education*, *59*(5), 428–441. doi:10.1177/0022487108324330

Kee, A. N. (2012). Feelings of preparedness among alternatively certified teachers: What is the role of program features? *Journal of Teacher Education*, *63*(1), 23–38. doi:10.1177/0022487111421933

Kerbrat-Orecchioni, C. (1990). *Les interactions verbales* (Vol. 1). Paris: Armand Colin.

Kersting, N. (2008). Using video clips of mathematics classroom instruction as item prompts to measure teachers' knowledge of teaching mathematics. *Educational and Psychological Measurement*, *68*(5), 845–861. doi:10.1177/0013164407313369

Kersting, N. B., Givvin, K. B., Sotelo, F. L., & Stigler, J. W. (2010). Teachers' analyses of classroom video predict student learning of mathematics: Further explorations of a novel measure of teacher knowledge. *Journal of Teacher Education*, *61*(1-2), 172–181. doi:10.1177/0022487109347875

Kirschner, P. A., & Karpinski, A. C. (2010). Facebook and academic performance. *Computers in Human Behavior*, *26*(6), 1237–1245. doi:10.1016/j.chb.2010.03.024

Kleinknecht, M., & Schneider, J. (2013). What do teachers think and feel when analyzing videos of themselves and other teachers teaching? *Teaching and Teacher Education*, *33*, 13–23. doi:10.1016/j.tate.2013.02.002

Kline, S., Stewart, K., & Murphy, M. (2006). Media literacy in the risk society: Toward a risk reduction strategy. *Canadian Journal of Education*, *29*(1), 131–153. doi:10.2307/20054150

Kobarg, M., Seidel, T., Prenzel, M., McCrae, B., & Walker, M. (2009, September). Patterns of science teaching and learning in an international comparison. In *PISA Research Conference*, Kiel (pp. 14–16).

Koc, Y., Peker, D., & Osmanoglu, A. (2009). Supporting teacher professional development through online video case study discussions: An assemblage of preservice and in service teachers and the case teacher. *Teaching and Teacher Education*, *25*(8), 1158–1168. doi:10.1016/j.tate.2009.02.020

Koellner, K., Jacobs, J., Borko, H., Schneider, C., Pittman, M. E., Eiteljorg, E., & Frykholm, J. (2007). The Problem-Solving Cycle: A model to support the development of teachers' professional knowledge. *Mathematical Thinking and Learning*, *9*(3), 273–303. doi:10.1080/10986060701360944

Kolås, L., Munkvold, R., & Nordseth, H. (2012). Evaluation and categorization of educational videos. In T. Bastiaens & G. Marks (Eds.), *Proceedings of E-Learn: World Conference on E-Learning in Corporate, Government, Healthcare, and Higher Education 2012* (pp. 648-657). Chesapeake, VA: Association for the Advancement of Computing in Education (AACE).

Koster, B., & Dengerink, J. J. (2008). Professional standards for teacher educators: How to deal with complexity ownership and function experience from the Netherlands. *European Journal of Teacher Education, 31*(2), 135–149. doi:10.1080/02619760802000115

Krajcik, J., Soloway, E., Blumenfeld, P., Marx, R. W., Ladewski, B. L., & Bos, N. D. et al.. (1996). The casebook of project practices: An example of an interactive multimedia system for professional development. *Journal of Computers in Mathematics and Science Teaching, 15*, 119–135.

Krammer, K., Ratzka, N., Klieme, E., Lipowsky, F., Pauli, C., & Reusser, K. (2006). Learning with classroom videos: Conception and first results of an online teacher-training program. *Zeitschrift für Didaktik der Mathematik, 38*(5), 422–432. doi:10.1007/BF02652803

Krone, A., Hamborg, K. C., & Gediga, G. (2002). About error-related emotional reactions in human-computer interaction. *Zeitschrift für Arbeits- und Organisationspsychologie, 46*(4), 185–200. doi:10.1026//0932-4089.46.4.185

Labate S, Pezzimenti L., & Rossi P.G. (2013). Oltre il costruttivismo. L'azione come spazio di mediazione. *Pedagogia e vita, 71*, 71-95.

Lambert, J. (2009). *Digital storytelling: capturing lives, creating community*. Berkeley, CA: Digital Diner Press.

Lampert, M. (2010). Learning Teaching in, from, and for Practice: What Do We Mean? *Journal of Teacher Education, 61*(1-2), 21–34. doi:10.1177/0022487109347321

Lampert, M., Franke, M. L., Kazemi, E., Ghousseini, H., Turrou, A. C., Beasley, H., & Crowe, K. (2013). Keeping It Complex: Using Rehearsals to Support Novice Teacher Learning of Ambitious Teaching. *Journal of Teacher Education, 64*(3), 226–243. doi:10.1177/0022487112473837

Lankshear, C., & Knobel, M. (2011). Nuevos Alfabetismos (3rd ed.). Madrid: Morata.

Larson, B. E., & Keiper, T. A. (2012). *Instructional strategies for middle and high school*. London: Routledge.

LaRue, E. M. (2012). Using Facebook as course management software: A case study. *Teaching and Learning in Nursing, 7*(17), 17–22. doi:10.1016/j.teln.2011.07.004

Lasagabaster, D., & Sierra, J. M. (2011). Classroom observation: Desirable conditions established by teachers. *European Journal of Teacher Education, 34*(4), 449–463. doi:10.1080/02619768.2011.587113

Laurilard, D. (2002). *Rethinking University Teaching*. London: Routledge. doi:10.4324/9780203304846

Laurillard, D. (2012). *Teaching as a Design Science. Building Pedagogical Patterns for Learning and Technology*. New York, N Y: Routledge.

Laurillard, D. (2012). *Teaching as a Design Science: Building Pedagogical Patterns for Learning and Technology*. New York, NY: Routledge.

Laurillard, D. (2014). *Insegnamento come scienza della progettazione*. Milano: FrancoAngeli.

Laveault, D., & Paquay, L. (Eds.). (2009). L'évaluation en salle de classes: des politiques aux pratiques. Mesure et évaluation en éducation en éducation, 32 (3).

Lave, J., & Wenger, E. (1991). *Situated learning: Legitimate peripheral participation*. Cambridge, UK: Cambridge University Press. doi:10.1017/CBO9780511815355

Lavolette, E., Venable, M. A., Gose, E., & Huang, E. (2010). Comparing Synchronous Virtual Classrooms: Student, Instructor and Course Designer Perspectives. *TechTrends*, *54*(5), 54–61. doi:10.1007/s11528-010-0437-9

Le Boterf, G. (2013). *Construire les compétences individuelles et collectives*. Paris, France: Eyrolles.

Le Fevre, D. M. (2004). Designing for teacher learning: video-based curriculum design. In J. Brophy (Ed.), *Using video in teacher education. Advances in research on teaching* (Vol. 10, pp. 235–258). Amsterdam: Elsevier. doi:10.1016/S1479-3687(03)10009-0

Leblanc, S. (2014). Vidéoformation et transformations de l'activitéprofessionnelle. *Activités (Vitry-sur-Seine)*, *11*(2), 143–171. http://www.activites.org/v11n2/v11n2.pdf

Leblanc, S., & Ria, L. (2014). Designing the *Néopass@ction* Platform Based on Modeling of Beginning Teachers' Activity. *Design and Technology Education*, *19*(2), 40–51.

Leblanc, S., Ria, L., Dieumegard, G., Serres, G., & Durand, M. (2008). Concevoir des dispositifs de formation professionnelle des enseignants à partir de l'analyse de l'activité dans une approche enactive. *Activités (Vitry-sur-Seine)*, *5*(1), 58–78. doi:10.4000/activites.1941

Lee (2005). Understanding and assessing preservice teachers' reflective thinking. *Teaching and Teacher Education, 21*, 699-715.

Lee, M., & Finger, G. (2010). *Developing a networked school community: A guide to realising the vision*. Victoria, Australia: ACER Press.

LeFevre, D. M. (2004). Designing for teacher learning: Video-based curriculum design. In J. Brophy (Ed.), *Using video in teacher education* (pp. 235–258). New York, NY: Elsevier.

Lefstein, A., & Snell, J. (in press). Classroom discourse: the promise and complexity of dialogic practice. In S. Ellis, E. McCartney, & J. Bourne (Eds.), *Insight and impact: Applied linguistics and the primary school*. Cambridge: Cambridge University Press. doi:10.1017/CBO9780511921605.018

Legge 107 (2015). Riforma del sistema nazionale di istruzione e formazione e delega per il riordino delle disposizioni legislative vigenti. *Gazzetta Ufficiale della Repubblica Italiana, S.G., 162*.

Lenoir, Y. (2012). La recherche collaborative entre recherche-action et recherche-partenariale: spécificités et implications pour la recherche en éducation. *Travaille et apprentissage, 9*, 13-39.

Leplat, J. (1997). *Regard sur l'activité en situation de travail - Contribution à la psychologie ergonomique*. Paris: PUF.

Lewin, K. (1951). *Field Theory in Social Science*. New York: Harper and Row.

Lewis, C. C., Perry, R. R., & Hurd, J. (2009). Improving mathematics instruction through lesson study: A theoretical model and North American case. *Journal of Mathematics Teacher Education*, *12*(4), 285–304. doi:10.1007/s10857-009-9102-7

Lewis, C., Perry, R., & Murata, A. (2006). How should research contribute to instructional improvement: The case of lesson study. *Educational Researcher*, *35*(3), 3–14. doi:10.3102/0013189X035003003

Liang, J. (2015). Live video classroom observation: an effective approach to reducing reactivity in collecting observational information for teacher professional development. *Journal of Education for Teaching*.

Lim, T., & Ismail, J. T. (2010). The use of Facebook for online discussions among distance learners. *Turkish Online Journal of Distance Education, 11*(4), 72–81.

Lin, N. (1999). Social networks and status attainment. *Annual Review of Sociology, 25*(1), 467–487. doi:10.1146/annurev.soc.25.1.467

Linston, M. (2015). The use of video analysis and the Knowledge Quartetin mathematics teacher education programmes. *International Journal of Mathematical Education in Science and Technology, 46*(1), 1–12. doi:10.1080/0020739X.2014.941423

Lipiansky, E. M. (1992). *Identité et communication.* Paris: PUF.

Llinares, S., & Valls, J. (2009). The building of pre-service primary teachers' knowledge of mathematics teaching: Interaction and online video case studies. *Instructional Science, 37*(3), 247–271. doi:10.1007/s11251-007-9043-4

Lonie, A.-L., & Andrews, T. (2009). Creating a Rich Learning Environment for Remote Post-Graduate Leaners. *Education in Rural Australia, 19*(1), 3–13.

Loomes, M., Shafarenko, A., & Loomes, M. (2002). Teaching mathematical explanation through audiographic technology. *Computers & Education, 38*(1– 3), 137–149

Looney, J. W. (2011). *Integrating formative and summative assessment: progress toward a seamless system?* OECD Education Working Paper 58. OECD Publishing.

Lussi Borer, V., & Muller, A., (2014). Connaître l'activité des eneseignants en formation sur la plateforme Néopass@ction. *Recherche et formation, 75*, 65-80.

Lussi Borer, V., Ria, L., Durand, M., & Muller, A. (2014). How Do Teachers Appropriate Learning Objects Through Critical Experiences? A Study of a Pilot In-School Collaborative Video Learning Lab. *Form@re, Open Journal per la formazione in rete, 14*(2), 63-74. Retrieved from http://www.fupress.net/index.php/formare/article/view/15137

Lussi Borer, V., Durand, M., & Yvon, F. (2015). *Analyse du travail et formation dans les métiers de l'éducation.* Louvain la Neuve: De Boek.

Lussi Borer, V., & Muller, A. (2014a). Quel apport/usage du « voir » pour le « faire » en formation des enseignants du secondaire. In L. Paquay, P. Perrenoud, M. Altet, J. Desjardins, & R. Etienne (Eds.), *Travail réel des enseignants et formation. Quelle référence au travail des enseignants dans les objectifs, les dispositifs et les pratiques?* (pp. 65–78). Bruxelles: De Boeck.

Lussi Borer, V., & Muller, A. (2014b). Exploiter le potentiel des processus de renormalisation en formation à l'enseignement. *Activités (Vitry-sur-Seine), 11*(2), 129–142. Retrieved from http://www.activites.org/v11n2/v11n2.pdf

Maccario, D. (2009). Sostenibilità del Programma Fenix in situazioni didattiche correnti. In C. Coggi (Ed.), Potenziamento cognitivo e motivazionale dei bambini in difficoltà. Il Progetto Fenix (pp. 331-351). Milano, Italia: Franco Angeli.

Madge, C., Meek, J., Wellens, J., & Hooley, T. (2009). Facebook, social integration and informal learning at university: 'It is more for socialising and talking to friends about work than for actually doing work'. *Learning, Media and Technology, 34*(2), 141–155. doi:10.1080/17439880902923606

Magnoler, P., & Iobbi, V. (2015). L'insegnamento agito. *Giornale italiano della ricerca educativa, 14*, 127-139.

Magnoler, P., Pacquola, M.C., & Tescaro, M. (2014), Knowledge in action for training. *Formazione, lavoro, persona, 12*, 1-13.

Magnoler, P. (2009). I dispositivi didattici e l'online. In P. G. Rossi (Ed.), *Tecnologia e costruzione di mondi. Post-costruttivismo, linguaggi e ambienti di apprendimento* (pp. 206–254). Roma: Armando Editore.

Magnoler, P. (2012). *Ricerca e formazione. La professionalizzazione degli insegnanti.* Lecce: Pensa Multimedia.

Maltinti, C. (2014). Il Lesson Study giapponese: un efficace modello cross-cultural. *Form@ re-Open Journal per la formazione in rete*, 14(2), 87–97.

Manca, S., & Ranieri, M. (2013). Is it a tool suitable for learning? A critical review of the literature on Facebook as a technology-enhanced learning environment. *Journal of Computer Assisted Learning*, 29(6), 487–504. doi:10.1111/jcal.12007

Maree, K., & Van Der Westhuizen, C. (2009). *Head start in designing research proposals in the social sciences.* Cape Town: Juta and Company Ltd.

Marsh, B., & Mitchell, N. (2014). The role of video in teacher professional development. *Teacher Development*, 18(3), 403–417. doi:10.1080/13664530.2014.938106

Marsh, B., Mitchell, N., & Adamczyk, P. (2010). Interactive video technology: Enhancing professional learning in initial teacher education. *Computers & Education*, 54(3), 742–748. doi:10.1016/j.compedu.2009.09.011

Martinand, J. L. (2001). Pratiques de référence et problématique de la référence curriculaire. In A. Terrisse (Ed.), *Didactique des disciplines. Les références au savoir* (pp. 179–224). Bruxelles: De Boeck Université.

Martinand, J.-L. (1989). Pratiques de référence, transposition didactique et savoirs professionnels en sciences et techniques. *Les Sciences de l'Education pour l'Ere Nouvelle*, 1-2, 23–35.

Martini, B. (2001). *Didattiche disciplinari. Aspetti teorici e metodologici.* Bologna: Pitagora.

Martini, B. (2006). *Formare ai saperi. Per una pedagogia della conoscenza.* Milano: FrancoAngeli.

Martini, B. (2011). *Pedagogia dei saperi. Problemi, luoghi e pratiche per l'educazione.* Milano: FrancoAngeli.

Masats, D., & Dooly, M. (2011). Rethinking the use of video in teacher education: A holistic approach. *Teaching and Teacher Education*, 27(7), 1151–1162. doi:10.1016/j.tate.2011.04.004

Mattozzi, I. (2005). *Un curricolo per la storia.* Bologna: Cappelli Editore.

Maturana, H. R., & Varela, F. G. (1980). *Autopoiesis and Cognition.* Dordrecht: Reidel. doi:10.1007/978-94-009-8947-4

Maturana, H. R., & Varela, F. J. (1987). *L'albero della conoscenza.* Milano: Garzanti.

Maturana, H. R., & Varela, F. J. (1987). *The tree of knowledge: The biological roots of human understanding.* New Science Library/Shambhala Publications.

Maubant, P., Lenoir, Y., Routhier, S., Auraujo Oliveira, A., Lisee, V., & Hassni, N., 2005, L'analyse des pratiques d'enseignement: le recours à la vidéoscopie, *Les dossiers des sciences de l'éducation*, 14, 61-93.

Maurice, M., Lowy, P., Girod, C., Irlande, J., Kempf, A., Moreau, M., & Zaidman, C. et al. (1983). *El video en la enseñanza.* Barcelona, Spain: Planeta.

Mayen, P. (1999). Les situations potentielles de développement. *Education permanente*, 139, 65-86.

Mazur, E. (1997). Peer Instruction: Getting Students to think in Class. In Edward F. Redish & John S. Rigden (Eds), The Changing Role of Physics Departments in Modern Universities (pp. 981-988). New York: Woodbury.

McCormack, A. C. (2001). Investigating the Impact of an Internship on the Classroom Management Beliefs of Preservice Teachers. *Professional Educator*, *23*(2), 11–22.

McCullagh, J. F. (2012). How can video supported reflection enhance teachers' professional development? *Cultural Studies of Science Education*, *7*(1), 137–152. doi:10.1007/s11422-012-9396-0

McDuffie, A. R., Foote, M. Q., Bolson, C., Turner, E. E., Aguirre, J. M., Bartell, T. G., & Land, T. et al. (2014). Using video analysis to support prospective K-8 teachers' noticing of students' multiple mathematical knowledge bases. *Journal of Mathematics Teacher Education*, *17*(3), 245–270. doi:10.1007/s10857-013-9257-0

McGarr, O. (2009). A review of podcasting in higher education: Its influence on the traditional lecture. *Australasian Journal of Educational Technology*, *25*(3), 309–321. doi:10.14742/ajet.1136

Merrill, M. D. (1983). Component display theory. In C. Reigeluth (Ed.), *Instructional Design Theories and Models*. Hillsdale, NJ: Erlbaum Associates.

Meskill, C., Mossop, J., DiAngelo, S., & Pasquale, R. K. (2002). Expert and novice teachers talking technology: Precepts, concepts, and misconcepts. *Language Learning & Technology*, *6*(3), 46–57.

Meyer, F. (2012). Les vidéos d'exemples de pratique pour susciter le changement. *Revue internationale de pédagogie de l'enseignement supérieur, 28*(2), 1-19.

Mezirow, J. (2000). *Learning as Transformation: Critical Perspectives on a Theory in Progress*. San Francisco, CA: Jossey-Bass Publishers.

Miles, M., Huberman, M., & Saldaña, J. (2014). *Qualitative Data Analysis. A methods Sourcebook*. Los Angeles, London, New Delhi, Singapore, Washington DC: Sage.

Miller, K., & Zhou, X. (2007). Learning from classroom video: what makes it compelling and what makes it hard. In R. Goldmann, R. Pea, B. Barron, & S. J. Derry (Eds.), *Video research in the learning sciences* (pp. 321–334). Mahwah, NJ: Lawrence Erlbaum.

Mishra, P., & Koehler, M. (2006). Technological pedagogical content knowledge: A framework for teacher knowledge. *Teachers College Record*, *108*(6), 1017–1054.

Mitchell, N., Marsh, B., Hobson, A. J., & Sorensen, P. (2010). 'Bringing theory to life': Findings from an evaluation of the use of interactive video within an initial teacher preparation programme. *Teacher Development*, *14*(1), 15–27. doi:10.1080/13664531003696543

Mitra, B., Lewin-Jones, J., Barrett, H., & Williamson, S. (2010). The use of video to enable deep learning. *Research in Post-Compulsory Education*, *15*(4), 405–414. doi:10.1080/13596748.2010.526802

MIUR. (2013). Avvio delle misure di accompagnamento delle Indicazioni nazionali 2012. Primi adempimenti e scadenze, Circolare Ministeriale n. 22. Retrieved from http://www.indicazioninazionali.it/documenti_Indicazioni_nazionali/CM_22_2013_Misure_Accompagnamento_IN.pdf

MIUR. (2014). Misure di accompagnamento per l'attuazione delle Indicazioni Nazionali per il curricolo (DM 254/2012) e per il rafforzamento delle conoscenze e delle competenze degli alunni (DM. 762/2014). Prosecuzione e avvio di nuove iniziative formative. Anno scolastico 2014-2015. Circolare Ministeriale n. 49. Retrieved from http://www.indicazioninazionali.it/documenti_Indicazioni_nazionali/CM_49_19-11-2014.pdf

Mollo, V., & Falzon, P. (2004). Auto- and Allo-confrontation as Tools for Reflective Activities. *Applied Ergonomics*, *35*(6), 531–540. doi:10.1016/j.apergo.2004.06.003 PMID:15374760

Mondada, L. (2008). « Production du savoir et interactions multimodales – Une étude de la modélisation spatiale comme activité pratique située et incarnée », *Revue d'anthropologie des connaissances,* 2(2), 219-266.

Mondada, L. (2012), « Organisation multimodale de la parole-en-interaction: pratiques incarnées d'introduction des référents », *Langue française,* 175, 129-147.

Montgomerie, T. C. (1987). Facilitating "Extended Campus" graduate education through electronic communication. *Canadian Journal of Educational Communication, 16*(3), 239–256.

Montù, V. (2015). La costruzione di una systematic review sulla ricerca con i bambini. *Formazione & Insegnamento. Rivista internazionale di Scienze dell'educazione e della formazione, 9*(1), 211–218.

Moore Johnson, S.The Project on the Next Generation of Teachers. (2004). *Finders and keepers: Helping new teachers survive and thrive in our schools.* San Francisco: Jossey Bass.

Moore, M., & Kearsley, G. (2012). *Distance Education: A Systems View of Online Learning.* Belmont, CA: Wadsworth, Cengage Learning.

Morcelini, M., & Rivoltella, P. C. (2007). La sapienza do comunicare: dieci anni di media education in Italia ed Europa. Trento: Erickson.

Morin, E. (1986). *La methode, 3: La connaissance de la connaissance.* Paris: ÉditionSeuil.

Morrisette, J. (2015). Une analyse interactionniste de la complémentarité des positions de savoir en recherche collabora-tive. *Carrefour, 39*(1), 103–118. doi:10.3917/cdle.039.0103

Mortari, L. (2007). *Cultura della ricerca e pedagogia.* Roma: Carocci.

Mortari, L. (2009). *Ricercare e riflettere. La formazione del docente professionista.* Roma: Carocci.

Mottet, G. (1996). Du voir au faire. Le trajet de la vidéo-formation, *Recherche et formation,* 23, 29-54.

Mottet, G. (1997). La vidéo, outil de constrction des compétences professionelles des einsegnants. In G.Mottet (Ed.). La vidéo-formation. Autres regards, autres pratiques (pp. 21-36). Paris: L'Harmanattan.

Mottet, G. (1997). *La vidéo-formation. Autres regards, autres pratiques.* Paris: L'Harmattan.

Muller, A., & Plazaola Giger, I. (Eds.). (2014). *Dispositions à agir, travail et formation.* Toulouse: Octarès.

Munoz, G. & Boivin, S. (2016). Accompagner les tuteurs à expliciter leur connaissance-en-acte. *Education permanente,* 206, 109-117.

Munoz, G., Minassian, L., & Vinatier, I. (2012). An analyzing of co-piloting in the teaching-learning process: a case study of science class debate. *WORK: A Journal of Prevention, Assessment, & Rehabilitation* (Special issue on Ergonomic Work Analysis and Training), 41, 187-194. http://iospress.metapress.com/content/l1683274520015h1/

Napoli, M. (2004). Mindfulness training for teachers: A pilot program. *Complementary Health Practice Review,* 9(1), 31–42.

National Governors Association Center for Best Practices, Council of Chief State School Officers. (2010). *Common Core State Standards (Mathematics).* Washington, DC: National Governors Association Center for Best Practices.

Newby, T. J. et al.. (2006). *Educational technology for teaching and learning* (3rd ed.). Englewood Cliffs, NJ: Pearson Merrill Prentice Hall.

Numa-Bocage, L., Marcel, J.-F., & Chaussecourte, P. (Eds.), (2014). L'observation des pratiques enseignantes, *Recherches en Éducation*, 19. Retrieved from http://www.recherches-en-education.net/IMG/pdf/REE-no19.pdf

O'Reilly, T. (2005). *What is web 2.0? Design patterns and business models for the next generation of software*. Retrieved from http://www.oreilly.com/pub/a/web2/archive/what-is-web-20.html

O'Sullivan, M. C. (2002). Action research and the transfer of reflective approaches to in-service education and training (INSET) for unqualified and underqualified primary teachers in Namibia. *Teaching and Teacher Education, 18*(5), 523–539. doi:10.1016/S0742-051X(02)00014-8

OECD. (2005). OECD Annual report 2005. Retrieved from http://www.oecd.org/about/34711139.pdf

OECD. (2012). Education at a Glance 2012: OECD indicators. Retrieved from http://www.oecd.org/edu/EAG%20 2012_e-book_EN_200912.pdf

OECD. (2012). *PISA 2012* Retrieved from http://www.oecd.org/pisa/keyfindings/pisa-2012-results.htm)

OECD. (2013). *PISA 2012 Assessment and Analytical Framework, PISA*. OECD Publishing.

OECD. (2015). *Mathematics performance (PISA) (indicators)* Retrieved from https://data.oecd.org/pisa/mathematics-performance-pisa.htm

OECD. (2015). *OECD Skills Outlook 2015: youth, skills and employability*. Retrieved from http://www.oecd-library. org/docserver/download/8714011e.pdf?expires=1443443835&id=id&accname=ocid195206&checksum=F738E31FE DCCBB3F972B655C3800656B

OECD. Organization for Economic Co-operation and Development. (2005). Teachers matter. Attracting, developing and retaining effective teachers. Paris: OECD Publishing. Retrieved from http://www.oecd.org/education/school/34990905.pdf

OECD. Organization for Economic Co-operation and Development. (2012). Teaching practices and pedagogical innovation: evidence from TALIS. Paris: OECD Publishing. Retrieved from http://www.oecd.org/education/school/TalisCeri%20 2012%20(tppi)--Ebook.pdf

Olsen, K. R., & Wølner, T. A. (2003). *Storyline for ungdomstrinnet*. Oslo: Universitetsforlaget.

Ombredane, A., & Faverge, J.-M. (1955). *L'analyse du travail*. Paris: PUF Organisation for Economic Co-operation and Development (OECD). (2014). *Education at a Glance 2014*. Retrieved from http://www.oecd.org/edu/Education-at-a-Glance-2014.pdf

Oppenheimer, S. (2003). [Interactive Map]. *Journey of mankind. The peopling of the world*. Retrieved from http://www. bradshawfoundation.com/journey/

Orland-Barak, L., & Yinon, H. (2007). When theory meets practice: What student teachers learn from guided reflection on their own classroom discourse. *Teaching and Teacher Education, 23*(6), 957–969. doi:10.1016/j.tate.2006.06.005

Orme, M. (1966). *The effects of modeling and feedback variables on the acquisition of a complex teaching strategy [Unpublished doctoral dissertation]*. Stanford, California: Stanford University.

Orungbemi, O. (2009). Awareness and use of teaching skills among primary school social studies teachers. *Sustainable Human Development Review, 1*(3), 127–138.

Özer, B. (2004). In-service training of teachers in Turkey at the beginning of the 2000s. *Journal of In-service Education, 30*(1), 89–100. doi:10.1080/13674580400200301

Ozonur, M. (2013). Sanal gerçeklik ortamı olarak ikincil yaşam (second life) uygulamalarının tasarlanması ve bu uygulamaların internet tabanlı uzaktan eğitim öğrencilerinin öğrenmeleri üzerindeki etkilerinin farklı değişkenler açısından incelenmesi [The design of Second Life applications as virtual world and examining the effects of these applications on the learning of the students attending internet-based distance education in terms of different variables] [Doctorate Thesis]. Mersin University: Mersin, Turkey.

Pachler, N. (Ed.). *Mobile Learning. Towards a Research Agend.* Retrieved from <http://www.wlecentre.ac.uk/cms/files/occasionalpapers/mobilelearning_pachler_2007.pdf>

Pajares, M. F. (1992). Teachers' beliefs and educational research: Cleaning up a messy construct. *Review of Educational Research, 62*(1), 307–332. doi:10.3102/00346543062003307

Palmer, D. J., Stough, L. M., Burdenski, T. K. Jr, & Gonzales, M. (2005). Identifying teacher expertise: An examination of researchers' decision making. *Educational Psychologist, 40*(1), 13–25. doi:10.1207/s15326985ep4001_2

Paquay, L., & Wagner, M.-C. (2006). Competenze professionali privilegiate negli stage in video-formazione. In Altet M., Charlier E., Paquay L., Perrenoud P. (Eds.), Formare gli insegnanti professionisti. Quali strategie? Quali competenze? (149-174). Roma: Armando.

Paquay, L., Altet, M., Charlier, E., & Perrenoud, Ph. (Dir.) (1996). Former des enseignants professionnels. Quelles stratégies? Quelles compétences? Bruxelles: Editions De Boeck.

Paquay, L., Van Nieuwenhoven, C., & Wouters, P. (Dir.) (2010). L'évaluation, levier du développement professionnel? Bruxelles: De Boeck-Université.

Park, J. (2008). Preparing secondary mathematics teachers in urban schools: Using video to develop understanding of equity-based discourse and classroom norms. University of California, Los Angeles.

Pascarella, E. T., Seifert, T. A., & Blaich, C. (2010). How effective are the NSSE benchmarks in predicting important educational outcomes? *Change: The Magazine of Higher Learning, 42*(1), 16–22. doi:10.1080/00091380903449060

Pastré, P. (1997), Didactique professionnelle et développement, *Psychologie française,* 42(1), 89-100.

Pastré, P. (2007). Activité et apprentissage en didactique pfosessionnelle. In M. Fabre & M. Durand (Eds.), Les situations de formation entre savoir, problems et activité (pp. 102-123). Paris, France: L'Harmattan.

Pastré, P. (2011). *La didactique professionnelle. Approche anthropologique du développement chez les adultes.* Paris: PUF.

Pastré, P. (2011). *La didactique professionnelle.* Paris: PUF. doi:10.3917/puf.faber.2011.01

Pastré, P., Mayen, P., & Vergnaud, G. (2006). La didactique professionnelle. *Revue Française de Pédagogie, 154,* 144–198.

Pearson (2012), *The Learning Courve, Lessons in Country. Report Performance in Education.* Retrieved from http://media.pearsonitalia.it/0.698971_1399648396.pdf

Peirce, C. S. (1978). *Ecrits sur le signe.* Paris: Seuil.

Pellegrini, M. (2014). La valutazione degli insegnanti nell'area OECD. *Form@re, Open Journal per la formazione in rete,* 4(14), 105-117.

Pellerey, M. (2005). Verso una nuova metodologia di ricerca educativa: La Ricerca basata su progetti (Design-Based-Research). *Orientamenti Pedagogici, 5*(52), 721–737.

Pellerey, M. (2014). La forza della realtà nell'agire educativo. *ECPSJournal, 9,* 63–81.

Perla, L. (2010). *Didattica dell'implicito. Ciò che l'insegnante non sa.* Brescia: La Scuola.

Perla, L. (2011). *L'eccellenza in cattedra. Dal saper insegnare alla conoscenza dell'insegnamento.* Milano: FrancoAngeli.

Perla, L. (2012). *Scrittura e tirocinio universitario. Una ricerca sulla documentazione.* Milano: FrancoAngeli.

Perla, L. (Ed.). (2014). *I nuovi Licei alla prova delle competenze. Guida alla progettazione nel biennio.* Lecce: Pensa Multimedia.

Perrenoud, P. (2001). Le travail sur l'habitus dans laformation des enseignants. Analyse des pratiques et prise de conscience. In L. Paquay, M. Altet, E. Charlier, & Ph., Perrenoud, (Eds.), Former des enseignants professionnels. Quelles stratégies? Quelles compétences? (pp. 181-208). Bruxelles: de Boeck.

Perrenoud, P. (2002). Dieci competenze per insegnare. Roma: Anicia. (Originale ed.: Perrenoud, P.) (1999). Dix nouvelles compétences pour enseigner. Paris: ESF.

Perrenoud, P. (2006). Il lavoro sull'habitus nella formazione degli insegnanti. Analisi delle pratiche e presa di coscienza. In Altet M., Charlier E., Paquay L., Perrenoud P. (Eds.), Formare gli insegnanti professionisti. Quali strategie? Quali competenze? (175-200). Roma: Armando.

Perrenoud, P. (1999). *Dix nouvelles compétences pour enseigner: invitation au voyage.* Paris: ESF.

Philipp, R. A. (2007). Mathematics teachers' beliefs and affect. In F. K. Lester (Ed.), Second handbook of research on mathematics teaching and learning (pp. 257-315). National Council of Teachers of Mathematics. Charlotte, NC: Information Age Publishing.

Philippot, T., & Niclot, D. (2009). La professionnalité des enseignants de l'école primaire en France: une démarche qualitative. In Actes du 2ème colloque international francophone sur les méthodes qualitative. Lille.

Piaget, J. & *al.* (1926). *La représentation du monde chez l'enfant.* Paris: F. Alcan

Piaget, J. (1936). *La naissance de l'intelligence chez l'enfant.* Paris, Neuchâtel: Delachaux & Niestlé.

Piaget, J. (1970). *L'épistémologie génétique.* Paris: PUF.

Piaget, J. (1974). *Réussir et comprendre.* Paris: PUF.

Pitler, H., Hubbell, E., & Kuhn, M. (2012). *Using technology with classroom instruction that works* (2nd ed.). Alexandria, VA: ASCD.

Poizat, G., Bailly, M. C., Seferdjeli, L., & Goudeaux, A. (2015). Analyse du travail et conception dans le cadre de recherches technologiques en formation: illustration sur le terrain de la radiologie médicale. In V. L. Bore, M. Durand, & F. Yvon (Eds.), *Analyse du travail et formation dans les métiers de l'éducation* (pp. 71–91). Louvain La Neuve: De Boeck.

Poizat, G., Salini, D., & Durand, M. (2013). Approche énactive de l'activité humaine, simplexité et conception de formations professionnelles. *Education Sciences &Society, 4*(1), 97–112.

Previtali, D. (2012). *Come valutare i docenti?* Brescia: La Scuola.

Putnam, R. T., & Borko, H. (2000). What do new views of knowledge and thinking have to say about research on teacher learning? *Educational Researcher, 29*(1), 4–15. doi:10.3102/0013189X029001004

Quiñones, M. A., Ford, J. K., & Teachout, M. S. (1995). The relationship between work experience and job performance: A conceptual and meta-analytic review. *Personnel Psychology, 48*(4), 887–910. doi:10.1111/j.1744-6570.1995.tb01785.x

Rabardel, P. (1995). *Les hommes et les technologies; approche cognitive des instruments contemporains.* Paris: Collins.

Rabardel, P. (2005). Instrument, activité et développement du pouvoir d'agir. In P. Lorino & R. Teulier (Eds.), *Entre connaissance et organisation: l'activité collective* (pp. 251–265). Paris: La Découverte.

Rabardel, P., & Pastré, P. (2005). *Modèles du sujet pour la conception*. Toulouse: Octarès.

Ray, B. B., & Powell, A. (2014). Preparing to teach with Flipped Classroom in teacher preparation programs. In J. Keengwe, G. Onchwari, & J. Oigara (Eds.), *Promoting active learning through the Flipped Classroom model*. Hershey, PA: IGI Global. doi:10.4018/978-1-4666-4987-3.ch001

Reia-Batista, V. (1995). Pedagogia da Comunicação, Cinema e Ensino. In *Educación y Medios de Comunicación en el Contexto Iberoamericano*. La Rabida: Universidade Internacional de Andalucia.

Reigeluth, C., & Stein, F. (1983). The elaboration theory of instruction. In C. Reigeluth (Ed.), *Instructional Design Theories and Models*. Hillsdale, NJ: Erlbaum Associates.

Reynolds, P. A., & Mason, R. (2002). On-line video media for continuing professional development in dentistry. *Computers & Education*, *39*(1), 65–97. doi:10.1016/S0360-1315(02)00026-X

Rézeau, J. (2004), *Médiatisation et médiation pédagogique dans un environnement multimédia - Le cas de l'apprentissage de l'anglais en Histoire de l'art à l'université* [Thèse de doctorat]. Université Victor Segalen Bordeaux 2.

Rhine, S., & Bryant, J. (2007). Enhancing pre-service teachers' reflective practice with digital video-based dialogue. *Reflective Practice*, *8*(3), 345–358. doi:10.1080/14623940701424884

Ria, L. (2015). Former les enseignants au 21ème siècle. Volume 1: établissement formateur et vidéoformation. Bruxelles: De Boeck.

Richardson, V., & Placier, P. (2002). Teacher change. In V. Richardson (Ed.), *Handbook of research on teaching* (4th ed.). Washington, DC: American Educational Research Association.

Riley, C. (2009). Teacher quality v teaching quality: What's the difference? *Innovations*, *8*, 6–9.

Rivoltella, P. C. (2005). Il cinema luogo di educazione, tra sacuola ed extra-escuola. In Malavasi, P., Polenghi, S. & Rivoltella, P.C (Eds), Cinema, pratiche formative, educazione. (pp. 67-88). Milano:Vita e Pensiero.

Rivoltella, P. C. (2008). Usare el cinema in scuola. In P. Ardizone & P.C. Rivoltella (Eds), Media e tecnologie per la didattica. Milano: V&P.

Rivoltella, P. C. (2014). Episodes of Situated Learning. A New Way to Teaching and Learning. *Research on Education and Media*, 6(2), 79-87. Retrieved fromhttp://ojs.pensamultimedia.it/index.php/rem_en/article/view/1070/1040

Rivoltella, P. C. (2012). *Neurodidattica. Insegnare al Cervello che Apprende*. Milano: Raffaello Cortina Editore.

Rivoltella, P. C. (2013). *Fare Didattica con gli EAS. Episodi di Apprendimento Situati*. Brescia: La Scuola.

Rivoltella, P. C. (2014). *La previsione*. Brescia: La Scuola.

Rivoltella, P. C. (2015). *Didattica inclusiva con gli EAS*. Brescia: La Scuola.

Rivoltella, P. C., & Rossi, P. G. (Eds.), (2012). *L'agiredidattico. Manualedell'insegnamento*. Brescia: La Scuola.

Rivoltella, P. C., & Rossi, P. G. (Eds.). (2012). *L'agire didattico.Manuale per l'insegnante*. Brescia, Italia: La Scuola.

Robinson, B. (2008). Using Distance Education and ICT to Improve Access, Equity and the Quality in Rural Teachers' Professional Development in Western China. *International Review of Research in Open and Distance Learning*, *9*(1), 1–17.

Roblyer, M. D., McDaniel, M., Webb, M., Herman, J., & Witty, J. V. (2010). Findings on Facebook in higher education: A comparison of college faculty and student uses and perceptions of social networking sites. *The Internet and Higher Education, 13*(3), 134–140. doi:10.1016/j.iheduc.2010.03.002

Roche, L., & Gal-Petitfaux, N. (2014, March). Design of an audiovisual device for preservice teachers' training. In *Society for Information Technology & Teacher Education International Conference* (Vol. 2014, No. 1, pp. 1313–1316).

Roehl, T. (2012). Disassembling the classroom–an ethnographic approach to the materiality of education. *Ethnography and Education, 7*(1), 109–126. doi:10.1080/17457823.2012.661591

Roeser, R. W., Skinner, E., Beers, J., & Jennings, P. A. (2012). Mindfulness training and teachers' professional development: An emerging area of research and practice. *Child Development Perspectives, 6*(2), 167–173. doi:10.1111/j.1750-8606.2012.00238.x

Rogalski, J. (2003). Y a-t-il un pilote dans la classe. *Recherches en didactique des mathématiques, 23*(3), 343–388.

Romano, M., & Schwartz, J. (2005). Exploring technology as a tool for eliciting and encouraging beginning teacher reflection. *Contemporary Issues in Technology & Teacher Education, 5*(2), 149–168.

Rosaen, C. L., Lundeberg, M., Cooper, M., Fritzen, A., & Terpstra, M. (2008). Noticing How Does Investigation of Video Records Change How Teachers Reflect on Their Experiences? *Journal of Teacher Education, 59*(4), 347–360. doi:10.1177/0022487108322128

Rosaen, C., Schram, P., & Herbel-Eisenmann, B. (2002). Using hypermedia technology to explore connections among mathematics, language, and literacy in teacher education. *Contemporary Issues in Technology & Teacher Education, 2,* 2–31.

Rossi P.G. (2015). Ripensare la ricerca educativa nell'ottica della professionalità docente e della generalizability. *Pedagogia Oggi,*(2), 49-64.

Rossi P.G. et al. (2015), The use of video recorded classes to develop teacher professionalism: the experimentation of a curriculum. *Je-LKS – Journal of e-Learning and Knowledge Society, 11* (2), 111-127.

Rossi P.G., Fedeli L., Biondi S., Magnoler P., Bramucci A., & Lancioni C. (2015). The use of video recorded classes to develop teacher professionalism: the experimentation of a curriculum. *Journal of e-Learning and Knowledge Society, 11* (2), 111-127.

Rossi, P. G., & Pezzimenti, L. (2012). La trasposizione didattica In P.C. Rivoltella, P.G. Rossi (Eds.), L'agire didattico. Manuale per l'insegnante (pp. 167-184). Brescia: La scuola.

Rossi, P.G., Magnoler, P., Giannandrea, L., Mangione, G. R., Pettenati, M.C., & Rosa, A. (2015). Il teacher portfolio per la formazione dei neo-assunti. *Pedagogia Oggi, 2.*

Rossi, P. G. (2011). *Didattica enattiva. Complessità, teorie dell'azione, professionalità docente.* Milano, Italia: Franco Angeli.

Rossi, P. G. (2013). *Didattica enattiva: complessità, teorie dell'azzione, professionalità docente.* Milano: Franco Angeli.

Rossi, P. G. (2014). Le tecnologie digitali per la progettazione didattica. *Journal Of Educational, Cultural Psychological Studies,* 2014, 113–133.

Rossi, P. G., & Pezzimenti, L. (2012). La trasposizione didattica. In P. C. Rivoltella & P. G. Rossi (Eds.), *L'agire didattico. Manuale per l'insegnante* (pp. 167–183). Milano: La Scuola.

Rossi, P. G., Prenna, V., Giannandrea, L., & Magnoler, P. (2013). Enactivism and Didactics. Some Research Lines. *Education Sciences & Society*, *1*, 37–57.

Rossi, P. G., & Toppano, E. (2009). *Progettare nella società della conoscenza*. Roma: Carocci.

Roth, K. J. (2009). Using video studies to transform science teaching and learning: results from the STeLLA professional development program. In T. Janik & T. Seidel (Eds.), *The power of video studies in investigating teaching and learning in the classroom* (pp. 243–258). Münster: Waxmann.

Roth, W. M. (2007). Epistemic mediation: Video data as filters for the objectification of teaching by teachers. In R. Goldman, R. Pea, B. Barron, & S. J. Derry (Eds.), *Video research in the learning sciences* (pp. 367–382). Mahwah, NJ: Lawrence Erlbaum Ass.

Rouis, S., Limayem, M., & Salehi-Sangari, E. (2011). Impact of Facebook Usage on Students' Academic Achievement: Role of Self-Regulation and Trust. *Electronic Journal of Research in Educational Psychology*, *9*(3), 961–994.

Rudd, D. P. II, & Rudd, D. P. (2014). The value of video in online instruction. *Journal of Instructional Pedagogies*, *13*(1), 1–7.

Ruiz-Primo, M. A., & Furtak, E. M. (2004). Informal formative assessment of students' Understanding of scientific inquiry. CSE – Center for the Study of Evaluation – Report 639, Los Angeles, CA.

Sabers, D., Cushing, K., & Berliner, D. (1991). Differences among teachers in a task characterized by simultaneity, multidimensionality and immediacy. *American Educational Research Journal*, *28*(1), 63–88.

Saiti, A., & Saitis, C. (2006). In-service training for teachers who work in full-day schools. Evidence from Greece 1. *European Journal of Teacher Education*, *29*(4), 455–470. doi:10.1080/02619760600944779

Salaün, M. (2010). *A l'épreuve de l'autochtonie. Penser la décolonisation de l'école. Une comparaison France/Etats-Unis (Nouvelle-Calédonie/Hawaï)*. Dossier d'Habilitation à Diriger des Recherches sous la direction d'Elisabeth Bautier, Université Paris 8 Saint-Denis.

Salaün, M. (2011). *Renforcer l'enseignement des langues et cultures polynésiennes à l'école élémentaire. Contribution à l'évaluation de l'expérimentation ECOLPOM en Polynésie Française: aspects sociolinguistiques, Rapport de recherche*. ANR.

Samurçay, R., & Rabardel, P. (2004). Modèles pour l'analyse de l'activité et des compétences, propositions. In R. Samurçay & P. Pastré (Eds.), *Recherches en didactique professionnelle* (pp. 163–180). Toulouse: Octarés.

Samurçay, R., & Rabardel, P. (2004). Modèles pour l'analyse de l'activité et des compétences. In R. Samurçay & P. Pastré (Eds.), *Recherches et pratiques en didactique professionnelle*. Toulouse: Octarès.

Sancar Tokmak, H., & Incikabi, L. (2012). Understanding expertise-based training effects on the software evaluation process of Mathematics Education teachers. *Educational Media International Journal*, *49*(4), 277–288. doi:10.1080/09523987.2012.741198

Sancar-Tokmak, H. (2013). Effects of Video-Supported Expertise-Based Training (XBT) on Preservice Science Teachers' Self-Efficacy Beliefs. *Eurasia Journal of Mathematics. Science & Technology Education*, *9*(2), 89–99. doi:10.12973/eurasia.2013.924a

Sancar-Tokmak, H., Baturay, H. M., & Fadde, P. (2013). Applying the context, input, process, product evaluation model for evaluation, research, and redesign of an online master's program. *The International Review of Research in Open and Distributed Learning*, *14*(3), 273–293.

Sancar-Tokmak, H., & Karakus, T. (2011). A Case Study on Contribution of Initial Teacher Training to Teaching Practice. *Contemporary Educational Technology Journal, 2*(4), 319–332.

Sandoval, A., & Bell, P. (2004). Design-Based research methods for Studying Leaning in Context: Introduction. *Educational Psychologist, 39*(4), 199–201. doi:10.1207/s15326985ep3904_1

Santagata, R. (2010), From Teacher Noticing to a Framework for Analyzing and Improving Classroom Lessons. In M. Sherin, R. Phillip e V. Jacobs (Eds.), Mathematics teacher noticing: Seeing through teachers' eyes (152-168). New York: Routledge.

Santagata, R. (2012). Un modello per l'utilizzo del video nella formazione professionale degli insegnanti. *Form@re-Open Journal per la formazione in rete, 12*(79), 58-63.

Santagata, R., & Guarino, J. (2011), Using video to teach future teachers to learn from teaching, in ZDM the International Journal of Mathematics Education, 43(1), 133–145. doi:10.1007/s11858-010-0292-3

Santagata, R., & Guarino, J. (2011). Using the video to teach future teachers to learn from teaching. *ZDM. The international Journal of Mathematics Education, 43*(1), 133-145.

Santagata, R., & Stürmer K. (2014). Video educazione: nuovi scenari per la formazione degli insegnanti. *Form@are, 14* (2), 4-6.

Santagata, R. (2009). Designing video-based professional development for mathematics teachers in low-performing schools. *Journal of Teacher Education, 60*(1), 38–51. doi:10.1177/0022487108328485

Santagata, R., & Angelici, G. (2010). Studying the impact of the *Lesson Analysis Framework* on pre-service teachers' ability to reflect on videos of classroom teaching. *Journal of Teacher Education, 61*(4), 339–349. doi:10.1177/0022487110369555

Santagata, R., & Guarino, J. (2011). Using video to teach future teachers to learn from teaching. *ZDM. The International Journal of Mathematics Education, 43*(1), 133–145.

Santagata, R., & Yeh, C. (2014). Learning to teach mathematics and to analyze teaching effectiveness: Evidence from a video-and practice-based approach. *Journal of Mathematics Teacher Education, 17*(6), 491–514. doi:10.1007/s10857-013-9263-2

Santagata, R., Zannoni, C., & Stigler, J. (2007). The role of lesson analysis in pre-service teacher education: An empirical investigation of teacher learning from a virtual video-based field experience. *Journal of Mathematics Teacher Education, 10*(2), 123–140. doi:10.1007/s10857-007-9029-9

Schifter, C. (2008). *Infusing technology into the classroom: Continuous practice improvement.* Hershey: Information Science Pub. doi:10.4018/978-1-59904-765-2

Schön, D. (1994). *Le praticien réflexif: à la recherche du savoir caché dans l'agir professionnel.* Montréal: Les éditions logiques.

Schön, D. A. (2006, trad. It.). Il professionista riflessivo: per una nuova epistemologia della pratica professionale. Bari: Deedalo.

Schon, D. A. (1983). *How professionals think in action. The Reflective Practitioner.* New York: Basic Books.

Schön, D. A. (1983). *The reflective practitioner: How professionals think in action.* New York, NY: Basic books.

Schuetze, H. G., & Sweet, R. (2003). *Integrating School and Workplace Learning in Canada: Principles and Practices of alternation Education and Training.* Montreal: McGill-Queen's University Press.

Schwan, S., & Riempp, R. (2004). The cognitive benefits of interactive videos: Learning to tie nautical knots. *Learning and Instruction, 14*(3), 293–305. doi:10.1016/j.learninstruc.2004.06.005

Schwartz, Y. (2007). Un bref aperçu de l'histoire du concept culturel d'activité. *Activités (Vitry-sur-Seine), 4*(2), 122–133. Retrieved from http://www.activites.org/v4n2/v4n2.pdf doi:10.4000/activites.1728

Schwindt, K. (2008). *Teachers observe instruction: Criteria for competent perception of instruction.* Münster, Germany: Waxmann.

Scriven, M. (1967). The metodology of evaluation. In R. E. Tyler, R. M. Gagnè, & M. Scriven (Eds.), *Perspecive of corriculum evaluation.* Chicago: AERA Monograph Series in Education.

Seago, N. (2004). Using video as an object of inquiry for mathematics teaching and learning. In J. Brophy (Ed.), *Using video in teacher education* (pp. 259–286). Oxford: Elsevier.

Seidel, T., Pehmer, A. K., & Kiemer, K. (2014). Facilitating collaborative teacher learning: The role of "mindfulness" in video-based teacher professional development programs. *Gruppendynamik und Organisationsberatung, 45*(3), 273–290. doi:10.1007/s11612-014-0248-0

Seidel, T., & Prenzel, M. (2007). How teachers perceive lessons- Assessing educational competencies by means of videos. *Zeitschrift fur Erziehungswissenschaft, 10*, 201–216.

Seidel, T., & Shavelson, R. J. (2007). Teaching effectiveness research in the past decade: The role of theory and research design in disentangling meta-analysis results. *Review of Educational Research, 77*(4), 454–499. doi:10.3102/0034654307310317

Seidel, T., & Stürmer, K. (2014). Modeling and Measuring the Structure of Professional Vision in Preservice Teachers. *American Educational Research Journal, 51*(4), 739–771. doi:10.3102/0002831214531321

Seidel, T., Stürmer, K., & Blomberg, G. (2010). *Observer: video-based tool to diagnose teachers' professional vision.* Munich: Technische Universität München.

Seidel, T., Stürmer, K., Blomberg, G., Kobarg, M., & Schwindt, K. (2011). Teacher learning from analysis of videotaped classroom situations: Does it make a difference whether teachers observe their own teaching or that of others? *Teaching and Teacher Education, 27*(2), 259–267. doi:10.1016/j.tate.2010.08.009

Seldin, P. (2004). *The Teacher Portfolio.* Bolton, MA: Anker Publishing.

Selwyn, N. (2009). Faceworking: Exploring students' education-related use of Facebook. *Learning, Media and Technology, 34*(2), 157–174. doi:10.1080/17439880902923622

Selwyn, N., & Grant, L. (2009). Researching the realities of social software use—an introduction. *Learning, Media and Technology, 34*(2), 79–86. doi:10.1080/17439880902921907

Sensevy, G. (2008). Le travail du professeur pour la théorie de l'action conjointe en didactique, *Recherche et formation, 57*, 39-50. Retrieved from http://rechercheformation.revues.org/822

Sergiovanni, T. J., & Starratt, R. J. (2007). *Supervision: A redefinition* (8th ed.). New York: McGraw Hill.

Shanahan, L. E., & Tochelli, A. L. (2014). Examining the use of video study groups for developing literacy pedagogical content knowledge of critical elements of strategy instruction with elementary teachers. *Literacy Research and Instruction, 53*(1), 1–24. doi:10.1080/19388071.2013.827764

Shavelson, R. J., Black, P., Wiliam, D., & Coffey, J. (2003, January). On aligning summative and formative functions in the design of large-scale assessment system. *Paper presented at theNational Research Council's workshop on Assessment in Support of Instruction and Learning.*

Shen, J. (2003). New teachers' certification status and attrition pattern. A survival analysis using The Baccalaureate and Beyond Longitudinal Study 1993–97. *Paper presented at theAERA annual meeting*, Chicago, IL.

Shephard, K. (2003). Questioning, promoting and evaluating the use of streaming video to support student learning. *British Journal of Educational Technology*, *34*(3), 295–308. doi:10.1111/1467-8535.00328

Sherin, M. G. (2001). Developing a professional vision of classroom events. In T. Wood, B. Scott Nelson, & J. Warfield (Eds.), Beyond classical pedagogy: Teaching elementary school mathematics (pp. 75–93). Hillsdale, NJ: Erlbaum

Sherin, M. G. (2004). New perspectives on the role of video in teacher education. In J. Brophy (Eds.), Using video in teacher education (pp. 1-27). New York: Emerald.

Sherin, M. G. (2004). New perspectives on the role of videoin teacher education. In J. Brophy (eds), Using video in teacher education (pp.1-27). New Yok: Elsevier.

Sherin, M. G., & Van Es, E. A. (2002). Using video to support teachers' ability to interpret classroom interactions. *Society for Information Technology & Teacher Education International Conference*, 2002(1), 2532-2536.

Sherin, M. G. (2001). Developing a professional vision of classroom events. In T. Wood, B. S. Nelson, & J. Warfield (Eds.), *Beyond classical pedagogy: Teaching elementary school mathematics* (pp. 75–93). Hillsdale, NJ: Erlbaum.

Sherin, M. G. (2004). New perspectives on the role of video in teacher education. In J. Brophy (Ed.), *Using video in teacher education* (pp. 1–27). Amsterdam: Elsevier.

Sherin, M. G. (2007). The development of teachers' professional vision in video clubs. In R. Goldman, R. Pea, B. Barron, & S. Derry (Eds.), *R. Goldman, R. Pea, B. Barron, & S. Derry, Video research in the learning sciences* (pp. 383–395). Hillsdale, NJ: Erlbaum.

Sherin, M. G. (2007). The development of teachers' professional vision in video clubs. In R. Goldman, R. Pea, B. Barron, & S. Derry (Eds.), *Video research in the learning sciences* (pp. 383–395). Hillsdale, NJ: Erlbaum.

Sherin, M. G., & Han, S. Y. (2004). Teacher learning in the context of a video club. *Teaching and Teacher Education*, *20*(2), 163–183. doi:10.1016/j.tate.2003.08.001

Sherin, M. G., Jacobs, V. R., & Philipp, R. A. (2011). *Mathematics teacher noticing: Seeing through teachers' eyes*. New York: Routledge.

Sherin, M. G., Linsenmeier, K. A., & van Es, E. A. (2009). Issues in the design of video clubs: Selecting video clips for teacher learning. *Journal of Teacher Education*, *60*(3), 213–230. doi:10.1177/0022487109336967

Sherin, M. G., Russ, R. S., Sherin, B. L., & Colestock, A. (2008). Professional Vision in Action: An Exploratory Study. *Issues in Teacher Education*, *17*(2), 27–46.

Sherin, M. G., Russ, R. S., Sherin, B. L., & Colestock, A. (2008). Professional Vision in Action: An Exploratory Study. *Teaching Education*, *17*(2), 27–46.

Sherin, M. G., & van Es, E. A. (2008). Effects of video club participation on teachers' professional vision. *Journal of Teacher Education*, *60*(1), 20–37. doi:10.1177/0022487108328155

Shön, D. A. (1993). *Il professionista riflessivo. Per una nuova epistemologia della pratica professionale*. Bari: Edizioni Dedalo.

Shulman, L. S. (1987). Knowledge and teaching: Foundations of the new reform. *Harvard Educational Review*, *57*(1), 1–22. doi:10.17763/haer.57.1.j463w79r56455411

Shulman, L. S. (2004). *The Wisdom of Practice: Essays on Teaching, Learning, and Learning to Teach*. San Francisco: Jossey-Bass.

Siemens, G. (2011). *Learning analytics: foundation for informed change in Higher Education*. Retrieved from http://www.slideshare.net/gsiemens/learning-analytics-educause

Siemens, G. (2005). Connectivism: A learning theory for the digital age. *International Journal of Instructional Technology and Distance Learning*, *2*(1). Retrieved from http://www.itdl.org/Journal/Jan_05/article01.htm

Smith, A. (2010). Home broadband. *Pew Internet & American Life Project*. Retrieved from http://www.pewinternet.org/topics/broadband/

Snoeyink, R. (2010). Using video self-analysis to improve the "withitness" of student teachers. *Journal of Computing in Teacher Education*, *26*(3), 101–110.

Sorlin, P. (1997). *Estetiche dell'audiovisivo*. Firenze: La Nuova Itália.

Spiro, R. J., Collins, B. P., & Ramchandran, A. (2007). Reflections on a post-Gutenberg epistemology of video use in ill-structured domains: fostering complex learning and cognitive flexibility. In R. Goldman, R. Pea, B. Barron, & S. J. Derry (Eds.), *Video research in the learning sciences* (pp. 93–100). Mahwah, NJ: Lawrence Erlbaum.

Stam, R. (2003). *Introdução à teoria do cinema*. Campinas: Papirus.

Star, J. R., & Strickland, S. K. (2008). Learning to observe: Using video to improve preservice mathematics teachers' ability to notice. *Journal of Mathematics Teacher Education*, *11*(2), 107–125. doi:10.1007/s10857-007-9063-7

Star, S. L. (1988). The structure of ill-structured solutions: Boundary objects and heterogeneous distributed problem solving. In M. Huhns & L. Gasser (Eds.), *Readings in distributed artificial intelligence* (Vol. II, pp. 37–54). Menlo Park, CA: Kaufman.

Star, S. L. (2010). This is Not a Boundary Object: Reflections on the Origin of a Concept. *Science, Technology & Human Values*, *35*(5), 601–617. doi:10.1177/0162243910377624

Stigler, J. W., & Hiebert, J. (1999). *The teaching gap: Best ideas from the world's teachers for improving education in the classroom*. New York, NY: Free Press.

Stockero, S. L. (2008). Using a video-based curriculum to develop a reflective stance in prospective mathematics teachers. *Journal of Mathematics Teacher Education*, *11*(5), 373–394. doi:10.1007/s10857-008-9079-7

Stockman, S. (2011). *How to shoot video that doesn't suck*. New York, NY: Workman Publishing Co.

Stokking, K., Leenders, F., de Jong, J., & van Tartwijk, J. (2003). From student to teacher: Reducing practice shock and early dropout in the teaching profession. *European Journal of Teacher Education*, *26*(3), 329–350. doi:10.1080/0261976032000128175

Strauss, A., & Corbin, J. (1998). *Basics of qualitative research. Techniques and procedures for developing grounded theory*. Thousand Oaks, CA: Sage Publications.

Strayer, J. F. (2007). *The effects of the classroom flip on the learning environment: A comparison of learning activity in a traditional classroom and a flip classroom that used an intelligent tutoring system*. The Ohio State University. Retrieved from http://etd.ohiolink.edu/send-pdf.cgi/Strayer%20Jeremy.pdf?osu1189523914

Strong-Wilson, T., Mitchell, C., Morrison, C., Radford, L., & Pithouse-Morgan, K. (2014). Looking Forward Through Looking Back: Using Digital Memory-work in Teaching for Transformation. In *Becoming teacher: Sites for teacher development in Canadian Teacher Education*, 442.

Stürmer, K., Könings, K. D., & Seidel, T. (2013). Declarative knowledge and professional vision in teacher education: Effect of courses in teaching and learning. *The British Journal of Educational Psychology, 83*(3), 467–483. doi:10.1111/j.2044-8279.2012.02075.x PMID:23822532

Stürmer, K., Seidel, T., & Schäfer, S. (2013). Changes in professional vision in the context of practice. *Gruppendynamik und Organisationsberatung, 44*(3), 339–355. doi:10.1007/s11612-013-0216-0

Sun, J., & van Es, E. A. (2015). An exploratory study of the influence that analyzing teaching has on pre-service teachers' classroom practice. *Journal of Teacher Education, 66*(3), 201–214. doi:10.1177/0022487115574103

Swan, K., & Hofer, M. (2014). *And Action! Directing documentaries in the social studies classroom.* Lanham, MA: Rowman & Littlefield.

Talis (2013). Results: An International Perspective on Teaching and Learning, OECD from http://www.oecd.org/edu/school/talis.htm

Tan, A. L., Tan, S. C., & Wettasinghe, C. M. (2011). Learning to be a science teacher: Reflections and lessons from video-based instruction. *Australasian Journal of Educational Technology, 27*(3), 446–462. doi:10.14742/ajet.954

Tap, P. Marquer sa différence, in J.C. Ruano-Borbalan (Ed.), L'identité: l'individu, le groupe, la société (pp. 65-68). Auxerre: Sciences Humaines.

Taylor, P., Ling, E., Ming, K., & Hui, C. (2013). Making learning visible in initial teacher education: A pedagogical characterisation scheme. *Educational Research for Policy and Practice, 12*(3), 193–209. doi:10.1007/s10671-012-9140-2

Theureau, J. (2002). Self Confrontation Interview as a Component of an Empirical and Technological Research Programme. Retrieved from http://www.coursdaction.fr/06-English/2002-JT-C93ENG.pdf

Theureau, J. (2004). *Le cours d'action: Méthode élémentaire.* Toulouse: Octarès.

Theureau, J. (2006). *Le cours d'action: méthode dévéloppée.* Toulouse: Octares.

Theureau, J. (2006). *Le cours d'action: Méthode développée.* Toulouse: Octarès.

Theureau, J. (2009). *Le cours d'action: méthode réfléchie.* Toulouse: Octares.

Tochon, F. (2007). From video cases to video pedagogy: a framework for video feedback and reflection in pedagogical research praxis. In R. Goldman, R. Pea, B. Barron, & S. J. Derry (Eds.), *Video research in the learning sciences* (pp. 53–65). Mahwah, NJ: Routledge.

Torgersen, G. E. (1998). *Læring med IT – Teori og metode for undervisning med informasjons- og kommunikasjonsteknologi.* Oslo: Opplysningsfilm.

Trinchero, R. (2002). *Manuale di ricerca educativa.* Milano: Franco Angeli.

Tripp, T., & Rich, P. (2012). Using video to analyze one's own teaching. *British Journal of Educational Technology, 43*(4), 678–704. doi:10.1111/j.1467-8535.2011.01234.x

Tufte, B., & Christensen, O. (2009). Midia-educação entre teoria e prática. *Perspectiva, 7*(1), 97–18.

UNESCO. International Institute for Educational Planning (2005) *Education reforms and teachers' unions: avenues for action.* Paris. Retrieved from http://unesdoc.unesco.org/images/0014/001410/141028e.pdf

Usluel, Y. K., & Mazman, S. G. (2009). Adoption of Web 2.0 tools in distance education. *Procedia: Social and Behavioral Sciences, 1*(1), 818–823. doi:10.1016/j.sbspro.2009.01.146

Usta, E., & Korkmaz, O. (2010). Öğretmen adaylarının bilgisayar yeterlikleri ve teknoloji kullanımına ilişkin algıları ile öğretmenlik mesleğine yonelik tutumları[Pre-service teachers' computer competencies, perception of technology use and attitudes toward teaching career]. *Uluslararası Insan Bilimleri Dergisi*, *7*(1), 1335–1349.

Van der Maren J.-M, & Yvon F. (2009). L'analyse du travail entre parole et action. *Recherches qualitative*, 7, 42-63.

Van der Maren, J.-M. (2006), Les recherches qualitatives: des critères variés de qualité en fonction des types de recherche. In L. Paquay, M. Crahay, J.-M. De Ketele (Eds.), L'analyse qualitative en éducation. Des pratique de recherche aux critères de qualité, (69-84). Bruxelles: De Boeck.

Van der Maren, J.-M. (2003). *La recherché appliqué en Pédagogie. Des modèles pour l'enseignement*. Bruxelles, Belgique: De Boeck.

Van der Maren, J.-M. (2014). *La recherché appliquée pour les professionnels. Éducation, (para)medical, travail social*. Bruxelles, Belgique: De Boeck.

Van Es, E. A., Stockero, S. L., Sherin, M. G., Van Zoest, L. R., & Dyer, E. (2015). Making the Most of Teacher Self-Captured Video. *Mathematics teacher educator, 1*(4), 6-19.

van Es, E. A. (2009). Participants' Roles in the Context of a Video Club. *Journal of the Learning Sciences, 18*(1), 100–137. doi:10.1080/10508400802581668

van Es, E. A. (2012). Examining the development of a teacher learning community: The case of a video club. *Teaching and Teacher Education, 28*(2), 182–192. doi:10.1016/j.tate.2011.09.005

Van Es, E. A., & Sherin, M. G. (2010). The influence of video clubs on teachers' thinking and practice. *Journal of Mathematics Teacher Education, 13*(2), 155–176. doi:10.1007/s10857-009-9130-3

van Es, E. A., Tunney, J., Goldsmith, L. T., & Seago, N. (2014). A framework for the facilitation of teachers' analysis of video. *Journal of Teacher Education, 65*(4), 340–356. doi:10.1177/0022487114534266

van Es, E., & Sherin, M. G. (2002). Learning to notice: Scaffolding new teachers' interpretations of classroom interactions. *Journal of Technology and Teacher Education, 10*(4), 571–596.

van Es, E., & Sherin, M. G. (2008). Mathematics teachers' ''learning to notice'' in the context of a video club. *Teaching and Teacher Education, 24*(2), 244–276. doi:10.1016/j.tate.2006.11.005

Vanhulle, S., Merhan, F., & Ronveaux, C. (2007). Du principe d'alternance aux alternances en formation des einsegnants et des adultes. In F. Merhan, C. Ronveaux, & S. Vanhulle (Eds.), *Alternances en formation* (pp. 7–45). Bruxelles: De Boeck.

Veeramani, R., & Bradley, S. (2008). *Insights regarding undergraduate preference for lecture capture*. Madison, WI: University of Wisconsin-Madison.

Veletsianos, G., & Navarrete, C. C. (2012). Online social networks as formal learning environments: learner experiences and activities. *The international Review of Research in Open and Distributed Learning, 13*(1). Retrieved from www.irrodl.org/index.php /irrodl/article/view/1078/2077

Verganud, G. (1990). La théorie des champs conceptuels. In Recherche en didactique des mathématiques, 10(2-3), 133-170.

Vergnaud, G. (2007). Représentation et activité: deux concepts associés. *Recherche en éducation*, 4, 9-22, http://www.recherches-en-education.net/IMG/pdf/REE-no4.pdf

Vergnaud, G. (2008). Culture et conceptualisation, *Carrefours de l'éducation*, 26, 83-98.

Vergnaud, G. (2011). Au fond de l'action, la conceptualization. In J.-M. Barbier (Ed.), Savoir Théoriques et savoir d'action (pp. 275-292). Paris, France: PUF (Presses Universitaires de France).

Vergnaud, G. (1990). La Théorie des champs conceptuels. *Recherches en Didactique des Mathématiques, 10*, 2–3, 134–169.

Vergnaud, G. (1990). La théorie des champs conceptuels. *Recherche en didactique des Mathématiques, 10*(2-3), 133–170.

Vergnaud, G. (1996). Au fond de l'action, la conceptualisation. In J. M. Barbier (Ed.), *Savoirs théoriques et savoirs d'action* (pp. 275–292). Paris: PUF.

Vergnaud, G. (1996). Au fond de l'action. La conceptualisation. In J. M. Barbier (Ed.), *Savoirs théoriques et savoires d'action*. Paris: PUF.

Vergnaud, G. (1999). Le développement cognitif de l'adulte. In P. Carré & P. Caspar (Eds.), *Traité des sciences et des techniques de la formation* (pp. 103–126). Paris: Dunod.

Vermersch, P. (1991). L'entretien d'explicitation. *Les cahiers de beaumont, 52 bis 53*, 63-70.

Vermersch, P. (1994). *L'entretien d'explicitation en formation initiale et en formation continue*. Paris: ESF.

Vermesh, P. (2011). *L'entretien d'explicitation*. Paris, France: ESF.

Vertecchi, B. (1976). *Valutazione formativa*. Torino: Loescher.

Veyrunes, P., Imbert, P., San Martin, J. (2014). L'appropriation d'un format pédagogique: l'exemple du contrat de travail individuel à l'école primaire. *Éducation et didactique, 8*(3), 81-94.

Veyrunes, P. (2015). Configuration de l'activité collective en classe et culture du métier dans la formation des einseignants. In V. Lussi Borer, M. Durand, & F. Yvon (Eds.), *Analyse du travail et formation dans les métiers de l'éducation* (pp. 33–48). Louvain la Neuve: De Boek.

Villeret, O., Munoz, G., & Boivin, S. (2014). Quelle créativité dans la conception de dispositifs de formation basés sur l'analyse de l'activité? Paper presented at the Colloque HEP (haute école pédagogique): *Créativité et apprentissage: un tandem à ré-inventer?* Lausanne, Vaud, 15 & 16 mai.

Vinatier I., Morrissette J. (2015). Les recherches collaboratives: enjeux et perspectives. *Carrefours de l'éducation*, 39, 137-170.

Vinatier, I. (2010). L'entretien de co-explicitation entre chercheur et enseignants: une voie d'émergence et d'expression du "sujet capable". *Recherches en éducation*, 1, 111-130.

Vinatier, I. (2011b). La recherche collaborative: Enjeux et fondement théoriques. In J. Y. Robin & I. Vinatier (Eds.), Conseiller et accompagner. Un défi pour la formation des enseignants (pp. 45-60). Paris, France: L'Harmattan.

Vinatier, I., & Pastré, P. (2007). Organisateurs de la pratique et/ou de l'activité enseignante. *Recherche et éducation, 56*, 95-108.

Vinatier, I., Fillietaz, L. & Kahn, S. (Coord.). (2012). Enjeux, forme et rôle des processus collaboratif entre chercheurs et professionnels de la formation: pour quelle efficacité? *Travail et apprentissage*, 9.

Vinatier, I. (2009). *Pour une didactique professionnelle de l'enseignement*. Rennes: PUR.

Vinatier, I. (2009). *Pour une didactique professionnelle del'enseignement*. Rennes: PUR.

Vinatier, I. (2011a). Comment penser la possibilité d' "apprendre des situations" pour des enseignants en formation: Une co-élaboration entre chercheur et praticiens? *Education Sciences & Society, 2*(1), 97–113.

Vinatier, I. (2013). *Le travail enseignant. Une approche par la didactique professionnelle*. Bruxelles: De Boeck.

Vinatier, I., & Altet, M. (Eds.), (2008). *Analyser et comprendre la pratique enseignante*. Rennes: PUR.

Von Cranach, M. (1982). *Goal-directed action*. London: Academic Press.

Walkowiak, T. A., Berry, R. Q., Meyer, J. P., Rimm-Kaufman, S. E., & Ottmar, E. R. (2014). Introducing an observational measure of standards-based mathematics teaching practices: *Evidence of validity and score reliability. Educational Studies in Mathematics, 85*(1), 109–128. doi:10.1007/s10649-013-9499-x

Wang, J., & Hartley, K. (2003). Video technology as a support for teacher education reform. *Journal of Technology and Teacher Education, 11*(1), 105–138.

Ward, B. E. (1970). A Survey of Microteaching in NCATE-Accredited Secondary Education Programs. Washington, D.C.: Office of Education (DHEW).

Ward, P., Suss, J., & Basevitch, I. (2009). Expertise and expert performance-based training (ExPerT) in complex domains. *Technology, Instruction. Cognition and Learning, 7*(2), 121–145.

Watson, D., Blakeley, B., & Abbott, C. (1998). Researching the use of communication technologies in teacher education. *Computers & Education, 10*(1-2), 15–21. doi:10.1016/S0360-1315(97)00074-2

Weeden, P., Winter, J., & Broadfoot, P. (2002). *Assessment. What's in it for schools. London: Routledge. Trad. It. Scalera, V. (2009). Valutazione per l'apprendimento nella scuola. Strategie per incrementare la qualità dell'offerta formativa*. Trento: Erickson. doi:10.4324/9780203468920

Wenger, E. (1998). *Communities of Practice: Learning, Meaning, and Identity*. Cambridge, UK: Cambridge University Press. doi:10.1017/CBO9780511803932

West, C. (2012). Developing reflective practitioners: Using video-cases in music teacher education. *Journal of Music Teacher Education, 22*(2), 11–19. doi:10.1177/1057083712437041

Woo, K., Gosper, M., McNeill, M., Preston, G., Green, D., & Phillips, R. (2008). Web-based lecture technologies: Blurring the boundaries between face-to-face and distance learning. *ALT-J Research in Learning Technology, 16*(2), 81–93. doi:10.1080/09687760802315895

Wu, C. C., & Kao, H. C. (2008). Streaming videos in peer assessment to support training pre-service teachers. *Journal of Educational Technology & Society, 11*(1), 45–55.

Xavier, I. (Ed.), (2003). A experiência do cinema: antologia. Rio de Janeiro: Graal: Embrafilme.

Yasmin, D. (2013). Application of the classification tree model in predicting learner dropout behaviour in open and distance learning. *Distance Education, 34*(2), 218–231. doi:10.1080/01587919.2013.793642

Yeh, C., & Santagata, R. (2015). Pre-Service Teachers' Learning to Generate Evidence-Based Hypotheses about the Impact of Mathematics Teaching on Learning. *Journal of Teacher Education, 66*(1), 21–34. doi:10.1177/0022487114549470

Yerrick, R., Ross, D., & Molebash, P. (2005). Too close for comfort: Real-time science teaching reflections via digital video editing. *Journal of Science Teacher Education, 16*(4), 351–375. doi:10.1007/s10972-005-1105-3

Yin, R. K. (1984). *Case study research: Design and methods*. Beverly Hills, CA: Sage Publication.

Yoshida, M. (1999). *Lesson study: an enthnographic investigation of school-based teacher development in Japan* [Unpublished doctoral dissertation]. University of Chicago, IL.

Youens, B., Smethem, L., & Sullivan, S. (2014). Promoting collaborative practice and reciprocity in initial teacher education: Realising a 'dialogic space' through video capture analysis. *Journal of Education for Teaching, 40*(2), 101–113. doi:10.1080/02607476.2013.871163

Zaccaï-Reyners, N. (2005). Fiction et typification. Contribution à une approche théorique de la transmission de l'expérience. *Methodos, 5*, 1–21. doi:10.4000/methodos.378

Zask, J. (2004). L'enquête sociale comme inter-objectivation. In B. Karsenti & L. Quéré (Eds.), *La croyance et l'enquête. Aux sources du pragmatisme* (pp. 141–163). Bruxelles: De Boeck.

Zeichner, K. (2010). Rethinking the connections between campus courses and field experiences in college and university-based teacher education. *Journal of Teacher Education, 61*(1), 89–99. doi:10.1177/0022487109347671

Zhang, D., Zhou, L., Briggs, R. O., & Nunamaker, J. F. Jr. (2006). Instructional video in e-learning: Assessing the impact of interactive video on learning effectiveness. *Information & Management, 43*(1), 15–27. doi:10.1016/j.im.2005.01.004

Zhang, M., Lundeberg, M., Koehler, M. J., & Eberhardt, J. (2011). Understanding affordances and challenges of three types of video for teacher professional development. *Teaching and Teacher Education, 27*(2), 454–462. doi:10.1016/j.tate.2010.09.015

Zingaro, D., & Oztok, M. (2012). Interaction in an Asynchronous Online Course: A Synthesis of Quantitative Predictors. *Journal of Asynchronous Learning Networks, 4*(16), 12.

About the Contributors

Pier Giuseppe Rossi is full professor at the department of Education, Cultural Heritage and Tourism at University of Macerata (Italy). He is the author of several books, book chapters and scientific articles in the field of Educational Technologies and Didactics.

Laura Fedeli has an MSc (Instructional Technology and Distance Education, USA) and a PhD in e-Learning, Knowledge Management and Psychology of Communication (Italy + EU label). She has been involved in a number of European projects dealing with e-learning, quality procedures and policies and the use of social media in education and teacher training. She is currently a lecturer at the University of Macerata (Italy) where she has been working since 2008.

* * *

Amélie Alletru teaches at the University of Nartes, France, where she is involved in pre-service and in-service teacher training at the ESPE (Superior School for Teaching and Education). She carries out Collaborative researches using an ethnographic approach, that focus on a co-analysis of teachers' effective practices in a multimodal perspective. She pays particular attention to the way practitioners can be accompanied in their professional development, in a Professional Didactics perspective, through analyzing their won professional activity, and be provided with conceptual tools in this very explicit ambition: analysis to the purpose of training. Aiming at understanding how a teacher's work activity is structured and conceptualized in situation, her PhD in Educational Sciences deals with a multimodal analysis of teachers' effective practices in a multilingual context (French Polynesia). She is a member of the CREN (Research in Education Centre of Nantes) team and of the OPÉEN&ReForm research group.

Giorgio Bolondi received his PhD in algebraic geometry. He is currently professor of Mathematics at Bologna University, where he teaches History of Mathematics and Math education. His main research interests are the impact of standardized assessment on teaching and learning processes, and the construction and implementation of task for math learning assessment. He has been the President of the Italian Commission for the teaching of Mathematics, has been involved in the definition of the Italian Math national curricula, and is currently member of the group responsible of the construction of the national tests for mathematics (Invalsi). He published more than one hundred of scientific papers (in complex analysis, algebraic geometry, history of mathematics, math education) and many books, and he has an intensive activity in pre-service and in-service teacher training. He has also been involved in several science popularization events.

Valérie Lussi Borer is senior lecturer and researcher at the Faculty of Psychology and Educational Sciences and at the University Institute of Teacher Education of the University of Geneva. Her research focuses on the analysis of teacher work activity, the use of video for preservice education and professional development of teachers and teacher professionalization in a socio- historical perspective. She is a member of the research team CRAFT (design, research, action, education, work) headed by Marc Durand. She is involved in primary and secondary preservice teacher education programs. She also contracted partnerships and conducted research with French departments and Swiss cantons ministries of Education to design video-artifact-based programs for teachers and school counselors' professional development called "Collaborative Video Learning Labs".

Pilar Colás-Bravo has a PhD of Science Education from the University of Seville, Spain. Professor of Research Methods and Diagnosis in Education at the University of Seville. Specialist in Methods Research in Education and Qualitative and Quantitative Research. Their lines of scientific and research projects focus on Innovation, Technology and Educational assessment. The quality of his scientific career is supported by the recognition of four Research Periods by the CNEAI (National Assessment of Research Activity). It belongs to the Research Group called "Evaluation and Educational Technology" (HUM-154). She collaborates with the National Agency for Quality Assessment and Accreditation (ANECA) as Expert for Accreditation of Teacher Education and the National Agency for Assessment and Planning under the Ministry of Science and Technology. She is a member of the Committee of Experts of the Youth Council of Spain, in Education.

Jesús Conde-Jiménez is Holder of Staff Training Grant (FPU), Spanish Ministry of Education at the University of Seville, Spain. He is currently doing his PhD thesis called *The mediation of ICT in creating learning environments and achieving digital competences*. He holds a Master in *Management, Evaluation and Quality of Training Institutions* (2011) and a degree in Psychopedagogy from the University of Seville (2008-2010). He is a research fellow of the Group *Research, Evaluation and Educational Technology* (GIETE, HUM154) since 2011, and has been teaching in the Department of Research Methods and Diagnosis in Education (MIDE) at the University of Seville. He has done research stays in *Arcola Research* (London, England) and in the *School of Engineering and Computing* in the *University of West of Scotland* (Paisley, Scotland). He has collaborated on several R+D projects, such as in the European project *Stay In: Student guidance at university for inclusion*. In addition, he has participated in national and international conferences, through communications and paper presentations. In addition, he has written several papers and book chapters.

José Antonio Contreras-Rosado has a PhD of Science Education from the University of Seville (Spain). He is currently Honorary Assistant in the Department of Teaching and Educational Organization at the University of Seville. Their lines of scientific and research projects focus on Innovation, Technology and ICT. He belongs to the Research Group called "Evaluation and Educational Technology" (HUM-154). He has collaborated on various projects of National and European research. He has participated in national and international conferences. He has published articles in scientific journals and book chapters.

Juan De Pablos-Pons has a Ph.D. in Science Education and is University Professor since 1995 in the area of Teaching and School Organization at the University of Seville. Head of the Research Group

Evaluation and Educational Technology linked to the Andalusian Research Program since 2000. The teaching is recognized for 7 six-year periods of teaching and research with 4 six-year research, recognized by the CNEAI (National Commission for Assessment Research activity). President of the University Network for Educational Technology (RUTE) since 2012. Also, he is Evaluator R+D projects from different national and regional agencies. His preferred research lines developed over the past ten years have been: ICT applied to education; education policies and the integration of ICT; teacher training. He has led numerous projects R+D on these topics. In the field of management, he serves as Dean of the Faculty of Education since 2009 until today. He is president-elect of the Conference of Deans of Andalusia of Educational Sciences. He collaborates with the National Agency for Quality Assessment and Accreditation (ANECA) for Accreditation of College Teacher and the National Evaluation Agency (ANEP), under the Ministry of Science and Technology, responsible for evaluating projects research belonging to the National Programs R+D (ANEP). In addition, he is scientific editor of specialized books on ICT and Education.

Monica Fantin, is a PhD in Education, is an Associate Professor in Education and Communication at the Federal University at Santa Catarina, Brazil. She coordinates the Research Group "Childhood, Communication, Culture and Art", UFSC/CNPq. She has published and edited some books and many articles about childhood, culture, media education, digital culture and teaching and learning education.

Federica Ferretti has her PhD in mathematics (thesis in mathematics education). For several years she has worked in Math education and teacher training. She is adjunct professor at the University of Bologna (UNIBO) and at the University of Bressanone (UNIBZ). She is a researcher at the Department of Mathematics and at the Department of Education Studies (UNIBO) and a manager in the LLP Comenius Project FAMT&L focused on formative assessment in Mathematics. Her main research interests are assessment's tools and classroom practices and the impact of evaluation in students learning process.

Alessandro Gimigliano has a PhD in Mathematics, Queens' University, Kingston, Canada. He is Full Professor at the Dept. of Mathematics, University of Bologna (Italy). His main field of research is Algebraic Geometry and he teaches Geometry and Basic Mathematics for the degree course of "Scienze della Formazione Primaria" (Teaching in Primary School degree).

Teresa González-Ramírez has a PhD of Science Education in the University of Seville, Spain. Associate Professor of Research Methods and Diagnosis in Education at the University of Seville. Associate Dean of Quality and Educational Innovation since 2009 at the Faculty of Science Education. Their lines of scientific work are ICT, Research and Evaluation. She has participated in international and national projects about ICT educational applications. She has led numerous projects about Educational Innovation: Creating a Technical Unit ECTS for teacher training: *Development, evaluation and certification of competencies (2007-2008), Creation of an observatory for innovation in the fields of Practicum for the development and evaluation of professional skills through portfolio (2005- 2006), Creation of methodological workshops for teacher training in European convergence (2005-2006) and evaluation of basic and specific competences for the formation of the evaluator at the university through the student portfolio (2004-2005).* She is scientific author and editor of several books and book chapters. Since 2010, she is evaluator at the Project Evaluation of Educational Innovation in Andalusia. Andalusian Evaluation Agency.

Janette Jovel received a Bachelor degree in Psychology and Sociology with a minor in Educational Studies from the University of California, Irvine and a Master's of Science in Education, Culture and Society from the University of Pennsylvania. Her research interests include issues affecting educational equity and opportunity with a focus on teachers' understanding and management of institutional and individual racism in the classroom.

Stefania Lovece has a PhD in Educational Sciences. She is currently Research fellow and Teaching tutor at the Department of Education Studies "Giovanni Maria Bertin" (University of Bologna) and has carried out research and management in the context of the LLP Comenius project FAMT & L aimed at the promotion of formative assessment to improve teaching. For several years she has carried out research and training on issues of education, educational technology, design and educational innovation in school, extracurricular contexts and professional training.

Daniela Maccario is an Associate Professor Methodologies of teaching and special education (M-PED/03) - University of Turin. She teaches Teaching methods and instructional design; Classroom management; Educational planning in social work. His main research field is the development of didactic models, with specific reference to teaching and educational interventions based on competencies (A scuola di competenze -2012- Torino: SEI). He is interested to study teaching and educational action as the core of professionalism of teachers and educators.

Patrizia Magnoler is a researcher in pedagogy. He has developed several studies on teacher education pre-service and in-service. He teaches in the graduate program in Primary Education. She is company secretary scientific research for teaching (Italian Society for Educational Research) and member of the research groups Opéen Reform. Its volume "Research and training" (2012) was awarded the pedagogy prize in 2014.

Giuseppina Rita Mangione is Researcher (tenured position) at INDIRE (National Institute of Documentation, Innovation and Educational Research). She is working on training and professional development for teachers in induction. She holds a Master's degree in online education and a PhD in Telematics and Information Society at University of Florence. She has been postdoctoral associate at the University of Salerno, working on e-learning and innovative educational methods. Her research interests include teachers' training, adaptive instruction and learning technologies. She conducts her research activities on innovative models in the school from the point of view of education and professional teacher development. She coordinates activities of observation of situated practices by analyzing the dimensions of new teaching and learning methodologies. She is author of several books and scientific papers.

Alain Muller is senior lecturer and researcher at the University Institute of Teacher Education of the University of Geneva. He is a member of the research team CRAFT (design, research, action, education, work) headed by Marc Durand and of the research team LIFE (Laboratory for Innovation and Education) headed by Olivier Maulini. He works in a pragmatic perspective on the analysis of teachers work activity and teacher education. He is involved in primary and secondary preservice teacher education programs. He also contracted partnerships and conducted research with French departments and Swiss cantons ministries of Education to design video-artifact-based programs for teachers and school counselors' professional development called "Collaborative Video Learning Labs".

Grégory Munoz works on the analysis of activity of professionnals, in particular teachers (Grangeat & Munoz, 2006; Specogna & Munoz, 2011; Munoz, Minassian & Vinatier, 2012; Villeret & Munoz, 2015), tutors and trainers, from the point of view of the ergonomic psychology and professional didactics, according to a genetic approach, wich try to clarify the concepts-in-action of the workers, in order to train and develop. On the other hand, his works are interested in alternation training (Gérard, Munoz & Rousseau, 2013) and into the mediations in action (Munoz & Boivin, 2016), in particular in training (Bruno & Munoz,2010), or in accreditation of prior learning of the experience (VAE)(Munoz, Sylvestre & Soulard, 2013). Within the analysis of activity, he tries to consider the systems of intruments of the workers (Munoz & Bourmaud, 2012; Munoz, Vidal-Gomel & Bourmaud, 2015).

Maila Pentucci is PhD in Education at the University of Macerata and human sciences teacher in secondary school. Her research deals with the processes of didactic transposition and mediation, particularly in the historical disciplines and the education technologies for teaching and learning systems. She collaborates with educational institutions and networks of schools for the in-service teachers training. Among his recent publications: "Le immagini nei libri di storia per la scuola primaria", in Form@re. Open Journal per la formazione in rete, n. 2(2015).

Loredana Perla is Full Professor in Special Education at the University of Bari "Aldo Moro" (Italy); she is Professor of Theory of Education, Analysis of Practices, Special Education and Enviromental Education. She is representative for national and international projects on teachers' training and competence development. She is Vice-president at Quality Assessment Unit, University of Bari "Aldo Moro" (Italy). She is a member of ISATT (International Study Association on Teachers and Teaching), Ideki (Information, Didactique, Documentation, Enseignement, Knowledge Kultur, Ingénierie) and she has been member of Opéen&ReForm (Observation des pratiques éducatives et enseignantes). Her fields of study are: Analysis of educational and professional practices. Her latest publications: L. Perla (eds) (2011). *L'eccellenza in cattedra. Dal saper insegnare alla conoscenza dell'insegnamento*, FrancoAngeli; L. Perla (eds) (2014). *I Nuovi Licei alla prova delle competenze. Guida alla progettazione nel biennio.* Lecce: Pensa Multimedia; L. Perla (Eds., con M.G. Riva) (2016). *L'Agire educativo. Manuale per educatori e operatori socio-assistenziali.*

Maria Chiara Pettenati is Research Director at INDIRE (National Institute of Documentation, Innovation and Educational Research) and Coordinator of the School Personnel Training Area. She holds an honours degree in Electronics Engineering (1996) and a PhD in Telematics and Information Society (2000) from the University of Florence. Between 2011 and 2013 she was Program Manager at the ICON Foundation (International Centre of Computational Neurophotonics) a non-profit research Foundation participated by LENS, IBM and the University of Florence. Until 2011 she was Research Assistant by the Telematics Laboratory of the Electronics and Telecommunications Department of the University of Florence and she held a course in Telematics e-learning Systems within the Post-graduate Master program in e-learning Techniques and Methods of the University of Florence. From 1997 to 1999, she was PhD visiting student by the Computer Science Department (DI - LITH Laboratory) of the EPFL (Swiss Federal Institute of Technology, Lausanne). Her current research interests deal with teachers' training (Induction and Continuous Professional Development), educational technologies, e-learning and e-knowledge.

Ljuba Pezzimenti has a PhD in psychological, sociological and e-learning sciences at University of Macerata (EU label). Her research interests concern the didactic transposition process, the relationship between didactic and disciplines, the didactic mediation, the analysis of educational practices, the teacher professionalism. She is currently a primary school teacher.

Angiline Powell is a teacher trainer at the University of Memphis, USA. She works primarily in the areas of mathematics education and technology integration.

Beverly B. Ray works with in-service teachers across the globe on issues of technology integration and social studies education. She works in the field of pre-service teacher training at Idaho State University.

Salvador Reyes-de-Cózar is a Ph.D student of Science Education from the University of Seville (Spain). He is currently Honorary Assistant in the Department of Research Methods and Diagnosis in Education at the University of Seville. Their lines of scientific and research projects focus on Innovation, Technology, Education assessment and Educational Engagement. He belongs to the Research Group called "Evaluation and Educational Technology" (HUM-154). He has collaborated on various projects of National and European research. He has participated in national and international conferences. He has published articles in scientific journals and book chapters.

Alessia Rosa is a Researcher (tenured position) at INDIRE (National Institute of Documentation, Innovation and Educational Research). She deals with models of professional teacher development and evaluation of teachers skills. She has been professor with a temporary appointment for the courses of Educational Technology and Educational Assessment at the University of Turin. She holds an honours degree in Educational Sciences and a PhD in Media Education from the University of Turin. Her research interests include teachers' training, assessment strategies and media education in formal and informal learning contexts. She managed several projects in the field of education, collaborating with international partners (NGOs, Universities and other Governmental bodies). She is author of several books and scientific papers.

Hatice Sancar Tokmak, PhD: Assoc. Prof. Dr. Sancar Tokmak is on the faculty in the Department of Computer Education and Instructional Technology at Mersin University since 2011. She has a Ph.D. (2010) in the Department of Computer Education and Instructional Technology from Middle East Technical University. Her research interests include Teacher Education, Evaluation / Design of Online Courses, and Educational Simulations / Simulators. She specifically interested in: - XBT (Expertise based training) or TPACK (technological-pedagogical- content knowledge) based course designs for improvement in teacher candidates' self-efficacy, confidence, and teaching practices about technology integration; - Educational games: integration to instruction; evaluation process; game design process. - Validation and use of educational simulations/simulators. - Macro-Micro Evaluation models use for Online Courses evaluation and design.

Rossella Santagata is Associate Professor at the School of Education, University of California, Irvine. Her research focuses on teacher preparation and professional development with particular attention to the teaching and learning of mathematics and the use of video as a tool to facilitate analysis of practice and teacher professional growth. She is author and co-author of numerous essays and scientific papers in this area.

Nunzia Schiavone has a PhD in Designing and Assessment of training processes at the University of Bari "Aldo Moro" (Italy); specialisation in autobiographical methodologies at the Free University of Autobiography, Anghiari (Arezzo, Italy); she is member of IDEKI Information, Didactique, Documentation, Emseignement, knowkedge, Ingènierie), SIREF (Italian Association for Educational Research), GRAPHEIN (Society of Writing Education); and partner of Siped (Italian Association of Pedagogy). Her fields of study are: Theories and practices of autobiographical writing education (keywords: autobiographical writing, Research, Humanities,Teacher Education); The documentation of teaching practices (didactic documentation, documentary writing, reflexivity, didactic practices, school assets); Pedagogy and didactics of the school: School pedagogy and didactics.

Ira Vannini received her PhD in Educational Research from "La Sapienza" University of Rome. She is Associate Professor at the Department of Education, University of Bologna (Italy). At the Faculty of Education, she teaches "Methodology of Educational Research" and "Theories and methods of planning and evaluation" in the undergraduate courses for pre-service teachers. At present, her research activities are focused on topics such as formative evaluation research and curricular planning in school and in vocational training; studies on teacher training also using technics of video-analysis in classroom; educational innovation monitoring in kindergarten, primary and secondary school; the relationship between teachers and school evaluation: use of formative assessment (mainly regarding mathematics teaching); the assessment and certification of skills, in e-learning contexts, too.

Cathery Yeh is an Assistant Professor at Chapman University. Her research explores pedagogy that leverages the learning opportunities of students and teachers, particularly in culturally and linguistically diverse communities and in the area of mathematics. This work is informed by her background as a teacher and teacher educator.

Index

A

aesthetic participation 4-5, 8, 17
alternation 2, 4, 16-18, 21, 55, 137
Analyse de Pratiques (Analysis of Practices) 4, 21
Analyse Plurielle (Plural Analysis) 21
Analysis 1-22, 46-47, 51-52, 54, 57-61, 64, 66, 127-128, 131-136, 138-139
art 1-3, 5-7, 10, 13-14

B

boundary object 9, 11, 14, 21

C

cinema 1-4, 7, 10, 13-14
Cinematographic-Educational Mediation 14, 17
co-analysis 1-2, 5-8, 60
Coding 5-7, 13, 133
Co-Explicitation (Joint Explication) 2, 4-7, 9-13, 17, 20-21
collaborative inquiry 1, 3, 5, 13
collaborative research 1-2, 5, 7, 12-13, 21
comparison 1, 4, 7-10, 12, 14, 17, 21, 48, 57-60, 66
Conceptualisation of Actions 20
culture 2-7, 9, 11, 13-15, 17-19, 49

D

Design Based Research-DBR 64
Dewey 1, 3-6, 10-11, 14, 138
Dialogic Video Cycle 1, 3, 10, 13, 22
didactic action 20, 47, 52-61, 64
didactic mediation 10, 12, 14, 20, 47, 55, 130
didactic transposition 1-3, 7-8, 17, 20

D

digital video 1-2, 26, 287
discussions 1-5, 7-9, 12-14, 58, 60, 286
dispositif 2-4, 7, 16-17, 21
Double Vraisemblance (Double Verisimilitude) 21

E

Educational Evaluation 18
educational mediation 4, 8-9, 18
Educational Social Platforms 26
Educational Video 26, 284
Emergent method of reviewing 2, 22
entretiens de co-explicitation 2, 7, 10, 20
experience 1-15, 17, 19, 45-47, 49, 51, 56-57, 59, 130, 138, 271-274, 276, 282, 285-286
Expertise-Based Training 1-3, 17

F

facilitator 1, 5, 10-11, 13-14
formative assessment 127-129, 131-135, 137, 139
framework 1-5, 7-13, 17, 19, 128, 131
Francophone ergonomics 3

H

habitus 1, 3-6, 13, 18, 21, 54
History didactics 1

I

ICT 4, 26
in-service training 1-7, 10, 12-13, 16-18, 22, 128, 133
Instructional Design Theories 17
Instructional Technology 8
intermediary processes 1

K

Knowledge Based Reasoning 22

L

Lesson Study 3, 10-12, 22
Life Long Learning 17
Lumière Minute 1-2, 10-15, 18

M

mathematics teaching 1-2, 7-10, 128, 134, 137
Media Education 1-6, 8, 18
Mimetism 7
multiliteracies 1-2, 9-10, 15, 18

N

Narrative Review 1, 22
new literacies 2, 9-10, 18
noticing 1-3, 5, 7, 9-10, 14, 17, 22, 271-272
Novice 1-4, 6, 9, 11, 17, 271-281, 284-287

O

observation 1-2, 4-15, 17, 21, 46, 52-57, 59-60, 130-139, 274
outil (tool) 21

P

participatory research 3, 64
Podcast-Based Learning 10, 26
practical knowledge 46, 65
Practice Based Research-PBR 65
pre-service teachers 1-5, 7-10, 13, 139, 286
professional development 1-7, 9, 11-13, 15, 17-18, 21, 61, 66, 272-274, 276, 285-287
professional growth 8-9, 13, 47
professional identity 1, 4, 6-9, 15-16, 20, 22
professional routines 64-65
professional self-assessment 3, 13, 18
Professional Vision and Development 1-7, 9-10, 14, 17, 21-22
professionalism 1-2, 4, 6-9, 11, 13, 16, 22, 130, 132, 137, 139
professionalization 6-7, 21-22, 45, 129, 131, 137

R

Recherche Collaborative (Collaborative Research) 3-4, 21
reflective practice 1, 3, 12
reflexivity 3, 5, 21, 138
representation 3, 9-11, 14, 47-48, 51, 53, 57, 60, 135
research-development 45, 47, 51, 54, 61, 65
research-training 1, 5-6, 18

S

school 1-22, 55, 128, 132, 135-136
self-assessment 1-4, 6, 10, 13-15, 18, 131-132
Self-Defense Mechanisms 9, 23
self-reflection tool 18
Situated Learning Episodes 1-2, 10, 18
social network 6, 8, 17, 26
Social Networking Site 1-8, 14-18, 26
Standards-Based Instruction 1, 13
student thinking 1-5, 8-9, 11, 13, 23
Study of Practices 18, 21

T

teacher education 1-2, 4-5, 8-10, 12-14, 17, 19, 272
teacher learning 1-2, 7, 10-11, 14
Teacher Practice 21
teacher professional development 2, 9, 11, 13
teacher training 1-7, 11, 13-18, 26, 54, 127, 132-134, 136-137, 139, 271-274, 276-277, 285-287
teachers' training 2, 10, 15, 21
teaching practices 1-9, 11, 13-14, 21, 51, 65, 132, 137-139
Teaching Video Club 1, 3, 10, 23
technology integration 7-8, 17
tool 1-7, 9-15, 17-18, 21, 50, 127-129, 131-136, 138, 271-272, 275-276, 287
topic segments 5-9, 13
TPACK (Technological Pedagogical Content Knowledge) 17
training models 1-3, 14, 18
triangulation 1-2, 7, 9, 11-13, 16-18, 22, 57

U

United States 2, 272, 280

Become an IRMA Member

Members of the **Information Resources Management Association (IRMA)** understand the importance of community within their field of study. The Information Resources Management Association is an ideal venue through which professionals, students, and academicians can convene and share the latest industry innovations and scholarly research that is changing the field of information science and technology. Become a member today and enjoy the benefits of membership as well as the opportunity to collaborate and network with fellow experts in the field.

IRMA Membership Benefits:

- **One FREE Journal Subscription**

- **30% Off Additional Journal Subscriptions**

- **20% Off Book Purchases**

- Updates on the latest events and research on Information Resources Management through the IRMA-L listserv.

- Updates on new open access and downloadable content added to Research IRM.

- A copy of the Information Technology Management Newsletter twice a year.

- A certificate of membership.

IRMA Membership $195

Scan code to visit irma-international.org and begin by selecting your free journal subscription.

Membership is good for one full year.

Printed in the United States
By Bookmasters